WILLIAM EMPSON

AMONG THE
MANDARINS

John Haffenden is Professor of English Literature at the University of Sheffield. His books include *The Life of John Berryman*, *W. H. Auden: The Critical Heritage*, *Viewpoints: Poets in Conversation*, and *Novelists in Interview*; and he has edited *Berryman's Shakespeare* and several collections of works by William Empson including the *Complete Poems*. He is a Fellow of the Royal Society of Literature, and has been a British Academy Research Reader.

WILLIAM EMPSON

AMONG THE
MANDARINS

JOHN HAFFENDEN

OXFORD
UNIVERSITY PRESS

OXFORD
UNIVERSITY PRESS

Great Clarendon Street, Oxford OX2 6DP

Oxford University Press is a department of the University of Oxford.
If furthers the University's objective of excellence in research, scholarship,
and education by publishing worldwide in

Oxford New York

Auckland Cape Town Dar es Salaam Hong Kong Karachi Kuala Lumpur
Madrid Melbourne Mexico City Nairobi New Delhi Shanghai Taipei Toronto

With offices in

Argentina Austria Brazil Chile Czech Republic France Greece
Guatemala Hungary Italy Japan Poland Portugal
Singapore South Korea Switzerland Thailand Turkey Ukraine Vietnam

Published in the United States
by Oxford University Press Inc., New York

© John Haffenden 2005

The moral rights of the author have been asserted
Database right Oxford University Press (maker)

First published 2005

British Library Cataloguing in Publication Data

Data available

Library of Congress Cataloging in Publication Data
Haffenden, John.
William Empson : among the Mandarins / John Haffenden.
p. cm.
Includes bibliographical references (p.) and index.
1. Empson, William, 1906– 2. Poets, English–20th century–Biography. 3. Criticism–Great Britain–
History–20th century. 4. British–China–History–20th century. 5. Critics–Great Britain–
Biography. I. Title.
PR6009.M7Z69 2005 801'.95'092–dc22 2004029385

ISBN 0–19–927659–5

1 3 5 7 9 10 8 6 4 2

Typeset by Kolam Information Services Pvt. Ltd., Pondicherry, India
Printed in Great Britain on acid-free paper by
Biddles Ltd., King's Lynn, Norfolk

ACKNOWLEDGEMENTS

I have incurred many debts while researching this biography, in Great Britain, the USA, China, and Japan. The task began, in some sort, as early as 1982, when I plucked up the courage to ask Sir William Empson whether he proposed to write his memoirs. 'Possibly, possibly,' he responded. 'Er, do you really think you will?' I pressed on (I had spent many weeks nerving myself to this moment). 'Oh, probably not,' he granted. 'Then would you mind if I begin to gather materials towards a biography...?' (Later I would discover a letter to his friend and publisher Ian Parsons, written long before I asked my impertinent question—on 16 January 1973—in which he anticipated, though with little enthusiasm, the far-off time when his life's work might be polished off and he could begin on an autobiography: 'When I am past anything else maybe I will be able to dictate my memoirs.') I don't recall whether it was that day or on a later occasion that he finally gave me his permission, which essentially consisted of a handwritten note requesting librarians and others to make available to me any letters or other papers in their control. I do remember asking him further, 'Perhaps you'd like to read my biography of John Berryman?' 'Oh, I've read it already,' he promptly came out. 'I read it with great interest and admiration... The only trouble is, these Americans seem to have kept all their letters and diaries. I haven't.' The last was said with a palpable note of glee. Some time after his death I was told he'd once expressed the view that his biography was now 'in safe hands', which I think has to be taken as one of his more accomplished and perhaps most mischievous ambiguities.

One other exchange of which I have a vivid memory is when I temerariously (I was braver in those days) asked him whether—given that I had undertaken to research his life even while he was still alive—he wanted any ground rules: whether I should draw short of investigating his private life (I did not then realize that even the Empsons' private life tended to be conducted in a rather public fashion). He was not much given to eye contact—he could often look hooded or abstracted, or roll his eyes over the ceiling while he considered a matter; or else he would appear to be directing his voice into the fur of the ginger cat, called just 'Cat', that sat on his lap—but on this occasion he looked me suddenly straight in the eye. 'Ground rules? Certainly not! Just get on with it.'

I thank him for his faith; so too Hetta, Lady Empson, for sustaining that unconditional trust over the years, and through many amusing and sometimes unnerving visits to her home at Studio House in Hampstead. Like so many biographers, I resolved at an early stage to try to avoid putting myself into too great a debt to my subject and his family, in case the ideal of disinterested scholarship should somehow be compromised in consequence. However, after quite a while—at a period when I was visiting Hampstead about once a month to spend a day or so going over some of the papers that Empson did happily leave stockpiled in his den—one evening proved to be so lavish with alcohol that I was almost incapable of making my way elsewhere for the night. I was bidden to sleep in William's bed. Later, while swimming on his bed and skimming through some of his notebooks, I suddenly spotted on the desk a tall, buff-coloured carton. Indulging the biographer's besetting nosiness, and somehow assuming in my grossly fuddled state that this mysterious package must contain something special like a bottle of malt whisky, I proceeded to pull up the tab, only to discover, with something approaching a galvanic shock, a label bearing the name 'WILLIAM EMPSON'. Worse still, at that precise moment, the door flew open and Hetta Empson's arm flashed out to seize the vessel from me. 'Whatever else you do, you're not sleeping with William!' she pronounced like a Wildean dowager. It turned out that she had forgotten for many weeks to collect his ashes from the crematorium: only on that day had she fulfilled that duty; and only in the small hours did she think that I might not wish to spend the night with my subject in quite such a state.

I am grateful to the Empson family for their long patience, their friendliness, and their tremendous hospitality, and for continuing to entrust me with this task after the death of Hetta Empson: primarily, Mogador Empson and Jacob Empson, and their wives; Simon Duval Smith, Saul Empson, Benjamin Empson, James Empson, the late Charles Empson, the late Sir Charles Empson, and the late Lady (Monica) Empson.

I am indebted to the British Academy for a Research Readership in 1989–91, and for a later grant-in-aid; and no less to the Arts Council of Great Britain, the Society of Authors, and the Research Fund of Sheffield

University for awards towards the costs of my research over the years. I simply could not have progressed with the job without such help.

Many libraries and other organizations and institutions have been equally generous in affording me accommodation, or in providing research facilities of one sort or another. I am eager first of all to thank the Houghton Library, Harvard University (custodian since 1986 of the Empson Papers), and in particular Leslie Morris (Curator of Manuscripts), Rodney G. Dennis (former Curator), and Elizabeth A. Falsey (who undertook the awesome job of preparing an inventory of the papers). I am deeply grateful too to the authorities of Peking University, Peking, who kindly hosted my initial visit in 1984; the British Embassy, Peking (Alan Maley, First Secretary, Cultural Section, British Embassy, and Martin Davidson; David Marler, Cultural Counsellor, British Council Representative in China); the British Council, London (Angela Udall, Leigh Gibson, Specialist Tours Department; Martin Carney; Adrian Johnson, Cultural Counsellor and British Council Representative, Peking); the British Embassy Cultural Department, the British Council, Tokyo (Katsumi Higashida); BBC Written Archives Centre, Caversham, Reading (Jacqueline Kavanagh, Written Archives Officer; Gwyniver Jones, Assistant-in-Charge, Enquiries; John Jordan, Enquiry Assistant); Beinecke Library, Yale University; British Film Institute; Department of Manuscripts, The British Library; Butler Library, Columbia University (Bernard Crystal, Librarian for Rare Books and Manuscripts; Kenneth A. Lohf, former Librarian); Chalmers Memorial Library, Kenyon College (Thomas B. Greenslade, College Archivist); Chatto & Windus; School Library, Eton College (M. C. Meredith); District Probate Registry, York; Embassy of the People's Republic of China (Ji Chaozhu, Ambassador; Chen Huaizhi, Cultural Department); Exeter University Library (Alistair Patterson); Goole Library; Haileybury College; Harry Ransom Humanities Research Center, University of Texas at Austin (Ellen S. Dunlap, Research Librarian; Cathy Henderson, Research Associate); Humberside County Record Office, Beverley; King's College, Cambridge; King's College, Cambridge (Dr Michael Halls, former archivist); the Library of Congress, Washington, DC; Magdalen College, Oxford; Magdalene College, Cambridge; Mills Memorial Library, McMaster University (Carl Spadoni, Research Collections Librarian); the National Archives, Washington, DC (Kathie Nicastro); Library/Information Service, National Sound Archive, British Library (Lee Taylor); Newnham College Library, Cambridge; Registrar of the Roll, Newnham College; North Yorkshire County Library, York; Princeton University Library (Jean F. Preston, Curator of Manuscripts);

the Public Record Office, London; Reading University Library (Michael Bott); Rockefeller Archive Centre, Tarrytown, New York; St John's College, Oxford; School of Oriental and African Studies, London; the Society of Authors; the *South China Morning Post*; Trinity College, Cambridge; the Library, University of Victoria, Canada (Chris Petter, University Archivist and Head of Special Collections); Victoria & Albert Museum Archives; Wilson Library, University of Minnesota; Winchester College (Dr Roger Custance, Archivist); Wren Library, Trinity College, Cambridge (Dr David McKitterick); Yorkshire County Archives, Beverley; and Yunnan Normal University, Kunming (which generously invited me to attend the celebrations in October 1988 marking the fiftieth anniversary of the Southwest Associated University).

Individuals who have most kindly afforded me information, advice and assistance in various capacities include Professor Peter Alexander, A. Alvarez, Sir Michael and Lady Atiyah, Dr Charles Aylmer, Professor Bao Zhi-yi, Jonathan Barker, Sebastian Barker, Robert J. Bertholf (Curator, The Poetry/Rare Books Collection, State University of New York at Buffalo), Andrew Best, the late Professor Bian Zhi Lin, the late Professor Max Black, Dr Sidney Bolt, the late Ronald Bottrall, Mrs Margaret Bottrall, Gordon Bowker, the late Professor Muriel Bradbrook, Baroness Brigstocke, Mrs J. J. Brodrick, Sally Brown, the late Arthur Calder-Marshall, James Campbell, Professor John Carey, Professor Owen Chadwick, Chang Chu-Tse (who generously undertook to be my cicerone in the city of Kunming in the spring of 1984), Professor Chao Chao-hsiung, Diana Chardin, Igor Chroustchoff, Chien Chung-shu, Ci Ji-wei, Patrick Clapham, Dr Colin Clark, Dr John Constable, the late Alistair Cooke, Arthur Cooper, Laura Pieters Cordy, Clive W. Cornell (W. Heffer & Sons Ltd), Sir Hugh Cortazzi, Jenny Cowan, Mrs C. Cruickshank (Archivist, Faber & Faber), Peter Currie, Dr Gordon Daniels, the late Hugh Sykes Davies, Professor Frank Day, the late Lord Devlin, Professor Martin Dodsworth, L. K. Duff, the late Elsie Duncan-Jones, Professor Katherine Duncan-Jones, Professor Svetlana Rimsky-Korsakov Dyer, H. J. Easterling, Professor Richard Eberhart, Mrs Valerie Eliot, the late D. J. Enright, Feng Cun-li, the late Professor Feng You-lan, the late Professor C. P. Fitzgerald, Dr Chris Fletcher, Professor Valerie Flint, Dr Shirley Foster, D. C. R. Francombe, Mrs Paddy Fraser, Mrs Rintaro Fukuhara, Professor David Fuller, John Fuller, Milla Gapanovich, Helen Gardner (Society of Authors), Margaret Gardiner, Professor Stephen Garrett, Kathleen Gibberd, the late Roma Gill, Reginald Goodchild, Adrian Goodman, Professor W. Terrence Gordon, T. W. Graham, Professor Gayle Greene,

Dr Eric Griffiths, Ruth Gunstone, Dr Michael Halls, the late Ian Hamilton, Jason Harding, Claire Harman, Selina Hastings, the late Professor Christopher Hawkes, Professor David Hawkes, the late Sir William Hayter, Geoffrey Hazelden, Professor He Zhao-wu, Christopher Heywood, Andrew and Geraldine Hillier, Charles Hobday, Professor Philip Hobsbaum, Anthony Hobson, Theodore Hofmann, Dr Eric Homberger, the late Michael Hope, the late Professor Graham Hough, Hsü Yuan-chung, Professor Huang Ming-yie, Professor Huang Zhong-hua, Allegra Huston, Professor Kazuo Irie, Professor Yukio Irie, Professor John Israel, Kevin Jackson, Mark Jacobs, Lord Jay, Elizabeth Jenkins, Dr Nicholas Jenkins, Mary-Lou Jennings, Ji Chaozhu, Professor Jin Di, Professor Jin Fa-xin, the late Professor Jin Yue Lin, James Joll, the late John Henry (David) Jones, Professor Kai Yuzuru, Professor Ryuichi Kajiki, Kang Hong-qiu, Paul Keegan, Anne Kelly, Professor Richard J. Kelly, Professor Sir Frank Kermode, Grace Margerie Key, the late David Kidd, Rev. H. P. Kingdon, Robert Lazarus, the late Sir Desmond Lee, the late Lady Lee, Dr E. S. Leedham-Green, the late Professor Peter Levi, the late Professor Li Funing, Professor Li Zhiwei, H. Lintott, the late Lord Listowel, Professor James J. Y. Liu, Mrs Liu Ruoduan, Liu Yuan Zi, Dr Richard Luckett, Jim McCue, Anne McDermid, the late Dr Eric Mackerness, the late Professor Ian MacKillop, Lachlan Mackinnon, Mrs Miriam MacIver, Alan and Robin Maclean, the late Professor Charles Madge, Dr D. H. Marrian, the late Jeremy Maule, Professor Giorgio Melchiori, M. C. Meredith, Mrs Sybil Meredith, M. F. Micklethwait, Seitoku Minagawa (Division of Administrative Affairs, University of Tsukuba), Mineo Moriya (*The Rising Generation*), Sir Jeremy Morse, Marjorie Mosby, Professor Andrew Motion, Professor Shigehisa Narita, Stella Mary Newton, Yoshio Nakano, Professor Christopher Norris, Professor Kazuo Ogawa, Sumie Okada, Timothy O'Sullivan, A. E. B. Owen, Dr Barbara Ozieblo, Maggie Fitzgerald, the late Ian Parsons, Lucy Pascocello (Rights and Permissions Manager, Harcourt Brace & Company), Mrs Peng Jing-fu, Peng Wen-lan, Dr Seamus Perry, David M. Petherbridge (General Manager, Ardsley Moat House, Barnsley), Dr David Pirie, Dr Kate Price, Edwin Pritchard, Qi Sheng-qiao, Qien Xuexi, Quan Hui-sien, the late Sir Peter Quennell, Dr E. A. Radice, Craig Raine, the late Dr Kathleen Raine, Peter Robinson, the late Theodore Redpath, the late Dorothea Richards, Professor Christopher Ricks, Susan Rieger, Professor Andrew Roberts, Professor Neil Roberts, Lisa A. Rodensky, Derek Roper, Sachiyo Round, the late Dr A. L. Rowse, Professor John Paul Russo, Ray Ryan, the late Dr George Rylands, James Sabben-Clare, Leo Salingar, John Saxby, Professor Eitaro Sayama,

Michael Schmidt, Mrs A. C. Scott, Debra Selinger, the late Martin Seymour-Smith, Dr C. J. Sharrock, Russell and Mary Sharrock, Mme Shen Baoqing, W. G. Shepherd, Professor Shui Tien-tung, John A. Simson, the late Norah Smallwood, the late Janet Adam Smith, Professor Nigel Smith, Richard C. Smith, Professor Soji Iwasaki, John D. Solomon, the late John Sparrow, the late Sir Stephen Spender, Lady Spender, Professor Jon Stallworthy, Professor Herbert Stern, the late Dr Alice Stewart, Professor and Mrs Harry Stoneback, Sun Yu-mei (my kind minder at Peking University), Alan Surridge, David Tang, Sir Keith Thomas, Mark Thompson, John L. Thorn, Anthony Thwaite, Nobuaki Tochigi, Professor Shigehito Toyama, the late Julian Trevelyan, Tuan Hui-sien, Jane Turner, Lindeth Vasey, John Vice, Dr Sue Vice, the late Igor Vinogradoff, the late Professor John Wain, William Wain, the late Earl Waldegrave, Lord Waldegrave, Stephen Wall, Jemma Walton, Wang Huan, Wang Min-yuan, Wang Ming-zhu, Professor Wang Shiren, Professor Wang Ting-bi, Professor Wang Zuo-liang, Dr George Watson, Andrew White, the late John Willett, Mrs Ann Willett, Hugh Williamson, Professor J. H. Willis, Jr., Professor John M. Willis, David Wilson, the late Robert Winter, Professor Lewis Wolpert, the late Basil Wright, Wu Bao Zhang, the late Professor Wu Fu-heng (President, Shandong University), Professor Wu Jing-rong, Professor Wu Ningkun, Air Marshal Sir Peter Wykeham, Professor Xu Guozhang, Professor Xu Yuan-zhong, the late Gladys Yang, Yang Xianyi, Professor Yang Yeh-chi, the late Professor Yang Zhouhan, Professor Shoichiro Yasuda, Mrs Vera Yorke, Yuan Chia-hua, Yuan Ke Jia, Professor Yuan Shiban, Professor Yu Da-zhen, Zhang Xiang-bao, Professor Zhou Jue-liang, Zhu Gheng-gong, Professor Zhu Guang-qian, and the late Lord Zuckerman.

Last but not least, I have learned a great deal over the years from my fellow critics and editors of Empson; and I should acknowledge in particular my sense of indebtedness to the work of John Constable, Frank Day, Terry Eagleton, Paul H. Fry, Philip and Averil Gardner, Philip Hobsbaum, James Jensen, the late John Henry Jones, Frank Kermode, Christopher Norris, Christopher Ricks, Lisa A. Rodensky, Roger Sale, Mark Thompson, and the late John Wain.

CONTENTS

LIST OF ILLUSTRATIONS

ABBREVIATIONS

Argufying	Empson, *Argufying: Essays on Literature and Culture* (London: Chatto & Windus, 1987)
Ambiguity	Empson, *Seven Types of Ambiguity* (London: Chatto & Windus, 1930; third edn., 1953)
Constable	John Constable (ed.), *Critical Essays on William Empson* (Aldershot: Scolar Press, 1993)
Complete Poems	*Complete Poems of William Empson* (London: Allen Lane, 2000)
EG	*Empson in Granta* (Tunbridge Wells: Foundling Press, 1993)
GS	Empson, *The Gathering Storm* (London: Faber & Faber, 1940)
Gill	R. Gill (ed.), *William Empson: The Man and His Work* (London: Routledge and Kegan Paul, 1974)
Houghton	William Empson Papers, Houghton Library, Harvard University
JH	John Haffenden
KMT	Kuomintang
Magdalene	I. A. Richards Papers, Old Library, Magdalene College, Cambridge
Milton's God	Empson, *Milton's God* (rev. edn.; Cambridge: Cambridge University Press, 1981)
Pastoral	Empson, *Some Versions of Pastoral*
Poems 1934	Empson, *Poems* (Tokyo, 1934)
Rodensky	Prefatory Note to *Pastoral* (Harmondsworth: Penguin, 1995)
SCW	Empson, *The Structure of Complex Words* (London: Chatto & Windus 1951; 3rd edn., 1977)
SSS	Empson, *The Strengths of Shakespeare's Shrew* (Sheffield: Sheffield Academic Press, 1996)

TLS	*Times Literary Supplement*
TUC	Trades Union Congress
WE	William Empson

CHRONOLOGY

1906   27 September: born at Yokefleet Hall, Howden, near Goole, Yorkshire; youngest child of Arthur Reginald Empson (landowner and squire) and his wife Laura Micklethwait; his siblings are John ('Jack', born 1891), Arthur (1892), Charles (1898), Maria Eleanor Katharine, known as 'Molly' (1902).

1914   16 May: death of eldest brother, a lieutenant in the Royal Flying Corps, in an aeroplane crash.

1914   Enrols at a preparatory school, Praetoria House School, near Folkestone, Kent, where mathematics becomes his forte.

1916   15 March: death of father, aged 63.

1920   Wins an entrance scholarship to Winchester College; specializes in mathematics and science; falls under 'the drug of Swinburne'. Writes first known poem, 'Mother, saying Anne good night', by 29 June, *aetat* 13.

1924   December: wins Milner Scholarship to Magdalene College, Cambridge.

1925   Wins English literature prize at Winchester; comes second (*proxime accessit*) to the future Labour MP Richard Crossman in competition for the Warden and Fellows' Prize for an English Essay (John Sparrow, future Warden of All Souls College, Oxford, is third).

        October: goes up to Cambridge, where his tutor for mathematics is A. S. Ramsey, father of the mathematical prodigy Frank Ramsey and the future Archbishop of Canterbury, Michael Ramsey. Joins humanist discussion society, The Heretics.

1926   February–March: T. S. Eliot delivers his Clark Lectures, 'The Metaphysical Poets of the Seventeenth Century', at Trinity College, Cambridge. Although Empson does not attend all the lectures, he benefits from informal conversations with Eliot. Participates in debates at the Union.

1926   12 June: publishes his first literary notice in *The Granta*.

1926   June: gains 1st class in Part I of the mathematical Tripos; awarded college prize.

1927   5 February: acts in a production at the Cambridge ADC of his one-act play, *Three Stories*, a melodrama.

1927   Begins reviewing film and theatre, as well as books, for *The Granta* and the *Cambridge Review*. For 1927–8, while still a student of mathematics, becomes 'Skipper' (literary editor) of *The Granta*.

June: publishes first poem at Cambridge, 'Poem about a Ball in the Nineteenth Century'; he is influenced by seventeenth-century metaphysical poetry, especially John Donne.

1928   June: Senior Optime (Upper Second) in Part II of the mathematical Tripos: a disappointing result.

October: registers for the English Tripos; tutored by I. A. Richards at Magdalene College; attends Richards's lectures on 'Practical Criticism'; begins work towards *Seven Types of Ambiguity*; becomes president of The Heretics.

November: launches avant-garde magazine, *Experiment*, co-edited with Jacob Bronowski, Humphrey Jennings, and Hugh Sykes Davies (it runs for seven issues, the last in May 1931).

1929   20 January: gives a talk at Cambridge on ambiguity in literature.

February: publishes 'Ambiguity in Shakespeare: Sonnet XVI' in *Experiment* (the essay will in due course form part of *Seven Types of Ambiguity*).

March: takes title role in *The Tragedy of Tragedies: or the Life and Death of Tom Thumb the Great* by Henry Fielding, in a production by the Cambridge Mummers.

June: gains first class with 'special distinction' in English Tripos; awarded a Magdalene college prize; elected to a Charles Kingsley Bye-Fellowship for 1929–30.

July: discovered by college porters to be in possession of contraceptives; an extraordinary meeting of the Governing Body of Magdalene College resolves to deprive Empson of his Bye-Fellowship and remove his name from the college books. Empson removes himself to 65 Marchmont Street, London, where he lives as a freelance writer for the next two years; he is cultivated by literary figures including T. S. Eliot, Virginia Woolf, Harold Monro, and Sylvia Townsend Warner.

October: *Letter IV* published by Heffer's of Cambridge. Six of the eighteen poems he has written to date feature in *Cambridge Poetry 1929*, published by Leonard and Virginia Woolf at the Hogarth Press.

November: publishes 'Some Notes on Mr Eliot' (a further preview of *Ambiguity*) in *Experiment*.

1930   November: *Seven Types of Ambiguity* published.

1931   29 August: begins three-year contract as a professor of English at Tokyo University of Literature and Science (Bunrika Daigaku); teaches also at Tokyo Imperial University.

1932   February: six poems are included in anthology, *New Signatures*, published by the Hogarth Press.

1934   *Poems*, in an edition of 100 copies, privately printed by The Fox & Daffodil Press, Kinuta-mura, near Tokyo

8 July: returns to London, where he spends the next three years as a freelance writer.

1935   May: *Poems* published in London.

October: *Some Versions of Pastoral* published.

Publishes translations into Basic English of two works by J. B. S. Haldane, *The Outlook of Science* and *Science and Well-Being*.

Gains MA, University of Cambridge.

1936   W. B. Yeats includes an Empson poem in the *Oxford Book of Modern Verse*; Michael Roberts picks six for *The Faber Book of Modern Verse*.

1937–8   August: takes up appointment at National Peking University, arriving just as the Japanese invade China; journeys through China with I. A. Richards and his wife; works with the exiled Peking universities—amalgamated as the Temporary University — from November 1937 to February 1938 on a mountain at Nan-Yueh, Hunan Province; journeys to Hong Kong.

1938–9   Continues university teaching with the National South-west Associated University in remote exile, first in the town of Mengtzu and then in Kunming, capital of Yunnan province, near the Indo-China (Vietnam) border. In the autumn of 1939, sets off to return home by way of the USA, where he spends a period in Cambridge, Mass. (broadcasting on Basic English).

1939   28 January: arrives back in England.

1940   26 June: joins the Monitoring Service of the BBC at Wood Norton Hall, near Evesham in Worcestershire, working as a sub-editor.

September: *The Gathering Storm* published in London.

1941   Transfers to the BBC Overseas Service in London, where he
        becomes a Talks Assistant and then Chinese Editor, organising
        talks to China and propaganda programmes for the Home
        Service; for two years, works alongside George Orwell.

1941   2 December: marries Hester Henrietta Crouse ('Hetta'), a South
        African artist, at St Stephen's Church, Hampstead, London.

1942   9 November: birth of first son, William Hendrik Mogador

1944   30 September: birth of second son, Jacob Arthur Calais.

1947–52 Teaches at National Peking University, his post being subsidized
        by the British Council; witnesses the civil war and the six-week
        siege of Peking late in 1948; the Communist takover and the
        inauguration of the People's Republic of China, including the
        beginnings of reform and 'thought control'.

1948   24 March: *The Collected Poems of William Empson* published in New
        York.

        July–August: teaches at Kenyon College Summer School, Gam-
        bier, Ohio, USA, on leave from Peking.

1950   Further summer visit to the Kenyon College Summer School.

1951   July: *The Structure of Complex Words* published in London.

1952   Summer: returns with family from China to England.

        15 December: *The Poems of William Empson* broadcast by BBC.

1953   October: takes up Chair of English Literature at the University
        of Sheffield, where he works for the next 18 years, with occa-
        sional sabbaticals at American and Canadian universities.

1954   May: Gresham Professor in Rhetoric, Gresham College, London,
        lecturing on 'The last Plays of Shakespeare and their Relation to
        the Elizabethan Theatre'.

        June–July: Fellow of the School of Letters, Indiana University,
        Bloomington, Indiana.

        27 October: *The Birth of Steel: A Light Masque* performed for Queen
        Elizabeth II at the University of Sheffield.

1955   29 September: *Collected Poems* published in London.

1961   February: *The Collected Poems of William Empson* (New York) issued
        in paperback.

1961   *Milton's God* published.

        William Empson Reading Selected Poems (*Listen* LPV3) issued.

1964   Autumn: Visiting Professor, English Department, University of
        Ghana, Legon, Accra, Ghana.

1968   Hon. D. Litt, University of East Anglia, Norwich.

        Ingram Merrill Foundation Award.

June–August: Visiting Professor, Department of English, State University of New York at Buffalo.

1971 Hon. D. Litt, University of Bristol

Summer: retires from University of Sheffield.

1972 January–February: gives Waynflete Lectures on 'The editorial choice of the text of a poem', at Magdalen College, Oxford.

Publishes *Coleridge's Verse: A Selection* (with David B. Pirie).

1973 Visiting Professor, York University, Toronto

1974 Lent Term: delivers Clark Lectures at Trinity College, Cambridge, on 'The Progress of Criticism'.

Hon. D. Litt., University of Sheffield.

Honorary member of the American Academy of Arts and Letters/The National Institute of Arts and Letters.

1974–5 Visiting Professor of English, Pennsylvania State University.

1976 Autumn: Visiting Professor, Department of English, University of Delaware, Newark, Delaware.

Fellow of the British Academy.

Honorary Fellow of the Modern Language Association of America.

1977 10 June: Hon. Litt. D., University of Cambridge.

1979 Knighted in New Year Honours for 'services to English literature'.

Elected Honorary Fellow, Magdalene College, Cambridge.

1982 January–April: Visiting Professor, University of Miami.

1984 15 April: dies in London.

Collected Poems reissued; *Using Biography* published.

1986 *The Royal Beasts and Other Works* and *Essays on Shakespeare* published.

1987 *Argufying: Essays on Literature and Culture* and *Faustus and the Censor: The English Faust-Book and Marlowe's 'Doctor Faustus'* published.

1993 *Essays on Renaissance Literature*, vol. 1: *Donne and the new astronomy*.

1994 *Essays on Renaissance Literature*, vol. 2: *The Drama*.

1996 *The Strengths of Shakespeare's Shrew: Essays, Memoirs and Reviews*.

2000 *Complete Poems of William Empson*

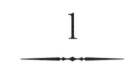

Introduction

Somebody had poor Julian Bell's great gushing Life and Letters
[*Essays, Poems and Letters* (London: The Hogarth Press, 1938)], it
would have offended him rather I think. But my word how he did
write letters. And what is this business of keeping letters? Do *you* keep
letters? It must be a widespread practice judging from biographies.
Rather an ugly one I think. It certainly couldn't be done in my
mother's house, where any writing left about (including two complete
plays of mine some time ago) gets immediately destroyed. Very
properly too, as I feel even when it turns out inconvenient. Do you
suppose for instance that all your correspondents are saving up the
letters for the life and letters? And do they get *paid* for this rather eerie
and passive piece of work? How unexpected people are. But perhaps
Julian's lot were more likely to do that kind of thing. Darwin
I remember, though, a different kind of man, said it had been a
great help to him never to destroy a single letter. By the way, what
on earth was the disease of Darwin? Was it simply neurotic? They
never say, and he seems a very unneurotic man otherwise.[1]

THESE amusingly high-minded observations by William Empson,
written to his friend John Hayward on 4 May 1939 (when he was
32), are at first glance disconcerting to his biographer. Surely no decent
person would deliberately save up anyone else's letters? It is hard enough
to keep tabs on one's own papers. The practice seems so distasteful that
only a base and perhaps even venal motive could underlie it. Maybe only
'Julian's lot'—a side glance at the Bloomsbury Group—could be quite so
egocentric and self-important as to indulge themselves in such an 'ugly' but
'widespread practice'. The phrasing makes it seem like a form of perfectly
horrid self-abuse. Yet the essential balance of Empson's feelings on the

matter, and his ambiguity of mind, emerge in the concluding remarks, where any whiff of priggishness is set aside in favour of hero-worship and direct human interest. The instinct for biographical enquiry proves irresistible. If the great Darwin preserved his correspondence, maybe there is after all much to be said for this unsavoury habit—and come to think of it, was Darwin 'simply neurotic'? It would be really interesting to know, but why has nobody told us the answer?

In truth, Empson dearly loved biographical enquiry; his own critical writings are rich with it. Whether he was investigating Shakespeare or Donne or George Herbert, or Rochester or Coleridge or Lewis Carroll, or even his much-admired contemporary Dylan Thomas, he invariably found himself working to situate the work in the context of the life, and to spell out all the human truths, and the conflicts, at the heart of the complex construct that is the work of literature. For him, the art and the life were not to be told apart, even if some of his own critics thought he was often tearing apart the pure, expressive, unanalysable beauty of a poem: reducing aesthetics to mechanics. It is therefore surprising, and ironic, that he has so often been regarded—and is still sometimes held up—as the founding father of what the American critic John Crowe Ransom was to christen the 'New Criticism': the critical theory which reckons that a work of literature is exclusively self-dependent, and not to be analysed in relation to the author's life and times, ideology, or intentions. The insistence upon the semantic autonomy of the text, treating the literary object as a self-enclosed or organic system of signs, was a theoretical notion which Empson dismissed as the 'print-centred or tea-tasting outlook'.[2] When in *Seven Types of Ambiguity* (1930) he analysed Herbert's 'The Sacrifice', for instance, he aimed to comprehend the poem as a site of live conflict between Christian doctrine and human judgement. The poem was not an academic toy, it was a 'machine' for struggling with a genuine moral issue; and the object of the analysis was 'to show the modes of action of poetical effect'.[3] Looking back in 1955, he was to maintain: 'if the poem was good, and if I could go at it the way I wanted to, nothing in the poem at all would be irrelevant by the time the critic had finished explaining it. I still think this a proper objective... To say that you won't be bothered with anything but the words on the page (and that you are within your rights, because the author didn't *intend* you to have any more) strikes me as petulant, like saying "of course I won't visit him unless he has first-class plumbing." If you cared enough you would. For one thing, you might want to know whether the author has really had the experience he describes...'[4] Indeed, it was in defiance of almost every modern critical theory—including New Criticism, Deconstruction, the death of the author, and the 'privileging' of the reader—that he gave the final volume he was to put together (it came out soon after his death in 1984) the knowingly provocative title *Using Biography*.

Like many academics of my generation, I was turned on to the idea of literary criticism in large part because of the prodigious discriminations laid out with such amplitude in *Seven Types of Ambiguity*, which I first read at school. A word, a phrase, a sentence, need not denote simply a singular idea, I learned: they were multiple in connotation and combination, fashioning (as it seemed) illimitable meanings—whether by design or serendipity, I did not then mind. In a great poem, semantics and syntax perform together, and layer meanings and implications; they comprise feelings, ideas, and attitudes under maximum and even explosive pressure. What Empson did with a poem showed unprecedented perspicacity; before the appearance of *Ambiguity* in 1930, no critic had ever written with such wooing detail of the effects of language, such searching and imaginative analysis, such sustained subtlety and insight. And in the beginning, his ability to discern and adjudicate scales of ambiguity gave a number of critics a great big shock. They reacted as if he had somehow violated the magical or quasi-mystical character of the work of literature: the thing of beauty, they feared, would no longer be a joy forever. Even Empson's mentor, I. A. Richards—who favoured feeling over thinking—employed a peculiarly ambiguous trope when he came to put on record, in a Festschrift (1974), his own equivocal appreciation of Empson's achievement: 'Long ago, when a bound copy of *Seven Types* first reached me (in Peking, it was) I used to press it on likely readers with this recommendation: "It will make you feel you are having a lovely go of influenza—high-fever fireworks, you know." '[5] Empson's work seemed to him so heady, so dizzying, he chose to liken the effect of reading it to feeling ill: it was in every sense faint praise.

Most contemporary critics admired the intellectual ingenuity and agility of the book, along with its capriciousness and an impiety that were yet disconcerting. All the same, it took about a decade, into the 1940s, for this revolutionary novelty to be fully relished and built upon—though the most elaborate recognition was to take place in the USA rather than in the UK. Kingsley Amis, for instance, was to recall in 1987 that at Oxford during the Second World War everybody seemed to be reading just two specific works of criticism: either *The Allegory of Love*, by C. S. Lewis, or else *Seven Types of Ambiguity*. 'I was in as deep as any; I went so far as to steal the Oxford Union library's copy of *Seven Types*, as the cognoscenti called it.

(It was out of print at the time [because of paper rationing], which I suppose both aggravates and extenuates the offence.) The feeling of illumination it gave, of helping you to see things in poetry you had had no idea were there—10 different reasons why Shakespeare's "bare ruined choirs" in Sonnet 73 was an appropriate phrase—is hard to recapture now...'[6] Likewise, Barbara Hardy recalled in 1982 (in a periodical series, 'The Critics Who Made Us'): 'what I remember most clearly, from student days at University College, London, in the 1940s, is first looking into *Seven Types of Ambiguity*. My sense of discovery and delight has not diminished over the years.' She went on:

In *Seven Types of Ambiguity* I found analysis—persistent, thorough, minute, clever, responsive, self-conscious, lucid, undogmatic, affective. It was exciting about literature, and it was exciting as literature. It was amusing, amused by itself. It was not closet criticism, but was written from an awareness of science, politics, psychology, and sex. It was ironic and sceptical. It had individuality of temperament, tone, and feeling.

Overcoming her apparently unqualified initial enthusiasm, she reflected further—and with a good deal of justice:

There was another important aspect of my response—disagreement. I had disagreed before, but not with anyone whose work I so admired. Empson seemed at times dangerously charming but flippant. I distrusted and enjoyed his levity... And at times he was unconvincing, even silly. He pursued nuance, implication, irony, and complexity beyond the bounds of critical common sense...

In sum, she remarked:

Empson provided that best stimulus, something to admire and something to question. He was alive, impassioned, and surprising, as he reminded us that literature is the product of individuality, intellect, and passion.[7]

In 1930, Empson was often taken to be almost too clever for his own good, an intellectual virtuoso who had the knack of balancing umpteen ambiguities on the pin of a word or a phrase, a point of lexis or a turn of grammar. He seemed so clever, in fact, he scarcely had time for evaluative judgements or moral reflections; certainly no room for spiritual convictions. What delighted his readers were his lightning glosses, his capacity to solve semantic and grammatical posers, to spin out the answers to poetic puzzles. Moreover, his engaging, witty personality was never in doubt. Throughout his career, in fact, there is the presence in his books of the great entertainer lavishly broadcasting as many scintillating jokes as sparkling critical jewels. In 1991, Professor Jonathan Bate was to assert a brave claim which is in fact irrefutably the case: 'Johnson, Hazlitt and Empson are the greatest English critics of their respective centuries not least because they are the funniest.'[8] No other critic of the century could match the spiritedness of his intelligence.

Yet underpinning the bravura critical analyses, and the stylistic sprezzatura, there was at all times a profoundly serious purposiveness which has not been reckoned with by Empson's critics as fully as it should be. As Professor Hardy discerned, there is an extraordinary passion to his work. Others appreciated it also: W. H. Auden, for instance, was to remark, in the late 1940s, that Empson 'really feels deeply about poetry...The man writes with such genuine passion for the books he's discussing.'[9] That passion for the poetry is apparent to anyone who takes the true measure of Empson's criticism, though it is surprising how often he has been accused of being a pure intellectual (whatever that might mean), so cerebral as to be virtually unemotional. But there is still more: above all else, there is an absolute and passionate emphasis in Empson's work on terms of opposition. Among the key terms throughout his critical writings are clash, conflict, contradiction, subplot, outsider, scapegoat, resistance, hidden, secret, dissent, isolation. For Empson, it is axiomatic that the writer is at odds with his society, and with official doctrine: the writer is at root the critic. The qualities he salutes most passionately of all are the independent intelligence and the covert judgement.

His critical career has popularly been reckoned to fall into roughly two halves, the first ending with *The Structure of Complex Words* (1951), the second appearing to forsake semantic interests in favour of chastising the aberrant morality of what he styled the 'Neo-Christian' school of critics. Even Empson felt that after writing three books covering the subject of literary ambiguity—*Seven Types of Ambiguity* (1930), *Some Versions of Pastoral* (1935), and *The Structure of Complex Words* (1951)—he had shifted ground in the post-war years from linguistics to ethics. 'There is in my later work what may look like a failure, I now see,' he wrote to Roger Sale,

in my practically giving up Ambiguity as a method of exegesis. I had better have explained myself there. Reviewers were telling me, as soon as *Ambiguity* came out, that not all poetry was ambiguous, and I could see that the method worked best where the authors had had some impulse or need for the process; but, as it had become my line, I went on slogging at it for two more books. Then I thought I had given a rounded view of the subject, and unless challenged to debate had no need to go on about it.[10]

However, just as many reviewers felt vexed by his practice of distilling the multiple meanings of poetry—the 'possible alternative reactions' to be derived from 'the full intention' of a poem[11]—so many were equally disconcerted when in *Some Versions of Pastoral* he discussed complete texts in terms not only of psychology but also of social relationships. In good poetry, he later stipulated, 'there is always an appeal to a background of human experience which is all the more present when it cannot be named'.[12] Thus his progression from types of ambiguity to versions of pastoral was far less the radical shift that contemporary readers suspected, more a natural development—since the pastoral convention operates like ambiguity against 'a background of conflict'. Pastoral functions as a critique—a mode of scepticism, independence of judgement, and even subversion—as much as it balances the conflicts within society. Where a poem is ambiguous in meaning because it externalizes the conflicts of the individual, pastoral likewise embraces the 'commotion' of social opposition within the 'calm' of its form. In *Some Versions of Pastoral* he therefore laid down this truth: 'the artist never is at one with any public.'[13]

The test cases of Empson's novel critical approach were his surprising, indeed shocking, analyses of Hopkins's 'The Windhover' and Herbert's 'The Sacrifice', where he argued that the authors had felt obliged to confront rather than to accommodate themselves to the comforting but pernicious paradoxes of Christian doctrine. That is to say, *Seven Types of Ambiguity* not only inaugurated a mode of submitting imaginative literature to the test of the discursive reason, it also culminated with two analyses that challenged Christian doctrine. In 1963, he reiterated:

I put 'The Sacrifice' last of the examples in my book, to stand for the most extreme kind of ambiguity, because it presents Jesus as at the same time forgiving his torturers and condemning them to eternal torture. It strikes me now that my attitude was what I have come to call 'neo-Christian'; happy to find such an extravagant specimen, I slapped the author on the back and egged him on to be even nastier...Clearer now about what the light illuminates, I am keen to stumble away from it.[14]

'It was in the air of Herbert's time that the paradoxes of Christianity were a moral embarrassment,' he commented.

Empson ultimately acquired massive publicity for his views on the wickedness of the Christian religion when he published *Milton's God* (1961), with his thesis essentially following in the footsteps of Voltaire, Samuel Butler, Gibbon, Buckle, and J. M. Robertson. The crux of his argument he left in no doubt at all, though subsequent critical misapprehensions forced him to repeat it again and again, as in this letter from 1967: 'Shelley found it plain that, the more he reverenced the Son who endured, the more he must execrate the Father who was satisfied by his pain.'[15] The snag in his approach, which certainly gave some reviewers the opportunity to scoff at the book, lay in the very fact that he confronted the Christian God through a work of literary imagination, on the questionable assumption that Milton's version of God could be identified with the 'truth' of the Gospel. Whereas C. S. Lewis, in *A Preface to 'Paradise Lost'* (1942), had persuasively argued for the orthodoxy of Milton's theology, other critics found poem and doctrine incommensurable and reasonably jibbed at Empson's evident equation. *Milton's God* thus contrived to run up against an unforeseeable but perhaps unsurmountable irony: that, as one notice deftly put it, 'Empson's every insult to God should prove a compliment to Milton'.[16] By arguing that Christianity was radically incoherent and morally ugly, Empson praised Milton for outstaring the embarrassments of the myth in poetry that was all the more brilliant because unblinking. Professor John Bayley discriminated the central irony of Empson's approach when he observed: 'Unlike most critics, Lewis and Empson make a steadfast claim for Milton's complete moral coherence.'[17] The 'obstacles to grasping' the power of the poem, Empson wrote later, 'come from the basic fallacies of the Christian religion, or indeed the whole previous cult of human sacrifice.'[18] And again: 'I am such an old academic that I agree with Blake and Shelley . . . I think the main points which have been found bad about *Paradise Lost* are precisely what made it so good, because they amount to a profound analysis of what is fundamentally wrong with the Christian God.'

In *Ambiguity* he addressed 'the class of readers' who agreed with him about 'certain effects' in poetry; not perceiving himself as a polemicist, he simply practised the close reading of literature in terms of what he considered 'depth psychology'. In his later years he resolved to reconstruct any and every kind of literary student—the mass of misreaders—for 'the intentions of the authors [they read],' he insisted in another letter, 'were very unlikely to be so nasty as those of your many-legged neo-Christian torture-worshippers.'[19]

Thus not only did Empson achieve the main feat of inventing modern literary criticism in English, he acted too as a cultural fifth-columnist, bravely and pig-headedly (some would say pixilatedly) challenging received doctrine in life and literature. 'It is a very good thing for a poet, one might say the ideal, to be saying something which is considered very shocking at the time,' he once pronounced in a letter.[20] That is surely true of his own work as a critic—he was intent upon the idea 'that a piece of writing which excited moral resistance might be a discovery in morals, a means of learning what was wrong with the existing system...'[21]—and much the same might be said of his own poems. The imaginative issues of his poetry were stirred by the human implications of modern science—astrophysics, biology, botany, chemistry, entomology, evolutionism, anthropology, and psychology. A poet abreast of his age, he avidly devoured the literature of the new science. In a letter to a Chinese acquaintance written in 1947 (at a time when he had virtually stopped writing his poetry), he would look back with wonder:

The point where I most disagree with you is about science. I should have thought that the present age had very little to boast about in any form of imaginative work except the scientific one, and it is obvious that a physicist like Einstein or Eddington is making superb uses of the imagination. A critic who cuts himself off from the only fertile part of the contemporary mind is I think unlikely to understand what good work feels like when it is new, and as far as my own work is concerned anyway I am sure I have always found the world-picture of the scientists much more stimulating and useable than that of any 'literary influence'.[22]

His apprehension of the place of the sciences in the modern world charged his poetry (according to his friend Kathleen Raine) with distressing questions about the way in which man tries 'to impose order on fields of knowledge and experience so contradictory as to threaten the mind that contains them with disorder—the compulsion, as Empson writes, to "learn a style from a despair" '.[23] The imagination he brought to the 1920s and 1930s 'had to adjust itself to a new scientific world-view at once alarming and inspiring,' Raine recalled. In the conviction that enormous shifts in scientific knowledge of the physical world must radically challenge received ethics, Empson treated the conflict in a spirit of painful perplexity. Like E. M. Forster when he worried that 'the post-war world of the '20s would not add up into sense,'[24] he took to his troubled heart the contradictions of his age. The big issue, in poetry as in life, was that science does not readily or even necessarily accommodate itself to human culture, ideas, or ethical structures: 'life involves maintaining oneself between contradictions that can't be solved by analysis,' as he famously said in his notes to the poem 'Bacchus'.

Empson never made very high claims for his poetry—he once called it 'too specialised'[25]—but his best poems (he remarked in an interview) are 'complicated in the way that life really is'.[26] Critics have from time to time accused Empson the poet—just as they accused Empson the critic—of being over-intellectualized, of compiling crossword-puzzle poems of such a brainy order that they seem virtually divorced from true lyric feeling. In fact, much of the poetry is driven by such emotions as fear and courage, and Empson went on record, in a published interview, to say that several of the poems he wrote at Cambridge were about 'boy being afraid of girl, as usual'; he stated elsewhere too that his poems came out of great 'isolation and suffering'. I have taken it as my brief as biographer to try to identify and understand both the intellectual passions and the emotional energies that inspired the poems; among them, his struggle with the dilemma of his sexual orientation, which meant that sometimes in the 1920s and 1930s he wrote 'girl' instead of 'boy'. In any case, intellectual passions are also matters of intense personal feeling. T. S. Eliot showed great discernment when he responded to a letter from A. L. Rowse carping at Empson's poetry, not with a tacit connivance at Rowse's view but with a tribute to the emotional tribulation that provoked the poetry:

I don't think I at all agree with you about Empson: I don't think that his tiresome metaphysicality (which I think, moreover, he is growing out of) is just 'cerebral' or due to a desire to impress with cleverness, but that it springs from a peculiarly twisted and tormented, but very painfully suffering soul. One can only guess.[27]

It is the biographer's business to attempt to resolve some of that guesswork.

Empson retired from Sheffield University in 1971; I arrived as a junior lecturer only in 1975. Thus I never enjoyed the privilege of working alongside him, though I can recall feeling bucked by the knowledge that this was the very place which had employed Empson: the man whom the late John Wain had justifiably called 'the finest literary critic the English-speaking world has had in our century'. In fact, I first met up with Empson only in the late 1970s, though I recall having been present at a poetry reading by him at Trinity College, Dublin, in the 1960s. (Unfortunately, he had caused great restlessness among his audience by mumbling and stumbling throughout his reading, to a point when a woman cried out with exasperation from the back of the hall, 'Speak up, you silly old fool!' Whole rows of necks shrank into their shoulders with the embarrassment of it all, though later I was tipped off that the outspoken woman had been Empson's wife—so that was all right.)

At Sheffield I would occasionally pick up stories about the eccentric Empson. One of the first remarks that came to my notice, I remember, was that he rode around on a red post office bicycle (his wife Hetta, who had preferred to live in London, I was told, would visit him driving a former ambulance). Before the age of the zip, and for want of a seamstress, he was often obliged to secure his flies with one or two safety pins. 'I am a proud man, but, good heavens,' he was said to have remarked, 'I'm not a vain man—vanity is silly.' He lived in an insanitary basement room (it became universally known as 'Empson's Burrow'), which contained just an iron bed (never blessed with sheets, only blankets), a table, one source of light, and a 14-inch electric fire; his usual tipple was guinness-and-gin, or Bloody Marys decanted from a medicine bottle. When he felt he really needed a bath, he would visit his colleague Francis Berry's desirable residence nearby. When invited to dinner by another colleague, he responded, 'No, to tell the truth, I don't like your wife's cooking'—adding, to soften the blow: 'Come to think of it, I don't like my wife's cooking either.' Although he could occasionally seem haughty and unnervingly candid, I was given to understand, he was in fact a man of modest kindliness, even quite shy, and with a childlike gentleness; only truly combative in his literary and ethical disputes with the likes of F. R. Leavis, T. S. Eliot, and Dame Helen Gardner.

His critical brilliance, his oblivious eccentricity, and his generosity won him esteem and affection. So did his humane instincts. During Faculty meetings he would often lose himself in doodling mathematical puzzles ('Doing sums,' he once explained, 'is a good substitute for masturbation'). At one meeting, however, when the Psychology Department brought forth a proposal for 'the devising of a system for the measurement of fear', Empson instantly queried: 'Is it intended that there should be laboratory experiments on animals or human beings?' (After very little further discussion, the proposal was put by.) His students and colleagues delighted in his literary acumen and his conversational asides, whether they took the form of a remark such as that the poet Hopkins was 'a gloomy Jesuit' or of the comment: 'We'd be mad to join the Common Market. Underneath us the ground is constipated with coal.' (He was not so quick to see the joke when a student audience at Kenyon College guffawed at his observation that the figures in Keats's 'Ode on a Grecian Urn' were 'glued to the pot'.)

But I think it was only after a few years of gathering occasional gossip at Sheffield that I suddenly became convinced I might write a biography of Empson; specifically, that is, when I came across, in the Festschrift for Empson, a parenthetical remark by I. A. Richards about the inspiring teacher and scholar-gipsy who had become, to coin a phrase, a legend in his own lifetime:

Would that somebody could tell adequately what Empson did through his long years in Peking! I saw enough to know but not enough to give any account. A man who can teach *Songs & Sonnets*, reassembling a text out of his head, does more than we easily realize for passionate young students of poetry.[28]

Indeed, not only was Empson a literary genius, I was presently to discover, he had also been quite an eccentric adventurer. I received his permission to start collecting materials towards a biography sometime in 1982, but it was only in March 1984 that I seriously embarked on my quest for Empson, when I set off for a few weeks to hunt down his quondam colleagues and students in China and Japan. 'I think I can only really help you when I'm dead,' Empson had once disconcertingly said to me (probably after I had hinted that there might be papers of use to me at the back of his drawers; understandably, he resisted the idea of digging about for mislaid old letters—he still had essays to get written or rewritten, he used to say, so anything else would have to wait).

His public life took him through many of the major political events of the modern world—the rise of imperialism in Japan, the Sino-Japanese war in China, wartime propaganda for the BBC, and the Chinese civil war and Communist takeover of Peking in 1949—and his friends, acquaintances, and critical sparring partners included I. A. Richards, J. B. S Haldane, Humphrey Jennings, George Orwell, John Crowe Ransom, Robert Lowell, and T. S. Eliot.

Not only was he one of the few great poet-critics to have true personal charisma, he was a man of astounding energy and curiosity, and a genuine eccentric who remained imperturbable in the face of all the extraordinary and even alarming things that would happen to him. The discovery of contraceptives in his possession by a prying bedmaker at Magdalene College, Cambridge, led to his being robbed of a promised Fellowship. Yet *Seven Types of Ambiguity*, drafted in part while he was still an under-graduate, transformed English literary criticism and brought him world-wide fame.

In 1931, at the age of 25, he became a lecturer in English at Tokyo University of Literature and Science, where he worked for three years in an ethos of perniciously developing nationalism: 'one feels the popular jingoism and official militarism like a weight on the back of the neck,' he observed.

In 1937 he went East again, to teach at Peking National University, where he arrived on a Japanese troop-train. He found himself in the thick of the Sino-Japanese war, refugeeing with the northern universities and enduring two years of what he described as 'the savage life and the fleas and the bombs'. He was in fact the only European to share the academic exodus with the Chinese academics, and stoically survived a poor diet, primitive living quarters, and even a personal assault by bandits in remote south-west China. Since there were no books for his students to study, he did indeed manage (as Richards later remarked) the feat of teaching his courses pretty much from memory, and his students—many of whom subsequently attained high positions in the People's Republic of China—revered him. He also gained a high-mettled status in the Chinese classical tradition of inebriated poets.

During the Second World War he went to work for the BBC, progressing by way of the Monitoring Department and what he himself styled the 'Liars' School' to become Chinese Editor, where he exhausted himself in the effort to maintain both shortwave radio broadcasts to China and propaganda features for the home audience. The effectiveness of his work for the BBC (where his friends included George Orwell) provoked the Nazi propagandist Hans Fritzsche to dub him a 'curly-headed Jew'.

Having acquired a wife and family, he returned to Peking in 1947; there he found himself caught up in the Communist siege of the city—he even crossed the fighting lines to deliver his weekly lecture on Shakespeare at a university outside the city walls—and he witnessed Mao Tse-tung's triumphant entry and the inaugural ceremonies of the People's Republic of China. 'I was there for the honeymoon between the universities and the communists,' he was to recall; 'we were being kept up to the mark rather firmly.' He left Peking in 1952, having witnessed the first stages of the so-called 'Thought Reform'—what he was later to describe as 'the dragooning of independent thought and the hysteria of the confession meetings'.

From 1953 he held the Chair of English Literature at Sheffield, where he involved himself more vigorously than ever before in public controversy, being spurred on by his desire to correct what he thought the wrongheaded orthodoxies of modern literary criticism. A reluctant metacritic, Empson nonetheless tackled the follies of his fellows with tremendous vigour, and gave them a thorough drubbing on various issues of principle and practice such as 'the cluster of Imagist beliefs', the Fallacy of Intentionalism, and 'neo-Christian' literary criticism. 'I was considered a bold appointment,' he acknowledged (with considerable ironical understatement) when he retired.

'It is of great importance now that writers and other artists should try to keep a certain worldmindedness,' he believed. 'Without the literatures you cannot have a sense of history...and nowadays we very much need the balancing-pole of not national but world history.' His own world-mindedness (strengthened by his sojourns in the Far East), and his passionate humanism, wit, and wisdom are fully in evidence in the story of his life. But perhaps one statement by Empson has impressed me above all else as I have lived with his life and work over the past many years; it seems to me so true of the man and his career that I think of it as a motto for his literary and cultural endeavours:

To become morally independent of one's formative society...is the grandest theme of all literature, because it is the only means of moral progress, the establishment of some higher ethical concept.[29]

It can be seen to begin with a rebellion against his own heritage and class.

2

In the Blood: Sir Richard Empson, Professor William, and John Henry

History is a record of the vicissitudes & the uncertainty of human affairs & of human Life. Often too the history of a Private family during a few years proves the same Position, as I have said is the case with Kingdoms.

The Revd John Empson to his son, John William,
27/8 October 1836[1]

WHEN the Reverend John Empson (1787–1861)—best known as the famous 'Flying Parson', because of his insatiable and nerveless passion for hunting—set himself to compose some verses to grace a memorial to his parents, he very slightly adapted a pair of couplets from William Cowper's poem 'On the Receipt of My Mother's Picture' (1790). The resulting tribute might have amused the most literary of his descendants with its unwonted ambiguity:

> Our boast is not that we deduce our birth
> From loins enthron'd, and rulers of the earth:
> But higher far our proud pretensions rise
> The sons of parents passed into the skies.[2]

What the Revd John was trying to convey was the faith that his clergyman father and his mother must have been assumed as saints into heaven; what he actually produced was a combination of bathos and spiritual swank.

There was a long-standing tradition of churchmanship in the family that would give small joy to the vehemently anti-Christian William Empson, the youngest of the Revd John's great-grandchildren. But there is actually little evidence to suggest that Empson took much interest in his churchy, landowning forebears. Being out of step with his squarsonical ancestry, he never, or at least never deliberately, traded on his place in English society. In any event, as the youngest of the five children of ageing parents, he stood to gain little from the family's territorial inheritance even if he had embraced its *mores* and convictions. So he was not given to flourishing the laurels of his lineage; and to that degree at least he was not dissimilar to the Flying Parson, who had written to his parents in 1832: 'To make antiquity of family a subject of Pride is ridiculous; to make it a topic of interesting research is allowable.'[3]

Equally, William Empson was not ungrateful for the fact that, as he put it in his later years, he had been given the right ticket in life. While not showing a trace of snobbery in his personal dealings, he always spoke, in person and on the page, with the unemphatic authority of the patrician voice; and he was capable of deploying in his literary criticism the odd personal anecdote which gives certain evidence of a comfortable patrimony—or in this case, as prompted by W. B. Yeats's poem 'Byzantium', his matrimony:

When I was small (born 1906) I was sometimes taken to visit a venerable great-aunt, and after tea she would bring out exquisitely preserved toys of an antiquity rivalling her own. Chief among them was the bird of Yeats in its great cage, wound up to sing by a massive key; a darkish green tree, as I remember, occupied most of the cage, and a quite small shimmering bird, whose beak would open and shut while the musical box in the basement was playing, perched carelessly upon a branch at one side. The whole affair glittered, but I cannot claim to have seen the Golden Bough; it was prettier than a gilt tree would have been; and of course the bird was not plumb on top of it, like Satan in Paradise. I remember being struck to hear my mother say, by way of praising the great age of the toy, that she remembered being shown it herself when she was a child after such a tea; and she and Yeats were born in the same year, 1865. I can raise no visual memory of the ones Queen Victoria presented to the Empress Dowager of China, which were on view in the Summer Palace [in Peking in the late 1940s] (the Communists preferred to show other treasures after a bit), but I remember thinking they were just like Aunt Lizzie's, only plastered with semi-precious stones. Considering the date (1873), when the Empress first sent an envoy to London, hers and Aunt Lizzie's and Yeats's were probably all made by the same firm.[4]

The background to such remarks is a world of gentility and privilege, a social order that Empson first took for granted and then turned away from.

A good deal is known about Empson's remarkable ancestors, including one, Richard the Roundhead (familiarly known as 'Stiff Dick'), who fought on the opposing side to his brother in the English Civil War. Another, Cornelius, was a friend of William Penn and established for himself a sizeable portion of territory in Pennsylvania. Such remote ancestors have no immediate bearing on the background and pedigree of William Empson, though their stories are rich and entertaining (see Appendix). Yet there is one piece of folklore that greatly amused him. Legend has it—and Empson liked to claim it during his schooldays[5]—that the family may be descended from the man who made their name notorious: Sir Richard Empson, the putatively wicked minister of Henry VII. Indeed, such was Sir Richard's reputation for infamy that no one even cared very much to try to sort out the facts and falsehoods of his career until as late as 1982—more than 470 years after his execution. Born in about 1450, the son of a gentleman of Towcester in Northamptonshire, Richard Empson successfully, and profitably, practised law and became a Justice of the Peace. In 1478 he was appointed to the office of attorney-general for the duchy of Lancaster, though he fell into inexplicable disfavour under the last Yorkist monarch (when he was even referred to as the 'late' attorney-general). But three weeks after the battle of Bosworth Field he enjoyed a fresh start under Henry Tudor and was again appointed attorney-general for Lancaster. He represented Northamptonshire in parliament from 1489 to 1504; in 1491 he was made Speaker of the House of Commons; and in 1505 he was finally selected by the king as chancellor of the duchy of Lancaster. He was also a central participant in the 'council learned in the law', a group of royal officers of state who held proceedings to determine suits involving the laws of the realm and the rights of the king.

His legendary ruthlessness, as retailed with acid prejudice by the chroniclers, arose from his zeal as royal debt collector and as an associate of Edmund Dudley (who was far more of a knave than he was). Mark R. Horovitz explains: 'A major responsibility pursued by Empson and his colleagues during the last years of Henry VII's reign involved the taking and prosecuting of written obligations, or bonds—legal instruments utilized by the law courts and the various departments of state. These "writings obligatory" placed a person in a legally constituted debt, be it for money, allegiance, the payment of farms and customs duties or the promise of good behaviour ("good abearing").' Empson's crime, if such it was, was extortion, or unscrupulous strictness, but nothing truly treasonable. 'Trained in the administration of the duchy of Lancaster, eager to follow the prosecution of the law as attorney-general and a member of the various conciliar courts, Empson's triumph as a leading Tudor minister was also the culmination of twenty years of expedient royal policy for ruling England.'

Within two days of the accession of Henry VIII, Empson and Dudley were arrested for treason. Separately arraigned, they were condemned to death, and presently hanged, drawn, and quartered on Tower Hill on 17 August 1510. 'That the names Dudley and Empson became convenient clichés for heavy exactions and legal chicanery is exemplified in a passage by Jonathan Swift [in "An Argument against Abolishing Christianity" (1708)]: "What if there be an old dormant Statute or two against [a man]? Are they not now obsolete to a Degree, that *Empson* and *Dudley* themselves, if they were now alive, would find it impossible to put them in Execution??" ' As the annalists noted with satisfaction too, 'Many opprobrious Rhimes were made in despite of Empson & Dudley &c.'[6] But Sir Richard Empson's biographer sums up his career in an indulgent or at least more tactful vein: 'It was perhaps the driving force in his life to make the laws of England profitable for his monarch. When Henry VII was dead and the cry for justice rang forth, all the loyalty and sedulity of a Tudor minister were of little profit to Richard Empson.'[7]

The name of Empson has resounded down the ages as a byword for avarice and cruelty. And so indeed the name came to be known to William Empson. Even Dylan Thomas shared the tease when in 1940 he came to assemble (with John Davenport) his modern dunciad, *The Death of the King's Canary*, by purporting to conceal the identity of his friend, whose poetry is mocked in the verse 'Request to Leda', behind the other dread name of Dudley.[8]

It is a paradoxically glamorous fancy to imagine oneself descended from a fabled villain. In the case of the Empsons' claim to descend from the wicked Sir Richard, it seems likely to be far more of a fancy than a fact. While Sir Richard was survived by two sons (the elder, Thomas, petitioned the King for the restoration of his father's estates, and his suit was granted by act of parliament 4. Hen. VIII) and three daughters, it is still necessary for us to admit at once, on the authority of the Windsor Herald, that Sir Richard Empson's family died out in the male line, leaving only heiresses, in the sixteenth century. (All the same, this elimination could have been fabricated, since sixteenth-century officers of arms were quite as skilled at scotching a family line as at moving people in the other direction.) Notwithstanding, it remains possible that the Yorkshire branch of the family is of collateral descent. In the family papers there is an incomplete and unsigned memorandum (written by 1856 at the latest) which puts on record the supposed connection in such a simple and seemingly disinterested fashion that it is tempting to credit the document as a piece of authentic oral history (for all that it includes several errors of fact) and not merely as a doctored family myth:

Sr. Richard Empson Prime Minister to King Henry 7th was born at Shinkley in Essington Ward in the County of Durham, he was a man of great parts and knighted by King Henry the 7th and made one of his Prime Ministers of State and Lord Dudley the other. They were both beheaded by King Henry the 8th when he came to the Crown.

Sr. Richard's son or grandson settled at Gowle Hall near Snayth in Yorkshire. There was George and Richard of this Family both of Gowle Brothers and in the Civil Wars George was engaged for King Charles the 1st and Richard (commonly called Stiff Dick) was engaged for the Parliament, so that there was a mortal hatred between them.

Still, the gap between the paragraphs quoted clearly betrays a missing link.

The second of the brothers of the Reverend John Empson (alias the Flying Parson) may very well be a crucial person in this story—and not only because he was prominent in the literary life of the nineteenth century, as a contributor to, and third editor of, the *Edinburgh Review*. Born in 1789, William Empson went to school at Winchester, where he became an intimate friend of Thomas Arnold, the future headmaster of Rugby (throughout life he ardently supported Arnold's literary, educational, and ecclesiastical views), and at Trinity College, Cambridge, where he commenced BA in 1812 and MA in 1815. He was called to the Bar by Lincoln's Inn, and until 1824 practised on the Midland circuit and Lincolnshire sessions, where he became friends with Thomas Denman (the future Lord Chief Justice) and his fellow Yorkshireman and Cambridge contemporary, William Wrightson, who was later MP successively for East Retford, Hull, and Northallerton (and notably author of the Corn Laws in 1843). He began to contribute to the *Edinburgh Review* in 1823, when Francis Jeffrey, afterwards his father-in-law, was still editor. Between that date and his death in 1852 he produced more than sixty substantial articles (some readers considered them flowery and long-winded: Thomas Carlyle and the testy Lord Brougham thought him a bad imitator of T. B. Macaulay)[9] on a multiplicity of subjects including the Alien Act, the condition of the poorer classes, negro slavery, domestic politics, poetry and biography, and literary topics in general. With Macaulay (who 'looked like a battering-ram,' said one of Empson's students in 1824),[10] Empson was a member of the first committee of the Anti-Slavery Society in 1823. 'Under whatever formal sanction a property in man may be legally instituted,' he avowed, 'it can never stand on that original and continuous moral right, which sanctifies a property in things.' By 1827 he was secretary to the African Institution. In 1843 he wrote a sympathetic assessment of Jeremy Bentham; and the next year a full-hearted memorial essay on Thomas Arnold. 'I do not think [Empson] ever loved or venerated a living creature so much as he does [Arnold's] memory,' observed Lord Jeffrey.[11]

In 1833 he wrote a carefully laudatory notice of the series of 'scientific' fables entitled *Illustrations of Political Economy*, by Harriet Martineau, with whom he later developed a cordial friendship—although she would repay him by patronizing his generosity at the expense of his intelligence:

We were never otherwise than perfectly friendly, though I could not help feeling that every year, and every experience, separated us more widely in regard to intellectual and moral sympathy. He was not, from the character of his mind, capable of having opinions; and he was, as is usual in such cases, disposed to be afraid of those who had. He was in a perpetual course of being swayed about by the companions of the day, on all matters but politics. There he was safe; for he was hedged in on every side by the dogmatic Whigs, who made him their chief dogmatist. He was full of literary knowledge;—an omnivorous reader with a weak intellectual digestion. He was not personally the wiser for his reading; but the profusion that he could pour out gave a certain charm to his conversation, and even to his articles, which had no other merit, except indeed that of a general kindliness of spirit.

The 'good Mr Empson' and 'the Jeffrey set', she thought, looked on her as 'romantic, high-flown, extravagant, and so forth.' She was right; unlike his brother John, William Empson was a man of his time. Martineau was ahead of hers; she was impatient of all well-meaning, ineffectual Whigs— including Lord Monteagle, who had been a like-minded friend of Empson's since their schooldays, and who rose to be Chancellor of the Exchequer. Today, it is true, Empson's encomium of her didactic stories reads like a piece of crashingly old-style condescension. 'The less women usually meddle with any thing which can be called public life out of their village, we are sure the better for all parties,' he proclaimed even in his opening paragraph (we recall that George Eliot set *Middlemarch* at the time of the Reform Bill). 'A deep sympathy with the precarious situation of their poorer neighbours, and an active benevolence in relieving the distressed, and in encouraging the virtuous, furnish them with a circle wide enough.' Indeed, a large part of his essay has the air of correcting a headstrong ward ('Does Miss Martineau really mean that the "right principle", on which the advantages of a gradation of "ranks in society" can practically depend, is "superior merit", and that, too, to be ascertained by universal suffrage?'), and sometimes smiling upon her *sottises*, her 'controverted opinions':

> If Miss Martineau really thinks that, at her time of life, and with her opportunities, she is competent to legislate for mankind anew on its most complicated institutions—that she can resettle the foundations and transmission of property— dispense with criminal law by doing away with the *crime* of punishment—alter the framework of society, so as to remove out of it the *disgrace* of indigence;—if she is looking forward to the period when actresses are to be above marrying secretaries of state, and typing up their papers,—and is ready with a millennium of her own, in which our ladies will have taken out of our monopolising hands the cares of Parliament and public life,—there is no knowing whither a mind, which has already got so high into the visionary empyrean, may ultimately soar.

Empson had a relentlessly ratiocinative turn of mind, trimmed with fanciful metaphors and aphoristic grace-notes. His conservative progressivism, built upon received wisdom, timidity, and cool logic, was not ready for the shock of what we would now identify as her excitable left-wing radicalism. Thus the best advice he could offer her was that she should let her 'peremptory and self-controlling reason' get the better of all this 'intellectual fever'. Yet it is good to know that Martineau was content: she found his review 'flattering'. (But perhaps it is useful to know, in addition, that it must have been Empson—and not Lord Jeffrey—who tampered with G. H. Lewes's review of Charlotte Brontë's novel *Shirley*, in the *Edinburgh Review* of 1850, so as to heighten its disrespect for women.)[12]

In 1823, when he began to send articles to the *Edinburgh Review*, he was appointed to the first council of the Royal Society of Literature; and it was nearly a quarter-century later that he attained the summit of his public life in literature, when he succeeded Macvey Napier as editor of the *Edinburgh*. Under both Napier and Empson, that periodical did indeed serve as the voice of the Whig Party; 'an unlooked-for failure in modesty and manners in good Mr. Empson spoiled the literary prospect,' opined Martineau (as she would); 'so that the review lost character and reputation quarter by quarter, while under his charge'. But the vivacious, versatile, over-voluble Lord Jeffrey ('Jeffrey has been here with his adjectives, who always travel with him,' as Sydney Smith was to quip) thought well of his editorial abilities— though he may have been a wee bit swayed by family partiality. Charles Darwin gallantly, or just whimsically, numbered Empson and Jeffrey among 'the geniuses';[13] and even Carlyle referred to Empson in 1831 as 'a man of some rank, and very considerable talent and learning'.[14] He certainly cultivated all the right people, including Wilberforce and the Lansdowne Set.

From 1824 to the very moment of his death, Empson was Professor of General Polity and the Laws of England at the East India College, Hailey-bury, in succession to Sir James Mackintosh. 'Pop' Malthus, Professor of Political Economy, a kind, placid, courteous figure, became his dearest friend, despite what Empson wittily called his 'ungracious doctrine'. Empson would in due course pay tribute to 'the great Master of Population' whose 'discretion and urbanity, his authority and attraction, made him the most enviable colleague that the members of a public body could ever wish to act with; and his union of the severe and gentle virtues was so rare and so complete, that he was equally the object of their admiration and their love.'

Empson was well versed in the details of the application of the laws in India; but better still, he imparted to his students the fundamental doctrines of moral science, the laws of nations, and the principles of ethics. He asseverated: 'It is impossible for teachers to maintain their authority as teachers, unless they show a due reverence for their office, by a scrupulous anxiety to maintain our confidence in the completeness and correctness of their knowledge, and in the soundness of their understanding.' The *Hertford Mercury* had good reason to praise his years of service as a teacher at Haileybury: 'To form the mind of those young men, many of whom, as magistrates and judges, were to affect the interests of thousands and millions, was to him a duty of a solemn, or rather of a sacred, kind. His students, when promoted in India, might be considered not only as representing English law and justice, but Christianity itself, in the minds of the Hindús and Mussulmáns.'[15] The students found him an amiable and estimable man—as one of them would say, 'He told us not only what the law, civil and criminal, was, but also what it ought to be'[16]—even though he would deliver his discursive and often mumbling lectures at a sprinting rate of speech that Sydney Smith made friendly fun of in society.

Charles Merivale, later Dean of Ely, would recollect that Empson's classes

> were a perpetual stream of suggestions and illustrations. His fluency was immense. He entered with inspiring zest into the political philosophy of the day, the theories of Paley and Mill, of the struggle between the old traditional opinions of our constitutional writers and the subversive discoveries of the new lights in Law, Politics, and Morals. The era of 1824 may be remembered as an epoch in our political history, when the spirit of Reform was just awakening and the Tory *régime* beginning to show the first signs of its approaching decline. Empson was a mild reformer himself, a Whig who had been long sighing on the shady side of political life and was hoping for happier times. He could not refrain from giving us a taste of his opinions . . . [17]

The passage of the Reform Bill in 1832 thrilled the cautious liberal William quite as much as it did his reformed and enlightened brother, the Revd John.

Professor Empson, said another pupil, 'was ever willing to assist those whom he thought in earnest, and usually a few men remained after lecture, when he would explain difficulties in his inimitable way—sometimes for twenty minutes or more. He was a little absent, and very kindly, of which lazy students sometimes took advantage. For instance, in the Hall at the Law examinations, one after the other would propose some difficulty in the paper, and so induce him unconsciously to explain nearly every question.'[18]

He even died at his desk. Surprisingly—in view of the energy he spent on his writing and teaching—he suffered from feeble health all his life, and often sought out spas and rest cures. However, in December 1852, after invigilating an examination in a cold hall he dreaded, he burst a blood vessel and went into a fatal decline. Yet as the *Gentleman's Magazine* noted: 'Notwithstanding his enfeebled state of health, he carefully went through the Examination papers, and assigned to each student his rank and position. No man ever fell more truly in the field of duty.'[19] In his last moments he made known his wish that his gravestone should add nothing to his name except the old faithful text, 'The Lord is my Shepherd, therefore I can lack nothing.'[20]

In 1838, at the advanced age of 49, he had married Charlotte, only child of his friend and colleague Francis Jeffrey (who was not old enough to be his father).[21] William loved the company of little children, as did his father-in-law, and Charlotte did not disappoint them: she produced five children in all—one boy and four girls—the last being born after a gap of eight years, in 1852, the year of William's demise at the age of 63. They were not strong stock: the first child died at 17 (after her father); the second perished in a year; and only the third lived precisely as long as her father, dying in 1906. Charlotte Empson was in fact sickly and neurotic; the nasty gossip Thomas Carlyle found her (admittedly after she was a widow) 'a morbidly shy kind of creature' who, he thought, had inherited a 'nervous infirmity, and indeed I think was partly lame of one arm ... abstruse, suspicious, timid, enthusiastic; and at length, on death of her parents and of her good old jargoning husband ... [she] became quite a morbid exclusive character'—living a withdrawn life among her children.[22] But William doted on his wife and children, even if he had to treat them like invalids, and his pedagogical and editorial labours left him all too little time for them. It is possible that he might have felt unconsciously threatened by a stronger woman: he liked to josh women as though they were small children. Even in an early letter to his new sister-in-law, he scarcely bothered to draw a line between teasing and patronizing; this was written nearly twenty years before he rallied Harriet Martineau in similar vein, so we may wonder whether he was not really feeling more fretful than flirtatious: '*we* have the making of Laws & of Opinions, & it is our Interest that you should be neither dull nor selfish: happy Women who are forc'd to be a little wise & now & then virtuous, in spite of yourselves. But there are those among you who think it very hard, who sigh for a Seat in Parliament or a Commission in the Guards: bold & manly Spirits who disdain the Distinction of a Side Saddle, & regret that in your most convivial Humours you are obliged to get drunk alone.' However that may be, it is notable that some of William and Charlotte Empson's children would pass almost all their time with the gratified grandparents at their home near Edinburgh.

The evidence of all surviving papers, including an extensive correspondence with Jeffrey and with Napier, indicates that William was a sweet-natured person, altogether generous and honourable; if he had a fault, it was that he was too obliging (the almost obsequious mannerliness of his letters we may acknowledge as an affectation of the period). Jeffrey assuredly prized his son-in-law, and praised to his face the gentleness of his disposition and the kindness of his heart. We can gather a good impression of his simple integrity and his charitableness even from an early letter to his beloved Aunt Sarah; this was written from Cambridge, *circa* 1812:

I understand that my Place in the Examination was sixth . . . You ask me how it happens that I stand higher than my late Equals. Examinations are but indifferent Tests of Merit when Men are nearly equal . . . Much depends on the State of Mind & Body at an Examination: much on the Chance of Subjects for Composition & Translation being such as you have before seen or thought of: & most of all in the comparative Labour & Care you may employ in the performing & revising the very Papers then before you. Wrightson & Rolfe have measured Swords with me for three Years past: we have fought our Ground step by step: & if either has gained an Advantage in one place, he has generally lost as much in some other: we ran so near that the Conqueror came in but by a neck, or (to speak in the Language of Algebra) by a quantity less than nothing. I am sorry they are not at present bracketted ever with me: for they who are ignorant of their real Merits will of course judge by Appearances, often delusive, & now particularly so. I am rais'd above them: to which I have no claim: but the next Examination will set all right. I trust I have no Envy. If it should prove so, I would forswear Competition for ever. There is nothing I hate worse, except Ingratitude, to which it has some similarity in its meanness. For every honourable object of Ambition within my reach I give my Friends notice I am a candidate: I tell them I will pass them if I can. If they pass me, why all that remains for a Philosopher & a Friend is to feel happy at their Success, & rejoice that their are so many cleverer Men than myself.[23]

That seems to be rather more than a pompous parroting of decency; indeed, it shows high-mindedness of an unusual order. To his friends, as to Harriet Martineau, he showed the deep kindliness of his spirit: he was just so nice.

Yet his brother, the Revd John, who was himself an old scapegrace, thought him mercenary and found him ungrateful. He wrote, for example, in March 1831: 'In my way from Rome he was brutal, but he was ill, & on arriving at Yokefleet was severe even to his pecuniary Mamma—a rare thing when William frowns on any One who "has much to leave".' Did John have good cause to hold a grudge, or was he jealous of his brother, the professor of polity and prominent man of letters? Or was it the other way round? Was William peculiarly severe and unpleasant to his eldest brother, perhaps because he could not forgive the Reverend John the bad behaviour of his earlier life—especially his shabby treatment of his wife, the early-doomed Margaret (who died at the age of 27, eighteen years before William, deep into middle age, came to marry his 'Charley')? The earliest evidence, in a letter of 1814 (the year the Revd John married Margaret), does not suggest that he disapproved of his brother's predilection for hunting. William wrote home happily that Christmas, during a visit to Paris: 'I have thought more than once of the mild open Weather that you might have in Nottinghamshire & the fair Tryal you would take of the Country: I thought of it with Pleasure, for as long as you hunt, I wish you to enjoy it. Whatever one does ought to be done well, to get at the right pleasure of it: & it is but too true that many men arrive at the End of a pretty long Life without having got further than the Surfaces, taking the Nuts in their Hand but never cracking them.'[24] But his good cheer in that letter does not prove that his opinion of his brother John gallivanting off across the country every day did not deteriorate over the next six years.

It is likely, however, that the problem was one of deeper moment. Not to make too much of a mystery out of this surmise, there is some evidence to suggest that the gallant William, then in his late twenties, had an affair with his sister-in-law Margaret. If that was the case, and indeed if he fell in love with her, it might just account for the fact that he (who never behaved badly to anyone else) was later curmudgeonly and cruel towards the brother who had married, neglected, and prematurely lost the very woman he himself had come to love too late. The chances are, then, that the Revd John might never have known the cause of his brother's ill conduct towards him.

But there is yet another piece of evidence we cannot ignore. On 10 January 1825, a month before the eighth birthday of his brother's child John William (who had been motherless for five years), William wrote a curiously touching, yearning poem to the boy. What is remarkable about the piece is that it is in fact a paean to the departed mother, his brother's deceased wife, whom he sorrowfully sees in the person of the child:

> Memory and Hope are round thee flinging
> My Boy, their deep contrasted Flowers.
> The Lark and Nightingale are singing
> Each their own Song within thy Bower,
> Whose Birthday's Aspect seems by Nature cast
> Bright for the future, holy o'er the past.
>
>   .   .   .   .
>
> Yet Memory stay—for more securely
> I clasp thee to my bounding Breast;
> And choosing thee I feel how surely
> I have laid my Soul in Rest,
> Mellowing & dearer growing day by day,
> Where none can now corrupt nor take away.
>
> Oh many a sweet & dear Remembrance
> Of Scenes fast fading from my Sight,
> A Look, or Manners slight resemblance
> Wakes & retouches into Light;
> Till Love, on Fancy leaning, smiles to trace
> Thy Mother beaming from thy youthful Face.
>
> At every Moment, whether playing
> Or in a calm half-thoughtful mood
> Some coaxing Lisp, some pretty Saying,
> Some comic Turn or Attitude
> Untwines the poppy Wreath where clusterd lie
> Dreams which may sleep awhile, but cannot die.
>
> For I could sit the Day and watch
> Upon thy Lips the waking Smile,
> Rise to the dimpling Cheeck & catch
> That Eye's bright Torch—whose beacon Pile
> Lights up thy Features—as on War's Surprize
> From Hill to Hill the flaming Signal flies.
>
> Thy careless and most innocent Speech
> Has something oft which makes me start
> And, while thou little heeds't, can reach

To shake the Fastness of my Heart
With a melodious and fairy Tone
I thought to hear again in Heaven alone.

One higher Likeness yet remaining,
Oh may thy growing years recall -
A Character above all feigning
Gracefully true and natural,
Serious yet sprightly, humble though refin'd,
Sweetness of Temper, Dignity of Mind:

For more transparent, airy, slight
Than lightest Cup from China's Land
Her Frame contain'd a Soul, which might
At once both soften and command:
Pure Feelings, melting at the Touch like Snow,
With Principles as firm as Rock below.

Memory & Hope, live on together!
Ye cannot, must not, shall not part:
Wing'd by the self-same angel's Feather
Your Shafts have sunk into my Heart:
One Bowl thus mingles your empassiond Wines,
That my Life drinks of both, or both resigns.

From the evidence of those verses, there can be little doubt that he had been in love with Margaret. Moreover, it seems reasonable to surmise from such a heart-wrenching poem that he was addressing his natural son. It is at least a possibility, never to be corroborated, that William Empson was in fact the great-grandchild of the first Professor William, whose life—in many respects—interestingly prefigured his own, including the course of his education, his life in literature, and even his enthusiasm for Bentham's utilitarianism. Of course this is principally a guess, and perhaps a slur on his reputation, though we may be sure that William adored his sister-in-law. Still it is tempting to fancy that the first famously literary Professor William Empson was the direct ancestor of the more illustrious Professor Sir William Empson of our era.

Of William Empson's grandfather, John William Empson, who was commonly known as 'G.P.' (for Grandpapa), we know less than of his forefathers—except that he too neglected or grew sick of his wife, Maria, felt guilty about his Yorkshire roots, and then did quite disastrously the wrong thing to assuage his guilt.[25] He was given a very churchy upbringing, under a special tutor named Mr Berry who did his best to propel his pupil along the proper path. But John William showed independence of mind: he was the first in four generations of Empsons to turn down a destiny in the Church. After taking his MA at Brasenose College, he married Maria Allen at the age of 25, and took his bride off for a honeymoon in Rome. But the couple never did see Rome: they got only as far as Paris, where the venal husband began to buy so many things—clocks and other *objets d'arts*—that they ran out of cash and had to return home to Yorkshire. For a while they tried to inhabit Blacktoft Grange, an outlying estate which his great-great-grandfather had acquired 85 years before. But that proved to be intolerable, and Maria peremptorily removed the family—their first child, John Henry, was born in 1843—to the markedly more amenable home ground of her side of the family. There they set up a home at Ripple Hall, near Tewkesbury, where John William served as a magistrate for County Worcester. Naturally, like the Revd John (who was still very much alive, albeit buried in his books), John William lived as a gentleman, but there was nothing *infra dignitatum* in such a station in life: it is a modern notion that a country landowner should live (let alone labour) on site. From the family property in the East Riding, he received rental income from the 1,924 acres in Bishopsoil, Metham, and Yokefleet, while his first cousin, William Henry, vicar of far-distant Wellow in Hampshire, profited from a further 1,359 acres. All the same, John William was yet squire of Yokefleet. According to John Bateman, squires were 'commoners owning between one and three thousand acres—who generally resided on their properties, performing valuable functions at the bottom end of the landowning hierarchy'[26]—and John William's inability to fulfil such functions, to shoulder his responsibilities as lord of the manor of Yokefleet (where there were over 200 inhabitants), troubled his conscience throughout his marriage. Indeed, there is a family story that after about a quarter-century of married life he opted to return to Yorkshire in his early fifties and to build a new manor house at Yokefleet simply because he could no longer stand the company of his wife.[27]

Whether or not he did really feel 'bound fast to an uncomplying discord of nature', he in fact survived his sentence and went back to Yorkshire only after Maria's death in January 1869—though it is assuredly the case that he had begun to build Yokefleet Hall a year before. Anyway, maybe it was the soft living and long boredom of his years at Ripple Hall that made him decide in favour of reviving his derelict squirarchical duties. Certainly the new Yokefleet Hall was fashioned so as to ensure that the prodigal lord should never suffer from boredom; it is a most masculine building. In a gentleman's residence, whether town or country, the billiard room is the male penetralia: it is a place for the chaps to chat and smoke. But at Yokefleet the entire building is constructed round the billiard table: the billiard room *is* the reception hall, with the principal staircase at one end of it, so that the obsessive pastime of John William's advanced years is eccentrically thrust in the face of every visitor. Probably designed by F. S. Brodrick (nephew of the more famous Cuthbert Brodrick, architect of Leeds Town Hall and the Grand Hotel in Scarborough), the house, which is approached by way of two gaily polychromatic lodges, is in High-Victorian Gothic, red brick with jazzy tilework.[28] The north front is an unprepossessing mess; but the pleasure of the place is the sudden surreal sight of ocean-going ships gliding by the bottom of the garden. The clean line of the high dykes of the river opposite Ousefleet and Whitgift makes for an abruptly artificial horizon backed by a swathe of pure sky. (The ground floor of the building is some 10 feet below sea level at high tide.) Moreover the south front of the hall, facing the river, has a more gracious, almost attractive, look than any of the other elevations: the deep red brick is dressed with stone mullions at the tall windows, and the whole structure is topped off by three great gables providing dark and chilly but fairly roomy servants' quarters.

Quite remarkably, however, within less than ten years of the completion of the building, the family was advertising for a tenant, at £400 a year. The published inventory affords a good account of this modest, well-accoutred country house in 1881:

Hall porch, entrance hall (used as a billiard room) 30ft by 20ft, with excellent table by Burroughs & Watts; drawing room 27ft by 11ft 6in and large bay, with grand pianoforte by Collard; communicating with ante-room 16ft by 12ft; and opening thence to the dining room 28ft by 16ft by 11ft 6in; gun room or smoking room 16ft by 11ft; seventeen principal and secondary bed and dressing rooms, box room, wardrobe room, fitted linen room, good bath room (hot and cold) with fire place, w.c.s and lavatory.

The Servants' Offices are store room; butler's pantry (with telephone to stables); servants' hall; kitchen 21ft by 15ft with range by Walter, and side oven; scullery (with range); capital larder; game ditto; beer and wine cellars etc.

Outside are coal cellar; laundry (not fitted); boot hole; wood house, and other necessaries. The water supply is pure and abundant (pumped daily into tanks), there being also a large soft water tank, and the drainage is in good order; the stabling consists of four stalls and four loose boxes (well fitted); harness and saddle rooms; two coach houses, wash box and copper; two mens' rooms over stable; large lofts etc.

There is also a lodge occupied by the keeper, the one at lodge gate being tenanted by coachman.

The pleasure grounds include the shrubberies to about 10 acres, and there is a good tennis lawn, while a small golfing ground could readily be made in the park.

Kitchen garden and small orchard (one gardener being employed). Included in the letting are two paddocks of about four acres, but if desired 20 acres of excellent grass land adjoining can be had at £2 per acre. The Shooting extends to about 3,000 acres, of which about 40 acres are covert, the average game bag for the last 5 years being 122 pheasants, 116 partridges, 164 hares, 263 rabbits, 10 duck, 22 snipe, 46 various. A great feature in the place is the wild-fowl shooting on the river, and also on artificially flooded land. There is also fishing (salmon netting), 3 miles of which runs with the property, and boating, there being a sailing boat and boat-house for the use of a tenant, and the river traffic all through the year. A steamer plies to and from Hull during the summer months. Hunting with three packs of hounds.

A Victoria and a Landau were also to be supplied, plus a donkey for mowing the lawn 'etc'.

Such is the house that John William Empson built for himself in his fifties, the house in which his grandson William, poet and critic, was to pass his earliest years. But it was never to be a happy home; and an obvious question has to be asked—why did the family desire to sublet this handsome new residence, crammed as it was with amenities, almost as soon as it was completed? The answer is a lesson in Victorian family lore.

In addition to John Henry, John William and Maria had four offspring: three girls—Margaret, Maria, and Ellen—and a spare son, Arthur Reginald, who appeared nearly a decade after their first-born, in 1853. John Henry followed his father to Eton and to Brasenose College, Oxford; then he became a barrister of the Inner Temple, and a magistrate for the East Riding—where he was living at the old Yokefleet Hall when he fell deeply in love with a girl who happened to be his distant cousin, Alice Lister Empson, from across the river at Ousefleet Grange. (Alice's father, Robert Cornelius Lister—who had taken the name of Empson—was a JP for County Lincoln and for the West Riding of Yorkshire; he owned both Ousefleet Grange and Goole Hall.) John Henry and Alice were married on 12 June 1867. It must have been with a view to handing over the property to his son and heir that John William set about to build the new house with lawns leading down to the river; it would be a place where he could play out his days at the billiard table and dandle his descendants. It was not so fated. Just eighteen months into marriage, Alice Empson died at the age of 22, in January 1869, after giving birth to a daughter.[29] John Henry was devastated: his mother had died on the first day of the New Year, so he had barely had time to bury her, let alone mourn her, before his wife perished of her terrible parturition (the baby was delivered on 24 January, and Alice passed away five days later). The child who survived her was christened Maria Alice: she would never marry, though she lived even through the Second World War. (Charles Empson, the most recent incumbent of the estate at Yokefleet, who was born in 1935, remembered being taken on an exeat from his prep school to visit the frail old Aunt Alice in a nursing home. If the estate had not been devised in tail male, she would have been outright heir.)

Like his grandfather the Revd John (who had been released from life just eight years earlier, at the age of 74), John Henry grieved for his wife a long age. His father, having lost his wife and his daughter-in-law, carried on building the new residence at Yokefleet, though it seems most likely that he had already lost heart in the idea of living there. In any event, he was not there to succour his son even by the final week of the next month, when his clerk of works wrote that he had managed to interest the doleful but polite John Henry in plans to alter the east end of the building: 'this seemed to be the only thing that attracted Mr John's attention on Thursday and he said "that will look very nice indeed, Mr Hull, it is a capital idea, it will do very well." '[30] John Henry was a widower for a decade. And then, at the ripening age of 35, he tried marriage for a second time, in July 1879. His new wife was an outstanding match for him: she was well born, and a widow. Fourth daughter of the Hon. William James Coventry (late Earl of Coventry), Mary Theresa Burdett had been the wife of George Seaham Tucker de Windt, Esq., of Dinnington, Northumberland. John Henry was thus doing a fine thing for his family by taking this particular second wife: he was lifting the Empsons, a family that had risen from the Yorkshire mud, into the rare air of nobility.

But things went frightfully ill yet again. John William, having built his modest red-brick pile on the warp of the Ouse, decided he could not bear to live there after all, and retired to Worcestershire. But he was not content to leave the place well alone: he was still bothered by a sense of guilt about his Yorkshire roots, his rights and obligations, and his bad conscience led him to bully his son to take up residence at Yokefleet Hall as a stand-in for the lord of the manor.[31] He even ordered his lawyers to enjoin his son to live on the land in his stead. By himself, John Henry might have bowed to such parental pressure. But the new wife would not have it: she took one look at Yokefleet and its environs, and deserted her marriage. Such at least is the family story; but there was probably much more to it than we can hope to recover—for she not only ran off from John Henry and the new house that his father had made into a millstone, she ran off with another man. Perhaps she had found that the Empsons had too little *ton* for her taste in mates, for her paramour was the Hon. Frederick Standish O'Grady, the future 6th Viscount Guillamore. The elopement, which took place after less than two years of marriage, stunned the Empson family; it was a foul blow to their name, their standing in society. Above all, it staggered the highly sensitive John Henry, who had never fully recovered his well-being in all the years since the early death of his true love, Alice: it broke his nerves, which were already stretched to screaming point between the opposed wills of father and wife.

Mary Theresa and O'Grady recognized the heinousnous of their offence, for they absconded halfway round the world—to Australia. Yet no matter the distance, the Empsons determined that honour must needs be satisfied. Since John Henry was in no fit state to do anything, John William dispatched his younger son—the 29-year-old Arthur Reginald— to give the aristocratic bounder the thrashing he deserved. Thus it was that Arthur Reginald came to write home from Sydney on 26 August 1881 that he had duly fulfilled his mission:

Mr dear Father,

When I went back on board the Lusitania on Tuesday (at Melbourne) 23rd inst morning I received a letter from Mr O'Grady saying that he had seen my name in the list of arrivals & that he was staying there (at Melbourne). I had just time to get my luggage off before the ship sailed, & went back to 'Scott's' where I had stayed the night before. A native of Melbourne, whose acquaintance I had made on board the Lusitania, gave me an introduction to his lawyer, a Mr Emmerton, a very good fellow. I wrote to O'Grady & fixed an appointment for the following day. On Wed (24th inst) I called at his hotel, taking the Melbourne lawyer with me. I found them both there. Mr Emmerton handed me the citations, & I duly served them. I then suggested to Emmerton that Mrs Empson should leave the room. I then had a short conversation with O'Grady, told him he was a . . . scoundrel, & broke a whale bone stick over him. The interview ended by Mr Emmerton pulling me out by the coat-tails . . .

Best love to all,

ever your affte Son

Arthur R Empson

P.S. The whale bone cost 12/6, but it was not strong enough. I ought to have bought one in London before I left.

At least the cad was not a coward: O'Grady did not try to run away from his come-uppance. And he did his duty insofar as he married Mary Theresa later that year. The beating he received from young Empson caused him no lasting harm, since he lived on for nearly half a century— though he and his ill-gotten wife produced no issue.

But Arthur also struck a grave note; remembering that he had left home while his elder brother was still in a bad mental state, he added to his letter:

'I am rather anxious about Johnny & shall feel much relieved at the news you will send to San Francisco'—where he was bound on the long way home. The news that eventually reached him was in fact utterly appalling: on 29 August, while visiting the town of Ilkley in north Yorkshire (presumably in an effort to recuperate his ruined spirits), John Henry shot himself. The son and heir was dead. He had not even waited to learn if his younger brother had done the business of trouncing the blackguard who ran off with his wife, and evidently he nursed no thought of the wife coming back.

Arthur Reginald, the runt who had displayed his mettle in upholding the honour of his elder brother, inherited everything by default. The youngest of a family of five children, he would go on to sire five children of his own—of whom the youngest was William Empson.

John Henry was buried alongside his first wife, Alice, in the churchyard at Blacktoft. The family tried to keep his tragic suicide a secret, but in practice it was kept only from succeeding generations of the family itself: the whole county seems to have known all about it, but not the children of the afflicted family. There is certainly no evidence at all to suggest that William Empson ever knew the fate of Uncle Johnny; and Charles Chesshyre Empson learned about the manner of his great-uncle's death only when he came to sort out some family papers in adult life. The horror that the circumstances of John Henry's death inspired in the immediate family explains why they proposed to sublet Yokefleet Hall later that same year: none of them, and certainly not 'G.P.' the paterfamilias John William himself, could face the idea of living in a place that may have been partly instrumental in the fate of the elder son.

They lost no time in commissioning local licensed valuers to draw up an inventory of the household furniture and effects of the deceased; delivered on 5 September, just one week after the death, it showed that he had owned the largest part of the furnishings, including curtains and rugs, as well as the necessities of the household—seventeen pairs of sheets, eleven toilet covers, table services, etc.—along with 330 bottles in the capacious, necessary cellar. (There is a story that after John Henry's tragic death G.P. walled up that part of the cellar in which his son had stored his liquor; but that one of the grandsons abused his sentimental gesture by breaking through the wall.) The father had made the son inhabit the house, whether he wanted it or not.

Yokefleet Hall was not let out to tenants. Instead, Arthur Reginald, who had shown his worth in a magnificent way, came into his own in every sense: he resolved to make a go of his inheritance, both house and estate.

By 1890, when he got married at the good age of 37, his wife discovered that her new establishment was to be shared not only with her father-in-law but with his two maiden sisters. (The middle sister, Maria Louisa, had died in 1882, and she was buried alongside her mother in Worcestershire.) This arrangement did not last long, for the aunts were presently pensioned off and went to live in Ireland; and John William—'G.P.'—died in 1893 at the age of 77.

Laura Empson was obviously proud to be able to tell her children how their father had finally tamed the wilful, bossy, and conscience-baffled 'G.P.' After dinner, she related, the old man would routinely and insinu-atingly compliment his son: 'Capital port, my boy! Capital port!' But Arthur Reginald would reply, quite unmoved, 'You're not having any more. Go to bed now!'—whereupon 'G.P.' would get up and toddle out of the room.[32] There was no doubt whatever that Arthur Reginald Emp-son had resolved to put his family back on track, and to manage its affairs at home in Yorkshire.

3

'A horrid little boy, airing my views'

I remember believing I should have to die in order to grow up, and thinking the prospect very disagreeable.

'Alice in Wonderland: The Child as Swain'

Literature is a social process, and also an attempt to reconcile the conflicts of an individual in whom those of society will be mirrored.

'Proletarian Literature', 1933

UNLIKE both his grandfather and his father, who deserted Yokefleet at the earliest opportunity, Arthur Reginald Empson felt a sense of belonging to this seemingly lost place in the levels of the Ouse. He was not born to it: he had spent his early years in Worcestershire, and as a younger brother he had of course no idea that the patrilineal succession would fall to him. But he was a natural countryman, and took an energetic interest in the agriculture of what outsiders might look upon as a dull, dank waste-land, as well as in its considerable sporting opportunities.

Since the little empire of the Empsons was founded on mud, one of the special features of the farmlands by the Ouse which delighted Arthur was the process of using mud to make the meadows, which then made money. Every so often, over a period of several months, sterile marshes would be magically transformed into fertile soil. Huge sluice gates, or 'cloughs', set into the bank of the high river enable the tide to engorge a vast dyke which funnels the tumbling tawny water into smaller channels or 'runs', with the result that there is a rapid, equal distribution over the area to be warped.

In the hour or less before the turn of the tide, and only in those few minutes when the water falls still, the wondrous warp—fine particles of mixed clay and sand—is evenly deposited right up to the embankment, before the ebb drains the water, leaving a gleaming slick and a salty tang in the air. The process is repeated every twelve hours for at least a year, and generally for eighteen months—the ideal period is two winters and one spring—until the rich alluvial deposit adds up to a depth of 18 inches or 2 feet. This 'warped' soil produces excellent crops of wheat and potatoes, as well as particularly remunerative mustard. The Blacktoft warping drain, which is 3 miles long and services a large part of the Yokefleet terrain, was in fact built in 1825—at the direction of Arthur's grandfather, the Revd John, who hated the featureless estate he inherited but had the sense to see that fertile silt meant solvency in such a place.[1]

Arthur was enchanted by this positively Marvellian metamorphosis of the sour flats first into a playground and then into ripe fields. On 13 May 1894, four years after his marriage (and with two sons already laid in the nest), he composed this poem in celebration of the shape-shifting meadows; a hymn to irrigation in three movements, it is entitled simply 'Warping':

> He stood and watched the weary waste
>   Disdainful geese flew screeching o'er
> Not e'en an ass would stoop to graze
>   The weeds and thistles that it bore.
>
> The rushing river pours; leaving behind
>   The wealth of many tides. Wild duck and snipe
> Plover and curlew feed. Salmon and eels
>   Abound. Deep through the mud the sportsman wades.
>
> Ah! Now he sees a different scene
>   Fair waving corn and scented bean
> Rich mustard and potato fields
>   The fruitful soil ungrudging yields.

William Empson was to become familiar with his father's sentiments, for those verses hung by the stairs at Yokefleet Hall; and he shared the old man's affection for the louring, luscious landscape in which he grew up. As an undergraduate, he would know enough about the demands of farming to review a volume with a truly leaden title: *British Farmers in Denmark*. 'I know parts of Yorkshire,' he lamented, 'that have actually gone back to swamp because the farmers couldn't agree to keep the banks mended.'[2]

But it was not just good husbandry that concerned him, he admitted: as far as the countryside was concerned, he was assuredly a 'sentimentalist'. It is hardly surprising, therefore, that one of his own earliest poems reflected his father's absorption in the mysterious picture that periodically engulfed the house at Yokefleet. The opening lines of 'Flighting for Duck' have no rival in Empson's poetry for their rapt, exact description of a natural scene:

> Egyptian banks, an avenue of clay,
> Define the drain between constructed marshes
> (Two silted lakes, silver and brown, with grass,
> Without background, far from hills, at evening).
> Its pomp makes a high road between their sheets
> (Mud shoals, a new alluvium, dabbled water,
> Shallow, and specked with thistles, not yet mastered)
> At the subdued triumph of whose end
> Two transept banks, the castle guard, meet it,
> Screening the deeper water they surround
> With even line of low but commanding pinetrees
> Dark but distinguished as a row of peacocks.
> The darker silhouette is where a barn
> Straddling two banks over a lesser channel
> Stands pillared upon treetrunks like a guildhall
> Empty, mudheaped, through which the alluvial scheme
> Flows temporary as the modern world.
> The mud's tough glue is drying our still feet.
> A mild but powerful flow moves through the flats
> Laden with soil to feed the further warping.

Whether he wrote his poem (first published in *Magdalene College Magazine* in December 1928) as almost a subliminal tribute to his father, it is just not possible to determine. All that he ever said about it, in 1951, was: 'The magazine of my college at Cambridge asked me for a poem, and as this seemed a gentlemanly sort of public I thought they would like a poem about shooting, so I turned one out.' It is interesting to note how closely the verses quoted echo his father's feelings for the locale—though he is more taken with details of engineering than with anything sheerly picturesque—but it is difficult to say if he inherited much of his father's talent or temperament, because all too little is known about the father.

Arthur Reginald was educated like his father at Eton and at Brasenose College, Oxford, where he commenced MA in 1870. After being called to the Bar, he became a magistrate for the East Riding and was chairman of the Howden Bench for many years.[3] In 1912 he became a member of the East Riding County Council as representative of the Laxton Division. He sat regularly at the Howden Police Court, and did his duty as a member of the Howden Board of Guardians and the Howden Rural District Council. In sum, he was everything one might expect. A short, stocky, amiable man with very full moustaches, he also relished dining, dancing, and theatre-going. After he took over the Yokefleet estates, he was a conscientious landlord, albeit of his time: being a gentleman, he did not do any of the farming himself. His second son was, strictly speaking, the first member of the family to take the land in hand (and that son would in turn refer to the old man as a good farmer). As his capable pastiche of eighteenth-century pastoral verse shows, he was a cultivated man, highly interested in the arts; in later years he would propel his offspring to lots of concerts and theat-ricals. He was also an ardent fisherman, and would go off on expeditions up the Norwegian coast. In addition, he took after his gamesome grand-father, the 'Flying Parson', to the extent that he loved riding rough: he would head his horse at anything. Also like the Revd John, however, he loved the bottle—according to one of his retainers, 'he drank like a fish'.[4] Indeed, that weakness probably accounts in large part for one of the few letters by Arthur Reginald Empson that have come down to us; addressed to the Revd Edward W. Simpson, on 23 April 1902, it shows him to be the very model of the immemorial country gentleman:

I must plead guilty to going to sleep during the aft. sermon. But that is a case of 'original sin' on my part, & not due to the preacher, or to the locus in quo. It is 'my custom always of an afternoon', if I am tempted to eat a heavy luncheon. . . .
    Yrs very truly
    Arthur R. Empson[5]

At the time of writing, he was in his fiftieth year; just four weeks earlier, his wife had given birth to their fourth child, a daughter. A middle-aged man with a young and burgeoning family, Arthur seems already to have lapsed into the role of stereotypical squire—given to port and portliness, and to posing as a prematurely old buffer at the mercy of his metabolism. It is notable that in the letter he excuses himself for falling asleep in church but offers no firm purpose of amendment. Holy Trinity at Blacktoft, just a brisk mile's walk along the lane from Yokefleet Hall, was his parish church, so Arthur Reginald usually took the family there as a matter of duty. But the homilies of the vicar, Mr Turner, must have matched the dreary character of his church, for the Empsons were always eager to leave before he got up to sermonize: they learned to deploy the trick of covering their

tracks with their children. 'We've got to go out—Charlie's being sick!' was
the signal for a smart evacuation of the family.[6]

Arthur had taken his time about getting married, and he chose wisely.
Laura Micklethwait was 25 to his 37; a slim, good-looking woman with
long, aquiline features, and frizzy hair which she took the trouble to tame,
she was sociable and chatty, with a ready sense of humour.[7] She laughed
uproariously when the children told her the rhyme, 'Mary had jam and
Mary had jelly—and Mary went home with a pain in her stomach.'[8] But
she could be argumentative: she was quite capable of flying into a rage
(and often engaged in thoroughly refreshing squabbles with her sister).
Clever without being intellectual, she was elegant, orderly, hospitable, and
practical. She liked to wear tweeds; she adored hunting; she was extremely
fond of bridge and gardening; she had talent as an amateur artist—she
could have gone far in that field with (as they say) a little training.
Moreover, she was brave; once, when staying by herself at Yokefleet, she
went up for the night and caught sight of a pair of boots protruding from
her bed: undaunted, she promptly snatched off the covers and pulled out a
tramp—who did not care to stay much longer. She was bred to be the lady
of a manor, with native graciousness.

Her father, who died only two years before her marriage, was Richard
Micklethwait, lord of the manor of Ardsley, in the valley of the Deane near
Barnsley, where the family lived at Ardsley House (a graceful house they
had built around 1750);[9] he had qualified in the law, he had been a JP for
the West Riding, and he had served as a captain in the West York Rifles.
The Micklethwait family had been landowners in Ardsley since the mid-
seventeenth century; in addition to farmlands, they owned brickworks and
a quarry, and had considerable interests in the Barnsley Main and Oaks
Collieries. In fact, the family must have been so wealthy by the late
Victorian period that it is quite surprising they do not appear in John
Bateman's *The Great Landowners of Great Britain and Ireland* (4th edn., 1883),
which does include the 2,059-acre estate of Yokefleet. In his will, Richard
Micklethwait appointed portions of £3,000 each for his two daughters, as
well as creating a further charge of £10,000 in their favour.[10] Laura was a
valuable match for Arthur in 1890.

Her brother, Richard Key Micklethwait, who succeeded to the honor-
ific title of 'Squire of Ardsley', served as a major in the Yorkshire Drag-
oons, and was later a prime mover in the establishment of a successful
working men's club and institute at Stairfoot; a popular figure in the
community, he died in 1908 at the age of 39.[11] Her nephew, Richard

G. Micklethwait (1896–1976), next squire in line, married the Hon. Ivy Stapleton, younger daughter of the 10th Baron Beaumont (and aunt of the present Duke of Norfolk); he farmed the family estates for many years, and claimed to have the first tuberculin-attested herd of cattle in South Yorkshire.[12] Her younger sister, Eleanor Frances (born in 1871), married in 1897 an army man of her own age who would rise to become Colonel (Hon. Major-General) Sir Llewelyn William Atcherley, CMG, CVO—but their chief abiding claim to fame is that they produced the celebrated flying twins, Richard and David (born in January 1904, three weeks after the Wright brothers' flight). In 1908 Colonel Atcherley was made Chief Constable of the West Riding, based in Wakefield, where the family lived in some style, with six indoor maids and a chauffeur; and after the world war he was appointed HM Inspector of Constabulary, being knighted in 1925. Thus William Empson's uncle was both a war hero and a chief of police. The adventurous, mischievous Atcherley twins, with their sister Grace Margery, would play with cousin William on monthly visits to Yokefleet, and when the Empsons caught the train or motored to their place. (Eleanor Frances, Lady Atcherley—'Nellie'—died in 1957 at the age of 85; Frances Eleanor, William Empson's grandmother, lasted till the age of 90.)

Whether by accident or by design, Arthur Reginald and Laura Empson produced five children over a leisurely fifteen-year period: John in 1891, Arthur in 1892, Charles in 1898, Maria Eleanor Katharine (Molly) in 1902, and finally William, who was born on 27 September 1906 and baptized at the Holy Trinity, Blacktoft, on 28 October.[13] Arthur Reginald was 'a funny little tub of a man—with all those large sons,' remarked one of the many Micklethwait aunts.[14] (William—'Bill'—the classic runt, did not match his brothers in height: they reared up to 6 feet and over.) Arthur Reginald was 53 when William was born, so his sister-in-law Nellie would coin an old wives' tale when she asserted that William was the son of an old man—which explained why he was so clever. William was to find out for himself that his parents had not expected to have any more children after Molly.

The significant gap between first-born and last meant that in practice the parents had to raise two generations of offspring. John—or Jack as he was called—had virtually grown up before William even started off to school. But Jack's life was to be cut short in a way that must have struck his father as grotesquely reminiscent of the doom of his own brother John Henry. Though afflicted with a severe stammer, Jack turned out to be a buoyant, energetic youth, fascinated by every sort of engine. An undated letter to his mother from Eton, where he loved being in the cadet corps, gives us an idea of his lively character (the family already owned a car, but he was determined they should keep up with the latest models):

I think you must inveigle Father over to the Show at Olympia this year, it is going on now & I believe some of the cars are very cheap. You might tell Granny I am doing my exercises regularly & I think my stammering is improving therefrom.

I saw the Kaiser & 'presented arms' in great style. I was standing near the gate through which he came & he had a huge grin on when he passed me, but I believe when he had got to the other end of the line the grin had quite come off & he had a vacant stare on instead. I expect he got rather bored. . . .

Best love to Father, M[olly], A[rthur], C[harles], Bill & yourself.

Best love your loving son,

Jack (!!!)[15]

Not being especially gifted as a scholar, he opted for a career in the army and so went on to Sandhurst; he was commissioned as a lieutenant in the 7th Royal Fusiliers. In 1912 his proud father threw a huge garden party to celebrate his coming of age, and the entire tenantry of Yokefleet—300 or 400 people—turned out to cheer the young master, the heir apparent. There was a marquee and a maypole; a sumptuous tea was served; there were fireworks in the evening; and the Gilberdyke Brass Band played popular tunes throughout the day. In the afternoon they arranged a cricket match between Married and Single, but only the Benedicts got in to bat, running up a score of 64, before rain stopped play. In fact, such was the ferocity of the squally weather that everyone had to squeeze into the famous billiard room for the speeches and presentations. The tenant farmers gave Jack a beautiful gold half-hunter engraved with monogram and crest; the cottagers a silver inkstand and candlestick; the indoor and outdoor staff of the Hall, led by Hatfield the butler, presented him with a silver cigar case. Among gifts from members of the family, he got a clock from Molly; while Aunt Alice—sole child of the son and heir who had shot himself—donated a present that would have seemed magnificent if only it had come from anyone but her—a pair of guns.[16]

Jack's first posting was less glamorous, let alone heroic, than he must have hoped for his military career. On 31 March 1912, a month after his twenty-first birthday, he wrote to his father from Whittington Barracks, Lichfield: 'At present we are stationed here in Staffordshire in reserve for Strike Duty. So far we have not actually been on duty in the mines but are in a state of perpetually standing in readiness in case we may be called on.

There are a lot of mines about 8 miles away in Cannock Chase where the miners have been rather rowdy & the West Yorks have been called out to look after them.'[17] Such rough duties must have encouraged him to leap at the opportunity to transfer from his regiment to the Royal Flying Corps: the romance of the air held out the prospect of far more fun than the business of bashing miners. After a period at the Central Flying School, he received his certificate at Brooklands on 7 January 1913 and joined no. 2 Squadron (stationed at Montrose) in time to see action in the Irish Command Manoeuvres. Then in 1914 it was ordained that the full squadron, commanded by Major Charles James Burke (an officer who was said to be 'utterly brave and determined, careless alike of danger and of ridicule'),[18] would fly south by set stages to its new base at Netheravon in Wiltshire; one stopover was to take place on the Knavesmire racecourse at York. Hence Laura Empson wrote to her sister on 6 May: 'We found Jack at Driffield Terrace [her mother's address in York]. He had come over to arrange landing grounds for the Montrose flying corps. He says the twelve aeroplanes and all their sheds and paraphernalia will arrive on Knavesmire on May 15 (Friday) and stay till Monday morning, on their way to Salisbury Plain. Why don't you motor to York on the Saturday and see them all?'[19]

Accordingly, in the early hours of 15 May, ten aircraft took off at ten-minute intervals from Seaton Carew, near Hartlepool, for the 70-mile leg to York. The weather looked fine as they set out. After passing over the Tees, they swung west of the Cleveland and Hambleton Hills and then followed the line of the Great North Road and the North-Eastern Railway. But all of a sudden they ran into appalling fog. Jack had no option but to head down for a blind landing: he smashed into the ground in a ploughed field, hurtled through a hawthorn hedge, and somersaulted into a further field on a lower level. The framework of his BE 2 biplane (no. 331) was splintered to matchwood; the wheels of the undercarriage, with the tyres torn off, lay 30 yards away. Jack and his 21-year-old mechanic were crushed under the buckled engine, their faces and bodies mutilated. No one witnessed the crash as it occurred, but at about 8 o'clock a milkman on his round raised the alarm when he caught sight of the sorry wreckage on a farm at Hutton Bonville, some 5 miles from Northallerton.[20]

In 1914 it was not unusual for aircraft to make forced landings, and in fact only three of the planes reached York that day. Number 332 ended up as a mangled wreck near Danby Wiske Station, on the North-Eastern Railway, but the crew got away with nothing more serious than an awful bruising; others reported their whereabouts as the anxious hours passed.

All too soon, however, the news was broken to the family gathered on the Knavesmire racecourse (including grandmother Micklethwait). Margery (Atcherley) Key, who was present that fateful day with her twin brothers, along with William Empson, remembers that someone gave Laura a drink of brandy—but she shook so badly that she spilled it all over herself.[21]

No one told the child Margery there had been a fatal accident, but her mother gave the twins a softened version of the terrible tidings. The boys had been starry-eyed about the future of flying from an early age, so now she decreed: 'This finishes flying for you two boys.' Yet as John Pudney related in *A Pride of Unicorns*, his biography of the brothers:

It was in fact a beginning and she lived on into another world in which Richard, holding the rank of Air Vice-Marshal, at the age of fifty broke the sound barrier— at a time (1954) when the supersonic frontier had not been crossed by many. David, who had also attained the rank of Air Vice-Marshal, had been reported missing two years earlier at the age of forty-eight, flying a Meteor jet... Yet for all these long years of close family unity and ardent filial devotion she never completely quelled the anxieties which stemmed from that May morning on the racecourse at Knavesmire. Throughout the flying careers of the Atcherley twins, she resolutely refused to watch them fly or even to see an aeroplane.[22]

While David was awarded the DFC (1942), DSO (1944), CBE (1946), and CB (1950), Richard, the dominant twin—who became known as 'Batchy' on account of his madcap exploits—won the AFC in 1940, and bar in 1942; and the Norwegian War Cross; he was also awarded the OBE (1941), CBE (1945), KBE (1956), and CB (1950).[23] The Micklethwait blood clearly had something especially wild in it, for the twins turned out to be every bit as unorthodox in the RAF as Empson was to be in academia. As the late Air Marshal Sir Peter Wykeham has written, they 'were a type of man whose ability, devotion to duty, and intensity of purpose allowed them to survive and prosper through careers studded with crashes, courts martial, and the type of gaffe which offended the more pompous heads of military and civil life'.[24] In later years, Empson knew that his first cousins had earned exuberant reputations as airmen, but he did not boast of the relationship.

William was not yet 8 when his biggest brother died. One might imagine that the dire event instilled in him a sense of fatalism. It seems far more likely, however, that he was not stricken by a deep sense of loss; after all, he had hardly known Jack as a brother, since Jack had gone off to Sandhurst before William grew conscious of anything much at all. He felt close to Charles and Molly, the siblings who were nearer his age—the ones he played with—and so did not feel badly deprived of a relationship which had never really had much of a chance to develop.

For the Empson parents, of course, it was a completely different story: they suffered terrible grief, even while having to put on a brave face for their younger children. Arthur Reginald had set the highest store by his first-born, and his loss seems to have knocked all the stuffing out of him. His brother had killed himself, and now his own son had been wiped out: it must have seemed to him that a fatal curse had fallen upon the family. The whole of Yokefleet turned out in sorrow for the funeral at Blacktoft, and the father headed a dragging black train of mourners home on foot.

Within just two years, on 15 March 1916, Arthur Reginald Empson died at the age of 63. He had lost a lot of weight in recent months, and was diagnosed (perhaps charitably) as diabetic;[25] it seems likely that he had continued to drink freely, which would have been a fatal folly. The death certificate records that he suffered a cerebral haemorrhage two days before the end. By his own choice, he was buried at Blacktoft, alongside his brother and son; and he was honoured with a famous funeral: the coffin, draped in a purple pall, was borne to the church on a farmer's rulley drawn by four black horses. As if in defiance of death, Molly wore a brilliant white dress with a blue sash: it could well have been intended for her fourteenth-birthday party the following week, but she wore it instead for her father's obsequies.[26]

In the knowledge that Yokefleet had been a cause of bitter anguish to his father and his brother (not to mention the forebears who had shunned the place), Arthur Reginald Empson had taken pains to 'settle' the estate. Specifically, he took advantage of the terms of the Settled Land Act 1882 to draw up a complex will with a simple intention: its purpose was both to secure the future management of the land and to ensure that all of his children benefited from the will.[27] In settling the land, he was creating a succession of interests—though each 'tenant for life' could still treat the estate as if it were held in fee simple. The tenant for life would act as the trustee of the estate, that is to say, in the interest of all beneficiaries; he could even convey the whole legal estate, at his own discretion, so long as he understood that he was still accountable to the other beneficiaries—who, in the event that the tenant for life thought it wisest to sell the land, would have an interest in the purchase-money just as they had originally held an interest in the land. Accordingly, in the major article of his will, dated 19 January 1909—it ran to 13 packed pages, with 29 articles in all—he bequeathed 'all the freehold lands and hereditaments' at his disposal to the use of my eldest son John Empson and my second son Arthur Empson and my third son Charles Empson and my fourth son William Empson and all my other sons born or to be born successively according to seniority for life with remainder immediately after the estate for life of each such son To the use of his first and other sons successively according to seniority in tail male and so that an elder of my sons and his first and other sons shall always take before a younger of my sons and his first and other sons . . .

—and so on, with daughter Molly 'and all my other daughters born or to be born' naturally taking the hindmost. Thus the rule of primogeniture still prevailed, and indeed the tenant for life might act as a limited owner in possession. But no tenant would be vested with outright ownership—he would be a 'highly interested' trustee; so too, no descendant would be totally disadvantaged by the accident of being younger. Thus the tenant for life would have to discharge the responsibilities of the estate while in possession—though he was paradoxically endowed with the discretionary power to convey the land in spite of not being vested in fee simple—and all of the beneficiaries would share in annuities or 'rent charges'. In William Empson's case, he would end up receiving £200 a year for life (he was to feel irked, years later, when he realized that this dividend might have been 'redeemed' for a lump sum equal to 25 years of rent charges: he could have made a fair income by investing £5,000 from an early age).

What is astonishing about the will is that it devised the estate in such terms for a period of 200 years, since a major consequence of the Settled Land Act of 1882 was the abolition of the concept of 'keeping the land in the family': an incumbent tenant for life could dispose of the property if he deemed it financially smart to do so. Yet Arthur Reginald must have felt he was putting everything right in drafting this will: he was seeking to determine the future prosperity of his estate, and at the same time he was protecting his heirs—all his descendants, born and unborn (and their spouses)—from an inheritance that might sometime turn into a nuisance. Nevertheless, if he planned to safeguard his offspring against a sense of jealousy or unfair exclusion, equally he was binding them to the estate by way of a will that made provision for a joint interest while cultivating collective possessiveness. There can be little doubt that Arthur Reginald Empson's primary motive was unexceptionable: he framed his will in the interests of his children, and his children's children, since all would retain a stake in the land. Yet there is something sinister, even hubristic, about seeking to ordain the future for 200 years. (The 1882 Act was in fact passed as the result of a period of agricultural depression, and yet paradoxically it smacks of Victorian confidence.) Clearly, for all that he hoped to determine that his descendants would hold their mutual interest in the land, Arthur Reginald was still a true son of his forefathers to the extent that he could not actually countenance the idea that the Yokefleet estate might ever pass out of the family.

This is made rigorously plain by an article in the will which provides that every person, without exception, who 'becomes entitled as tenant for life or as tenant in tail male or in tail by purchase to the possession or to the receipt of the rents and profits of the premises hereby settled' shall 'use and bear the surname and arms of Empson'. (He did not know that he himself was not even entitled to bear those arms.) If anybody who was otherwise entitled to become tenant should refuse or neglect to take the name after a year, they would forfeit their rights: 'the premises hereby settled shall immediately go to the person next in remainder'—it would be as if 'that person were dead and there were a general failure of issue'; likewise for anyone who was born with the surname and relinquished it. Such intransigence in the matter of perpetuating the family name evinces a degree of pride—pride of person, pride of place in the community—which the Empson family could not be said to have earned in generations of restive residence in Yokefleet. To coin a phrase, Arthur Reginald must have got it from his father. But the issue was primarily one of self-pride: it seems to be characteristic of his conceit, for example, that he was intent on bequeathing his property and personalty exclusively to the children of his loins. He seemed highly unwilling to spare much else for anyone else. To his surviving sister Margaret, still a spinster (the youngest of his three sisters died in December 1908, the month before the will was signed), he devised £100 *tout court*: it was precisely as much as he left to his second cousin Charles William (who would still have the decency, ten years later, to will his wealth, including Blacktoft Grange, back to his cousins in Yorkshire); the same too as he bequeathed to each of his executors—his cousin Sir John Poynder Dickson-Poynder, Baronet, of Hartham Park, Wiltshire,[28] and George William Lloyd, of Stockton Hall, York—for their trouble in proving the will and accepting the trusts. What is more, he seemed to be loath to admit that he owed a moral debt to his niece Maria Alice, the child of his deceased elder brother (who was just 40 when he signed the will), for he left her only the same trifling legacy of £100—an insulting gesture, a tip. As William Empson was to remark many years later, when he looked into his father's complex will, 'Alice must have been furious to get only £100.'[29] In truth, the father's intention must have been far less to shirk the claims of those outside his immediate family who might otherwise feel entitled to a portion of his estate than to leave as much as possible to his children—just as any good father would wish. All the same, William not unreasonably felt that his father had done ill by the alienated niece.

William was 9 when his father died, and he did not speak of him in later years. (Nor, according to Monica Empson, did his brother Charles.) We can only guess at the reasons why he found no occasion to mention his father. Maybe the father, who by all accounts was a very kind man (the young Charles would happily trail him round the farm), made little impression on his youngest child; maybe William was repressing feelings which he never articulated even to himself. Yet he was not uninterested in the figure of the father: even in a review of the published facsimile of the drafts of T. S. Eliot's *The Waste Land* (1971), he proposed the unusual critical insight, 'Eliot wanted to grouse about his father.'[30] But it would be wrong to suggest that he suffered from an obsession or aversion in respect of the father—except in so far as fatherhood meant dogmatism, which he would always meet with contumacy. With regard to his own father's will— it is one of the few documents by the man that has come down to us—he observed once, albeit disingenuously: 'My father, we need not deny, wrote a rather silly will, in a jovial manner, but he expected the Trustees to make bold investments for his children, who were still young; rather dashingly, he suggests South American [Argentinian] railways, which at the time were a speculation.'[31] But the context of those remarks is a creative misreading of the character of the will, which is in truth neither jovial nor dashing but grimly calculating. William never quite comprehended the ins and outs of his father's will, but in later years he did come to feel that the trustees had not garnered the fruits of shrewd investment that the family had a right to expect. Actually, he was not in the least concerned on his own account; he was temperamentally incapable of mastering strategies for sound financial management—or he could not be bothered. He felt agitated only when his sister ran into difficulties, or when it seemed to him, quite often mistakenly, that his own offspring might be done out of their rights.[32]

It is one of life's natural little ironies that once he had children of his own he should become anxious about the legacy he would be able to will to them, especially when his own negligence or inattentiveness might be the cause of their inheriting less than they should. Yet as a youth of left-wing leanings he had tended to sniff at the anticipatory acquisitiveness—the sheer greed—of the dying hand: his father's testamentary prudence. As the Settled Land Act 1882 allowed, Arthur Reginald Empson declared that the trustees of his Will should administer his estate for 200 years 'upon trust that they shall as and when occasion shall arise . . . grant or procure to be granted a lease or leases of all or any part of the coal and other minerals within and under the hereditaments'. Since Arthur had married into a big coal-owning family, it is not in the least surprising or disreputable that he should wish his descendants to benefit from any natural resources in the bowels of his property. In a way he was right, because the Selby Field, about 15 miles from Yokefleet, is part of the Barnsley drift. Before the nationalization of the coal-mining industry, the father would obviously project a long profit from mining his lands. The very idea depends on the archaic 'legal fiction' that where you own land, you also own that portion of the sky above your property—the 'airspace'—as well as the earth down to the centre: in cross-section, that is to say, your notional rights are wedge-shaped, with the apex at the earth's core. If William was too young to have realized at first hand that his father had mines and money in mind—perhaps with something approaching a manic intensity—other members of the family must have muttered about this preoccupation in the years following his death—because William would write a poem on the subject when he came to be 22. 'Legal Fiction', published at Cambridge in 1928, Empson would later call a political poem—very relevantly so—for it is a suave indictment of the kind of territorial imperative upon which his father's will had so rapaciously insisted:

> Law makes long spokes of the short stakes of men.
> Your well fenced out real estate of mind
> No high flat of the nomad citizen
> Looks over, or train leaves behind.
>
> Your rights extend under and above your claim
> Without bound; you own land in Heaven and Hell;
> Your part of earth's surface and mass the same,
> Of all cosmos' volume, and all stars as well.
>
> Your rights reach down where all owners meet, in Hell's
> Pointed exclusive conclave, at earth's centre
> (Your spun farm's root still on that axis dwells):
> And up, through galaxies, a growing sector.
>
> You are nomad yet; the lighthouse beam you own
> Flashes, like Lucifer, through the firmament.
> Earth's axis varies; your dark central cone
> Wavers, a candle's shadow, at the end.

Empson hardly ever commented on this lucid poem, but he did speak of it at one reading late in life. He was the son, he explained, 'of a Yorkshire landowner who actually did, as he grew older, get more and more puzzled by the belief that some wicked coal mine was sending tunnels under his land ... It was extraordinarily difficult to prove that anyone was mining under his land, and so claim royalties; it occupied his mind a good deal.' While that gloss is genial if mocking, the poem is in fact designed to be a severe satire on the father, who is the type of Ozymandias; in particular, the cadence of the concluding lines, delayed by two caesurae, spells out a *memento mori*. The sure implication of the poem is that the father is to be disparaged for the diabolical presumption of his proprietary jealousy. Although it is generalized by including the reader in the second person, its autobiographical subtext identifies the father as the anonymous 'you' who stands reproved. Thus one may say with reasonable confidence that Empson had come to feel estranged from his father—or rather, perhaps, from the capitalist culture his father was moved to perpetuate in his will.

Arthur, a year younger than John, was not 22 when his brother's death made him the heir of the family; on the father's death in 1916, he became the eldest male, at the age of 24. Even before that eventuality, he seemed to William to be virtually a parental figure, not someone to play with. As William would write to his third brother, Charles, in about 1973, 'Since I was a child, I have greatly admired Arthur for his strict sense of justice and complete lack of favouritism; I suppose chiefly because Mother told me he was like that ...'[33] Such terms of reference quite clearly reveal the roles they assumed—by nature or circumstance—one to another, from an early age.

But Arthur, like John, left home while William was still a child. After school at Charterhouse, he went direct to the Royal Military Academy at Woolwich; and before the age of 21 he was stationed in Ireland with the Royal Field Artillery—supposedly helping to pacify the Irish but actually more concerned with enjoying himself on a good mount. 'I don't believe the Government will do much coercing of Ulster,' he wrote home; 'they daren't even squash Mrs Pankhurst.'[34] Yet having determined to make his career in the army, he was not in the least shy of fighting; indeed, as the war in Europe became imminent, he ventured: 'I hope we don't back out of it if there is a general bust-up, as one would imagine that Russia and France would be quite a match for Germany and Austria; I don't believe the Germans are worth much anyway, though they do bounce such a lot.'[35]

Posted as a subaltern (a second lieutenant, on 14 shillings a day) to 116 Battery, 26th Brigade, 1st Division, he saw relentless action for the greatest part of the war in the fields of Flanders; at Ypres, at Loos, along the Aisne: muck, cold, blood, flailing offensives, nightmare retreats. Throughout the horrors he witnessed—the nerve-flailing, deafening cannonades, the sick, soggy days of digging trenches, saps, and salients—he remained the stalwart English gentleman, imbued with all the sangfroid of legend. 'We fired about 1500 rounds of ammunition in the battery yesterday,' he wrote to his mother early on (21 October 1915). 'We were all quite hoarse with shouting & deaf with the noise. We had our "baptism" of fire but it was the C. of E. method, not total immersion!!'[36] On 9 December that year: 'Some of my under-clothes, notably pants, have been destroyed by shell fire, not "shot from under me" like Aunt Mabel's groom's six horses, but hanging out to dry after a wash.'[37] Nothing ever came near to cracking his redoubtable spirit; early the next year he reported home, 'We have been having a lot of fun lately firing at Germans digging in the open, especially at one particular house which is an observing station or else a battalion headquarters and from which they all rush out to a dug-out when we get a shot close to it; and a ridiculous German pipsqueak gun which fires at our bit of trench, gives "the spice of danger" which they say makes a sport . . . P.S. I have purchased a Gramophone which warbles to us every evening.'[38] In all the dozens of letters he posted home, if he touched on the conditions of the war, he did not voice a trace of discontent or self-pity. On 31 July 1917, for instance, he was to write, 'Really one begins to feel the greatest contempt for shells after a bit; if you do get caught in the open & lie down flat whenever you hear one coming, the odds are on your side even when quite a big one bursts within 20 yards of you.'[39] And even in the miasmal, mud-mired field of battle he found a poignant, even sardonic reminder of home: 'The trenches are very like the warping just now. The mud reaches up to one's calf but is quite the stickiest stuff I've ever met—like warp that's just beginning to dry.'[40]

On 18 August 1916 he was severely wounded by a shard of shrapnel that lodged in his chest, and was invalided home to London. From the Royal Herbert Hospital he wrote with brave humour to his mother (who had buried Arthur Reginald only five months before): 'They have at last discovered the bit of shrapnel and have made a gallant attempt to extract it this morning but without any success; so I have to have what old man Smith calls a whiff tomorrow morning.'[41] The operation passed off well; but his full recuperation took some months, so he was temporarily posted to the 4th Army Artillery School, chafing all the while: 'I feel very sick at being here while it's going on; I've been in all the real "pushes" so far . . .'[42] In 1917 he returned to active duty with the 51st Battery, 39th Brigade. 'The Daily Mail Continental cheerfully remarks that if we can only hold out till next year when the Yanks will be in, all may yet be well,' he joked on 29 July. 'Surely this is a pessimistic view of the general situation!'[43]

Within a month, on 23 August, his mother received a dread telegram from the War Office: 'Deeply regret to inform you that Lieut. A. Empson R. F. A. 29th Brigade was killed in action August 21st. The Army Council express their sympathy.'[44] Almost a fortnight later, on 5 September, there followed the regulation telegram from Buckingham Palace, signed by the Keeper of the Privy Purse: 'The King & Queen deeply regret the loss you and the Army have sustained by the death of your son in the service of his country. Their Majesties truly sympathise with you in your sorrow.'[45] Yet the 19-year-old Charles Empson, who had recently volunteered as a cadet at Woolwich, noticed a significant discrepancy; he had received letters from Arthur which post-dated the supposed death: decidedly, they had been dated by Arthur—not a day or so later by the censor. A flurry of enquiries took place, agonizing days passed. Then the secretary of the War Office telegraphed on 11 September: 'Glad to inform you that report of death of Lieut. Empson incorrect. Letter follows.'[46] And finally Arthur himself wrote on 14 September, naturally to say that reports of his death had been greatly exaggerated. His letter is a typically Empsonian exercise in laconicism:

My dear Mother

Just a line to let you know that if anybody has been reporting me dead, missing or sick lately, he is misinformed . . .

Rather a good move of the King to send telegrams of condolence to *all* the next of kin! Earning his salary, I suppose.

Please give my love to Grannie; I hope you are all quite well.

Your loving son

Arthur[47]

There had been a confusion of corpses in France, it seems.

Arthur was assuredly the born soldier: dedicated to the service of his country, loyal to his troops, unflinching, brave beyond measure. Having being taken for dead in 1917, the next year he received a richly merited accolade for his gallantry in the face of the enemy: he was awarded both the Military Cross and the Belgian Croix de Guerre. Though proud of the medals, and of the Mons ribbon he also received, modesty prevented him from showing off; he sought no privileges but simply went on soldiering till the war drew to its right end. 'We were just beginning a battle which had every sign of being rather a sticky one, when this glorious news came in,' he saluted the armistice on 11 November 1918. 'We feel we ought to celebrate it in some way but don't quite know how.'[48]

On 22 November he and his fellows rode into Brussels to witness King Albert's official entry. All the restaurants were closed, as they found to their dismay; but the proprietor of 'a very swell place'—'the typical restaurateur of the best type—fat, with small imperial, and bald head'—treated them to a magnificent lunch *en famille* ('une petite soupe,' he had proposed), complete with sherry, claret, champagne, and cognac—

upon which, 'mighty merry' as Mr Pepys has it, we sallied forth with Henri and another small son to the Grande Place to see the King make his bow from the Hotel de Ville which is an extraordinary fine building. We had to wait two hours before he appeared with the Queen & a small princess person, whereupon we all sang something about 'Le Roi, la Loi, la Liberté' & departed.

Do you remember the evening in Amsterdam when the Princess Wilhelmina was born? Well, it was the same sort of thing last night, only more so. Crowds of people in all the main squares & streets, with soldiers of all nationalities... [T]hree elderly nuns accosted us, the eldest saying 'Americains?—Nong, Angly' whereupon they each extracted the right flag, waved it above their heads and shouted 'Ip ip Ourah' which I thought was rather a comic touch.[49]

By the end of November his division, slowly advancing eastwards, had reached only as far as Louvain; but at last on 13 December they officially marched into Cologne and across the Rhine. Weary, cold, and underfed, Arthur was amazed to find, when he had tea at the largest hotel he came across in Cologne, 'a band, huge crowds of well-dressed fat looking people and chocolate cakes ad. lib.'[50]

In another letter he reflected more darkly, 'I wonder if after this war, the "pomp and circumstance of glorious war" etc. *legend* will crop up again and people forget about the reality. Even now people are beginning to talk about their experiences as if they had rather enjoyed them.'[51] One might be forgiven, reading his letters from the front, for thinking that he had rather enjoyed himself a good deal of the time. But the truth is that he was a most staunch, resilient character, resolute in his refusal to retail either melodrama or false heroics: he would naturally shelter his mother and family from the most ghastly stories, even if not from all the worries. The blood of the Empsons was in that respect traditionally British: cool, tough, stoical, matter-of-fact, preferring bluffness and banter to bombast, not unemotional but not very readily demonstrative.

In November 1917 Charles Empson, Arthur's junior by six years, was given his first posting—to India. Arthur's letter in response to that news is quite casual, affable, and unsensational—but by no means insensitive:

Dear Charles
    Many thanks for your letter.
    I'm at present living in a pill box, the men being in derelict tanks. When it rains the water rises & is at present 1 foot deep in here. In spite of all, I'm

beginning to get quite a sentimental affection for the old place, and to look upon it as home—be it never so 'umble etc. We bail out furiously during our spare time and this morning I tried to work a system of drainage outside, but we were so continually coming upon dead Bosche in various stages of decay that we had to give it up.

I hope you have good luck in India and will be able to justify the purchase of the gun. I'm afraid I can give you no wrinkles, never having been in the Shiny [ocean] myself—though I *have* heard that it's a mistake to play poker on board ship until you quite understand the difference between a flush & a straight.

I'm afraid there is no hope of my getting leave to see you off as events are transpiring hereabouts.

There used to be a rule in India not to imbibe spirituous liquors before sundown but perhaps the march of science has done away with all that.

Well cheerio, good luck.

    Your affect. brother

        Arthur[52]

The dryly humorous, seemingly offhand, tone should not be mistaken for lack of feeling. ('I have seen a pipe,' Arthur wrote home while anxiously waiting for news of his brother's arrival in India, 'which I thought should cheer Charley's declining years and shall send it to him when he arrives.')[53] It is the understated style—clear-headed, determinedly genial and wry, disdaining fuss and nonsense—in which William Empson learned to think: the classically controlled British style.

Arthur rose to the rank of major by the end of the war. Yet his war was not over, for he was presently posted to the Army of the Black Sea—with the task, as he put it, of 'cowing Constantinople'. By the close of 1920, however, he came to realize that his destiny was no longer to fight the good fight overseas but take up his unwanted inheritance at Yokefleet—especially since his mother was about to move out of the unmanageable Hall into a convenient house on the public highway in Fulford, near York. Arthur and Jack had been very close as children, so Arthur was stricken when Jack perished. In time he had to admit that it was his doom to run the estate, though it would turn into a terrible grind for him as the years passed. And somehow, understandably, it soured him: in later years he would now and then refer to 'my good father' in very sarcastic tones.[54] He never married, though he once got as far as proposing to a distant cousin in the drawing-room at Yokefleet. 'We'll live in London,' she said. 'You'll live here,' he replied.[55] So that was that. Something of a puritan, and—at least with advancing years—critical of the behaviour of others, he was also canny about money, though less mean than economical. But he was a fine, dutiful son: he was well capable of cycling from Yokefleet to York when his mother fell ill. Like William, he was gloriously untidy; like his brother too, he did not miss a thing.[56]

Moreover, along with the rest of the family, Arthur had a great sense of humour—his finest grace. He was well able to take a tease, as one tale shows. In the tradition of the 'Flying Parson', Arthur enjoyed riding to hounds; he kept two hunters and rode with the Holderness Hunt. One of his hunters, a large chestnut called 'Yokefleet', he eventually sold to the Metropolitan Police in London; whereupon the next time anyone saw Yokefleet, the gelding had the honour of bearing the Duke of Edinburgh at the first Trooping of the Colour after the Coronation. But Yokefleet behaved very badly and almost unseated the Duke; it was the first time the Duke had been seen on a horse at any such occasion, so he was made to look very foolish. Reports of his mount's friskiness, with photographs, even featured in the newspapers in the USA, where Charles and Monica Empson were based at the British Embassy in Washington. Arthur, who had missed the news, was thus amazed to receive a terse telegram, 'Deplore behaviour of Yokefleet': amazed, but then—just as soon as he cracked the meaning of this missive—irresistibly, guffawingly amused.[57]

'The family works very well if you don't force it, but to look for soul-mates there is a form of incest,' Empson wrote in 1928.[58] Allowing for the wide span of their ages—fifteen years is longer than a lifetime to a child—the brothers and their sister got on together very well indeed. Despite the succession of crises the family suffered in his early years—the death of his eldest brother, the father's death, Arthur's near-fatal wounding—all of which occurred before he reached the age of 10, William's childhood was delightful and active. His brothers and sister were not the sort to make a drama out of a crisis: they were outgoing, sportive children for whom the estate at Yokefleet constituted a swell adventure playground.

A pretty little child with yellow curls, William was quite the ordinary baby. He would cry when his nursery governess, who sat next to him at the luncheon table, made him eat up his potato skins. Later on, when the Atcherley family came to visit, Charles (William's senior by eight years) would go and climb trees with Lucy Atcherley, the eldest of the cousins; and from up on high they would yell at Margery Atcherley and William, who were thrown upon one another's company, 'Go away, you children! We don't want you!' William liked Margery, but he liked her best of all on casual terms: on one trip to Scarborough, where all of the children built sandcastles, he suddenly hit her with his spade; when asked why he had turned so nasty, he said simply, 'I don't like Margery in her best clothes.'[59]

Every summer there would be a number of trips to the Yorkshire seaside, where William grew to pride himself on attaining the age when he could endure and finally even enjoy the full career of the homicidal Punch. 'It was quite frequent on the sands, as I remember,' he was to recall fifty years afterwards,

for one of the kids to bellow because 'Punch' was too hard to take, and this unfortunate would be carried away by its nurse; but the elder children, when I was one, proud that they could take it, would laugh on till the final hanging of Punch as their Victorian parents had done at the same age. I have been secretly afraid of the theatre ever since, but I feel I know what it is about.[60]

The cousins shared many other games, such as doing battle to be king of the castle (the Empson children felt decidedly snooty when they were able to produce a real sword-stick). On the other hand, William did not like any rough carry-ons. 'I am not a tough guy,' he would write much later in life; 'even when young I disliked horse-play, and still more being horse-played upon...'[61] Other rather more ambiguous treats included being taken to the pantomime (many years afterwards, he would still remember that the Fairy Queen in the panto was always made to utter bad verse)[62] and being subjected to dancing lessons: as he was to write in a later year, 'the profession of Eng. Lit. has become a farcically rigid convention, like being taught The Lancer when I was a little boy. That did not last long, though it seemed eternal at the time.'[63] Yet another cousin, Muriel Micklethwait, recalls that William was exceptionally good at making up games. Once, he made everyone pile books round the floor so as to frame a scenic route for an imaginary railway track: a tennis ball, or a ping-pong ball, did duty for the train, being shunted round this curiously-conjured obstacle course. But then his mother burst into the room and sent the books flying; the magic railway simply disappeared. William, his cousin reflects, seemed to have an 'extra loop' in his brain. Even as a grown-up he would not forget the secrets of a happy childhood: one day, for instance, to the great glee of Muriel's son, he stood on his hands and said the boy could have anything that fell out of his pockets.[64]

In the tradition of the Flying Parson, Arthur Reginald Empson was a keen sportsman; he hunted with both the Holderness and the York and Ainsty packs. His wife loved horses too, and hunting. (Indeed, William once snooped in his mother's diary and learnt that she had gone hunting just three days after his birth—such was her impatience to discharge the baby and resume her riding. He learned too, apparently from the same source, that he was not a planned child.)[65] Not surprisingly, William had to follow his parents into the saddle, but as a horseman he invariably displayed more valour than expertise. Nevertheless, he really did know how to manage a mount, at least in theory; he could tell a martingale from a bearing-rein.[66] In a later year, when *Brideshead Revisited* was being filmed for a television adaptation at Castle Howard (12 miles to the north-east of York), a colleague at the University of Sheffield happened to ask if he had ever visited the place: and Empson was not being affected when he responded, 'Yes, I used to go hunting there.' Similarly, it was personal experience, not pretentiousness, which enabled him to remark in *Seven Types of Ambiguity*, quite incidentally: 'Horses . . . display mettle by a continual expression of timidity.'[67] He would be every bit as brave, while exercising a good deal more skill, when he came to take up skiing, which gave him enormous pleasure.

But severe myopia meant that he could never be any sort of shot: he was Shakespeare's 'creeping fowler' in a rather dismal sense. Molly, who was a terrific tomboy and capable sportswoman, once resoundingly announced when they got home, 'William's bag today was a keeper, a cow and an owl!'[68] Though a tease, it might have stung him rather sharply in such a settled country family. (On occasion, Molly, for want of anything better to do, would go off and take potshots at rats in the stables: a latterday Annie Oakley.) Likewise, a family retainer remembers to this day that William 'couldn't hit a pig in a passage!' He would love to have been a good shot, he told his sister-in-law Monica; so he must have felt less than equal to his family's expectations. Yet Margery Atcherley recalls that all of the Empsons tended to be slapdash, and bad at holding the line. 'William once almost shot my husband.'[69] All the same, William always savoured the country, and the countryman's lot; it was bred into him to respect the know-how, hard work, and rough play of the landsman.[70] These verses from the poem 'Flighting for Duck' show his alert appreciation of Nature's loveliest turns while waiting for flights of duck on the crepuscular marsh:

> 'What was that drumming in the sky? What cry
> Squawked from the rustled bushes a reply?
> Was it near? Are they coming?
> Could you hear?' Sound travels a good way by night;
> That farm dog barking's half a mile away.
> But when the swarms gathering for food repay us
> This hint of anti-aircraft is disarmed
> And as the fleets at a shot reascend
> The eye orders their incredible chaos
> (The stars are moving like these duck, but slower,

Sublime, their tails absurd, their voices harsh)
And analyses into groups the crowds.
Two surfaces of birds, higher and lower,
Rise up and cross each other and distend
As one flight to the river turns, alarmed.
They are out of shot, and like the turning clouds
From meditative cigarettes amuse.
Manure in smoke over the fructuant marsh,
Curled vapour, incense from the cult of Ouse.

Bang. Bang. Two duck blur 'mid the social crew;
For man created, to man's larder due.
With plump or splash on the new-nurtured field
To Reason's arm they proper homage yield.
'The well-taught dogs wait but the voice to run,
Eager, and conscious of the murd'ring gun.'

Then the closing lines express a sense of cosmic awe, with vague stirrings of
the metaphysics of death; night's onset becomes a mesmeric emblem of the
very end of all:

Starlit, mistcircled, one whole pearl embrowned,
An even dusked silver of earth and sky
Held me, dazzled with cobwebs, staring round.
The black band of my hat leapt to my eye.
Alone in sight not coloured like the ground
It lit, like a struck match, everything by.

In a way, 'Flighting for Duck' offers a metaphysical comment on the more
simply marvelling 'Warping' that his father had written in 1894.

Now and then, William played tennis, but his weak eyes again meant he
could not be any good at it.[71] Thus his favourite outdoor recreation was the
simplest sort of exercise: he walked with vigour from an early age, and even
in advanced years he set a cracking pace that few could match.

William's next eldest brother, eight years his senior, was not destined to
exercise much of an influence over him. Charles was sent off to a prep
school called Praetoria House, outside Folkestone—he would journey to
and fro by a tramp steamer out of Goole (it carried coal to Kent, and Kent
coal back to Yorkshire)[72]—and then in 1912, when William was turning 6,
he won a mathematics scholarship to Harrow. By the time he left school, in
haste and against parental opposition, to take part in the war, Charles was
head of his house and in the sixth form.[73] At any rate, as well as being
intelligent and august, he was famous for his utter silences, and so made

little impression on the baby of the family. It had been a major event in his early years (as his wife was later told) when Molly was able to report, after the young folk returned from a party together, 'Yes, it was a very good party—even Charlie spoke!'[74]

And so it fell out that for want of fatherly or strong fraternal influence William was thrown upon the women of the family, especially the women on his mother's side of the family—whose views and values he soon grew to question and (more often than not) disrelish. The sportful, forthright Molly was good company for outdoor pursuits:[75] she was like a whole team of girl guides wrapped up in one person. Once, she took William camping out on the moors, with a horse to carry their baggage, but a gale wrecked their tent. 'It's all experience,' remarked the unflappable Molly.[76] That was the no-nonsense sort she was. At her boarding school, the recently founded Queen Ethelburga's in Harrogate, she excelled in the jolly-hockey-sticks stakes. Arthur Empson evidently had the true measure of his sister when he wrote home from the front in Flanders: 'I've just had a letter from Molly, apparently she is a fag! and remarks that her hands are smarting through doing fielding-practice! I'd no idea that Girls' Schools went in for all that sort of thing, but it ought to suit Molly.'[77] Like the good older sister she was (her cousin Margery noted), Molly always supported William—more even than she backed up Charles, to whom she was otherwise closer in spirit.[78]

Still, the bracing outdoors was not all in all for William in the way it was for Molly. From an early age he felt the need to stretch his intellect. Molly's affinity with him did not extend to his intense bookishness, so he shared his developing love for the written word with Margery Atcherley, who was bidden to furnish information about the fascinating business of writing: he asked her once, while still very young, 'What's a paragraph?' He would get out a book even before he could read, Margery remembers. The goodly supply of reading matter at Yokefleet Hall, which still housed much of the library lovingly assembled by the Flying Parson, must have helped William to cultivate his ferocious independence of mind, which he was never shy of voicing—even as a child (though he was not loquacious, it was a family in which everyone argued like mad). As he was to recall in a later year, 'When I was a horrid little boy, airing my views, grown-ups would sometimes say, in their rotund Edwardian manner, "Well, and who put that into your head?" I thought it very rude of them.'[79] If he enjoyed prattling from an early age, however, he was apparently just as sharp at listening to the curious conversational topics that grown-ups chose to air in the drawing-room, as well as (quite surprisingly) their various accents, if we can credit a memory he claimed at the age of 60:

Within living memory, if you were talking about pedigrees to someone proud of long descent from a royal bastard, it was essential to begin the word like 'bat', not like 'barn'; otherwise you would be suspected of low jeering at a subject which demanded reverence. I have heard this going on, and it is not likely to have been a Victorian invention, as that age was little plagued by royal bastards.[80]

What he heard (or overheard) was probably just a Yorkshire accent—though the short 'a' (as spoken by Lord Curzon) was certainly regarded as superior before 'RP' or the public school accent were ever heard.[81] But one can hardly begin to guess at the identity of whoever it was that his parents entertained who bragged about the thin blue blood in his veins.

Partly perhaps because he was significantly the junior of the brood, and because of the circumstances of his early years, he often felt like an outsider—a spectator, even an anthropologist—looking in on his family with a mixture of fondness and estrangement. His grandmother, for instance, struck him as so unreconstructed in her attitudes that she stood for a sadly fossilized Victorianism. For her, it seems, Christian sentiment was a white racial reserve, the prerogative of Empire; at Christmas 1930, shortly after the publication of his first book *Seven Types of Ambiguity*, Empson related to a friend this example of the old lady's views:

My grandmother lectured me for nearly an hour about a pamphlet she wants somebody to write, and as I can apparently make a publishing firm publish anything I had better do it for her—at once, before I go out of fashion, she explained. It is to tell the white races that they must unite and suppress the black races.[82]

Such sentiments were routine for someone of her generation and class, but her progressive grandson evidently considered them sufficiently scandalous or risible to be worth reporting in a postcard. Throughout his early years, William felt that his days in Yorkshire were lived among relics of a lost era, specimens of a species whose assumptions he did not wish to share—especially after he found out at his public school that politics really did have to do with rotten principles and social ills.

Most children at boarding school experience a feeling of asynchronism when they go home for the holidays, a troubling sense that things are out of step. Empson felt this gap in quite a high degree—because his parents were somewhat older than the average, and because his brothers (if not his sister) were old enough to be breasting adulthood while he was still a child. The aunts of the family, his mother's sisters, often struck him as surviving out of time, like figures in faience which would shatter if they were ever truly exposed to the twentieth century. On one occasion, in fact, he was so astonished by the passage of time that he felt impelled to type this memorandum about the sudden withering of a bygone beauty:

I have seen written in criticism that the final Guermantes party in Proust is incredible; people never grow old suddenly like that. The machinery of the novel presumes ten years while the teller sat in hospital. But I would like to tell an anecdote on this point, reporting a speaker who wholly agreed with that criticism. The last time I had seen the most beautiful, much the most beautiful, of my aunts she had sallied into a drawingroom as a public triumph, so vastly more beautiful than either of her daughters that it could not have helped teasing those fine and handsome and quite all-right women. This time I saw her, as an undergraduate, it was just that the lit lamp seen in the dark had become the empty lamp seen in the day; some mysterious force had failed; there is no question of make-up when the thing lost is so real. She was as delightful as ever. I was horrified; it had taken about a year and a half. And then, if you please, she began being pleasant to me by saying that she didn't follow most modern writing, but she did love Proust, and the only thing she couldn't quite swallow in Proust (apart from *all* the males turning out perverts, a just criticism) was this surprise at the end about everybody seeming old. How old was he when he died? she said, quite a young man when he died, I believe, not more than fortyfive, he can't have seen that happen, not at fortyfive. I just remember being repulsed after lunch when she went to have a good gossip with my mother in the garden, so I must have wanted more. The desires of the young are insatiable, and I wanted every word she said, and still do if she reads these lines. But for all that I was glutted with horror and with the truth of Proust.

As for his 'admirable mamma', he loved her dearly. But even so, she seemed a strange being. To a degree, the course of his development took the form, as it does for many children, of rebelling against the parent's expectations and values. His mother's sense of her own station in life—her conservatism, her genteel prerogatives—was an embarrassment. He remarked in a rather pretentious diary he kept for a brief while as an undergraduate, with specific reference to his mother's particular, precautionary ways as he observed them during a vacation: 'the pleasure that women take in locking up their houses, that passionate and tidy hugging, or nocturnal gustation of their estate, is borne [*sic*] of an enthusiasm I cannot follow...'[83] He was thus designating that he preferred to be a free spirit, untrammelled by pride of ownership—or responsibility. Not to be labelled or judged in terms of rank or class, I am a bohemian, a social idealist, the young Empson appeared to declare. Yet he understood the pattern of her behaviour—the cultural paradigm—well enough; it was her all-too-ready, and indeed resourceful, compliance with the conventions of her class that gave him pause.

When we were small [he noted in his diary in about 1925–6] mamma used to say about Christmas presents, our mechanical affections to aunts never seen in flesh, who might leave money at last to someone that if there was a blot, or dear for darling 'You've got to get it right, you know, people are awfully queer'. 'She'll get awfully huffy, you've no idea.' When I was told I was offended about something, I would take offence. What do you take me for, an *aunt* or something? Mamma (person not principle) was very subtle, she was mainly on the side of the aunts really, and people reasonably were queer. But to deal with our child's logic she judged plainly the system she thought in, we must go through the motions, and might think at pleasure.

Hollow gestures, empty manners, dead show: such, it occasionally seemed to him, was the stock-in-trade of the landowning, lording, anachronistic class that his mother embodied and expected to perpetuate. 'You mustn't expose a servant to temptation' was one of her best *Sententiae pueriles*, but William must have found it a condescending saw. Throughout his early years and into young manhood, one of the most dislikable aspects of his mother's demeanour was the very fact that she would weigh other people by their breeding. She was a snob, and not loath to show it.

My Mum was a Tory and a terrific class-addict [he recalled in 1973], so that I could bring nobody to her house except people I didnt like...[84]

For the young William, this would not have been a neutral feature of life at home: it must have felt oppressive. The phrase 'to her house' may or may not be significant in this respect; while such a locution could be seen to imply that he had distanced himself from the domestic environment in which he grew up, it could equally well suggest that he always thought of The White House, Fulford, just outside York, as strictly his mother's house—the house to which the doughty, tweedy, clever widow moved after the death of her husband[85]—whereas 'home' for him naturally meant the Hall, the place of his birth and earliest years. At any rate, William was a *rara avis* in the social world of the Empsons, past and present. He loved, especially when at university, to associate with individualistic, odd, wild kinds of people: those who bowed to no norms; writers, artists, socialists; eccentrics, misfits, rebels. He enjoyed acquaintances who neither owned nor laid claim to their place in society. By nature and vocation he stood aside from the stereotypes of his class and upbringing. And yet it seems likely too that he gradually, consciously, came to accentuate the oddity, the zany, in himself, so as to stress his own difference—his distance from the snooty, presumptive culture of his parent's sector of the upper class. Once, while visiting his mother at the White House, he was asked out to a dinner-dance; but since he did not have a dinner jacket, he just donned a macintosh and acted as if he was quite indifferent to the impropriety of his get-up. (Another day, she noticed, he had tied up his shoes with string.) So perhaps, at times, there was a signal, even if only half-conscious, touch of defiance in his eccentricity, his deviation from convention. Yet there was something genuinely special about his style of mind and eye; on another occasion, for example, he suddenly observed, without looking for effect, 'Those stripes on the curtains have every colour you can see on an egg.'

His cousin Margery Key recalls him once walking all the way from Fulford into York with one foot on the kerb and one in the gutter— but that was more probably just William being William, the man of mind, rapt in algebraic abstraction or literary analysis.

Thus it is not in the least surprising that one of his Cambridge friends, Desmond Lee, the classicist and future Headmaster of Winchester College, should write of Empson (*c*.1928) in his unpublished memoirs,

> He was fond of his family . . . But his family found him difficult to understand, and he found communication with them difficult, saying to me once that fond as he was of them, when he visited them it was 'like being in the company of steam engines'. You recognised their merits but had little in common.[86]

The family were very nice to each other (Empson's sister-in-law Monica— Charles's wife—likewise recalled for me), but they were inclined to mock William in a friendly way.[87] It was hardly surprising.

'I can't read his books,' Mrs Empson once declared apropos her son— though she was assuredly very proud of him, and of his achievements in that line. In any event, she set him no model of literary endeavour—and it seems that she had little feeling for the theatre: as he was to recall in 1968, 'I remember my mother when I was a boy remarking that she had once been taken to see *Macbeth*, long long ago, and it turned out to be the most appalling melodrama—"I was quite shocked," she said placidly.'[88] If he left any manuscripts lying around the house, his mother would just throw them out: a stray sheet of paper was simply a piece of untidiness. He would admit to his friend John Hayward, even at the age of 32, 'in my mother's house . . . any writing left about (including two complete plays of mine some time ago) gets immediately destroyed'. Perhaps feeling he had been too damning of his mother's ruthless philistinism, her insensitivity to the written word, he added with huge generosity of spirit: 'Very properly too, as I feel even when it turns out inconvenient.'[89]

Accordingly, it was his own precocious curiosity, his greed for reading, that brought about what we can only call his first—literal—'gut reaction':

When I was a little boy, about eight I think, I read a story in my sister's *Girl's Own Paper* about a catty girl who accused another of tightlacing, whereas the truth was, the story explained, that all these girls, including the catty one, were ill and in pain because they had to tightlace. I crept away sweating with horror, but feeling I had learned an important truth about the way people behave.[90]

He would also quite incidentally remember, when writing to his mother in 1938, 'the only thing I heard about China as a child was descriptions of Chinese tortures from poor Miss St George [presumably a mad governess], which always made me sick, and I never dared complain about it.'[91] What appalled him was that any culture could find value in inflicting pain upon an individual. It upset him just as much that his own mother, for example, should suffer herself to wear stays at the bidding of her society as that the Christian God should be pleased and appeased by the sacrifice of his Son. Indeed, it was to become an article of Empson's humanist faith that sadism is the major evil of mankind.

One of the most deep-rooted convictions of Empson's life, enunciated at length and with the utmost passion in *Milton's God*, was his contempt for Christianity, which he tagged 'the torture-worship'. In particular, he scorned the doctrine of the Trinity, the consubstantiality of the Son with the Father, as nothing but an article of evasion, so to speak, a sophistical formulation devised to overcome a morally repellent alternative. 'The doctrine of the Trinity is necessary, or the Father appears too evil in his "satisfaction" at the crucifixion of his Son,' he wrote with devastating logic. 'But to present Jesus as one with the Father only turns him into a hypocrite; when he prays for his enemies to be forgiven, he knows under his other title he will take revenge.' Thus it is particularly interesting, with regard to estimating the influence upon the adult Empson of events and impressions from his childhood, that he was given to understand his own father was of his mind vis-à-vis the doctrinal trick of Trinitarianism:

The Creed of St Athanasius (my mother told me as a boy that my father threatened the Vicar to walk out if it was read, but unfortunately happened to be asleep when the occasion arose) amounts to saying that the Father and the Son both are and are not identical, and that you will go to Hell unless you believe both. Christians have always been encouraged to recognize the negative half of this paradox by the insistent metaphors about money, which led them through their natural exasperation into persecution of the Jews. Terms such as 'redemption', deep into human experience though they undoubtedly plunge, are metaphors drawn from the slave-market. It is hard to call up the identity of Father and Son at such points, and envisage God as driving a hard bargain with himself before he agrees to torture himself to death out of love for mankind . . . Only if this God had a craving to torture his Son could the Son bargain with him about it. In return for those three hours of ecstasy, the Father would give up the pleasure of torturing for all eternity a small proportion of mankind; though such a tiny proportion, it has usually been agreed, that his eternal pleasure can scarcely be diminished.[92]

It is not possible to say just when he was thunderstruck by the gross significance of the Sacrifice that is crucial to Christian doctrine, but it may have been soon after he discovered the appalling truth of tightlacing: the connection between those two horrors is obvious—even if, at first blush, seemingly bathetic. Though not squeamish, Empson was hypersensitive, especially with regard to the causing of pain. But it is unlikely that Laura Empson took the time to discuss the Christian religion with her son, even if he had one day insisted on pointing out to her the fallacies of the faith. The widow Empson would have accepted Christianity as a natural part of life, just as normal and necessary as stout shoes and a trug for gardening: not as a thing you could do without or seriously scoff at. (William would sit cleaning his nails while in church, a cousin recalls—out of indifference or defiance, either way a gesture of some sort.)

But William was gravely affected by what he thought the incoherence, the radical dishonesty and moral ugliness, of Christianity. His inability to talk to his mother about his misgivings, the reasons why he had no choice but to reject her faith, served only to cap the great wall that separated him from her time-honoured values. Laura Empson's faith in Christ was of a piece with her Conservatism: to doubt her God would feel like failing her place in society. At any rate, just as the poem 'Legal Fiction' stands in some sort for a criticism of Empson's father, so 'To an Old Lady' depicts his mother as another alien phenomenon: in her case, as a planet apart. (Not surprisingly, both poems—written in 1928, after Empson attained his majority—are imbued with the idioms and imagery of *Paradise Lost*.)

> Ripeness is all; her in her cooling planet
> Revere; do not presume to think her wasted.
> Project her no projectile, plan nor man it;
> Gods cool in turn, by the sun long outlasted.
>
> Our earth alone given no name of god
> Gives, too, no hold for such a leap to aid her;
> Landing, you break some palace and seem odd;
> Bees sting their need, the keeper's queen invader.
>
> No, to your telescope; spy out the land;
> Watch while her ritual is still to see,

> Still stand her temples emptying in the sand
> Whose waves o'erthrew their crumbled tracery;
>
> Still stand uncalled-on her soul's appanage;
> Much social detail whose successor fades,
> Wit used to run a house and to play Bridge,
> And tragic fervour, to dismiss her maids.
>
> Years her precession do not throw from gear.
> She reads a compass certain of her pole;
> Confident, finds no confines on her sphere,
> Whose failing crops are in her sole control.
>
> Stars how much further from me fill my night.
> Strange that she too should be inaccessible,
> Who shares my sun. He curtains her from sight,
> And but in darkness is she visible.

An extraordinary poem, it is at once tribute and lamentation. However much we honour her, the poem says, mother still inhabits another world: the poet and the parent find no common ground. So the generation gap goes on for ever. (When Empson's mother read this poem, it does not surprise us to know, she naturally assumed that it was about *her mother*— such is the perennial divide between parents and children.)

In answer to a correspondent in 1973, Empson observed about the certain link between 'To an Old Lady' and the Christian faith he spurned:

The religion has always seemed to me just black horror, or already did when I was a schoolboy, long before writing these poems. Perhaps I ought to have said so, but my friends took it for granted. I felt bad about other things, but freedom from the torture-worship was a bit of clear gain.

[Mother] was not a sanctimonious woman, and it seemed clear to me that the Martians would not call their own planet by the name of a god, whereas they would call the earth after some quite unexpected god. Still, it is true she was a Christian and I wasn't, and it might have been easier to talk to her if I had been. I wouldn't mind having thought of that, and if I did it doesn't give the holy boys much to crow over. The bang in the last line, 'but in darkness', was meant to imply: 'It's only when you're in real trouble that you see the old woman at her best', and this was written before I was thrown out of Cambridge, when I thought her behaviour justified my tribute. I ought to have put this in the notes, but was shy about it.[93]

For Empson as a child, and certainly as a modern young man, not having his mother's social and religious certainties, the world was up in the air: the future had to be forged without reliance on things past. As he put it in the notes published along with his poem (taking care to generalize this issue),

'*Our earth* without a god's name such as the other planets have is compared to some body of people (absurd to say "the present generation") without fundamental beliefs as a basis for action.' Empson's choice was to head his own way in life, separate from the expectations of his family.

Some critics of his work have tended to see his stance on Christianity as unreasonable, excessive, even hysterical; in sum, they spy a bigot. In his later years, they believe, he became bitterly negative, even virulently destructive, in his views. But any such interpretation of his career is a mistake. On the strongest natural and moral grounds he felt sickened by the practice of cruelty: appalled at the perverse notion of the Father in Heaven being 'well pleased' at witnessing the sufferings of his Son, the Christ. 'To say I hate God seems to me an example of pretending that Christianity is the only religion,' he protested in a letter; 'I hate Moloch, the god who was satisfied by crucifying his son.'[94] He would not acquiesce in the idea that the Christian faith is little more than a function of civility, a gentle facet of the English social order—as his mother would almost certainly have held. On the contrary, his scorn for this particular God could summon both logic and history to witness.

S. G. F. Brandon, for example, in *The Judgment of the Dead* (1967)—which Empson reviewed some six years after publishing *Milton's God*—gave an objective assessment of the meaning and implications of Christ's ministry in terms that in no way shirk the issues that goaded Empson. Starting out from the eschatalogical tradition of Jewish apocalyptic belief that the Messiah would reward his faithful servants with everlasting bliss and damn his enemies to eternal torment, Brandon observes, Catholic Christianity emerged as 'a salvation-religion centred on a saviour-god'. Notwithstanding the increasing stress that the historical Church laid on a wholesome soteri-ology, however, 'Christ appears [in the liturgy] in two different, and logically contradictory roles, namely, as the Saviour and the Judge of mankind.'

We are naturally shocked [Brandon goes on] at the readiness with which earlier generations of Christians believed that the larger part of mankind would ultim-ately be doomed to hell. Their attitude, however, was logical; for Christian eschatology taught that faith in Christ was essential to salvation . . . The dilemma of modern Christian theology is that of shedding the mythology of an ancient eschatology and its rigorist exclusiveness which involves contemplating the eternal damnation of most of mankind, while maintaining faith in Christ as the unique Saviour of men.

His conclusion is therefore inescapable (though it is difficult to judge whether he is implying an argument for more rigour or deep regret):

'because belief in judgment after death, with its eternal consequences of Heaven or Hell, constitute[s] the "teeth" or ultimate authentication of the Christian ethic, that belief has now become practically even more necessary than it was before.' In any event, he adds a footnote that presses home the terrible irony that this religion of merciful redemption somehow requires the sanction of everlasting punishment: 'Ideally, of course, the Christian moral code should be practised for love of God, and not for the hope of gaining Heaven or escaping Hell. Nevertheless, the validity of that code depends logically upon an ultimate distinction, made by God, between the just and the unjust.'[95]

Empson's opinion of such a blackmailing doctrine was contemptuous. 'A man who believes in Hell can't help relating the prospect of it to his feelings about life in general,' he maintained. So it may be the ultimate irony of his early years that his own mother dearly believed in Hell; at least it is evidence of the sorry gulf between mother and son, as between Empson and the majority of his forebears. Mrs Empson was occasionally heard to complain about her local vicar, a liberal: 'I go to church in order to be told I'll go to Hell if I'm not good—and he never tells me that!'[96]

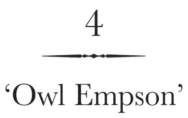

4

'Owl Empson'

[W]hen I was a little boy I was very afraid I might not have the courage which I knew life to demand of me . . .

Milton's God, 89

Prep School: bombs, stripes, maths

Just why his parents sent him so far away to school is a mystery. There were perfectly good prep schools within convenient range of home; and yet at the age of $7\frac{1}{2}$ he was posted off to an unhistoric redbrick institution on the south coast.

Praetoria House School stood on the western outskirts of Folkestone, near to Shorncliffe camp where troops were assembled before embarking for France. German pilots braved the Channel from Belgium, piloting small planes called *Taubes* ('Crows') with the intention of dropping a few bombs on London: if they had any left over after the dicey run across Kent and Sussex, or failed to reach the capital, they would dump their lethal cargo on Shorncliffe, Folkestone, or Dover. The school headmaster, as soon as he detected the high-pitched hum of an aeroplane, would fetch out a whistle that sounded like a siren and give several loud blasts; everyone would drop everything and make a mad dash for the air-raid shelter under the cricket pavilion. This little drama held an obvious appeal for the new boy from Yorkshire in the summer of 1915. 'The most eventful and most happy day here was on the 12th [June] (Saturday),' he wrote to his sister Molly on the Sunday (obligatory letter-writing day). 'We had a cricket-match against another school that day, and the "dug-out" whistle went some time between 8 and 10 o'clock. It was jolly good fun waking up I can tell you, I took quite a long time to do it (= wake up).'[1] But the excitement must have palled when the alarm was raised several times a day. His brother Arthur wrote home on 13 June, with kindly thoughts from out of Flanders fields: 'I am sorry to hear that William is so down in the mouth but his first term will soon be over now.'[2]

Praetoria House was owned by the headmaster, Maurice Roderick, a stout, balding, jovial Welshman, affectionately known as 'Old Mo', and his equally easy-going South African wife; their own son attended the school, and a daughter came to help at the worst times of the war. In order to run their establishment of about fifty noisy and potentially riotous children, they were assisted by four masters—all of them invalided out of the services—and one cleric, plus two delightful mistresses to help with the juniors. This teaching team managed to create a fairly scholarly forcing house. Marks and form places would be given out every week, and regularity ruled the day. Though a pleasant and usually reasonable man, Old Mo evidently frowned on any attempt to spoil the boys in his charge. William had to tip off soft sister Molly in one of his first letters: 'P.S. We are not allowed any other eatables sent from home except fruit'[3]—though it appears that sweet-eating was not entirely excluded, and the chief thing was to share the luck of one's tuck. 'I am allowed cakes if it is divided among the boys.'[4] On Sundays they were taken for long country walks in strict crocodile formation. 'Molly and Charley are mistaken in thinking that you choose a partner and squirm about as much as you like,' William briefed his mother, 'you have to go in line during walks.'[5] He would sign himself off with prim dignity, 'With love, William Empson', or else simply: 'so goodbye. W. Empson.'

Discipline was maintained by a system of slips. Every teacher had two books, the size and shape of a cheque book, one pink and one blue. Good work or behaviour was rewarded with a pink slip known as a 'Star', but misdemeanours were recorded in the blue book, and the culprit was issued with a blue slip ominously called a 'Stripe'. These had to be shown up to the headmaster in his study, every day at 6 p.m., and if blue outnumbered pink, trouble was in store. First offenders were set 'squares': numbers from 9 to 1 were written down, and below them 1 to 9—all of which had to be multiplied together and then divided by some other unimaginable figure. These mind-wrenching feats had to be done in spare time, and reams of paper would be consumed. However, repeated production of blue slips resulted in a beating: Old Mo would vigorously apply a stout leather slipper to the bare bottom of the malefactor, who was bent over an old leather armchair. Even before the first stroke had been laid on, the victim would set up a huge howling, and Old Mo would address him as 'sir'—no doubt expecting the child would see fit to take it like a man. 'Will you do it again, sir?' 'You are lazy and disobedient, sir.'

An even-tempered little chap, William betrayed no signs of homesickness or insecurity—even after the death of his father in 1916. His mother was too matter-of-fact to encourage in her child any indulgence of temperament; it was more important simply to get on with life and its obligations. The tough old stock of the Empsons would see you through, and William was brought up to know that one should show resilience and scorn self-pity. Furthermore, privilege was inextricable from duty. On top of that, he had learned that he was an afterthought of the family, an extra burden for his mother; and experience showed that Molly afforded him the best love of all. All the ambition of the parents had been lavished upon the three elder brothers. William was small for his age, myopic, and hopelessly equipped by nature more for private study than for public service. His mother loved him, and believed in him; but still, as he understood, he had a lot to live up to. This combination of factors made him a sober but game boy, and reflective ahead of his years. As one of his contemporaries would remember, 'Whereas most of the pupils were noisy, mischievous, rushing down corridors and fighting each other when released, W.E. remained calm and aloof.'[6] But he was not perceived as either a brainy brat or a bully's butt. 'I think he was quite popular if only for the reason that—unlike many of his contemporaries—he never sought popularity. He might well have been involved in such minor escapades as making apple pie beds or tying shoe laces together, but I cannot imagine him putting glue on a master's chair!'[7] He was phlegmatic, unfastidious, and modestly confident. When he wrote to his mother during his first summer at the school, for example, 'Do not think we are still wearing stiff collars and long trousers', it was not at all in a spirit of priggishness but merely to signal that no fuss needed to be made.[8] William understood the run of the thing, and had everything under control. He had no talent for games, and few other available recreations; he was even thrown out of the school choir ('and now cackle mournfully away to myself in a corner,' he added with evident glee).[9] But he was not a rebel, and approached his every next task with due seriousness. 'We have exams this week,' he wrote home in November 1915, for example, and, without pausing even to hint at his feelings on the subject, went straight on: 'There is going to be a concert for the convalescent soldiers. I am going to recite a peice [*sic*] called "Bravo".'[10] But equally he could be as excitedly boyish as the next man: 'P.S. I have seen two air-ships (not Zeppilins [*sic*]) since I came here.'[11]

Academically, he did well from the start. On 5 December 1915 he began his weekly letter home: 'If no news is good news, I have the best place possible this week.' Overcoming the nonsense of that opening, he explained: 'I am top in exams. Exams;-Composition 86. (I was top in it). Geometry 44. English Grammer [*sic*] 69. Geography 47. Arithmetic 80. History 43. Latin Gram. 54. Latin Exercise [and] Latin translation 111. Script 72. French Gram. 66. French Translation 74.'[12] He stayed at the top throughout his five years at the school, despite the fact that it presently became distractingly nomadic. As the bombing became more frequent (one bomb fell on a girls' school next door), the school was transplanted to a grim mansion in Matlock Bath, Derbyshire. Then, after about a year, it came south again, to Manor House, Horsham, which afforded much more suitable accommodation; and finally, after the armistice, it went back to Folkestone. But William was a natural student, raptly inquisitive, and unperturbed by having to go from pillar to post. (Indeed it became a feature of his life that he could read and write literally anywhere: he would live like a pig in a world of his own, and the only thing that really bothered him was noise.)

In particular, the wonders of science excited his curiosity at a young age. 'There is a lot of scientific books in the library, and I have read a lot of them,' he told his mother in an early missive, not as a boast but merely for information. ' "The romance of the animal world," and "The Romance of Insect Life," (by Edmund Selous). Then I am reading "The romance of animal arts and crafts," by H. Coupin & J. Lea. They are quite good, I like Edmund Selous's [books] best.'[13] Perhaps it is not surprising that Maurice Roderick soon had occasion to tell the assembled school about an essay that Empson had written on the subject of 'Instinct in Animals'. The piece was remarkable for a boy of his age, more like the work of a man of 21, said Old Mo; it was duly published in the school magazine.[14]

Though not a man to show any favouritism, Roderick must nevertheless have felt gratified to find that Empson had a flair for his pet subject, mathematics, which he taught very thoroughly indeed. In the year 1918–19 Empson joined the first (top) form, where he and two other bright young things—Hazelden and Flurscheim—were taken by the Headmaster as a separate class for mathematics. 'We took the Common Entrance papers for practice,' Geoffrey Hazelden recalled for me, 'and were expected to get 100%, which I believe we did as often as not.'[15] Empson's work was atrociously untidy, and he was conscious of it ('Excuse bad writing and spelling with a touch of generosity,' he remarked in one letter home),[16] and yet he must have got the right answers, because Old Mo accepted it. That summer, Hazelden won the top scholarship to Cheltenham, chiefly on account of his mathematics, while Empson—who was his junior by a year—still had another year to go. The Headmaster explained to Mrs Empson in May 1919, 'He is not up to the standard this year, but will be certain of a Scholarship next year. I am anxious for him to try Winchester next year, but Harrow comes before Winchester . . . He has improved his writing a little during the holidays. I hope he will continue to do so.'[17] Mr Roderick kept up the pressure on the promising 12-year-old, yet again telling his mother in April the next year: 'I feel pretty certain that William will get a scholarship. William is working very well, but he is still careless, but improving.'[18]

We do not know what happened to the Headmaster's hopes for Harrow, but the child carelessly contracted measles at a time coinciding with the exceptionally demanding scholarship examination for Winchester—the toughest entrance examination in the country—which he took with another boy from Praetoria House School. His mother promised that he could go on a skiing holiday to Switzerland if he landed a place, which was a tremendous incentive for him. 'The exams finished yesterday,' he wrote home on a postcard on 11 June, 'and we are now "resting" in the nursery again . . . We will hear to-morrow, and wire if there's any luck. The measles are going by degrees, but there's about ten left still. The next boy wants the pen now, so Goodbye William.'[19] The following day, the Second Master of Winchester advised Mrs Empson that her son had been placed tenth on the roll for entrance to College (he was three places higher than R. H. S. Crossman, the future Labour Cabinet Minister), and was elected to a scholarship by the Warden and Fellows.[20] The scholarship afforded an invaluable remission of fees: William worked out that he could pay his way through school (tuition and boarding fees would amount to £13 a term) with the investment income on the sum of £300 that his great-aunt left him at this time. He therefore counted his lucky stars in exemplary fashion:

Well, I succeeded with an effort. Last year the tenth boy wouldn't have got in. We met the boy who had been turned down for 9th on the list, because their were just 8 vacancies. He must have felt sick! The other boys must have been silly asses to have pushed me up so. I made an awful hash of some of the papers. Cobbe (the other boy who went up with me) hasn't heard yet, as he is a War scholar and the only one up. We met another boy who got a schol at Winchester from P.H.S. He was rather a superior gentleman, but awfully decent to us . . . We had to make up English verse. A sonnet on a submarine(!) An aeroplane journey from London to Paris! The happiest day I ever spent(!) I hope there were no budding genii in the neighbourhood!

I suppose this means Switzerland! I've afraid I've been terribly lucky.
   Best love
      William—wondering why?[21]

Apart from the long-lost essay on 'Instinct in Animals', and perhaps his
sonnet on a submarine, there was little evidence in his prep school career
of a literary genius in the making—mathematics was his forte—apart from
one original poetic effort that he penned at Praetoria House for a boy who
was a year or two his junior. John A. Simson was not only younger, he
figured among the academic 'sediment' of the school, while Empson
seemed to him so far advanced as to be virtually middle-aged; Simson
has remembered too: 'I was shy and not at all self-confident, and probably
found W.E. a congenial pal.'[22] For his part, Empson may have gone out of
his way to make a chum of a poorly favoured young chap, knowing what it
felt like to be the baby of the family; certainly it redounds to his credit that
he did not disdain his juniors. When Simson asked him to pen something
in his autograph book, Empson composed a witty piece of doggerel which
strikingly adumbrates his mature aversion to the Christian religion. Written by 29 June, just as he was on the brink of leaving Praetoria House (at
the age of 13), it is his first known poem:

> Mother, saying Anne good night,
> Feared the dark would cause her fright.
> 'Four angels guard you,' low she said,
> 'One at the foot and one at the head—'
>
> 'Mother—quick—the pillow!!—There!!!
> Missed that angel, skimmed his hair.
> Never mind, we'll get the next.
> Ooh! but angels make me vexed!!'
>
> Mother, shocked, gasped feebly 'Anne!!!'
> (A pillow disabled the water-can.)
> Said Anne, 'I won't have things in white
> Chant prayers about my bed all night.'

'William the Wykehamist'

Empson seems to have experienced no difficulty at all in fitting in to the
austerely privileged life that had evolved at Winchester during the 526 years
since the first election of seventy 'poor and needy' (*pauperes et indigentes*)
scholars entered into possession of William of Wykeham's Foundation.[23]

His mother took him down for the start of term; and then he was handed over to his *pater*, a scholar of a year's standing who would indoctrinate him in the ways of the little world of Winchester, including the scholars' morning hymn *Jam lucis orto sidere* ('the first two words pronounced in the Old English, the last in the Italian style; and why? Well, that is the rule'),[24] the school song *Domum* and the Graces—and certainly not forgetting the so-called 'notions', the school's enormous, peculiar vocabulary or dialect. The process of conning notions took about a fortnight, during which time he would be exempted from 'sweat', that is, fagging (performing menial chores, e.g. polishing shoes, at the bidding of seniors; a boy was 'in sweat' for two years). He would then be examined by the prefects in the so-called 'Notion Examina' (the convenient but perhaps tiresome trick of abbreviating certain words is itself a 'notion'), and probably beaten for his errors, along with the *pater* who had failed to teach him adequately.[25] There was also an initiation ceremony to be endured.

Empson took it all in good spirit; he was keen to belong to this select society, and obviously reckoned that the business of joining was purely a formality, not an occasion for personal affront. This letter, dating from 16 September 1920, a day or so after his arrival, shows just how readily, even buoyantly, he assumed to himself the character of the college:

Dear Mother,

I am sitting in one of the seats in the middle of the room, after all, as the man who had my place refused to leave it. However, I daresay he knew what he was about. When I left you I came back to the college and found everybody parading the courtyard place in twos, after tea. I had tea, and couldn't get a partner for some time, but Philips—the boy we were talking to—came to my rescue. They have a lovely arrangement in the mornings. You go into the bathroom in your pyjamas with a towel. The baths have cold water running through them. You kneel and wash your face, then splash the water backwards over the rest of you (taking off the pyjamas, of course). It wakes you up beautifully! I went through the usual ceremony today on Hill. First, you run uphill in a body till you see the tops of a clump of trees: then you shout out 'The Feathers' and fall flat. Next, you are blindfolded and have to walk out of the wood. Then you run round a maze cut in the turf. After that, you run down a dry moat, up on the other side, and fall flat on your face, kissing the ground in front of you, and putting a peice [*sic*] of white chalk into a cross made out of them [Domum Cross]. After that you walk over a plank over the river and back. It used to be much thinner and slippery with moss on, but they changed it this time as it had almost worn out. Great indignations! Then I came home, had an ice at the tuck-shop, and wrote this. They are all very friendly here, and not sniffy a bit. Howell, the boy I knew (otherwise my totherite) left last term, but as he was apparently very unpopular no harm's done. So far we have only had one lesson, but when once we had found the way there it was fairly easy. They wanted to know whether I was to learn Greek. *I* didn't know, and as I couldn't tell them what I was going to be I was rather a puzzler. I will be 'talked over'. I had to buy some ink and a pot (11d), but otherwise I have been all right so far. This letter had better do for Molly as well. We haven't played any games yet. Switzerland is still a long way off.

 Yours sincerely
 William the Wykehamist
 (with best love from me)[26]

In Wiccamical parlance, 'man'—as he uses it in the first sentence—means a boy in the school. Not all boys are men. (The Headmaster, whom William of Wykeham designated as 'hired and dismissible', was 'Head Man'; other masters are known as dons, as at the university. The affectation of this usage may well explain why Empson would later playfully reverse the process and refer to undergraduates as 'children', although it may be the case that he was happily prolonging as much as protesting against the game.) He had evidently started off well, even down to using the term 'totherite' to refer to a boy at a school other than Winchester; though he had yet to learn both that 'the courtyard place' is properly Chamber Court (paved not with flagstones but with 'sands'), the medieval flint-and-stone collegiate enclosure in which he would study, eat, and sleep for the next five years, and that the near hill crowned with a 'clump' of Scotch firs and beeches is called 'Hills', albeit a single hill (the name of St Catherine's Hill, the school's stomping ground, is first abbreviated and then augmented with a superfluous terminal *s*, for boys' own unfathomable reasons).[27]

'Nor was a man recognized as a true Wykehamist,' wrote John D'Ewes Firth (alias 'Budge'), a Housemaster and historian of Winchester, 'until he had... been beaten twice. He did not have to wait long for this last qualification.' Empson was beaten 'rather too often', as he himself lamented, the first time in company with Richard Crossman. 'We were new boys together, and from the day we both got beaten for writing and circulating a lampoon on the prefects it was clear to me that Empson was the kind of light-hearted genius and academic "lifeman" that Winchester occasionally produces as a reaction against its standard type.'[28] Like the legendary Sydney Smith, who opposed boy rule and suffered himself to be made Prefect of Hall (Head Boy), and who 'in old age shuddered at the recollection of Winchester',[29] and like his later hero Jeremy Bentham, Empson loathed the practice of corporal punishment; physical cruelty seemed to him the major evil of the world, exceeding any other perversity. Prefects at

Winchester were entitled to flog their juniors with a ground-ash with split ends (it could draw blood, and was kept in water for suppleness),[30] in spite of the fact that the Founder's Statutes charged the Headmaster 'in castigando modum nequaquam excedat'.[31] ('Ah,' the Headmaster told the new House Prefects in 1922, 'if yer see any little beast shouting filth about the corridors, yer must just tund [beat] him out of hand, that's all.') Empson, at least during his first years at the school, thought the system 'very brutal':[32] moral sensitivity and sharp experience convinced him that it was a gross feature of an educational system for adults to instruct children to inflict pain on one another. Boldly enough, he made his position clear in his third year, when he contributed to a school debate on the motion 'The Public School system is not in accordance with the needs of to-day'; *The Wykehamist* reported this flat interjection: 'W. Empson demanded a substitute for corporal punishment.'[33] But in a later year he would readily acknowledge that even the beatings could not impair his opinion of the school as a whole, which he thought outstanding. 'Winchester I am sure is not as dreadful as it was when the child Empson took a vow while in fear that he would never deny that it was good,' he was to write to Sir Desmond Lee, a Cambridge intimate who had become Headmaster of Winchester. He did not mean that the high praise he would give the school was actually worthless because it was offered under a self-enforced oath; he meant that Winchester was excellent *in spite of* the corporal punishment it licensed in his day. 'Please,' he told Lee, 'the whole point of this is that I did not just accept being tortured; the child fought against it; but the child could easily realise that it was being carried up in an aeroplane high above the world, from which in the end it could fall like a hawk.'[34] Not being a snob, not a bit of it, he did not mean that the public school cachet gave him a first-class ticket for life. The image of the hawk, reminiscent of Hopkins or Auden, is peculiarly appropriate: Empson believed he should give every credit to Winchester for being such a superb educational 'machine' that it not only winged the child aloft but empowered him to fly unaided; it developed all his faculties, and gave him the confidence to use them to the full. He simply despised, and refused to be quelled by, overbearing and tyrannical behaviour of any sort: 'speaking as an English schoolchild,' he wrote the year after leaving school, 'I don't like the dominating Anglo-Saxon, we used to call it "prefectitis".'[35]

Indeed, so far from being intimidated by the prefectorial system, both his few surviving letters and the testimony of his contemporaries go to show that he thoroughly relished his time in college. Sparky from the start, this early letter to 'his ultra-angelic MA' expresses his enthusiasm not only for the fountain pen his mother had sent him, and for the 10/- he had got from 'Granny' (who had aptly 'adressed' him, he said, as 'Darting William'), but for Wiccamical life in general: 'Thanks awfully! The pen is magnificent! The filling apparatus is superb!!! ... I have nearly finished my probatory first fortnight, after which I will be a real, though hardly life-size Wickhamist. I have started on your pound of sweets. Molly's Marsh Mallows are Most 'Mazingly Masticatable! We have finished about two layers.'[36] He was obviously feeling fairly fizzy.

The 'We' in question was not royal, it was the eleven or twelve boys with whom he shared chambers, a day-room downstairs and a dormitory upstairs. William of Wykeham's Foundation Deed, executed in 1382, had directed that the scholars in his college were to be aged from 8 to 12, and fit for advancement principally as priests and civil servants. By William Empson's day there were still exactly seventy scholars, but aged from 13 to 18, and few of them had an eye on the Church. Of the full complement of about 450 boys at the school, the vast majority were so-called Commoners; they lived in Houses, and looked across the gulf fixed between their preponderance and the elite of college as at what Lord Jay (a Commoner contemporary) has called 'a strange breed like black men or Etonians'.[37] Scholars lived in the famously original fourteenth-century buildings, and were themselves divided into yet smaller, tightly knit groups so as to fit into the six principal 'chambers'. In these narrow groups, which were changed at least once a year, the ages were fully mixed, with an 18-year-old senior prefect studying, sleeping, eating, and playing compulsory games, all at the same prescribed times, alongside the most raw and insecure new boy. For the purposes of games and the Officer Training Corps, college comprised two units, College East and College West. Empson was in College East,[38] but his poor eyesight meant that he could never be useful to his side; instead, he would often go rowing for exercise.[39] As Michael Hope (an Empson contemporary) recalled, life in college was extremely hierarchical. 'In each Chamber every individual from senior prefect to the lowest junior had his status, his duties, his privileges and in the case of a prefect his powers.' There were three or four prefects to each chamber, just over a quarter of the total number of scholars. It was an unsoftened, remarkably public kind of existence. In the downstairs chambers each boy had his own open-sided stall (known as a 'Toys' or 'Toyes'), containing a cupboard, shelves, a fixed 'slab' or writing desk, and a stool, where all his worldly possessions (apart from clothes) were kept. Even the prefects only had a larger open space that was hemmed in—for each 'place'—by two or three tables; and the centrepiece of the room was a large table at which the prefects had their tea. 'The upstairs dormitories were equally spartan in furniture. There was virtually no opportunity for a private conversation with one's friend except by going for a walk or on a bicycle ride.'[40]

What with all this public exposure, the possibilities of any sexual activity were strictly curtailed, even though the school considered it very bad form for a 'man' to go around without a *socius* (companion). Not infrequently during his first year, Empson went for Sunday walks with Andrew White, an exact contemporary who was said to have 'a florid complexion & singularly cacophonous voice'; also for Leave-Out-Day 'expedis'.[41] The Founder was a celibate priest who commanded that no woman should ever enter Outer Gate. Michael Hope recalled, however, 'No doubt there were emotional, even passionate, affairs among the boys, but physical caresses, let alone buggery, were in my experience impossible.' Sir William Hayter, future British Ambassador to Moscow and Warden of New College, Oxford, who was Empson's senior by a year, confirmed that in his time at Winchester 'homosexual couplings' were exceptional, though one boy was obviously homosexual.[42]

The Headmaster for the most part of Empson's time at the school—that is, until 1924—was Montague John Rendall, a Harrovian who rapturously dedicated his life to Winchester: he was 'unencumbered with wives, children, etc.'[43] The presence of youth filled him with 'ecstasy', he would tell a junior master; and again, with unbelievable sincerity: 'For more than thirty years I have entered my classroom with joy.' A first-class classicist and inspirational teacher, Monty was an idealist, an enthusiast, a gentleman in all his dealings, and a magnificently calculating performer. 'Life in his presence became more exciting, more vivid, more coloured,' 'Budge' Firth would write in eulogy.[44] A vain, self-conscious, self-dramatizing man, he affected a shaggy Edwardian moustache and normally wore an oversized and shapeless double-breasted jacket of heavy cloth, with his tie not knotted but dragged through a tie-ring; and on high days and holidays he would top off this peculiar ensemble with a bowler hat. 'It is significant', Firth noted, 'that his chronic weakness of the throat had no organic cause, but was due to his forced and over-elaborate pronunciation. This was—as he said of the Gentlemen Commoners whose portraits hang in the Second Master's dining-room—"Fop-pic, ah, full of fop-dom".'[45] Equally he was humble, a natural solitary, and a devout Christian who exercised a simple moral influence over those in his charge. However, being so romantic and flamboyant, and so embarrassingly eccentric (he was not above using his stiff shirt-cuffs as memo pads, or prolonging the chant in chapel when everyone else had finished), he was regarded by many boys as an old phoney; and by 1920, when he was 57, he had become, or at least appeared to be, vague and absent-minded, which compounded the absurd element in his monumental personality. To others—including a number of Empson's generation—he could seem a distant, Olympian figure. Yet the genuineness of his passion for poetry, music, and art (especially of the Italian Renaissance, for he had studied with Bernard Berenson)[46] was deeply infectious, even if it tended to be somewhat sentimental. Hence Kenneth Clark in his autobiography would extol Rendall's 'magnificent presence, large romantic eyes, and flourishing moustache, his speech as a kind of incantation, as of a poet reading his own works and punctuated by unpredictable snorts'.[47] Michael Hope confirmed that Rendall 'must have had a pervasive if indirect influence on us all'—however rummy he seemed at the time.[48]

'His classroom was radiant with light,' wrote Budge Firth, who seems to have adored him (Firth seemed even to enjoy the embarrassment of being mocked by the Head Man, as when Rendall twitted him for 'having added a new word to the Greek language').[49] Even while he was Headmaster, Rendall took a large share in the teaching of Senior Division, for he had resolved that Winchester should maintain its tradition of being 'par excellence the classical school'; and in fact the number of boys learning Greek never fell below 50 per cent during his tenure of office.[50] (When a Greek play was being studied, a master would have the whole text by heart.)[51] 'His Aristophanes hours were pure rollicking joy, especially when he sang the choruses aloud, not without some prodigious manipulation of the scansion,' chortled Firth. 'But above all did he excel in the interpretation of Plato.'[52]

Monty Rendall won many schoolboy hearts, it seems, principally with his active sense of humour. He could not function properly without the constant stimulus and inspiration of laughter. As James Sabben-Clare (a recent headmaster) has written, 'little boys brought up on a severely grammatical approach to Latin poetry could not help being startled by remarks like "Ah used to sing me Horace in the early morning on the hills of northern Italy" followed by a strange mooing noise that was his idea of a suitable chant for the lyrics'. Indeed, several of his pupils agreed that his single most endearing quality was his ability to oust solemnity with laughter: he was 'so marvellously, so intoxicatingly, so memorably, so splendidly funny'. He also took some lessons in Divinity (compulsory for all boys), which he was far from comprehending in depth: in particular, certain passages from the knottier Epistles of St Paul clearly confounded him, so that he would exclaim with majestic bafflement: 'Ah, there is a great and glorious thought behind this bony bit, and at the proper time and place I shall not burke it.'[53] A Winchester Annalist has put on record these further examples of his style: 'Ah, there are some passages of a *rare* and *sing*ular beauty in the book of JO*NAH*.' (Here, unexplicably, there were sounds of suppressed amusement from a corner of the room, and he continued:) 'Aghchhh! Ah will not have levity! Ah know pughvectly well what there is in the book of Jonah: in fact, ah know it better than you do!' And again, when quite obviously stumped for words: 'Ah, the whole question of the AtoneMENT is very deep.'

Perhaps it was partly in an attempt to rag Rendall's lessons in Divinity that Empson designed a little cardboard puppet show of the story of Jonah, which he rendered in verses of his own. Sad to say, only a single couplet survives for the delectation of posterity; it was held in mind for more than sixty years by the eminent agricultural economist Dr Colin Clark (who was the closest friend the loner Empson made at Winchester):

> Useful gourd to shelter my head
> Without this gourd I would soon be dead.

Clark would act as showman, attracting audiences to watch Empson's performances.[54]

'During the Confirmation term each year Rendall took all the candidates together Sunday by Sunday, and also gave to each an individual interview,' Firth recorded. 'Many boys were helped by the earnestness of his message and his approach.' Empson, though he could not duck out of the obligatory Confirmation (his mother would not wish it), would not have welcomed the Headmaster's attention in this respect; even less because Rendall evidently had a weak head on the subject of Christianity, as his hagiographer conceded: 'He was not well qualified to resolve religious difficulties of a fundamental nature. "If any scientist tells you your faith is nonsense," he once said, "you can give him short shrift, that's all." '[55] According to Colin Clark, Empson was keen to discuss religion, and once suggested that God created man because he felt lonely.[56] Another contemporary, later the Revd H. P. Kingdon, remembered Empson commenting critically on the Prayer Book response, 'Give peace in our time, O Lord . . . for it is Thou only who fighteth for us.'[57] However, in line with his disgust for corporal punishment, he had already decided to reject with outright contempt any sacrificial religion. Christianity is an evil religion, he concluded at school, a loathsome system of torture-worship which has a pernicious effect on the moral views of its adherents—and, as he was to discover years later, on modern literary criticism. 'While at school,' he would recall in *Milton's God*, 'I was made to read *Ecce Homo* by Sir John Seeley (1866), a life of Jesus which explains that, when he was confronted with the woman taken in adultery and wrote with his finger in the sand, he was merely doodling to hide his blushes; then the book makes some arch comments on his sexual innocence, as if by Barrie about Peter Pan. I thought this in such bad taste as to be positively blasphemous, which rather surprised me as I did not believe in the religion.'[58] He had made up his mind early, and was not afraid to speak it. His antipathy was made public at the very latest by his third year at Winchester, 1922–3, when the fuming 15-year-old got up to speak on a 'Deba Sa' (Debating Society) motion, 'This House condemns the Sentiment Vox Populi Vox Dei'. His contribution is recorded in *The Wykehamist* for 18 May 1923: 'W. Empson asserted that "Vox Dei" meant the voice of a god, with a small "g", and that Vox Populi was just as much Vox Dei as the worship of any Greek or other deities, as it requires votaries and sometimes human sacrifice.'[59]

If only he had known, he might well have felt more sympathetic towards the dear, formidable Headmaster who had idolized his own mother and who admitted that he too winced at the thought of the Christ in torment. 'If the Cross has always stood for the symbol of Christianity,' Rendall once wrote, 'yet from the thirteenth century onwards, and indeed from an earlier date, it was to a large extent superseded by the Representation of the Virgin and Child. It seems as though the world had demanded some less painful emblem of Christianity than the Cross.' On the other hand, maybe Rendall and Empson did have a frank exchange on the subject; and yet it seems unlikely, since the Headmaster had acknowledged favourites among the boys—'those who were brilliant, attractive, and vital'. In earlier years Rendall had been taken by figures such as Raymond Asquith ('tall, upright, athletic, strongly but lightly built . . . gifted with infinite humour and utter fascination') and Arnold Toynbee ('a most white soul'). From among Empson's contemporaries he singled out the brilliant and charismatic Crossman, assuredly the cynosure of his generation. Nevertheless, if one were now to suppose that Rendall was actually a repressed homosexual, that is precisely what he remained. Budge Firth, in his memoir of his mentor, insisted that the Head Man's 'tendency' to cultivate favourites among the boys 'was always kept within strict limits. Moral earnestness was fundamental to him; there was never any real danger that it would be more than superficially overlaid.'[60] It is obvious from that last equivocal phrase that Firth acknowledged the suspicion, and knew it was mistaken. However much Rendall felt for his glorious boys, he left them innocent of his ardour—though Sir William Hayter, who thought him something of a charlatan, claimed that he never recovered from the shock of having been placed on Monty Rendall's knee and kissed by him.[61] 'The word manliness was often on his lips' in sermons, it has been said, 'but he used it in some sense which almost excluded the implications of virility. The manliness Rendall preached had to be pure and wholesome . . . '[62] Be that as it may, Empson did not figure in the charmed circle: he was small for his age, and scruffy, with steel-rimmed spectacles secured with a bit of wire or cobbled together with tape (he referred to his glasses, which he was always losing, as his 'Soit', and one of his nicknames was 'Owl Empson');[63] and he had birdlike gestures and voice, as well as a persistent eczemic boil on the top of his head which one of his friends christened 'the venerable pile'.[64] In sum, Empers—as he was invariably known—was not a very debonair or comely little man.

In theory he would have fallen more thoroughly under the influence of the Revd A. T. P. Williams (familiarly known as 'Bill'), who was the Second Master until becoming Head in 1924, at the age of 36. Originally known as the *Hostiarius* or Usher, the 'Second Man' had particular charge of College and lodged hard by his boys in the north-west corner of Chamber Court; in addition, he was the Headmaster's curate.[65] 'It is a post that kings or angels might covet,' Raymond Asquith once remarked to Monty Rendall. Dr Alwyn Terrell Petre Williams was large in every sense: large of stature and voice, he was an outstanding scholar and a happy, courteous and kindly man, 'always on the side of order, learning and useful occupation and opposed to cruelty and muddle'.[66] His qualities were so considerable that his future career might have followed almost as a matter of course: Dean of Christ Church, Bishop of Durham, Bishop of Winchester, Chairman of the Committee which prepared the New English Bible. It was he who abolished the use of the ground-ash as an instrument of punishment at Winchester (in 1926, the year after Empson left the school), following a wincing incident involving Richard Crossman. Williams replaced the ash with a cane that was promptly accorded the sobriquet 'little Willy'.[67] As a historian (whence his Commoner nickname 'History Bill'), he relished the human comedy and enlivened lessons with wordplay, coining similes and sayings of all sorts, often of a debunking nature. People 'pomped around' or 'woffled', he would say; or 'nullification hove on the horizon like a sort of new fowl.' But in his other dealings with the boys he felt reserved, and was in practice a fairly remote figure. As a Second Chamber annalist observed in a warm memoir, 'Though responsible for the lives and welfare of seventy boys, he did extraordinarily little about us in College, only intervening when he was obliged to but normally leaving us to run ourselves.' On one of the few occasions when he did intrude into the Chamber, he discovered the boys playing a harmless game of cricket, which incensed him—and yet all he did about it was to exclaim 'Beasts!' and then withdraw. 'He hardly ever ventured into upstairs chambers,' added the annalist, 'except on Sunday after early service when senior men sometimes took a long lie. With the righteousness of the early-riser Bill would stride into the chamber in his top-hat with his Sunday frock-coat swaying behind him, seize the sleeper's bedclothes with one hand, whip them off him, and stalk out again with an "Up, SLOTH".'[68] Despite Williams's remoteness from Chambers, his prefects were usually able men, so the time-honoured system of College self-government worked pretty well on the whole: juniors would behave themselves for fear of seniors, and so on and so forth.

If the comparatively young Second Master, Dr A. T. P. Williams, inspired such trust and affection in the boys, a still younger master made an even more invigorating impression on Empson and his peers. Spencer Leeson, who had entered College as a scholar in 1905 and returned to teach there in September 1924, 'flung himself with tremendous zeal and abandon into the work, riotously happy, enjoying every moment of his time with the boys, making friends on all sides, full of fun and laughter, and universally beloved'.[69] Though afflicted with a hoarse stammer at moments of high emotion (often attained), nothing impeded the zest with which he turned his classroom into an open forum. As an Empson contemporary recalled, 'Those who were present at the first hour he took as an assistant master...are not likely to forget it. Having never taught before he may have found it an ordeal to begin with Senior Division, Sixth Book; if so he did not show it, his usual stammer was well under control except for a slight difficulty over "the poet Browning", and it was one of the most stimulating hours his hearers can ever have spent.'[70] Michael Hope remembered likewise: 'Leeson was very different at this time from the dog-collared clergyman and bishop that he turned into later...[H]e treated senior boys almost as equals, encouraged discussion of all kinds of topics, aesthetic, historical, philosophic; even religion could be analysed, criticised and discussed without too much offence.'[71] He was such a 'warm and gay' character, according to a devoted memoir, that he would play 'frivolous party games with supreme skill'; and with respect to a later period, when he became Headmaster: 'One always felt that he was afraid lest his natural inclination might lead him to relax discipline too much for the good of the school or the nature of his office.'[72] Even so:

Empson would remember an occasion when for some reason he did apparently abandon all restraint during his first year as a schoolmaster: Leeson was 'carried naked in a bath tub round Chamber Court while passages were read aloud from his private diary,' Empson related.[73] It is difficult to imagine that such a jest was not assisted by something a little more intoxicating than the high spirits of a bunch of untethered school-boys. Nevertheless, the older Empson was prompt to enter this tribute to the young master who had enlarged his understanding: 'he was an excellent teacher to me, and of course to the whole class, really a generous mind...'[74] In later years Leeson became first Headmaster of Winchester and afterwards Bishop of Peterborough, when he was 'very critical of orthodoxy and much inclined to Modernism';[75] all the same, Empson might have been inclined to agree with the Oxford don, a Leeson contemporary, who claimed that he had 'a mind rotted by religion'.

Empson was indebted for his academic opportunity at the school to Monty Rendall's predecessor as Headmaster, the Reverend Hubert Murray Burge, who had succeeded in his aim of alleviating the tyranny of the Classics only in the very first decade of this century. Burge did away with compulsory Greek: this astonishing breach with tradition meant that a boy might 'reach the highest Divisions of the School without being an expert in two ancient languages', and so 'proclaimed that henceforward it would be respectable not to be a classic'.[76] Sabben-Clare explains further: he 'introduced for all boys in Senior Part (roughly equivalent to a modern Lower Sixth) a "staple" which included Latin and Maths, and a little bit of Science, History, and Divinity; the other nine periods a week offered a choice of more Classics, or Modern Languages, or Maths and Science'.[77] Rendall, who ruefully spoke of the New Curriculum as his 'inheritance', further divided the whole of the so-called Middle Part, i.e., seven classical 'divisions' (or forms), into Greek and English sets for five hours a week; though he felt gratified to report that the vast majority of the boys still did Greek. (Amateurism died a belated death: as late as 1916 Rendall wrote in his Annual Report, 'I hope that many of our classical and mathematical masters alike will add a scientific subject before they settle down to teach, just as they add a foreign tongue.')[78]

Empson had taken no Greek at his prep school, so he was at once relieved and eager to tackle the Mathematics-and-Science option. He showed very high promise from the start, but it was presently suspected that he might let himself down with imprecise and scrabbly work, and after just two terms at the school he was placed only thirteenth out of twenty-two boys in the class. 'He is very inaccurate as a classic, but his intelligence in other respects is considerable,' said his report for Common Time (Easter Term) 1921. 'He possesses a quantity of general but somewhat confused information.' While he was deemed to be 'Quick but inaccurate' in Science, the quality of his Maths was marvellous: he came first in a set of eighteen boys, though the master commented colourlessly: 'Has done very well: should make his work more attractive to examine.' As for English, he performed notably well, coming second out of a set of twenty, and the master remarked with enthusiasm, 'English writing most intelligent & original'—but of course that counted for much less than his lax Latin. Dr Williams, the Second Master, summed up his performance with these words: 'Conduct excellent. I hope he will work away at accuracy *now* when it is easier to attain than he will find it later. Clearly he has good general ability, and must not spoil it.' All the same, Monty Rendall the Head Man inevitably exhorted young Empson to rise to his own predilection: 'His place is low: I hope he will strengthen his Classics by a real effort.'

Notwithstanding, for nearly a hundred years Mathematics had been the second most important subject on the curriculum; it is the school's strongest subject to this day. In Empson's time it was lifted to an unparalleled height, as James Sabben-Clare has related, 'by the arrival of C. V. Durell who by his work and writings dominated the teaching of Mathematics up and down the country for the first half of the century. Durell was rather an austere person, not easily befriended; his brief excursion into housemastering was not a success. But he had a brilliant mind and a genius for exposition, best displayed in his thirty or more textbooks which have been used in their millions all over the world.'[79] As principal 'Mathma don', Clement Vavasor Durell was acknowledged as a great teacher (any incomprehension on the part of his pupils would make him squeal with indignation); he was just too shy to be chummy, though he would do his best to be genial and encouraging to boys who were good at Maths (such as the prodigious F. P. Ramsey—elder brother of the future Archbishop of Canterbury—who won an Exhibition to Cambridge just as Empson entered college, and who wrote *The Foundations of Mathematics* before his untimely death in 1930, at the age of 26). It did not help matters that 'Clem' Durell had a very hard, loud, lisping voice, speaking as if he had a potato in his mouth, with the result that he was nicknamed 'The Tout'. Most boys found him so overbearing that he seemed simply comic. Even Empson, who duly turned out to be one of his star pupils, remarked that he could not imagine Durell discharging his House-don's duty of giving 'Confirma jaws' to the 'Confirmendi' in his House.[80] But Durell did manage quite successfully to teach his charges all about Einstein.

Andrew White has commented, 'any mathematician who was not more than ordinarily good at Classics was inevitably a good deal of an odd bird'.[81] Empson, as the only boy to get a Mathematics scholarship without Greek, was surely the oddest bird of all; only one other member of his Roll, E. A. Radice, showed a lasting interest in Mathematics, and he certainly carried on with Classics—as did Richard Wilberforce (a descendant of Samuel Wilberforce, a bishop who earned the nickname 'Soapy Sam' for his ecclesiastical slipperiness), later a Lord of Appeal in Ordinary. Radice went to exactly the same classes as Empson throughout their time at school; he was up to his rival in algebra, he remembers, but not in geometry.[82] But Empson was also devoted to 'Stinks' (Chemistry), which was thought to be a very low pursuit. 'When the first proper Science division was constituted in 1921,' writes Sabben-Clare, 'it was regarded as somewhat below the salt, and a newly appointed College Officer who was a scientist had to accept a nominal transfer to the Classics ladder in order to give him the dignity befitting his station.'[83] Empson evidently thrived on being the odd man out: through the whole of one term, for instance, while he was engaged on a thrilling chemical experiment, he went round with a bottle containing some coloured liquid and asked all and sundry if they could detect any change in colour compared with the week before.[84] However, his application paid off handsomely: at the end of his school career the Chemistry don would report that he had 'shown more originality and initiative and even a more delicate touch'. His Mathma don said he had been 'reading more advanced work: & making something of it'—though he also mentioned a continuing handicap: 'He is a little apt, I think, to gloss over difficulties.' Moreover, Dr Williams, enjoying his first session as Headmaster, continued to tag him as a clever but queer fish: 'He has a good deal of originality and enterprise: I hope he is learning also to discipline his vagaries.'[85] The exact nature of the waywardness was anyone's guess, but presumably the Head Man considered Empson too idiosyncratic to be entirely tractable.

Notwithstanding the school's minimal misgivings about his demeanour, in December 1924 he was elected to a Milner Scholarship (worth £80 a year) at Magdalene College, Cambridge—where his brother Charles had studied—commencing the following October.[86]

E. A. Radice, who also won a mathematical award—in his case to Magdalen College, Oxford—has saliently observed: 'It may be a testimony to the breadth of Winchester education in those days that we both should have abandoned mathematics, he for English Studies and I to take my finals at Oxford in Classical Greats and later to become an economist.'[87] Nowadays it would indeed be unusual to switch from Maths to English in the middle of the journey of one's undergraduate career, but for Empson and his peers it was not such an extraordinary leap. In any event, his talent for English had certainly been spotted at Winchester, for the English master commented on his performance, 'I expect much of him and am seldom disappointed. I hope he will continue to keep his range wide.' Empson also raised the English Lit. prize in his last Common Time (Easter Term), and the Second Master wrote of him in consequence:

He has been doing useful work and has not wasted his time. I am glad he showed his literary capacity in achieving a creditable performance in English Lit. Exam[n].

He has a distinctly enterprising intellect, but must remember that his opinions on the big questions of life can still be only tentative and experimental. 'Youth shows but half', and he must learn to 'prize the doubt, low kinds exist without'.[88]

Furthermore, in his final term he put in for the Warden and Fellows' Prize for an English Essay. The prize actually fell to Crossman; but Empson was named *proxime accessit* and managed to best John Sparrow ('Honourably mentioned'),[89] the future Warden of All Souls, who was a year his senior and never a close friend, and who had proved to be so precocious as a scholar that two years earlier, at the age of 16, he had published an edition of Donne's *Devotions upon Emergent Occasions*. (According to the 'Second Chamber Annals' composed by a senior boy, John Sparrow was at once 'a clever little lick' and 'very, very spree [cheeky] indeed'; and A. L. Rowse would later put the young Sparrow into verse—

> . . . a precocious boy,
> Broad brow, falling lick of hair, firm chin,
> Always alert to be amused, a quip
> Ready on lip, and intermittent charm.[90]

A budding aesthete, Sparrow disdained Empson, as he later intimated to me, less on intellectual than on artistic grounds: he thought him a rough, repulsive beast. A few years later, in 1930, they would go to open war—a war waged, as it were, between Oxford and Cambridge—over the value to English studies of I. A. Richards's *Practical Criticism*; naturally, Sparrow stood for cultivated appreciation over close critical analysis.[91]) Thus it is not so astonishing that Empson should have switched from Maths to English after taking his first degree at Cambridge; it was not a Pauline conversion. What was remarkable, however, is that he could achieve so much so soon after he did so.

And yet he was always a beaver at his books. While still at school he discovered Proust, and the science fiction of H. G. Wells, and Aldous

Huxley; and the new psychology as well as pure old science: he was much impressed, for example, by the eloquent materialism of *Psyche's Lamp*, by Robert Briffault (who subsequently appeared in the news as a writer of pornography).[92] He was deeply influenced in the direction of psychology, and psychoanalysis, by a senior pal named Carew A. Meredith, a very able mathematician who was also, in spite of his name, a fervent Irish nationalist. Empson was to stay in touch with Meredith through his Cambridge years and beyond.

As for poetry, 'I was intoxicated by Swinburne as a schoolboy,' he would always readily admit. In particular, as Colin Clark remembered, he was intensely moved by 'The Garden of Proserpine', which he would recite with fervour.[93]

> She waits for each and other,
>   She waits for all men born;
> Forgets the earth her mother,
>   The life of fruits and corn;
> And spring and seed and swallow
> Take wing for her and follow
> Where summer song rings hollow
>   And flowers are put to scorn.

Nevertheless, being 'a slave to the drug of Swinburne' did not mean that he entertained sado-masochistic ambitions of his own, for he had every reason to divorce the poetry from the belief. The sadistic or masochistic passages in the first series of Swinburne's *Poems and Ballads* 'are frightfully good poetry though morally most undesirable,' he would stipulate in 1969.

No doubt positive virtues in Swinburne, such as readiness to take a dare, are part of what the reader admires; and I do not expect that the verses do actual harm. I was devoted to them as a schoolboy, when I was being beaten rather too often; and it was quite clear to me that this literary taste did nothing to make one enjoy being beaten. (Can the poet really have been removed from Eton because he proved that he did? What a triumph that would be!) But I cannot help regarding sadism very glumly, as the only perversion really deserving the name, and it seems important to get clear that one can appreciate the poetry without sharing the mental disease.

Even so, as a schoolboy, he may have felt, albeit unconsciously, that Swinburne's paeans of perversity answered to his own distress, that there was a song for his pains.

It is possible too that he wrote some poems of his own while in college, but most of the evidence seems to suggest otherwise. Sad to say, the only verses which could possibly be by Empson are those published as 'Four Epigrams' (see appendix in *Complete Poems*) in *The Wykehamist* (27 May 1925); but—to put the case a bit more warmly—it is possible that Empson did write them. On the other hand, it has to be admitted that the attribution was in a later year denied by his college friend Ian Parsons; effectively denied too by a number of his other contemporaries—John Sparrow, Sir William Hayter, Lord Wilberforce—all of whom told Sir Jeremy Morse in 1989 that they did not think of him as a poet at Winchester. 'He was my junior prefect in Sixth that year, and I think, though of course one can't be sure at this remote time, that I should have known if he was sending poems to the Wykehamist,' wrote Hayter.[94] Douglas Jay wrote heaps of poems, as did Richard Crossman (who favoured big, broad effects, and once tried not very successfully to imitate T. S. Eliot); and John Sparrow was touched by the Muse—as the Second Chamber Annalist put it, Sparrow 'was known to write quite good English Verse on occasions and was a great deal cleverer than one would judge from results'. But none of them has any recollection of Empers pretending to poetry.

However much he feared being 'tunded' (beaten), his peers remember him as perky, game, and self-sufficient; enigmatically clever; a very odd chap in his harmlessly abstracted way; neither bashful nor much of a talker; but always buoyant, terribly busy about his curious interests, and invariably quite happy. Some boys would think rather better of him (English social distinctions being what they are) for the fact that he rode to hounds with the York and Ainstie—even though they did call him 'Woggy'. On the other hand, his hopelessness at 'Athla' (sports) did not really matter a whit, for the chief determinant of status was a man's academic position in college, not his athletic prowess—or even seniority of age. In any case, Empson was far from being a natural butt, a weakling or sissy. On the contrary, as E. A. Radice remembers, he was tough and quite energetic: 'he turned up late at the start of the under-sixteen 3-mile steeplechase but insisted on running the course (quite fast too!). He got in last, amid great cheers, affectionate rather than ironic, for he was something of a school mascot.'[95]

In truth, he was aware that his contemporaries thought him a standing curiosity: a dishevelled, quasi-comic eccentric.[96] When a contemporary tried to epitomize him in the so-called 'Second Chamber Annals', he was almost at a loss for words and indeed saved him up for the final word; 'Empson was amazing' was all he could find to say. But Empson shrewdly defended his difference by acting up to the role in which others cast him. Surely it was not by chance that when 'Bill' Williams, as Second Master, mounted a production of Marlowe's *Dr Faustus* in College Hall on

31 March 1924, Empson was given the part of Clown, and paired with another, senior 'character' as Wagner, C. E. Stevens, scholar and athlete (and future fellow of Magdalen College, Oxford), who had earned the nickname 'Tom Brown' after arriving at Winchester in Eton get-up and top hat. (Empson appeared too as the sixth of the Seven Deadly Sins, that is, Sloth; the Seventh, being Lechery, was of course cut for schoolboy performance.) The part of Dr Faustus was taken by Christopher Hawkes, and Mephistophiles by Richard Crossman, who was reported to have afforded 'a good picture of a soul tormented by remorse and driven on by necessity to do evil'; Hayter was both the Cardinal of Lorraine and an Evil Angel, Sparrow aptly a Knight and a Scholar.

Empson's principal appearance as the Clown—who is named Robin in a variant text—was noticed by *The Wykehamist* with these anonymous words: 'The scene between *Wagner* (Stevens), *Faustus*' servant, and a *Clown* (Empson) was well acted, though we feel that *Wagner*'s part was not acted quite as Marlowe intended: this scene was, of course, only written to relieve the tension of the play and as such perhaps could not fail to be unreal.' He could also bask in the paradoxical commendation that 'a great deal was demanded of the smaller parts, as they had to relieve the tension, and yet not obtrude too much upon the central theme'.[97] Moreover, in the opinion of Christopher Hawkes, who thought of Empson as 'a freak and a character... a huge joke' and who had a hand in casting the production (which might go some way to explain why he himself took the leading role), Empson 'made himself, for a schoolboy character-actor, extremely funny'.[98] Probably any adolescent, if he is not unduly shy, would relish being licensed to utter such mischief as this speech (Empson accentuated the impishness by speaking in a particularly juvenile voice):

How? A Christian fellow to a dog or a cat, a mouse or a rat? No, no, sir, if you turn me into anything, let it be in the likeness of a little, pretty, frisking flea, that I may be here and there and everywhere. O, I'll tickle the pretty wenches' plackets! I'll be amongst them, i'faith.

But maybe the part was expurgated for Wiccamical consumption.

At any rate, the conventional view of the play, as *The Wykehamist* stated, is that the comic exchanges between Wagner and Robin the Clown are meant merely to ape Faustus' aspirations. Wagner is the tragic hero's zany, the merry mimic, carefree in his diabolical conjuring, and Robin little more than a coarse rustic, at most a scabrous parodist. What Dr Faustus is to Wagner, his master and his mentor, Wagner would be unto the foolish Robin: 'Well, wilt thou serve me? and I'll make thee go like *Qui mihi*

discipulus?' Nearly half a century later, however, when Empson came to
write about the play at length, he argued that the subplot in which he had
featured at school had a more valuable function than that of crudely
mocking Faustus' vicious desires and deeds. Sickened by the muddle
of the surviving texts of *Dr Faustus*—in particular the 'harmful' status of
the B-text—and by the sanctimoniousness of many of its critics, Empson
attempted to reconstruct the whole play against the background of its
known sources, the hermetic tradition, Marlowe's likeliest intentions, and
theatrical expectations. The result, posthumously published as *Faustus and
the Censor* (1987), is a radical rereading, putting the cat among the pietists.
Faustus must no longer be seen as an overreaching dope who deserves
eternal punishment: he is reinstated as a true Renaissance hero, a resourceful and roguish magician who 'lives next door to Punch' and
makes a business deal with the 'freelance' Mephistophiles. Robin the
Clown plays a vital role in rescuing him from a vile doom. Modern literary
critics, Empson was to write, 'think the function of the comic scenes is to
jeer at the hero. These poverty-struck lousy criminals are obviously loathsome, and plainly Robin does what Faust does; he is meant therefore to
imply that Faust, whose familiar devils are his lice, is sickening too. But
logically it is just as possible to argue the other way; plainly Robin, who is
always fun, does not deserve eternal torture, and the play assures us that he
is soon released . . .; therefore Faust, who has not really done anything
worse, and has taken to a life of fun, does not deserve it either.' While it
would be fanciful to suggest that Empson laid the ground of his thesis as a
17-year-old schoolboy at Winchester, it would not be too much to observe
that he must have felt a deep sense of identification both with Robin
the clown, the spirited fool, and with Marlowe the freethinker, even at
that age and especially in that place. The qualities he admired in Robin
are initiative and enterprise; so it is quite possible that he was unconsciously depicting something of himself, young and old, in this later
account of Marlowe's attitude towards the clown he created: 'What is
called his homosexuality is basically a political sentiment, though he was
likely enough to act upon it personally. He admires young men who use
their wits, and such strength as they have, against a society which appears
closed to them; he wishes them luck. It is automatic for him to back Robin;
and indeed, if the exploits of Robin had been told at greater length, by
another author, he would seem a good deal of a hero.' In such terms, there
is probably an unwitting element of self-description in the way he chose to
characterize both Marlowe and Robin. A large part of Robin's charm is
his brave resourceful wit. He is 'unpuncturable,' Empson believed.

Just so, Colin Clark would always remember that Empson himself was not affected by being thought of as a peculiar character at Winchester—'owing to his imperturbable good nature'.[99] Even though he erred on the solitary side, he loved to go around and exchange ideas with everybody possible. He always wanted to find out what everyone thought. As Sir William Hayter recalled, he was tirelessly enquiring and interested, unexpected in his own ideas, and not a bit boring. On one occasion, he even asked Hayter if he planned to get married, adding an observation that is certainly curious for a youngster of his age: 'You should—you're good stock.'[100] The sweet temper, and the surprising humility, with which he approached his friends are apparent in the (sadly few) loose leaves of a journal that survives among his papers. Although these passages are not dated, they seem to relate to the beginning of his very last Common Time (Easter Term), when he was assigned to a new chamber.

Thursday. This is fearfully enjoyable. I had not expected to be so smitten by Chamber Court; the rich and cool, soothing and piercing beauty is like a pint of beer after a ten mile tramp in May; gray subtle stable Chamber Court with lemon yellow gas lamps. I could talk to people in College...I bounced about saying more than I meant, and repeating myself, till told to go away...How delightfully on the spot this is, with William Hayter...in the same house, and all College—a good chunk of the real world—waiting for me in the back yard. Am tired, and pinkily pleased with everybody...

Friday. Went all round College, not staying very long in any one place, the welcome never quite exhausted: perhaps [John] Willis, last chamber but one, had had almost enough before he sent me away. I paddled in to VIth to see Oscar Knowles, who had just sent me away, I was going, when Crossman opening an eye called me back. 'Did you do that because you seriously wanted me to?' I said. 'I never do anything for any other reason,' he promised me. I paid him the extravagant compliment of believing him, and talked for the time he allowed me, till a quarter to twelve. I say this to reassure myself.

Passing the Second Master on the way up to bed, I dropped in to say Goodnight. 'Where have you been all this time?' 'Oh talking to people.' He looked surprised and worried. 'I hope you aren't keeping them awake, you know, examinas and so on.' 'I don't think they'd stand me if they didn't want to, they are ready enough to be rude when they're tired of me' I said. 'I'm sure they're very polite.' I tried to back myself up a little...The Second Man is a splendid person with no nuances of manner, he has a most refreshing and civilised way of telling you what he means (not adapted to psychological diaries). He showed his feeling about my staying on very clearly...(I am not indifferent to his having told me he thought well of me last half, anyway)...Probably I am writing all this because [Carew] Meredith told me I had a sweet disposition.

'He is evidently leading a happy life in College,' wrote the Second Master as Empson's school career drew towards a close, 'and I usually find him in excellent spirits and good company.'[101] He did truly relish the sharp-minded fellowship that Winchester afforded him, and would have been sure to endorse these remarks by Budge Firth: 'Seventy picked brains always living together must be a permanent intellectual leaven... College men are not always universally popular, especially in their early days. They are sometimes precocious, no doubt. But most of those who have spent five or six years in College may probably feel that they never expect to live in such a wonderful community again.'[102] Empson could not have agreed more: though a quiet boy, with few close friends, he believed that the conversation of the scholars was a rare blessing.[103]

Winchester in his time offered 'the best available education, and we kids in College said so,' he would volunteer in a later year. 'We thought it was entirely because of ourselves, not a bit because our teachers were very properly dishing out [a] good education... a thing we seldom denied... [W]e thought we were under our own steam, and it was only good luck to have a fairly good teacher...'[104] John Willis, later a Professor of Classics (who was apparently, according to the Second Chamber annalist of the day, 'apt to take himself somewhat too seriously'), confirms that 'the masters took very little notice of us and we of them. Ours was a "boy" society—in which, as I remember, we discussed most of the pressing problems of "life" and "religion"—before we had experienced them!'[105]

Dressed in their distinctive outfit—long serge black gown and sleeved waistcoat, with striped trousers—the scholars knew themselves to be 'in some sense an élite, in others looked down upon,' as Michael Hope would recall. 'One developed a defensive, slightly contemptuous, attitude to the rest of the world, and a fair ration of priggishness. Eccentricity of dress or behaviour was frowned upon and indeed severely punished. Eccentricity of interests or viewpoint was tolerated, perhaps even encouraged, to an extent which was almost unthinkable in a public school at that time. Unfashionable, even outrageous, opinions could be expressed and were debated; they would not be ruled out of court as long as it was clear that the holder was sincere in his views.'[106]

Winchester's collegiate life offered obvious advantages in this respect, and Empson certainly grabbed them. In his case, it is no exaggeration to say that many of his adult convictions—on religion, science, and psychology—were primed at school, very often by simply arguing with his fellows. Dissent became a point of honour, since a natural scepticism led him to speak up for unorthodoxy and subversion against what is now called the Establishment. Though the scion of a landowning family, and genuinely enjoying his privileged education, he turned to the left in politics. His political outlook was probably encouraged by the powerful personality of Richard Crossman, whom a Second Chamber Annalist (during the session 1925–6) hailed as 'the most striking figure of his epoch'.[107] Michael Hope spoke for the majority who willy-nilly bowed to Crossman's pre-eminence: 'Very large for his age, clumsy but powerful, with a loud voice when he chose to use it, he was the natural focus and leader of any gathering. He is remembered now for his left-wing political views, and no doubt these influenced a number of us, myself included. But what is sometimes forgotten is his infectious enthusiasm for all kinds of poetry, architecture, and music; I don't think painting appealed to him much, but his advocacy of Shelley and of Mozart was just as compelling as his support for the nationalisation of the banks or the Covenant of the League of Nations.'[108] Empson's deference to Crossman is obvious in the words of his short-lived journal quoted above; and perhaps it was under Crossman's influence that he introduced into his own Chamber a gramophone on which he played, in addition to some ephemeral music, Beethoven's Kreutzer Sonata[109] (he showed little feeling for music in adult life). It may also be indicative of his sense of inferiority to the other man that in after years he believed that Crossman was about a year older than himself, whereas 'the acknowledged leader of his roll' was actually three months younger than Empson. In fact, however, Empson had independently decided in favour of turning left in his political views, with just a little help from his own bookishness. The most important work he had ever read was *The Ragged Trousered Philanthropists*, he once announced to E. A. Radice, who was himself very interested in Labour politics. 'I had the feeling that the book was a revelation to him,' Radice has remarked, 'and that he had undergone some sort of conversion in his social and political thinking.'[110]

The public dimension of the boys' private discussions took the form of the regular sessions of the Debating Society (Deba Sa), in which Empson was not loth to blazon his opinions. As written up by *The Wykehamist*, his speeches may appear to have the air of ritual dissent, to be taken with a routine pinch of salt, but there can be little doubt that he had considered his contributions with due seriousness. Since he was nervous of public speaking, only a sense of moral pressure could have urged him to his feet. Furthermore, he was consistent in opposing attitudes founded on privilege or paternalism, elitism or imperialism. Given the first-class opportunities available to the men of Winchester, and the burdens of office they naturally expected to shoulder in due time, a number of the questions at issue had an immediate bearing on the political views that this generation would seek to impress upon the world. In December 1924, for example, the motion was proposed, 'In the opinion of this House, His Majesty's Government should continue the Imperial Policy of its predecessors'; and Empson sniped at the idea with a single intervention: 'W. Empson asserted strongly that we were militarists and always had been.'[111] The following February, the same anxious issue turned up in an alternative formulation: 'That a strong British Empire is the only hope of world peace.' Empson felt a longer liberal homily was in order:

W. Empson said that he disliked criticism of the motion: he then criticized it. What was a strong British Empire and what was world peace? Men go to war because they are stupid and quarrelsome. Against such natures you can do nothing: if men are mentally blind, nothing will stop them wanting war, except curing their blindness: it is not a British Empire but Education that is the hope of world peace. He declared that the Empire could of itself do nothing: it was an instrument like a train for travelling from one state to another. But like a train it can be used for going in the opposite direction, not from war to peace, but from peace to war. In it the seeds of dissension are sown: it has been built up on two principles, either of planting a few whites on an industrialized coloured population, or of killing off the coloured peoples and trying to plant an imported white population in their place: but this is never successfully accomplished: look at the emptiness of tropical Australia, and of Canada: we cannot live in many of our Colonies ourselves and will not allow anyone else to. Further, our alien police force has an irritating effect on the natives.[112]

Interestingly, the motion was lost by 26 votes to 18: so maybe the House had been moved by Empson's enlightened words.

Coming much closer to home, when the Society met (in November 1924) to discuss the motion that 'The Public School system does not serve the best interests of the nation', he tried out a satirical strategy: he sought to criticize the Public School ethos in the name of public service.

W. Empson said that when Mr. Sanderson was Headmaster of Oundle, he tried to undermine that everlasting spirit of competition which was so great a disadvantage of Public Schools. At Oundle people worked together and made useful things for the public service, without always trying to cut their neighbours out. This principle should be more widely applied; even in games, which were supposed to encourage the team spirit, the spirit of competition was to be found. Why, indeed, should he be forced to waste his time upon games, especially upon cricket, where nothing ever happened? He would go singing to the treadmill, a form of exercise which he believed to be of some physical value.

The Public Schools were said to produce leaders; but these were in reality men who wished, in their last years here, to have things done for them by other people, and afterwards became country gentlemen—a type no doubt delightful but one which the country could no longer afford to support. He hoped that much would be done to open up the Public Schools to the lower classes, but meanwhile he advised them to drop their self-satisfaction and to think out their patriotism more deeply.[113]

'This speech was delivered too fast,' said the anonymous reporter, 'but was full of brilliant humour and shrewd criticism.' Indeed, his sentiments were neither exceptional nor objectionable: after all, he did not advocate the abolition of Public Schools, he simply asserted the pointlessness of competitive sports and appealed to the guilty conscience of his privileged peers. Although the vote went against the motion, the opponents of the motion were not an overwhelming majority: the house split 27 to 19.

It is a tribute to Empson's pluck that he would publicly espouse ideas that might have seemed provocative or even offensive, and not fear the wrath of those in authority; a tribute too to the school that invited and respected his criticism. None of his fellows or masters was so fatuous as to allege that he was a deeply ungrateful son and pupil, or that only a schoolboy who was so unassailably privileged could afford to carp at his advantages. He had no doubt at all about the quality and value of the educational system enjoyed at Winchester: as he put it in a later year, 'every child had the right ticket, which wasn't fussed about'. There were no grounds for ingratitude. Also, he said, the effect of having several White Russians enrolled in College on a post-war Government scheme was enormously beneficial—'if only because they helped the vain children to feel that they had all the world at their feet'.[114]

In the face of his budding radical views, it may seem like an irony of his career at Winchester that when William Hayter became Prefect of Hall (Head of the School) for the session 1924–5, which he found 'curiously elating', he selected Empson as one of his so-called 'inferiors'—that is, to be a prefect, along with John Willis. (Hayter 'has a sweet gentleness entirely his own,' it was written at the time. 'Such is his tolerance, that even the continued and irritating effervescences of his two prefects [Empson and Willis] but rarely ruffled him.'[115] For his part, Empson was utterly delighted to be able to recall, thirty years later, that 'Hayter got through a year in office without allowing any beating at all.'[116]) But it was perfectly consistent for Empson to emerge at the top of a school in which he had gained so enormously from the system of mutual stimulation. The school was so good, he thought, everyone should have the chance to go there: the problem was to vanquish the stratifications of society. Moreover, such was his lasting high opinion of the corporate brilliance he had imbibed for five years that he was genuinely shocked when Crossman chose to declare in a book review as late as 1954: 'For six years I fought first for survival and then for success, according to rules which barred very few holds.'[117] Such remarks amounted to perverse revisionism, Empson maintained, and he promptly mocked Crossman's mendacity in a published letter: 'I thought we spent all our time talking our heads off, educating one another in a delightful manner but rather inclined to be above any struggle. I remember him as talking for victory a bit, but it never occurred to me he imagined he had anything to fight for; apart from passing his exams.'[118]

He was very happily paying a debt of honour when he spoke up in that way, for he had also written, in a private letter:

I must never deny what I felt at the time, that the other children (not the teachers at all) were giving me such a ripping education that it equipped a man to go anywhere in the world alone, from leaving school on.[119]

It is sometimes said of Wykehamists, for reasons which quite escape me, that they all turn out the same. 'If anyone says that again,' said Dr Williams, Second Master and Headmaster in Empson's day, 'just throw a melon at him.'[120] In the summer of 1925, few denizens of Winchester College reckoned that Empson would amount to very much in later life. None anticipated that his name would presently be known around the world. If anyone had tried to forecast a winner from among Empson's fellows, naturally they would have gone for Richard Crossman, who was destined to follow in the footsteps of Stafford Cripps and Oswald Mosley; or Hugh Gaitskell, a Commoner to whom his housemaster had said, 'You'll be Prime Minister one day' (he was nearly right).[121] It would have seemed improbable that Empson could measure up to the likes of H. A. L. Fisher, Arnold Toynbee, or the legendary George Leigh Mallory, who had 'climbed new mountains' and died even while Empson was at school. Certainly it would have been unthinkable that Empson would turn out to be one of the greatest writers in the history of Winchester. Among his predecessors in the literary line, there were Nicholas Udall, the 'cheery rogue and nimble turncoat' who as a student made an oration in praise of drunkenness, and who composed the first English comedy, *Ralph Roister Doister*; Sir Thomas Browne; Thomas Otway; Edward Young, who coined the best apothegm ever penned by a Wykehamist, 'Procrastination is the thief of time'; William Collins, whose 'Ode to Evening' was then thought to be 'the greatest Wiccamical contribution to English culture';[122] Joseph Warton; Thomas Warton; Anthony Trollope, who was so miserable at the school that he had to be taken away; Matthew Arnold; and we must not forget his father, Thomas Arnold—close friend of the earlier William Empson (editor of the *Edinburgh Review*)—who 'saved and remade the public schools'. And then there was Lionel Johnson, the rhymer of whom it was said in College, 'That man Johnson is an awfully good man; why, he is a Buddhist and drinks eau-de-cologne in his toys',[123] and who died before time 'By falling from a highstool in a pub', as some other poet said. So far from rivalling such fabled figures, Empson was not known to entertain any creative urge at all. In fact, if his contemporaries had voiced any opinion on the question, they would have foretold for him a talented but by no means distinguished career—perhaps, for all that he was an oddball, he would do really quite well in the way of the stereotypical Old Wykehamist, the Civil Servant.

Even Empson himself feared that life after College might be downhill all the way, as he later wrote:

It was a commonplace to say that a man worsened a good deal when he went to the university. Not the great step from the university to the world, but just leaving Winchester for Oxford or Cambridge, was where we thought a man . . . lost the cutting edge of his intellectual purity.[124]

5

'Did I, I wonder, talk too much?'

MAGDALENE College in 1925 was just emerging from an extremely long period in the doldrums.[1] Established as a Benedictine Monks' Hostel in 1428,[2] the institution became, at an uncertain date in the last quarter of the fifteenth century, Buckingham College (in tribute to its lay benefactor, Henry Stafford, second Duke of Buckingham); then in 1542 it was refounded by Thomas, Lord Audley—who had 'presided over the trials of Sir Thomas More and Anne Boleyn, and helped Henry VIII to get rid of two other wives, as well as Thomas Cromwell'—as the College of St Mary Magdalene, with the motto *Garde ta foy* ('Keep faith'). After the initial piecemeal development of its modest red-brick First Court, and the protracted building of a seventeenth-century gem, the Pepys Building, the fortunes of the place languished for two centuries. Nothing was built in the eighteenth century; and, as a college historian has noted, during the middle fifty years of that century the total number of undergraduates in residence sometimes fell below double figures. Little changed during the nineteenth century, and in the first decade of the twentieth century it had just forty undergraduates on its books, together with only five fellows.

The advent of A. C. Benson, as a fellow from 1904 and as Master from 1915, enabled the college to recover from its long nadir. A literary critic, belletrist, and diarist of a remarkable order (he 'observed naughtily, subtly, wittily, passively, on occasion with a feline caress,' Owen Chadwick has choicely written;[3] and we are dubiously indebted to Benson also for the words of 'Land of Hope and Glory'), he was the complete Edwardian dilettante (being waited upon by an elderly servant named Hunting), and a devotee of gossip. Dignified, shy, humorous, incessantly hospitable, he was not only a superb Master but a patron who worked hard to make improvements both to the fabric and to the scholarship of his college. 'The undergraduates of Magdalene,' it has been said, 'used to say about their Master that he spent the morning doing nothing and spent the afternoon writing about what he had done in the morning.' In fact, among his far-sighted actions he secured the teaching services of I. A. Richards (1893–1979), who would in time become Empson's mentor; and indeed it was Benson who elected Empson to a scholarship.

A former Eton master, he was assiduous in trawling the public schools. Of the sixty-five entrants in Empson's year, ten were assuredly from Eton, but the remainder represented a fair mix of schools, with three Wykeham-ists including Empson. One of his favourite pupils was a product of Winchester, George Leigh Mallory, who had matriculated in 1905 and died on Mount Everest in 1924; so it was possibly by way of being a private tribute that Benson that year gave a Milner Scholarship in Maths and Physics to a Wykehamist.[4] Also, though himself a classic, Benson was a friend of Sir Arthur Quiller-Couch ('Q'), who was for many years King Edward VII Professor of English Literature, and he had lectured on Milton (Benson's big library would in due course form the nucleus of the English Faculty Library). Although Empson must have made his acquaint-ance while being scrutinized for a scholarship, he is not mentioned in Benson's prodigious and polished diary; and Benson died in June 1925, four months before Empson came up.

His successor as Master, A. B. Ramsay, former Lower Master of Eton— a man whom Benson had derided as 'a poky, narrow-minded, parochial, stubborn, pig-headed little fellow... *totally* devoid of inspiration'—would take up residence in January 1926.[5] A grave and religious but reputedly kindly,[6] and even, in some quarters, gentle figure, with a love of classics, cricket, and chess, Ramsay (who tended to treat Magdalene as a finishing school for Etonians) was to find little in common with Empson. As his obituarist would note in the *Magdalene College Record*, 'The rather rule-less nature of Magdalene was a surprise to the Ram when he first came here.'[7] Far from being a modernizer, therefore, 'he was actually bent on retrogression in many respects'—he would even try to reinstitute com-pulsory Chapel—and many undergraduates considered him 'soggy and sanctimonious'.[8] His tenure as Master was to last for twenty-one years.

The few famous alumni were less obscure than the history of the college might lead one to expect. They included Archbishop Ussher of Armagh (1567), co-founder of Trinity College Dublin; Henry Dunster (1627), first president, benefactor, and true founder of Harvard University; Samuel Pepys (1651); the 8th Marquis of Queensberry (1864), formulator of the Boxing Rules and later persecutor of Oscar Wilde; Charles Stewart Parnell

(1865), leader of the Irish Parliamentary Party 1880–90; and Charles Kingsley (1838), who became Regius Professor of Modern History 1860–9 but who is better known to this day as author of *The Water Babies*. More recent graduates included Kingsley Martin, future editor of the *New Statesman*, J. R. Ackerley, novelist and literary editor of *The Listener*, and Geoffrey Webb, who was to be Slade Professor of Fine Art twice over. Very likely, at least as a freshman, Empson knew little or nothing of his predecessors in college, though some of their faces would look down from the shadows as he partook of candlelit dinners in the pine-panelled Hall (it was probably by way of being a deliberate policy that neither Queensberry nor Parnell were hung there), followed by 'green or gray' coffee in the Common Room.[9] But he knew that his brother Charles had preceded him by two student generations, graduating in 1922; and Charles would set him an example of enterprise for the rest of his life.

Like the majority of his peers, Empson regarded the college as a less restricted version of school, a residential club for young gentlemen who wished to develop their faculties in intimate association with one another and with as little interference as possible from directors of studies and dons in general. At his matriculation he was given a customary admonition by the praelector of the college: 'If a Fellow asks you to lunch, leave at 2.15 p.m.; unless the general conversation is particularly interesting when you may leave at 2.25 p.m.'; but he would overlook such etiquette. His sitting-room and bedroom in First Court, a battlemented and ivy-clad enclosure, gave a southerly view of a string of mature chestnut trees alongside the River Cam; and in comparison with the confinement he was used to at Winchester his rooms were prodigally spacious. In addition, he had no incentive either to be tidy or to exercise foresight: the fire would be laid each morning by his bedmaker, who carried coal-buckets up to all the rooms on her staircase, filled the scuttles, and saw to other necessary chores including emptying the chamberpots. (There were no lavatories or bathrooms, only washstands; so that for all bodily functions which required plumbing, the bursting, dirty denizens—as Frank West, Bishop of Taunton, would merrily recall sixty years on—'had to walk from our rooms across two courts in all weathers to a rather ramshackle building known euphemistically as Third Court').[10] Also in the morning, the bedder would bring hot water for the gentleman's shaving, lay out his shirt and tie, and clean his shoes. However, to judge from all accounts and photographs, the scruffy Empson must soon have foresworn the services of a bedder, or have exhausted her patience. 'Cooked breakfast, lunch and tea could be procured from Goodfellow, the red-faced butler,' old Bishop West would warmly remember as well. 'These meals were brought round to our rooms on a tray covered with a green baize cloth, on the head of a kitchen-boy.'[11] (Breakfast and lunch were always sent out from the kitchens.) Thus there was little for many a chap to do other than loll around in his set of rooms, take tea with buttered toast or crumpets from Matthews, swot at his books with an effortless air, and gad about with his fellows. Noel Blakiston, devoted correspondent of his Eton schoolfriend Cyril Connolly and a future Keeper of the Public Record Office, occupied rooms on the same staircase and became friendly with Empson.

But Empson was temperamentally incapable of being idle. Nervously energetic, he was always in a hurry, scurrying to a supervision, dashing like a demon possessed over the cast-iron Cam Bridge into town, or just chattering to his chums. It is impossible to know how much time he devoted to his academic pursuits, he gave so much of himself to other activities. Longing to be accepted into interesting circles, especially the fast set of the intellectual elite, keen to make special friends, and game for the luck of a party, often he would find himself amidst a crowd of loud young men who were perhaps over-indulging in alcohol (though not as a rule in the early days) and almost certainly boorish, boring, or pretentious. This entry in the loose leaves of an occasional diary he kept during his first year features an entertaining and kind-hearted contemporary named Walter S. Wigglesworth (who would go on to be an eminent ecclesiastical lawyer and a benefactor of Magdalene, but who was esteemed among his college contemporaries principally as 'the always high-spirited high-churchman, whose delight was to blaspheme in a ghastly Northern accent'):[12]

Horsey party in my rooms drinking a quiet lemon. Monstrous noise, things thrown out of the window, no conversation but one dirty story—by a Wykeham-ist, I am proud to say, and rather good. I like and admire these people very much but there is no doubt they bore me. Wigglesworth, for instance, is a quite Shakespearean buffoon, the literary pun in English French German Latin and Greek is bawled with the most vigorous good-humour, but I am dreadfully bored by it all the same.

Although he was left feeling supercilious in that gathering (probably because he could not match the learned gags), there is no reason to doubt that he could reduce himself to a similar silliness on other occasions.

A typical sequence of entries from his first-year diary shows how he was constantly chasing a wide spread of culture with the best of them (his taste in reading ran from E. F. Benson and Max Beerbohm to the new, forbidden fruit of Joyce's *Ulysses*); it shows too that he was determined not to be fooled by posing—least of all his own:

Friday. [Mark] Hartland Thomas suggested to me the reason why E. F. Benson's novels make a grand passion the only way of attaining the Inner Inwardness: that he knew he was incapable of one himself, and it was given, as out of reach, a halo. His sterility factor, working on the edge of consciousness, produced an erotic sentimentalism.

Audley Society's paper on Gilles de Rais. Consider.

Saturday. Read Ulysses to [Hartland] Thomas for 4½ hours; two chapters.

Sunday. I have a superficial air of great intelligence, which seems peculiarly adapted for getting halfway up the back stairs. Apparently the Plectron Club, which I appear to have joined, is rather exclusive and concerned with dramatic criticism. What do *I* know about it? And how on earth did I get there? People like Philip, who actually act, may with some point be dining with Earnest [*sic*] Thesiger and joining the Plectron Club, but I am there like a fish, talkative, in champagne.

He made some patterns in tautology with such words as 'art' 'realism' and what not. I can chatter tautologies too; a cat may look at a king; a cat, that is, has some neatness and available capacity, for strictly domestic purposes, a king is a practical man of detail, using judgement over real people. It is silly to talk in this evening's abstractions.

He said male actors in female parts were the right thing for Cambridge, where people like them better; they are less surprising and more attractive. How solid, how convincing. (The moral young Edward II who didn't want to kiss him; joke.)

In many respects, Empson's prototype might have been Stephen Dedalus in *A Portrait of the Artist as a Young Man.* The painful self-awareness, the fascination with analysing his own ideas and behaviour, even when done with a measure of self-irony, was by turns perplexed, pompous and priggish:

I squit up and down with various emotions and enthusiasms which, so far as I can judge, are callow, fleeting, and absurd. It is the business of my mind to focus them sharply, and judge them without favour; not to repress them with contempt or distaste. Perhaps one should expect a passive self-knowledge to deepen slowly the impulses which are its object, perhaps not. In either case the conscious fidgeting of one's better judgement should not be allowed to interfere with purpose and activity, or it may kill them altogether. The really impeccable people like William Hayter tend to do nothing at all.

Perhaps that is the crux about 'insincerity'. One must, on paper, feel an emotion strongly and without conflict see the absurdity of it at the same time. If any situation had his whole attention, that is the attitude he would take up ... A person who is wholly in earnest, and only of one mind in a matter is either not sufficiently wide awake or too stupid to think at all. I am here considering only the question of motive, and one's private judgement of whether it is worth making a fuss about; there is also of course the question of method, and one's private judgement of whether this is the right way to set about it. But it is possible to remember that one had decided on a course of action as best after weighing the evidence; whereas one's actuating emotion is an immediate and fluctuating affair which must always be observed and judged on the spot. One is quite often sincere in both senses at once about one's method, but only about one's emotion when filled with the breath of God ...

It is not difficult to see why he was belabouring himself for the lack of calm decisiveness in his life: he happened to be thinking about William Hayter, who had seemed to be so mature and well-balanced at Winchester, and feeling envious. Thus he found it a self-consolatory activity to write two ponderous and partly snide paragraphs to explain to himself why it was a good idea to be in two minds at once about everything. Of course he was not exceptional in this kind of carry-on: just the typically sharp-minded, self-conscious undergraduate. It seems typical too of Empson the adolescent atheist that when he felt like scoffing at his religious acquaintances he accused them of indulging in 'spiritual masturbation'.

What is not so typical is that he was not merely self-absorbed, he was absorbed too in the getting of knowledge—and not just from the curriculum. He read everything in sight.

His supervisor for Mathematics was A. S. Ramsey, a long-standing fellow of Magdalene (he had been appointed to a college lectureship in 1897) and a staunch noncomformist who worshipped at Emmanuel Congregational chapel. He was appointed Steward in 1900, College and Pepys Librarian in the same year; and he became Bursar in 1904. He was also President (Vice-Master) of the college, in succession to A. C. Benson, and Senior Tutor from 1912 to 1927. But few students could approach his rooms in the Pepys Building with a light heart. According to Owen Chadwick, 'He was a good mathematical teacher and he wrote a number of text-books, some of which went on selling into the 1980s. To the outward eye he was austere, even bleak. Colleagues and pupils thought of him as formidable; a few found him frightening, a few found him affable ...'[13] His younger son, Michael, Empson's senior by two years—a bright but ungainly youth with a sing-song voice who entered Magdalene in 1923—was given rooms directly above his silent, sober father's, and next door to a like-minded Liberal, Selwyn Lloyd.[14] Though destined to become Archbishop of

Canterbury (1961–74), Michael Ramsey's charity was strained by a long-
standing disaffection for his father (whom he would imitate to hilarious
perfection for the benefit of his fellows). 'I think that at the subconscious
and half-conscious levels he was a heavy weight upon me of a perhaps
oppressive or repressive kind,' Michael Ramsey would concede. 'In later
life I was made unnecessarily unhappy by my religious divergence from his
position.' Yet A. S. Ramsey may have shown Empson a fair deal of the dry
kindness in his nature. Or maybe the more outgoing Mrs Ramsey—who
had studied history at Oxford (where she had known Lewis Carroll), and
was a Socialist and a suffragette, being active after the First World War in
the cooperative movement and the Labour Party—softened the impress of
her husband. 'On Sundays she would invite a group of Magdalene undergraduates to lunch and they would stay till tea; then another group still
larger came to tea... [H]er face was interesting and intelligent and attractive. Her personality was magnetic.'[15]

Certainly Empson would do well in Mathematics during his first year,
though that may have been in part because he was drawing on a natural
talent. Yet he had a particular enthusiasm for algebra, which was among
Ramsey's specialisms, so perhaps they did hit it off together. In a much later
year, I. A. Richards was to put on record Ramsey's conversational remark,
made at the time when Empson abandoned maths for English, that 'Empson was one of the best mathematicians he'd ever had and he was sorry he
was leaving mathematics.'[16] Other topics for Part I of the Mathematical
Tripos included Mechanics (on which Ramsey lectured, in addition to
Algebra and Trigonometry), Calculus, Dynamics, Electricity, Optics, and
Hydrostatics—as well as Solid Geometry and Theory of Equations, which
were taught in King's College by Ramsey's elder son Frank (1903–30), who
was indisputably a mathematical and philosophical prodigy.

It is possible that Empson fell for a while under the influence of Frank
Ramsey: from the very beginning of his undergraduate career he was
reading G. E. Moore and Ludwig Wittgenstein, and worrying concepts
of meaning, beauty, emotion, and value. Yet it is also just as likely that he
devoured Moore and Wittgenstein because they were a fundamental part
of the *Zeitgeist* for a live-minded student.[17] In the few pages of the diary he
kept during his first year, for example, he penned a paragraph disputing a
point of definition with a Magdalene contemporary named W. G. Fordham; young Empson is exercised here by the pleasures of epistemology:

Fordham takes a view of Wittgenstein I think untrue. He is 'cynical' in the sense
Wittgenstein himself exploded. He said that an emotion was a fact; God is not 'in'

the world; God is not in a religious emotion. In so far as an emotion is treated as a fact which can be handled in proposition, it is colourless like other objects. That in the emotion which cannot be stated in a proposition, which shows itself, which is not 'how' but 'is', that may have value, I should have thought. 'The world is the totality of facts, not of things.' Emotion is a thing.

Also, very early on, he was concerned to formulate a definition of the power of mathematics under the rubric of aesthetic value, which shows he was resisting any suspicion that it might be necessary to divorce his own set subject from the philosophical and literary ferment that had been un-leashed in Cambridge of late. In the following passage he is toying with terminology taken principally from Wittgenstein's *Tractatus Logico-Philoso-phicus*, which he read in the first English translation (1922)—by C. K. Ogden, with the assistance of Frank Ramsey—as well as from *The Foun-dations of Aesthetics* (1922), by Ogden, I. A. Richards, and James Wood; his earnest desire to reconcile the disciplines almost certainly goes to show how hard he was trying to resolve a tension he had discovered in himself:

The view of mathematics as an exalted exposition of beauty does not conflict with Wittgenstein. A mathematical equation is a logical form, either a definition or a platitude, and all logical propositions are of equal value. But mathematics is self-evident only to the perfect mind, that is a mind which can grasp every aspect of a situation at once, that is can see at a glance the purport of all possible combinations of the fundamental propositions of a situation. The human mind can only grasp a limited number of aspects; any given mathematical notation draws the attention to some particular method (that is, series of combinations) as the most simple and fruitful. The aesthetic value of a mathematical process lies in the handling of the complex logical forms so as to vary the most natural selection of conclusions; in this way the power of the mind appears to be enlarged, so as to have a logical grasp on situations of greater complexity. A perpetual slight surprise, which on the next moment's consideration is turned to a richer acceptance, was what Aristotle found most fundamental to exalted beauty. This pleasure is inherent in the method of mathematics. The school of aesthetic appreciation whose high praise is 'how amusing' lays stress on the slight surprise, not on the acceptance of a richer, that is a more complex and suggestive, unity. It is right as far as it goes.

Not for Empson was there any gulf between the two cultures. All the same, he was trying to reassure himself that he might have his cake and eat it; that he could pursue mathematics—and perhaps philosophy—as well as keep up with advances in literary study. In addition, he was immensely attracted to the science of astrophysics, which had just been flooded with novelties. 'An Einstein universe is in equilibrium, but its equilibrium is unstable,' wrote Sir Arthur Eddington, Plumian Professor of Astronomy

(Empson would attend his lectures for the Special Board for Mathematics, along with those by Sir Ernest Rutherford). Empson was a true child of his time: even as he shifted his academic interests towards literature, he felt all the while every bit as stimulated by the discoveries of physics and astronomy as by I. A. Richards's enquiries, in *The Principles of Literary Criticism* (1924), into the value of literature. From Richards too he would learn of the prime importance of 'equilibrium' or 'balance', and of the self-completing character of literary creation and reception. In the meantime, before he discovered his true *métier*, Empson felt in himself a tremendous amount of strain and instability, of contradictory attractions, as he pursued at one and the same time the perfection of mathematics, the logical propositions of Wittgenstein, and the theory of 'the systematisation of impulses' propounded by Richards. Rarely can a student have felt such a multitude of ideas tugging him in several directions.

Not the least of his interests was psychology, which he had discovered at Winchester when his senior friend Carew A. Meredith urged him to read Robert Briffault; and he himself seized upon Freud, the new cicerone of the secrets of the unconscious mind. Carew Meredith, a small, gnomelike figure with a grin like a Cheshire cat and a pronounced Dublin accent (good for reading aloud from Joyce),[18] had proceeded in 1922 from Winchester to Trinity College, where he became the first Mathematical student to take a double first and a 'B star' in two years. Naturally he was one of the first people Empson sought out in Cambridge. Meredith duly introduced him to other friends: one such was J. D. Solomon (a student of geology), who would remember Empson as 'a rather short, round-faced youth with a ruddy complexion and an owlish expression. There was always a tone of something like mockery in his voice, although its timbre was fruity, appropriate to the Yorkshire fox-hunting squirearchy which I believe was his background.'[19] If it was Meredith's influence which partly persuaded Empson to specialize in mathematics in the first place, his enthusiasm for psychology helped to make Empson a fit pupil for I. A. Richards.

Even at the very start of his undergraduate career, Empson became fascinated by the recent Richards, notably *Principles of Literary Criticism*, and he argued about his ideas with Meredith and with his new friend, Fordham (an ardent Liberal and a frequent speaker at the Union who was destined to build up a thriving practice at the Criminal Bar). This passage from Empson's early jottings, in particular the references to 'the valuable emotions' and 'the vital sources of impulse', shows that even in his first session at university he was playing around with his future mentor's elusive psychological terms of reference:

So many of these people are driven to take a purely moralistic objection to their emotions, especially religious ones. Meredith had told me Fordham could not argue, and became inexplicably annoyed when he failed to do so. Fordham agreed with me that the corrosive analysis of Meredith gives one a feeling of being killed altogether, one has to cut and run after a time. The reason is that one feels the valuable emotions to be themselves at stake; the mind is not easily able to maintain critical self-knowledge without tampering with the vital sources of impulse. Mysticism is so naked without mythology. Fordham said that emotion and reason were much the same; reason was an emotion; there is the logical impulse. The two things interact, but they are distinct. Logic itself cannot provide an impulse, even the impulse to be logical. Without impulses there is no life, if logical analysis must, when carried far enough, put impulse to one side and show that there is no value, then logical analysis will kill us all. But there is no reason why, or way how, it *should* show or do anything of the kind.

The lucubrations of the 19-year-old Empson may seem slippery to the point of intellectual imposture; but it is often the case with the precocious adolescent that the intuitive intelligence outruns the discursive faculty, that lickety-split wit lacks patience with labouring sense. Since the energetic Richards was a leading figure in the happy growth of English studies at Cambridge, and was attached to Magdalene College, Empson would have needed no prompting to get hold of his work; but Meredith's infectious enthusiasm for psychology may have clinched Empson's sense of commitment.

There is no doubt that during his first year Empson allied himself to the principles of literary criticism laid out by I. A. Richards, and notably to his Theory of Value. In the very first literary notice he wrote for *The Granta*, on 12 June 1926, 'The Romantic Rationalist'—a review of *Reason and Romanticism* by Herbert Read—he observed that Read's 'toying with revealed truth is not really very strange . . . The divine revelation is only a quick way of recognizing Mr Richards' scale of values . . .' Not content with that endorsement of Richards, he went on to make this profession of faith in the local hero: '[Mr Read's] aesthetic theories, in the main, are true and valuable, especially when Mr Richards has stated them already.'[20]

Carew Meredith must also have introduced him to the society known as the Heretics. Publicly inaugurated in 1909, when it was addressed both by Jane Harrison (her paper, *Heresy and Humanity*, was later published) and by J. E. McTaggart, this discussion group had an amazing record for attracting eminent speakers. Its primary aim, according to the Laws devised by the founder C. K. Ogden, was 'to promote discussion on problems of religion, philosophy, and art'; and membership was made conditional upon rejecting 'all appeal to authority in the discussion of religious questions'. Honorary members included G. Lowes Dickinson, J. M. Keynes, G. E. Moore, Bertrand Russell (who had advised a meeting of the society that the Ten Commandments were like the customary rubric for a ten-question examination paper: 'only six need be attempted'), Bernard Shaw (who expounded his views on the Future of Religion), Eileen Power, and G. M. Trevelyan. C. K. Ogden, the first secretary of the society, took over as president in his third undergraduate year (1911) and continued so until 1924; during that time he organized talks by celebrities such as Bertrand Russell, Marie Stopes ('Birth Control'), E. M. Forster ('Anonymity'), Julian Huxley, G. G. Coulton ('Super Heresy'), F. M. Cornford ('Religion in the University'), G. E. Moore ('Some Problems of Ethics'), Lytton Strachey ('Art and Indecency'), as well as Edith Sitwell and Clive Bell. Virginia Woolf gave a version of the paper subsequently published as *Mr Bennett and Mrs Brown* (Empson was probably present on that occasion); J. B. S. Haldane took for his topics 'Callinicus' and 'Daedalus' (both later published in the *Cambridge Magazine*, of which Ogden was founder, proprietor, and editor); and I. A. Richards spoke of 'Emotion and Art'. As P. Sargant Florence would later observe, 'the Heretics were "natural" humanists in discussing morality without religion.'[21] Empson was naturally eager to join a society which set no bar on the candid discussion of religion, philosophy, and art, as well as (in course of time) anthropology, social history, psychology, sociology, and economics.

On occasion, the Sunday meetings seemed to afford Empson little more than the opportunity to crow with youthful arrogance, as when he set down in his diary this rebuke to a speaker who had clearly never read his G. E. Moore: 'Miserable little man lecturing the Heretics; why, he didn't even know the difference between a sensation and a sense-datum.'[22] The reason for such a private display of irritation is simple: since he was self-admittedly timid, and not yet bold enough to tackle an irritating speaker face-to-face, he had to go away and unbottle himself on paper. Just so, another day he harumphed back to his rooms and wrote:

A revivalist at the Heretics—'What shall we do with the parson[?]'—he foamed at the mouth, but did not know. He could not see that his own 'non-theological' services were organized religion, which assumed some dogmas, and performed some ritual. Soames [Jenyns] afterwards thought it more unselfish to preach than to create, and that God is Love. That phrase means God is an enthusiasm for the divine, or Himself; unless it means that personal relations (Freud) are the only matters of interest (but cf. Robinson Crusoe). It refers to the truth that man is a gregarious animal, and so it's not irrelevant, but see Marcel Proust on the opposition of friendship to intellectual integrity. In a man's private life, he must isolate so many things and say 'these are the value, and I shall chase', but not in his theory of the universe must he draw any such limitation.

In worrying the old saw that 'God is Love' without reference to E. M. Forster, it may be that Empson himself had not yet read *A Passage to India* (published in June 1924). But the kind of formula represented by the doctrinal assertion 'God is Love'—which Empson later styled an 'Existence Assertion'—is the sort of hypostatization of grammar that he would tax for many years, even until he devised the chapters 'Statements in Words' and 'A is B' for *The Structure of Complex Words*.[23] In the gnomic statement 'God is Love', he was to take pains to suggest (or rather explain with firm tact),

> *God* keeps its old referent—he appears as the same person we were calling God before, even if the new property which is imputed to him is a decisively important one; but *love* is both ideal (the best kind of love) and extremely general (all the love in the world). The reason why 'Love is God' feels puzzling is that we are not sure which definite idea to take about love, how much sex to put into it for instance, nor yet how we are to generalise or diffuse the idea of God; the slogan is likely to mean some kind of pantheism, but we cannot tell what till we hear more.

It is fascinating to note that the same analytical and expository cast of mind, albeit unpoised and less penetrating, was already in evidence in Empson's very first undergraduate year. But the young critic is twitchy and curt, flicking his rapier, and self-preening (casually flashing his powers of reference: Freud, Defoe, Proust); and he falls short of the inclusive good manners of the adult. He distinguishes just two possible explanations for the meaning of 'God is Love'—(*a*) God is the ultimate narcissist; (*b*) sex makes the world go round—before thrusting on. All the same, as he eases up from his irritation with empty chatter about religious rituals (which would invariably make him feel sick with the thought of blood sacrifice), his deeper good nature finds it important to put on record the thought that while the individual has to make exigent decisions on questions of personal value, it is important always to be open-minded on the larger philosophical issues.

What is clear is that Empson must have benefited to a high degree from paying close attention to the range of speakers who addressed the Heretics during the four years of his Cambridge career. In 1926–7, for example, he heard papers by writers as various as Wyndham Lewis, Richard Hughes, Herbert Read, and Leonard Woolf, and he had the chance to speak with them in person. Dr Joseph Needham, later Master of Gonville & Caius College, maintained 'under the text the "Limitations of Optick Glasses" that scientific and religious glasses might, each used alone, be equally fallacious'; C. D. Broad spoke on Francis Bacon; Bronislaw Malinowski on 'Heterodox Professions of a Schismatic Anthropologist'. (Sadly, D. H. Lawrence turned down an invitation to speak to the Heretics in 1926.)[24] With respect to Empson's later interest in semantics, and in explicating the hidden agenda of words—the 'compacted doctrines' or subversive implications that the language so often encapsulates—it is valuable too to learn from P. Sargant Florence: 'Certainly the philosophy of many of us Heretics began with the analysis of words.' Thus it is hardly surprising to find that by his fourth year, 1928–9, Empson had become so involved with the Heretics that he was to hold the position of president; his own guest speakers during that session were to include Rose Macaulay, Denis Arundell, S. R. Slavson, and Anthony Asquith. (In a later year Empson suggested to me that it would be valuable to find the minute-books of the society, but I have not been able to do so.) In what turned out to be his final term at the university he even arranged for Wittgenstein, who had recently returned to Cambridge, to present a paper on Ethics;[25] but Empson himself missed the talk, given in October 1929, only because he had been cast out of Magdalene three months before.

He chose not to go to T. S. Eliot's Clark Lectures, 'The Metaphysical Poets of the Seventeenth Century' (given at Trinity College in February and March 1926)—'on the sole and sufficient ground, as he thought, that in his undergraduate days he attended no lectures'.[26] (He was only doing as he had learned from others: I. A. Richards liked to inform his pupils that lectures were a curious survival from pre-Caxton days and that they should go to very few.) In a later year he would write in tribute to Eliot, with a hint of cheekiness: 'I feel, like most other verse writers of my generation, that I do not know for certain how much of my own mind he invented, let alone how much of it is a reaction against him or indeed a consequence of misreading him. He has a very penetrating influence, perhaps not unlike an east wind.' Of course he had read *The Waste Land* (1922), and the essays of *The Sacred Wood* (1920), which together secured for Eliot a pre-eminent authority as poet and critic; a prestige enhanced by Eliot's editorials in *The Criterion*, the periodical he had founded in 1922. But there is no way of telling if Empson had worked out a considered opinion of Eliot by the beginning of 1926; it would not seem likely. It is unlikely too, though not impossible, that he had as yet read I. A. Richards's essay 'Mr Eliot's Poems' (in the *New Statesman* that February), which vexingly extolled *The*

Waste Land and 'The Hollow Men' as conveying 'purely a music of ideas' whose effects are really not available to intellectual analysis but may somehow 'in us . . . combine into a coherent whole of feeling and attitude and produce a peculiar liberation of the will'. Nor would he realize, since he had not yet become a pupil of Richards, that Richards was a friend of Eliot's. In a later year again, he would take severe issue with Eliot's depreciatory final thoughts on Donne, who was in part the subject of the Clark Lectures (Empson assuredly read Donne's poetry during his first year in college). In 1932 Eliot would make the unsupported assertion, 'Donne was, I insist, no sceptic'—a ruling which riled Empson: Eliot had taken up his lasting stand as the literary high priest of the Christian religion. But there was little hint of such a reactionary view of Donne being adopted by the Eliot of 1926; and we may safely presume that in 1926 Empson would have counted himself among those who, in Richards's words, found in Eliot's poetry, particularly *The Waste Land*, 'a clearer, fuller realization of their plight, the plight of a whole generation, than they find elsewhere'.

On his visits to Cambridge, Eliot 'was prepared to receive undergraduates after breakfast on Thursdays [actually, Wednesdays],' Empson was to recall years later. Though he declined to attend the lectures, Empson was keenly to the fore of the flock of students who paid informal court to the poet (though he recorded in his diary notes that he completely forgot to attend the last—'well worth hearing'—of Eliot's four audiences); and he noted down that Eliot recommended them to read the sermons of Lancelot Andrewes. According to George Watson's account of Eliot's appearances in Cambridge, Empson remained 'impressed to the end of his life by the seriousness with which he listened to questions and arguments, and the earnestness of his answers'.[27] But meeting Mr Eliot could be a discomforting experience, even for someone like Richards who had won his friendship. Two years later, in February 1928, Dorothea Richards jotted down in her diary this vignette of an Eliot visit: he 'came up the stairs looking to me very gaunt & grim—as if he had burnt himself out. His queer coloured, strangely piercing eyes in a pale face are the most striking thing about him. He is pale with special wrinkles which run horizontally across his forehead & his nose is delicately Jewish. He doesn't understand all I say nor do we him. His questions are surprising—disconcerting because so simple, sometimes almost inane. We talked of skye scrapers—of Canada & drinking—we took the initiative.'[28]

What did Empson carry away from what he pointedly termed the *grande levées* [*sic*]—the Wednesday-morning meetings—of 1926?[29] One gem that

Eliot let fall gave him much encouragement: 'As a young man I snatched
at any chance to hear wisdom drop from Mr T. S. Eliot,' he was to recall in
1957, 'and he once remarked that the test of a true poet is that he writes
about experiences before they have happened to him; I felt I had once
passed this test, though I forget now in which poem.'[30] More substantively,
a brief memoir by Empson catches the awkward and punctiliously enunciated measure of Eliot's conversation:

At the first of these very awed gatherings someone [John Hayward] asked him
what he thought of Proust. 'I have not read Proust,' was the deliberate reply. How
the conversation was picked up again is beyond conjecture, but no one cared to
plumb into the motives of his abstinence. It was felt to be a rather impressive trait
in this powerful character. Next week a new member of the group asked what he
thought of the translation of Proust by Scott Moncrieff, and Eliot delivered a very
weighty, and rather long, tribute to that work. It was not enough, he said, to say
that it was better than the original in many single passages; it was his impression
that the translation was at no point inferior to the original (which, to be sure, was
often careless French), either in accuracy of detail or in the general impression of
the whole. We were startled by so much loquacity from the silent master rather
than by any disagreement with what he had said before; in fact it seemed quite
clear to me what Eliot meant—he did not consider he had 'read' a book unless he
had written copious notes about it and so on. I no longer feel sure that this was
what he meant, but I am still quite sure that he was not merely lying to impress the
children; maybe at the earlier meeting he hadn't bothered to listen to what they
were saying.[31]

However, Ronald Schuchard, in his edition of Eliot's Clark lectures,
comments on Empson's curious account: 'Empson evidently misheard or
misremembered the dialogue: Eliot may not have read "the last volume"
of Proust, but he had certainly read and formed an impression of earlier
work before the Cambridge visit.'[32] Otherwise, as Schuchard also points
out, Empson paid impressively close attention to Eliot's infomal remarks:

At the coffee-circle following Lecture VI, Empson also listened well to Eliot's
discussion of Shelley's careless use of imagery in 'To a Skylark' and in a chorus of
Hellas. Four years later, the attentive Empson reconstructed the discussion in his
Seven Types of Ambiguity (1930). To illustrate the fifth type of ambiguity, in which 'for
instance, there is a simile which applies to nothing exactly, but lies half-way
between two things when the author is moving from one to the other', he returned
to the fifth stanza of 'To a Skylark', 'about which Mr. Eliot started a discussion.
I am afraid more points were brought out than I remembered.

> Keen as are the arrows
> Of that silver sphere

> Whose intense lamp narrows
>   In the white dawn clear,
> Until we hardly see, we feel that it is there.

'Mr. Eliot claimed not to know what the *sphere* was', Empson recalled as he began his own analysis of the ambiguities, and Eliot 'complained that Shelley had mixed up' night and day in the poem (p. 157). Further, pointing to lines from the chorus of *Hellas* ('The earth doth like a snake renew / Her winter weeds outworn'), 'Mr. Eliot said that *snakes* do not *renew* their cast skins, and do not cast them at the end of *winter*; and that a seventeenth-century poet would have known his mind on such points' (p. 159). Empson, in his attempt to justify Shelley's 'bad natural history', was moved to 'agree very heartily with what Mr. Eliot was saying at the time . . . this muddle of ideas clogging an apparently simple lyrical flow may be explained, but is not therefore justified; and it is evident that a hearty appetite for this and the following type of ambiguity would apologise for, would be able to extract pleasure from, very bad poetry indeed' (p. 160). Thus did Eliot unwittingly impress his critical imagination on Richards' dauntless student during the coffee mornings.[33]

Empson's own sophisticated memoir, written twenty-two years after the event, managed at once to pay tribute to Eliot's majesty and to leave the impression that the writer of it has delivered a gently glancing blow. By that date, Empson believed he had reason to resent the authority of Eliot's opinions, not least because his *ex cathedra* pronouncements had hushed the defiant originality of young Jack Donne, deadening his radicalism in the eyes of generations of students. But Empson never changed his mind about the importance of Eliot's own early poetry, most especially *The Waste Land.*

Forty-eight years later, when he visited Cambridge to deliver his own (disappointing) Clark Lectures under the catch-all title 'The Progress of Criticism', he would remember and seek to emulate the decent example set by Eliot when he decided that he should make himself available to personal enquirers after each of his six lectures. 'How much to advertise these meetings for questions,' he wondered in a letter, 'is an abstruse question. Probably there is a University Calendar for the term giving all kinds of minor events? It could say I will be in my room at Magdalene from 3.00 the day after each lecture to answer questions, not necessarily about the lectures. I will say that in the lectures anyway. But it seems better not to have the offer billed, on posters, because that (for the first few times) might attract people who only felt curiosity.'[34] His apprehensiveness about such audiences may also have caught an echo from Eliot's rather nervous privy appearances.

If Empson was deeply uncomfortable about public speaking at this stage of his career, it is surprising to find that, starting in his second term, he forced himself to speak on several occasions at the Union, the University debating society—until he decided it was not worth all the torment and the fear. But a fair part of the reason why he put himself through the misery of giving what turned out to be a handful of muttering speeches is plain. He wanted both to be known and to be successful, and he knew that the Union offered a sure route to celebrity. In the smaller pond of Winchester he had done fairly well at debating, which gratified (albeit masochistically) the shy chap's desire to put himself forward. At Cambridge it must have seemed that with one heroic speech he could bound from reserved non-entity to celebrity. He had no reason to doubt his own intelligence and wit. As for public speaking, however, his bravery was greater than his better judgement. His generation boasted a number of fine speakers including a senior Magdalene man, Selwyn Lloyd, who in turn—as his biographer has related—picked out three outstanding speakers among his contemporaries: 'The first was Michael Ramsey ("tough and critical in debate and already an orator"), the second, Patrick Devlin ("a brilliant debater who never gave a point away, a keen politician, ambitious and one would have guessed then a natural selection for an outstanding parliamentary career") and the third, Gilbert Harding ("he had a rumbustious manner all his own"). The Union was seen, not least by its own members, as a House of Commons in embryo . . . '[35]

In fact Empson nearly failed to screw up his courage to make his maiden speech; as he recorded in his journal, 'I have been made to feel very grim and full of purpose in revolt against the futility of the Union, where I bobbed up and down for four hours or so without delivering myself of my timid crew of quips, not being a personal friend of the President.' Thereupon, perhaps partly by way of frustrated reaction, he resolved for the moment to commit his energies to another route to immortal fame, that of scientific research; the following words come directly after those last quoted:

I wish next holidays to use St Peter's laboratory in a serious attack on jellies; it depends whether they have a sliding microscope. If so I shall get to the bottom of the LT relation if it is in my power, and shall devise some method of attack on the lateral gap-teeth. Lord make me worthy of what is so arduous and so noble, and while you are about it don't let Smith + read my diary, I don't wish to be laughed at about this at all.

I see no reason to believe that knowledge about jellies is in any way absolutely desirable; it seems possible enough that my excitement about them is due to vanity, caprice, or perverted sexuality. I don't care a hoot . . .

What, if anything, came of his ambitious attempt to get to the bottom of jellies is not known.

On other days he adopted toward the debates the facetiousness that is typical of generations of undergraduates. 'Fordham, met at Union, sat by me, a great pleasure; not till I had had time to take the first speeches seriously; emotional plums plopped about; Indians on liberty and the homeland, fine cosmic raving. Many coloured persons on the Tory side of the house. When sitting with Fordham aesthetic appreciation must be of the fashionable "amusing" order; jokes of speakers and their self-contradictions only are beautiful.'

He spoke at the Union for the first time on 26 January 1926, to the motion 'That the Victorians were greater than ourselves'. The student magazine *The Granta* commented with unexpected generosity that he 'was making, we presume, a maiden speech; when he becomes less nervous and not so tied to his written word, he will be very good indeed.'[36] Michael Ramsey, who by virtue of being President of the Union for the Lent Term was required to write up the debates for the *Cambridge Review*, set down a few kindly words about his college contemporary: 'Mr Empson in a very amusing and clever speech defended Victorian dignity. It was a genuine thing, so why shouldn't they be proud of it?'[37] A week later, Empson contributed his aesthetic penn'orth in speaking against the motion 'That the existing standards of living impede the progress of civilization'. Ramsey duly reported a claim that is utterly of its time: 'Mr Empson defended luxury. It was largely artistic and so justified itself.'[38]

He had another go on 25 May, when the motion was a provocative piece of elitism: 'That from the point of view of the permanent progress of the Nation, Compulsory Free Education is a mistake.' Refusing to rise to the obvious bait, on this occasion Empson jumped ahead of his time in arguing that vocational training has just as much merit as an academic education. *The Granta* reckoned he had improved as a debater: Mr Empson, it noted, 'disliked education being based on a literary standard. One of the better contributions to the evening's discussion.'[39] On the other hand, according to H. G. G. Herklots (Union President for the Easter Term), Gilbert Harding of Queen's suitably 'deplored the weeping sentimentalism of socialism, and in the same breath declared himself a socialist. It seemed queer.'[40] Herklots saluted Empson's 'socialistic' contribution with a gloss in the *Cambridge Review* that opens with a self-referring sentence and goes on so bluntly as to give little idea of the no-doubt-persuasive eloquence of the speech itself: 'The education at present in vogue is the wrong kind of education. A literary education will not make a good craftsman. Mr Empson is always interesting.'

Hugh Herklots (Trinity Hall) had in fact befriended Empson, a fact which would have given a big boost to his self-possession as a public speaker—especially since Empson had developed a big crush on Herklots. Empson seems to have become infatuated with the older man (b. 1903) soon after coming up; and no doubt Herklots's twofold eminence—at the Union (where he was Secretary in Michaelmas Term, Vice-President in Lent, President in Easter) and at *The Granta*, of which he was editor for the session 1925–6—endowed him with extra charisma. This sequence of entries from Empson's diary, which is not meant to be as comic as it now seems, would appear to mark the beginning of the unavailing affair:[41]

Wednesday. I went to a Christian lecture on China and bought a pamphlet. Have carried away no new information but (for the moment) rather stronger feelings. I asked the great Herklots the way in; he sat by me, was most intimate and charming as a matter of course, and invited me to tea tomorrow. I had eaten too much and my heart was quite touched. Does he do that to everybody who ever sits next to him? ... Gloria in excelsis, how am I watched over and guarded by the loving care of God.

Thursday. Dull charity tea at Herklots'. He is a Christian, which explains much (though one must be careful not to insist on cause and effect in these matters). He is a 'nice playful man'; without religious backing this would be a decayed nervous mannerism, now he dances before the high altar and is hale and sane. But to do it he has to be a Christian, to cramp his mind with absurd historical theories, and a nasty moralism, and to herd with people who are shocked by what he does with the high altar. This is sad. Without being good-looking he is at times a vision, and the no doubt Platonic pawings are to be enjoyed.

A prospective ordinand, Herklots was 'playful' to the extent of penning and even publishing poems such as 'Ignorance', which begins:

> Is it enough that I have heard
>   Music from out a star,
> Music unheard by other men,
>   Inviolate, afar?[42]

No doubt the verse says much for the state of his soul; it does not say much for his judgement. To be fair, he enjoyed an evidently deserved reputation for his 'attractive and unusual make-up' and his 'comic spirit' (as a contemporary related); and in 1926 he published a book of poems and essays, under the title *Jack of All Trades*, which—according to *The Granta*—truly reflected 'the accent of his voice, the peculiar gesture accompanying the words'. The reviewer, who was obviously acquainted with the intellectually agile and immensely personable Herklots, went on: 'A wider circle will like the happy whimsical turn of mind and phrase, the light-hearted absurdity, the mental gambolling.'[43] (Two of his poems had even appeared in *Life*.) 'Were you so fortunate as to be asked to tea,' wrote *The Granta* in a profile of Herklots—the universal hero—'especially if it were in the winter terms, you would hear such tales of adventure as had rarely come your way, for none can talk so charmingly of himself as Hugh . . .'[44] Thus he must have been quite delightful to be with; even more so to be smitten with.

Accordingly, in the next relevant entry of Empson's diary, the author of the affair is understandably overcome by rapture:

Tuesday [10th]. Tea with Herklots (ecstatic) and horsey rowing men, no doubt Christians. When I saw him in the street I felt as if somebody was pulling in my waist and hauling up my laces; perhaps a tickling and lightness just over the kidneys is what I mean. During tea I sat still and lapped him up (not but what I talked all the time) and made rabbit-eyes ever so; he goodnaturedly pawed at me. Now I feel as if I'd run five miles, my legs stiff, with muscles felt separately like dead branches, and sleepy, to speak at the Union. How dignified of my legs, not the sort of thing I should have thought of myself. I suppose it *is* because I sat rigid in the excitement of his beauty, like young women watching the heroes on the films. Where is my peroration? I had not realized I was in love so deeply.

Wednesday. From T. S. Eliot Levée to midnight Christians, there has been nothing but conversation this day.

What happened next was that Empson realized that his desires could scarcely be confined to one object. Consequently, he started to spin a theory of selfless love—which would be somehow both vicarious and voyeuristic, and which would find pleasure in a kind of inactive happy triangle. The following formulation very interestingly anticipates by many years his exposition of the *ménage-à-trois* that he believed James Joyce inscribed in *Ulysses* (it is possible that the young Empson had already read Joyce's play *Exiles*):

Friday. Found myself, during concert, taking great pleasure in furtively watching the fresh young (elder?) Clutton Brock during love-songs. It is an oddly altruistic lewdness, homosexual in origin and heterosexual by proxy. 'Unselfish'; on the analogy of the old maids who join leagues for enforcing purity among the young, I suppose you might say my feeling came from too much masturbation, I was jealous of his virginity and wanted to see him lose it. (You can always give a fact a hard name without altering its 'scientific' relations.) My mission in life; God has called me at last. The Book of the Happy Bawd. In the same way, my feeling for Herklots would become an almost wholly static satisfaction if he was to marry and I was in love with his wife.[45]

Hugh Herklots married in 1930. He became a clergyman. He ended his career as Moderator of the Church Colleges of Education and the

Residentiary Canon of Peterborough. There is no evidence whatsoever to suggest that he reciprocated Empson's upheaval of feelings at Cambridge. But he was quite friendly enough to suggest during his term of office as President of the Union that Empson should put himself forward in June for election to the Standing Committee. It was a fond idea, and nothing more: Empson was not only *not* elected, he polled what may well have been a record for the lowest number of votes—39.[46]

At the Union on 9 November 1926 (the second month of his second academic year), Empson actually opened the opposition to a fetching motion: 'That this House deplores the prominence given to questions of sex in the post-war novel'. The celebrity guest speakers were J. C. Squire, poet, critic, essayist, parodist, founder of the *London Mercury,* sometime literary editor of the *New Statesman,* chief literary critic of the *Observer,* and butt of both Bloomsbury and the Sitwells (speaking for the motion), and on the other side the novelist Compton Mackenzie. Empson worked himself into such a state of dread that he quite forgot to welcome the eminent visitors; instead, he came immediately to the motion. The President of the Union this session was no less a rising personage than the red-haired Patrick Devlin (Christ's), the future Baron Devlin of West Wick, who reported judiciously for the *Cambridge Review*:

Mr Empson contended that the modern novel was but a reflection of the modern mind. It was ridiculous to suppose that the novelist could omit from his theme one of the primary topics which the public were discussing. The art for art's sake novel had gone for ever. Mr Empson said some very clever things *sotto voce*, but he never secured the attention of the House. The audience was far larger than anyone expected, and Mr Empson had not the experience to cope with it, nor is his style sufficiently declamatory.[47]

While J. C. Squire attempted to counter Empson's argument by claiming that the manner in which sex was recounted in the modern novel was a 'manufactured' commodity, Compton Mackenzie 'completely carried the House' with an intensely witty speech on behalf of sincerity; he blamed journalists for drawing attention to the sex question in the modern novel, and strongly denied that the youth of today were corrupted by it. Selwyn Lloyd spoke third on Empson's side. The motion was lost by 86 votes (210 to 296).

Perhaps it was something to be written out of the ranks of advocacy by a future Lord of Appeal in Ordinary.[48] *The Granta* totally agreed with Devlin's assessment of Empson's shortcomings as orator: 'It was difficult to follow Mr Empson's argument because, besides being at times inaudible, he entirely failed to establish contact between himself and the House, for whom he was altogether too subtle.'[49] All the same, Devlin did put Empson's name down for election to the Committee the next Term, though probably as a matter of form rather than from conviction (and yet again Empson would not be elected).

After his sorry showing at the debate on the prominence of sex in fiction, Empson was still reeling with embarrassment and defiance three weeks later. He poured out his self-commiseration in a diary entry for 2 December 1926; it added up to a renunciation of the misbegotten idea of making his name at the Union, and it showed that the bright adolescent was not yet a man (it seems fair to judge too that his large and ebullient friend Hartland Thomas, who is mentioned here, was less sympathetic than patronizing):

A little time ago I made a speech on the paper at the Union and it was very bad. For all that Devlin has put me down again to stand for the Committee and perhaps now I have been advertised a little I shan't be bum of the poll.

Sitting at Debates I feel ploughed across, I feel my disagreement, scorn, fear . . . like a flat stretched network of each twisted nerve. They creep with dead concepts and vote for the emancipated side. I know no intelligent person who has anything to do with them, and my reasons for getting mixed up there are in a dismal apologetic make-shift idea for publicity. Pigs.

After my fiasco speech I decided what had really happened was I spurned their insincerity, compliments, flauntings, grappled with the problem at issue and turned starkly from their calling. 'Now I have shown you how men should think, I have flung the gauntlet . . . and spat finally at your faculty. I have borne my witness and shall not come again.'

Thomas said that was a very natural and proper attitude, why didn't I go and cross my name out? It was very irritating of him not to ask me whether I wanted it. Paper pride, I should be firm with the Union.

. . . But to me, I am a fool . . . to me it is too plain and predetermined a reaction, and I do not know whether I shall vote for myself or not.

It was perhaps Empson's 'fiasco speech' that *The Granta* was to recall some two-and-a-half years later, when it ribbed him in a profile which has the awful ring of embarrassing authenticity:

Accused of Union speaking the wretched man [Empson] broke down and confessed all, and said it was only long ago in the heat of his youth, and he had promised his mother never to do it again. Of his deeply-rooted addiction to this practice at one time, however, witness an historic scene which we can ourselves call to mind: the crowded, eager, impatient house, bursting at intervals into uncontrollable salvoes of coughing and somnolent as is its wont, except for occasional fainting fits; the gloomy, bitter, and intense faces of the visitors wondering what they had come for and trying to remember their epigrams; the nervous determination of the secretary, finding that it would soon be too late to get through the set speakers; and the bright, unconscious face of our hero still babbling precisely though unintelligibly, suffering himself to be led quietly from the rostrum by a friend, and pausing only to collect his sock-suspenders.[50]

All the same, it says a good deal for Empson's strength of character that he was not so utterly abashed by his poor showing in November 1926 that he would shrink from speaking ever again at the Union. On 25 October 1927 (at the beginning of his third year) he spoke in opposition to the motion 'That this House sees only degeneration in Modern Literature'. In a speech that the *Cambridge Review* found 'entertaining', he winsomely suggested that 'modern literature is trying all the time; even if it fails, that is no reason for condemning it'. *The Granta*'s account was at once gratifyingly candid and loyally affectionate:

The motion was opposed by MR WILLIAM EMPSON, the remarkable Skipper [literary editor] of this paper. His matter was profound and his manner delightfully weird, and both were sufficiently esoteric to make the result obscure. The Union was not unnaturally baffled, and we sat with our faces flat, blank and unmoved. The reporter of the *Cambridge Daily News* went home with lines on his brow, and had to content himself with the remark that 'to be perfectly frank, his arguments were much too obscure to permit of a paragraph summary'. One cannot help remembering, however, some clever remarks about the Joyces and Steins of this world, and an important point, that was never afterwards answered, that the crowning literature of our age is scientific, and scientific literature is not decadent.[51]

The House took warmly to his side, and the motion was voted down by 185 votes to 54.

If speaking of sex finally killed off his career at the Union, his own sexual career did not die in the bud. Herklots apart, there were many other young men—'charming creatures,' he termed them—to be chased and enjoyed. Like so many of his generation who passed their formative years sequestered in all-male institutions, he understandably sought satisfaction first from his own sex.[52] There was nothing unusual or untoward about it; and probably—however much he may have dreamed of buggery—he settled happily for petting or mutual masturbation where he could get it. Also like so many male children of his generation, he tended to take an instrumental view of sex; it was just a matter of easing the libido, like scratching an insistent itch. The muddling thing was affection or love, which would often be inspired only to cause pain and confusion.

The following entry in his diary is fairly characteristic of the 19-year-old Empson, torn between forthright desire, emotional involvement, and the requisite dash of cynical posing:

Thursday. Smith turned up in my rooms; I find I am not indifferent. As if he was a large and unclean spider, unreasonable fear behind a strong disgust. I had to play football so was able to take to my heels. Poor plump Smith, I must be a chaste boy. Funny that while masturbating last night I thought pleasurably of perversions with him. How Aldous Huxley.

By 12 June he was pondering his ambivalent feelings for another youth, who had introduced another problem into his life:

Found myself in the specifically moral situation this evening. It would be nice to kiss that Lochlann child—how tiresome of him to use that scent—but if I do it will mean seeing a lot too much of him. He is wholly uninteresting. Wishing to kiss him is a Lust of the Flesh. I hugged him casually and was more friendly than usual, being undecided. Or would it, I wonder, have shocked and driven him away?

Lochlann was indeed available for some sort of sexual activity, it seems; the problem was both how to make use of him and how to get rid of him, for he turned out to be a social and intellectual liability. Empson's prose churned under the dilemma, awash with a scalding contempt that may have been borrowed to a degree from his reading in Wyndham Lewis:

I used to imagine with luxury a charming boy who could be pulled up through my window in the evening, and he should fill my heart with the tingling of his beauty, my flesh be effervescent and my skin singing . . . I lie beside him and masturbate with placidity, and he could be let down again in the small hours. Then we got a rope, and Lochlann insisted on being pulled up. He filled the bill exactly, and I am sure hoped (with the greatest delicacy and shrinking) for a quate refayned embrace. I had to sit up till the small hours when he chose to be let down. I did not really want to, I knew there was no other way of getting back my peace of mind. My dreamt-of bumboy, Onan-child too far, was an alert and lively small creature who would have been a capable enough male when he grew up. The homosexuality which seduces children is a healthy and convenient side-show . . . He fills me with such fury and that I don't say anything, I feel rather sick and he talks along. He has absolutely no mental grasp on anything . . . He is very soft and pretty and goodnatured, wants to be pawed and played with and is in no way male at all. He is Mr Bloom's nightmare [in Joyce's *Ulysses*]—'the new womanly man—a dear man, a dear person.' Ever such a pure, clean boy, of course, he spoke with indignation of homosexual young men with painted faces, and made ten emotional statements he considers an argument about their being unnatural. He has Wyndham Lewis's shaman 'delicacy' . . . He stands for the breakdown of male logic and male will, for the post-war exhausted 'niceness', for the screwed-up virility of a dour Scotchman, like Lewis's Siberians, rejected; in fact he stands wherever you like to put him, poor little fool, the problem at the moment is that he *will* stand in my room.

Presumably he resolved this distasteful problem of lust and self-loathing by inducing a crisis in the relationship, since the name of Lochlann is never again mentioned in his papers.

Whatever the degree of distress such friendships and passions caused him, he continued to feel the draw of homosexuality, and to find it natural. In truth, even when he eventually discovered the pleasures of women, their company and sexuality, he did not make any complete break from men to women: he always left open the by-way of bisexuality.

On Tuesday, 4 May 1926, the second day of the General Strike, Empson had even proposed to proselytize for bisexuality at a Union debate on the motion 'That the Youth of today is degenerate.' Yet he failed to do so—not because he lost his nerve but only because the debate was cut short. Selwyn Lloyd, in proposing the motion, 'claimed that modern youths were physically feeble and lacked the creative spirit'; he was seconded by the guest speaker of the evening, A. M. Ludovici, author of *Lysistrata* (1924) and *Woman: A Vindication* (1923; reissued 1926), who proclaimed—or so it was written—'A self-controlled personality was like unto a damp match which would not light. The extreme absorbtivity [*sic*] of modern youth was most dangerous. The essence of character was resistance.' The fourth speaker was the far from degenerate Michael Ramsey, who (according to *The Granta*) made 'a brilliant series of debating points at the expense of the hon. proposer and third speaker. Excellent.' Thereupon the House divided, the motion was lost by 57 votes, and everyone rushed off to listen to the radio.[53]

Empson felt frustrated; he had read enough of the works of Ludovici to know that he advocated a conventional kind of virility, the unremitting pursuit of the female by the male. Empson, who resolved to believe in a Greek idea of the fundamental importance of male bonding, wrote rather petulantly in his journal that night:

We are in the middle of a grave national crisis. It prevented [Gerald] Sparrow [an ex-President] from speaking at the Union, and made the debate end at a quarter to ten. And for why? Because we all wanted to hear the latest news: the recruiting stations are crowded, the food services are normal, the Wessex tram drivers have returned to work...I wanted to speak against Ludovici and the Heterosexual Healthiness; the natural man does not need 96 women, he is male for a honeymoon, and then while the woman plans the autumn baby the man swings back to the homosexual, he wants men-friends, a social evening, 'civilisation'; they have both had enough of it. A purely heterosexual man is dangerously uncivilised. 'Can you blame the theatre-managers?' asked Noel Coward 'they've their wives and mistresses to look after.' To make sure the family, Freud has shown, we took sex aside and turned it Oedipose [*sic*]; to make sure civilisation, the focus has shifted again, and we 'love our neighbours'. Civilisation is not a plurality of harems...

To argue against heterosexual hunger and promiscuity on the grounds that he happened to prefer the company of men was not persuasive. It is easy to spot an element of contemptuousness in his reference to the woman planning 'the autumn baby'. And yet there is nothing really sinister about a young man who is prepared to admit that he dreads the prospect of domestic entrapment. Naturally Empson was frightened of women, and he knew it.

Indeed, a good deal of his early poetry is possessed by the subject of love and desire. But love always suffers its ambivalences and its fears; perhaps most especially—in his case—because of the conflict he experienced in his sexual appetites. Attracted towards both men and women, he found distrust, disappointment, and potential despair only a hair's breadth away from desire. In later years, when asked about the predominant topics of his early verses, he was never reluctant to declare that his biggest subject was that of the unsatisfactory love affair—with 'boy being afraid of girl, as usual'. In particular, he said it of 'The Ants' ('the first poem I thought worth keeping'),[54] which he was to place first in his *Collected Poems*. In a letter of 1957 he offered this gloss: 'The ants' tunnels are compared to the London Underground, which has advertisements for patent medicines on the walls and a special ventilation system... Surely the pity is felt quite as much for man as for ants. It is meant to be a love-poem; the woman's mind and sympathies are the open air, and seem unmeritable, even if safe to reach, so that the lover is like city workers in their tube.'[55] Similarly, to another critic, he wrote in 1967: 'In *The Ants*... it occurred to me that the queer habits of these ants were like an unsatisfactory love-affair with a person revered but not understood (to which as a student I was sadly prone). I described the ants, making the parallel as far as I could see it... The onset of neurotic (uncaused) fear seemed to me a probable result...'[56] Three years later, he declared in a letter to another correspondent: 'I thought I said *all* my student love-poems were about "boy afraid of girl", not "The Ants" especially...'[57]—so it seems fair to extrapolate from the example of this poem.

'The Ants' takes the form of a Petrarchan sonnet, which would suggest that it belongs to the tradition of chivalric poetry; and yet this curious 'love' poem focuses on the self-involved ants ('we ants') as they succour and milk 'honey-dew' from the aphids (parasites) that serve them by sapping sustenance from the garden. Self-protective concealment is all in all to these male ants, for everything else is a threat: their buried life enables them to cower away from the outer world, the perils of the open air ('the tube-station . . . is too close to the dangerous surface of the planet', as the poet explained to his correspondent in 1957). The poem ironically compliments woman as denizen of daylight and the natural order, while man—inhumed in his anxiously defended world—shrinks from what she represents into his sublimating regimen. However, it is perhaps the allusion in line 10 to *Samson Agonistes*—'How small a chink lets in how dire a foe'—which really presses home the point that the worst threat of all is woman, the ultimate predator. One has only to compare the complaint by Samson to which Empson's phrase perhaps alludes, 'What boots it at one gate to make defence, | And at another to let in the foe | Effeminately vanquished?' (ll. 560–2), to appreciate the force with which the poem depicts woman as the enemy.[58] To the time-serving underground man, woman is the Satan in his Eden; the female is thus dreaded as much as desired. This notion that the young man must have perceived females as threatening as much as frightening is reinforced by the likelihood that the line incorporates yet another possible allusion: the most apt point of origin. In *Venus and Adonis*, Shakespeare gives a funny, sexy, and pathetic account of how Venus lays amorous—lustful—siege to a shy, priggish, and possibly high-principled mortal youth:

> Full gently now she takes him by the hand,
> A lily prisoned in a jail of snow,
> Or ivory in an alabaster band,
> So white a friend ingirts so white a foe!

Needless to say, the youth resists the female, and pays a price for doing so. But at least, in Empson's poem as in Shakespeare's, the woman is a goddess.

    With regard to another poem, 'Arachne', Empson's characterization of Arachne, in his own note, as 'disastrously proud' is a highly personal interpretation of the story related in *Metamorphoses*. It is not a moral to which Ovid draws especial attention. If anything, Ovid seems to have been more troubled by 'divine injustice', as G. Karl Galinsky notes: 'Minerva is prompted by sheer envy . . . Minerva's moral indignation about the subject of Arachne's tapestry, the divine loves, is not developed . . . In his description of her end Ovid clearly manipulates our sympathies towards Arachne. The goddess smites her violently (*percussit*) and repeatedly . . . Arachne is *infelix* but remains courageous . . . '[59] All the same, Empson puts his stress on Arachne's supposed pride—probably for a reason which has to do with hurt male pride, offended masculinity. It is a poem which does seem (as Empson came to realize) to rebuke the woman. The last stanza figures the girl as too avid in her sexual ambitions, perhaps even promiscuous ('vain | Hydroptic'); in any event as (in every sense) a consumer of men. Accordingly, since she is represented as such a rampant, impatient spider, for her to end the affair, to terminate loving, would be to deny herself satisfaction. Whereas most of the poem argues for interdependency between male and female, for complementarity, this shocking shift in the final lines is unwittingly offensive, as Empson came to consider it—less a threat than an insult. He omitted 'Arachne' when he recorded his poems for a disc in 1959 (as he remarked to Christopher Ricks in 1963), 'because I'd come to think that it was in rather bad taste. It's boy being afraid of girl, as usual, but it's boy being too rude to girl. I thought it had rather a nasty feeling, that's why I left it out.'[60]

As for the General Strike, which perhaps saved him from making a fool of himself at the Union debate on that day in May 1926, Empson was firmly on the side of labour against capital. He thought it a scandal that the coal-owners should offer the miners nothing but reduced pay and a longer working day. Unlike many commentators, he did not see any revolutionary impetus behind the decision of the General Council of the Trades Union Congress (TUC) to give this industrial dispute a political dimension. It did not seem unconstitutional for the leaders of the working classes to hold the elected government and the country to ransom. For its part, the government of Mr Baldwin was anyway acting for the owners, he believed; so the workers had a right to react as a body to its obvious bid to destroy their organized bargaining power. The issue seemed clear-cut. But Empson was not as naive as he was idealistic; he showed some shrewdness in his reckoning of the situation, for one of the first questions he posed is 'How can they hope to beat the Government?' His diary for 5 May continues with a rather well-judged assessment of the situation, although the first statement here was to prove unfounded—at least in the immediate future:

If the Government, a word often used for the owners, no doubt rightly, wins, the industry will be dealt with on a national scale (that point the miners have already won). Various expensive measures will be taken, old mines run at a loss abandoned, and new plant elsewhere installed. The reduced pay, and that is all anyone is fighting over, will come in. The power of the Trades Unions will be seriously set back, I don't know how much, or with what effect on the Labour party. Socialism is likely to gain by the weakening of its extremely unsocial backers.

From the point of view of his life as an undergraduate, however, he had to admit that it all seemed a bit of a lark. Nor was it hard for him to square an apparent contradiction: he would both give his support to the strikers and volunteer to help the country. Thus his diary follows the course of the strike with concern, though pretty much in the holiday humour that the majority of students experienced:

The tripos is in three weeks or so, a fairly acute stage of the strike according to the prophets . . . May Week is in five weeks; that will be the starvation week if we hold out till then. Will that take precedence, I wonder? Death or Dancing? These romantic pleasures! . . .

I have been saying for some time . . . I mean to go and join the Blackleggers tomorrow. O. M. S. [Organization for the Maintenance of Supplies, the puta- tively non-Government committee] Fascist . . .

Thursday 6th. Hartland Thomas' bedder is very much worried because of the strike, it weighs her down and she goes about looking sad. It doesn't have that effect on me, or indeed on us, at all . . . I signed on at the Guildhall today; everybody has done that, as an unskilled porter or what not. One might go up to the station and see if there is anything to be done, in the morning. [Michael] Ramsey thinks it all very panicky and unregulated, but a great many people even from Magdalene have 'found jobs'. I cant 'find jobs', now or later, for a short life or a long vacation. [J. D.] Solomon's Father, who refused the son a car (go and do some work) to 'aid the strikers', said that the breaking of the Trades Unions would be the best thing possible for Socialism. The Government is starting some men on a fortnight's training in the 'skilled' trades; they mean to hold out, and the Unions are supposed to be wavering . . . Smith and the young 'British Workers' say the Government brought on the strike of their own accord, to break the Unions once for all. Is it relevant to the real difficulties of the country, and if so are they wise? I wish I had a political opinion, it would flavour these meaty days.

Friday 7th May. Out of 80 buses put on the London streets, 47 are already out of action. Picketing, adds the *British Gazette* [the emergency Government news- paper edited by Winston Churchill], is on quite small scale and of no serious importance. It is raining hard and my bedder tells me it feels as if everything was dead (Cf the Nocturnal on St Lucie's Day). I wish one had the high seriousness of one's bedder . . . I believe more and more the Government knows what it's about; astute and evil-minded men; Mr [A. J.] Cook [Secretary of the Miners' Feder- ation] has publicly no hope against them . . .

Ramsey hopes to assist his mother in showing the strikers round the colleges; Herklots will lecture to them on coffeehouses; the idea is to keep them from brooding... There is a notice up that we are to wait quietly in Cambridge, and there shall be many jobs that only such as we can grasp, and to these in good time shall we be summoned. Well, well, there's no one the men obey like an officer, they know a gentleman when they see one; breeding tells. We shall be sent to sit on grim miners' heads, calmly, as a ruling caste, and with the authority of the squires. I haven't sat on anybody's head for years.

There seems to be no doubt it was the Government that broke off negotiations, and rather insolently turned the lights off, locked the door, and went to bed [at about 12. 30 in the morning of Monday, 3 May]; they heard about that *Daily Mail* highhandedness, and saw their way. I think they knew what they were about, I know I don't...

Saturday...

Various bishops have put their heads together, and concocted a fearfully strong magic for the occasion [an appeal for the resumption of negotiations, published on 8 May in the *British Worker* and *The Times*, but not in the government organ, Winston Churchill's *British Gazette*]. The Archbishop of Canterbury itself is speaking on the wireless tomorrow; they are rather in favour of the miners, I believe, for the shoddier reasons...

Sunday. The strikers have played a football match with the policemen, so the wireless has hooted, and came off 2–1. The special constable arrangements are being done with alarming efficiency; it's quite logical and legal, indeed the Government usually is (as Lady Macbeth pointed out). The Archbishop of Canterbury is going to be allowed his whack on the hooter this evening, but the clergy, in appealing for arbitration before the strike ends, have been sat on. £200,000 have been sent to the Unions from Russia; the cheque was returned. That information comes from my 'British Worker'[61] ... The foreign press is congratulating us on the common sense, good nature, and so on, of both sides. Is it a virtue? a degeneracy? a joke?

I saw fifty motor cars along the Backs [Queens Road] today, waiting in line with a double rank beside them of men with suitcases, bound for some centre of disturbance unknown. They had just had speeches by General Costello, and cheers, and now there were sergeant-majors and fearful military efficiency; a large crowd watching...

Monday. The Senate will decide today what we are going to do; Tripos, long vac term, so on...

'It is absurd for Mr Baldwin to say he is fighting to a finish; to what finish is he fighting?' That is the *New Statesman* in a good slashing but rare edition. Nobody wants a strike, the Government forced one on the country at a stage when the owners, like good canny men, were offering ridiculous wages, and not wanting to be beaten down before the real bargaining began. Under those circumstances 'to talk of an attack on the Constitution is mere slush.' Yes, but the question has an answer. He wants to 'break the Trades Unions.'

I think more and more that the miners are in the right; and I still think my original attitude about portering is the best one...

—The Trades Unions wish to maintain essential services, or say so. It is thus not unreasonable in their supporters to assist in giving them what they want...

One way or another, we are in a gang and shall go in a day or two.

But it was all over within two days. And in the event, unlike some of his Magdalene contemporaries, including Selwyn Lloyd and J. E. H. Blackie (future Chief Inspector of the Ministry of Education) who had been posted to the East End of London where they earned £2. 5s. 0d. for their work, he did not get to witness any exciting action. He had declined to sign on as a special constable, only for portering. Hence, even three years later, in May 1929, *The Granta* was to tease him in a profile: 'During the Great Strike... he exerted his critical faculties, and had just matured an elaborate scheme for doing active work on behalf of both parties simultaneously, when it came to its regretted and premature end.'[62]

On Wednesday 12 May, when the strike was called off by the General Council of the TUC, against the express wishes of the miners, there was a widespread misapprehension that the government had agreed to the terms of a memorandum drafted by Sir Herbert Samuel—'in which it was proposed that no wage cuts should be made without some assurances that "the measures of re-organization proposed by the Committee will be effectively adopted". A Mines National Board with an independent chairman should be set up to seek a final settlement. The Board would prepare a simplified wage agreement which would not affect the wages of the lower-paid men, and it would fix "reasonable figures, below which the wage of no class of labour should be reduced in any circumstances".'[63] There was in fact no such settlement; the TUC had surrendered without making terms. As the *British Gazette* trumpeted that day: 'Unconditional Withdrawal of Notices by TUC'.

Empson promptly drafted his own memorandum, headed 'Revolution in England', pointing up some of the miserable ironies of the strike and ending with his misunderstanding that a wretched settlement had been reached—which would ironically have been far less damaging to the cause of collective labour than the capitulation which the TUC had agreed:

I   A *general* strike has occurred against a *democratic* government.
II   Large numbers of miners on strike enlisted as voluntary railwaymen, and some railwayman became special constables, to keep *themselves* quiet.
III   The parties at war played football matches with one another.

IV   The strikers prevented themselves from stating their case publicly by
     suppressing all newspapers; then the newspapers of both sides were
     printed as usual under different names.
V   If the miners had run out of food, they could have gone to the local
     Guardians and demanded some. This contingency was neither suggested
     nor provided for, as it was obviously not part of the game.
VI   The Conservative Party nationalized a newspaper and a system of
     feeding the country; the Socialist strikers indignantly denied themselves
     any political intentions at all.
VII The end of the strike came when the strikers allowed the Government the
     pleasures of a triumph, in return for a secret promise, intended for
     immediate non-official publication, that they should be given everything
     they were fighting for.

But it did not take him long to realize that the outcome of the strike was
even more appalling than he had been given to believe at first. 'I can't
understand it,' he wrote, perfectly reasonably, on the Wednesday evening;
'the official view of the Labour Party is that the Unions surrendered
unconditionally, on condition in secret that the Government gave them
all they wanted...But, if so, why are the miners still out? And isn't it
suicidal of the Trades Unions, to toss away so much prestige?' The miners'
strike actually went on for six months, and then broke down in hunger and
despair. The government was delighted to be able to boast that, even if the
TUC and the miners had accepted the terms of the Samuel Memorandum, Sir Herbert Samuel and Mr Baldwin had never actually discussed
the contents of the Memorandum; so that it would have had no standing as
the basis for an official settlement.

   Many strikers felt betrayed by their unions. Empson felt more disturbed
by the cruel disingenuousness of the government. Almost certainly, he
believed, Baldwin had let Samuel go through the exercise of appearing to
negotiate while resolving never to end the dispute in any other way than by
the total defeat of the TUC. The government's intransigence, as Empson
saw it, in the face of the desperation and anger of the workers confirmed
him in his lifelong support of socialism.

   Several months later, in February 1928, in a review of *The Sleeping Sword*
by Barbara Goolden, he made his position plain when he gave all credit to
the author for her stylish prose but none for her rotten politics:

There have been many authors in the past who are immensely stirring in the
display of opinions with which one at no point agrees. It is not then that Mrs
Goolden's wartime sentiments, or the way she throws them at you, are so simple-
hearted or so wicked. In fact, her using the late Strike as an apocalypse because

the young men went and drove trams, so that the great heart of England *must* be still beating, in spite of all these horrid Dagoes and Epstein, and the way Bulldog Drummond, when one looks round one's young friends, seems to be so rare—her using that to finish the book with, instead of telling you it fizzled out, seemed to me a fine and intelligent piece of structure . . .

No; it seems disastrous that ladies of this type should be politically so powerful, but they write, as a matter of fact, rather well.[64]

6

'Mr Empson gave a very competent performance': The Multiple Man of Letters

'THE General Strike is over,' wrote Empson on Wednesday, 12 May. 'I am disappointed, there was some hope of stopping mathematics, of being forced to do something active which might rouse crude enthusiasm and physical satisfaction, and some intellectual initiative. But no, the miners are the kindliest of men, and my door is closed. Incidentally I suppose it has been a great disaster politically, we shall yet see.'

There is no other indication in his papers that he had come to regard mathematics as a stagnant or enervating course of study, or that he needed to be prodded out of inertia. Admittedly, nearly two years after this, he made one reference to the difficulty of mathematics; reviewing a book entitled *Hermes, or the Future of Chemistry*, by T. W. Jones—who observed that matters like 'hydrolysis, catalysis, degrees of freedom and what-not are all *almost* "synonymous with life"'—Empson would protest: 'I must say I should put degrees of freedom among the things less like life, myself; there is a widespread belief that the answer possesses free-will if the sum is hard, a belief more gratifying to chemists than to mathematicians.'[1] But that was just a good joke—sums that will not work out can naturally appear to have a cussed mind of their own—with no suggestion of any personal frustration.

Indeed, he duly gained the expected First Class result in Part I of the Mathematical Tripos in 1926 (this achievement, it has to be said, was not exceptional: the majority of mathematicians—fifty-two candidates in Empson's year—got firsts at this stage);[2] and he was one of a mathematical

threesome to receive a college prize: 'books to the amount of £2. 12s. 6d'.[3]
All the same, during his second year he committed more and more of his
energies to literature and journalism, where he exerted vast intellectual
initiative and discovered much excitement, though the process did not
involve any wholesale translation of interest from the sciences to the arts.

He broke surface first as a playwright. Indeed, a few references in his
journal suggest that he became involved in the theatre even in the first year
of his undergraduate career. Against a date given simply as 'Sunday 8th',
for instance, there occurs the tantalizingly terse entry: 'Wrote sadist play.'
(It is well known that he could produce work at an exceptionally fast speed,
but that sounds preternatural even by his standards.) Then on 4 March
1926 he wrote, 'I have had in mind, for a week or so . . . the idea of a play';
and yet even that entry goes on disappointingly, 'I shall take the easier step
of describing it here'—though it does include a full outline of the play he
would never write.

Three Stories, a one-act melodrama in five scenes that he did bring to
completion, was performed on 5 February 1927 in a season of 'Nursery'
productions at the Amateur Dramatic Company (ADC). It was part of a
triple bill, though only one of the other plays was an original piece: *Dragons:
A Symbolic Play* was by Basil Wright—the future film director, Governor of
the British Film Institute, and President of the International Association
of Documentary Film Producers—who also acted in his own production
(a two-hander, with the other role, tantalizingly described as 'A Man in a
Bowler Hat', being taken by Humphrey Jennings).[4] In conversation with me,
Wright would recall his own play as 'exceedingly turgid', an unconscious
attempt to proclaim his homosexuality. '*Dragons* created a scandal among the
older dons because they thought I was doing it on purpose—saying I was
queer—but in fact I was doing it by mistake.'[5] However, according to an
unkindly but perhaps canny notice in *The Granta*, *Dragons* was 'all about what
a young man of seventeen ought to know. We can praise him for what for the
moment we will call sincerity, and for fearlessly proclaiming a high standard
of University life; but his fantasy was somewhat loose and his dialogue
somewhat dull, so that often his play seemed held together by Mr Hartland
Thomas's virile scenery.'[6] (The *Cambridge Review* seconded that sad assessment of Wright's brave effort: 'the play . . . was so obscurely portentous, as to
be almost unintelligible . . . The dialogue was very poor.')[7]

However, *The Granta* went on,

Mr Empson of Magdalene's play, *Three Stories*, was quite another thing. He had
achieved an almost complete mastery of his Oedipus complex, and used it for very

intelligent purposes. A theme of the rebellion of an idealist young man led from excellent Shavian comedy to plain, honest melodrama, and was framed within romantic scenes in heroic couplets and contrasted with a scientific disquisition fathered on to Dracula. It sounds very complicated, but, if we interpreted it rightly, it amounted to something like this: that the ethical problems of life differ from the scientific problems only if one conceives them romantically, and even then, the apparent romanticism achieved, they become scientific again. The last line of the play, in which the hero, having slain his business-like ogre, is compelled to proclaim himself a 'managing young man', we thought a triumph.

The piece opens and closes with a crop of mock-heroic speeches in which a youthful knight with the unlikely name of Gerald arrives to free a fettered princess who rejoices in an equally unromantic name, Margery (played by William Connell). 'Which way has walked this conjuror I kill? | Princess Princess, tell me, I will, I will,' he pledges. The scene then dissolves into the modern world which occupies the best part of the play: the book-lined study of number 5, Cheshire Avenue. Gerald is personal secretary to a bullying old buffer, a rich popular author named James (played by Empson himself); Margery is James's wife, whom the angry young Gerald is determined to carry off to a better life than that of her putative servility. This scene ends with Margery's bored but compromised and venal admission to Gerald, 'I do think I should be happier with you because it's quite true what you say, there seems to be no doubt the old man's reasonably impotent and I'm a nice natural girl, we might even run to a baby or two. But listen to me, Gerald, we must have lots of money, quite half as much as James has got, I don't mind how you get it, only we must be quite safe about it and I mustn't be cut off from some sort of intelligent society. If you can do all that, Gerald, though I'm a very contented young woman anyway, I'll come. Mind you, whether I'd say that if I thought you were in the least bit likely to *do* it, is another question.'

Then, in the middle of this supposedly single-act play, like an errant entr'acte, comes a scene in which another young man, with the generic name of Smith, is seeking to escape from Dracula's castle. Empson would later explain the double-plot device, perhaps anticipating his essay on 'Double Plots' in *Some Versions of Pastoral*: 'the basic structural idea of the play was to take a story and interpose a scene of apparently total irrelevance in the middle.' (The word *apparently* is significant, one trusts.) Dracula, it turns out, can summon the wolves of the wilderness to do his bidding; and this queer talent quite confounds his prisoner, who favours not a supernatural but a rational account of things:

SMITH The scientist, Dracula, can only live in a very odd universe indeed. And to start with, it must be in some way impersonal, it must obey a law and not a master. You don't know what you are saying; it matters, Dracula, you must tell me at once.

DRACULA I must tell you, must I, whether the universe is the sort of universe you would like it to be?

SMITH Or a tuppeny nightmare, a sick man's fancy we couldn't trust while we were sleeping. Must I be afraid of the dark again, and when you're dead will the bogeys get you? Oh, is the world sound, Dracula, can we sleep tonight?

DRACULA My friends, I have my plans, and I think you are beaten. But there's no doubt, *I* shall sleep all right.

SMITH Saved again. I say, thanks awfully, Dracula, you've quite set me up again; if you'd gone on putting across the wicked fairy business I'd have knuckled under altogether.

Smith may be satisfied with Dracula's equivocal response, but the audience is permitted to doubt whether the wizard has really admitted an explanation of the universe which would satisfy a sceptical scientist.

Yet we are given no time to ponder that puzzle before being thrown back into the Shavian world of smug James, flighty Margery, and fretful Gerald. Time has moved on; and Gerald, it transpires, has attempted to steal some money from James by forging a cheque—a gesture which everyone agrees was puerile rather than principled. But Gerald proves his integrity by producing a gun and shooting not himself as we might fear but James; whereupon Margery reverts to her mode as 'Princess' and hails the Childe Gerald who has slain her 'ogre' with his 'sword'.

Thus the true theme of Empson's funny little play is emancipation. If the Dracula scene depicts an ambiguous liberation from the world of supernatural superstition, the Gerald–Margery–James imbroglio scoffs at the world of bourgeois convention. The mythic, the romantic, the scientific, the ethical: each aspect in some way mirrors the others, however skewed; and the 'message' of the play is that one must deride all folly and imposture—fairy tales and false scales of values. Both the deadly Dracula and the rich, cold-hearted James are conjurors: they pretend to be masters of the universe. Or at least the play is laced with the strains of scientism and socialism—though sheer good fun is certainly more to the fore than any concerted radicalism.

According to the *Cambridge Review*, 'Scene II was the best thing in this play: a very excellent light comedy scene, displaying real sense of the stage, in which the dialogue sparkled merrily.' The reviewer's judgement was good: scene ii, in which Gerald and Margery chaff one another, shows

Empson at his spry best; he makes the thing fairly skip along with topical and literary references that the audience would be sure to know and delight in. When Margery ribs Gerald for being jealous, for example, he protests: 'Rubbish, you don't know what jealousy is. I'm not personally jealous, at all. I see you with a quite cold and detached horror, as one of the thousands of victims of this commercial civilisation, the clever savoury wellsexed young women who moulder complacently, *queens* of virtue, beside bored and impotent old grandfathers who oughtn't to be let leer at them from behind railings.'

She gaily retorts: 'Sesame and lilies. Beautiful, Gerald.' *Sesame and Lilies* is the collection of three lectures by John Ruskin; and Margery is referring to the second of them, 'Lilies: Of Queen's Gardens' (i.e. woman's sphere), which starts off quite reasonably by scorning 'the idea that woman is only the shadow and attendant image of her lord, owing him a thoughtless and servile obedience'. However, when Ruskin proceeds to define the 'true place and power' of 'womanly mind and virtue', he merely reiterates, and without irony, the received Victorian wisdom that a woman plays a secondary and essentially supportive role. 'She must be enduringly, incorruptibly good; instinctively, infallibly wise—wise, not for self-development, but for self-renunciation,' he proposes—so proving that male idealism can be a truly insulting instrument. As for her studies, 'All such knowledge should be given her as may enable her to understand, and even to aid, the work of men ... [A] girl's education should be nearly, in its course and material of study, the same as a boy's, but quite differently directed ... [S]peaking broadly, a man ought to know any language or science he learns, thoroughly—while a woman ought to know the same language, or science, only so far as may enable her to sympathise in her husband's pleasures, and in those of his best friends.' Furthermore, she is not suited to consider or to pronounce upon questions of theology; and she must be saved from 'the sore temptation of novel reading', because of 'its overwrought interest' (that is, a 'romance' can be too exciting, and might give her ideas beyond hearth and home). There is no doubt that Ruskin felt strongly about his exhortations; at one point he even commits himself to this extraordinary ambivalent outburst: 'the whole system of society, as respects the mode of establishing them in life, is one rotten plague of cowardice and imposture—cowardice, in not daring to let them live, or love, except as their neighbours choose; and imposture, in bringing, for the purposes of our own pride, the full glow of the world's worst vanity upon a girl's eyes ...'[8] In the context of Empson's play, therefore, Margery's deft riposte serves to say to Gerald: silly man, now you've declared yourself a modern Ruskin, making a ridiculous, condescending pronouncement on the question of what's good for women. This riposte had all the more edge in a university where the 'undergraduette' had still not been granted a status equal to that of her male counterpart; and it was further honed in the ADC production—which was directed by none other than Mr Mark Hartland Thomas, who also designed the scenery, costumes, and lighting— by the fact that the part of Margery was taken by a man (women, not being full members of the university, were banned from taking part in university theatre productions).

Empson enriches the ambiguity by having Gerald huff: '*I* don't want you, you can go to bed with the gardener's boy if you like, but do for God's sake stop titivating that propertied old eunuch and calling it a quiet life'; to which Margery smartly responds: 'But of course I agree with you, Gerald. In fact, it's rather the pious thing to say just now, isn't it. Ludovici and all that. In fact at Girton they gave us a positive course of lectures entitled "*Go* to bed with the gardener's boy, or Virtue its own reward". And I'm sure I'm a nice natural girl and always careful to do what the earnest people tell me.' In May 1926, at the start of the General Strike, Empson had been denied the opportunity to attack the robust heterosexuality of A. M. Ludovici; and now he finds his mocking occasion. The male actor advocates going to bed with a boy, while guying a woman who favours Ludovici's straight line on sex. The audience surely cackled at the *double entendre* ('a theatre with boys acting as girls must be expected to extract fun from the charms of the boys,' as Empson would later observe),[9] though the joke must have been on a goodly number of them.

'Margery, don't be brutal, what are you snubbing me for?' Gerald whines. She responds adroitly, showing off her studied Modernism by giving him a little lesson in metacriticism:

MARGERY I think we are a little at odds on the tub-thumping issue Gerald. I know it sounds very vigorous and intelligent to walk up and down and use a lot of rude words, but it's very distracting and a little tiresome. I mean, it isn't as if I hadn't read the books you keep quoting all the time.

GERALD But of course I keep quoting, Margery. This civilisation has a very bad conscience, and we *all* know it, but we're *all* actuated by the people who say so. What else can I do but quote them; they all quote each other, don't they?

MARGERY Well, if you're frankly quoting, you should do it gracefully, allusively and flatly, with a lot of little prepositions and no fuss. You should assume they've read it, and give tabloids.

GERALD But I'm not *thinking* in tabloids, I don't *feel* like a literary allusion. Why should I go -

MARGERY Use defensive satire in case anybody wants to laugh at you, always talk as if you won't think the same next week, and say 'of course' to avoid drama.

GERALD But I don't *want* to. Can't you see the two things don't *mean* the same?

Naturally, on hearing Gerald mention the word 'mean', Margery responds as if by reflex by citing another tome that was totally *à la mode*—*The Meaning of Meaning*, by C. K. Ogden, I. A. Richards, and James Wood—which Empson could assume a fair portion of his audience would at least have tried to read before recoiling in a state of muddlement similar to these tusslers:[10]

MARGERY Things don't mean things, Gerald, you know you aren't allowed to use that word.

GERALD Sorry. I mean they don't refer to the same reference.

MARGERY Of course they couldn't have just the same reference, Gerald, or we couldn't tell them apart.

GERALD Margery, I'm crying to you for help, I open my inmost heart to you, and all you do is to sit with your head in a cupboard and talk like the Mad Teaparty.

Thus *Three Stories* was a witty skit, obviously delightful to a young and like-minded audience; and salted with just enough social criticism to satisfy a deep need in Empson's carelessly (and consistently) rebellious nature. As *The Granta* opined with some pomp, 'It was pleasant to find a new dramatist experimenting with a complicated technique, with one, too, which seems admirably suited for the production of a modern play; and perhaps still more so to find him at the same time not unskilful of dialogue and repartée, to keep the audience attentive and bemused.' It also gave Empson, who took the part of James, a further opportunity to disport himself in public; and it marked the acting debut of a Winchester contemporary, Ian Parsons (Empson's future publisher, and F. R. Leavis's), who played Gerald. The *Cambridge Review* observed: 'Mr Empson gave a very competent performance as the novelist in his own play. Mr I. M. Parsons shows distinct promise as a juvenile.' *The Granta* wholly agreed: '*Three Stories* also pleased us, because it proved to the world the merits of Mr I. M. Parsons as an actor'—though it declined to offer any opinion of Empson's turn on the boards.[11]

It was probably as a direct result of writing and acting in his own play that he felt ready and willing to review theatre and cinema for both *The Granta* and the *Cambridge Review* (starting with the movies in 1927, he was reviewing both film and theatre by 1928–9). For the session 1927–8, when he was in his third year as a student of mathematics, he acted as 'Skipper' or literary editor of *The Granta*. The friends he commissioned to write reviews found him amusing and provocative. Among others, he asked Basil Wright to review films for *The Granta*, encouraging him to make his pieces lively or impish. 'Write a review in the wrong style for film criticism,' he would urge; or: 'Write a totally unintelligible review of the latest Hollywood film.' Anything to *épater le bourgeois*.[12] Empson looked like a mina bird, Wright remarked, and he dressed abominably; but the chief thing one really noted about him was his marvellous incisiveness of mind.

Empson's own output was remarkable, a tribute to his powers of assimilation and responsiveness. James Jensen has provided this helpful précis: 'The bulk of Empson's contributions to *Granta* consists of about sixty book reviews of widely varying interest and length—only a few run to much more than five hundred words and a good many are only one or two sentences long. In addition... there are about fifteen movie and drama reviews, also uneven in character, but occasionally quite provocative, plus some clowning and riddling material of no particular consequence. Though books of literary or esthetic value predominate among those he reviewed, they by no means constitute a monopoly; the list includes such titles as *British Farmers in Denmark*, *Sex Relations without Marriage*, and *ABC of Adler's Psychology*. Indeed, extended examples of close verbal analysis, at least in the serious way we now think of it, would be an absurd anomaly in the hearty, gamesome pages of *Granta*. The atmosphere of the magazine is highly precocious but unstable, wavering between formidable gravity and witty or impudent lightheartedness which does not always escape silliness, nor always try to. Yet nearly all Empson's reviews exhibit an air of alert knowledgeableness, an easy habituation to the critical context...'[13] (The total of Empson's book reviews is now believed to be seventy.)[14]

Although Empson took the immature art of film seriously, and did not think it a crude medium, it gave him many opportunities to flex his wit—usually at the expense of ham acting. Haddon Mason in *Palaver*, for example, 'looked like a rabbit with adenoids'; and with respect to Lillian Gish in *La Bohème* he observed: 'when starved down for the sad parts she looks like something not of this world, a mouse with a blue nose, for instance; and she has a most statuesque way of draping the lips when on the deathbed, it is done by blowing from inside. There were yards of film while she just held it there.'[15] But not all his remarks were the stuff of undergraduate jocularity. When he went to *The Circus*, for instance, he hoped to find that Chaplin had gone back to good old 'custard-pie' comedy, 'without any of the haunting pathos of [the] masochistic period': 'This stress on the peculiarity of Chaplin in his world, and the way the other characters tell you what to think of him, is a serious weakness, contracted during the time he was throwing up everything for pathos and wanted to make himself look as lonely as possible.' It says much for Empson's sensitivity that he saw the silent hero as not just endearingly sad but as painful in his solitude. Maybe he found it threatening, though it seems more likely that he had come to think of Chaplin's winsome posturing as self-indulgent. Notwithstanding, he remarked, *The Circus* 'does seem to include and justify all that he has yet achieved.' Moreover, he was alive to the techniques of cinema, as when he observed, incidentally but perceptively, 'Chaplin...still takes no interest in photography as such.'[16]

Basil Wright would later remark—in *The Long View* (1976), his classic handbook on international cinema—that the actor H. B. Warner 'looked like a large and amiable dog' when playing Christ in Cecil B. De Mille's *King of Kings* (1927). Perhaps he was unconsciously remembering Empson's analysis of the film, with the buttonholing technique that would become an Empson trademark being put to keen early use, in the *Cambridge Review* for 19 October 1928:

> The Christ in films (except for the one that reduced him to his halo, like the Cheshire cat) is always made dog-like; you can read anything into the faces of dogs; they are reverent yet non-denominational. I never remember this one showing any definite expression, except in that delightful bit about rendering unto Caesar some money presented him by a fish; then he looked like Bernard Shaw. But it is a good dog-face; it is first seen, as a climax, through the eyes of one of those superb gnathic slum children, with cheekbones, you know, and a mouth like Elsa Lanchester; she works her way through the crowd and there is some most noble trick filming about healing her blindness; and in casting the Seven Devils out of the Magdalene (always a cheering person for the producer) he did actually look convincing. But they will try to show him actually overturning the tables of the money-changers, a thing that no spaniel wrapped in blankets can possibly do without losing its dignity...

However, having charmed the reader with this much chummy chat, just so much tolerable daring, he was not shy of voicing his opinion of Christianity itself; in the middle of the very next sentence he hits the faith hard in the solar plexus: 'there seems little religion in a drawn-out sanctimonious gloating, over tortures whose theological interest is not once adumbrated.'[17] The accusation, which even here is obviously more earnest than impudent, would become a major critical refrain in his later career.

Similarly, when reviewing *The Magic Flame*—a film that Martin Dodsworth has fairly called 'a preposterous Ruritanean drama'[18]—in which

Ronald Colman appears as both an honest clown and a 'wicked young Count', Empson becomes so captivated by the process of spelling out the psychology of the doubling in the film that he draws very near to enunciating the theory to be found in his later essay on 'Double Plots'. 'What is displayed on the tragi-comic stage is a sort of marriage of the myths of heroic and pastoral, a thing felt as fundamental to both and necessary to the health of society,' he would write in *Some Versions of Pastoral*.[19] In October 1928, his struggle to put the complex into the simple when analysing the plot and theme of *The Magic Flame* touches upon the same trick of pastoral, the myth of atonement:

Making the same actor take two parts at once is one of the odd advantages of the cinema, which will always act as a focus of interest because one is curious to know how it was done; and the trick has sufficient point to sustain interest once focussed, through suggesting it all symbolizes an inner conflict, making of one man the whole milieu of the story, and being well suited to the dream-like, 'psychological', 'being taken out of yourself', and as it were expatriated attitude towards the arts, which now in general for economic, political, and moral reasons, and in the cinema in particular, from the nature both of its public and its medium, takes the place of say Jane Austen's more well-balanced interest in the reactions of a whole family or tribe...A novelty of technique can seldom have been more fully mastered...

The excitement with which one follows this absurd story, the impression of profound and tortuous motivation given by an immaculate couple who never do anything but the proper thing, the way each episodic twist of the plot manages, forming a sort of pun with its official function, to body out a grand and quite unmentioned organism of tragedy, hangs altogether, I think, on the hint given by the double part. You are given a notion, probably unjustified, that if you could undo the censoring dream-work, recover the desires and jealousies of the two (not three) people in the original impulse of the story, it would turn out to be something very elaborate and explanatory which could not otherwise have been staged; and this belief in a 'real', a less ridiculous story hidden, as one would oneself hide, without understanding, such a thing, behind it, gives it weight and pathos, like a generalization.

This rather facile mystification, too (we are so easily bounced nowadays), must be why the happy ending seems quite satisfying...I am told there are two endings sent round with such films now; the Tragic and the Comic Muses hover above them, and the manager takes his choice. If so I was happy in my manager; it is a civilised and Euripidean gesture, and leads naturally to the National Anthem, that after Tragedy has risen to her full and in this case somewhat cloudy grandeur, Romance, the dedicatee of these temples, should be given decent homage, and made deus ex machina.[20]

One of the most striking things about the piece is that Empson, even as he labours to keep his grammar in order, can hardly credit his own insights; he seems embarrassed by them, fearing that he is reading too much into the effects of the film. The essay is peppered with disclaimers. He is taken by the idea of the other life, the secret sharer, but feels shy of it. Yet in trying to distil what he understands by the strategic relation in the film of the high and the low, the haughty and the humble, as they are jointly expressed by the one actor, and in seeking to explain it all by way of Freudian psychology (as in the concept of 'the censoring dream-work'), he suddenly realizes that the device of doubling does serve for reconciliation, psychological and social. The perception that 'one man' can stand for 'the whole milieu of the story', as he phrases it, anticipates this central concept of the essay on 'Double Plots': 'Such an identification of one person with the whole moral, social, and at last physical order, was the standing device of the metaphysicals...'[21] Thus his early review, albeit faltering and self-doubting, reads the film as a form of metaphysical poetry, and so anticipates a rule that Empson would learn only later from an essay on metaphysical poetry by James Smith—'that the metaphysical conceit was always built out of the immediate realisation of a philosophical problem such as that of the One and the Many.'[22] (Incidentally, Empson may perhaps be credited too with coining the concept of alienation; except that he calls it 'expatriation'—clearly a less catchy term.)[23]

One other film which especially excited his imagination was *Metropolis*, the great study of dehumanization directed by Fritz Lang for Universum Film Aktiengesellschaft (UFA). 'Of course everybody will see this,' he wrote in *The Granta*; 'it is a feast I cannot review in detail... The story has been much maligned, partly from its simple solution of all possible economic problems... For Metropolis is the Greek city state... [O]bviously... we had to kill the inventor, and purge our suspicion of contrivances.' Obviously too, Empson could not judge the film as a forecast of Nazi regimentation; and yet he registered the conflict between the sheer beauty of industrial order and its inhumanity—'the contrast between that exhilaration of the imagination one finds in their mechanical forms... and the wooden deadness of drilled workers.'[24] Likewise, he was quick to see the point of another UFA film, *Berlin*, a documentary by Walter Ruttmann. '[The producers] wanted to lay bare the works, the economics, the whole order of a great city; to show it opening like a flower and going through a composed cycle, to show you its functions, its explanation, its organism, to make you fall down and worship a power and glory of the world. That was put across very ably.'[25] However, when Desmond Flower, in a letter to the

Cambridge Review, took issue with Empson's interpretation—'The whole film seems . . . to protest against mechanisation, like "Metropolis" '—Empson fairly, if sarcastically, defended his analysis:

There is a notion now, spread by Wyndham Lewis, that one should not study a contemporary movement without 'protesting'; in his case, it is a rowdy substitute for criticism. Now, large factory cities are no doubt inconvenient in many ways, but to say that *Berlin* 'protests' against them is surely a libel; it is far more seriously engaged in elaborating their peculiar beauty. I am sure Mr Flower was fascinated and invigorated, like myself, both by the particular shots of bottle and type-setting machines, and by the sense of the whole city as a far more elaborate and (of course) not in the least 'disorganised' organism; I suppose then that while enjoying their beauty he purged his feelings, with a true Puritan 'protest', by making them the villain of the piece; his excited disapproval, in fact, made even the stray cats into evidence of mechanisation; there they were, slinking; up to no good, I'll be bound.[26]

With regard to the intention of *Berlin*, he was right; after all, it was subtitled *Symphony of a Great City*. But Desmond Flower was the more percipient in arguing that the film excited a sinister political effect. Yet Empson was by no means blind to the chilling metaphorical implications of *Metropolis* and *Berlin*. Two years later, in fact, he would concoct a rather poor poem with the telling title 'UFA Nightmare' (which he chose not to include in *Collected Poems*). A fraught and impenetrable piece, transposing the immense machine of *Metropolis* to the engine room of a ship, the poem begins:

> Gramophony. Telephony. Photophony.
> The mighty handles and persensate dials
> That rule my liner multi-implicate
> Ring round, Stonehenge, a wide cold concrete room.

Although he tended to think of *Metropolis* as representing the excesses of Victorian industrialism, not as a preview of the modern totalitarian state, he perceived the dark truthfulness, the frightening possibilities, it figured. This can be seen in his notice of *The Way the World is Going*, the book in which H. G. Wells, with his perennial faith in rational progress, wrote off *Metropolis* as the world's silliest film. It had to be acknowledged, Empson argued, that imaginatively appalling things, scientific and political, were already at work in the world:

[H. G. Wells's] remarks are crucial as far as they go; that [*Metropolis*] was not about the future at all, but an imaginative playing in pictures with economics of about fifty years ago, was of course quite true, and one bore it in mind in watching; that it was silly could only be said by one who, whose literary generation in fact, took no interest in Art. To a generation which does, the world is odder than Mr Wells's, perhaps less strenuous and less sensible.[27]

He had equally firm views on the theatre. He believed in writers more than in directors; respect for the text was vital. He believed that the theatre was properly a place of artificial convention, not of misplaced naturalism. And he believed that while there is room for all kinds of experimentation, monkeying for its own sake should be off limits. The genre of theatre stood closer to the lyric poem, with which it shared thrift and punch, than to the more capacious form of story-telling that is the special province of the novel. The dramatist, he wrote, has always 'got to drive in the points of dramatic interest by some more immediate appeal than narrative and the audience's touching belief that the stage is realistic; the Galsworthy play, at once grim and uncertain, a pattern drawn in broken lines with ruler and compasses, is depressing to see.'[28]

He was happy to enjoy a production which was sheerly entertaining, with no pretensions, especially when it did not tax the mind and spirit at a time when they were fully preoccupied—as when taking his Maths finals. *Madame Pepita* quite fitted the bill for the Tripos week of 1928: 'There is a clear complicated plot; no disturbing ideas . . . a technique so adequate that even when working in a whirl, it is a pleasure to sit and listen to (the play begins by putting the happy ending clearly in your mind and introduces a series of difficulties); characters that state their type at once and produce an effect of epigram when they vary slightly from it . . . [L]ike the Church of Rome, they have their limitations, but they never let you down; and a bouquet should be handed to Mr Gray . . . '[29] In the absence of television, sex, or drugs, obviously that production at the new Festival Theatre on the Newmarket Road was gentle and relaxing. But he had no time for pointless gimmickry.

The Festival Theatre, as Julian Trevelyan was to recall, 'was a new venture directed by Terence Gray, an almost mythical figure, shy to the point of embarrassing everyone around him, who could occasionally be seen moving through the foyers, a tall, handsome man with a black beard. He had decorated the place in black and emerald green, and many of the ideas that have become accepted conventions of the theatre, were here tried out by him for the first time. He had built an apron-stage, with a cyclorama, and the sets were composed of various arrangements of wooden blocks, known then as "units".'[30]

However, when Gray modernized a classic (that is, bowdlerized it), even during an otherwise idle time like May Week, Empson felt irritated at the result, which had turned out to be more like a revue than an intelligent production of Aristophanes' *The Birds*. The haughty cadence of Empson's put-down is superb: 'I suppose people just want a romp at this time of year; something amusing and brightly coloured to look at, and a play of quite casual fantasy with about the proportion of not at all disturbing politics that you get at a music-hall . . . So there is quite a lot to go for, if you don't take any pedantic interest in Aristophanes, if you don't mind the extreme thinness of the language and humour . . . and if you like watching very amusing and capable people performing heroically at the last minute a gay but casual charade.'[31]

In November 1928, Gray's Festival Theatre production of *As You Like It* (in which the star-struck young Trevelyan played his oboe behind the scenes) earned a similar shapely brickbat.[32] Empson, who was by now a signed-up student of English Literature, defended the Bard against those who would do him wrong:

I can explain my feelings so little about this I must just say what they were; I was terribly depressed, and spent some time after I had got home hunting through the text to see if I could find all the Beauty which must surely have been cut. But no, the cutting was fairly tactful; involving chiefly the rather self-supporting dialectics which were so important a part of the Elizabethan attitude to poetry. Why is it that seeing Shakespeare or Beaumont at the Festival Theatre is like hearing your love-letters read out in a divorce court; you feel keenly only your own past lack of judgment, and it might all have been written by Sir James Barrie?

Partly because the guts are taken out (I insist on believing this is really a good play); one ought to feel it was *brave* of them all to romp like that; Nature was not really kindly, and Nurse not in reserve . . . This dramatic poetry continually centres round objects, food or a sword. I cannot think what is in a producer's mind when he wants to leave them out; certainly no understanding of the poetry . . . It is extraordinary what castration can be effected by the Festival Theatre's tricks of production.

Partly because nobody said the verse as if it was verse at all. (Alan Wheatley is almost an exception to this.) It is true they didn't say it as if it was verse written in the last century, one must be grateful for that. But after hearing Madame Lopokova [Mrs Maynard Keynes] recite Shakespeare properly last week my ear was still expecting to hear him said *both* as if it was poetry *and* as if the meaning was of some importance.[33]

On the other hand, he welcomed worthwhile novelty. *The Hairy Ape*, by Eugene O'Neill, he thought a play of energy and intelligence. What was valuable about the work was not merely its political correctness as 'a protest against the present structure of society on behalf of... the Worker' (though it managed a tremendous feat in that respect: 'This is the only play I know with a working-class communist who holds forth which does not seem trivial or embarrassing'), but that it gave 'body to the central notion, showing it from enough points of view to make one feel something in the real world is being considered.'[34] He had no higher praise than that; it is what the greatest literature achieved—and the best criticism to a corresponding degree.

What emerges most strongly from his book reviews (the majority of them written while he was 'Skipper' or literary editor of *The Granta*, in 1927–8) is a conviction as to the sympathetic power of the imagination, its capacity to embrace difference, strangeness, and wonder. What most disappoints him in a piece of writing is a failure of the requisite imaginative exertion. After giving due credit, for example, to the qualities of E. M. Forster's lectures collected in *Aspects of the Novel* (such as the achievement of style, exquisitely characterized as 'the little soft pat of butter that surely, on second thoughts, has been doped with brandy'), he is obliged firmly to lament 'the common-sense limitations' of Forster's criticism.

An attempt, successful or not, to include all possible attitudes, to turn upon a given situation every tool, however irrelevant or disconnected, of the contemporary mind, would be far too strenuous and metaphysical an exertion.[35]

Written in October 1927, when Empson had only just embarked upon his last year of reading Mathematics, those words amount to a radical manifesto for the kind of literary criticism he would produce in *Seven Types of Ambiguity*—and indeed for the kind of poetry he would soon start publishing. Thus it is not surprising that he should comment on Richard Church's collection of precious poems, *Mood without Measure*: 'Psyche is there all right; she sidles round her pin... One cannot but respect this sensitive, terrible aesthetic conscience; Mr Church's delicacy and integrity are not exercised in vain, but really, one feels, a poet must be more sure he has something to say.'[36]

He had no quarrel with lyric poetry; on the contrary, he loved it. To cite a notable example, the level of the translations by Humbert Wolfe (*Others Abide*) and Arthur Waley (*Poems from the Chinese*), he considered 'extraordinarily high. Mr Wolfe and Mr Waley... produce poems that, in their wealth and delicacy, stand very high among the original work of this in no way lyrical period.'[37] It was poems that posed as exquisite *per se* that rattled him.

So, in the temporary absence of the lyric impulse in the modern age, he suggested in a review of *The Secret of Father Brown*, by G. K. Chesterton: 'I wish more poets would write detective stories, but they could hardly produce effects more lyrical, or state a more vivid view of life, than these.'[38]

Whatever the subject matter, imagination is all: it expands the reader's powers. Wyndham Lewis's stories in *The Wild Body* 'gratify our strong and critical curiosity about alien modes of feeling, our need for the flying buttress of sympathy with systems other than our own.' That is splendidly phrased; so is the reason Empson brings forward to persuade his student audience that Lewis's stories are good—'neurotic egotist though he is, and painful though it is to read his accounts of himself as flaying in conversation some crippled mind. What he has is the humour Eliot claimed for Marlowe, he exhilarates by describing people with strong, able, well-marked systems of habits, absurdly unlike one's own.' But the true genius of the review comes in this next sentence: 'It gives a sort of courage, and it makes you feel more competent, even to have imagined them.'[39]

He has just the same expectations of the scientist. In *The Life of the White Ant*, Empson keenly observes, Maurice Maeterlinck 'has taken upon himself one of the artist's new, important, and honourable functions, that of digesting the discoveries of the scientist into an emotionally available form'—and again the specification applies best of all to Empson's own poetry. In spite of assembling 'many strange facts,' however, M. Maeterlinck fails in his ultimate duty: 'the work itself calls for a more desperate effort of imagination. It is no use, for instance, wondering ... whether it must not be very sad to be blind, when they [the ants] are so perfectly sure of their world, and can communicate with such nicety. The life of a termite, as he interprets it, is one of vivid but unrelieved horror ... It is hard to suppose a termite would agree.'[40] (In quite the same way, Empson believed, it is a stultifying fallacy to treat all history as if it were contemporary history: 'never to imagine a period, a system of ideas, as a whole, actually to regard it as vivid and imaginative not to do so, is not to give the man-in-the-street the telescope of history at all.')

As a mathematician with a strong interest in the physical sciences, Empson was naturally adept at settling pseudo-scientific hash. A study of the work of the psychiatrist Alfred Adler (author of a watershed paper with a worrying title, 'The Inferiority of Organs') inspired him to open an otherwise hostile review with this just and homely tribute to Freud:

Professor Freud elaborates theories to fit particular neuroses with which he has had to deal, and then says that though of course that is not the whole of the matter, these processes probably play a large part in the average mind. It is no use at all to say he must be wrong because his mind is saturated with sex; you might as well say a plumber must be wrong because his mind is saturated with lead piping; he may not know the price of the furniture, but he is certainly competent to find where the pipes go, even if he says a really modern house has pipes running all over, and some American houses are given away with the plumbing. He has his methods of finding out, anybody can watch them, and it is with great pleasure of the ordinary novel-reading type that you join the hunt on your own pony.

As for Philippe Mairet's attempt to extrapolate good ideas from Adler's work, Empson believes that Adler has written up nothing but 'crude little sermons':

an honest sermon bases its ejaculations and conclusions on an idea of what is good, and on claiming to know that it is true. You can no more 'derive' an idea of the good from psychology than you can from plumbing, nor has Professor Adler tried to, he has just picked up the most respectable ideas of the good that lay handy, and stolen fire from the scientific altar to put them across.

Freud's beliefs may be all nonsense, but if they are true they are an addition to human knowledge. The beliefs peculiar to Professor Adler... it is merely muddling to call 'scientific' at all.[41]

A collection of essays entitled *Mind*, edited by R. J. S. M'Dowell, earns this impatiently flippant opening declaration: 'The scientists spend a great deal of their time discussing with an extreme lack of subtlety whether they are Materialists or not. One after another they take bellyflops into the sea of philosophy, and say mind and matter are essentially One; or not more than one and a half, anyway. It is of historical interest only.' But then Empson leaves off fashioning a witty metaphor so as to offer a more constructive opinion (it is the mark of the instinctively expert reviewer, who knows he must first entertain in order to engage his reader with the development of his theme):

Any simple relation which may be proposed between subject and object leads at once to an infinite regression; the relation is known therefore not to be of the ordinary sort. The only analogy so far proposed is that of a mathematical limit; it is mysterious; but there is no reason to despair of cataloguing its more important properties, and knowing to what variations they may give rise. If the scientists met the problem in the course of their work, they would rise to the occasion splendidly. As it is, they use placid and depressing bludgeons.[42]

Likewise, any work in favour of the Christian religion was sure to earn an unflinching rebuke from the brave reviewer. When H. G. Wood attempted to upbraid Bertrand Russell for not being a Christian, Empson took pains to praise what he called Russell's 'English way of thinking'—the ability to be 'subtle only where it seems interesting' as well as not 'pained by crudity elsewhere'; the elegance of his work, and his freedom from verbiage. Only a fool would underestimate the depth of Russell's thought. Empson dealt out a similar dose of scientific logic to crush a false argument:

Mr Wood, when he is not, to his own frankly confessed shame, indulging in casual and rather witty nagging, . . . [will often] call a dilemma trivial when it has much in reserve. For instance, both in the First Cause argument for the existence of God, and in the crux about whether goodness is created by God, so that it is not for him absolute and he is not good, or independent of God, so that he is subject of it, Mr Wood is betrayed by Mr Russell's chattiness into mixing up before in time with before in logic, and then complaining of superficiality.[43]

The impertinent arrogance of Christians infuriated him. In response to a volume called *The Quest of Religion*, by C. E. Raven, he catechized the outrageous presumptuousness of the proselytizer: 'Would it be for Canon Raven to dogmatize about the finality of Jesus for an Australian aborigine, or an anthropological research student? He tacitly would avoid doing so, I gather, for an inhabitant of Mars. (The Church of Rome, of course, is in no such difficulty, Martians are capable of sin or beatitude only on the Martian, and not till membership of the Church is offered to them, on the divine, plane.) . . . How far is the Personality of Jesus . . . essential to this extremely tenuous creed?' It seemed to be a sick necessity for Christians to be shy about the cruelty of their religion. Even Thornton Wilder, in his limpid fable *The Bridge of San Luis Rey*—which is about 'the conflict in the writer between the heartlessness of Nature and the loving care of God'— takes refuge in this tactic. 'When Mr Wilder takes his subject seriously he is magnificent,' wrote Empson with much justice; 'but he is continually exploiting his style to make an escape from his subject into whimsicality.'[44] (Harold Acton too published a fable at this time, but in his case it had simply nothing but style to recommend it; and once again Empson was not shy of saying so: 'I confess I was able to get through *Cornelian*, but it is pretty dim stuff. It combines the most dismal qualities of the Sitwells and the nineties, of snarling and snobbery. There is no ingenuity.')[45] With regard to the essays collected in *Proper Studies*, by Aldous Huxley (whose 'gay hurt rapid novels' he greatly admired), Empson lamented: 'it is the pseudo-

Catholic bias makes him put things, only worth restating from both sides with the right proportion, too simply; as in the statement that the nerve specialist is a surrogate of the priest, showing that priests are missed; such a specialist obviously does a small part of the priest's job better, the only question is how far you should specialize, and it is not discussed.'[46]

Empson's 'alertness to multiple points of view deepens his humanity, as well as making his critical procedures endlessly subtle'. John Carey's description (in 1974) of the humane and commodious nature of Empson's critical writing is astute. The character of the criticism was by no means an accidental achievement, for Empson had set out what amounted to a deliberate programme even during his second year as an undergraduate. Not surprisingly, the goal of the new criticism, as he formulated it in his review of Forster's *Aspects of the Novel* in October 1927, corresponds with remarkable exactness to the strategy and the qualities that John Carey commended in the later work. The important point then was to make an 'attempt, successful or not, to include all possible attitudes, to turn upon a given situation every tool, however irrelevant or disconnected, of the contemporary mind...'[47]

Empson may be said to have come of age as a critic within six months of drafting that intoxicating and ambitious brief, with a review of *Blue Trousers*, the classic novel by Lady Murasaki (translated by Arthur Waley). The rich comedy of the fiction, and its 'architectual qualities', excited him to rehearse its success with a virtuoso critical performance: it is by far the fullest book review he wrote at Cambridge, a cascade of ideas and insights. The piece is fully Empsonian, and is worth quoting at length, from the helter-skelter inventory of the second paragraph (which is a single 300-word sentence) right to the end:

The critic, in giving way to boundless superlatives, might seem to be led astray by accidental qualities; by the romantic fantasy gratification in a hero of matchless beauty, charm which (we are told) had never been seen in the world before, rich with imperial scents (the privilege of his house), master of palaces four hundred yards square, of vast gardens adorned with forgotten cunning, and pathways of finely powdered jade, of numberless concubines, each of whom, when going on a journey as unostentatiously as possible, takes twenty coaches (and the number of outriders is extremely small), of uncounted mysterious and guilty secrets, such as the paternity of the Emperor, and of endless details of polite versifying; by the Wordsworthian air of simple truth, with which all this Vathek detail is carried off, and without which, even from so courtly an authoress, it would be too crude to please; by the curiosity continually excited as to what exactly the customs were, and how they worked, the shock of being reminded that these witty and cultivated women were entirely secluded, and the difficulty of finding out, for instance, Genji's methods of governing, or the nature of the Labour troubles so often hinted at; by the mingled sense of our civilization's inferiority in these extremes of delicacy, and of the practical Westerners' superiority to so 'quaint' and flower-chattering a people, from which we are startled back into fantasy identification with Genji when (filling an awkward pause) he embarks on a discourse about plum-blossom or novel-writing, or the limitations of their social love-poetry, making criticisms that seem so naturally one's own; indeed, by the modernity of the conversation of all the characters; one is continually thinking 'Waley *must* have made that up,' and then finding it woven incidentally into the next paragraph.

It may be such factors as these, superimposed on the original novel, that make it such a continual delight to read, and so liable to be rated too highly. But there are in this volume three or four comedies of situation; between Genji, his new child wife, and his chief concubine (what gross farce it sounds); about Yugiri, the faithful lover, now in domestication; and about the marrying off of Tamakatsura, who was prevented by a sad accident from entering the Emperor's household; in each of these one is dizzy with the subtlety of the writing, with each clause, each placidly given detail, there is a new twist to the dialogue, a different construction is put upon the relations of these always charming people. There is nothing exotic about it, it is what the western novel has done continually, but it is done supremely here.[48]

James Jensen has perceptively remarked, 'Perhaps the only reason this is not an even more obvious example of Empsonian analysis is that it is concerned not with the so-called "accidental qualities" of particular words and phrases in lyric poetry but with these qualities as they are produced by the broader structural components of the novel—setting, characterization, tone. Nonetheless, the basic technique is sufficiently recognizable: within the unity of a single sentence [the first paragraph quoted above] he lists five main sources of the novel's appeal (romantic gratification, Wordsworthian tone, cultural exoticism, tension between superiority and inferiority, sophisticated dialogue), amassing under each source varied but illustrative specimens of response designed to reproduce in concentrated form something of the actual sentient texture of the entire novel.'[49] That is, he looks at the novel from enough points of view to make one feel that something in the real world is being considered.

And yet probably the most astonishing thing of all is that Empson had not even started officially to read English literature when he wrote that brilliant piece: he was just a week away from tackling Part II of the Mathematical Tripos (in which Frank Ramsey was one of his examiners). Perhaps it is not surprising that he turned out only Senior Optime (Upper Second), and not a Wrangler (First).[50] There was no prize this time round.

7

'His presence spellbound us all': The *Experiment* Group

'ᴮILL Empson is very earnest about the *Experiment*,' wrote the *Cambridge Gownsman* (an undergraduate periodical edited at the time by a loyal and evidently well-advised Magdalene man) in October 1928.[1]

Such was the reputation Empson won with the poems he published in the summer of 1928—they included 'To an Old Lady', 'Invitation to Juno', 'Relativity' (later retitled 'The World's End'), and 'Inhabitants' (later 'Value is in Activity')—it was probably inevitable that he should have become involved in founding a literary magazine by the time he began officially to study English. The group of like-minded undergraduates who brought *Experiment* into being in November 1928 included Jacob Bronowski (who had come up to Jesus College in 1927, also as a mathematician), Humphrey Jennings (painter, poet, designer, who was reading English at Pembroke), and Hugh Sykes Davies (St John's), as well as Viscount Ennismore, a saturnine and permanently black-garbed figure who preferred to call himself by his family name, William Hare (future Earl of Listowel, last Secretary of State for India and Burma in the Labour government, and Governor-General of Ghana). Although 'plain Mr Hare' often hosted meetings in his rooms at Magdalene, and indeed funded the publishing venture, he was so taken up with Labour Party politics and philosophy[2] that the lion's share of the editorial work of *Experiment* fell to Bronowski and Empson—in truth, probably more to Bronowski than to Empson. Yet another mathematician, Max Black (reading mathematics at Queen's), future Professor of Philosophy and Humane Letters at Cornell University, who had undertaken to be business manager, somehow devised the title of the magazine after much wrangling. Misha Black (who had no connection with Cambridge University other than through his older brother, and who was later knighted for his services to industrial design) drew a cover design in thrustingly geometrical-modernistic green-and-black;[3] and the launch was hailed with 'Laudatory Verses' in *The Granta* beginning:

> Hail to thee, *Experiment!*
> We applaud thee, Heaven-sent;
> By five pious hands conveyed—
> Anonymous and undisplayed.[4]

Experiment, as its title indicated, was dedicated to modernist experimentation. Its policy, as proclaimed in an archly phrased editorial in the first issue (we may doubt whether Empson composed it), was 'to gather all and none but the not yet too ripe fruits of art, science and philosophy'. If Cambridge, as Empson suggested, was suffering from 'anxiety neurosis', *Experiment* was to seek to display its myriad manifestations. In the event, this zestful little magazine would run for just seven issues over four years, with the last appearing in May 1931 (Empson had editorial control only for the first three issues); and it fulfilled its aims to a remarkable degree, publishing verse of all sorts, critical essays, fiction, portraits, reproductions, translations, photographs by Cartier-Bresson, paintings by Braque and Ernst, and articles on everything from biochemistry to art and theatre design. Every genre and medium that was new and vital (and very little that could be called phoney with the benefit of hindsight) filled out its pages—and Bronowski even had the cocksureness to reject a proposed submission by Ezra Pound.[5] Bronowski was to receive letters from both T. S. Eliot and James Joyce congratulating him on his editorial achievement, and a selection of the work first published in *Experiment*, including pieces by Empson, would be reprinted by Eugene Jolas in his acclaimed little magazine *transition* (Paris, 1930)—though T. H. White (albeit a contributor) complained that *Experiment* 'contained large numbers of lamentably clever young gentlemen talking clap-trap more obviously than any congeries of the nineties'.[6] One of the most exhilarating pieces to appear in the magazine was Empson's own essay with the modest title 'A Note on W. H. Auden's *Paid on Both Sides*' (Spring 1931); so featured in the very last issue, it seemed fittingly to sum up his contemporaries' restless quest for coherence, for focus and purpose, personal and political, amid the stresses of post-war change:

[T]he play is 'about the antinomies of the will, about the problems involved in the attempt to change radically a working system . . .

One reason the scheme is so impressive is that it puts psychoanalysis and surrealism and all that, all the irrationalist tendencies which are so essential a part of the machinery of present-day thought, into their proper place; they are made part of the normal and rational tragic form, and indeed what constitutes the tragic situation. One feels as if at the crisis of many, perhaps better, tragedies, it is just this machinery which has been covertly employed. Within its scale (twenty-seven pages) there is the gamut of all the ways we have of thinking about the matter; it has the sort of completeness that makes a work seem to define the attitude of a generation.[7]

Like Empson, Jacob Bronowski (1908–74) believed that 'doing science was as natural as breathing or writing poetry'[8]—though Empson was later to say that Bronowski was sensible 'to have stuck to his sums'.[9] Born in Poland, he had arrived in England in 1920, speaking no English; his family lived in Whitechapel, in the East End of London, where he went to school. Just seven years later, in the autumn of 1927, he had won a scholarship to Cambridge. Empson, who was then in his final year of Mathematics, introduced this tyro to a wider literary circle. It was at Empson's instigation, for instance, that 'Bruno' scampered through a copy of Joyce's *Ulysses* in little more than a day, so as to be able to take part in a closet seminar on the banned novel that Empson presented on 12 March 1928. (In 1925 F. R. Leavis had been called to account by the Vice-Chancellor for making use in his classes of *Ulysses*, which had been banned from Britain in December 1922[10]—though I. A. Richards continued to lecture on Joyce with seeming impunity.) 'Our heroes were James Joyce, and D. H. Lawrence,' Bronowski would remember years later. 'There was a considerable division between the James Joyce faction and the D. H. Lawrence faction, because the James Joyce faction thought sex was "wonderful but private", and the D. H. Lawrence faction thought sex was "pretty good but public".'[11] Empson had no difficulty in persuading him to join the Joyce faction—at least for a time.

Though Empson's junior in years, the brilliant, self-conceited Bronowski soon caught up with the leaders of the intellectual avant-garde; as Julian Trevelyan was to recall, he was 'a dynamic gnome who cheerfully ordered our lives for us, and for whom we were generally prepared to die'.[12] A short, rather ill-favoured man with stiffly upstanding black hair, Bronowski wittily endeared himself to another acquaintance, Desmond Lee, who was blessed with good looks, blue eyes, and blond hair, by remarking of him: 'His appearance is against him.' He would also say, of Empson: 'he was not quite as good a mathematician as I, but a better poet.' That last statement was made in a radio broadcast in 1973; yet forty-five years earlier, one may suspect, the attention-seeking young Bronowski suffered from a dose of jealousy, since his only recorded opinion of his co-editor's poetry at the time is this single sentence, which is at best ambiguous and at worst derogatory (from an article on 'Poetry at the Universities'): 'Mr Empson achieves directness of thought on the principle of the modern definition of number, by using the aggregate for the essence.'[13] (Alistair Cooke met Bronowski on the day they both enrolled at the university Chess Club; Bronowski asked of him, in his highly fricative accent, 'Do you play classical or rrrromantic?' Devastated by the question—he thought he simply played chess—Cooke never again turned up at the club.[14] Bruno 'was pompous and determinedly intellectual before and during the *Experiment* period,' Cooke was to recall; though he presently became close friends with Bronowski and discovered his warmth and showy merriment. Others found him loudly self-opinionated.)

Bronowski and Empson ('Bronowski already spoke in the editorial plural,' Kathleen Raine noted)[15] were quick to keep each other up to editorial scratch, as one anecdote may illustrate. T. H. White—who was reading Modern Languages, and wore blue velvet plus fours, and who had already acquired a certain reputation as a poet (he had put out a little volume of verses entitled *Loved Helen*), but who would become famous as author of *The Once and Future King*—was Skipper of *The Granta* for 1928–9; he was a good friend of Bronowski, as well as of Ian Parsons, though not of Empson (which may explain why Empson contributed only one review to *The Granta* during his last year at Cambridge). In any event, when Bronowski showed 'Timothy' White the proofs of the first issue of *Experiment*,

he was suddenly overcome with jealousy and decided that he must appear. So he gave me a poem—I now suspect that he wrote it hastily while I was out of the room, but at that time I was more innocent and accepted it as pure gold. He gave me a poem which was just long enough to fill a space that we had on one page. And I dashed round to Empson full of enthusiasm and said 'We have a poem by Timothy White'. Empson wasn't very fond of Timothy White, because at that time they were the two poets who could claim to have something of an established reputation in Cambridge. So Empson looked at this poem with a certain cynical distaste, and the poem which was about mules contained a line which cast some biological aspersions on the function of mules and referred to them as 'the gelded mules'. And Empson looked at that in that slightly head-in-the-air way that he has, and said 'Gelding the lily, don't you think? Gelding the lily.' That's always been my favourite piece of literary criticism.[16]

'I sold my first copy [of *Experiment*], at the first meeting of the Heretics Society,' Bronowski would recall after forty-four years, 'to Rose Macaulay, who was even at that age a marvellous old lady looking exactly like an elderly crane. And speaking much the same tones.'[17] (Like all young people, Bronowski obviously thought his elders much older than they really were. Rose Macaulay—author of the recent, witheringly comic satire on snobbery, *Keeping Up Appearances*, which Empson found a painful book[18]—was only 48.) Empson, having officially embarked upon studies in English, had taken up the office of President of the Heretics as well as his editorial job for *Experiment*; and Macaulay was his very first guest speaker. Other speakers that autumn included Jacob Faithful (author of a book on bisexuality), who spoke on the subject of 'Psychology and Religion', Denis Arundell on 'Producing', S. R. Slavson on 'Raising our Educational Standards', and Anthony Asquith (an old Wykehamist) on 'Films'. *The Granta* affords us the only known glimpse of Empson in his capacity as President—primed, anxious, intense:

[T]he interesting creature is on view every Sunday evening in the Conservative Club Rooms [in Falcon Yard, Petty Cury] on payment of a nominal fee—(we do not mean that the fee is small: merely that it is unpaid)—where he may be seen preening himself before his catch, and glowering at the assembled Heretics; the student, if fortunate, may even be able to catch the faint, indignant squeak which means he has asked a question designed to annoy the lecturer.[19]

Of the full pride of editors of *Experiment*, Hugh Sykes Davies was the cub. He had just come up to St John's with a scholarship in Classics; and after attaining a first class in the Classical Tripos Part I in 1930, Hugh Sykes (as he was then called) would go on to win a first with distinction in Part II of the English Tripos in 1931, when he became Jebb Student. *Realism in the Drama* won him the Le Bas essay prize for 1933. For two years he was a member of the Cambridge Conversazione Society ('the Apostles')—Anthony Blunt and Guy Burgess were fellow members and friends—and he would join the Communist Party in 1937, in reaction to the Spanish Civil War (though he left it after the Second World War). Having been made a Fellow of St John's in 1933, three years later he was appointed a University Lecturer in English—and so he remained for the next forty years. But in the Michaelmas Term of 1928, when *Experiment* was launched, he must have been looked upon by Bronowski and Empson as primarily an apprentice. Yet he continued to be a principal editor of the magazine for a good while after Empson was deprived of his career in Cambridge. 'We were the main editors...and we did, in a sense, form a circle,' Sykes

Davies would remember. 'But among us there was no doubt that Bill Empson was a genius. He was the chap who would last—we have been perfectly right about that.'[20]

The true third of the editorial trio was supposed to have been Humphrey Jennings (Pembroke)—who at that time showed less interest in the film-making for which he was to become renowned than in painting, scenography, and poetry. Already in 1927 he had skilfully designed the scenery for Dennis Arundell's spectacular production of Purcell's *King Arthur*, 'one of the most memorable of Cambridge musical productions';[21] and in 1928 he would design the ADC set for the first public performance in Britain of Stravinsky's *The Soldier's Tale*, with Michael Redgrave as the Soldier and Lydia Lopokova as the Princess, produced by Dennis Arundell, conducted by Boris Ord, and with costumes by Duncan Grant. In practice, then, Jennings was more passionate about designing scenery for the theatre (he contributed 'Design and the Theatre' to the first number of *Experiment*) than about the business of running a magazine; so he took less of an editorial part than Bronowski and Empson—though it did fall to his lot to look after the art side of the thing.

Just under a year younger than Empson, Jennings radiated charisma; he was an elegant man with a mane of brushed but uncontrollable yellow hair, a lean face, and longish, fleshy nose. Like Empson and in due course Sykes Davies, he read English, and he presently gained a first with special distinction. But in October 1929, just as he began doctoral research on Thomas Gray,[22] Jennings would take what was regarded as the quite extraordinary step of getting married. His wife Cicely was beautiful and serene, and a gifted cook; and the couple though poor lived in style. Unlike most students, as Bronowski would recall, 'Jennings was not at all a conformist; he was the most wonderful eccentric that I have ever met; he was totally unaware of the fact that every gesture that he made was outrageous.'[23] What enthralled his friends, however, was that he possessed the knack of orating with erudite zest; the world of wondrous learning seemed his to conjure and command. 'He had a manner which was full of what I can only call impersonal excitement,' Bronowski acutely observed; 'he always came alive in conversation, but what gave him life was the conversation, not the people.'[24] Trevelyan too was won over by his magical aplomb: 'Humphrey's was a prodigious intelligence; he devoured books, and as a dialectician he seemed invincible. He introduced us all to contemporary French painting through the medium of *Cahiers d'Art* and through various books on Picasso. He was alive to the ever-changing value of "contemporariness" in art, and the word *weltanschauung* was used much by us at the time . . . I can remember great monologues from Humphrey on Petrarch's triumphs, on the Chinese sage Chuang-Tzu, on the Industrial Revolution, and on Picasso.'[25] (In later years Jennings produced several pioneering documentaries including *London Can Take It, Listen to Britain*, and *A Diary for Timothy*, the last with a commentary written by E. M. Forster. Lindsay Anderson has fairly described him as 'the only real poet the British cinema has yet produced'. But he died too soon, at the age of 42, after falling from a cliff while reconnoitring film locations on Poros. He recovered a posthumous celebrity with the publication in 1985 of *Pandaemonium*, a long-devised anthology embracing over 200 years of appalling and inspiriting writings of all descriptions on the machine age.)[26]

Empson readily submitted himself to the spell of the rhapsodic young Jennings, and would in due course write a self-revealing memoir of him that is worth quoting here at length. Looking back in 1973, Empson begins by hitching one of Jennings's hobby-horses to his own continuing counter-campaign:

I wish I could remember more of the things Humphrey Jennings used to say, when we were both undergraduates studying English at Cambridge, because some of them might even now be useful bits of ammunition; but anyhow I remember their main trend. This was towards the end of the twenties, just before the great wave of self-righteous dismalness broke into 'Eng-Lit' as a result of the Great Slump; as a result of the steady supply of other disasters, I need hardly add, that inundation has never yet receded. So it was heady bouncing talk, though almost entirely about the art and literature of the sixteenth and seventeenth centuries. He talked about other things to other people, but in this area we had interests in common, and I think he would have agreed that they were fundamental to his world-view as a whole. Western man was still working out the Renaissance, and what you made of that had to appear in your popular films and your abstract paintings. The theory that the Renaissance never occurred had perhaps already been invented, but he would have brushed it aside as a minor but typical 'treason of the clerks'. 'Triumphs, Triumphs, it's all Triumphs'—I actually do remember him saying that, with a breezy gesture, in the middle of a non-stop harangue of documentation. Very few years after (and this is one of the points where his infuriatingly accidental death did so much harm), it became a standard doctrine of 'Eng-Lit' that Pride is the source of all sin, and trying to learn any kind of knowledge or skill, how to blow your nose for example, is obviously a bad case of Pride; therefore whenever you meet a Renaissance work praising a man for some notable ability or competence you should realise, since the Renaissance never occurred, that the author was being satirical, and meant you to consign the man to Hell for it. The play of *Dr Faustus* has actually been destroyed by this extremely nasty line of talk; students are made to read a corrupt text, intended to satisfy fanatics with a craving to torture witches, and are told that this is what Marlowe wrote, or arranged for someone else to write. Humphrey would never have put up with such stuff, if only he had been around.

Even at the time, there is no need to deny, I reflected that not all Renaissance men could have been triumphing all the time, especially since most of their triumphs were over one another. The very Triumphs of Petrarch, which were his basic text, have I think a triumph of Death over some other abstraction before the final triumph of Heaven over Death which allows to the series a quieting and dignified close. But as man is a profoundly social creature most of his experience is 'sympathetic', each man imagining in himself the experience he observes in another man; hence the process of triumph can be singled out as the most formative and significant one within a particular society. This could easily become a bad thing, and Renaissance characters seem to fall back deliberately on their medieval tradition when they wish to avoid being fatuously or offensively progressive, but this does not prevent the line of difference between the two periods from remaining a real one. As we still in the main accept the Renaissance map of values or sympathies, a question arises how it can best be used in the popular arts, or at least whether possible harm can be avoided, indeed whether there is a margin there for manipulation. Such is the way the lad Humphrey was approaching the popular arts, and I do not know that anyone has had the nerve to do it since.

There was only one time when I saw him often and long, a performance by the Marlowe Society of *Fair Maid of the West*. This heroic girl sailed to America and made the rough types do much better there; my impression is that she founded the British Empire, but in any case she behaved like the Queen: 'Elizabeth—there's virtue in that name!' Humphrey was the Fair Maid; I had a walking-on part, and forget whether I said anything, but there was never a dull moment. He was on the tall side and lanky, or what I think is meant by gangling; there were no rumours of his giving homosexuality a trial, whereas our friends would have seen no need to be discreet if he had; but anyway, the absence of sex in his treatment of the part was what you would expect of the Fair Maid, who was more in the line of Joan of Arc than of the Queen. But he was immensely queenly. Of course, female actors were then simply forbidden, so that his taking the part was not all out of the way; even so, the force and naturalness of the result struck me as needing an explanation. 'Don't poke, Humphrey' the producer would say (whoever can the producer have been? An older man, and one felt they hardly existed); this was a very classy phrase, usually needing to be said to a future duchess before she attended her first Hunt Ball. Often he would stand very upright and glare straight at the audience, or smile at it graciously; but then he would withdraw into himself, and the long neck would protrude horizontally, while he gazed at the floor. How often did he do this in his own clothes, I wondered, without being noticed? The play went off very well, and I wish my memory was less capricious about it. But I felt I solved the sex-problem of Humphrey; the reason why the part suited him was that, though quite unaffectedly a leader, he was not at all a bully. He was not interested in 'mastering' people, or 'possessing' them, let alone frightening or bribing them—in fact, he was rather unconscious of other people, except as an audience; he did have a good deal of consciousness of whether he was swinging round his audience to vote on his side. It is in a way a saintly quality, and I daresay I had been taught to admire it by the Julius Caesar of Bernard Shaw, though I am pretty sure I did not think of the parallel at the time. Of course women, like men, are often bullies and possessive, and some can fight, but the position of a woman leading the councils of a group of armed men selected for fight makes the contrast sharp. Evidently too this quality might do a bit to quieten the Renaissance feeling of Triumph, which at times fell so low as a simple jeering at a defeated enemy. . . .

His theory about the Renaissance approval for Triumph was the sort of thing that especially needs presenting in a documented written text, so that you can find what holes need to be stopped in it, where it is liable to give bad advice, or instead might be a rough medicine for an emergency. He understood that very well, and here I have to make a painful confession. He posted me (when I was living in Bloomsbury) a long statement of the theory, which I had asked for because it might help me in writing *Ambiguity*, and I probably did use it though I can't now say where. At the end of this document, which he had clearly written straight down, he added casually: 'You might hold onto this, because I don't think I have written it all down anywhere else.' I am extremely sorry that I did not do what I was told, but the random stroke of his death was beyond foreseeing, and at the time I was sure that he would write down a better version of it soon after. All the same, to lose it was a betrayal, and I must never blame my own friends for betraying me, if I could do that to him.[27]

Empson did not in fact betray his friend in that fashion; he kept the letter in spite of his own itinerant life and untidy habits. But he was wrong to think that Jennings might write out a fuller, more coordinated version of the theory. As Bronowski would remark, Jennings 'was always too inventive in his reading of poetry, too subtle and too nimble-minded, to get down on the page all that he wanted to say—and did say in conversation'.[28] On Jennings's death in 1950, T. S. Eliot was to recall 'his extraordinary liveliness of mind and conversational powers'; and much earlier, on 3 April 1934, he had chosen to compare the capabilities, and the achieved work, of Empson and Jennings, observing that the latter 'didn't give me the impression of having a mind anywhere near the class of Empson's, although extraordinarily clever'.[29]

Other bright writers quickly lined up alongside the editors of *Experiment*. Out of the blue during the long vacation of 1928 there arrived at Empson's door an essay on Valéry and Hopkins by one E. E. Phare—later better known as the scholar and critic Elsie Duncan-Jones—whom he presumed to be a man ('at that time such a mistake gave pleasure'—or so she said later). But Elsie Elizabeth Phare, a Newnhamite who was known to Jennings and T. H. White, had attended the 'momentous' classes given by the rather shy, 'thin, ethereal' and Shelley-like Dr Leavis;[30] and she had done exceptionally well in the English Tripos that summer, receiving a Special Distinction in Part I. (A fellow Newnhamite, Q. D. ('Queenie') Roth, who would be translated into Mrs F. R. Leavis the following year, had gained a Special Distinction in Part II; so had L. C. Knights, who was later Empson's predecessor in the Chair of English Literature at Sheffield.) I. A. Richards wrote the gifted E. E. Phare a testimonial beginning 'Miss Phare, whose record in the English Tripos has been the most distinguished yet achieved by a woman *or by a man*—'; and Dr Leavis likewise informed her tutor: 'Miss Phare would get anything she wanted.' Miss Minna Steele Smith (Newnham tutor), with her thick spectacles and her hair that looked for all the world like wool, hugged Miss Phare and cried with delight, 'What a joy you are!' In Part II E. E. Phare would gain a Distinction, alongside Jennings, Ronald Bottrall, G. W. Rossetti, and T. H. White (who perhaps used her as a 'lightning-conductor', she told me, because he was reluctant to admit to his homosexuality),[31] and she was the first woman to win the Chancellor's Medal for English Verse.

At the start of her final year, however, Elsie was simply delighted to have her critical piece accepted for the first number of *Experiment* by William Empson—'admired of us all'—who praised her too 'for selling 30 copies of that issue in Newnham alone (Newnhamites were very loyal). He called on me once in my room in college and patiently explained some of his poems . . . Everybody in that little "coterie", as my tutor, not quite approvingly, called it, I think felt the pre-eminence of "Bill". I remember vividly a grey afternoon—we must have ceased to be undergraduates, for it was after the publication of *Seven Types of Ambiguity*—when Humphrey [Jennings] leant lazily against the chimney piece, perhaps in Pembroke, expressing general discontent; then he said with great emphasis, "I wish Bill would write another book".' As for herself, she regarded Empson—who wallowed in 'hairbrush-and-butter' rooms—as a *lusus naturae*, even when she came to know him a little better. (In a later year he would put himself in debt to her work on Andrew Marvell, and to her personal generosity.)

A latecomer to the list of contributors to *Experiment*, and only the second woman to earn that giddy privilege, was Kathleen Raine (reading Natural Sciences at Girton), whom Julian Trevelyan extolled as 'slight and beautiful as a flower'[32]—and with a sharp intellect to boot. Brought up to think of poetry as a matter of soulful effusion—though she was well aware that the cultural atmosphere of Cambridge had recently been recomposed into what she later called a 'medium of Bloomsbury humanism, Freudianism, Wittgenstein's and Russell's positivism, behaviourism, Marxism, Imagism'[33]—she was yet astonished at the modernity of Empson's poem 'Camping Out', which appeared in the second issue of *Experiment* (February 1929). Where was the love in such a poem, she asked herself? Well, as she later glossed that very poem, 'one might say that the incidentalness of sex (or love) and the anguish arising therefrom, *is* his theme. When the beloved is no more than the surface-tensions and viscosities of a chemical compound of 98 per cent water (of which a textbook of the time alleged even the Archbishop of Canterbury to be composed; which being so of course so much for his beliefs—but then why not Marx or Bertrand Russell?) so much for that for which the soul pines.'[34] In 1929 she had little understanding that poems could address such substantive issues; all the same, Raine did submit to the awesome poet and editor of *Experiment* the few poems she had written, and was overjoyed to be invited to lunch.

When I saw William Empson for the first time, he was reclining upon a window-sill of his rooms in the first court of Magdalene. I remember the impression he made upon me—as upon all of us—of contained mental energy, as of a flame whose outline remains constant while its substance is undergoing continual transformation at a temperature at which only intellectual salamanders could hope to live. This impression of perpetual self-consuming mental intensity produced a kind of shock; through no intention or will to impress; for William was simply himself at all times. William came down from the window-sill and brought in the College lunch from the window-box where it was keeping cool (or hot). I seem to remember there was another guest; but in any company William was the one remembered. Never I think had 'Bill' any wish to excel, lead, dominate, involve or otherwise exert power; he was at all times, on the contrary, mild, impersonal, indifferent to the impression he made to the point of absent-mindedness. Nevertheless his presence spellbound us all. His shapely head, his fine features, his eyes, full lustrous poet's eyes but short-sighted behind glasses and nervously evading a direct look (I always mistrust people who look you straight in the face) was the head, in any gathering, that seemed the focus of all eyes. His mannered speech too charmed us; those Wykehamical intonations slurred and stressed into a kind of incantation, even when he was not declaiming poetry; which he did with frightening intensity, like one possessed.

He was beardless that year; but on a long vacation grew his first beard (I think on a skiing holiday in Switzerland) which added to the daimonic energy of his appearance. His mother (I remember his telling us) had offered him ten pounds to remove the beard; and he had written her that 'since no one had offered him a larger sum to keep it on' he was obliged to accept her offer. So the beard went; but not the instinct for that mandarin form of barbarity, which did assert itself later, as we all know.[35]

'The Editors of *Experiment* never took me seriously as a poet, of course,' Raine was to write, much later in life, 'although they all, in turn, looked me over'.[36] That does not seem to be a fair insinuation—at least not with respect to Empson. He did publish two of her poems in the third issue (May 1929) of *Experiment*—'Atticus' and 'Hymn for the B.V.M.'—although admittedly they were not the 'immature and personal' pieces she had penned in her first year at Girton but what Muriel Bradbrook (a Girton contemporary) later called 'mythological exercises' influenced by T. S. Eliot ('We disregarded his theology,' Raine herself was later to say; 'yet a generation saturated in Atheism, Freudianism and Marxism inhabited, as we inhabited no other poem, Eliot's *The Waste Land*').[37] If Raine was cultivated by the editors of *Experiment*, as she later implied, more for her femininity than for her gifts as a poet, it may have been that they were simply responding to her self-presentation. For she inhabited too the Girton of Rosamond Lehmann's *Dusty Answer*, a novel which—as she admitted with a deep exhalation even then—spoke for her own hopes, her own swoons. 'The phrase "godlike young men" was current in Girton; and only half in irony, after all. Neither in Florence nor in Athens, nor in Murasaki's Kyoto, could our young aristocracy have been surpassed in that well-bred grace of good looks enhanced by good manners, and by the possessors' own carefree assurance of their own godlikeness. We loved our lords.'[38] It must be evident from the account of her first meeting with Empson quoted above that she was all but infatuated with him, that he became for her a kind of Shelleyan deity incarnate. In return he tended to idealize her, though not to idolize her. She had grace and beauty, and was self-beguiled; from her first year at Girton she had been led to think herself attractive—which

turned my head completely for a time; for it is hard, at eighteen, to grasp the truth that to be loved for our beauty is not to be loved at all. We expect to be treated as the goddess whose reflected image we bear; we think we are ourselves that goddess. When at the end of my third year I had no idea where to go or what to do, William Empson's idea was that my face would adorn the cinema-screen and he sent photographs of me to his old school friend, Anthony Asquith. The photographs were well received, but nothing of course came of it.[39]

That Empson also took her to call on I. A. Richards (who became his Director of Studies in English in the autumn of 1928) would suggest that he regarded her as something more than merely a 'looker'. And surely there must have been something ethereal about their relationship. He did not see her as a sex object; rather she was someone whose beauty and personality inspired in him a sense of reverence. She was too good to be true, too pure to be touched. Even some twenty-three years later, in 1952, he would publicly describe her as 'a rather saintly character'.[40] In any event, if Empson's incandescent, impersonal intellect made him figure in her eyes as some sort of god, the deity had other avatars; as Raine acknowledged in her memoirs, 'I think I learned more, in those years, from the inspired talk of Humphrey Jennings than from any other person. I see him, in memory, as an incarnation of Blake's Los, spirit of prophecy; whom in appearance... he much resembled.'[41]

Among other early contributors to the new magazine *Experiment* were J. L. Sweeney, Louis Le Breton, Ormerod Greenwood, Gerald Noxon, James Reeves, John Solomon, and the American poet Richard Eberhart (whom Bronowski found 'wild but delightful'); as well as E. M. Wilson, future Professor of Spanish at Cambridge, whom Empson urged to translate the poem *Soledades* by Don Luis de Góngora. In fact, Empson published in *Experiment* the first fragments of Wilson's translation; and Wilson was to write to him in 1930—when most of the translation was finished, and at a moment when T. S. Eliot had just accepted an extract for the *Criterion*—'If the whole is published may I dedicate it in part to you? You first suggested the work, and I think your poems have had their influence on my method of versifying, with Milton & Dryden.'[42]

Wilson also felt much indebted to Empson for enabling him to become the friend of another highly entertaining Magdalene figure, John Hugo Edgar Puempin Marks, who had been brought up in Spain and was bilingual in English and Spanish. Marks was editor of *The Granta* in 1928–9, and encouraged Empson to write a handful of (now dated) humorous sketches on the theme of the adventures of a character called Slumberbottom. In the 1930s he would translate the first novels, *Voyage au bout de la nuit* and *Mort à crédit*, of Louis-Ferdinand Céline (who hailed him, 'O Espagnol de Londres, Don Juan des Brumes'), as well as works by René Clair, Sacha Guitry, and Jean Malaquais. During the war he was to be responsible for setting up the BBC Iberian service, and from 1943 to 1953 was the *Times* correspondent in Madrid.[43] Empson delighted in vigorous, amusing personalities, and the 20-year-old Marks, a gifted, confident, raunchy fellow, did not disappoint him; as it was reported at the end of this friend's stint as editor, '*The Granta* office was never a dull place when Marks had the chair...'[44]

Whatever the sparkling talent that Empson and his co-editors attracted to their magazine, *Experiment* yet had some competition as an outlet for the young writers of Cambridge. *The Venture*—the title alone Empson and his chums considered far too Georgian—was edited by Michael Redgrave and Robin Fedden (who were also both at Magdalene), with help from the witty and sophisticated 'Apostle' Anthony Blunt (Trinity), who had already won himself a reputation as an art critic and so 'lent a real and much-needed note of distinction'.[45] Resisting the modernism of T. S. Eliot and the scientism of I. A. Richards, *The Venture* was 'more traditional, and subscribed more or less to the current Bloomsbury ideology,' Julian Trevelyan noted. John Lehmann took the view that *The Venture* occupied the political 'centre' of the Cambridge poetic renaissance, while *Experiment* stood for the 'extreme left'. He also provided this pen portrait of the young Redgrave, who took Modern Languages for a year before moving over to English in 1929: 'Tall, slim, with curly chestnut hair and a romantic profile, he was an engaging embodiment of the ideal conception of what a young poet should look like and how he should behave; but the stage was in his blood—and would out.'[46] Another acquaintance described Redgrave, cutely, as 'flower-like and detached'.[47] But Redgrave and Fedden gathered an interesting mix of contributions for their pleasingly packaged magazine: a short poem by J. R. Ackerley, a short story by Clemence Dane, a sonnet by John Drinkwater, and poems as well as woodcuts by John Lehmann (*Experiment* preferred to use reproductions of paintings by abstract and surrealist artists). Other notable contributors included Julian Bell (the son of Clive and Vanessa Bell who was to be killed in the Spanish Civil War), Basil Wright, John Davenport, Malcolm Lowry, and again a certain E. E. Phare. Redgrave published a fragment of prose by himself, 'The Widows' ('I was much given to fragments in those days'),[48] and worked hard to publicize his literary magazine in the face of the competition from *Experiment*, which first came out in the same month, November 1928. 'I hired a barrow with a large poster to be parked in various strategic spots, and a dozen sandwichmen were paid to walk up and down King's Parade.' Yet Redgrave did later admit that the rival magazine almost eclipsed *The Venture*—though 'I thought poorly of some of the poems which our competitors had printed: Empson's "She cleaned her teeth into the lake" [i.e. 'Camping Out', which opens with the arresting line 'And now she cleans her teeth into the lake'], for instance, seemed too self-consciously anti-poetic.' Even so, he gracefully conceded, '*Experiment*...was genuinely experimental. In its light *The Venture* was shown clearly to be what it was—a farrago of juvenile trifles.'[49]

Most other contemporaries could not help but admit the supremacy of Empson's work. Trevelyan vividly hailed the master: 'by far the most brilliant member of the *Experiment* group was William Empson whom we all, to some degree, worshipped. He rolled his great eyes round and round as he read his poems, looking like the mythical dog with eyes like saucers in Anderson's *Tinderbox.*' Empson read the poems, Trevelyan went on, 'in a low drone, accenting suddenly unexpected words to bring out some hidden cross meaning. For he was already at work on his *magnum opus*, "The Seven Types of Ambiguity", and he would find in our most innocent remarks, multiple meanings of which we were not at all aware. For his ingenious and incisive mind left us all feeling pretty silly.'[50] Even John Lehmann, who was committed to the rival *The Venture*, doffed his cap to Empson's work in *Experiment*, most notably to 'Camping Out', the poem that Redgrave found repellently anti-poetic—albeit with a reservation expressed in an inappropriate metaphor:

by far the most interesting of all the contributions were those by William Empson, including the extraordinary early poem *Camping Out*, which begins, 'And now she cleans her teeth into the lake'. Nothing more original was produced in our time, and yet these rare blooms had poison in the stalk for those who plucked them. I was fascinated by their formal skill, the poetic discipline which controlled the off-hand conversational manner, giving it a subtle texture and music; not, however, having received, as Empson had, a training in mathematics or science, I was all too often baffled by the extended specialist metaphors which he carried through with sure cunning; and I looked with a suspicious and unbelieving eye on those of my friends who claimed that they understood them. No such frustrations arose about the extracts which Empson also allowed to appear in *Experiment* from the book on which he was at work, *Seven Types of Ambiguity*, which I still consider one of the cardinal books of my initiation into the deeper mysteries of poetry, as important for me then as Robert Graves's *On English Poetry* had been at an earlier stage.[51]

Empson's prominence as a poet was both reconfirmed and advertised on the national stage by the appearance of *Cambridge Poetry 1929*, which was published by Leonard and Virginia Woolf at the Hogarth Press. A sampler of pieces by twenty-three Cambridge undergraduates of the day, including Julian Bell, Ronald Bottrall, Richard Eberhart, John Lehmann, Michael Redgrave, James Reeves, Hugh Sykes, and Basil Wright—and not forgetting the only woman to be represented in the anthology, E. E. Phare (Kathleen Raine was still waiting in the wings)—the volume made up the supposed rivalry between the local magazines and their contributors so as to gather together a panoply of shining talent. In terms of numerical representation, the three undergraduate editors of the volume—Christopher 'Kit' Saltmarshe (Magdalene), John Davenport (Corpus), and Basil Wright (Corpus)—recognized that Empson and T. H. White deserved the largest share, with six poems each. Of Empson's modest published output—just eighteen poems by the beginning of 1929—they reprinted a full third: 'Part of Mandevil's Travels', 'To an Old Lady', 'Villanelle', 'Letter', 'Legal Fiction', 'Arachne'. Both Davenport and Wright had appeared only in *The Venture*, not in *Experiment*, and might have been tempted to favour the conservative sect of versifiers; but it is clear that Saltmarshe functioned as editor-in-chief of the anthology and ensured that the poems were chosen solely on the basis of merit (and in alphabetical order).[52] Saltmarshe and Wright limited themselves to three poems each, and Davenport appeared with just one—albeit the longest in the collection, 'Dying Gladiator', which is saturated in T. S. Eliot and Ezra Pound.

The year 1929 also saw Empson's first solo appearance. *Letter IV*, which was written by May and published that autumn by W. Heffer & Sons of Cambridge, was the first in a series of booklets—'single, hitherto unpublished poems by Cambridge poets of established reputation'—called *Songs for Sixpence*, edited by Jacob Bronowski and J. M. Reeves.[53] The print run was a generous 1,000 copies; and while it is not known how many were sold, a quantity were definitely pulped in the 1930s. But Empson may well have felt relieved that the poem attracted so little attention at the time, for he presently became dissatisfied with it and chose to reissue it only a good while later, in revised form, for the American edition of *Collected Poems* (1949).

Perhaps it was through his witty and agreeable friend 'Kit' Saltmarshe that Empson first met John Davenport (1910–63), who was ostensibly reading History but actually making a dazzling reputation for himself as bibliophile, linguist, poet, pianist, art connoisseur, boxer, and boozer. Yet the burly, brilliant, entertaining Davenport needed no introduction; as Trevelyan remarked, he 'became an institution from the moment he arrived . . . His rooms at Corpus, lined with books, all of which one wanted to read, were a perpetual meeting-place for gregarious souls like myself. Fat, witty, bibulous, charming, bawdy, with a vast storehouse of a mind out of which nothing escapes, John has remained much the same throughout the years. With him was often to be found Malcolm Lowry, either leaning through the bar at the Maypole, or strumming on his banjo.'[54] (As well as co-editing *Cambridge Poetry 1929*, Muriel Bradbrook noted, Davenport 'wrote the Footlights Revue for 1932, *Laughing at Love*, to which Lowry contributed lyrics and in which he made a stage appearance'.) Redgrave later styled Davenport 'the Coleridge of our circle'—for at least one reason: he would end up wasting his intellectual promise with alcohol abuse. But Empson delighted in the Davenport he got to know at Cambridge, for his learning, his shrewdness, his wit, his boisterous sociability. The gifted, difficult Davenport was also an excellent talent-spotter: he was one of the first to celebrate Isak Dinesen, and he was to give constant support to Dylan Thomas.[55]

It was possibly through Davenport that Empson came to be included in the circle of young intellectuals—including Michael Redgrave, Sykes Davies, and Kathleen Raine—which would meet up at Roebuck House, the rambling, comfortable home (in the Cambridge suburb of Old Chesterton) of the brilliant biochemist J. B. S. Haldane (1892–1964) and his wife Charlotte (1894–1969), who was a journalist and novelist in her own right. Dark-haired and pretty, Charlotte was a firm-minded feminist of 35; she liked to cultivate writers, philosophers, and musicians. Her husband, who seems to have considered her glittering courtiers primarily pariahs, called the gatherings 'Chatty's addled salon'.[56] Empson admired her quite well enough to respond with teasing gallantry when she requested him to write a poem on her birthday. 'To Charlotte Haldane' (published posthumously) is written in terza rima, as if by Dante to a new Beatrice; the poet transposes his blank inability to offer satisfactory praise to the woman into a beautifully speechless, if Eliotesque, paean:[57]

> A task of terror. I must first dissent
> From all the frankness which such themes intend,
> And all who blame and who commend.
>
> What insolence and what abandonment
> To claim at large that one has known a friend,
> And, knowing, could in thought amend;
>
> That all her value, in such knowing pent,
> One dare show her, and say no more was meant,
> 'Madame, l'addition,' on one paper penned.
>
> And would I sum you to your end,
> Even to reign, myself, God at your judgment,
> And so assure you what he best can send?

Empson relished the opportunity to get out of Magdalene and to share the rich ripe talk of an evening at Charlotte's open house. Since the garden of Roebuck House ran right down to the Cam, he loved also to go for a swim there on a summer's day. However, although Empson enjoyed the company of Charlotte and her friends, he had a further incentive for calling at the house: he felt a deep admiration for J. B. S. Haldane's work in genetics, and for the sheer clarity of his essays in scientific popularization. (Haldane's collection entitled *Possible Worlds* had become one of his cardinal texts as soon as it appeared in 1927; and in 1935 Empson would skilfully translate into Basic English (see Chapter 11) two of Haldane's monographs, *The Outlook of Science* and *Science and Well-Being*.) It was worth braving the gruffness of the formidable Professor 'Jack' Haldane, with his balding block of a head and penetrating eyes, to catch a few of his words. Even if Empson had been informed that Haldane 'detested' the crew who danced attendance upon his wife (as he purported to do), he would not have been deterred from dropping by. Indeed, in a memoir that he sketched for a BBC programme soon after Haldane's death in 1965, Empson reported that the notoriously short-tempered professor would respond with courteous interest whenever the whipper-snapper Empson said his piece. No matter his offensive reputation, Haldane had breadth of mind and spirit—and nothing was more creditable than that.

He was an all-round learned man, a scientist who as an undergraduate had done well at Greats, and as well as this classical and philosophical education was always liable to quote from Hindu or Icelandic epics or what not. This of course made him exciting to talk to, and people are rather fond of saying, when such a man dies, that there can never be another one, because the field of knowledge has become too big. I expect they will go on cropping up. Such a man does not really know everything, and isn't tempted to pretend he does; he has looked up information on a variety of subjects, always sticking to the point of view which made him curious about that subject to start with. You may say, he has his own picture, and knows where everything fits in. There is nothing in the growth of modern knowledge to make that impossible any longer, I think. It is just that few people try, because the pressure makes them specialise from their schooldays, and many experts are liable to attack anyone who climbs the hedge into their field. It also takes a bit of self-confidence, naturally, and it seems to take considerable bodily strength, though I am not sure why. Haldane remarks in one of the essays that, when he was getting back to work after the First World War [when he had served in France and Iraq], he found he had acquired a craving for bodily exercise, which he hadn't time for; so he fought this as if it were a drug habit, and found after six months that he was able to go on with his reading without interruption . . . When I was an undergraduate in Cambridge, and he was Professor of Genetics there, his wife Charlotte was a generous hostess for the children [undergraduates] and he would talk to us for short periods, or join the swimming at the end of the garden. I think this gave me the right angle on the rudeness which was perhaps his most famous trait. It was mainly a refusal to be bored, hurrying the discussion on to where it would get interesting; he quite expected to be answered back, and had no presumption that a child's ideas would be wrong— plainly, he was curious to know what we did think, perhaps as part of a social inquiry, but at that age one will put up with a lot for being taken seriously at all. One was willing enough to talk back, though secretly glad it was soon over. His obvious courage, and the presumption that his opinions would challenge ortho- doxy, were always present; a brotherly gruffness was the only suitable tone. This was not unusual in the twenties; I remember a speaker at the Heretics, who was being heckled by a student, and the student was observed to blench and feel that his line of objection had better stop, and the man stroked his patriarchal beard and said: 'Continue, young man; do not be imposed upon by these white hairs.' Probably his [the student's] opinions were dull enough [at this point, Empson censored a snobbish reflex in his own script, cutting out the words 'I expect he came from a Garden City']; they have left no impression on my mind. But then, I am very bad at remembering conversation, and have found that if I appear to succeed I am only inventing; all I can say is that, when you are told Haldane was rude in talk, you should remember he had lived on, like so many of us, into a smaller-minded age.[58]

It seems likely that Empson took something from the example: a little of the 'brotherly gruffness', a good deal of the curiosity and large-mindedness.

Exactly when Empson joined the ranks of Charlotte Haldane's gentle-man-callers is difficult to ascertain. Not before the summer of 1929 would be a good guess. John Davenport was four years his junior, and first met Empson—or so it would seem—early in the academic year 1928–9, when he and his co-editors were putting together the contents of *Cambridge Poetry 1929*. Malcolm Lowry matriculated at St Catharine's only in the Michael-mas Term of 1929, and promptly paid a visit to Davenport in his rooms at Corpus 'with all the solemnity of a Frenchman seeking election to the academy'. With his golden hair, electric blue eyes, compact, muscular body, and the roughneck manner of a sailor on shore leave, the shy Lowry—who went armed with a tenor ukulele—became Davenport's regular drinking companion; and in Lowry's case it was definitely Daven-port who introduced him to Charlotte Haldane at Roebuck House. 'Though he needed a drink in order to speak at all, Lowry wanted very badly to be a tough guy, to prove he was tough and could take it,' said Charlotte Haldane years later. 'I felt at once there was a strong streak of infantilism in him.' In truth she was quickly taken with what she called 'his clumsy masculinity' and fictionalized him in her novel *I Bring Not Peace* (London, 1932). As his biographer has said, while Lowry probably became 'shyly and chastely infatuated with Charlotte,' it is equally likely that 'she was clearly—and not so chastely—infatuated with him'. As to her other *saloniers*, Lowry announced that he abhorred 'the preponderance of homo-sexuals'.

It is certain that Empson knew Lowry at Roebuck House; and yet Empson had been 'effectually "sent down" ' (as M. C. Bradbrook nicely put it) in the summer of 1929, for reasons which will be examined presently. So it is evident that Empson must have paid several return visits after July 1929—at least enough to leave some people with the impression that he was still in residence. Thus Empson and Lowry were seen in company together in the months following the autumn of 1929, and their talents and dispositions were compared by friends as if they were contemporaries— even though Empson had been thrown out of Cambridge in the summer before Lowry rolled up. Kathleen Raine, for instance, thought Lowry belonged to the category of 'genius' (along with Humphrey Jennings), for all that Empson—who was 'among us in the full blaze of his glory'—had peerless powers of mind:

William was able brilliantly to articulate a student's intellectual and emotional experience. As between William's brilliant gift of discursive intellect and Mal-colm's inarticulate, profound feeling and intuitive insight, William's, at that time, impressed us more. Or must I say, impressed me more. Impressed me in part because William's brilliance frightened me and made me feel inferior; whereas Malcolm did not frighten; he was too shy, too vulnerable, to overawe . . . [59]

Similarly, Hugh Sykes Davies later seemed to think that Empson, Bronowski, and he had still made up the editorial team when Lowry's piece called 'Port Swettenham' (an extract from chapter 5 of his novel *Ultramarine*) was published in *Experiment* no. 5 in February 1930. But Sykes Davies and Bronowski were in fact the sole editors at that time, with Gerald Noxon (son of the High Commissioner for Ontario, and a student of modern languages at Cambridge) as their publisher. Kathleen Raine later made out that she failed while at Cambridge to value Lowry's gifts of 'feeling and imagination' because she had been awestruck by Empson's rationalism; of course, she said, 'Bill had no great opinion of him.'[60] But she was wrong to make that assertion, for Empson endorsed Sykes Davies's and Bronowski's enthusiasm for the newcomer, and thought more highly of Lowry than of any other contributor to *Experiment*—not even excluding Bronowski, T. H. White, and Humphrey Jennings. We can be sure of his high opinion of the gentle genius of St Catharine's because in 1933 Empson was to write to John Hayward, without pretence or prompting: 'Has anything been heard of Malcolm Lowrie [*sic*], the best of that Experiment lot, who wrote short stories about the sea?'[61]

We know too that Lowry reciprocated Empson's good opinion, because Empson once whimsically retailed a curious compliment that Lowry gave him. It sounds so extravagant, we must hope it was authentic:

He said (we were both students at Cambridge, and I rather think we and others were swimming...at the bottom of J. B. S. Haldane's garden) that he would already have killed himself if he had not got my poetry to read. I thought this was just the way to talk, and felt pretty sure that nobody had said it to T. S. Eliot. But it did not lead to any greater intimacy; very likely through my fault...I think his life was ruined by a mistaken critical theory, and I am very sorry we never discussed it when we were lads together. Or perhaps I should say ashamed.[62]

Although Empson did not enlarge on that statement, probably the 'mistaken critical theory' he had in mind is to be identified with this observation about Lowry by John Davenport: 'The weakness and the strength of his novels lies in the fact that he can only create *himself*.'[63] But equally Empson was to remark with great keenness, in a very much later year, that he did not admire the adult Lowry's 'seeming somehow to make a virtue of alcoholism', for it was no boasting matter—he had felt the danger of alcoholism for himself, said Empson in his old age (*aetat* 75), and saw nothing in it to be proud of.[64] (It is interesting to note too that Empson also spoke as if he and Lowry were up at the same time; whereas he would have had almost no chance to get to know him better.)

Lowry's tribute was perhaps the most startling to come Empson's way, but it was by no means exceptional. The American Richard Eberhart—a potential rival who read English at St John's in 1927–9—may have been just a little sentimental when he chose to celebrate Empson's poetry in 1944; but if even a portion of this bouquet is a reliable report, it says a great deal for the state of Empson's repute in 1929:

In Cambridge everybody talked about Empson's poetry. His poems challenged the mind, seemed to defy the understanding; they amused and they enchanted; and even then they afforded a kind of parlor game, whiling away lively hours of puzzlement at many a dinner party. The shock and impact of this new kind of poetry were so considerable that people at that time had no way to measure its contemporary or timeless value. They were amazed by it. Eliot was already enthroned. The 'Oxford Group' [W. H. Auden and his Oxford contemporaries] had not yet got fully under way. And Cambridge was buzzing with activity.[65]

To be sure, Eberhart was not cheering the poems merely with the benefit of hindsight: in the early 1930s he enthusiastically corresponded with I. A. Richards on the subject of Empson's most exacting—least enticing?—poem, 'Bacchus'.[66]

Nor was the buzzing confined to undergraduate friends including Eberhart, Wright, Bronowski, Sykes Davies, Jennings, E. E. Phare, Raine, Davenport, Saltmarshe, Lowry, Marks, Wilson. When the publication of *Cambridge Poetry 1929* made the dons sit up and take notice, they too enunciated their approval of Empson's poems, which they spotted as the outstanding contribution to the volume. F. R Leavis wrote in the *Cambridge Review*:

> He is an original poet who has studied the right poets (the right ones for him) in the right way. His poems have a tough intellectual content (his interest in the ideas and the sciences, and his way of using his erudition, remind us of Donne—safely), and they evince an intense preoccupation with technique. These characteristics result sometimes in what seems to me an unprofitable obscurity, in faults like those common to the Metaphysicals... But Mr Empson commands respect. Three of his poems, *To an Old Lady*, *Villanelle*, and *Arachne*, raise no doubts at all in me: there is a compelling drive behind them.[67]

Three years later, in the 'Epilogue' to his influential *New Bearings in English Poetry* (1932), Leavis placed Empson's 'remarkable' poems in the choice tradition of John Donne and T. S. Eliot:

> Mr Empson's poetry is quite unlike Mr Eliot's, but without the creative stir and the reorientation produced by Mr Eliot it would not have been written... [and] he has clearly learnt a great deal from Donne. And his debt to Donne is at the same time a debt to Mr Eliot... Mr Empson's importance is that he is a very intelligent man with an intense interest, not only in emotions and words, but also in ideas and the sciences, and that he has acquired enough mastery of technique to write poetry in which all this is apparent...
>
> But it will not do to let this reference to Donne imply a misleading account of Mr Empson. He is very original: not only his ideas but his attitude towards them and his treatment of them are modern. The wit for which his poetry is remarkable is modern, and highly characteristic... [A]ll Mr Empson's poems are worth attention. He is often difficult, and sometimes, I think, unjustifiably so; but his verse always has a rich and strongly characteristic life, for he is as intensely interested in his technique as in his ideas.[68]

Perhaps that encomium does not say all that much; in truth, it says just one thing two or three times: that Empson was strong on both ideas and technique (though Leavis presents no illustrative or analytical detail to show quite what he meant). Yet Leavis says it with warm conviction; and the Leavis *imprimatur* was worth having in 1932, even though the 'Epilogue' to *New Bearings* goes on to give many more pages of enthusiastic description to the work of Ronald Bottrall. (In 1950, Leavis would assert that both Empson and Bottrall had failed 'to develop, or to develop satisfactorily').[69] But there is no doubt that Leavis felt sincerely enthusiastic for Empson's poetry in the early years, and acknowledged its brilliant originality— whatever the influences the young poet had absorbed. Indeed, he began to cite Empson's poetry in his classes.[70]

He was just as enthusiastic—at the beginning of the 1930s—about Empson's work in prose, *Seven Types of Ambiguity*, which he saluted on a number of occasions—as in an article on 'Criticism of the Year' (1931), where he praised the volume as 'the most important critical book of the year . . . one of the most important . . . in the language; written by a first-class mind.'[71] Indeed, he felt he might profit by the association: in a 1931 letter to Ian Parsons outlining his then prospective book *New Bearings in Modern Poetry* (as he had provisionally entitled it), Leavis choicely wound up with this declaration:

I should like to take the opportunity of congratulating you on Empson's book. It's magnificent, and is, I am quite sure, going to be a classic. I'm pushing it as hotly as is discreet in lectures and supervision, and have sent it to various parts of the world.

It's a book that I confess (I'm afraid this is not modest) I should like to be in company with.[72]

That unqualified tribute was not just a safe private gambit written out of self-interest; Leavis was fully as good as his word the following year, when he ordained Empson's book as a touchstone of critical talent:

Further education in analysis may be derived from Mr. W. Empson's *Seven Types of Ambiguity*; those who are capable for learning from it are capable of reading it critically, and those who are not capable of learning from it were not intended by Nature for an 'advanced education in letters.'[73]

The buzz of interest in Empson's startlingly original poetry extended beyond the Faculty of English. Even Ludwig Wittgenstein was tipped off about Empson, and felt eager to learn about his poetry. In a later year Leavis told a story that seems to have been meant to emphasize what he called 'something like an antipathy of temperament' between Wittgenstein (whose interest in English literature 'had remained rudimentary', Leavis alleged) and himself. Yet this anecdote certainly redounds to the credit both of Wittgenstein and of Empson:

He said to me once (it must have been soon after his return to Cambridge): 'Do you know a man called Empson?' I replied: 'No, but I've just come on him in *Cambridge Poetry 1929*, which I've reviewed for *The Cambridge Review*.' 'Is he any good?' 'It's surprising,' I said, 'but there are six poems of his in the book, and they are all poems and very distinctive.' 'What are they like?' asked Wittgenstein. I replied that there was little point in my describing them, since he didn't know enough about English poetry. 'If you like them,' he said, 'you can describe them.' So I started: 'You know Donne?' No, he didn't know Donne. I had been going to say that Empson, I had heard, had come up from Winchester with an award in mathematics and for his Second Part had gone over to English [Empson had actually completed Part II of the mathematical Tripos before going over to English] and, working for the Tripos, had read closely Donne's *Songs and Sonnets*, which was a set text. Baulked, I made a few lame observations about the nature of the conceit, and gave up. 'I should like to see his poems,' said Wittgenstein. 'You can,' I answered; 'I'll bring you the book.' 'I'll come round to yours,' he said. He did soon after, and went to the point at once: 'Where's that anthology? Read me his best poem.' The book was handy; opening it, I said, with 'Legal Fictions' ['Legal Fiction'] before my eyes: 'I don't know whether this is his best poem, but it will do.' When I had read it, Wittgenstein said, 'Explain it!' So I began to do so, taking the first line first. 'Oh! I understand that,' he interrupted, and, looking over my arm at the text, 'But what does this mean?' He pointed two or three lines on. At the third or fourth interruption of the same kind I shut the book, and said, 'I'm not playing.' 'It's perfectly plain that you don't understand the poem in the least,' he said. 'Give me the book.' I complied, and sure enough, without any difficulty, he went through the poem, explaining the analogical structure that I should have explained myself, if he had allowed me.[74]

If Leavis collapsed when Wittgenstein put him through his critical paces, there is a further fine irony underlying the fact that Wittgenstein could so readily appreciate and explain Empson's poetry. In an earlier year, most probably in 1926, when he was first attempting to write poetry, Empson had reflected on the apathetic contemporary response to what he called

the closing tautology of Wittgenstein [in the *Tractatus Logico-Philosophicus*]; 'Whereof one cannot speak, thereof one must remain silent.' The detachment of that phrase from its context is the weakness of our generation. Could not Romeo be written? Were the Songs and Sonets what cannot be said? What philosophy cannot state, art lays open. But philosophy has only just found out that it cannot state, all that we have no art to lay open.[75]

Those words perhaps mark the moment at which Empson determined to write poetry. Imaginative literature should encompass more than the philosopher's dream of expounding; a complex art must reach the parts that conceptual thought falls short of. In that sense, Empson's poetry stands for an attempt to meet the challenge of Wittgenstein's aphorism, the philosopher's ruling on the limits of language.

8

The Making of *Seven Types of Ambiguity*: Influence and Integrity

Critics, as 'barking dogs' . . . are of two sorts: those who merely relieve themselves against the flower of beauty, and those, less continent, who afterwards scratch it up. I myself, I must confess, aspire to the second of these classes; unexplained beauty arouses an irritation in me, a sense that this would be a good place to scratch; the reasons that make a line of verse likely to give pleasure, I believe, are like the reasons for anything else; one can reason about them . . .

Seven Types of Ambiguity (1930), 9

M URIEL Bradbrook, an Empson contemporary who later became Professor of English at Cambridge, and Mistress of Girton College, has written:

The briefest definition of Cambridge English would be: Contemporary, Comparative, College-based. We never troubled ourselves unduly about 'covering the syllabus'; yet while Richards was at Cambridge, there was true balance between the centripetal force of his lectures and the more intimate college teaching. There was a general feeling that a student ought to have his wits stretched. We tended to prefer the difficult poets—Donne, or Marvell, or Eliot. 'Strenuous' was a word of praise. We were not very charitable to fools. The over-earnest young woman whom C. S. Lewis depicts in *Rehabilitations* (p. 97) is myself.

The Cambridge of Wittgenstein, Richards, Empson, Leavis and [A. P.] Rossiter was not cosy or permissive; it was craggy and opinionated. Richards could smite vigorously in defence of a good cause; once when Empson, in a talk at the A.D.C., was being persistently heckled in a nasty way, Richards suddenly turned round with vigour and interjected at the irrelevant interruptor, 'And if a sunstroke hit you on the back of the neck, you'd be dead!'

Ivor Richards cannot be met adequately through his books alone. To hear him read aloud is the best education in poetry; his voice, melancholy, show-cadenced, sinks with an emphatic fall to clench his argument. His impish humour, his personal courtesy and his surprising union of the authoritative and the mischievous are more fully shown in talk, lectures . . . [1]

Any account of Empson's critical work must begin and end with Richards, for his career constitutes in many ways a fifty-year debate, and sometimes a dispute, with his mentor. Commentators sometimes assume that the lines of influence all run in one direction, from Richards to Empson, but it should be said that in many of his writings after 1930 Richards is responding to Empson's published and private views, and attempting to adjust his own position by definition against Empson's.

'Up to 1923,' wrote E. M. W. Tillyard, 'no lecturer destined to a permanent appointment in the English Faculty had taken the English Tripos.'[2] Richards was no exception. Eight years younger than Ezra Pound, five years younger than T. S. Eliot, he was born in 1893, which also made him two years older than F. R. Leavis and thirteen years older than Empson—old enough to be a brother, if not another father. After starting a degree in history at Magdalene, he grew sick of the subject after just a year and turned to moral sciences, for which he was tutored first by the idealist philosopher J. M. E. McTaggart and then by the logician W. E. Johnson, though his 'master'—his 'old dominator'—was the philosopher of mind and objectivism and the proponent of goodness, G. E. Moore, author of *Principia Ethica* (1903): 'I spent seven years studying under him and have ever since been reacting to his influence,' he remarked. He gained a first in Part I of the Moral Sciences Tripos; but then he suffered a severe bout of tuberculosis from which he took a long while to recover, mountaineering in Wales and in the Alps (for a time he seriously considered a career as a mountain guide on the Isle of Skye). Towards the end of the war, the ever-optimistic Richards took up biology and chemistry, with a view to going into medicine and eventually psychoanalysis; but the delightful and irrepressible Mansfield Forbes, Fellow of Clare and saintly 'genius', happily diverted him with an invitation to lecture for the English School on 'The Principles of Literary Criticism' and 'The Contemporary Novel'. 'All I know about him is that he's got a First in Moral Science and has a red nose,' said Professor H. M. Chadwick in 1919. 'But Forbes says he's all right, and I've put him on the lecture list.'[3] In 1922 Magdalene appointed him Lecturer in English and Moral Sciences (£100 a year plus tuitional fees—that is, 15*s.* paid by each student attending three or more of his lectures), and four years later elected him to a fellowship, which afforded between £350 and £400 a year. Also in 1926, in accordance with a decree of the University Commissioners, he was made a University Lecturer, with tenure and a stipend of £250.[4] He married Dorothea Pilley in Honolulu that December.

Though something of a late starter, he worked fast and accomplished the most remarkable work of his career by the time he reached his late thirties. In 1918 he teamed up with the daunting polymath C. K. Ogden, co-authoring *The Foundations of Aesthetics* (1922; with James Wood as their 'chief instigator') and *The Meaning of Meaning* (1923); and he was sole author of two works, *Principles of Literary Criticism* (1924) and *Science and Poetry* (1926), which secured his place at the forefront of literary and semantic studies. (By 1943, as his biographer John Paul Russo notes, *Principles of Literary Criticism*, which Richards later dubbed 'a sermon disguised in the fashionable scientific language of the time', had gone through seven British printings and sold 10,500 copies.)[5] His generative contribution to the emergence of the English Tripos, which came of age in 1926 when it passed from the control of the Special Board for Medieval and Modern Languages to that of the Board of the English Faculty, has been well attested; although the spry and watchful F. R. Leavis, who became one of six Probationary Faculty Lecturers in 1927,[6] would much later write him down in an ill-written phrase: 'his part in the alliance with Forbes that established as a recognized thing the need to cultivate sensibility in a discipline of intelligence directed upon words, rhythm and "imagery"— language in its poetically creative use—was necessary.'[7] But Manny Forbes, the kind and effervescent recruiting officer (whom Leavis acknowledged as his own benefactor), knew that Richards was 'necessary' to him in a more vital sense than Leavis's slipshod bathos suggests: together they begot the structure and the style of modern English studies—with help from two progressive former 'classics', the King Edward VII Professor of English Literature, Sir Arthur Quiller-Couch (Q, who held perennial classes on Aristotle's *Poetics* and who once remarked in a lecture, 'I fill a place, I know it') and the self-styled 'political factotum' E. M. W. Tillyard (who formerly specialized in Archaeology and Greek ceramics, and who lectured on criticism from Classical to Neoclassic). According to Tillyard, in his suave, sly account of Cambridge English, *The Muse Unchained* (1958),[8] Professor Chadwick, the shy but heroic philologist who had in fact initiated the transformation of English at Cambridge (he thought it an agonizingly pointless exercise for the average student to be forced to con his subject), 'trusted Forbes and me entirely and was willing to support anything we proposed. Q did not bother to initiate things but he liked to be consulted. If I could bring myself to spend long enough over consultation, Q ended by agreeing to anything that Forbes, Richards and I had decided was desirable.' Mansfield Forbes in particular, Tillyard went on, 'supplied a general distinction, both aesthetic and moral, rarely found in universities'; and yet he 'needed Richards through whom to work'. Richards for his part 'owed an incalculable amount to Forbes's inspiring faith and vitality and in matters of taste he relied on the sureness of Forbes's intuitions and the breadth of his reading. What Richards most contributed was leadership and a policy.'

Richards had two main aims:

first to supplant the easy-going and vaguely laudatory criticism that was still largely the vogue by something more rigorous, and secondly to apply the science of psychology to the processes of making and enjoying literature.[9]

Richards's capacities as a lecturer have earned an exceptional *réclame* in memoirs, fiction, and folklore. He has been described as 'spell-binding'— 'partly because we could not fail to notice that he was breaking not only chalk but new ground,' said Joan Bennett (also Girton)[10]—'impersonal' and 'electrifying', though also, strangely, toneless and unostentatious, as well as 'dry but expressive' in his delivery. Looking hawklike, with an emperor's skull, Richards was given to covering every bit of the blackboard with diagrams and arrows. In particular, the lectures that turned into *Principles of Literary Criticism* dazzled everyone with their novelty. Christopher Isherwood would rhapsodize in retrospect, 'Here, at last, was the prophet we had been waiting for—this pale, mild, muscular, curly-headed young man who announced in his plaintive baa-lamb voice: "According to me, it's quite possible that, in fifty years' time, people will have stopped writing poetry altogether..." ... But, to us, he was infinitely more than a brilliant new literary critic: he was our guide, our evangelist, who revealed to us, in a succession of astounding lightning flashes, the entire expanse of the Modern World...We became behaviourists, materialists, atheists.'[11] In 1925, when Richards delivered the first of his series of lectures with the odd and impudent title 'Practical Criticism', the Examination Hall was packed with 120 undergraduates from English and other disciplines. Mansfield Forbes was often there; so too E. M. W. Tillyard; the redoubtable Miss Hilda Murray; H. S. (Stanley) Bennett and Joan Bennett; and F. R. Leavis; along with other bigwigs including on occasion T. S. Eliot—who is believed to have handed in one of the 'protocols' on the undated and unattributed poems that were the meat of the course.[12] After taking an extended leave (March 1926–September 1927), Richards gave the course again in 1927–8, when a remarkable generation of students—including Muriel Bradbrook, E. E. Phare, Jacob Bronowski, Humphrey Jennings, Hugh Sykes, Alistair Cooke, and others of Empson's acquaintance—all flocked to have their feeble efforts flayed by the prophet, and to be fledged anew as practising critics.

'These occasions,' said Bradbrook, 'felt like a cross between a Welsh revivalist meeting—for Richards shows some very Welsh qualities as an orator—and the British Association's lectures in Elementary Science.'[13] They could also be comical, though not always intentionally so, as Alistair Cooke would recall. Richards, who held firm views on verse speaking, enjoined his audience 'not to colour the verse with any hint of the reader's personality; to be a neutral channel. He then read to us the poem [featured in *Practical Criticism*] by, I think, G. H. Luce and began, in his high querulous whine: "*Climb*, cloud, and *pen*cil all the blue With your mira*cu*-lous stockade; The earth will have her *joy* of you And *limn* your beauty till it fade." The emphases were about as personal as Richards's own voice, and every cadence ended, not with a bang or a dying fall, but with a rising inflection, as if for a petulant question. It was all very funny and totally idiosyncratic.'[14]

It is difficult to know whether Empson attended the 1927–8 course of 'Practical Criticism' lectures on anything like a regular basis. Richards published in *Practical Criticism* 387 so-called 'protocols', in whole or in part, out of about 1,000 that were submitted for his adjudication between 1925 and 1928, and he approved of about 30 of them.[15] As Joan Bennett observed with due rue, the majority of the written exercises exhibit 'the strange, comical, dreadful evidence of how poems can be mis-read'.[16] But the map of misreadings that Richards surveyed made Empson cringe with discomfort—in sorrow more than irritation. As criticism, Empson said in his first remarks on Richards's collection of invariably cock-eyed written comments, the protocols were 'bad': 'They are tedious and sometimes facetious; they display to the bitter end what it would be more merciful to hide; I confess I could not attend the original lectures because I found them embarrassing for that reason. But this is not a thing I am proud of...'[17] All the same, there is evidence to suggest that Empson did attend at least a few of the lectures in 1928. Among other witnesses, Alistair Cooke, who attended all the 'Practical Criticism' lectures, remembers feeling 'very bucked to hear [Richards] say that only two of the people who'd turned in their "protocols" had spotted the incurable cocksureness

of Edna St Vincent Millay's sentimentality [in Poem V, the sonnet beginning 'What's this of death, from you who will never die']. Mine is 5.8, and
of course the witty and devastating one is on p. 79, and is Empson.'[18] Yet
two other authorities are equally sure that protocol 5.81 was submitted by
someone else: Joan Bennett believes it is 'in the inimitable impressionistic
hand of Manny Forbes';[19] and Hugh Carey, author of a memoir of
Mansfield Forbes, thinks likewise.[20] (In any case the flamboyant facetiousness of 5.81 does not sound like Empson, who might have given more
thought than most of the protocol-writers to the satirical edge of the phrase
'your unimpeachable body'—one other protocol, 5.71, guessed at the
'sneering' implications of the epithet, though without truly weighing
them—and so realized that the poem may be a supposedly consolatory
address by a sarcastic woman to an absurdly vain man. It is curious that
Richards should have praised 5.81 for its 'detailed observation of the
matter and manner of the poem', when in fact it goes in for little more
than self-applause.) This is not to accuse Alistair Cooke of misrepresentation, only to suggest that he may have laboured under a misapprehension.
Nor is it to accuse Empson of lying: what he must have meant is that he
had dropped in to one of the lectures of the first series—that is, strictly
speaking, the 'original lectures' of 1925–6 (when he also chose *not* to go to
T. S. Eliot's Clark Lectures in early 1926)—and found the experience so
awful that he shied away from all public displays of practical criticism for
the rest of that session. Empson did not deny that he had been present at
some lectures in the 1928 series; and indeed he later testified to the
excitement that greeted Richards whenever he set out his wares: 'more
people would at times come to his lectures than the hall would hold, and he
would then lecture in the street outside; somebody said that this had not
happened since the Middle Ages, and at any rate he was regarded as a man
with a message.'[21] Richards, Empson heartily agreed with Bradbrook, 'was
a spellbinder, not at all shy about being Welsh'.[22] Nevertheless, he
reaffirmed in a letter of 5 November 1970: 'I didn't contribute any protocols, feeling shy about the process, though I went to one or two of the
lectures. I didn't realise that Richards was right till after he had stopped
teaching me—my friends thought him absurd and regarded me as a source
of comic anecdotes about my tutorials under him. The young are always
wrong and I suppose need to be.'[23]

Empson did not go to many lectures in general, or not as many as his
friends frequented (as Elsie Duncan-Jones has reported, 'they were social
events, for one thing'). In any event he left no recorded remarks about
A. B. Cook's lectures on Greek tragedy; G. G. Coulton on medieval

life and thought in relation to medieval literature; Stanley Bennett on Shakespeare; Mrs Bennett on eighteenth-century prose; G. G. Coulton on 'Life and Thought, 1066–1550'; T. R. Henn on 'Stage Development in the English Drama from the Morality to the Restoration'; Enid Welsford on the Renaissance; Basil Willey on the English Moralists; L. J. Potts on seventeenth-century English comedy; or even Dr F. R. Leavis (whom he always called 'Mr Leavis') on eighteenth-century literature. But he did happily go along to hear at least one celebrity, as he was to recall at Cambridge after nearly half a century, in 1974, by way of introducing his own Clark Lectures: 'When I was a student here I heard E. M. Forster giving *Aspects of the Novel* as a series of Clark Lectures [spring 1927], and I thought they were a model; never noisy or rude, but continually amusing and even exciting, and one's attention was kept at stretch to hear the asides, which were mainly remarks about other writers, but they always seemed strictly part of the discussion.'[24] Forty-six years later, when preparing his own Clark Lectures for delivery in 1974, Empson would recall just so: 'E. M. Forster gave the ideal Clark Lectures; his lectures, with a few by Richards, are about the only ones that I remember from my time at Cambridge.'[25]

Since Richards discouraged his students from attending lectures—indeed, it was official Faculty policy that a student 'need not attend many lectures, for the preparation for this Tripos depends less on teaching and more on the student's private reading than that required for any other Honours Examination'[26]—Empson was presumably happy to pass up the opportunity to patronize the exquisite show of Richards's most notable opponent, F. L. Lucas of King's, whose *Tragedy*—the book of his elegant and well-attended but critically slight series of lectures on 'Tragedy Ancient and Modern in relation to Aristotle's *Poetics*'—was rubbished by an Empson contemporary, T. H. White, in *The Granta*.[27] Elsie Duncan-Jones recalls too, 'Dr Leavis had warned us against writing in the rather purple style, epigrammatic and bitter, adopted by F. L. Lucas. I am glad to think that we were perhaps not wholly docile.'[28] Mansfield Forbes too was prone to speak of Lucas as 'sowing the fields with puffed wheat'.[29] There is certain evidence, on the other hand, to suggest that curiosity did drive Empson to a performance by one visiting celebrity, Gertrude Stein, who in 1926 delivered her famous—and famously, stupefyingly reiterative—lecture entitled 'Composition as Explanation'.[30] However, even if he did not actually go to the lecture, he took pains to read it when it appeared later that year from 'Leonard and Virginia Woolf at the Hogarth Press'. He must have thought Stein quite modern enough to emulate—for several months afterwards, he would occasionally deploy in his published reviews one of the key words from her lecture, 'equilibration'—and in June 1927 he would publish an odd prose poem, 'Poem about a Ball in the Nineteenth Century', which he confessed to modelling on her efforts.[31]

However, if Empson neglected most university lectures for the sake of his supervisor, it does not seem likely that he would have neglected the brilliantly entertaining lectures of Richards's close collaborator—the agent of his ascendancy—Mansfield Forbes, whom Basil Willey extolled: '[F]or sheer brilliance, unexpectedness, insight and originality, these lectures were unrivalled. They were also extremely funny... In more ways than one Forbes was a Coleridgean type; his lectures were a tissue of digressions; they eddied, but progressed little and had little orientation... But none of this mattered; Manny had a truly seminal mind, an imagination from which ours caught fire, and an extraordinary sureness of taste and rightness of judgment.'[32] Forbes was capable of teasing a single sonnet by Wordsworth, 'Surprised by joy', for weeks at a time; so it is not surprising that the young Richards should have followed suit—according to Queenie Roth's gossip, 'Richards believes in studying poetry intensively and will spend a whole term's lectures on two lines.'[33] Thus it was honest and wholly appropriate for Richards to write in the copy of *Practical Criticism* that he gave to Forbes—'you are responsible more than anyone for its having been written'—since (as Graham Hough would later remark without especial prejudice) Richards's method of Practical Criticism 'was in large part a systematization of Forbes's practice'.[34]

At least we can be sure that Empson did not on the whole like lectures, because he said so—ironically, in a notice of *A Lecture on Lectures*, by Sir Arthur Quiller-Couch, written while he was still a student of mathematics in March 1928. The piece is short enough to be quoted in full (it says much in a small compass, with the first sentence being particularly nicely phrased); while he obviously held no high opinion of the popular Q, he was prepared to give the time of day to other 'lecturers on English' so long as they were lively performers—not unlike (we may suppose) I. A. Richards:

This little book very gracefully says the little there is to say in favour of spoken lectures, as an introduction to a series in which various people's spoken lectures, by being printed, are undermined. Lectures are suited to a display of personality and of mental trapeze-work; so that lecturers on English and mathematics, at any rate, have some chance of putting up a fairly good music-hall show.[35]

How apt it was, then, that forty-five years later he was to write to Gareth Jones, Senior Tutor of Trinity College, Cambridge, in connection with the

arrangements for his own long-awaited appearance as Clark Lecturer:
'The lectures, I hope you agree, ought to be striking and entertaining . . .'[36]

Empson had read Richards—*The Meaning of Meaning, Principles of Literary
Criticism,* and *Science and Poetry*—in his first year at Magdalene, when he was
intending mathematics. Not only did he read Richards the theorist of
aesthetics, from the start he allied himself to the theory: he declared his
allegiance in *The Granta* in June 1926, when he ironically complimented
Herbert Read's aesthetic theories as being 'in the main . . . true and valuable, especially when Mr Richards has stated them already.'[37] He was
referring to Richards's so-called 'Theory of Value' (as rehearsed in the
'value chapters' of *Principles of Literary Criticism* (1924) which Richards later
regarded as 'rather the hardest, longest, most sustained thinking I had to
do' up till then).[38] In truth, Empson would worry Richards's pragmatic
principles for the rest of his life; his responsiveness to Richards's aesthetic
theory links the final chapter of *Seven Types of Ambiguity* (1930) and
'A Doctrine of Aesthetics' (1949), for example, as well as 'Death and its
Desires' (1933) and 'Literary Criticism and the Christian Revival' (1966).
'Nothing less than our whole sense of man's history and destiny is involved
in our final decision as to value,' Richards wrote in *Principles of Literary
Criticism*—a claim which Empson implicitly heeded throughout his career.
'To set up as a critic is to set up as a judge of values . . . For the arts are an
appraisal of existence,' he added in a ringing challenge.[39]

Richards's emotive theory of value centred upon what he called 'the
effort to attain maximum satisfaction through coherent systematization'—
'the systematization of impulses'.[40] Positive 'impulses' he termed 'appetencies', and anything which worked to satisfy such impulses must be
regarded as good or valuable. The full and ordered life necessarily maxi-
mized its varied satisfactions and minimized suppression and sacrifice.
Given such a goal, the individual's accession to a life of self-realization
and self-knowledge, it is poetry that must take up the role of religion for the
modern world. We must use poetry—'the most important repository of our
standards'—as 'a means for reorganising ourselves'.[41] Its intrinsic, vital,
and self-justifying function is to engender 'the best life . . . that in which as
much as possible of our possible personality is engaged'.[42] In short, the
beauty of poetry is to beget mental harmony: the good. John Paul Russo
characterizes this ideal of the good as 'an enlightened, critical eudaemon-
ism'.[43] In *The Foundations of Aesthetics* (1922; written with C. K. Ogden and
James Wood), Richards had taken the psychological term *synaesthesis* (not to
be confused with the literary term *synaesthesia*) to stand for the state of

aesthetic equilibrium thus engendered. 'A complete systematisation must take the form of such an adjustment as will preserve free play to every impulse, with entire avoidance of frustration.' This synthetic-dynamic principle of equilibrium 'brings into play all our faculties...Through no other experience can the full richness and complexity of our environment be realised. The ultimate value of equilibrium is that it is better to be fully than partially alive.'[44] Despite the obvious frailties of his rhetoric in such early writings, Richards more or less retained the theory of impulses in his later criticism, varying only the term he used to define the crucial 'mode of systematisation': 'synaesthesis', 'interinanimation', and 'feedback', and 'feedforward'.

Throughout his undergraduate career and up to the publication of *Seven Types of Ambiguity*, Empson seemed staunch in his loyalty to the doctrine, claiming without further exploration in 1930 that Richards had 'produced a workable theory of aesthetic value'. Yet he registered misgivings from quite an early stage, and by 1937 reserved judgement in describing it as 'a police theory [which] helps you to stop the narrower theories from obstructing your practice'. By 1950, in 'The Verbal Analysis', he seemed momentarily to surrender his faith to scepticism:

I do not deny that it may be a splendid thing to have a grand synthesis of human experience, a single coherent Theory of Value which could be applied to all works of art and presumably to all human situations; but it seems hardly reasonable to grumble, in the present state of affairs, that nobody has provided one; and if it did exist it would clearly be a philosophical synthesis rather than a literary one.

Earlier in the same piece he proposed his own practice of the 'depth analysis' of poetry as 'probably the best way out of this limiting critical impasse'—the impasse created by

the idea that poetry is good in proportion as it is complicated, or simply hard to construe; it seems quite a common delusion, and always shocks me when expressed. And yet I suppose it is very near my own position; in any case it joins on to I. A. Richards' Theory of Value as the satisfaction of more impulses rather than less, and T. S. Eliot's struggle to find a poetic idiom adequate to the complexity of modern life.

Making shifts between moral philosophy and psychology, Richards really begged as many questions as he contrived answers; his references seemed to be interchangeable.[45] Richards's biographer candidly defines the issue: 'Where he should have been proximate, he was definitive; where he should have challenged, he was clamorous. It is hard to be both tentative and inspiring.'[46] Among the problems posed by Richards's epistemology are the mercurial meanings of his terms for psychological wholeness—such as 'impulse', 'attitude', 'tension', 'opposition', and 'equilibrium'. Is 'impulse', for instance, psychological or philosophical? Is the aesthetic theory a matter of utterance or analysis, creativity or reception? 'The impulse theory provides no real explanation of the genesis or nature of attitudes,' laments Jerome P. Schiller. 'It simply assures us that Richards believed them to be central to the reading of poetry.'[47] Empson proposed to put his own qualms directly to I. A. Richards in 1933: 'I don't understand whether an impulse is defined as physiological or not. If it is I don't understand what its satisfaction is.'[48] More recently, John Needham has pointed out the deficiency of the general theory of value when it is applied to poetry:

Richards himself seems to be implicitly aware of the difficulty, because when he is presenting his general theory of value he talks straightforwardly of the 'satisfaction of appetencies', but when he is applying it to poetry he uses, not 'satisfaction', but words like 'balancing', 'reconciliation', 'adjustment', 'resolution', and so on... 'Impulse', as he defines it, is a useful term for Richards because it enables him, albeit unjustifiably, to slide from stimulus to response and back again as the needs of the moment dictate; but it brings him into intolerable difficulties. As his insights into the complexity of poetic *language* develop, he has to re-formulate the general theory of complexity in terms of a creative account of the mind, rather than a stimulus-response account.[49]

According to Russo, Richards had simply assumed the licence to have it both ways: 'his terms for psychological wholeness served almost equally well for literary analysis... This dual functioning of terms allowed Richards to slide between mind and poem and to understand and define one quite literally in terms of the other.'[50] The question goes on begging.

Richards did appear to believe, at least initially, that literary criticism was an auxiliary mode of psychology. 'I was someone really saturated in psychology and neurology making a book about the literary approaches,' he later said.[51] His aesthetic theory made use of a neurophysiological model derived from the work of C. S. Sherrington, though he refrained from acknowledging as much at the time. 'I just translated Shelley into Sherrington,' he casually admitted in 1970.[52] 'A polyvalent term in Richards,' says Russo, '*impulse* may refer to a whole spectrum of events or to any one of many separate events along it. Impulses are the vehicles on which a host of other elements—sensations, images, emotions, references—ride piggyback through the mind. At one end of the spectrum the impulse is the physiochemical happening . . .'[53] Such a presupposition would go far to explain the paucity of critical analysis in Richards's writings; as Russo has frankly observed, 'Richards was eighty-one when he published his first book of practical criticism, *Beyond*.'[54] (It certainly incited Empson to try to make good the neglect with his close 'practical' readings of poetry.) In *Practical Criticism* in particular, as John Needham regrets, 'the doctrine of equilibrium inhibits a fruitful development of Richards' work on poetic language.'[55]

According to the theory of value, poetry—which Richards later exalted as 'the supreme organ of the mind's self-ordering growth'[56]—can literally 'save' us:[57] it will replace religion by relegating any Magical view of the world and enthroning a fundamental secularism. Richards arrived at this doctrine by way of making a distinction between the language employed for enunciating true beliefs (essentially, scientific verities) and the language of poetry, which comprises 'pseudo-statements'. Pseudo-statements are 'not necessarily false,' he quite reasonably explained, but 'merely a form of words whose scientific truth or falsity is irrelevant to the purpose in hand.' Thus his argument runs:

Countless pseudo-statements—about God, about the universe, about human nature, the relations of mind to mind, about the soul, its rank and destiny—pseudo-statements which are pivotal points in the organization of the mind, vital to its well-being, have suddenly become, for sincere, honest and informed minds, impossible to believe as for centuries they have been believed . . .

This is the contemporary situation. The remedy . . . is to cut our pseudo-statements free from that kind of belief which is appropriate to verified statements. So released they will be changed, of course, but they can still be the main instruments by which we order our attitudes to one another and to the world.[58]

In short, belief in God (for example) is far less actual than fictional. T. S. Eliot deprecated this sort of secular salvationism as a boss shot; it seemed to him scarcely more than a revival of Matthew Arnold's views on Literature and Dogma: 'it is like saying that the wall-paper will save us when the walls have crumbled,' Eliot twitted his friend. But strangely enough, even though that brilliant image might appear to demolish Richards's aberration, Eliot still brought himself to concede, earlier in his review of *Science and Poetry*, that the theory

is probably quite true. Nevertheless it is only one aspect; it is a psychological theory of value, but we must also have a moral theory of value. The two are incompatible, but both must be held, and that is just the problem. If I believe, as I do believe, that the chief distinction of man is to glorify God and enjoy Him for ever, Mr Richards' theory of value is inadequate: my advantage is that I can believe my own and his too, whereas he is limited to his own.[59]

Not surprisingly, Empson felt baffled by Eliot's claim that he could readily accommodate both his own faith in the transcendent truths of the Christian religion and a doctrine of value which to all intents and purposes profaned it.[60]

Empson accordingly sought to strengthen the foundations of the doctrine, to stop the holes in Richards's rhetoric of assertion (and hence in his theory); and he believed he could best do so by challenging it. If it makes any sort of claim to universal validity, he felt, Richards's argument for a humanistic standard of valuation—which amounted to an argument for irreligion—must be capable of accounting for other cultures and religions. When Richards judged that traditional beliefs about God and Destiny should properly be levelled to the status of pseudo-statements, for example, he had clearly fixed his sights on the Christian conception of Heaven. Empson publicly, though sympathetically, put in question the effectively wholesale anti-religiosity of that judgement by way of the wider angle of an Appendix in *The Structure of Complex Words*. ' "Theories of Value" is a brilliant essay,' Empson's bibliographer Frank Day has rightly suggested, 'broad in understanding and eloquent in expression. It is one of the best things Empson has written and deserves to be more widely discussed, especially by those interested in Stanley Fish's notion of interpretive communities. Unless one insists that a value system has to be externally grounded—as I suppose [Hugh] Kenner does—...then Empson's rational appeal to community should be esteemed for its avoidance of egoism. If it's ultimately judged to be a sleight-of-hand trick in logic, then it's at least as convincing a magic show as any other under the big tent.'[61]

Empson was teaching in Japan from 1931 to 1934 when he started working towards the essay entitled 'Theories of Value', so he found it both convenient and fascinating to submit Richards's theory to the best local test, the Buddhist religion. In *The Foundations of Aesthetics* Richards had denied that synaesthesis could mean 'Nirvana, Ecstasy, Sublimation or At-oneness with Nature';[62] but Empson argued that the construction nowadays put upon the concept of Nirvana—that it stands for 'a re-absorption into the Absolute' (exactly the same alternative to the Christian concept of godhead for which he would argue from the 1950s onwards)—

brings [Buddhism] into line with a mystical strain within all the great religions, one which has usually been at loggerheads with the offer of Heaven; and there

I think we find the great historical antagonist of anything like the Richards Theory of Value—that is, of any self-fulfilment theory. It is opposed to any such theory not because it is pessimistic but because it does not believe in the individual. I cannot pretend that I have any capacity to act as a go-between in this quarrel . . . [I]f the Theory of value merely recommends the satisfaction of the human creature, whatever makes it really satisfied, Professor Richards need not be as secure against the religions as he intended to be. What satisfied the most impulses might turn out to be the same as what was to the glory of God or even as what tended to Nirvana.[63]

There is ultimately 'something of a notional Buddhism lurking in Empson's strenuously rational humanism,' Harold Beaver has observed in a notable essay review.[64] Indeed; and one of the aspects of Buddhism that Empson particularly favoured—as an essay called 'Death and its Desires' (1933) makes clear in its preliminary exploration of the arguments of 'Theories of Value'—was what he called its 'rationalizing escape from the fear of death [which] is carried so far that there is much less sense of tragedy and of the fascination of a sacrificial death than in Christianity with its certainly immortal individuals.' If any culture necessarily values the purposes of life by its estimate of the meaning of death, one certain attraction of Buddhism is that it seemed to resolve the paradox of at once doubting immortality and planning for a better life on earth. Buddhist art, it seemed to Empson, expressed just such 'a fundamental contradiction between death and a completely satisfying life'. Even in a radio broadcast on the subject of 'Life', written in Basic English for Station WRUL (Boston) in 1939, he felt duty bound to bring up Buddhism as the most heartening rival to Christianity—and it is noticeable that on this topic his tone heightens with enthusiasm, and his rhythm seems even to mime the 'Fire Sermon' itself:[65]

This is the teaching that went across all the East of Asia and by only touching a country made it strong. It seemed beautiful, it seemed safe, it seemed a new way of living and a good one and it gave fruit to millions of men. And this is what it said, and it said DEATH, there is no other possible good thing but death, and it said that very clearly. The facts about the behaviour of men are very much stranger than they seem to us. And so it is important to say . . . that almost all the effects of the Fire Sermon were good effects. For example, hundreds of thousands of men have been burned while still living in the name of Jesus, and probably no man has been so burned in the name of Buddha. But the Buddha said things that gave much more reason for burning, much more hate of common living, much more poison, if you are looking at the simple words, than the words of Christ. But in fact they did no damage. As a question of history, where these words came they did good.

(Because of that astounding paradox, Empson appropriately brings into play in 'Death and its Desires' the analogous psychological dimension of Freud's proposition in *Beyond the Pleasure Principle* (1920) that '*the end of all life is death*'—a formulation which Freud based on the natural observation that organic life can be seen ironically to desire it own demise: that is, it actually aims at self-extinction.)[66]

What particularly exercised Empson about Richards's Theory of Value was that its best case appeared to hinge on a distinction between 'balance' or 'equilibrium' and 'irresolution' or 'deadlock' (in which two or more conflicting states of mind fail to resolve)—as here in *Principles of Literary Criticism*: 'The equilibrium of opposed impulses, which we suspect to be the ground-plan of the most valuable aesthetic responses, brings into play far more of our personality than is possible in experiences of a more defined emotion... [W]hat happens is the exact opposite of a deadlock, for compared to the experience of great poetry every other state of mind is one of bafflement.'[67] Empson felt vexed that Richards's language appeared to polarize satisfaction and frustration, pleasure and pain, in a way that was linguistically beguiling but scarcely tenable in actual fact. 'It looks, however, as if there is one chink through which a Buddhist conclusion might creep into the arguments of Professor Richards; his rather mysterious distinction between a deadlock (which is bad) and a balance (which is good),' he wrote in 'Theories of Value'[68] (and again when reviewing a reissue of *The Foundations of Aesthetics*). As he phrased his objection to Richards in his draft letter (written in a Peking bar) of 2 April 1933—again with reference to the alternative perspective offered by Buddhism—

pain (I understand) is not an essential opposite of pleasure but a separate biological invention. The Buddhist position seems to be that pain is a result as well as cause of pleasure, that pleasure is essentially misleading because it is a creator of desire that eventually leads to pain. But this is mere assertion made convincing by seeming to invoke the removal-of-stimulus idea only (and backed up by transmigration): clearly some people escape from this life (supposing it is their only one) without getting much pain out of their pleasures. (Fatuous these terms are: the air as I write is full of pain and despair from a Russian prostitute being very slowly turned out of the bar—everybody having to collect the money and ornaments she has flung all over the floor, so that she is tremendously in command of the situation). But if pain is quite separate from pleasure it seems even less likely that the satisfaction and frustration of an impulse are (other things being equal) of equal and opposite value, which is (apparently) needed for your theory.

Moreover, even though the Theory of Value was in no sense hedonistic, Richards put it forward in the language of behaviourist psychology that he had learnt from John Watson and hence made value look like an essentially unconscious gain: a form of involuntarism.[69] Empson's rational humanism prohibited a state of unknowing. As far as he was concerned, any theory of value must afford a sense of deliberate responsibility: it must strike a fully conscious, rationalistic balance between 'charity and a sense of social values', for the ultimate criterion is 'more nearly a political one'. By way of obvious logical example, he suggests,

[behaviourists] would say that having an appetite for dinner, feeling sure you will get it, and getting it, is of negative value (or null as a limit): because a need has been unsatisfied and then merely satisfied after an interval. Obviously there is positive pleasure at both stages. It seems to me that there is positive pleasure in appetite because the creature is (a) conscious (b) capable of knowledge...

And so follows the crux of his argument—it informs all his writings on poetic and human value, most notably including his onslaught against Christianity—'it is the intellectuality of the creature that turns a state of need into a state of pleasure.'

Empson thus became intent on turning what he regarded as Richards's theory of an essentially passive (because behaviouristic) acquisition of value into a statement of supremely conscious apprehension. 'It seems clear that consciousness is somehow involved in value, because if there was no consciousness we would at any rate feel there was no value,' he declared in April 1933. Nonetheless, though he worried Richards's Theory of Value only in order to make it in every sense more purposeful, he continually endorsed Richards's secular morality—the morality he derived from Jeremy Bentham's concept of the individual as a 'trustee for the community'. Richards's theory of the fullest satisfaction of positive impulses (or 'appetencies') essentially constituted a reprise of Bentham's utilitarian proposition that some kind of 'moral arithmetic' can determine the value of the pleasurable and the good, which is in itself socially serviceable and not self-serving. Following J. S. Mill, Henry Sidgwick, and Bertrand Russell, Richards expressed the utilitarian ethic in this form in *Principles of Literary Criticism*:

the only reason which can be given for not satisfying a desire is that more important desires will thereby be thwarted. Thus morals become purely prudential, and ethical codes merely the expression of the most general scheme of expediency to which an individual or race has attained... Particularly is this so with regard to those satisfactions which require humane, sympathetic, and friendly relations between individuals. The charge of egoism, or selfishness, can be brought against a naturalistic or utilitarian morality such as this only by over-looking the importance of these satisfactions in any well-balanced life.[70]

Empson, continually seeking to apply such a pragmatic principle in his own life and writings, reaffirmed in 'The Hammer's Ring', his 1973 tribute to Richards: 'The idea of making a calculation to secure the greatest happiness for the greatest number is inherently absurd, but it seems the only picture we can offer.' Among the best reasons for supporting this 'Calculable Value' theory, he believed, is the necessity both to avoid arrogantly self-confirming critical judgements (that is, what Matthew Arnold called the fallacy of the 'personal estimate')—'the only alternatives to Bentham are arty and smarty moralising,' wrote Empson; 'giving unreasoned importance either to a whim of one's own or to the whim of a social clique'—and to appreciate different world-views without cultural prepossession:

The main purpose of reading imaginative literature is to grasp a wide variety of experience, imagining people with codes and customs very unlike our own; and it cannot be done except in a Benthamite manner, that is, by thinking 'how would such a code or custom work out?'[71]

Kenneth Burke's accusation against Empson that *Milton's God* 'deflects attention from the central relationship between religion and the social order' could hardly be farther from the mark, because Empson's high concern with social morality (which is evident even in his work of the 1930s, especially in *Some Versions of Pastoral*) led him to repudiate a religion which served only to damage a decent sense of life and literature. Richards utterly agreed.[72] The Christian God offered humankind nothing more than a casuistical contract; whereas for Empson, as Frank Day has rightly observed, 'the bedrock of systems of value is human rationality'.[73]

But if putatively neo-Christian critics offended authorial integrity by bleeding works of literature of their rational conflicts and moral resist-ances, perhaps the worst charge that can be made against Empson is that he too indulged a *parti pris*: making his critical findings a function of his moral expectations. Where the New Criticism virtually hypostatized the concepts of semantic autonomy and intrinsic value, Empson disdained formalism and insisted upon authorial rationality and critical common sense. If he could not be disinterested, however, he endeavoured always to resist reductivism, whether Christian or New Critical—the constrictions of doctrinaire morality or tidy theory. 'Mr Empson, perhaps, will never elaborate a critical, political or metaphysical system,' his friend Michael

Roberts perhaps advisedly forecast in 1936.[74] Instinct told Empson that to
enunciate any theory was to impose illogical and unnecessary limits on
critical and ethical enquiry. Iconoclastic but never anarchistic, he stood
out for the dignity of social order and the prerogative of individual human
reason. If he also eschewed the call to proclaim a critical creed, however,
reserving to his own practice all the rights of pragmatism, still it can be
seen from the bulk of his work that he avows at least an implicit theory of
the creative imagination itself. By definition, he judged, the best literature
is rationally protestant, often dissentient and rebellious, the expression not
of neurosis but of real mental conflict, and it externalizes the specific case
in a publicly accountable form. Empson's theory (if it is one) thus works to
emancipate the human mind from dogma and to make literature continuous with all human experience.

In the post-war years he would come more and more to believe that 'the
whole of "Eng. Lit." as a University subject needs to return to the
Benthamite position'[75]—very much for the reason that the liberation of
the author cannot be achieved unless the critic is made equally free, and
vice versa. In 1949, in 'A Doctrine of Aesthetics', he wrote, 'Perhaps the
real test of an aesthetic theory, at any rate while so little is known about the
matter, is how far it frees the individual to use his own taste and judgement; it must be judged in practice rather than abstract truth.' In so doing,
he reaffirmed the principle he had avouched at the outset of his career: 'the
crucial judgement lies with taste,' he insisted in 1936; 'it is hard to feel that
an adequate theory of literary criticism, if obtained, would be much more
than a device for stopping inadequate theories from getting in your way.'
He reiterated the sentiment in 1961, in 'Rhythm and Imagery in English
Poetry': 'It is not even clear that you want a theory, because its findings
must always be subject to the judgment of taste.' Yet to the end of his
career he applauded Richards's Theory of Value, even while remaining
doubtful that it had really and permanently defined the good effects of an
aesthetic experience. Critics who ignore it, he felt, inevitably offend against
the fundamental Benthamite spirit of capacious generosity. 'It was a fatal
step, I always think,' he wrote in a letter of 1959,

when Leavis began attacking Richards' Theory of Value, which however hard to
express properly is an essential plank in his platform; Leavis has never shown any
philosophical grasp of mind, and took for granted that he could strut about on the
rest of the platform without ever falling through the hole. The effect has been to
turn his intensely moral line of criticism into a quaintly snobbish one, full of the
airs and graces of an elite concerned to win social prestige, though this is much
opposed to his real background and sympathies.[76]

Certainly Richards stuck to his guns; in an unpublished 'Preface to a second edition' written on the flyleaf of his copy of *Principles of Literary Criticism,* he reiterated: 'It is indeed one of my main contentions that apart from such an ethical and psychological basis as I have outlined, Criticism must remain without principles.'[77]

Studying a literature, Empson similarly stressed in 1959, 'is frivolous unless related to judgements of value, experience of life, some kind of trying out [of] the different kinds of attitude or world-view so as to decide which are good ones.' It was exactly the same fine conviction he had voiced twenty-five years earlier, in 1934, while still finding his way as critic and teacher. In 'Teaching Literature', written for his students in Japan in the early 1930s, he stipulated that the benefits a student gains from literature are—in addition to pleasure—'fullness or breadth of emotional life, independence of mind and a sense of proportion'.

Richards's 'basic theory,' Empson noted in a letter to Richards's biographer in 1982, 'is a defense against absolutisms; it is not a thing you can extract rules from. He would have liked it to, or at least to give useful advice, and when he arrived at these formulations was hoping that Psychology would show the way, but hope soon became dim.' And Empson went on, loyal to the end: 'Of course I think there ought to be practical deductions, and probably would be by now if his work had been better understood.'[78]

Probably the most valuable remarks Empson made about his relationship with Richards, his sense of indebtedness, and the reservations he felt it necessary to enter, figure in an obituary piece written for the *London Review of Books.* Three points are worth extracting from the heart of this memoir. The first reports, as already noted, that by 1928 Empson had read and assimilated the aesthetic theories of the early Richards—on meaning, beauty, value—and had come to regard them as stable doctrine rather than provocative hot news:

Professor Basil Willey, in a *festschrift* for the eightieth birthday of Richards (1973), said that he not only founded modern literary criticism but supplied it with a vocabulary which has become accepted currency for so long that its origin is often forgotten. I now think this is true, but it was not clear to me when he was my supervisor. Willey was present at the first lectures by Richards at Cambridge, which became the *Principles* (1924), whereas I (then a math student) attended one or two of the lectures which became *Practical Criticism* (1929). His position had become familiar. My literary faction (Bronowski, for instance) accepted Richards as a great liberator who had made our work possible: but he kept telling us that each of his doctrines was only common sense, and that somebody had said it in the eighteenth century. Like the Mona Lisa of Pater, we imagined ourselves to be older than the rock on which we sat.[79]

The second point shows that while he accepted the aesthetic-pragmatic theory of value, even as a student he harboured misgivings about the freight of psychology and neurophysiology—the talk of 'impulses', 'appetencies', 'synaesthesis'—that Richards was attempting to import into literary criticism.[80] The scientific Richards, Empson goes on to say in his memoir,

was then expecting an intellectual revolution from psychology. While I was having a weekly supervision from Richards, in my final year, I was listening to the James Smith group, who favoured T. S. Eliot and Original Sin. After each of his supervisions, as I remember, though I had enjoyed and learned from them enormously, I would goad the enemy by reporting some theologically absurd remark, typical of an expert on Scientism. Within a year, I was defending him in some periodical against a particularly gross attack, so I was not actively disloyal; but it would be a mistake to suppose that Cambridge ever agreed on a monolithic acceptance of the view of Richards... [H]is analytic power always made people regard him as an extremist. (p. 227)[81]

He was not owning up to an early ambivalence, and his private disloyalty, only after Richards's death; he never denied this point of disagreement. In 1966, for example, he included in a published comment on an article entitled 'The Construction of *Seven Types of Ambiguity*', by James Jensen, this confession: 'I really was much influenced by Richards, but I thought it proper to learn from both sides, and would probably have said that I was on the side opposed to him. I am not sure when I decided that he had been quite right... when I positively chose the side of "scientism", though it wasn't till I began teaching in a Christian country that I realised the active harm done by the religion. The logical mysteries about "scientism" are certainly there, and part of the mystery about its truth, but that gives no excuse for worshipping the Devil instead.'

However, the final and most telling point to be highlighted in his obituary essay on Richards is a limiting judgement.

And yet most of what he was saying [in the 'Practical Criticism' lectures] was negative... He was concerned with a bafflement about what happens when people read, or about the aesthetic experience in general; it is important to realise that they are usually reading wrong, but apart from that, when is the effect a good one?... But the only definite part of the programme, it seems fair to say, was the removal of obstacles. (p. 227)

The astutely paradoxical observation that the 'definite' aspect of Richards's work on Practical Criticism was 'negative', being concerned with 'the removal of obstacles', does not imply that Richards brought matters to a dead end. On the contrary, he created an opportunity. As Empson likewise remarked in his contribution to the Richards Festschrift, 'The spell had been useful, as an incitement to action in young people who were just going to choose a field of work; it held open a glimmering entry to a royal garden, or an escape route which would entirely transform common experience, or at least ordinary theoretical problems.'[82] But Empson's observations do imply a query: why didn't Richards produce the critical analyses for which he had prepared the ground?

The short answer is simple: if Richards was the theorist, Empson was the practitioner—though not, it has to be said, according to Richards's guidelines.[83] The justification for that assertion must address the question of what Empson's writings owed to Richards's example and canons of criticism, along with the extent to which—with deep respect—he really had to beg to differ.

In addition to his qualms about the validity of the scientific terminology and the quasi-behaviouristic character of Richards's Theory of Value (which he otherwise endorsed to the nth degree), there was one area of disagreement that vexed Empson still more deeply. It was an issue on which Richards assumed a position that offended a principle of communication, Empson believed. Richards had argued in *Science and Poetry* (1926) that 'thought is not the prime factor' in poetry. 'Misunderstanding and under-estimation of poetry are mainly due to over-insistence on the thought in separation from the rest . . . It is never what a poem *says* which matters, but what it *is*.'[84] That pronouncement is a variant of Archibald MacLeish's 'poeticized' modernist dictum 'A poem should not mean | But be' (the last verset of 'Ars Poetica'), which Empson deplored for its perverse anti-rationalism. As Richards's biographer, John Paul Russo, puts the matter in an ugly phrase, Richards 'lowers the "idea" quotient' in poetry; and '[i]n this respect he was of his age: the revolt against intellect began towards the end of the nineteenth century in such thinkers as Nietzsche, James, and Bergson and intensified after World War I.'[85] The early Richards 'deliberately minimized the "sense" variable in a poem'.[86] Against this teaching, much of Empson's criticism worked hard to repair the rupture that Richards appeared to have introduced between 'emotive' and 'referential' (assertive and verifiable) language; between feeling and sense in a poem.[87] In literature, Empson argued, 'the medium is close to the discursive reason, and to cut them apart is unnatural'.[88] He later observed too, in *The Structure of Complex Words*, 'The trouble I think is that Professor Richards conceives the Sense of a word in a given use as something single, however "elaborate", and therefore thinks that anything beyond that Sense has got to be explained in terms of feelings, and feelings of course are Emotions, or Tones. But much of what appears to us as a "feeling" (as is obvious in the case of a complex metaphor) will in fact be quite an elaborate structure of related meanings. The mere fact that we can talk straight ahead and get the grammar in order shows that we must be doing a lot more rational planning about the process of talk than we have to notice in detail' (pp. 56–7). In response to that claim, Richards jotted these comments on the flyleaf of his copy of Empson's book: 'Disagreements with IAR? e.g. pp. 56–7. These seem, in the theoretic chapters (1 & 2) [which are pointedly accorded the binary titles "State-ments in Words" and "Feelings in Words", as if in deference to Richards] to be well-worth study. My feeling is that W.E. is almost always right in dissenting from what he takes I.A.R. to be saying, but nearly invariably wrong about that. In many instances, the two seem to be trying to say much the same thing in different ways. In others, some chance phrase of mine leads him to suppose in me a view I would violently disown . . .'[89]

But Empson can scarcely be blamed for any of his supposed misunder-standings—if such they were.[90] Christopher Isherwood was left in no doubt as to the gospel Richards purveyed in his lectures, and bowed to the prophet's bidding. 'In our conversation, we substituted the word "emotive" for the word beautiful.'[91] So too, Edward Upward—just like Empson—felt incensed by the false distinction that Richards laboured. B. K. Wilshaw, the 'amazing genius' who stands in for Richards in Upward's novel *No Home but the Struggle*, considered 'that poetry was "emotive", "emotive" being the key-word he habitually used to convey his view that poetry was concerned essentially with states of feeling, in contradistinction to science which was "intellectual" and was concerned with objective reality . . . His view that a poetic statement could not have any external "referent" was, as I came to realise before long, central to his whole poetic theory.'[92] Upward chastises Wilshaw's mistake on no fewer than three separate occasions in the novel. Empson combated the same error for twenty years.

Richards had been 'slightly wrong' in making a distinction between the affective and the referential modes of language, Empson would later explain in an indulgently understated letter, and he himself had 'intended to restore the unity . . . What Richards and I both recognized was that analysis must be able [to] say when language is used dishonestly, as when a demagogue attempts to cheat his hearers by exploiting the emotive uses of words so as to prevent them from following up the referential uses.'[93]

But Richards's unstable early rhetoric was a tremendous irritant to Empson. John Paul Russo seeks to note the gravity of this point of disagreement: 'Empson began by weighting the "sense" component in poetry more heavily, and this turned out to reveal deeper differences as their careers advanced. From *Seven Types* to "Argufying in Poetry" (1963) and the late controversies, Empson carried a rationalist standard and insisted on logical equivalence in poetry. As Richards explained [in informal conversation with Russo in 1978], "Empson was a mathematician and hence he took the quantitative side of things. Likes to think in terms of equations—Cambridge-type." '[94] That is fair enough as far as it goes; but it is not correct to say simply that Empson put more stress on sense than on feeling in poetry. As far as Empson was concerned, it was Richards who put too much weight on the supremacy of feeling; Empson himself had been concerned to hold the equation steady. What Empson looked for, he insisted in May 1930 (ironically enough, in an article defending *Practical Criticism* against a contemptuous attack in an Oxford periodical by his old school acquaintance John Sparrow), was 'organic coherence', the atonement of sense and feeling: indistinguishability. Accordingly, even as he pitted his wits against Sparrow, he ticked off Richards: 'Feeling and thought are not separate objects; in one of their senses they are more like an inside and an outside.'[95] This was not a mean, incidental matter. One of the major critical prescriptions of Richards's *Practical Criticism* runs as follows: 'Language—and pre-eminently language as it is used in poetry—has not one but several tasks to perform simultaneously.'[96] It is surprising to note that Richards uses the word 'simultaneously' at this point, since the burden of his argument serves to say that the reader cannot apprehend such a fusion of functions at one time; so that 'four types of meaning' (as he puts it) have to be distinguished: Sense, Feeling, Tone, Intention. There can be little doubt that this divisive idea had been impressed upon Empson for some months before the publication of *Practical Criticism*. Mrs Richards noted in her diary 'Ivor's lecture' on 25 October 1928: 'The big room crowded out, people sitting on the floor, me perched on a tressle with a dozen others at the back, over 200 present. All about *Meaning* being divided into Sense. Feeling. Tone. Intention. A great clarifier.' The difficulty of making out the sense of a poem, Richards decreed, is as nothing in comparison with trying to grasp the 'will-o'-the-wisp' of feeling.[97] The solution is to undertake 'two kinds of paraphrasing ... the one to exhibit the sense of a poem, the other to portray its feeling' (pp. 223–4). Notwithstanding that proposition, he wrote, 'we do not yet know how to analyse' feeling (p. 217). Nonetheless, the language itself is a 'repository, a record' of feeling, and 'our power of interpreting the psychological records embodied in words is increasing and capable of immense increase in the future. Among the means to this end a combination or co-operation of psychology and literary analysis, or criticism, seems the most hopeful' (pp. 218–19).

Empson rebuffs this simplistic, tidy taxonomy in chapter 8 of *Seven Types of Ambiguity*—in which he otherwise consolidates many of the principles set out (in 'Part III: Analysis') of *Practical Criticism*, including the nature of beliefs in poetry ('you have to be a person who is liable to act as if they were true,' wrote Empson, alluding to Hans Vaihinger's *Philosophy of As/If* (1911); while Richards presently deployed the deft phrase 'imaginative assent'). A conceptual apparatus that seeks to separate Sense, Feeling, Tone, and Intention will not do, Empson argued; to divide is to spoil, to misrepresent:

[T]he process of apprehension, both of the poem and of its analysis, is not at all like reading a list ... People remember a complex notion as a sort of feeling that involves facts and judgments ... But to state the fact and the judgment (the thought and the feeling) separately, as two different relevant matters, is a bad way of suggesting how they are combined; it makes the reader apprehend as two things what he must, in fact, apprehend as one thing.[98]

By way of reproving Richards's notion that psychology and literary criticism might combine to unearth the repository of feelings buried in language, he added: 'Detailed analysis of this kind might be excellent as psychology, but it would hardly be literary criticism' (p. 238). But the primary thing, he reiterated in the next paragraph, is co-instantaneity and not disintegration: '[T]o say a thing in two parts is different in incalculable ways from saying it as a unit ... [T]he only way of not giving something heterogeneous is to give something which is at every point a compound' (pp. 238–9).

In 1947 Stanley Edgar Hyman acutely observed that while Richards had often put on record his enormous admiration for Empson's poetry, 'nowhere in his books does [he] more than mention Empson's criticism or quote briefly from it, to my knowledge.' There was little change in that less-than-due regard for the next twenty-five years—until, that is, Richards came to write a curiously equivocal tribute for the Empson Festschrift in 1974. In 'Semantic Frontiersman' he ducks and weaves around the prospect of saying something sensible about *Complex Words* (as the editor of the volume had asked him to do); and even when he does offer his tribute, he manages at once to give and to take away. *Seven Types of Ambiguity* and *The*

Structure of Complex Words, he says, assuredly did ' "raise the standards" ' of
the elucidative commentary on literature'. But that obeisance must needs
be qualified, it seems:

> In saying that Empson's best work in elucidative comment 'raised the standards'
> I have obviously to guard against misapprehensions. I am *not* saying that people in
> general, after studying him, did such work better—became more enterprising and
> effective. Far from it ... And I am *not* saying that *all* of Empson's elucidative (or
> would-be elucidative) writing is on this new high level. I am saying only that at his
> best he is able to point out, describe, and make evident co-operations and
> interactions among meanings on a scale and with a subtlety and resource not to
> be found in previous critics.[99]

And so he goes on, betraying all the signs of penning a decidedly constrained testimonial, or like a parody of a pedant. Empson may be a
virtuoso, but he is generally lacking in 'reconstitutive or seminal powers'
(p. 101). Most of the work in *Ambiguity* and *Complex Words*, Richards alleges,
'is *experimentation in paraphrase*' (p. 106; Richards' italics)—which is surely a
palpable slight, for Empson was doing far more than merely follow the
recommendation that Richards himself made in *Practical Criticism*. But
what is especially noteworthy is that Richards ends up rubbing the very
spot where an old sore smarted after all those years: 'the referential and
emotive functions can maintain their "unity and married calm" (as Shakespeare's Ulysses has it) only by preserving their due independence'
(p. 108).

In view of Empson's misgivings about the critical relevance of 'scientism'
(including neurophysiology) to poetry, and his vexation with Richards's
anti-rationalist postulate that 'It is never what a poem *says* which matters,
but what it *is*' (including the unwarranted privileging of feeling over sense),
a further key question becomes unavoidable: did *Seven Types of Ambiguity*
actually owe all that much to Richards, whether as theorist or as critic? No
one who knew Richards as a teacher, or heard him lecture, disputes that he
was a great analyst of poetry. His biographer Russo sings a paean on this
theme: 'In his practical criticism Richards had a microscopic eye, a gift for
a literary critic perhaps even greater than theoretical brilliance. He is the
Leeuwenhoek of criticism; to him were finer optics given ... For those who
heard him lecture, he left the indelible impression of having gazed upon
the ultimate particles of poetry.'[100] However, on the evidence of the works
by Richards that were available to Empson in 1928, and even by 1929, one
might take leave to question the fulsomeness of that praise. Hugh Carey

remarks that the commentary in *Practical Criticism* is 'somewhat indeterminate'. Similarly, where W. H. N. Hotopf once ventured to observe that Richards's 'comments on the more valuable poems are generally oblique,' he receives a dusty response from Russo: 'This misses the point of Richards' exercise; he was not claiming to do "close readings" of entire poems; he was correcting misreadings, and his comments are quite specific.'[101]

All the same, it seems fair to ask why Richards did not provide a model of 'practical criticism' in the book of that title. Equally it would be fair for a defendant to answer that Richards could not offer such a 'working model' because he knew the identities of the authors of the poems used for the exercise, as well as their dates: not only would it have been far too easy, too swanky, to trump the writers of the 'protocols' on that score, it would have violated the (specious) principle of textual objectivity to which he adhered. But then again, a plaintiff might say, it would have been a straightforward matter for Richards himself to sit some sort of 'unseen' test administered by a third party. As things stand in *Practical Criticism*, he has the advantage (even if it is not of his seeking) over the students who took his course: willy-nilly he had access to information that was extraneous to the set poems.[102] Nevertheless, we must graciously accept that Richards was a master analyst. Joan Bennett firmly reported that he 'was an exciting and trustworthy interpreter partly because his response to each poem was not only intellectually alert but also intuitive and strongly felt'.[103] But his exegetical gems were reserved for the lecture hall, it seems; books were for theory, not interpretation. In any case, he was averse to the interventionism that practical analysis stood for: 'Richards thought that most literary glosses failed to perform the same clarifying function served by good theory.'[104] In sum, if anyone wanted 'practical' criticism, they should do it for themselves.

In truth, anyone who desires to show posterity that the early Richards really could do a bit of practical criticism must needs turn to one of the few places where he does have a go, on page 215 of *Practical Criticism*: it is an explication of G. H. Luce's line about clouds at sunset—'O frail steel tissues of the sun'—which Richards himself (who misquotes the line) offered as 'a fairly detailed analysis'. John Paul Russo claims that this passage 'exemplifies the close reading method as it stood in 1929':

'Tissue', to begin with the noun, has a double sense; firstly, 'cloth of steel' in extension from 'cloth of gold' or 'cloth of silver', the cold, metallic, inorganic quality of the fabric being perhaps important; secondly, 'thin, soft, transparent' as with tissue-paper. 'Steel' is also present as a sense-metaphor of Aristotle's second kind, when the transference is from *species* to *genus*, steel a particular kind of strong material being used to stand for any material strong enough to hold together, as it appears, the immensity of the cloud-structure. The colour suggestion of 'steel' is also relevant. 'Frail' echoes the semi-transparency of 'tissue', the diaphanousness, and the impending dissolution too. 'Of the sun' it may be added runs parallel to 'of the silk worm' [a phrase which does not figure in the poem], i. e., produced by the sun. I give such an elaborate explanation partly because of the many readers (10.42) who had difficulty in making out this line.[105]

What is quite evident from the context is that Richards found it pretty tiresome to have to explain even thus much. Yet Russo, intent upon proving that Richards had it in mind to illuminate an ambiguity in Luce's line of poetry, has no compunction about supplying rather more than the gloss that Richards offered: ' "Frail" is the opposite of steel-like; hard steel the opposite of soft tissue; tissue is midway between opacity and transparency; the organic dissolution of the "sprawling domes" of clouds in the prior line undoes the mechanical erection of an immense edifice. The double senses of the words elicit equilibrium in response out of the structures in the text.'[106] I do not pretend to understand what that last sentence means; but it is clear that Russo makes a different point from the original. Richards is concerned only to convince his audience that in all likelihood they *felt* it was a good line of poetry *before* they came to under-stand it: 'It will be agreed that the sense here is intricate, and that when it is analysed out it shows a rational correspondence with the feeling which those readers who accept the line as one of the felicities of the poem may be supposed to have experienced... How far does this logical structure which appears to him while reading seem the source of the feeling of the words? Does it not rather remain in a vague background, more a possi-bility than an actuality?' (pp. 214–15). For Richards, then, the sense of the line is an aftertaste—at best, it functions as a chaser to the feeling of the poem: 'a feeling that is quite pertinent seems often to precede any clear grasping of the sense' (p. 216). In any event, he was really not explaining the workings of ambiguity in poetry.

Furthermore, Richards himself well knew—several months before pub-lishing his reluctant gloss on Luce's line (with its incidental ambiguity that Russo belatedly pins down on his behalf)—that Empson had brought forth, at remarkable speed, a sustained argument about seven types of ambiguity, along with detailed analyses. Jacob Bronowski recorded in his diary the fact that Empson gave a talk on ambiguity as early as 20 January 1929;[107] and Dorothea Richards noted in her diary for 5 May 1929: 'Went on to Empson's paper on *Ambiguity* which he gabled through. All came back with Elsie Elizabeth [Phare], Marks, Saltmarshe, Empson & Hallihan [an American pupil of Richards'].' (The Hispanist Edward M. Wilson would later express gratitude not so much to I. A. Richards for his 'practical' theories as to Empson for the great exegetical leap of ambiguity, and for those early talks; he was to tell Empson in 1957, 'My great debt to you is that your conversation, your lecture to the [H]eretics and your *Ambiguity* taught me to see what was down on the paper before me.')[108] The first publication of all this work by Empson appeared in February 1929, in the periodical *Experiment* (co-edited by Empson), which prinked itself out in the wonderful analysis of ambiguity of syntax (double meaning) in Shakespeare's Sonnet XVI that would go straight into *Seven Types*: truly, that piece exemplifies the method of close reading as it stood in 1929.[109]

Still, Russo is keen to give his man the credit for virtually everything—including the machinery of poetic ambiguity that Empson first deployed:

Seven Types contains Richards' influence in its kernel idea, structure, method, terms, and conclusions. The kernel idea combines contextualism with the notion that ambiguities can be plotted in 'stages of advancing logical disorder.' This is a step beyond the insight towards which Richards had groped for a decade, and which he had stated succinctly in *Practical Criticism*: 'ambiguity in fact is systematic.' ... What Richards had attempted to do with 'emotion,' 'beauty,' and 'meaning,' Empson performed on ambiguity ... (p. 526)

Every aspect of ambiguity taken up in *Practical Criticism* received extensive elaboration in succeeding years. First, the search for multiple meanings and their 'systematic interlocking ambiguity' became the hallmark of 'close reading' and the New Criticism, threatening to become an end in itself in the hands of Richards' disciples ... In view of subsequent trends—Empson's ambiguity [etc.]—Richards' promotion of ambiguity from a minor to a major—*the* major—literary device was a historic moment in criticism. (pp. 279–80)

Russo's work is comprehensive and erudite, but these passages are misleading to a severe degree. For one obvious matter, Empson was by no means concerned to define the meaning of 'ambiguity' in the way that Richards proposed to define the meanings of 'emotion', 'beauty', and 'meaning'. Far from defining 'ambiguity' as an abstract term, he sought to describe some versions of the behaviour of ambiguity in poetry—the ambiguous effects, chiefly lexical and syntactical, as inscribed, consciously or unconsciously, in particular poems.

Whatever else Richards meant by the term 'ambiguity' when he used it in his early writings, he did not mean what Empson took it to mean. In

Principles of Literary Criticism (1924) he insisted, for example: 'Ambiguity in a poem . . . may be the fault of the poet or of the reader.'[110] Again, when John Middleton Murry was to complain that *The Waste Land* offended 'the most elementary canon of good writing' by being ambiguous in its 'immediate effect', Richards seemed to accept the charge only to suggest that the reader gets over the problem with a little more application: 'Even the most careful and responsive reader must re-read and do hard work before the poem forms itself clearly and unambiguously in his mind.'[111] As Russo glosses Richards's point here, 'the final effect is some kind of clarity in which the ambiguities are resolved.' That is not Empson's position at all: he is not looking to *settle* ambiguities, as if they represent some kind of literary indigestion, but to celebrate the polysemy of poetry, its weft and warp of mixed meanings. Likewise, the phrase from *Practical Criticism* that Russo takes to be a clincher—'Ambiguity in fact is systematic' (p. 10)— Richards is in fact applying *not* to poetic language but to the language of criticism, those rhetorical reach-me-downs—the 'omnipresent ambiguity of abstract terms' (p. 344), 'the inevitable ambiguity of almost all verbal formulae' (p. 341)—that do duty for the genuine discriminations that are the 'choice of our whole personality'. Richards quite rightly laments the ambiguity of such abstractions: 'Words like "sincerity", "truth", "senti-mentality", "expression", "belief", "form", "significance", and "meaning" itself, seem to those who rely on them to hit the mark repeatedly in an almost miraculous fashion. But this is only because a cloud of heterogeneous missiles instead of a single meaning is discharged on each occasion . . .' (p. 300).

Still Russo seeks to reinforce the suggestion that Richards is actually concerned with ambiguity in poetic expression by offering this gloss on another passage from *Practical Criticism*: 'Poetic language is even more ambiguous because of its compression; it does many things discursive language either does not do or does only by "spatializing" its ideas.'[112] Yet again, however, on looking up the reference, one finds that Richards is discussing *not* ambiguity but rather the density, the amplitude, of 'ideas' in poetry (which is not the same thing), and the consequent difficulties of analysis: 'the compression of poetic language tends to obstruct the discursive intelligence that works by spreading ideas out and separating their parts.'[113] ('Spatializing' is not his word: it is Russo's.)

Most important of all, Russo's exaltation of Richards as the discoverer and champion of ambiguity in poetry effectively gives the lie to Empson's own account, written in 1966, of his complex relationship with Richards:

Richards was tutoring me for the First Part of the English Tripos, not to write a book, and he made sure I had looked round the field; I seem to remember a number of bad essays about novels. Two hours may have been spent on ambiguity, but not more . . . I would not have allowed Richards to give me 'prolonged tuition' about how to write my book, because I disagreed with him in principle . . .

Empson was so deeply versed in Richards's writings, and not reluctant to give credit where it was due, that one ought to respect his testimony. (One may compare, for example, this acknowledgement in *Ambiguity*: 'most of what I find to say about Shakespeare has been copied out of the Arden text.')[114] If he had truly believed himself to be developing an idea discovered by Richards, he would have said so. Apart from that act of trust, we have the authority of Richards's own admission, in *Practical Criticism*, that he had not yet found a way fully to fathom the behaviour of ambiguity in poetry, whether cognitive or conative—let alone as a coefficient phenomenon: 'Words, as we all recognise, are as ambiguous in their feeling as in their sense; but, though we can track down their equivocations of sense to some extent, we are comparatively helpless with their ambiguities of feeling.'

As for the issue of 'principle' on which Empson said he disagreed with Richards at the time, Russo has reasonably suggested that it might have concerned the psychoanalytical tricks (the so-called 'Depth Psychology') that Empson borrowed from Freud and put to use in *Ambiguity*;[115] but it may well have been Empson's initial ambivalence vis-à-vis the place of 'scientism' in literary criticism; or again his disgruntlement with Richards for proposing to split the atom of sense-and-feeling in poetry; or even a combination of those three factors. Empson might have realized too that the theory of poetry-as-conflict which he personally espoused had no validity in Richards's scheme of value other than in the unsatisfactory category of 'deadlock'.

Richards held supervisions in his bohemian, sparsely furnished teaching room on the third floor of a rickety old building at 1 Free School Lane. The heater stood not in the fireplace but alongside two wicker chairs in the middle of the room; the fireplace was adorned with photographs of mountains; the parti-coloured (predominantly orange) walls seemed to be papered with jottings—a collage of quotations that were so much easier to spot than if they had been entered tidily into notebooks. Margaret Gardiner, who waited on Richards in this milieu, has left a memorable account of it all:

If he was in when you called to see him, he would offer you tea and hand you biscuits in the lid of a biscuit tin; if he was out, you could catch up on what he had been thinking about because he had the habit of leaning out of his chair and scribbling his ideas on the wall. I was told—although the existence of the crowded bookshelves belied this—that he so strongly disapproved of possessions that he would tear each page out of a book after reading it, scrumple it up and toss it into the waste-paper basket.

In spite of all the adulation that came his way, there was nothing in the least bit bigsy about Richards. He had a way of seizing upon any shred of interest in what others said, however banal, and transmuting it into a new and exciting idea. It was, I think, this rare and generous gift that made him such a splendid teacher: he was able to make one feel—and therefore perhaps even to become—more intelligent and interesting than one really was. He was always encouraging, never impatient or sarcastic.[116]

There is no record of the 'bad essays about novels' that Empson read up; but it seems likely that among others he and Richards discussed *The Turn of the Screw* and *Heart of Darkness*, which were among Richards's favourite texts; of poetry, probably Donne, Hardy, Hopkins, and Yeats in particular (Richards did not like the early Yeats, but enormously admired *The Tower*, 1928); and otherwise, as Empson said, the curriculum for Part I of the Tripos. Whatever the text, these supervisions were concentrated, vibrant, voluble affairs. Forty-five years later, Richards could still recall the day 'when Empson suddenly ended a supervision by leaping from his chair to shout through his mirth. "Metaphysical poetry! Why, we've been *talking* metaphysical poetry all the morning!" '[117] In her diary for 14 November 1928, Dorothea Richards gives us this glimpse of the gaucherie of her husband's prize pupil and his fellows (and perhaps especially their awkwardness in the unaccustomed presence of a grown-up female):

Three young men to tea—very shy—[J. H. P.] Marks is the half-Spaniard & the most mature—he has an air of savoir faire—though they all tend to jump about a good deal in school boy fashion—[Christopher] Saltmarshe—wears a grey suit, pink ties & a trailing manner—was *so* shy that he couldn't get his words out properly & he is publishing a current Cambridge book of verse [*Cambridge Poetry 1929*]. Redgrave the actor, poet looks the completest child & had a quite bewitch-ing charm. He didn't say much—they none of them did—because Ivor's head ached & he got a monologue going at such a rate that he simply daren't stop for fear of a silence:—so nobody else dared to speak. After coaching Empson—a boorish person who glares at nothing as if I didn't exist & he wished he didn't, when I come into the room—Ivor came home & went to bed to nurse his cold—

It is hardly surprising to learn that Richards found it a huge relief when his most intensely clever student asked if he could go about his own business for a while:

William Empson made his name first with *Seven Types of Ambiguity*, a book which came into being more or less in the following fashion [he recalled in 1940]. He had been a mathematician at Cambridge and switched over for his last year to English. As he was at Magdalene, this made me his Director of Studies. He seemed to have read more English Literature than I had, and to have read it more recently and better, so our roles were soon in some danger of becoming reversed. At about his third visit he brought up the games of interpretation which Laura Riding and Robert Graves had been playing with the unpunctuated form of 'The expense of spirit in a waste of shame.' Taking the sonnet as a conjuror takes his hat, he produced an endless swarm of lively rabbits from it and ended by 'You could do that with any poetry, couldn't you?' This was a Godsend to a Director of Studies, so I said, 'You'd better go off and do it, hadn't you?' A week later he said he was still slapping away at it on his typewriter. Would I mind if he just went on with that? Not a bit. The following week there he was with a thick wad of very illegible typescript under his arm—the central 30,000 words or so of the book. [In fact, it was about 15,000 words.] I can't think of any literary criticism written since which seems likely to have as persistent and as distinctive an influence. If you read much of it at once, you will think you are sickening for 'flu'; but read a little *with care* and your reading habits may be altered—for the better, I believe.[118]

That account differs in no significant particular from the acknowledgement Empson made in a prefatory note added to the first edition of *Ambiguity*:

Mr I. A. Richards, then my supervisor for the first part of the English Tripos, told me to write this essay, and various things to put in it; my indebtedness to him is as great as such a thing ever should be. And I derive the method I am using from Miss Laura Riding's and Mr Robert Graves' analysis of a Shakespeare Sonnet

 The expense of spirit in a waste of shame,
in *A Survey of Modernist Poetry.*

As James Jensen remarked, 'What *does* a teacher do when confronted with an unprecedented talent mounted upon a sheer access of enthusiasm?' Yet we must note, in Richards's genially ironic piece, the scepticism of the phrase 'the games of interpretation', which seems to suggest that his pupil was seeking to go in for a possibly pointless mode of pure play (as against the play of feeling on which Richards focused attention), along with his remark that reading a little too much Empson can leave one feeling feverishly ill; so too, in Empson's preface, the curiously equivocal words in which he acknowledges a debt that is 'as great as such a thing ever should be'. Such canny phrases are I think explained by Empson's preface to the second edition of *Ambiguity* (London, 1947, p. viii):

I was surprised there was so little of the book I should prefer to change. My attitude in writing it was that an honest man erected the ignoring of 'tact' into a point of honour. Apart from trailing my coat about minor controversies, I claimed at the start that I would use the term 'ambiguity' to mean anything I liked, and repeatedly told the reader that the distinctions between the Seven Types which he was asked to study would not be worth the attention of a profounder thinker. As for the truth of the theory which was to be stated in an irritating manner, I remember saying to Professor I. A. Richards in a 'supervision' (he was then my teacher and gave me crucial help and encouragement) that all the possible mistakes along this line ought to be heaped up and published, so that one could sit back and wait to see which were the real mistakes later on.

It is evident that he must have felt impishly disingenuous from the start. What Richards reckoned to be a mistaken line of criticism, Empson took with full seriousness. That last paragraph as it stands is mock modest (as Roger Sale was perhaps the first to remark);[119] and indeed the very next sentence caps it by cocking a snook at the stimulating disincentive of his old teacher: 'Sixteen years later I find myself prepared to stand by nearly the whole heap.'

The quintessence of the theory of ambiguity according to Empson may have been incited by I. A. Richards, but actually it owes just as much, if not more, to the work of Sigmund Freud and Robert Graves. Empson enunciated just what he had in mind when the young Newnhamite star Elsie Phare submitted to him, in his capacity as co-editor of *Experiment*, an article entitled 'Valéry and Gerard Hopkins' (a version of which was published in the first issue in November 1928). Empson dispatched his response in September, but by way of mining his own vein of interest. This is crucial:

Commentators on Shakespeare will imply 'the man is being obscure again', and give three things in the notes, some one of which they think the word 'means'; usually the effect of the passage involves the word meaning all three and more. Passages in 'The Windhover' in the same way mean both the opposites created by their context, it seems plain; Richards said that once, and then edged away from it.
　'Buckle' [in the sestet of 'The Windhover'] means at once girt about you, like a belt, for war, and/or buckled like a bicycle-wheel, smashed by accident and no longer working. 'Here' means at once either the bird or the fire. It is a trick often

used in poetry, and always in jokes, to express two systems of values, an agony or indecision of judgement. Freud and Ambivalence, in fact, I wish you had driven that home . . . [120]

Both paragraphs of that letter would find their place, with remarkably little change, in *Seven Types of Ambiguity*. The first part, about the superabundance of meanings in Shakespeare, figures in the discussion of the second type of ambiguity (second edition, p. 81); and the second, concerning the conflicts of opposites in Hopkins, in Empson's discussion of the seventh type, which is the acme of ambiguity—'the most ambiguous that can be conceived'. This ultimate type amounts to 'full contradiction', a point of apparently utter irrationality or at least diametric opposition. Such a binary opposition 'occurs when the two meanings of the word, the two values of the ambiguity, are the two opposite meanings defined by the context, so that the total effect is to show a fundamental division in the writer's mind'.[121]

The element that Empson calls 'Freud and Ambivalence' enters into the scheme of the seventh type because, as he explains in *Ambiguity*, opposites 'are an important element in the Freudian analysis of dreams': the analysis whereby opposition at least signifies dissatisfaction. 'In more serious cases, causing wider emotional reverberation, such as are likely to be reflected in language, in poetry, or in dreams, it marks a centre of conflict . . . ' As an extension of this proposition—that dreams unify opposites, or show them as one thing, or even represent 'any element whatever by the opposite wish'—Freud had chanced in 1910 on a pamphlet by the philologist Karl Abel, *Über den Gegensinn der Urworte* (published in 1884), which he said first enlightened him as to 'the strange tendency of the dream-work to disregard negation and to express contraries by identical means of representation'. In a number of languages, Egyptian, Semitic, and Indo-European, he noted, there are relics of the primitive world in which a number of words have two meanings: 'one of which says the exact opposite of the other'. But what may strike us now as a lexical peculiarity, the sheer absurdity of words which unite antithetical meanings, came about because our very conceptions arise from comparison. Primitive man, according to Abel, 'only gradually learnt to separate the two sides of the antithesis and think of the one without conscious comparison with the other.' Whereupon Freud, in ' "The Antithetical Sense of Primal Words" ' (his review of Abel's book), took this peculiarity of the contradictory meanings that seem to be a habitual phenomenon in primitive languages as 'a confirmation of our supposition in regard to the regressive, archaic character of thought-expression in dreams'.[122]

Empson, who considered that such words are equally 'to be expected from a rather sophisticated state of language and of feeling', drew upon Freud's piece for his description of the seventh type of poetic ambiguity (pp. 194–5)—the sort that combines 'two opposite meanings defined by their context' and is unable to arbitrate between them, thus marking an absolute contradiction. But earlier still, he described this formulation in a further missive to Phare, who had questioned the terse assertion in his first letter that the verb 'Buckle' in 'The Windhover' necessarily carries all its possible meanings at once—however irresolute or torn with conflict it leaves the final effect of the poem. Taking Freud on the nature of opposites as his sole text, without qualification, Empson explained his steely view in the first week of October 1928 (it is worth noting that this was just before he began to be supervised by Richards; he wrote from his home in York, prior to the start of the academic year):

You say the two meanings of buckle are simply two, and can be held together in the ordinary way. But they *are* the opposites created by the context; the life strung to activity, the life broken and made static. (The fact is, this idea of opposites is a factitious one; you can string, as it were, a scale, between any two points.) All that makes them opposites is the poet's wish to connect them, the variety of impulses which make one suggest the other. In the obscure field where images take effect in poetry, they are the most natural form of two meanings joined in one word. P, if you like, is the opposite of not P, but they both state the outline between them. Primitive languages have the same word for two opposites; you state, as it were, the scale of grey, and whether you mean black or white is conveyed incidentally. 'Not' is a late and strange human invention, used with a variety of meanings whenever the thinker found himself in a difficulty. And in the dream-world considered by analysis, opposites of a certain kind are regarded as interchangeable, both referring to the same more elaborate state. 'Of a certain kind' certainly seems important; common sense, any orderly attitude to the world, is so dependent on distinctions, and if any conclusion might safely be negated you would have No conclusion at all. But that it is effective in poetry, and, as I say, jokes, I must say I believe.

You say the poem then consists of two alternate meanings, according to which meanings you take. It would consist of many more. But as the meanings are all connected with one another, and make—rather pitifully perhaps— different statements about the same situation under the same sets of impulses, they produce a very rounded and grand unity. You might as well say contrapuntal writing was several different tunes—you might certainly say it to me anyway, as I always find it a question of listening to one and letting the others take effect. But the others *do* take effect, especially of course when you know it better.[123]

For Richards, the idea that conflicts in poetry might add up to a total contradiction—wherein 'the two meanings of the word, the two values of the ambiguity, are the two opposite meanings defined by their context, so that the total effect is to show a fundamental division in the writer's mind'—was intolerable.[124] Whatever the refractoriness of the 'impulses' that constitute it, Richards believed, the true poem must finally effect a 'coherent systematization' of those impulses: the requisite balance or equilibrium. 'A complete systematisation must take the form of such an adjustment as will preserve free play to every impulse, with entire avoidance of frustration.' Empson stressed that he was at odds with Richards on this issue when he added to *Ambiguity* this footnote: 'It may be said that the contradiction must somehow form a larger unity if the final effect is to be satisfying. But the onus of reconciliation can be laid very heavily on the receiving end.' Richards's predicate in *Principles of Literary Criticism* and *Practical Criticism* is that the poem, if it is to be valuable, has to be a point of organization, of harmonization; so that always in a poem, if it truly possesses value, there is an order, a wholeness, a portion of goodness, to which the reader, despite difficulties and distractions, must duly respond. In consequence, 'when the conflict resolves itself, when the obstruction goes down or the crumple is straightened out . . . the mind clears, and new energy wells up; after the pause a collectedness supervenes; behind our rejection or acceptance (even of a minor poem) we feel the sanction and authority of the self-completing spirit.'[125] As against that beautiful notion, that idealism, Empson offered a more commonsensical, humane, available reckoning: 'human life is so much a matter of juggling with contradictory impulses (Christian-worldly, sociable-independent, and such-like) that one is accustomed to thinking people are probably sensible if they follow first one, then the other, of two such courses; any inconsistency that it seems possible to act upon shows that they are in possession of the right number of principles, and have a fair title to humanity.'

Undoubtedly, that passage from *Ambiguity* is a refreshing quaff of realism. But it was not promulgated just to fit the thesis of ambiguity. Empson had spoken in such terms for months before he came to think of filling up his book, most notably when—in his capacity as literary editor of *The Granta*, and while still a mathematical student—he reviewed a volume happily entitled *Opposite Things*, by M. Carta Sturge, in March 1928:

Extremely often, in dealing with the world, one arrives at two ideas or ways of dealing with things which both work and are needed, but which entirely contradict one another. Very often in the past a new idea or way of dealing with things has been found, which includes the two old ones, and when you think back to them as particular cases they 'obviously' don't contradict any more. Scientific examples not yet resolved are the static and dynamic atom models, the corpuscular and wave theories of light. I can't at the moment think of any already resolved, one forgets them because they no longer seem contradictory.

Miss Sturge is expounding this very important process with reference to Hegel; but she is not much concerned with him; she could get it out of the practise of scientists, recent mathematical logic, primitive languages, the doctrine of the Trinity, the corresponding Eastern ideas, and, in fact, out of anything of any importance.[126]

It is precisely this recognition that he had already made a chief theme of his own poetry. He would spell it out in the notes to a later poem, 'Bacchus': 'life involves maintaining oneself between contradictions that can't be solved by analysis'—an observation which has its counterpart in *Ambiguity*: 'The object of life, after all, is not to understand things, but to maintain one's defences and equilibrium and live as well as one can; it is not only maiden aunts who are placed like this.' In the terms of that last sentence, of course, Richards would have been quite in sympathy with Empson's theory, for the notion of preserving a dynamic balance or equilibrium was his own. Empson, in his analysis of Herbert's 'The Sacrifice', makes use of Richards's key terms to explain both the motivation and the effect of the poem: 'the contradictory impulses that are held in equilibrium by the doctrine of atonement'—the Christian Atonement—create 'a luminous juxtaposition'.[127] What is so astonishing about the poem is that Herbert—never relaxing his stanzaic and rhythmic scheme (a frame, as Empson superbly characterizes it, 'of monotonous and rather naive pathos, of fixity of doctrinal outlook, of heartrending and straightforward grandeur')—magnificently accepts what Empson regards as an abhorrent 'theological system' that lashes together the love of God and an unspeakable retributiveness. '[T]he various sets of conflicts in the Christian doctrine of the Sacrifice are stated with an assured and easy simplicity, a reliable and unassuming grandeur, extraordinary in any material, but unique as achieved by successive fireworks of contradiction, and a mind jumping like a flea.'[128]

For example, the distasteful central paradox of the Christian religion—the 'fusion of the love of Christ and the vindictive terrors of the sacrificial idea'—is made to feature in 'The Sacrifice' at the moment when the Christ counsels 'his dear friends not to weep for him, for *because* he has wept for both, when in his agony they abandoned him, they will need their tears for themselves.'

> Weep not dear friends, since I for both have wept
> When all my tears were blood, the while you slept,
> Your tears for your own fortunes should be kept.
>   Was ever grief like mine?

Likewise, Empson shows, Herbert foregrounds a similar complexity, a sense of complicity, in this stanza:

> Behold they spit on me in scornful wise
> Who with his spittle gave the blind man eyes,
> Leaving his blindness to mine enemies.
>   Was ever grief like mine?

Empson's commentary on the stanza not only explains its grim paradox, it also adumbrates a central insight of his later analysis of pastoral. 'Leaving his blindness wilfully, the conceit implies [of the blind man], as a cruel judgment upon my enemies, that they should in consequence spit upon me and so commit sin. (Father, forgive them, for they know not what they do.) These two events are contrasted, but that they should spit upon me is itself a healing; by it they distinguish me as scapegoat, and assure my triumph and their redemption; and spitting, in both cases, was to mark my unity with man.'[129]

However, to the extent that Herbert seems to accept the contradictory theology of Christianity 'so completely', Empson frankly concedes, 'the poem is outside the "conflict" theory of poetry; it assumes, as does its theology, the existence of conflicts, but its business is to state a generalised solution of them.'[130] To that extent, in other words, the poem accords with Richards's postulate of 'balance' or 'equilibrium'—both as inherent value and as affect. For Herbert, it would appear, 'no mutual frustration of impulses remained';[131] and his poem may thus be deemed to arouse 'tendencies towards self-completion'. With respect to this poem, therefore, Empson did put Richards's principle into his own words when he noted that Herbert's strong-minded accommodation of 'the theological system' of Christianity operates 'as a releasing and reassuring condition'.[132] Yet, at heart, Empson was always loath to concede so much.

John Paul Russo argues, with respect to the desideratum of 'reconciliation' in poetry, that Empson is like Richards in showing 'that the objective text has coherences in form and subject matter that may offer paths to resolving the conflicts it arouses'.[133] But that is not what Empson meant, at all. For him, the ultimate in ambiguity is created by the poem which makes two or more statements, or expresses two or more attitudes, that cannot be reconciled (this is what Richards would call a deadlock): that is, the poem in which the attainment of a state of composure or equilibrium would mean evasion, amelioration, or mitigation.[134]

Certainly Richards asserted that an artist's 'experiences, those at least which give value to his work, represent conciliations of impulses which in most minds are still confused, intertrammelled and conflicting'.[135] Yet he had at one time, earlier in his career, seemed to comprehend (if not to endorse and to prove to be 'valuable') the extreme case of ambiguity that comes under the head of the seventh type, the type in which 'full contradiction' shows a 'fundamental division in the writer's mind'. As Empson crucially pointed out in his first letter to Phare, 'Passages in "The Windhover" . . . mean both the opposites created by their context, it seems plain; Richards said that once, and then edged away from it.' Richards had indeed said it, in an article on Hopkins dating from 1926—it was one of the first attempts to take stock of Hopkins's newly emerging poetry. Russo calls the article 'not really' a close reading at all, but a 'general' study; but that does the piece less than justice.[136] In an effort to make some 'suggestions toward elucidation' of 'The Windhover' (this sonnet was not a critical chestnut at that date), Richards paused to figure out the possible meanings of its latter half, from the close of the octet through the sestet:

> . . . My heart in hiding
>   Stirred for a bird,—the achieve of, the mastery of the thing!
> Brute beauty and valour and act, oh, air, pride, plume, here
>   Buckle! AND the fire that breaks from thee then, a billion
> Times told lovelier, more dangerous, O my chevalier!
>   No wonder of it: shéer plód makes plough down sillion
> Shine, and blue-bleak embers, ah my dear,
>   Fall, gall themselves, and gash gold-vermillion.

'Why in hiding? Hiding from what? . . . What is the greater danger and what the less?' asks Richards.

I should say the poet's heart is in hiding from Life, has chosen a safer way, and that the greater danger is the greater exposure to temptation and error that a more adventurous, less sheltered course (sheltered by Faith?) brings with it. Another, equally plausible reading would be this: renouncing the glamour of the outer life of adventure the poet transfers its qualities of audacity to the inner life ('here' is the bosom, the inner consciousness.) The greater danger is that to which the moral hero is exposed. Both readings may be combined, but pages of prose would be required for a paraphrase of the result.

The only conclusion Richards feels able to draw is that this combination of 'plausible readings' ('meanings', Empson would say) results in a poem of 'unappeased discontent' (which is the same as what Empson meant by his phrase 'fundamental division'). The poet in Hopkins, Richards goes on, 'was often oppressed and stifled by the priest. In this case the conflict which seems to lie behind and prompt all Hopkins' better poems is temporarily resolved through a stoic acceptance of sacrifice.' There may appear to be a little contradiction, a wobble of logic, in the suggestion that an 'unappeased discontent' is (at one and the same time) 'temporarily resolved'; but that need not detain us, for Richards ends up by stressing: 'His is a poetry of divided and equal passions—which very nearly makes a new thing out of a new fusion of them both.'[137] In sum, as Russo glosses Richards's regretful summary, Hopkins strives for 'inclusion' and yet fails.[138]

Thus Empson was put on notice that 'The Windhover' should represent the apex of ambiguity. As a connoisseur of conflict, however, he saw no reason to regret the turbulently self-divided character of the poem; on the contrary, he felt, it achieves a thrilling tension. In *Ambiguity* (where he gives full credit to Richards's pioneering essay), he analyses the poem with a loving fascination that requires quotation at fair length. This extract shows how he brought to fruition the germ of the idea that he had first dispatched to Elsie Phare in September 1928:[139]

Confronted suddenly with the active physical beauty of the bird, he conceives it as the opposite of his patient spiritual renunciation; the statements of the poem appear to insist that his own life is superior, but he cannot decisively judge between them, and holds both with agony in his mind. *My heart in hiding* would seem to imply that the *more dangerous* life is that of the Windhover, but the last three lines insist it is *no wonder* that the life of renunciation should be the more *lovely*. *Buckle* admits of two tenses and two meanings: 'they do buckle here,' or 'come, and buckle yourself here'; *buckle* like a military belt, for the discipline of heroic action, and *buckle* like a bicycle wheel, 'make useless, distorted, and incapable of its natural motion.' *Here* may mean 'in the case of the bird,' or 'in the case of the Jesuit'; *then* 'when you have become like the bird,' or 'when you have become like the Jesuit.' *Chevalier* personifies either physical or spiritual activity; Christ riding to Jerusalem, or the cavalryman ready for the charge; Pegasus, or the Windhover.

Thus in the first three lines of the sestet we seem to have a clear case of the Freudian use of opposites, where two things thought of as incompatible, but desired intensely by different systems of judgments, are spoken of simultaneously by words applying to both; both desires are thus given a transient and exhausting satisfaction, and the two systems of judgment are forced into open conflict before the reader . . . The last three lines, which profess to come to a single judgment on the matter, convey the conflict more strongly and more beautifully.

In short, the poem does not achieve a state in which impulses are reconciled. 'Impulses which commonly interfere with one another and are conflicting, independent and mutually distractive,' wrote Richards, in the poet 'combine into a stable poise.' But where Richards, with his pious view of poetic purposes, of the poem and its beneficial properties, berated Hopkins for allowing frustration and a lack of appeasement to infect 'The Windhover', Empson found the evidence of opposition and conflict to be an enrichment of the work, a mark of truth to life. (It may have been on account of the undoubted power of Empson's argument that as the years passed Richards gave up insisting on the idea of poetic value as an 'equilibrium of opposed impulses' and began to talk in terms of 'oppositions and collaborations among words'.[140])

While I. A. Richards did probably more than anyone else in the 1920s to promote the theory of the analysis of literature, Empson would presently discover for himself a practical approach he could use, a method he would make his own. Laura Riding and Robert Graves, in *A Survey of Modernist Poetry* (London, 1927), compared two versions of Shakespeare's Sonnet 129—*Th'expence of Spirit in a waste of shame*—the 'original' printing from the Quarto of 1609, with its enticing feast of punctuation and orthography, and the eighteenth-century recension that has become the standard text (as in Quiller-Couch's *Oxford Book of English Verse* (London, 1900)). According to an adage that may be taken as a motto for the whole exercise, their purpose was zestfully paradoxical: 'Making poetry easy for the reader should mean showing clearly that it is difficult.' The editor who doctored the initial spelling and punctuation of Shakespeare's sonnet, they argue, did grave damage; he aborted its pregnancy: 'The effect of this revised punctuation has been to restrict meanings to special interpretations of special words. Shakespeare's punctuation allows the variety of meanings he actually intends; if we must choose any one meaning, then we owe it to Shakespeare to choose at least one he intended and one embracing as many meanings as possible, that is, the most difficult meaning. It is always the most difficult meaning that is the most final.' The permutative provocations of Shakespeare's spelling and syntax give rise to a plural signification, a mass of tenable meanings. 'All these alternate meanings acting on each other, and even other possible interpretations of words and phrases, make as it were a furiously dynamic cross-word puzzle which can be read in many directions at once, none of the senses being incompatible with any others.'[141]

Naturally Empson was enthused by the prospect of besporting what Riding and Graves termed the 'intensified inbreeding of words' in poetry.

We know he had read *A Survey of Modernist Poetry* at the latest by 11 May 1928, because that was when he reviewed a book of criticism that suffered in comparison, *Words and Poetry*, by George Rylands (it was surely not by coincidence that this latter piece appeared alongside the wonderfully heady review of *Blue Trousers* by Lady Murasaki that was the summit of his term as Skipper of *The Granta*):

> The Robert Graves' school of criticism is only impressive when the analysis it employs becomes so elaborate as to score a rhetorical triumph; when each word in the line is given four or five meanings, four or five reasons for sounding right and suggesting the right things. Dazzled by the difficulty of holding it all in your mind at once, you feel this at any rate is complicated enough, as many factors as these could make up a result apparently magical and incalculable. Mr Rylands, however, is seldom bringing off the trick with sufficient concentration . . . [142]

He was evidently referring to *A Survey of Modernist Poetry*, by Riding and Graves, because in none of his previous works had Graves orchestrated quite such an elaborate analysis as of the Shakespeare sonnet in that volume. But it is not obvious why Empson should refer merely to the 'Robert Graves' school of criticism', unless he was tacitly acknowledging that he felt he had already put himself to school to the analytical ingenuity of Graves's approach: no one else had yet thought to deal out the flush of meanings that Riding and Graves managed in *A Survey*. That being the case, however, why did Empson not credit Laura Riding as co-author of the method?

The influence of the 'Graves–Riding' exegesis of Sonnet 129 is everywhere apparent in *Seven Types of Ambiguity*, perhaps nowhere more so than in the discussion of the second type. 'An example of the second type of ambiguity, in word or syntax, occurs when two or more meanings are resolved into one.' Indeed it seems likely that in the Michaelmas Term of 1928, when Richards told him to go ahead with the task of gathering together his happy 'heap' of ambiguities, Empson first looked at the way in which alternative meanings often manage to become reconciled: two or more meanings from which 'an ordinary good reading can extract one resultant'. Not only is Chapter 2 the longest in *Ambiguity*, it includes an example that is little different from the first piece he ever printed on the subject, 'Ambiguity in Shakespeare: Sonnet XVI' (*Experiment*, February 1929)—which is quite obviously modelled on the Graves–Riding analysis of Sonnet 129. 'Ambiguity in Shakespeare' actually opens so very briskly that it seems less a poised introduction than an impatient declaration of intent: 'This is taken out of an essay on the *Seven Types of Ambiguity*. It is an example of the second type: "two or more meanings which all combine to a single mood and intention of the writer." '[143] Likewise, the second chapter of *Ambiguity* incorporates another trial piece that came out in 1929, 'Some Notes on Mr Eliot', an analysis of the double meanings created by the confusion of past participles and active verbs in passages from *The Waste Land* and 'Whispers of Immortality'.[144] Since the only other extract Empson printed in advance of the book was a version of the climactic discussion of Herbert's 'The Sacrifice', it is reasonable to deduce that he started out by looking at the very extremes of ambiguity—that is, type 2, which manifests reconciliation, and type 7, sheer conflict.

When Empson brought out *Seven Types of Ambiguity* in 1930, he initially repeated the seemingly gratuitous error he had committed two years before: he appeared to forget that *A Survey of Modernist Poetry* was written *not* by Robert Graves alone but by Graves and Laura Riding (the American poet who had begun to collaborate with Graves in 1926). But such a gaffe in a big book was more conspicuous than an oversight in a little review. As soon as Graves heard that Empson had omitted to credit the joint authorship of *A Survey*—a volume which even (redundantly? anxiously?) included a 'Note' to stress 'This book represents a word-by-word collaboration' (p. 5)—he protested to Chatto & Windus, Empson's publishers, alleging that Empson's mistake was no mere formality: it was a stupendous insult to his co-author. Whereupon Empson willingly issued the erratum slip with the full acknowledgement already quoted.[145] Not so long after, in a private letter of 29 January 1934, Graves would similarly—loyally and consistently (though perhaps equivocally?)—write to the Cambridge don Audrey Attwater, 'it is simply untrue that I ever made any such analysis of any particular sonnet. I could not have done so, because it was Laura Riding who originated this exegetic method...We worked the whole thing out together at great labour and in pursuance of LR's idea, in the Spring of 1926.'[146] And yet, as time went on, Empson seemed to wish to compound his original fault or offence. In the second, revised edition of *Ambiguity* (London, 1947), he chose to drop altogether his salutation to the analysis of Shakespeare's sonnet 129 that had featured in *A Survey*; instead, in a bold new preface, he acknowledged simply 'in passing' that Robert Graves 'is, so far as I know, the inventor of the method I was using here' (p. xiv). Graves and Riding were perennially enraged by what they regarded as Empson's bare-faced discourtesy.[147] If he did owe a debt to the pioneering prestidigitation of the co-authors Graves and Riding, why was he so caddish as to be loath to admit the fullness of his debt—and even to suppress it?

As late as 1970 Laura Riding returned to the issue by initiating a recriminatory correspondence with Chatto & Windus. I do not know what had incited her to take up the cudgels again after a lapse of decades, but we may be thankful for the exchange that ensued—because it goaded Empson at last into justifying himself. He proceeded to explain in full—and not without a seasoning of spite—why he had felt indebted above all to Robert Graves. He responded to Riding on 25 August that year:

I had been greatly struck by the following passage [from the chapter 'Conflict of Emotions'], in a book, *On English Poetry*, written by Robert Graves alone (1922):

> When Lady Macbeth, sleep-walking, complains that 'all the perfumes of Arabia will not sweeten this little hand,' these perfumes are not merely typically sweet smells to drown the reek of blood. They represent also her ambitions for the luxury of a Queen, and the conflict of luxurious ambition against fate and damnation is as one-sided as ever [before]. Or take Webster's most famous line in his Duchess of Malfi:
>
>> Cover her face; mine eyes dazzle; she died young.
>
> spoken by Ferdinand over the Duchess' body; and that word 'dazzle' does duty for two emotions at once, sun-dazzled awe at loveliness, tear-dazzled grief for early death.

Two emotions but not two senses of the word, one might think, and yet the two processes of dazzling are quite different. Anyway he is mainly concerned in the book with the Conflict Theory of poetry, that it is a healing process through the confrontation of opposed impulses. This is the necessary background for a theory of poetical ambiguity, which he was approaching. He had reached it by 1926, with *Impenetrability, or the Proper Habit of English*:

> For instance, in Keats's *Eve of St Agnes*, Madeline is described in 'her soft and chilly nest', 'clasped like a missal where swart paynims pray', where 'clasped' means 'fastened with a clasp of holiness' or 'held lovingly in the hands', if the Paynims are held to be converted, but also, without prejudice, 'shut and coldly neglected' if the Paynims are held to be unconverted. . . . (quotation from a novel) . . . 'To acknowledge salty hospitality' is in one sense to acknowledge the social obligation of good manners which eating a host's salt implies in most countries. But it is also a comment on the absence of goodwill, in the sense that 'salty' means 'sterile'. In a third sense it is to comment on the host's dry humour in recognising and making fun of his guest's discomfiture, for 'Attic salt' is a well-known synonym for wit. When such a concentration of forces can be exerted at a single point in literature, then, in Humpty Dumpty's words, 'there's glory for you'—using glory in yet another sense than the many we have defined.

These of course are striking examples of the full process, where alternative possible meanings in a word are used together to handle a complex situation.

I felt that I ought to make some wholehearted acknowledgement of the inspiration they had given me.

But these passages, I thought, though they were really very decisive looked a bit scrappy, and when I got round to reading *A Survey of Modernist Poetry* (1927) I felt that the long treatment of the 'lust in action' sonnet would be the right thing to mention in my acknowledgement. It dealt with a complete poem, as I was by this time trying to do, and it had a cumulative weight and impressiveness. What I thought about the collaborator I do not remember, but I suppose these few pages, so very unlike the rest of the book, seemed to me such an evident further step by the mind of Robert Graves that no collaborator could disagree. But I do not deny that it was very foolish of me, if I thought so. When Chatto's told me they had received an enormous letter from Robert Graves denouncing me for a plot against women I found the accusation too absurd to be painful, but I urged Chatto's to put in an erratum slip, giving the correct authorship; not that they needed urging . . .

In the second edition of course I had to omit the reference to the *Survey of Modernist Poetry*, because the original reference to it had been a clumsy mistake, intended to make the little compliment to Robert Graves specific and intelligible, even though slightly untrue. I don't deny that you may hold the priority for the ideas in question, but I deny that I learnt them from you, and the only point of these little 'credits' is for an author to give his sources. Besides, after the fantastic accusations of Robert Graves, I had to stick to what I believed to be literal truth or I might appear to confess by yielding. However, at this distance of time, I no longer feel quite so certain; I wish I knew when I read your analysis of 'lust in action'. I would not rush to it, as I did not consider myself a 'modernist' poet or feel keen on arguments to defend them, but surely, looking at the dates, I must have read it before I wrote my book. The analysis uses the idea of ambiguity by syntax, which may need to be made plain by unusual punctuation; I used this in my book a good deal, and it seems quite possible that I derived it from the analysis of 'lust in action'. If you assure me that you invented it, and not Robert Graves, I grant that I may be in your debt so far; I don't remember any case of Robert Graves using ambiguity of syntax in his previous writing. It seems an obvious thing to add, when you are already using ambiguity of lexicon, but one so often doesn't see the obvious.

All the same, the whole affair seems to me very puzzling. Whyever was it that neither you nor Robert Graves used the technique again, having brought it to such a pitch? And, if you despise it so much as your letters imply, whyever are you so keen to have priority in it?

Of course, it was silly (as he recognized) to give a passing thought at that late date to the evasive and false idea that he might not have read *Survey* before writing *Ambiguity* (it was published in November 1927, and Empson had even reviewed it in *The Granta* in May the following year). Moreover, as for his claim that he had really meant all along to give thanks for the inspiration provided by passages from the earlier works of Graves—passages that can indeed look a trifle 'scrappy' when plucked out of context—Riding found it vile and spurious: such a feeble claim was just a 'dodging', a 'juggling outside the margins of the relevant,' she chided.[148] In fact, in a series of gawky, ill-composed letters, she went on to upbraid Empson at dizzying length for his vain shifts.

Graves, for his part, evidently enjoyed, or fooled himself into enjoying, a continuing pride in the same two pieces of analysis that Empson cited as an influence on his own theory of ambiguity—the comments on Lady Macbeth's 'perfumes of Arabia' speech, and on Ferdinand's great line from *The Duchess of Malfi*—for in 1949 he took care to resurrect them from the general neglect of his early critical writings and to reprint them, in revised form, in a volume of his collected essays called *The Common Asphodel*. But Riding, while wigging Empson on 11 November 1970, claimed to think nothing of the 'thin pickings' he adduced from the early Graves:

The rather cock-eyed identification of the perfumes as perfumes and as ambitions and the conflict of them with fate, etc., is a juvenile literalness as to perfumes amplified with the loosest sort of loading on of psychological analysis of the temper that was beginning to be current, and literarily current, at the time of the creation of this, by your reconstructon, archetype of *your* method.[149]

As to Ferdinand's gasping, searingly beautiful speech over the corpse of the Duchess of Malfi, Riding went on, both Graves's gloss and Empson's comments on that gloss were 'soft-minded':

There are not two processes of dazzling, nor does the word do duty for two emotions at once. First: we have, simply, here, an intransitive verb stating the undergoing of the eyes of an indistinctness of vision of the order caused by, or associable with, brightness shining into them. And that statement, a brevity by itself, in a line of three distinct brevities, stops there. Mr. Graves messes around with it to load it with a double connotation in order to swell the magnificence of the line, a connotation of a double emotion, also thus mucking up the meaning of 'dazzle' with tear-made blurriness, and also postulating an absurd possibility of a two-in-one instantaneity of eyes experiencing at once a vision-disturbing forth-shining and a vision-disturbing tears-spurt. This is unworthy appreciation-of-poetry comment, clumsy fine-points pointing-out, crude literary sentimentality; I call it unworthy in respect to the line—the line deserves better.

On 13 December 1970, Riding returned to her scarcely literate assault on what she termed Empson's 'early-Graves alibi'—specifically to demolish the second of his supposedly sham points of influence, from *Impenetrability*

(1926). No one, she wrote with unabashed abandon, 'could have thought that there was any worth of hide-and-seek stratagem of mock-defence in sober-faced pointing to what you point to in your second citing—for turning the table and putting me on the defensive'.[150]

This last infelicitous letter went unfinished, but she finally sent it off towards the end of April 1971. In the interim, however, Empson was reminded that in 1966 an American critic, James Jensen, had published a conjectural but very notable article 'The Construction of *Seven Types of Ambiguity*' (*Modern Language Quarterly*, 27, pp. 243–59). At the time when he accepted Jensen's article, William H. Matchett, the editor of the periodical, had reasonably thought that it would add interest, the principals being still alive, to have their comments on the piece; so he had written to Graves, Richards, and Empson, and each of them did add a comment. (Unhappily, Matchett failed to contact Riding, but only because he could find no up-to-the-minute information about her and came to the fatal conclusion that she was dead.) But in 1971, when Empson was directed back to Jensen's essay and its appendices, he discovered—much to his gratification—that Graves had actually made an admission as follows:

I was, I believe, responsible for most of the detailed examination of poems in *A Survey of Modernist Poetry*—for example showing the complex implications of Sonnet 129 before its eighteenth-century repunctuation...

In view of that explicit late disclosure, whether tergiversation or recantation, by Graves (which Empson all too vauntingly dubbed a 'confession'), Empson felt he could reply with undisguised offensiveness to Riding's complaints by saying that he had undoubtedly been stupid to forget that 'the legal authorship' of the *Survey* should be 'acknowledged jointly' in *Seven Types of Ambiguity*. But he had not done so, he said,

because it seemed to me obvious that this one chapter was written by Graves alone, in view of his style and previous writing; the rest of the book was written in an entirely different style. He now admits that I was right, and surely that is the end of it...

Your claim to have put the energy into the theory has much more substance; but then, did it only do harm to the theory? This is a basically interesting question; often asked before, in a way. For instance a book 'Interpretation in Shakespeare's Sonnets' (1963) by Milton Landry, which happens to be here. You and Robert Graves are rather scolded for the 'expense of spirit' essay, and so am I for being led astray by it. (p. 168 and elsewhere.) The discovery of ambiguous syntax he finds particularly harmful.

I am inclined to say something more radical; that the 'expense of spirit' example works against the original intention of Robert Graves. He had developed a Conflict Theory of poetry, soon after the war, and went on to consider the verbal means by which conflict finds expression. But your analysis makes Shakespeare in the Sonnet very single-minded, improbably single-minded. I have never seen anyone agree with the decision of you and Graves here to retain the garbled line:

A bliss in proof and prov'd and very woe,

which you said meant that Shakespeare hated the whole process of this love-affair, even the moments of bodily pleasure—it was all woe together, and that was what he meant in the previous line by saying all the stages were 'extreme'. But surely this word need only mean it was *either* great excitement, or pleasure, or suffering; and your reading is proved wrong by the line that comes next:

A bliss in proof, and, prov'd, a very woe,
Before, a joy propos'd, behind, a dream.

I remember an essay of yours, printed about that time [in *Anarchism Is Not Enough*, 1928], called 'The Damned Thing', which expressed great resentment at being saddled with any sexual equipment at all, and found everything to do with it merely unpleasant. Instead of Shakespeare expressing mixed feelings, in fact, such as he obviously had usually, however cross he felt at the moment, you make him express *nothing but* loathing for the whole condition of normal life. This did not need any subtlety of language; in fact, it is hard to see why he did not express it more plainly. I do not think I imitated this fault in my book, or not much, but I did use quite a bit of 'ambiguity of syntax', which I now think a very dubious thing, and perhaps one which actually cannot occur in the sharp form needed to express a conflict. Anyway it is always a temptation to the analyst, because it gives him a big extra chance of forcing in his own ideas against the surface intention of the poem.

When I came to do the second edition, in 1946, I had become inclined to cut these cases out, having already been warned against them, but I did not want to alter the book too much. You understand, it had kept up a small though steady sale for sixteen years, all the time carrying the erratum slip saying that you and Robert Graves were joint authors of the book *Modernist Poetry* (and hence presumably of the 'expense of spirit' chapter). But in the new edition, as I had come to think that that analysis had been a bad influence, I merely fitted into the new Introduction a 'credit' to Robert Graves, leaving it to be assumed that this referred to the earlier books when he was not writing in collaboration. This was entirely within my rights, and it seemed to me that my silence was charitable.

You express contempt for men who cry, when I quote to you the sentence by Robert Graves about the *Duchess of Malfi*. But you were not being asked to admire the character of Ferdinand, who has just had his sister murdered out of incestuous jealousy, and will next refuse to pay the murderer and turn into a werewolf. He is a hysteric, not a stoic; I bet he cried. Anyway, his character is patiently shown as extremely mixed-up, and I have always thought that the Graves comment throws a great deal of light on why the famous line (Mine eyes dazzle) has been so often praised. Your remark betrays a great lack of sympathy (I have to feel) with what he was trying to do, all along, in his earlier work on these verbal points; and that is why I still believe that you really did have an influence on the 'expense of spirit' chapter, as you claim, though he now says he was 'responsible for most of the detailed examination of poems (in the book), for example showing the complex implications of Sonnet 129...' After he had followed your advice, I am led to think, he felt the whole area into which I ignorantly blundered as one of intense irritation, and that is why he never did any more work of that kind, ever again.

If Empson had momentarily forgotten Jensen's 1966 piece on *Ambiguity*, and in particular Graves's claim that he was 'responsible for most of the detailed examination of poems in *A Survey*', including that of Sonnet 129 (which is significantly at variance with the authors' original insistence that the *Survey* comprised 'a word-by-word collaboration'), Riding knew nothing whatever of the Jensen article and its appended comments until the day she received Empson's letter of 29 April 1971. Naturally, and understandably, she felt incensed at Graves's betrayal—all the more so because Empson had reported it to her with such crowing prejudice. 'It seems to me appropriate,' she wrote in a prolix, incoherent letter to the editor of the *Modern Language Quarterly* (which he solemnly published in all its unedited, self-exposing silliness), 'to record that, without public statement of mine, recognition of my intellectually and verbally sensitive hand within the glove of the *Survey* method has been mounting, with perception of its connection, via Mr. Empson's hobby-horse use of it, with the "New Criticism," which tried to make real horse-flesh of it... [T]he quadruple contribution of which Mr. Graves' letter was part, contained, besides misrepresentations as to my work and personal life of his unctuous provision, aspersions on my authorial credit and general respectability of intellect.' With regard to her 'entitlement to be named first author [of *A Survey*], or, even, a substantially working second', she went on, any reader can see 'the difference between the variations-on-literary-interpretation-stereotypes freshened with still new psychological ideas, that was Mr. Graves' pre-*Survey* critical equipment, and the critical qualities of that book of proximity of presence to the word-totality of a poem—the predominating ones at least—...'[151]

While Riding promised 'some speakings of my own on those September 1966 theorizings, judgements, depictions' (in *Modern Language Quarterly*), she actually published nothing further of a substantive nature—probably, to be fair to her, because she had been ill, not from any hiccough of conviction—only extravagant counter-claims. In the *Denver Quarterly* (Winter 1974), for instance, she baldly asseverated, *pace* Graves: 'Mr Empson's book applied a method original to that work [*A Survey*], and originating with myself (it has become necessary to tell, because of Mr Empson's initial dishonoring, and Mr Graves' ultimate dishonoring, of my part in the book) . . . '[152]

For reasons of their own, therefore, both Graves and Riding laid claim to the writing of the analysis of Sonnet 129 in the *Survey*. This need not concern us much, except to note that when Riding's ex-husband, Louis Gottschalk, visited Graves and Riding in 1926—at a time when they were supposed to have been bonded in collaboration—he suspected even then that the balance of their contributions was uneven. Joyce Piell Wexler, who is in general sympathetic to Riding and her work, has candidly reported, in *Laura Riding's Pursuit of Truth*: 'Since Riding kept reiterating that her work with Graves was a full collaboration, while Graves insisted on nothing, Gottschalk concluded she protested too much.'[153] In any event, Riding persisted in castigating both Graves and Empson, in public and in private. She told Empson in May 1971, 'You differ from Mr. Graves in being an improviser of fabrications, while he is, privately and professionally, a liar; you also are what you are privately and professionally.'[154] Empson might have been forgiven for failing to see the difference. As Martin Seymour-Smith adjudged, the attacks that Riding mounted in various periodicals in her later years 'are of no interest, and have no factual value'.[155]

Robert Graves, for his part, picked over an old quarrel with himself—largely, it would seem, because he was annoyed by an observation made by James Jensen in 'The Construction of *Seven Types of Ambiguity*'. 'Graves had become initiated in the techniques of analysis in spite of himself, as a victim of shell shock and a patient of the psychologist W. H. R. Rivers,' wrote Jensen. 'Adopting an approximately Freudian method of treatment, Rivers stressed the value of close analysis of unconscious conflicts as they were elaborated in disguised conscious form in dreams and poems. A good part of Graves's literary career in the early twenties was accordingly spent in writing and analyzing poems to relieve his unconscious emotional conflicts and in adapting Rivers' theories to the contexts of criticism.' Whereupon Graves, in his published comment on Jensen's essay, sought to correct this notable error of fact: 'I was never a patient of Dr. W. H. [R.] Rivers . . . But he and his colleague Dr. Henry Head [a neurologist who had treated Graves for neurasthenia] . . . were my friends and for a while I accepted their general theory of a "subconscious self" . . . but not Freud's deformation of it. No Freudian I . . . ' Yet as Seymour-Smith has reported, Graves did in fact derive his knowledge of Freud from Rivers and Head, who made use of a modified Freudianism, as well as from a hasty perusal of the poor translation of *The Interpretation of Dreams* that had appeared in 1913; 'he therefore tends to attribute to Freud himself the excesses of some of his disciples.' Furthermore, Graves admired Rivers's work *Instinct and the Unconscious*, and gave it full credit in his *Poetic Unreason* (1925). In any case, there is no doubt about the upshot: 'His final position on the way poetry comes into existence does have an affinity with Freud's views.' Thus when Graves in 1966 chose to disavow the influence of Freud on his critical writings of the 1920s, he was perhaps forgetting that in the Introduction to *The Common Asphodel: Collected Essays on Poetry 1922–1949* (1949) he had already recorded with candour:

As a neurasthenic, I was interested in the newly expounded Freudian theory: when presented with English reserve and common sense by W. H. R. Rivers, who did not regard sex as the sole impulse in dream-making or assume that dream-symbols are constant, it appealed to me as reasonable. I applied his case-history method of accounting for emotional dreams to the understanding of romantic poems, my own and others', and found it apt enough; though poems were obviously complicated, I wrote, by 'the secondary elaboration that the poet gives them when no longer in a self-hypnotized condition.' My findings are recorded in *On English Poetry* (1922), in the final chapter of *The Meaning of Dreams* (1924), and again in *Poetic Unreason* (1925).[156]

I. A. Richards deplored psychoanalytical criticism ('on anti-biographical grounds,' as his biographer reminds us). 'Whatever psycho-analysts may aver,' Richards insisted in *Principles of Literary Criticism*, 'the mental processes of the poet are not a very profitable ground for investigation. They offer far too happy a hunting-ground for uncontrollable conjecture.' And he went on specifically to scold Robert Graves for his 'thoroughgoing Freudian onslaught' as a critic.[157] Empson could not pretend he had not been warned about Richards's opposition.

Pace the critics who suggest that Empson's analyses of ambiguity owed most of all to Richards's method of what he styled 'multiple definition', the first occasion on which Empson actually made use of that method is in a letter of February 1933—assuredly in response to the recommendations Richards set out in *Mencius on the Mind* (1932)—well over two years after publishing *Ambiguity*. But even in this letter, it is amusing to see, Empson teases Richards by citing Freudianism as opposite to Godhead in the context of reviewing a scale of value according to Yeats:

There was a point about the use of the word *dream* in Yeats which I should like to try and remember for you.

1) vision from God telling absolute truth

2) conception of a way to live, write a poem, or solve a definite problem.

3) conception of something valuable in terms of beliefs which one can no longer believe.

4) state of reverie in which one is protected so that such conceptions may be hoped from it.

5) state of reverie useful as example.

6) daydream admitted to be debilitating.

7) Freudian dream that sets to work unconscious forces admitted as lower, but claimed as a source of knowledge of oneself.

7 gets back to the 'mysterious forces' of 1 and 2. The 'romantic' Yeats manner always implies 'You've got to be high-toned if you're to read this: I don't write for the sort of man who thinks I mean a *nasty* dream—and if he does think that about *my* dreams he's probably wrong.' In his later use of *dream* he includes all the meanings—

> The soul remembering its loneliness
> Shudders in many cradles
>   —business man etc—
>   cradle within cradle and all in flight and all
> Deformed because there is no deformity
> But saves us from a dream
>   [cf. 'The Phases of the Moon']

1-4: saves us from a conception of value—which would involve painful effort. 5-7: saves us from a conception of desire which would jolt us out of the order at present achieved.

Very tactful of him to keep his language and leave room for the Freudians in it: the dream is no longer necessarily admired.

If Robert Graves in subsequent years denied the crypto-Freudianism of his first writings, Empson would never go further than to regret the Freudianism that had infected his own earliest criticism. Even though he had partly couched his analysis of Herbert's 'The Sacrifice' in Freudian terms, he later maintained, his analysis of the contradictions posed in the poem was still correct. Readers should not seek to dodge the true meaning of the poem just because the critic Empson had overindulged himself in the way he had chosen to explicate it. Herbert had not been addressing a peculiar problem of a psychological order. 'I meant, and still think,' Empson emphasized in 1953, 'that Herbert felt the paradox of the vengeful God of Love to be an extremely severe strain, as it has increasingly been felt to be since he wrote. That was why, in treating a traditional theme, he had to heighten the paradoxes till a reader is forced to wonder whether they will manage to balance.'[158] Earlier still, in the second edition of *Ambiguity*, he had similarly stressed this claim: 'my last example of the last type of ambiguity was not concerned with neurotic disunion but with a fully public theological poem. However, I want now to express my regret that the topical interest of Freud distracted me from giving adequate representation in the seventh chapter to the poetry of straightforward mental conflict...'[159]

He may not have been happy in retrospect with the Freudian element that informed some of his earliest criticism, or with the method of analysing ambiguity by lexicon that he adopted from Graves's description of Sonnet 129. All the same, Empson's greatest debt to Graves certainly did pre-date *A Survey of Modernist Poetry*. To prove the point, one has only to cite this single sentence from *Ambiguity*: 'There is a variety of the "conflict" theory of poetry which says that a poet must always be concerned with some difference of opinion or habit between different parts of his community; different social classes, ways of life, or modes of thought; that he must be several sorts of men at once, and reconcile his tribe in his own person' (p. 112). That passage could not have been written except as a specific reference to Graves's early (pre-Riding) definition, published in 1925, of 'the typical poet... the poet in the fullest sense' as one who 'must stand in the middle of the larger society to which he belongs and reconcile in his poetry the conflicting views of every group, trade, class and interest in that society...'[160] Furthermore, on a couple of pages from an early notebook covered with jottings and other references headed 'Mencius' (which dates these particular notes to 1932), Empson specifically referred himself to 'Graves social conflict e. g. Rivers'—again, that is, to the pre-Riding writings. However much Riding sought in later years to deride Graves's comments on Lady Macbeth's 'perfumes of Arabia' speech, or on Ferdinand's heart-stopping line in *The Duchess of Malfi*, Empson really must have been telling the truth when he said that such passages in Graves's first writings (albeit they 'looked a bit scrappy') had indeed inspired his interest in ambiguity.

In conclusion, one may say: Empson's work on ambiguity answered somewhat less to Richards's theory of equilibrium than to Graves's argument that the best poetry is the fruit of conflict. As far as Empson always believed, creative conflicts generate ambiguous effects. Hence it was clearly with the example of the early Graves in mind that Empson wrote in his Introduction to the second edition of *Ambiguity*:

I believe that rather little good poetry has been written in recent years, and . . . the effort of writing a good bit of verse has in almost every case been carried through almost as a clinical thing; it was done only to save the man's sanity. Excedingly good verse has been written under those conditions in earlier centuries as well as our own, but only to externalise the conflict of an individual. (p. ix)

The key development is that whereas Graves's dictum was sociological, and even political, Empson stresses in his response a clear psychological note.

9

'Those Particular Vices': Crisis, Expulsion, and Aftermath

FOLLOWING Empson's death in 1984, the *Magdalene College Magazine and Record* published an obituary by 'A.S.' (Arthur Sale) which included this bland and negligent sentence:

In 1931 after election as a Bye-Fellow but before taking up his position, he was appointed to a Chair of English Literature in Tokyo and his close association with Magdalene ceased for some 45 years.[1]

Just so, whether innocently or ingeniously, Sale got everything wrong, managing to minimize or overlook just about every melodramatic particular of Empson's exclusion from the college, which took place in the summer vacation of 1929—just one year into his study for the English Tripos.

The session 1928–9 had been a splendidly busy one for him, the start of a brilliant career. The college had allowed him to move on to a second degree despite the fact that his final result in the Maths Tripos fell short of stardom (although his scholarship was not renewed for a fourth year).[2] I. A. Richards was to recall for a radio programme in celebration of Empson's achievements, broadcast as late as 1977, that A. S. Ramsey, Empson's supervisor for Maths, told him 'that Empson was one of the best mathematicians he'd ever had and he was sorry he was leaving mathematics'.[3] His fame as a poet, and Richards's awed reports of his amazing work on literary ambiguity, must have reassured the Governing Body that they had done well to let him proceed with his studies.

He also busied himself with numerous other activities; among them, as Dorothea Richards noted in her diary for 18 May 1929—a month before he sat Part I of the English Tripos—he became 'much absorbed in [B]asic English'. (As it was reported, he was amused to find that, as far as he could determine, when employing the helpfully reductive methods of Basic English, a chap could not ask his girl 'Do you love me?', but had to say 'Will you do things of sex with me?')[4] He also held office as president of the Heretics. In addition, surprisingly, he found time in mid-March to take the title role for a three-night run of *The Tragedy of Tragedies: or the Life and Death of Tom Thumb the Great*, by Henry Fielding; this was the first production (with Empson got up in a 'creation of sack-cloth' by no less an artist than Humphrey Jennings) of a group called the Mummers, which was founded by the gangling Alistair Cooke as the first mixed ('co-ed') dramatic society at Cambridge.[5] Barbara Nixon played Huncamunca, Erik Chitty the King, and Cooke himself Lord Grizzle. Michael Redgrave, who was lauded as the leading light of the Marlowe Society, suggested in the *Cambridge Review* that the leading players (not including Empson) might seek to join one of the older dramatic societies (none of which, of course, admitted women on the stage) so that 'the Mummers might confidently cease to be'; he observed too, with all the cruel wit of the student critic: 'Mr Cooke, as the villain, was certainly acquainted with all the tricks, but, I regret, could perform none of them.'[6] (That casual sting lodged hard and deep in Cooke's memory.) As to Empson's final appearance on the boards, *The Granta* remarked with a suitably indulgent double edge that *Tom Thumb* 'is a burlesque directed against the heroic tragedies popular in [Fielding's] time. The whole cast recognized the burlesque, Mr Empson particularly its direction. Only those who know Mr Empson, or share his particular sense of the quaint, could enjoy his acting; but his interpretation was by far the most intelligent.'[7]

To Alistair Cooke's surprise, Empson played no part in the social life of the production. He came to rehearsals, took direction, and disappeared in a flash. Similarly, when Empson was a book critic of *The Granta*, he would simply appear in the magazine's tiny office in King Street, drop off his copy without a word, and vanish. He did not even turn out to the *Granta* teas, which were held on a regular basis in the editor's digs. Thus, as far as Cooke was concerned, Empson seemed to be 'all head', especially since his circle, including Bronowski and Jennings, were 'terrifyingly highbrow'.[8] 'I never saw him show emotion of any kind,' Cooke would recall for me; 'a passing nod on the street was about the limit of his affability'; and in another place: 'I'm afraid in all candour I have to add that Empson was just about the coldest human being I have ever met. I admired his writing (and his early poetry) immeasurably: he had a beautiful rapier of a brain, but in my personal contacts with him he was an icicle that never melted. Of course, this is not to imply that he wasn't capable of deep emotion: *Seven Types* offers ample proof of it, especially on Herbert and the metaphysical poets. Probably, the chemistry between us was negligible. I'm sure that with close friends he was a vastly different human.'[9] Naturally it is possible that Empson felt disdainful of idle chatter, or perhaps he took against Cooke; yet it is just as likely that he treated others in just the same detached way as he did Cooke. Throughout his life he cultivated few close friends, other than those who spontaneously looked after his needs (though he would certainly not see a relationship in that way), and never tried to set aside intellectual activity (even during an engrossingly congenial dinner party, when he would occasionally leave the table to go and type out something that had been simmering in his mind). Though very far from unsociable, he was shy, and for the best part of his life used alcohol to boost *bonhomie*. Thus he preferred acquaintanceship to friendship; occasional companions, especially those with wide-ranging interests, who shared his passion for an exchange of ideas or information, rather than intimates who might well expect emotional and moral energy of him, if not commitment. Nonetheless, Empson's tone of voice, his high, clipped enunciation, could leave casual acquaintances with an impression of chill aloofness—which may serve to explain the curious allusion in a silly article, 'The Bridge Street Coffee House' by a wit styled 'Obadiah Pompony', published in the *Magdalene College Magazine* in December 1928, to 'one, whom they called *E-mp—n*, who gave utterance in tones of staccato Indifference . . .'[10] Above all else, however, he was hyperexcited in mind and behaviour: he was observed always to be careering off somewhere.

Nonetheless, Empson did attend one of the annual *Granta* dinners for the scanty staff of the magazine. Alistair Cooke vividly remembered the occasion because Empson got very drunk and 'saw no reason why', as he announced, one should not eat a tulip (there was a vase of them decorating the table), and proceeded to do just that, petal by petal. 'Fairly soon after he had bowed to our goggling admiration, he threw up.' Empson also accepted an invitation by Cooke to a dinner in Jesus College where an unrecorded celebrity of the day gave a numbing talk after the meal. 'I've forgotten everything about a tedious evening,' Cooke would recall, 'except Empson's remark, delivered in a whisper as the boredom stretched on: "You can always shut your eyes and think of buggery." '

Empson was infatuated with one particularly handsome young man during the academic year 1928–9, though his desire was never to be fulfilled.

His series of 'Letter' poems was to be addressed to a friend named Desmond Lee (1908–93), a tall, blond, elegant, striking-looking man, who took firsts in both parts of the Classical Tripos.[11] While the first four poems in the series date from his last year at Cambridge, 'Letter V' was produced in Tokyo in the early 1930s, which suggests that he languished after Lee for a considerable period. ('Letter VI', the last of the series, was written as late as the occasion of Lee's marriage on 23 March 1935, and was not published during Empson's lifetime.) According to Lee's own account of their relationship, this series of poems came about after he happened to quote to his friend Pascal's resonant declaration, '*Le silence éternel des ces espaces infinis m'effraie*' ('The eternal silence of these infinite spaces [the heavens] terrifies me', *Pensées*, iii. 206), only to discover that Empson profoundly disagreed with the sentiment—and the first poem became Empson's argumentative response (Pascal's remark is cited in line 2). As soon as Empson completed each of the 'Letters', he would send Lee a typescript (with the exception of 'Letter VI', which he kept to himself).

'Letter I' is a teasing love poem. It begins by referring to the loved one's irrational terror of the dark, which he has expressed by way of endorsing Pascal's horror of the vacant interstellar spaces. The poet calls this emptiness between stars 'That net-work without fish, that mere | Extended idleness', picking up Eddington's observations that 'space is *like* a network of distances . . . a self-supporting system of linkage which can be contemplated without reference to extraneous linkages', and that 'The system of the stars is floating in an ocean . . . a placid ocean'.[12]

The poem goes on to argue in the second stanza that

> I approve, myself, dark spaces between stars;
> All privacy's their gift; they carry glances
> Through gulfs; and as for messages . . .
>   .   .   .   .   .   .
> . . . they are a wise go-between,
> And say what they think common-sense has seen.

In other words, space is seen as salutary—though an utter darkness, not really threatening—for it maintains individuality (of stars as of people) and provides linkage and an area for communication.

While the third stanza begins with apparently dark dubiety, asking if two potential lovers are in fact directly connected by space—which is 'warped' in non-Euclidean geometry—or by common sense, its final questions sound baleful but can be taken as reassuring:

> Where is that darkness that gives light its place?
> Or where such darkness as would hide your face?

Empson once wrote in a review, 'any serious attempt at establishing a relativity turns out to establish an absolute; in the case of Einstein the velocity of light.'[13] So too, in this poem, the absolute darkness the beloved friend fears is established by the implied fact of absolute light. Oblivion being so unlikely, kind consolation is always at hand.

Further, continuing his argument into the final stanza, he answers for the possible fate of our humble star, the sun:

> Our jovial sun, if he avoids exploding
> (These times are critical), will cease to grin,
> Will lose your circumambient foreboding;
> Loose the full radiance his mass can win
> While packed with mass holds all that radiance in;
> Flame far too hot not to seem utter cold
> And hide a tumult never to be told.

In *Possible Worlds* (1929), J. B. S. Haldane had mentioned the remote chance that the sun might explode.[14] The poem was written some ten years before scientists produced the true equations for the nuclear processes of the sun, but even in 1928 it was known that the sun was, as Empson says, 'packed with mass'—some 2,000 quadrillion tons of energy, enough to sustain the sun's radiation for 15 billion years.

Indeed the final couplet of the poem wittily clinches the argument, drawing the beloved's attention to the fact that the poet's passion is not unlike the energy of the sun. He must turn Lee's attention away from his fear of the stellar spaces and towards his own fear of expressing love. The fate of the sun, after all, could well be that of B Sirius (the so-called Companion of Sirius), a white dwarf which has bags of energy but no radiation. 'What is its temperature?' asks Eddington.

If you measure temperature by radiating power its temperature is absolute zero, since the radiation is nil; if you measure temperature by the average speed of molecules its temperature is the highest attainable by matter. The final fate of the white dwarf is to become at the same time the hottest and the coldest matter in the universe . . . Because the star is intensely hot it has enough energy to cool down if it wants to; because it is so intensely cold it has stopped radiating and no longer wants to grow any colder. (*Stars and Atoms*, 127)

Empson frames that extraordinary paradox in a witty conceit—a version, if you like, of wishing not to blow hot and cold but to consummate his love—which should certainly serve to beguile the beloved away from metaphysical anguish to the dilemma of his desire; like the Sun, he might 'Flame far too hot not to seem utter cold | And hide a tumult never to be told'.

How to deal with personal despair is similarly the true subject of Empson's poem 'Letter V'. It is about the elusiveness of the desired friend both as a physical person and as a metaphysical subject. It is also a self-addressed poem, suggesting to the poet—who finds the universe alienating and the friend a stranger—that he should turn hankering into happening. Since we are invited by Eddington and other physicists to believe that matter is no more than a 'fortuitous concourse of atoms',[15] the poem employs the conceit of trying to get hold of the lover in those terms. 'Not locus if you will but envelope,' it begins,

> Paths of light not atoms of good form;
> Such tangent praise, less crashing, not less warm,
> May gain more intimacy for less hope.

As Empson explains in his notes to the poem, 'A locus defines a surface by points and an envelope defines it by tangents.' While science insists that materially the loved one is not quite that which he might appear to be to the eager and bashful poet, and that you need a mathematical calculus truly to locate a material body, the poet turns the scientific grammar into a courtly compliment. The object of his desire may be engaged in social fencing, evading his physical advances—according to the scientists, you would need tensors to get hold of him[16]—but the poet suggests they might gain 'more intimacy for less hope': 'less hope of getting to bed together',[17] perhaps, but that should at least afford them the opportunity of (as the saying has it) 'really getting to know each other'. He then develops the compliment by saying,

> You are the map only of the divine states
> You, made, nor known, nor knowing in, make known.
> Yet if I love you but as Cause unknown
> Cause has at least the Form that has been shown.

Though unapproachable, as Empson says in the sleeve notes of his recording of *Selected Poems*,[18] the loved one has a Divine Form (in every sense: all puns are intentional). Is he real or evidence of the Ideal? The argument here, again according to Empson, is that 'there must at least be a structure in the external world corresponding to our sense-impressions'. He perceives the beloved as comely, in other words, whether he is to be taken as

evidence of divine creativity or as a material accident, the chance arrangement of the lines of moving electrons.

In short, the poem is gamesome—and actually very affectionate, as
Empson himself thought it—while at the same time discussing fundamental ideas. Empson is at once describing and wooing the elusive lover and
describing an important metaphysical concept: the terms from seduction
and the terms from physical science are interchangeable. The game
includes a challenge to a notion the Imagists held dear. Empson wrote in
a review some ten years later (1941):

Tennyson believed in immortality because his heart felt it, evidently sense-datum
of visceral type. Sense-data become opinions rather than perceptions . . . [S]ome
people say atoms have dim sensations—is it logically possible for me to be an
atom? The objection to assertions about matter is that we can't conceivably
observe it. How are we better off by reducing it to sense-data, which we can't
conceive ourselves as having? Here again, we know less about the sense-data than
we do about the things.[19]

That is to say, poetry which professes to offer the truth of sense perceptions
should think twice—it operates on the level of truth-of-feeling or intuition—because it is subject to physical laws which are beyond the grasp of
such 'perceptions'.

In terms of Empson's poem, the argument is concluded by resting on the
Kantian conviction that this is at least a world which can be 'observed by
the creatures it contains'. You may not ultimately be what you seem to be,
Empson tells his friend, but my understanding and common sense inform
me that I can describe what I see of you, and hope to hold you:

> These lines you grant me may invert to points;
> Or paired, poor grazing misses, at your joints,
> Cross you on painless arrows to the wall.

'Letter V' offers itself in the dignity of formal quatrains. The poet
compliments his friend as his muse—since Lee grants him the lines of the
poem even as he baffles him with the obliquity or evasiveness represented
by the lines of mathematical calculus—but the description is charged with
just enough aggression to suggest that he retains the sexual initiative: 'These
lines you grant me may invert to points', after all, and 'Cross you on painless
arrows to the wall'. That is to say, Lee might become a martyr to his
desire—a St Sebastian immunized by his love—but at least the lines of
his poem might win him by pinning him down. The poet obviously
appreciated that the figure of St Sebastian is a homosexual icon.[20]

'Letter VI', which comprises an awkwardly expressed and in parts inchoate set of stanzas, reflects:

> Terrified by the purity of your dry beauty
> Dry tough and fresh as the grass on chalk downs—
> The metaphor now seems stale to me only because
> It drove me younger to as empty a love—
> I have not dared mention to you even the ideal
> Version of love sent neatly in typescript
> Not altered before publication
> And drowned on meeting in my interminable yattering conversation.
>   My life's more weak than this traditional theme.

Though Empson clearly felt intense homoerotic feelings for his handsome but shy young friend, there was apparently no overt declaration of inter- est—or at least no totally unambiguous pass. However, while Lee was obviously not unaware of Empson's hankerings, he simply refused to acknowledge them: he would not meet Empson on such terms. He was to write, in his unpublished 'Autobiographical Notes, started in 1984': 'I do not think anyone has known that I was the addressee, nor do I think it is of great consequence. The last letter was accompanied by a note saying he would not "bother me" with any more.' Yet Lee also included in his memoirs the interesting remark, 'Retrospectively I think I probably felt that they [the poems] would introduce an intensity into our relations which was not appropriate in day-to-day affairs.' On the typescript of his 'Autobiographical Notes', Lee struck out the last clause (following 'which') and substituted by hand the phrase 'and which neither of us wanted'.[21]

One supposedly 'trivial' incident, as recorded by Lee himself, suggests that Empson experienced occasional spasms of jealousy; this anecdote, probably dating from the same year, also features in Lee's draft memoirs:

A party of us went up the river in punts. We got beyond Byron's Pool and, if I remember rightly, had lunch. And I don't think it is merely the sentimentalising of memory to say it was a gorgeous summer day. One member of the party (there must have been six or seven of us) was a notorious pansy of the day, Malcolm Grigg. He always very much dressed the part, with broad-brimmed velour hats and the like ... What Malcolm was wearing that day I do not remember in detail, but ... after lunch Bill obviously got sick of his peacocking around and, with no warning, pushed him into the river on the brink of which he was unwisely standing. We fished him out quickly enough and then Bill, in a curiously charac- teristic gesture, stripped off his own clothes, gave them to Malcolm for the return journey, and tucked a towel round his own waist. The rest of the party were clearly unwilling to travel back with him so clad; he was a formidable character and probably slightly tight, as were we all. So the job fell to me (I thought the others were being rather pusillanimous) and the two of us returned together in one of the punts, Bill punting most of the way clad only in his towel. I do not remember the end of the journey or how Bill got back to Magdalene . . . I know that Bill behaved as perfectly as anyone could in that predicament, and that my own feelings were of amusement and a certain admiration at the way Bill carried the whole incident off.

The incident is clearly susceptible to the interpretation that, once Empson had (spontaneously?) humiliated—doused—a rival, he could himself take up the ultra-masculine role ('formidable', 'punting most of the way', behaving 'perfectly') while indulging in an apparently innocent, yet most conspicuous, narcissistic display which assuredly served to captivate the attention of the lone male gaze. Lee would 'always remember' that day, he noted. It is very likely the same occasion that Empson was also to remember in 'Letter VI: A Marriage'; among other cherished recollections of Lee, the poem suspires:

> I remember only once bathing in the sight of your eyes
> Paying some attention to this bloodless series
> —One would think to the first—the grey eyes open
> Large milky lit fastened steadily on me
> Not knowing what to think of what might come next
> Supposing I was ever to stop haranguing the tea party;
>   There is a social weight on the traditional theme.

> It seemed to me impossible to admit that such a signal
> (Of which I was certain, which you would now certainly deny)
> So dissolving and so noble, had been even recognized,
> Still less, having sent them [the poems] to their owner out of a
>   clownish honesty,
> To make sensual capital out of writings
> Of a sort so much lectured on
> As to be practised with decency only for clinical purposes.
>   Life is allied to this traditional theme.

In a published response to a questionnaire in 1976, Empson was to observe among other matters: 'The deep intention [of a work of literature] may often be a thing the author himself is doubtful about . . . Obviously you need to think about his "biography", his formative experiences . . . Why ever not? . . . [A] real subject may be almost hidden behind a protective cover subject.'[22] (In another place, he accepted the critical proposition: 'you might want to know whether the author has really had the experience he describes, or is writing "conventionally"...')[23] The 'real subject' of the 'Letter' series may be said to be a desire for Desmond Lee, the only begetter of the letters; the 'protective cover subject' is the fearful desire of a 'boy' for a 'girl'. In truth, however, the discovery of the concealed identity of the beloved in these poems makes little difference to one's interpretation of them; like any poem—in this case, like any love poem—they are validated, and must be explicated and evaluated, not by their being encoded in a personal fashion but by their generic or universalizing power. Actually, the feeling of despair figures extensively in Empson's poetry—the despair of union in homosexual love is just one aspect of this theme—but it is not simply solipsistic; it has much more to do with writing poetry, as Empson himself put it in an early review, 'about a profound nervous dissatisfaction'—what he called the 'fully digested despair'[24] which can stand the test of a larger context, the metaphysical examination. In a review of A. E. Housman's *Last Poems* he observed:

It is true I think that all Despair Poetry needs a good deal of 'distance' (of the poet from the theme); you can only call despair a profound general truth when you are looking beyond all the practical particulars, which might well have been hopeful if the man had been stronger; and in a personal story, even a half-told one, you cannot do this easily... But there seems no decent ground for calling all Despair Poetry about love sentimental... It wants as its apparent theme a case of love with great practical obstacles, such as those of class and sex, because the despair has to seem sensible before this curious jump is made and it is called a universal truth.[25]

The great practical obstacle at the back of the 'Letter' series was Empson's desire for a fellow student who did not reciprocate his feelings, who refused to respond to him; their 'universal truths' are evidently larger.

But he had more than male bliss and buggery on his mind. Without reneging on his homosexual inclinations, he had begun to penetrate the world of women—with quite a vengeance, it seems. According to his contemporary Muriel Bradbrook, he took to playing the field; and she was also given to understand that 'Those who knew said his relations with women went wrong all the time.' (Those who knew, Professor Bradbrook told me, included Kathleen Raine.)[26] Probably he did not yet appreciate what most moved women, or he was not prepared to meet their differing needs. Almost certainly, he liked the act without attachment; and with male partners he was used to a quick exchange, the rub with a chum, the helping hand of mutual masturbation—with no questions begged or recriminations uttered. Hugh Sykes Davies claimed that one of Empson's girlfriends said, 'He used a girl like a lavatory';[27] but there is no other evidence to suggest that he used women in such a crude, unmanly, exploitative fashion: the remark is merely vulgarity aspiring to facetiousness.

To be sure, Empson did go out with women during his final year at college: we know this because a condom was to be the cause of his undoing as an aspiring fellow; and we know the identity of his first true lover. Elizabeth Wiskemann, the youngest daughter of a German emigré, was seven years his senior. Born on 13 August 1899, in Kent, she had won an Exhibition to Newnham College, where she gained a first in Part II of the History Tripos in 1921 (when Empson was 15; he would come up to Cambridge four years later). Thereafter she held a Gilchrist Research Studentship in 1924–5 while working for a doctorate on 'Napoleon and the Roman Question', but she was bitterly disappointed when her thesis gained her only an M.Litt. in 1927. Thus it was during the ensuing year or so, while taking stock of her life and trying to decide whether or not to give up the prospect of an academic career for herself, that she came to know her gifted junior, the eccentric, egregious Empson.

A small woman with rounded face, deep coral in complexion, thrusting jaw, and pale brown hair which she liked to bob, Elizabeth Wiskemann was not altogether good-looking (indeed, her face was just a little hairy—which led to her being occasionally and cruelly known as 'The Whisk'). Nevertheless, she had real attractions, most notably a vivacious and even flamboyant personality coupled with a devouring interest in European culture. An authentic intellectual and exuberant conversationalist, she knew how to charm and had a flair for cultivating distinguished people; equally, she was something of a snob, prone to push herself forward, selective in her attachments. (Among her other enthusiasms, she had a passion for the Bloomsbury circle and all it stood for.) She was very kind to the people she collected, but could be abrasive and unkind to the less favoured. All the same, if she could sometimes be prickly and quick to take offence, she was essentially a vigorous, ambitious, sensitive, and warm-hearted person who strove to meet the highest standards of intellectual endeavour.[28] 'Her interest in individuals and her lively social conscience', wrote L. K. Duff (who knew her well), 'combined with views on human duties and rights deriving, through nineteenth-century liberalism, from the *philosophes* of the eighteenth-century Enlightenment. Her spiritual home was perhaps among the radical (and anti-clerical) liberals of 1848.' The attraction for Empson of such a vital, intelligent older woman was obvious, especially since she would have been well able to take the initiative.

Throughout his life Empson appreciated resourceful, independent, competent women: women who would not exhibit any obvious need to lean on him. He was drawn to strength of will, uncomplicated vigour, self-sufficiency, and not to passiveness or pliancy. Delicate femininity was not so fetching to him.

There can be no doubt that the relationship was important to Empson, a matter for proper public acknowledgement, because he chose to give a lunch party in order formally to introduce his partner to his English tutor, who had already assumed a quasi-paternal role in his life—even though Richards was only thirteen years his senior. On 22 February 1929 the diary that Ivor and Dorothea Richards kept in common includes the entry: '1. To Empson & met Elizabeth Wiskermann [*sic*]'—which is fascinatingly followed by this note: '4. Walked to Leavis & [Queenie] Roth' (the latter being the future Mrs F. R. Leavis). It was quite a day for flies on the wall and biographers; although—as is always the way with such things—the intimate details of Empson's relationship with Elizabeth Wiskemann have died with the flies.

Whatever the intensity of this love affair, and the time it took up, his work did not suffer in the slightest. He was primed like a gun for Part I of the English Tripos—the examiners that summer were a lustrous array: E. M. W. Tillyard, F. L. Lucas, L. J. Potts, T. R. Henn, and H. M. R. Murray, with F. P. Wilson (Oxon.) as external examiner—and he presently carried off a 'special distinction' (it was an accolade also attained that year by the shy but brilliant Muriel Bradbrook, future Mistress of Girton College).[29] Indeed, with hindsight it might seem as if the paper with the dauntingly terse title 'Essay' might well have been set with Empson in mind: Question 5 invited a response to the broad proposition 'Great art is always complex'.[30] It is not known whether Empson did actually tackle that topic—rather than, say, 'Decadence in literature' or the ever-exasperating 'How far is English literature suitable as a University subject?' But there is yet in existence a sort of belated examiner's report in the form of a reference written by E. M. W. Tillyard, twenty-three years after the event—when Empson came to apply for the Chair of English Literature at Sheffield University:

I never taught him but I examined him in the Tripos, and I shall never forget the brilliance of his papers . . . He began as a scholar in mathematics and he has the logical penetration of the mathematician. In a certain kind of close literary analysis he has no equal. On the other hand his short flights are better than his long; and it was significant that his essay paper in the Tripos was illorganised as a whole and much inferior to his other papers.[31]

W. G. Shepherd, who was an undergraduate at Jesus College in the 1950s, relates an anecdote told him by Tillyard, who was then Master: 'In what Tillyard thought an unwonted access of frankness, the examiners confided to each other that they did not really understand Empson's essay—nor the quotations in it from his own poems. Invoking a rarely used rule, they summoned Empson to meet them, and invited him to explain his essay. He did so confidently, fluently, and at length. Having thanked and dismissed him, the examiners found they were considerably mystified—they "wished he would explain his explanation." They concluded, however, that Empson was clearly highly intelligent and full of knowledge—and should be awarded the highest marks. So that's what they did.'[32]

Not only did Empson win a Magdalene College prize for English, he was unanimously elected on 15 June to a Charles Kingsley Bye-Fellowship, with an emolument of £150, for the year 1929–30.[33] (The polymath C. K. Ogden, extraordinary begetter of Basic English, had been appointed Kingsley Bye-Fellow only the year before.)[34] I. A. Richards took deep pleasure in being the first to give Empson the tremendous news. Presently, on 20 June, Empson formally assigned himself, in age-old Latin formula, to the 'sodality' of the college.

Just seven weeks later, he was effectively 'sent down' by the fellows who had just appointed him a junior member of their College.[35] The entry in *College Orders and Memoranda 1907–1946* reads: 'It was resolved that William Empson be deprived of his Bye-Fellowship and that his name be at once removed from the College Books.' That stark sentence was signed the same day by A. B. Ramsay (Master) and A. S. Ramsey (President), and then by the seven Fellows in attendance: V. S. Vernon-Jones (Senior Tutor), Talbot Peel, Stephen Gaselee, F. R. Salter, Francis H. H. Clark (Dean), F. McD. F. Turner, and F. R. F. Scott (Junior Tutor).[36] The only other official record of Empson's catastrophe is that written up in the Minutes of the Governing Body over two months later, on 7 October, by A. S. Ramsey: 'After an adjournment to the following day and as a result of certain investigations it was resolved nem. con. that Mr. W. Empson's Bye-Fellowship should cease forthwith and his name be removed from the College Books.' (Two fellows of the college, Richard Luckett and Ronald Hyam, who have pieced together a candid account of the entire episode, remark in respect of this minute—perhaps with a touch of defensive partiality—'It should be noted that the decision to deprive him of his Fellowship was only "resolved": that is to say, it was *not* an agreed and unanimous decision.'[37]) Empson was to have no direct dealings with

Magdalene until the college elected Professor Sir William Empson (as he had become) to an Honorary Fellowship exactly fifty years later, in 1979.

It seems most strange, as the King of France said of Cordelia, that he whom even but now was their best object, the argument of their praise, should commit a thing so monstrous to dismantle so many folds of favour. Precisely what happened that July 1929 has become the stuff of legend, with as many versions as there were gossips to embroider them. But certain facts are patent. Empson had been lodging for a time, possibly for the full year, in a college hostel called Kingsley House, in the Chesterton Road, where he seems to have carried on in a free-and-easy, not to say licentious, way; he came and went just as it suited him, and he had even introduced a woman—almost certainly Elizabeth Wiskemann—and made love to her in his room. Upon his election as bye-fellow, he was given rooms in Magdalene College proper; but even as his bags were about to be carried across the road, a servant, or 'gyp', found that he had some contraceptives in his possession. Empson had been disastrously careless. And yet his inadvertence might not have been particularly damaging in itself except for the fact that the servant gossiped about it to other servants, who in turn noised the news about town. Since a public scandal appeared to be imminent, the Master (who was to take up the high office of Vice-Chancellor the following year) decided to convene an extraordinary meeting of the Governing Body in order to put it down. But the Governing Body, so far from dealing out a token punishment and a deft hushing-up, decided in its collective wisdom to exact the most severe penalty available to it—both to deprive Empson of his bye-fellowship and to remove his name from the college books (as the University Statutes empowered it to do, since sexual misconduct was deemed to be a university offence). Even his tutorial file was forthwith destroyed, so that as far as Magdalene was concerned, it should be as if he had never been there. They could not rescind his university degree, but in all other respects he was to be a non-person.[38] This ruthless decision meant too that he could no longer reside within the town bounds.

As fate would have it, I. A. Richards was not available to ward off this foul disaster. On 2 July, he and his wife, both dedicated mountaineers, had left for the Bernese Oberland, from where they were to journey, via the Trans-Siberian railway, to spend a year at Peking National University; they finally got back to Cambridge on 15 October 1931—and by that time Empson himself had gone away for three years. In the event, it was not until the impossibly late date of 29 September 1929 that Richards learned, in a letter from an undergraduate in America, that Empson had been thrust out of Magdalene. Bubbling with frustration, he dispatched a missive, at once accusing and seeking clarification, to his old mentor, Frank Salter, Fellow in History:

Do let me know what has happened. I'm v. much concerned & feel that something v. serious must have occurred for the College to have taken such a serious & public step. I'm sorry for the College's sake which I *think* has lost one of the really big chances, & for E. sake who loses his academic chance & for my own for I had been looking forward to getting some work out of him on my own linguistic stuff. I'm v. anxious to know what happened to make it impossible to hush up whatever may have arisen. I'm worried to think it must have all occurred in the Long [Vacation] when most of the Fellows would have been away. I do hope you were there. As you know I distrust very much the Master's pre-20th century Bachelor School Master's feeling, & his autocratic leanings. I do hope something unjust & unjustifiable has not occurred. I haven't any real facts & so cannot judge but at present I feel so indignant that I never want to come back. Has the Master any idea of the lives of half the young men he sees every day. To have made a preposterous example of our best man, without contriving some tactful way round, seems madness.[39]

The staunch Salter, a nonconformist and a Liberal (he stood for parliament in 1924), who was known to relish rumbustious party games with his tutees, and whose independence of view was not in question, replied in gratifying detail on 10 November:[40]

Dear Richards,
...As regards the Empson business,—I often thought of writing when I was abroad in the summer, but I was always expecting to hear from you (thinking that WE wd. be sure to write to you himself) & thought I would wait till I heard how much you knew already. The position actually is this, (and you ought, naturally, to use all this with discretion as details of what has happened at a G.B. meeting mustn't be widely divulged.)—The Master announced at our afternoon meeting on St Mary M's day that certain facts had come to his notice. They were of 2 kinds: (a) that in moving WE's things from Kingsley House to College various birthcontrol mechanisms had been discovered, *and* (b) (and this is what the outside public who have heard, God knows how, something of the situation, don't seem to have heard) that he had been in the habit of having a woman in his rooms late in the evening, sometimes staying till nearly 12.00, sometimes with his door locked and that on one occasion at least (more, if I remember right) they had, when the door was *not* locked, been found by Mrs Tingey in a compromising attitude. The Master saw WE early next morning and reported to an adjourned meeting of the G.B. who thereupon resolved (not unanimously) to take away the Bye Fellowship, as they are empowered to do by Statute in case of conduct judged disgraceful, and remove his name from the

books of the College. WE had not denied having used the birthcontrol gadgets but said that he had never used them actually in Kingsley House.

What went wrong at that adjourned meeting was, first, that we had the wrong people there, or rather, the right people absent, and, second, that we took the decision too hastily. Neither Piccoli, Gaselee nor King were present; an adjournment of a day would, I think, have made us *all* move rather further to the left, so to speak. Those who were rather vaguely unhappy & baffled would have become much more determined not to do anything drastic and some at least even of the others wd. have been rather less uncompromisingly rigid.

From the evidence point of view, if WE had denied everything, as he might well have done ('got them for a friend', 'got them out of curiosity' etc) I still think that the majority of the G. B. wd. have considered the case proved & acted no otherwise than they did.

What has got to be remembered is that sexual misconduct *is* a University offence & that when detected in an undergraduate, it leads almost invariably to his expulsion; as long as this is so, it is not unreasonable to expect senior members of a College to conform, or for us to find it a bit difficult to continue an offender in residence. A great deal of harm had been done in this case by the entirely unnecessary publicity which had already been given it. Mrs Tingey had in my opinion erred very greatly in not reporting the visits of the woman (as regards which she had, I think, a real grievance) *at once*, in which case [F. R. Fairfax] Scott, as WE's tutor, would have told him not to be an ass, & nothing further would have happened, or, at any rate, come to our notice.[41] As it was, the undergraduates in Kingsley House had apparently for some time past considered it already established &, not happening to like WE, made comments whenever the woman appeared. In the next place, everyone connected with the staff, pretty well, had a good look, and no doubt a good giggle, at the birth control things. Mrs Tingey fetched her husband: when Empson's stuff was taken across to College, the porters & buttery staff also had their attention drawn to them. The Bursar (damn him!) talked a lot of muck about our duty to the staff, removing the stain from the College at once & telling the staff that we had done so, etc. and this, which made some of us very angry indeed, carried some weight with others. There was a rigid block, considerably more than a mere majority of those present, who took the completely oldfashioned view of things and were determined to exact the maximum penalty (removal from books of College) with this degree of consistency that this has, rather stupidly, been done in the past to all undergraduate offenders along these lines. Consequently those of us who didn't agree were *forced* to go part of the way with the majority in the hopes of saving *something* and we tried to compromise on leaving Cambridge and loss of title of ByeFellow, while keeping emolument and name on the books. This would have made it possible for him to receive financial help towards literary research in London & also made it not impossible for him to get some kind of a character if hc put in for the Civil Service or the like. This, however, was defeated by a large majority (Turner and I being, as a matter of fact, the only two who voted for it) and the rigid folk genuinely, I think, thought it immoral even to consider such mitigation of punishment. If we had adjourned for a day & thought things out more thoroughly, Turner and I would probably have been less willing even to compromise at all and would have made more of a fuss, but I doubt whether it wd. have affected the ultimate issue: Scott, I think, now tends to think that we exacted the greatest penalty we even possibly cd. for what was not the greatest possible offence, and is therefore *somewhat* regretful, but I don't think the others are at all. Needless to say the possible parallel with Shelley & Univ. was brought forward, and I was heavily sat on for suggesting that it was almost impossible for a certain element of selfright-eousness & hypocrisy not to enter in to our judgments. What I had particularly in mind was the probable private lives of many of our most popular young men (*your* point) and the fact that at the Feast the night before (made horrible to most of us by thinking what was hanging over the unconscious Empson's head) we had all warmly welcomed 3 old Magdalene men, (who had been asked because 2 of them were staying as guests with the 3rd. who happened then to be living in Cambridge) about whose past (or present) I would be prepared to wager heavily but who had been more discreet than WE in their conduct. I do think that WE had been terribly silly and, much though I dislike the way the thing came to light, I am inclined to think that in the circumstances, Colleges being rather different from ordinary life, it was almost necessary for him to leave Cambridge, for the time at least. I am also wildly annoyed at the way in which some folk are now talking in Cambridge, without (a) knowing all the facts, (b) realising that their views on sexual relations are neither those officially held by the Univ. rules nor those held by anything like the majority of dons; so that I don't think that in similar circumstances many Governing Bodies would have disregarded the affair al-together, although they *might* not (though many *would*) have inflicted quite the same punishment.

The Master, I ought to say, behaved quite well. He was very anxious for anything to be said for WE that cd. be said, and he did not himself take any line at all, leaving everything in the hands of the meeting, although (I suspect) quite agreeing with their decision. But he said nothing at all to influence us either way. Turner and I (as it happened) V. J. [V. S. Vernon-Jones] had some heated words with the Bursar, because he would keep bringing in servants' gossip and vague reported assertions, one of which led to an extremely unpleasant investi-gation later in the Long Vac., which resulted in the clearing of the character of 2 suspected undergraduates, but not before a lot of harm had been done; and even now (as rather unlucky circumstances had it) I don't think it has got through to the porters that their characters *have been cleared* but merely that the case isn't proved. Nor, I think, has it been properly rubbed in to the porters that their business is to report things, if they think anything is wrong, and not themselves form judgments upon them and repeat them among themselves & to undergraduates in general gossip. Still less that if they *don't* report a thing (as in this case, which only came to light rather casually months after) it is entirely wrong for them to go on gossiping about it and treating it as if it had been not merely reported but also proved. But of this (which has been a very disquieting business) I will write again another time . . .

Ever yours

FRS

Frank Salter was writing more than three months after the meeting, and his memory was not infallible: he forgot, for instance, that Stephen Gaselee had been present at the meeting. Yet there seems to be no reason to doubt the principal facts, or the sincerity, of his report. All the same, given that Salter and only one other colleague tried to press for a compromise which finally failed to win the day, the Master must have decreed—or concurred—that, in view of the onerousness of the case, it was essential for the meeting to reach a unanimous verdict. And so it was achieved: the Governing Body resolved—as the President's subsequent minute recorded—*nemine contradicente*—to cancel Empson's fellowship and to expunge his name from the books. I. A. Richards was later inclined to take the view that the Bursar was the major villain in the case—Talbot Peel (fellow in Engineering and a nonconformist lay preacher) must have done his utmost to foment resistance to any plea for leniency, he believed—a view which would seem to be supported by Salter's account of how Peel ('damn him!') had 'talked a lot of muck' at the terrible hanging meeting.

Yet it is surprising to learn from Salter's letter that Empson was not popular with his fellow lodgers in Kingsley House. For all his known cleverness, he never affected superiority; and in most social dealings he was invariably direct and friendly. 'He was brisk, quick-moving, florid,' Richard Eberhart fondly remarked. Even a casual friend recalls of Empson: 'For all his erudition and completely disorganised way of life, he was the friendliest of men, with simple tastes and no "poetic" airs or graces.'[42] Thus in June 1929, which turned out to be his last full month at the university, his college magazine would make him the object of a piece of obviously affectionate satire—a 'Headmaster's Report': 'I hear from his form master that Bill has been caught writing poetry again this term, but I think that more games will soon knock that nonsense out of him . . . [H]e seems very destructive with his logarithm tables and often scribbles wantonly in his books.'[43] The anonymous writer could feel confident that his contemporaries would enjoy the private joke about their local genius— who does not appear to have aroused any great jealousy with his heady repute as mathematician and littérateur. At worst, therefore, it would seem

that the scruffy, scurrying, high-voiced, short-sighted, book-bolting Empson was a figure of friendly fun, and no man's foe. That same month, for
example, his college magazine published a sketch purporting to canvas
views on the coming General Election (which in fact returned, to Empson's
satisfaction, the first Labour government with an outright majority), and
managed rather well to lampoon his distracted, twittering demeanour and
tricks of speech: 'Mr Empson, the Obscurantist Candidate, received us in a
charming négligé of plain crushed marocaine, picked out with a delightful
motif of old gin stains. "Surely"; he said, "I don't pretend to know about
politics, and I suppose if they want to have an Election, no one can stop
them... but I've not heard what Mr Eliot thinks about it all... tell me
what is the vote and do you really?" '[44] (The sartorial details were meant to
be read as a reminder that the vague, unwordly poet habitually turned
himself out in a state of acute disarray.)

On the other hand, he had no time for rules and regulations; though not
a hell-raiser, roaring boy, or aristocrat, he was negligent of authority and
acted as if he was a law unto himself. Toeing a line was not for him: limits
tempt the trespasser. But this is not to say that he was exceptional in his
waywardness, only that he could not abide the meek or the dutiful. Like
any undergraduate with the necessary bit of nerve, he would ignore
curfews and stay out late, shinning back over the wall in the small hours;
in truth, he acquired something of a reputation for his skill at scrambling
back into bounds. Yet he was not above minding his manners at such
times. During the Long Vac Term of 1928, for example, Stephen Garrett
(a future Fellow and Professor of Mycology who was then one of only two
students at Magdalene reading for the Natural Science Tripos) happened
to occupy a set of rooms in the Old Lodge which formed one of the regular
routes for climbing into college after the gate was closed at 10 p.m. Many
students would scuttle through his rooms in this way, with just a passing
'Thank-you'. Only once did anyone ever pause to pass the time of night
with him—Empson chatted with him for twenty minutes or so. Garrett
was impressed by Empson's charm and courtesy; he appreciated it all the
more because, as a scientist, he was not in the social swim at the college.[45]
However, not everyone was so tolerant of Empson's gadding, as we may
gather from a teasing article about him (one of a series on 'Those in
Authority') published in *The Granta* in May 1929. After first dismissing
Empson's early career as of no interest to anyone, the piece touches just
as briefly on another matter: 'Nor have his powers of climbing into
his College, nor even his (abruptly curtailed) powers of climbing into his
present apartment, been put to any use that need detain our readers.'[46]

Empson must have been nabbed, perhaps once too often, by the proctors; but there is no hard information to tell us more. Possibly he had been gated on pain of stiff penalty—which makes it all the more remarkable that he managed to spirit a woman into his rooms at Kingsley House.

Yet it does seem likely too that he had the ill luck to lodge at his hostel with a particularly priggish set, who would of course sneer at his doings. All the same, his way of life would almost certainly have taxed the goodwill of any close neighbour. His rooms were a monument to sordidness, an environmental disaster, a health hazard (one friend remembers his 'jam-besprinkled records').[47] The chaps from *The Granta* were not exaggerating when they told of the horripilant spectacle they encountered at Kingsley House:

The poet was alone when we entered; lying in a welter of banana-skins, mathematical instruments, and abandoned pieces of paper, singing as he worked, and automatically writing with his left hand, he was patiently sucking some beer-stains out of the carpet. Sheets of vulgar fractions and chromatic cast-offs littered the floor on all sides, and it was only above the flood level of ink that we were able to distinguish the familiar details of the College-furnished apartment. 'Bill,' as he is affectionately called in the Mess, turned his back upon us with ready bonhomie. 'Either you're going to help or you aren't—I suppose,' he said. 'He that gathereth with me scattereth abroad.' We waited till he had Dried Up.[48]

Apart from the squalor of his rooms, it appears, for many months his unseemly carry-on had been a cause of exasperation to his long-suffering bedder, Mrs Tingey. Back in March, for instance, when Cambridge had been gripped by a frost of record severity, *Magdalene College Magazine* chose to publish burlesques—written by Michael Redgrave—of some of the predictable reactions by the better-known characters about the place. Empson was given to utter, with the scientist's airy curiosity, 'What's this about "cooling planets"?'[49] For Mrs Tingey, the awful weather brought in its wake the paradoxical boon that at least her wildest charge had been forced to curtail one show of his oddball behaviour: 'It's terrible, isn't it, but it stopped that Mr Empson from having his bath at three in the morning.' Joking apart, however, if it was the case that Empson and his girl had sometime left the door open, whereupon Mrs Tingey had discovered them in 'a compromising attitude', she might have felt she had something to resent and so seized the chance to get her own back against Empson's ungentlemanly, insulting conduct. For his part, he always took it particularly hard that his bedmaker had spent time prying into his papers: some of his letters must have been entered in evidence against him at the extraordinary meeting of the Governing Body.[50]

All the same, whatever the actual background of the case, Empson had little doubt that the otherwise gentle Master of Magdalene manifested a dark personal interest in hounding the culprit out of his college. Ramsay, he felt, arraigned him with all the zeal of an inquisitor from a bygone age. To I. A. Richards Empson relayed the devastating news in this fashion:

You wanted to be the first, I remember, to tell me I had been given a Bye-Fellowship, and I want to be the first to tell you it has been taken away again. I left some contraceptives in a drawer when my things were being moved; with criminal carelessness; I remember being no more than amused when I found they had been stolen, I didn't understand what was going on, in the way of collecting gossip and so forth, at all. As for the Body, they obeyed their own rules, poor creatures; I should like to, but cannot, feel indignation at the workings of a system with whose principles I disagree....

I don't know how much details would amuse you. The Master (with an air of melancholy conviction) told me that anybody who had ever touched a French letter, no matter when or why, could ever again be allowed with safety in the company of young men, because he was sure in some subtle way, however little he himself wished it, to pollute their innocence; and this in spite of the fact that his own intellectual powers would have been destroyed. As an act of grace I was allowed to poison the air of Magdalene for a day after my exposure, and this gave time for several of my judges to come and explain that I must mind and not bear a grudge, or that what they had done would be the best thing for me in the end, or that 'personally' they thought their own actions a Great Pity, or that though they were not addicted to Those Particular Vices (I wept with rage when this was said to me) I was to understand they had extremely Broad Minds.

And in a subsequent letter he responded to Richards's closer enquiries:

You ask me who made gossip; I think none was necessary. The porters told the Master they had found contraceptives, and he was very excited, and anxious to get the place purged of such things. (I think he had told them beforehand to be sure and let him know of anything they could find.) His argument to *me* was that I had caused scandal, but I think he was relying on the imagination of Mrs Tingey.

I think it very lucky you weren't in Cambridge for the row; you would only have shocked the Master, and incurred the consequences your colleagues seemed so afraid of.[51]

As such remarks show, he would not even try to hide or overcome his bitter dismay at the college's decision to dismiss him; but this is not to say that he was making up the sanctimonious utterances of the Master as he reported them to Richards, or indeed the humbug and self-deception of certain members of the Governing Body. (In a later year, Hugh Sykes Davies told me that one of the fellows was overheard to proclaim, as he came away from the extraordinary meeting, 'We can't have muckers like that in this society!'—but that report may be apocryphal and is in any case uncorroborated.) Other reports, albeit secondhand, blame the Master for directing the Governing Body to sacrifice Empson to his anachronistic rule. Professor Muriel Bradbrook, whose judgement could never be dismissed as negligible or merely mischievous, believed that Ramsay must have dictated the decision to rescind Empson's junior fellowship. In a memoir she wrote too that Empson 'suffered under an unusually authoritarian constitution and a Master who was Nonconformist, of a joylessness that offered a very ready target for the barbed wit of Queenie Leavis and others'.[52] Independently confirming Professor Bradbrook's allusion, Michael Tanner has written that at a dinner party with the Leavises in the late 1960s,

Mrs Leavis did most of the talking, keeping up a remarkable flow of anecdote, and laughing a great deal, her mirth often being occasioned by remembrances of prudery and priggishness. I recall her account of how an extremely distinguished literary critic was discovered by his bedmaker to be keeping condoms in his bedside table . . . and how they were taken to the Master of his College, 'one of those innocent classics who composed Latin verses about schoolboys bathing nude', and that he had to have explained to him what the condoms were for.[53]

Notwithstanding the rearguard rigour of his mind, it is to the Master's credit that he allowed Empson to speak to the board in his own defence: he did not condemn him out of hand, out of hearing. (F. R. Salter, in his letter to I. A. Richards, observes that the Master interviewed Empson and conveyed his findings to the Governing Body; but evidently Empson was permitted to address the board in person.) 'I'm afraid I don't know who was at the Meeting, except for the obvious people,' Empson remarked a few weeks later; 'they were hidden away in the dark rather, and I was concentrating on my little speech.' Unfortunately, there is no detailed record of what he found to say—though it is nice to imagine that he had enough of the Yorkshireman's brass neck to ask, as legend has it, 'Would you prefer me to go in for buggery?'[54] What we do know is that he admitted to having made use of condoms—he elsewhere disclosed that the wicked 'birthcontrol mechanisms' so vaguely referred to by F. R. Salter were none other than 'a French letter'—though never at Kingsley House. But maybe a piece of his literary criticism, dating from 1954, gives us a more precise sense of the tact he tried to exercise before the college board on that awful day in June 1929. Cassio, Othello's fresh lieutenant, is led into a drunken affray of which he is ashamed, and yet pride seems to prevent him from presenting his case before his master. Empson came to assess Cassio's situation like this: 'it is true Cassio could have pleaded his agony at length in person the next morning, but his unwillingness to do so seems to me ordinary decency, a mild form of the honor doctrine which is still current. Absolute lack of pride isn't thought agreeable ... The way he could get through his trouble was by firmly demanding this interview, and telling the truth coolly, and asking with concern what actual harm had been done; what goes wrong is not his excessive pride but his excessive self-abasement (nowadays he would be considered too young for the job).'[55] It seems quite likely that Empson was in part recalling his own plight from twenty-five years earlier when he wrote that mild evaluation of Cassio's predicament; and certainly it is a safe bet to imagine that, so far from pleading his agony, the naturally ruddy-faced but impenitent Empson had spoken up for the cool truth as he saw it at the time—and not for what he elsewhere scorned as the 'working lie'.

'Let me rein in my growing bitterness (it has all been my own fault, and I ought to have taken decent care of another person's interests if not of my own),' he reproved himself in his first letter to Richards. In truth, he took successful pains to conceal the identity of his lover Elizabeth Wiskemann: her name never came out at the time, and even their closest friends had to guess at the right person, so she suffered no taint of disrepute from the affair. Empson behaved honourably in screening her from exposure or scandal. (Ironically—at least according to Julian Trevelyan, who became a close friend of hers—Wiskemann herself 'would tell everybody that all that fuss about the French letters was on her account'.[56]) Nor did the catastrophe that befell him in any way injure her future. Her own failure to gain a Cambridge Ph.D. seems to have been the sole determining factor behind her decision to embark on a career as a journalist on the European continent. (In later years she would mention 'her gratitude to Cambridge for its training in veracity and exactitude'.[57]) A redoubtable woman who never did marry, she pursued a most remarkable career. 'If I had remained an academic specializing in the nineteenth century, I suppose my life would have been considerably duller than it became,' she later wrote.[58] While she continued to coach Cambridge students for a few years, she spent much of the early 1930s in Germany, observing and writing on German affairs for the *New Statesman* and other periodicals, constantly warning of the extent of the Nazi menace. Following the publication in 1935 of two articles that were particularly hostile to National Socialism, Hitler's police placed her under observation, and then, in Berlin in July 1936, she was detained at the Gestapo headquarters on Prinz Albrecht-strasse. Though familiar with Nazi methods of interrogation and intimidation, she revealed nothing of what she knew of German intelligence and plans. 'Do for heaven's sake look round,' she told herself, 'you're in a place of unusual interest'; and indeed, by studying the maps on the walls of the Nazi headquarters, she gathered a great deal about Hitler's policy of eastward expansion. Once released from detention, she was expelled from Germany and spent the remainder of the 1930s in those countries of central and south-eastern Europe that were falling prey to Nazi influence. In 1937, at the behest of the Royal Institute of International Affairs, she started on her first book, *Czechs and Germans*; it was followed by *Undeclared War* in 1939. She also afforded unsparing help to refugees from Hitler. During the war she was Assistant Press Attaché at the British Legation in Switzerland, charged with the perilous mission of collecting non-military intelligence about the whole of enemy-occupied Europe: she was one of the first to send in reports about the Nazi death camps and about Tito's partisan movement in Yugoslavia. Her invaluable work put her on the Nazi Black List. Though she won no honours for her wartime services, she was very proud to receive an honorary D.Litt. from Oxford in 1965, when the public orator properly described her as both 'a Cassandra who lived to record the war she had foretold' and 'a historian who had obtained international recognition'. Her later works include *The Rome-Berlin Axis* (1949), *Germany's Eastern Neighbours* (1956), and a volume of memoirs, *The Europe I Saw* (1968). From 1958 to 1961 she was Montague Burton Professor of International Relations at Edinburgh University, and from 1961 to 1964 a tutor in Modern European History at the University of Sussex. Yet at the end, harrowed by failing sight, and jealous of her self-reliance, she took her own life in London in July 1971—the very month in which Empson retired from teaching at the age of 65.

Whether or not, if Empson had survived his crisis at Cambridge, these fiercely intelligent, independent-minded individuals would have come together as a married or working couple (fit to rival the Leavises in their prime) is impossible to guess. Still, it is quite reasonable at least to infer that the severance of Empson's career at Cambridge did not immediately and forever mar relations between the flagrant pair. Sir Desmond Lee, in his unpublished memoirs, recorded an anecdote that may well be the final word on the state of the relationship between Bill Empson and Betty Wiskemann, but it is brilliantly suggestive:

In 1930 I went to Germany to try to learn the language. I started in Munich . . . and then moved on for a few days in Salzburg. There I found Bill. I can remember few details. I do not think the meeting had been pre-arranged and I do not remember how we met or where we stayed, though I remember going to a concert. I was due to go on to Vienna and to a brief visit to Wittgenstein and Bill decided to come with me, though of course he could not be included in the visit to Wittgenstein. I remember staying for a couple of nights in a small hotel near the station and having a quick look round Vienna; but then I had to leave him. This I did with some trepidation. My own German was rudimentary; his was simply non-existent. But he was not in the least perturbed.[59]

Empson must have gone to Germany that summer in the first place to escort Elizabeth Wiskemann to her new life; it is not likely that he would otherwise be chanced upon, solo in Salzburg, unless he had travelled on there after leaving Betty in Berlin. But when and how their relationship finally came to an end cannot be established. Having said that much, however, it must also be said that the trip to Germany and Austria turned out to be a double boon for Empson, a coincidence which was simply not to be missed. The opportunity to share a bedroom with the long-desired but uninterested Desmond Lee was the only feature of the trip that Empson ever saw fit to put on record, in these sorry closing lines of 'Letter VI':

> One of these poems at least occurred, long after being written.
> In the next bed to you in a pub in Vienna
> I watched the moon shadow of the window upright
> Walk clear across neck and face, in perhaps half an hour,
> Continually illuminating new beauties,
> Placing in you one minute after another everything
> I know of admirable in the history of man.
>   There is not much more in this traditional theme.
>
> I as in one instant felt during that time
> By a trick with time I have known otherwise
> Only in the absurd race of an ill-designed chemistry examination
> Where the quarters struck consecutively; but that I won;
> Perhaps inversely too in the still photograph
> Of shooting a snipe, already behind me, before I knew I had tried
> —I am trying to remember triumphs—
>   What else but this is the traditional theme?
>
> Maintained one exhausting ecstasy
> Interrupted only at moments by a nuisance
> A foam of self-consciousness and delight, through which I now
>   know that this occurred.
> As the shadow passed to your hair, leaving only truth, I spoke.
> You woke and understood this at once. A porcine

Expression of complacent pleasure
Rounded with a fine clang my series
Before you turned over and hid the face under the bedclothes.
    One could fit this into the traditional theme.

Empson's first mock-heroic response to being thrown out of Cambridge was to pen some verses entitled 'Warning to Undergraduates', putting to good use the octosyllabic couplets of Samuel Butler's burlesque *Hudibras*. Written within a few weeks of the fell event itself, but published only after his death, it is testimony to Empson's buoyant generosity of spirit that he could so quickly translate a painfully humiliating setback into a form of 'smilingness' (to borrow Byron's word)—as in these key passages:

My friends who have not yet gone down
From that strange cackling little town,
Attend, before you burn your boats,
To these few simple College Notes.

Lock up whatever it appears
Might give a celibate ideas.
You'd best import your own stout box;
They keep the keys of College locks
(Not that they wish, especially, to;
It is their duty, and they do).

Remember what a porter's for;
He hears *ad portam*, at the door;
He carries (*portat*) as he ought
(Dons love a Latin pun, with port)
All tales and all exciting letters
Straight to the councils of his betters
(Not that he wishes so to thrill;
But it's his duty, and he will).

Remember that a bedder's dreams
Are very active on such themes.
Don't let her fancies loose one minute
(Take most care when there's nothing in it).
'Don't clear the table, please, today,
Till we have started for the play.'
—She'll know what *that* means, right away...
See where the chaste good dons in rows
(A squinting, lily-like repose)
Have heard more tattle than one knows.

See where the Majesty of Cambridge towers;
Gives orders far beyond his powers;
Wields the unwieldy keys of Hell,
And shoos you from the town as well.
See, peeping, anxious, and discreet,
And listening for each other's feet,
Your various *kinderhearted* judges;
They hope you will not bear them grudges.
Their friendship is now much enhanced.
You must not think they're not advanced.
Their minds are desperately broad;
They sat in terror on the festive Board
And damned you hardly of their own accord.

His erstwhile fellows were not minded to take a lesson from his misfortune; they did what students always do when one of their number is made a victim: they put on a demonstration. Some felt it proper to make a protest because they felt a kind of veneration for him; others just enjoyed creating a stink. Michael Redgrave, who claimed in his autobiography that he 'had come to admire Empson tremendously', observed that 'all literary Cambridge exploded' as soon as the next academic year got under way. 'John Davenport, Hugh Sykes Davies, and I hired the Masonic Hall. Dressed *à la Bohème*, with a jug of beer on a candle-lit table, three mugs, and a pile of manuscripts, we read or declaimed Empson's poems for the best part of an afternoon before an enthusiastically partisan audience.'[60] The event even warranted a notice in *Cambridge Review* ('several of these poems do not lend themselves to recitation, [but] the effect was on the whole interesting and attractive'),[61] though it also stirred up petty jealousies among the littérateurs. Ralph Parker (of Corpus Christi), a budding Communist, gossiped in a letter to Elsie Phare: 'Bronowski amazed me by his arrogance. He's been boycotted, I believe: things came to a head when at the silly little reading of Bill's poems in the Masonic Hall, by Hugh S[ykes] John D[avenport] & Michael R[edgrave], (quite unsponsored by Bill): Bronowski, rising to ask if he might read the latest poem of Bill's, received by him on that day, was announced by John as "that busy little man from Jesus". So now he is railing against Hugh & John and all, except for his curious underworld gang in Jesus. "Bill, of course, is interested in practical criticism: I entirely in theoretical criticism, and I've been trying to get round the college on that score." (Does that mean he's trying for a fellowship[?]).'[62] So it's all a question of perspective: what seemed like a momentous manifestation of solidarity to one participant struck a witness as a 'silly little reading of Bill's poems'. Julian Trevelyan relayed the news to Wittgenstein, who was very upset.

Other protests took the usual jejune forms beloved by undergraduates. Max Black, for example, remembers that he and Empson 'must both have been members of the Labour Club, since I wrote a rhymed skit about the Master of Magdalene that was performed at the usual Christmas party'.[63] Much later in life, another friend, Ronald Bottrall, would write these light verses in Empson's honour:

> Betrayed by the head porter, ostracized by dons,
> Missing the pros, he was sentenced by the cons,
> A lamentable case of academic *mores*
> Prompted by puritan envy and trumped-up stories.

But Empson's disaster was not to be trivialized: nothing so outrageous, it would be argued (as Salter noted in his letter to Richards), had taken place since Shelley was thrown out of University College, Oxford, in 1811—technically for losing his nerve and so refusing to admit his authorship of the theological polemic *The Necessity of Atheism*.[64] Again, fifty-three years before, a national-prize-winning student, George Gissing, was expelled from Owens College (the future University of Manchester) for stealing money from his classmates to help support his mistress, an alcoholic prostitute named Marianne Helen ('Nell') Harrison; and he served a sentence of a month's hard labour (without remission).[65] But at least Gissing did commit a genuine crime, no matter the mitigating circumstances which the authorities in his case chose to put out of court. In comparison with such precedents, Empson must be considered to have been far more wronged than wrong-doing; and he himself grudged so too—'in many ways,' he wrote candidly to his junior friend Julian Trevelyan, 'it is very distressing that I have been so careless and so ill-used . . . '[66] ('He made no bones about being hurt,' Trevelyan was to recall for me, 'but he accepted things as they were.') He left other friends in no doubt that he felt dashed by the affair; defiant and prone to rebelliousness.

The national literary grapevine crackled with corresponding outrage. The distinguished writer David Garnett, for instance, wrote to Virginia Woolf's nephew Julian Bell (who was incidentally no enthusiast for what he regarded as Empson's intolerably obscure poetry) on 4 September:

I am naturally in a great fizz of indignation about the Cambridge scandal—but I can scarcely believe the reports I hear. Do you know Empson? Do you know if any remedy exists or if anything can be done to the Master of Magdalen[e]?

It seems to me there ought to be [be] a public protest for it is altogether too fanciful if the story I hear is true & it is merely the possession of French letters for which he loses a fellowship.[67]

For a while, for want of any possible career, it seemed that Empson might have to go into exile (quite like Gissing), though he favoured the gamble of freelance journalism. 'I am writing up Ambiguity in the country and feeling very puzzled about my future,' he wrote to Richards from the family home in Yorkshire. 'Would I be at all wise to creep into the Civil Service on any "character" the Master's charity would allow me (I have behaved politely to him; I thought him shockingly unscrupulous), or would I be at all wise to go and live in a garret, as I should like to do, go on with what I think worth doing, and take small journalist jobs if I can get them?' He then collected himself enough to go on, correctly:

It can so easily become despicable, don't you think, to hang about London starving and taking an interest in Art; one *ought* to be ambitious; and to refuse all solid jobs at my age is to prepare for oneself a great deal of bitterness and impotence in twenty years time.[68]

In fact, he felt so shaken by the catastrophe that his first desire was for a change of scene to clear his mind. He went off to Spain for a month, in company with John Marks, and took an interest in everything from blanched scenery to bullfighting and the treading of grapes.

No one was more exercised on Empson's behalf than his mentor, who dispatched numerous missives to his literary associates. At his request, C. K. Ogden agreed to counsel the outcast prize pupil, who reported back to Richards:

I have seen Mr Ogden, who was very brisk and seemed to think nothing impossible; he made me write to Mr Haldane and ask him to write to Mr Keynes and ask him to write to Mr Tawney and ask him to let me lecture to the W.E.A. So I have done that, and shall use your very generous testimonial (for which I must thank you very warmly) just to write to the W.E.A. myself at the same time; it seems a good thing to have done, if possible.

The suggestion that he approach J. B. S. Haldane, whom he had already met via Charlotte Haldane's 'salon' at Roebuck House, could not have been more apt. In 1925 J. B. S. Haldane had been found guilty of acting as co-respondent in the divorce proceedings of the then Charlotte Burghes; whereupon the *Sex Viri* (the 'Six Wise Men' sitting under the Vice-Chancellor), to whom he readily announced his responsibility, found him guilty of 'gross immorality' under Statute B, Chapter XI, Section 7, and so deprived him of his post as Reader in Biochemistry at the University of Cambridge. (When Haldane gave the *Sex Viri* the sobriquet 'Sex Weary', they reconstituted themselves as the *Septem Viri*.) The following year he won reinstatement on appeal. But no college would elect him to a fellowship: he would finally choose to resign in 1932, and later took up the position of Professor of Biochemistry in London. How suitable it was, then, that Empson should have this stout personage on his side when he was ejected from Cambridge on the mere suspicion of immorality. Haldane wrote to John Maynard Keynes with all the righteous, fighting energy he had learned from personal trial:

This letter is intended to serve as an introduction for my friend Mr. W. Empson B. A. Empson took a first in English Pt. II, following a second in Maths Pt II. He appears to me to be rather a good poet, and has a general education, which is rare. You will remember that he was given a by-fellowship at Magdalene.

He happened to be in possession of some contraceptives, which were stolen from him by one of the college servants, and presented to the master. He admitted having used articles of this type in the past, and was deprived of his post. I tried to make him fight the matter, but he would not, as he feared that the name of the woman in the case would come up.

He is now looking for a job, while writing a great work on literary criticism. I suggested that you might be able to help him. He appears to be a hard case, I understand that, in order to stay at Magdalene, he had turned down an offer of a fellowship elsewhere. But an academic career is now closed to him, though he is eminently suited for one, and not at all suited for any other sort. In his place, I should have brought a criminal charge against the vice-chancellor for receiving stolen goods. However he wouldn't, not being a pugnacious person.

I shouldn't write to you, in spite of the hardness of his case, unless I thought he was a very good man at his job. I. A. Richards, whose opinion is worth more, will support this statement.

Actually, it was not the intrepid J. B. S. Haldane who helped Empson to decide the next step in his guttering career; it was Charlotte Haldane who, when he carried his woes to Roebuck House, swiftly clarified the situation. (Magdalene's resolution to exclude Empson meant that technically he could no longer reside within the city of Cambridge, but the Haldanes' home—to which he removed himself for a while in the first instance—lay in Old Chesterton, beyond the city boundary.) Naturally he was upset, he told her, especially as he had a book to write: *Seven Types of Ambiguity*. When she asked him if he had any money, he responded: 'Only about £200 a year.' That was enough, she maintained; he should get himself a cheap room somewhere in London and write his book.[69] And that is just what he did—but not before he had obeyed one further directive. C. K. Ogden sought to get him a job at Birmingham University through the good offices of his friend Philip Sargant Florence, Professor of Commerce, who lived in a thronging house near the campus at Edgbaston. However, as Walter Allen tells the story—admittedly at second hand—'Empson arrived at Highfield for a weekend, with a toothbrush and a pair of pyjamas, and stayed for six months. Indefatigable in good works, Florence hoped to get Empson a job in the English Department and persuaded de Selincourt to come to tea and meet his protégé. Empson greeted him by telling him he had just read the most wonderful book, which he urged him to read. "And what is that?" de Selincourt asked. "*The Sexual Life of Savages* by Bronislaw Malinowski," Empson replied. There was no job for Empson in the English School at Birmingham.'[70] The story has ripened through its recitals—especially as regards the length of Empson's stay at Florence's house, a detail which belongs to folklore—but the gist of it rings true. Despite his lack of success at Birmingham, Empson was very willing to put in for another chance that Richards raised with him at this time, a post at Leeds University (unlike F. R. Leavis, who seems to have regarded the suggestion of the very same job at Leeds as little better than a slight).[71] He accordingly wrote to I. A. Richards in the autumn,

My family insisted on writing to Mr Ramsay to find whether he would give me a 'character' for the Civil Service, and apparently he has said he will. (The only letter I have seen says fairly definitely he won't.) So I suppose he wouldn't actually kick me out of Leeds University either. The Civil Service exam begins next August; and it would involve learning all the mathematics I have forgotten, with more; it is not the sort of examination I could do well, nor the sort of work I should do well if I got in. On the other hand August is the last chance.

I am fairly sure I am right not to go in.

If it was possible to go to Leeds I should be very glad, I think . . .

Please tell Mrs Richards she was quite right in thinking I should want to get away from the English, but my impulses are not so powerful as to drive me to China, and I was satisfied by a month in Spain.

She suggested Leeds; I wonder whether you would advise this; whether there are likely to be any vacancies; and how much I should depend on keeping my past dark—it doesn't seem to be very dark; I was told my Case had been mentioned to the International Sex Convention by somebody on the staff of the Yorkshire Post.

However there is no great hurry at the moment; I really seem to be living within my income.

In the event, as career opportunities failed to yield fruit, he was to spend nearly two years trying to live within his income in London. He rented a fair-sized first-floor room at 65 Marchmont Street (near Russell Square), a house owned by an engagingly bohemian doctor named Gilbert Back,[72] who was a consultant at one of the London hospitals. Mrs Back, christened Doris Russell, was an attractive, flamboyant person. Thirty years old, and always known as 'Jonny', she cut a fetching figure, tall and rakish, with raven black hair. She has been well described in a biography of the poet Edgell Rickword, who became her second husband: 'Energetic, resourceful, uncalculating and utterly without self-pity...she spoke abruptly like an officer's wife and swore like a trooper, yet when necessary she could act the lady to perfection ("Where are my fucking gloves? I've got to go to tea with the bloody vicar," she was once heard to say.)...Living with her, a friend has said, "was a little like dwelling on the lower slopes of a volcano"...'[73] Jack Lindsay's book *Franfrolica and After* talks about 'tiger women'—fierce, independent women—and Jonny was just such a woman. She was quite the sort of robust and strikingly handsome woman that the new lodger always admired. Some flavour of Empson's first days at Gillie and Jonny Back's is afforded by a letter from Ralph Parker to Elsie Phare, written on 15 November:

More, though, of Bill, who is as excited about everything as ever. I feel his intricate research, though not fantastic, is likely to make us all giggle too much. He is living in Bloomsbury in a large room, beautifully furnished above the waist level, below a sea of books, bread, hair brushes and dirty towels. On his first night his landlady was flung down the stairs into his room—a young thing, a doctor's wife—and Bill, lacking tea, which would have saved the situation—sat on a packing case, wondering whether this happened every night—how many beds there were in the house (for she said her man would kill her)—but [?driving] her back to her husband.[74]

Unfortunately, most of his days in London passed without melodrama. He would spend much of the working day in the British Museum Library, where he was admitted on 19 October, specifically—for the record—to study seventeenth-century English literature.[75] Yet mandatory forays to the pubs of Fitzrovia enabled him to consolidate his acquaintance in the literary world. But he was not at all loath to entertain at home. Among his notable guests, Sylvia Townsend Warner recorded in her diary for 11 April 1930 this delightful evening at Empson's digs:

I dined with W. Empson. I had gone a little frightened, fearing it might be a party of intellectual young things; but it was as though he had foreseen that I was a timid grandmother, for when I arrived it was to a very untidy room, with bottles and books on the floor, a delicious smell of frying, a saucepan of twopenny soup on a gas-ring and Mr Empson cavalier seul. So nothing could have been pleasanter. He had learned to cook because his sister runs Girl Guides, which led me to refer to 'the meteor flag of England'. He was extremely flabbergasted with the adjective, no doubt it would seem more striking to a scientist. We argued quite naturally about Eliot, and Windham Lewis and Richardson, and I found myself making gaffes quite comfortably. The argument was that I complained that W.L. had A Message. He was of the opinion that poets should have a message, should be in touch with real life. I didn't see then, but I do know [?now] that they should be so much in touch etc that they don't want to alter it. It is a drawing-room or study contact with real life which wants to move the groundsel off the landscape. Then he showed me Mr Ogden's sheet of practical [Basic] English, the vocabulary in six columns, with a translation of Job's warhorse into Ogden from which Job's warhorse emerged pretty unscathed. Then we talked about fish. According to his country lore eels are made from the tail-hairs of a white stallion. Then he explained his R. 101 to me: helium, the ur, unassimilable gas, first used for lifting airships, afterwards nitrogen, more common, and explosive, being a mixer—so when we use love to lift the soul, it is a mixer gas, and we must be careful accordingly, love better for getting on with our fellows. He told me that gravity was framed by the influence of *all* the stars. Then he talked extremely well about bull-fights, and then it was time for me to go home. I liked him very much. O, I forgot his picture of Newton: a thin haunted owl looking out of the hoary ivy-bush of its own hair, with rapacious, claw-like fingers: a most passionate face, that made me feel that the *principia* must be a real thing and not just a laudable epoch in history.[76]

From among his Cambridge friends he kept up perhaps best of all with the editor, bibliophile, and critic John Hayward, who had graduated from King's in 1927 and who thereafter, though bound to a wheelchair at his Kensington flat, enjoyed an eminent position in the literary life of London. Ronald Bottrall, who greatly admired Empson's work as poet and critic, has left a 'versified' account of visiting Empson at 'his Marchmont Street abode'—as he styles his bedsit with grand irony—

> Hands always inky.
> One entered skating on a kipper bone
> And heavily collapsed on a commode
> Garnished with scraps of egg and bacon.
> Refreshed by tepid beer
> Served in smeared tooth glasses
> One settled down to hear
> The youthful sage spinning his paradoxes.[77]

Empson would see a fair amount too of the tall, rangy, bespectacled figure of the critic and poet Michael Roberts, who according to John Lehmann looked like 'a giraffe that had taken to the serious life of learning, perhaps a university don of a giraffe. His gaze was sharp, rather formidable; but the rare, contracted smile that played across the strange zoo face was decidedly sympathetic...'[78] Empson, who found him less appealing and more stereotypically dour—'an angular ugly-ish Scotch sort of young man, very steady, no vices, rather lacking in joie de vivre for my taste; but of course very well-informed about English literature'[79]—had good reason to appreciate his literary perspicaciousness when Roberts picked out six of his poems for inclusion in the celebrated anthology *New Signatures* (published by the Hogarth Press in February 1932), which also blazoned work by eight other poets including W. H. Auden, C. Day-Lewis, Stephen Spender, William Plomer, and Julian Bell. A deeply political anthologist, Michael Roberts tried in his preface (or, better, manifesto) to promulgate the idea of a new generation or group whose work burned with revolutionary ardour; yet, although Auden, Day-Lewis, and Spender were assuredly political, there was really less unanimity of purpose in the collection than Roberts sought to proclaim. Notwithstanding, the anthology was a signal achievement, as J. H. Willis, Jr. has observed: 'The poems in *New Signatures* vigorously announced the arrival of a second generation of modernist poets on the Hogarth list. [T]he press was once more, if briefly, on the leading edge of modern poetry, a position not enjoyed since the Woolfs had hand printed Eliot's *Waste Land* in 1923.'[80]

Of an evening, Empson would particularly like to spend time at the Fitzroy Tavern in Percy Street (at least until its early closing time of 10.30), across the Tottenham Court Road, even though it was far from being his local. Run by a large, sweet-natured, and generous man named 'Papa' Kleinfeld, the Fitzroy featured a long saloon bar, a pianola, and sawdust on the floor. First World War recruiting posters adorned the walls. The artist and bibber Nina Hamnett, dubbed the 'Queen of Bohemia', held court at the Fitzroy Tavern; and Augustus John compared it to Clapham Junction. As Hamnett's biographer has remarked, 'Sickert, Duncan Grant, Vanessa Bell, Matthew Smith and Rex Whistler all lived in Fitzroy Street in the thirties. Fitzrovia acquired a more literary character as it became the favourite meeting-place for a new generation of poets, writers and editors such as Dylan Thomas, Stephen Spender, Louis MacNeice, William Empson, Geoffrey Grigson, Arthur Calder-Marshall and Keidrych Rhys. A whole society of artists and writers congregated there; not so much the fashionable and successful but the young and struggling, the rising stars as well as the hangers-on, the drop-outs and alcoholics, who either lived there or went there every night.'[81]

It was at the Fitzroy that Empson would hang on the chronically taciturn lips of the then famous Edgell Rickword, as he was to recall nearly fifty years on:

There was a time, around 1929, when Edgell Rickword was the Sage of the Fitzroy Tavern in Charlotte Street, much jostled by other sages, and very un-assertive, indeed he could hardly be got to speak, and then hardly above a whisper, but he was the real one, if you happened to know. John Davenport knew, and advised a few other Cambridge students, including myself; we felt that a visit to London had to include looking for him there. I remember straining my ears, and of course I often succeeded in hearing him, but I cannot remember anything he said. This is the less odd because what he said was remarkable for its studied moderation, and respected for that, even by us.[82]

In 1931, probably as a result of those indulgent encounters, Empson was invited to write a critique of the work of Virginia Woolf for a volume called *Scrutinies II*, edited by Rickword. His article on Woolf was quite scrupulously respectful, to some extent (as he later freely conceded) because the *grand dame* figured among the personages he had naturally sought to cultivate on his arrival in London. As a budding hack, he needed all the influential contacts he could get, and in any case he felt provoked by her work: he found the associative detail deployed in her fiction more suitable for lyric poetry. Woolf's graphic and very friendly assessment of her idiosyncratic young visitor, who had probably taken a drink or two to embolden himself before his august audience, features in two of her letters to her nephews, both written on 17 February 1930. To her nephew Clive Bell, she related succinctly: 'Mr Empson came to see us. A raucous youth, but I think rather impressive and as red as a turkey, which I like.' For Quentin Bell, she described Empson as 'a black and red sort of rook, very truculent, and refreshing. None of your etiolated, sophisticated, damp, spotted, you know what I mean...'[83] He struck others of his elders in similar fashion, as clever, assertive, vocal, and capable. Edmund Blunden, whom he met around this time—and whom he would always remember for his 'small shining eyes'—considered him a stimulating personality: 'a man of great possibilities'.[84]

Harold Monro, poet, publisher, and proprietor of the Poetry Bookshop, was another living legend whom Empson much admired. With his gentle, reserved demeanour, and a melancholy countenance that gave him the appearance (as John Drinkwater remarked) of a 'dejected Guards officer', Monro dedicated himself to the cause of poetry, fostering a free exchange of ideas between poets of diverse schools. At the height of his fortunes he had run his bookshop at 35 Devonshire Street; but declining business obliged him to move in 1926 to new premises at 38 Great Russell Street (almost directly opposite the British Museum), which Monro and his wife did out in shocking pinks and purples, with bright red window-frames; by the time Empson arrived on the scene the business was operating out of the back side of the same building, on Willoughby Street.[85] On Monro's death in March 1932, Empson was to write his obituary for a Japanese periodical in a vein that exhibited a high degree of respect and sad personal regard:

He stood for the old Bohemian tradition, still strong, they say, in the nineties, by which all sorts of literary people would meet each other as a matter of course: one knew that he would be in some special pub on Wednesdays, and that there would be other people there worth meeting; he had the good humour, and power of enjoyment, and power of scorn, which can keep such a thing going ... He carried with him in his last years an air of rich emotional life, which he had enough range of talk to sustain in all companies.

And he was a practising poet, a man who would be rung up by a daily paper and asked for something to help save a site for a hospital; I remember his boasting with great amusement and pleasure that he was given an hour to write something about some Royal Wedding. One may think the result was bad, but it shows there was some contact between a reputable writer and the larger reading public; most poets now who can be taken as seriously as Harold Monro cannot imagine themselves doing such a thing. I feel that with his death the poet in England will become even more isolated than before.[86]

The congenial and peculiarly British bohemian life of sordid bedsitting rooms, shabby clothes, beermugs brimming with cigarette butts and mantled in ash, loud pubs and good fellowship suited Empson to perfection; so did the support of other writers. Yet not everyone was to be accosted in casual barside manner. T. S. Eliot, poet, critic, editor of *The Criterion*, and director of Faber & Faber, who was the prize contact, had to be approached with due regard for dignity and deference. Empson had met Eliot at the breakfasts after the Clark lectures in 1926, and again when Eliot gave a paper to the Heretics during Empson's presidency, but he really could not count for much on so slight an acquaintance. But I. A. Richards lost no time in doing the necessary honours; he wrote from Tsing hua University in Peking in September 1929:

Dear Eliot,

I've just heard today from the best man I've ever had at Cambridge, William Empson, that Magdalene after giving him a Bye Fellowship largely under pressure from me have taken it away on the ground of some indiscretion with a feminine direction. I don't know any details but am most indignant.

He talks of coming up to London and working at the things he is interested in. This covers a good deal of 16th and 17th Century poetry and all sorts of things besides. I think he is a quite exceptionally good poet. *Cambridge Poetry 1929* will allow you to judge of this. He is a very ready hand with a pen and can produce new and valuable ideas about books within a very short time of first handling them. So he could be made great use of in reviewing. I'd always weigh his opinions as carefully as anyone's. I've told him that I would write to you in case you could help him to any journalism. I think he has a *small* private income. Don't mention to him that I have told you of his disaster...

Kind regards from us both to your wife and yourself.

Ever yours

I. A. R.[87]

Eliot proved to be a generous patron to Empson, inviting him to undertake a number of reviews for *The Criterion*.

Around 1930 I was sometimes allowed into Eliot's office to find books for review, and into the weekly At Home in the Poetry Bookshop or nearby, which Eliot attended [Empson was to recall after Eliot's death]. I was much impressed by the chalk-white face with the swollen purple lips, and felt confident that he had been brooding over the Crucifixion all night, or some other holy terror. But I never spoke to him about his religion, and might be asked now whether I have any evidence for this interpretation of his appearance. Well, it all seemed consistent. Literary gatherings talk a good deal about the sexual lives of other writers, and Eliot always welcomed any report of a crackup in these affairs, as a mercy in disguise; I thought at first it was a kind of joke, but it came out firmly and steadily. 'The greater torment / Of love satisfied' was a quite practical doctrine to him.[88]

While Empson thought Eliot's attitude towards broken relationships afforded him a sure but unwonted insight into the 'monstrosity' of the Christian religion that Eliot had come to profess, it seems quite likely that Eliot's expressed attitude arose out of bitter reflections upon the state of his own marriage.

A more fond and genuinely amusing anecdote is given in a piece that he wrote for a sixtieth-birthday Festschrift bestowed on Eliot. 'The Style of the Master' also manages to toy with self-mockery:

My most impressive memory is of walking up Kingsway with him after some lunch, probably about 1930, when finding myself alone with the great man I felt it opportune to raise a practical question which had been giving me a little anxiety. 'Do you really think it necessary, Mr Eliot,' I broke out, 'as you said in the preface to the Pound anthology, for a poet to write verse at least every week.' He was preparing to cross into Russell Square, eyeing the traffic both ways, and we were dodging it as his slow reply proceeded. 'I had in mind Pound when I wrote that passage,' began the deep sad voice, and there was a considerable pause. 'Taking the question in general, I should say, in the case of many poets, that the most important thing for them to do . . . is to write as little as possible.' The gravity of the last phrase was so pure as to give it an almost lyrical quality. A reader may be tempted to suppose that this was a snub or at least a joke, but I still do not believe it was; and at the time it seemed to me not only very wise but a very satisfactory answer. He had taken quite a weight off my mind.[89]

In terms of his close personal relations, the months after Empson's expulsion from Cambridge found him struggling with the divergent inclinations of his sexuality. Though still attracted to men, he was now equally inclined to seek out the company of women, to pursue pleasures of the kind he had experienced with Elizabeth Wiskemann. A passage from a review written over twenty years later gives an insight into his feeling of opening up to 'normal' relations with women:

I remember noticing in the Twenties [that is, the turn of the 1930s], when my mental eyes were peeping open, a rather curious tone about love taken at times by (for instance) Peter Quennell and Edgell Rickword as well as Graves, authors unlike in every other way. They wanted to combat a fashion for male homosexuality among intellectuals, a thing which was becoming tiresome for the boys as well as the girls, and they did this by saying it was sentimental to love other young men (because so reliably agreeable and comforting) whereas any man worth the name would take on a woman (because she would be certain to crucify him after stripping him of all his goods). This has always seemed to me a farcical way to recommend normal life, and if you really had a society in which women were as bad as that I would seriously think a man the more manly for rejecting them. You cannot simply set up a booth offering nothing but blood, toil, tears and sweat; there has to be some other influence, however unreasonable, before the crowd will surge after their leader. This local male revolt against women was chiefly a backwash from their recent liberation—they tended to put their demands too high.[90]

While that extract conveys all the good sense of hindsight, there is uncorroborated evidence that in the 1930s he had to do battle with the demons of misogyny in his own nature; he did not yet seem to know how to conduct himself with respect to women. Not far from his digs lived an old schoolfriend, Carew Meredith, whom he seems to have adulated, and possibly desired, at Winchester. Two years older than Empson, Meredith had made rapid progress through Cambridge and graduated in 1924. Nonetheless, the two men had managed to keep up over the years, and by the time Empson came to lodge in Marchmont Street, Meredith and his wife Sybil were living in a basement flat nearby in Mecklenburgh Square, which became a venue for fairly frequent parties (at which psychoanalysis was a standard topic of conversation). John D. Solomon, who had been up at Cambridge with Empson, and who was living just a few doors away in Marchmont Street (where Empson had found digs for him), formed the definite impression that Meredith's influence on Empson was, at least in their earlier years, 'probably homosexual in nature'. Meredith was charming, entertaining, disputatious, and often exasperating. As his wife was to recall, 'he could always stand embarrassing positions where other people would die'. Sybil Meredith's most abiding and shocking memory of Empson is that he apparently tried to strangle her during a party that he threw to launch *Seven Types of Ambiguity* in October 1930. Another man, she recalled, had to pull him off; and she was left feeling (in her own words) 'black and blue'. It was, she maintained, 'a ghastly experience'; and she could gather no immediate cause for the sudden terrible onslaught: 'he just disliked me.'[91] There are no surviving witnesses to the incident, and no other record of it, but there is also no good reason to doubt Mrs Meredith's allegation. It is scarcely possible to explain such an assault and battery—let alone explain it away. To say the least, Empson must have been dreadfully drunk to unleash violence against a woman; but whether this incident speaks for a deep-seated animosity towards women in general or only to Sybil herself is not to be discovered. However, it does seem possible that his action was the expression of a sudden sexual jealousy: his unconscious motive may have been that he wanted Carew Meredith for himself, and virulently resented Sybil for taking possession in marriage of his idolized friend. Whatever the cause, his conduct may indicate that he was undergoing an upheaval in his sexual orientation which caused him—if the story is true—to behave intolerably.

An altogether more fulfilling relationship came about when Solomon introduced Empson to another friend, a student doctor, though even this loving friendship was to be cut short—for an interim that was to last for many years—by a sadly baffling misunderstanding. Born on 4 October 1906, Alice Naish was just a week younger than Empson.[92] The third of eight children, she had grown up in Sheffield, where her parents, who were remarkable individuals in their own rights, both worked as doctors. (Her father, Ernest, had taken his degree at Trinity College, Cambridge, where he became friends with Bertrand Russell, and he was to cap his career by being appointed, at the age of 60, Professor of Medicine at Sheffield University; he was also President of the British Paediatric Association.

Among their various achievements, the parents set up the first infant welfare clinic in Sheffield.) After spending her early years at Sheffield Girls' High School and at St Leonard's (a boarding school in St Andrews, Scotland), Alice won a scholarship to study medicine at Girton College, Cambridge, where she took her MB. Her years at Girton (1926–9) coincided with Empson's at Magdalene, but they never met in Cambridge— even though one of her best friends, Margery, was the sister of Frank Ramsey, the famous son of Empson's tutor for maths. Kathleen Raine was another good friend of hers; and she was friendly too with Maynard Keynes's brother Geoffrey (later renowned as a bibliophile and editor). While Alice loved her time at Cambridge, her induction to the medical school had proved to be a shocking experience: she was obliged on her first day at lectures to endure a barracking from the men in her class. 'There were four women and 300 men in my class. As I came into the lecture theatre and took my first step the men started to slowly stamp their feet in unison. I had to walk down the steps, to run the gauntlet, to sit on the front row with the other girls, along with one other person [a Nigerian]— I would never make friends with any medical student; I was having nothing to do with these "scum", I said to myself.'[93] The experience confirmed her as a feminist, and put extra steel in her soul. She gained a first in the Natural Science Tripos, and—unusually for a woman—stayed on for a year to take a second Science Tripos. Being courageous and persistent, she had developed an absolute determination to create a career for herself; and she soon realized that medicine was destined to be her life. However, when her father discovered that the medical establishment in Sheffield had voted against having women serving as residents in hospitals, Alice, with her father's backing, looked elsewhere and landed a position as junior resident at the Royal Free Hospital in London. 'I was drawn to medicine less by the desire to heal than by an interest in science,' she admitted. She was dedicated to her independence, and to earning her own living. But she discovered to her surprise that she had a gift for clinical work and was especially skilled at diagnosis: she went on to win all the student prizes.

At Cambridge, she had met a man named Ludovick Stewart and presently agreed, while still a student, to become engaged to him. (The Stewarts were a prominent family in Cambridge, and Alice and Ludovick were pushed into one another's arms by his mother.)[94] All the same, she told her fiancé, she would not be married until she had completed her residency. 'The more I got involved with my work, the more I realized how much I was going to have to give up. I very nearly didn't get married.

Married women were not highly eligible for jobs. A married woman was thought of as someone to produce babies . . . I remember I very nearly ran away from being engaged because I wanted to go on with medicine. And I think it was sheer cowardice that stopped me doing it.' Ludovick presently took a job as a schoolmaster at Uppingham, and Alice pursued her new-found love of medicine.

In the meantime, however, she was introduced to Empson and instantly hit it off with him. They went to the cinema together, and to concerts at the Queen's Hall. They had supper with Empson's landlord, Gilbert Back, whom Alice found an entertaining man, a good conversationalist—though he would never speak about his work as a doctor. At other times they would simply walk all over London, or Empson would deconstruct the advertisements in the 'nostrum-plastered' underground.[95] 'He taught me to see things differently, to look at the world in a new way,' Alice told her biographer.[96] He was keen to tell her about his work and ideas; and he would cite lines from his poems which he thought applicable to her. Empson felt 'absolutely devastated' by the Cambridge affair, he told her: he minded it dreadfully, and didn't know what to do. He was rebellious, and seemed even to reject his family background, though she believed there was a strong relationship between Empson and his mother—'he was a Benjamin, her favourite.' Alice realized too that he was 'undoubtedly bisexual', but thought it not in the least unusual. 'When I was up at Cambridge, ordinary undergraduates wouldn't be seen dead with a woman student; even if they weren't homosexual, they pretended to be.' On the other hand, this made him undemanding company in one respect, as she told me: he 'had none of the graces that go with being oversexed. He wasn't the nasty grabbing sort. It was very deep in his philosophy that you never do anything unless it's mutually enjoyable.' Equally, if he did not appear to ask much of her, he seemed to take little trouble to pay court to her in a conventional fashion—or maybe he really didn't know how to. They always went back to his digs, never to hers—'but that again is just like William'.

Despite his casual demeanour, he was deeply attracted to her; he liked her intelligence and sharp curiosity, her tough-mindedness, her disregard for frivolous femininity, her briskness, her quick dry wit. She was intoxicated by him. 'I think I was very humble about myself at that time,' she reflected. 'From the very beginning I had been impressed by this very clever chap.' So eventually they had sex in his camp bed. But, unhappily, it turned out to be a one-night stand. The next day, Alice worried herself sick about what had taken place. She feared not only for what Empson might be thinking of her, but for two-timing her fiancé. 'I was in a terrible mess. It was so foreign to one's ideas, so wicked, to sleep with him; and besides I was playing at double-cross.' But instead of going back to Marchmont Street and trying to sort it out with him, she simply stayed away and took all the guilt upon herself. 'I was bitterly ashamed. I kept away. Look what I'd done! I'd let everybody down. I had gone off without explaining, and knew he must feel I'd been an absolute cad.' She worried too that he might reject her even if she did go back. 'I had all sorts of silly ideas, including the idea that William wouldn't want to go to bed with me again.' Finally, she started walking up and down Marchmont Street, trying to nerve herself to call on him—or to run into him in the street. And then the worst thing of all occurred: she saw him walking towards her—and he appeared to cut her dead. She would not see him again for ten years. 'To this day,' she remarked to me in 1992—even eight years after his death—'I don't even know if he just didn't see me. But I've got that clear vision.' The chances are that Empson, being terribly short-sighted and habitually abstracted, did not see her. But then again, he may have been embarrassed to see her just like that. In any event, it turned out just at this moment that Alice's fiancé got the sack from Uppingham School, so she came to think it a fateful thing that her relationship with Empson had coincidentally collapsed. She felt it would be unfair on Ludovick to lose his job and his girl at one and the same time: she therefore stuck to her word and was to marry him in 1933, and to bear him two children (including a daughter who was also to become a doctor, as did a niece: the family 'once filled a whole page of the British medical directory,' Alice proclaimed).

As the years advanced, Alice Stewart was to become a pioneer in radiation epidemiology, the youngest woman ever to be elected a Fellow of the Royal College of Physicians, and Reader in Social Medicine at the University of Oxford (and a professorial fellow of Lady Margaret Hall). In 1956 her research with the Oxford Survey of Childhood Cancers, which she ran from 1953 to 1979 (compiling a nationwide register of 22,400 childhood cancer deaths—the largest such database in the world), was to demonstrate that prenatal X-rays were causing childhood leukaemia. In 1974, after her official retirement from Oxford at the age of 68, she was to become Senior Research Fellow at Birmingham University, winning grants to a total of $2 million from the Three Mile Island Public Health Fund and continuously enhancing her reputation as, to quote the *New York Times*, 'perhaps the Energy Department's most influential and feared scientific critic':[97] a world authority on low-level radiation, and most highly respected of all in the USA. In 1985 she was elected a Fellow of the Royal College of Social Medicine and Public Health. She was nominated for the Nobel Prize, and in 1986 (the year of the Chernobyl accident) she received the Right Livelihood Award—the 'Alternative Nobel', as the media call it—which is awarded by the Swedish Parliament on the day before the Nobel Prize to honour those who have signally contributed to the betterment of society; Alice Stewart's award, for 'work on practical and exemplary solutions to the most urgent problems of today', was for the sum of £16,000 ($25,000). 'For vision and work,' reads the citation, 'forming an essential contribution to making life more whole, healing our planet and uplifting humanity.'[98] (Despite the prestige of this international award, the British Embassy would not send a car to pick her up at the airport, and only one newspaper in the UK carried the news of Alice's achievement, the *Yorkshire Post*—'and that's because the Right Livelihood has its headquarters in Bradford,' Alice noted. 'But I don't think it was mentioned anywhere else in England.') In 1991 she was awarded in Carpi, Italy, the Ramazzini Prize for epidemiology; and in 1996 she was featured as one of three pioneer women scientists in a Channel 4 TV documentary, 'Sex and the Scientist: Our Brilliant Careers'. Lastly, in September 1996, just a little short of her ninetieth birthday, she was appointed to an honorary professorship at Birmingham University for a period of five years. She died in Oxford on 23 June 2002, having been dedicated to the end to the furtherance of her daily research.

In the face of professional setbacks and sometimes ruthless official opposition, the quality that kept her going was—as she was happy to declare—her 'latent conceit'. 'I know that I am going to be right. I have known this for some time. It may not happen in my lifetime—in fact, it probably won't—but it will be found that we were on the right track. You'd be surprised how comforting that is.' In later years, William Empson and Alice Stewart were to recover a loving and supportive relationship. Yet he never offered to explain to her what he thought had happened between them in 1931; and she had the instinct never to ask him. From 1952 till his death in 1984, Empson was to be her lover and helpmate, albeit on a part-time basis (since he was working in Sheffield, and she in Birmingham; she would visit him at his digs in the north, or he would go down for weekends at her country cottage in Oxfordshire); on one occasion he would even draft for her a letter to *The Times* on the subject of smoking and cancer which was to be published over her name. She would become a deeply loved part of his life, and he of hers.

The single permanent triumph of the years immediately following Empson's departure from Cambridge—though even this certain achievement was to be ambiguous in its immediate critical reception, and so scarcely beneficial to his career prospects—was the publication of *Seven Types of Ambiguity* in 1930.

10

Seven Types of Ambiguity: The Critical Reception

I would like to tell you a secret 35 years old, about Ambiguity, but I can't think of one ... I was much supported by my pals then (Brunowski for instance) and rather enjoyed having attackers, whose folly was an interesting branch of study. I suppose a lot of the reviews praised the book more than it deserved, but that wouldn't occur to me at the time, and I thought I was attacked. The most extravagant piece of praise came from J H P Marks, who said with Spanish magnificence that one could tell (say, on meeting them at lunch) how many chapters each of our friends had read so far, as they modelled themselves upon each revelation in turn. We had been reading the *Tale of Genji,* and perhaps these compliments came from Lady Murasaki rather than Gongora.

Letter to Christopher Ricks, 31 January 1966

'I was thinking of offering a grammatico-critical essay to the Hogarth called the Seven Types of Ambiguity,' Empson wrote in June 1929 to his friend Ian Parsons (who had gone down from Cambridge to become an editor at Chatto & Windus): 'you don't do small essays (15,000 words) do you?'[1] It was the first outside news of a literary study that would eventually be hailed as the most transformative critical achievement of the century. Empson's youthful volume 'was to revolutionise the study of literature in the English-speaking world,' as Professor John Carey has correctly stated.[2] By July Empson found, seemingly to his own surprise: 'Ambiguity is growing on my hands ...'[3] In a postcard dispatched on 2 July, he confidently projected: 'Shall let you have Ambiguity in six weeks or so from now.' But the book did not get finished quite so soon. After having been sent packing by Magdalene, he resumed work over the summer at the family home in Yorkshire (prior to moving to London later in the year); whereupon it doubled in length in just a few weeks. 'I am trying to finish Ambiguity (it is over 60,000 words by now) and get it published,' he confided to Richards in the autumn, 'but I am much hampered by a doubt as to whether any of it is true. I feel that if it (Ambiguity, not its untruth) attracted notice, my position would be stronger.'[4]

In the event, the bulk of the book was delivered to the publishers by the end of the year, with the remainder following by April 1930: all told, it added up to about 90,000 words. 'I have just offered *a* finished version of Ambiguity to Chattos, to ask them how it ought to be altered,' Empson told his mentor. 'It is a very amateurish sort of book . . .' The very first reader to see the full text of *Ambiguity* was actually Charles Prentice, the senior partner of Chatto's—'a man of extraordinarily perceptive taste,' as Parsons related in a later year; 'and I well remember his coming in and saying that he'd read it at a sitting, and had stayed up until 2 a.m. to finish it.'[5] Parsons was therefore eager to publish this unprecedented work ('Your self-generatory style—if I may call it!—seems to me just suited to this kind of analysis'),[6] and so towards the end of July he wrote again: 'I am so glad to hear that Ambiguity is progressing so swiftly and satisfactorily, and I am already very anxious to discover your seven varieties . . .'[7]

On 13 April 1930, *Seven Types of Ambiguity* was finally accepted for publication by Chatto & Windus (with an advance of £25, and royalty terms that are magnificent by today's standards: 15 per cent on the first 6,000 copies sold, 20 per cent thereafter); 2,000 sets of sheets were printed, and the book came out on 6 November (500 sets of the sheets were destined for an American edition to be published by Harcourt, Brace, Inc. in 1931);[8] it was priced at 7s. 6d. Yet subscription sales amounted to only 146 copies by late in 1930, which did not augur well—in fact, it took more than a decade to sell the first 1,500 copies.[9] Still, the reviews of *Ambiguity* were extensive—though some of the notices admitted a feeling of being intellectually winded, and others were even aggressively defensive. A critical star had arrived, and no one could doubt his generative genius.[10] F. R. Leavis hailed him in the *Cambridge Review*: 'His book is the work of a mind that is fully alive in this age, and such a book has a very unusual importance.'[11] From Peking, I. A. Richards recommended the work to T. S. Eliot, though in a fashion that may be thought to salute his pupil's promise more than this present accomplishment: 'Empson's book has just arrived, and, looking hastily through it, I am more than ever convinced that, in spite of all his youthful exuberance (overdoing it), he has the goods and the pen with which to deliver them. Do look into it yourself.'[12]

Empson's critics have always insisted that he had much to answer for, not the least that he was far too 'ingenious'—a slighting term as the reviewers used it. His interpretations showed inspirited insight, along with a dubiously applicable methodology, but offered no real theory of literature. He was highly skilled at operating his self-designed 'machinery' but essayed few judgements of value or critical conclusions. Empson's friend James Smith, for instance, warned in *The Criterion* in July 1931 of the 'danger that...judgements of values will be forgotten'.[13] While the analytical results showed remarkable, keen perceptiveness in Empson himself, his critics alleged, his methods more frequently induced a form of irresponsibility or delinquency in their author (and at a later date in his supposed epigoni among the so-called 'New Critics'). T. Earle Welby, in a piece entitled 'Time to Make a Stand' (*Week-End Review*, 3 January 1931), protested with virtual seriousness that the 'remarkable young recruit' was 'so mischievously promising...that he must be extinguished, if possible, forthwith.' (Thirty-five years later, Empson could still recall that notice, though he misremembered the reviewer's name: 'Maybe P. H. Newby wrote a particularly funny attack.'[14])

'Reviewers were telling me, as soon as *Ambiguity* came out,' Empson was to write to one of a later generation of critics, Roger Sale, 'that not all poetry was ambiguous, and I could see that the method worked best where the authors had had some impulse or need for the process ...'[15] If it is now widely agreed that his taxonomy, or scale (or hierarchy, if it is one) of the seven types of ambiguity—seven representing a convenient and workable range rather than an absolute figure—did not yield a universally applicable system of classification, at the time of its first publication the book provoked most outrage with the very suggestion, and indeed the amply persuasive demonstration, that poetic effects could be elucidated through the scrutiny of diction, tropes, grammar, and syntax; that a poem is a compound of analysable meaning. John Middleton Murry made the case for the defence in the *Times Literary Supplement* (18 December 1930): 'a poem is a poem not least by virtue of its power to ward off these vagaries of the intellect. It is to some degree an incantation ... For, paradoxical though it must sound, the poem and the words which compose the poem are not the same thing, by the same necessity that an organic whole is not the same thing as the sum of its parts.'[16] To put it bluntly, Empson had the nerve to show that poetry may (and probably always does) add up to pragmatic sense. A poem comprises complex concepts, not just univocal discourse and approximate sounds; and it is available to analysis as much as to being introsumed in the passive fashion of affective-appreciative description— 'that humble readiness to receive the impress of a poem in its totality,' as Welby protectively styled the latter.[17]

But the first amazement or affront came down to two pertinent objections. First, his approach seemed to bypass judgements of value, and he had in any case been too prodigal in his (potentially uncontrolled) associative and sometimes impressionistic interpretations. Second, he too often worried the parts without reference to the whole—dissecting a sentence or a section in place of a full poem—so that local effects of word and phrase were called to do duty for a fully contextualized account. In sum, he was capable of working out a proliferation of possible (and, as it seemed to him, invariably fetching) ambiguous meanings but with too little regard to their relevance to the literary work as a whole. As Elder Olson later asserted the case, Empson could be accused of confounding 'potential with actual meaning'—the obvious danger was of over-reading—and in any case what Empson took to be 'the definitive property of poetry, ambiguity... [was] not a poetic principle; it [was] the rationalization of an opinion ...Empson's hypothesis...neither implies the data nor is implied by them.'[18]

With all its partly undisciplined enthusiasm, *Seven Types of Ambiguity* does indeed establish the 'phenomenon' of ambiguity more as critical performance than as poetic principle. Despite its numerical organization, it offers less a methodology than Empson's own methodized brilliance. While he never retracted his opinion that ambiguity was inherent in all good poetry, the question as to whether it is in fact a necessary and even defining property of all poetry must remain in question.[19] His claim apropos ambiguity most likely falls into the category of what E. D. Hirsch Jr. has termed 'broad genre theory'; it is a 'value-preference'.[20] (Given that the catch-all term 'ambiguity'—for which Empson admitted the widest possible definition—may be thought to carry suggestions of weakness or vacillation, certain rival critics have occasionally sponsored more positive terms, though none has managed to catch hold of the scope of the concept quite as well as ambiguity; Philip Wheelwright, for example, coined the term *plurisignation*: that is, multiple meaning or complexity.[21]) But what Empson did manage with consummate success was to reveal and unfold innumerable cases where ambiguity has a significant presence and fundamental effect. 'The class of readers I addressed in *Ambiguity* were those

interested in this subject, explaining how an agreed effect was obtained,'
he would explain in 1971.[22] Not prescribing but explicating. Yet if he
believed that he was simply setting out the working parts of a radical
though obscure machine—the modes of action of poetical effect—many
reviewers charged him with drowning in his own incontinence (he had
only himself to blame for introducing the metaphor in his very first
chapter)—or else in what Muriel Bradbrook discriminated as his gusto
and his friskiness. In their judgement, he multiplied exuberant (and sometimes dissociated and unfocused) explicatory possibilities to the point of
redundancy.[23] 'I recognised in the book,' Empson responded in a weak
passage of his preface to the second edition, 'that one does not want merely
irrelevant ambiguities, and I should claim to have had some success in
keeping them out. To be sure, the question how far unintended or even
unwanted extra meanings do in fact impose themselves, and thereby drag
our minds out of their path in spite of our best efforts to prevent it, is
obviously a legitimate one; and some of the answers may be important. But
it is not one I was much concerned with in this book' (p. xiii). As the years
passed, he would choose now and then to take refuge in *l'esprit de l'escalier*—
as when he remarked that 'some kinds of error are best avoided if you just
jump at the thing'[24]—but by the 1950s he was to resume his characteristic
combativeness in defending his position: 'if the poem was good, and if I
could go at it the way I wanted to,' he wrote in an important review essay
entitled 'Still the Strange Necessity', 'nothing in the poem at all would be
irrelevant by the time the critic had finished explaining. I still think this a
proper objective . . . '[25]

    He never had much regard for the importance of proclaiming a theory,
a code of critical practice. In 'The Verbal Analysis' (1950)—an essay that
stands out as a profession of his continuing faith—he would claim: 'a critic
ought to trust his own nose, like the hunting dog, and if he lets any kind of
theory or principle distract him from that, he is not doing his work. This
does seem to me the deepest truth about the matter . . . '[26] Yet any critic
who refuses to legislate on ways and means, let alone ends, might well slip
up on analytical rigour and so fall foul of irresponsible amateurishness; and
several readers charged Empson accordingly. Cleanth Brooks, for instance, was to slate him as 'an incorrigible amateur'.[27] Yet on two matters
Empson remained staunch. While other critics may choose to make value
judgements, he felt in no way obliged to do so: 'to assess the value of the
poem as a whole is not the primary purpose of [my] kind of criticism, or at
any rate ought only to emerge from the analysis as a whole.'[28] Second, on
the crucial issue of ambiguity, he regarded it as axiomatic that poetry is not

merely a matter of bearing witness to beauty or conjuring an epiphany; nor is it necessarily the product of personal assurance or composure. On the contrary, it is normally and by definition a complex and condensed mode of utterance, a kind which requires the poet to address deep personal, social, psychological, or ideological conflicts and to have comprehended alternative and invariably conflicting forms of expression, attitude, or ideology. Ambiguity connotes opposition. How else does one explain (he was to ask by way of climaxing his preface to the second edition) the cause of the presence in poetry of 'so straddling a commotion and so broad a calm'?[29] If a poem is answerable to intelligence, it does not consist of merely emotive statements: it speaks a grammar of invariably plural and probably conflicted meanings.

'I got interested as an undergraduate in the verbal analysis of literary effects,' he would tell a radio audience in 1939.

This is only a part of literary criticism, because the interest is the quasi-scientific one of showing how a literary effect is produced. It does not in itself give a judgement of value. It assumes an agreement, among those who seem most likely to know, as to what effect a given bit of writing produces, and goes on to argue that this can only have been produced by a curious but demonstrable process of interlocking and interacting structures of meaning. You may later get judgements of value from this line of approach, but it does not start with them. The fundamental idea in this sort of criticism is that the human mind (as a fact of psychology) does not naturally assume *one* structure of grammar in a sentence, or *one* sense to each word, or even one structure of implication within the single word, from the relations between that word's possible senses. In the casual use of language which goes straight ahead, and also in the literary reading which tastes the possibilities, the human mind has *more* grasp of the structure of the possible meanings than it has when trying to weigh the sense of the words carefully... But the full logical analysis of what seems a casual literary experience is not merely not single; it is often so complicated that it seems tedious and very improbable. Now if you accept this rather paradoxical theory, and I convinced myself that it worked, then the whole question of criticism looks rather different. All criticism since Aristotle has assumed that some understanding, of how a bit of literature works on you, makes you appreciate it better. But on this view there is a good deal to understand. So... I was... trying in a blind way to work out a handy machine for analysis...

So often when Empson speaks of ambiguity or complexity of meaning in poetry, he invokes considerations of 'associated meanings' or the claims of doctrine: that intimate connection distinguishes his aims from those of the strict grammarian or linguistician. Geoffrey Strickland, in 'The Criticism of William Empson', asserted that his 'theory of ambiguity and complexity is largely technical. It is concerned with analysis rather than with judgement.'[30] But to suggest that judgement or evaluation is the only alternative to technical analysis is to scorch the rich territory in-between. Empson himself sniffed at the very idea of laying down 'rules for critics';[31] he travelled at will all the way from technique to interpretation. All the same, at every stage he was baited for his supposed trespasses; and he felt honour bound to answer every challenge, acknowledging that his opponents often made strong cases. 'Controversy demands imagination,' he foresaw as early as 1931; 'you must try to understand your opponent's position, so that you can select the things worth talking about; so that you can find the root of his errors, or of your disagreement with him.'[32]

In addition to the accusation that he offered no judgements of value in his early work—which he answered with the not altogether satisfactory assurance that he would hardly have bothered to expound his chosen examples unless he had believed them to be good poetry—critics have most commonly levelled against him the charge that in *Ambiguity* in particular he flourished all too many 'possible alternative reactions' (his own words).[33] The critically promiscuous juvenile scored some hits but also several misses: he paid too little attention to questions of both authorial aim and literary and historical relevance. According to R. G. Cox in a review of the second edition, 'His characteristic fault, the lack of control by any over-riding sense of relevance, comes out interestingly in his very first example, the note on "Bare ruined choirs, where late the sweet birds sang" [Shakespeare, Sonnet 73].'[34] Empson conceded in a BBC broadcast, *Literary Opinion*, on 20 October 1954:

The argument which seems to me strongest, in these literary critics who say that Empson is absurd, is that they say the overall effect of a piece of writing, the general intention of the author, is what decides what you make of a particular line. The critic mustn't pick on one line and get astonishingly irrelevant meanings out of it, because that isn't what anybody does if he is reading properly. Yes, but I never denied that; and I have been able to argue back, three or four times, never leaving out a serious attack, that I *was* considering the whole background, all the time, and that was why I thought the extra meanings fitted in. The three main cases have been a line in a Shakespeare Sonnet, and a poem by George Herbert ['The Sacrifice'], and a poem by Gerard Manley Hopkins ['The Windhover'] . . . I know I made mistakes, but you can't laugh the whole method off; it can still stand up even when the fashion changes.

His mistakes included the capricious habit of misquoting from memory.[35]

F. W. Bateson (in an article adopting Matthew Arnold's title 'The Function of Criticism at the Present Time', and in correspondence arising out of it) borrowed the accusation that Edmund Wilson had levelled at T. S. Eliot's criticism—that it was 'fundamentally non-historical'—in order to tax Empson for manifesting a 'defective contextual sense' when he invented 'the by now almost notorious list of reasons, ten in all' for linking Shakespeare's boughs with ruined monasteries. 'The real critical error is more fundamental,' Bateson claimed. 'It is simply that the line on which Empson expatiates is not a separate sentence or even a separate subordinate clause. It is a verbal fragment that is, strictly speaking, *unintelligible* when lifted like this out of its syntactic context.' Empson's response was in that instance not very convincing, his final comment brave though perhaps a little bruised: 'The intention of this passage, which came early in my old *Ambiguity*, before the real problems began, was just to show what putting in some background is like; in Shakespeare's time, the ruins of monasteries must have been a prominent feature, so that *any* contemporary reader would easily think of this meaning for the line—it isn't a question of the peculiar mind of Shakespeare. I don't think it need have startled people into either kisses or kicks to have me offer this placid example of a bit of background.'[36] In other cases he returned with a far more assertive and convincing defence, in particular on Herbert's 'The Sacrifice' and Hopkins's 'The Windhover'.[37]

The most damaging later charge, which is almost always based on the youthful excesses of *Seven Types of Ambiguity*, was to give him issue in the form of the so-called New Criticism—John Crowe Ransom must take responsibility for settling the paternity case in his book *The New Criticism* (1941)—and its succeeding 'schools', including Deconstructionism, all of which Empson fiercely resented and disclaimed.[38] As late as 1986 John Carey recycled in the *Sunday Times* a commonplace misrepresentation with this casual report of *Seven Types of Ambiguity* (unqualified by any consideration of Empson's later position):

Essentially what this book showed was that if you were ingenious enough you could find alternative meanings which no one, least of all the poet, had suspected before. Consequently you could rewrite the whole canon of literature an almost infinite number of times. There was no longer any question of looking for a final or 'authorial' meaning—the critic's job was to extract those meanings that would appeal to his public...

One aspect of this approach is that the author ceases to matter, since literature is no longer regarded as the expression of a personality. For Empson this was an advantage.[39]

The truth is that Empson felt appalled at what he termed those 'bother-headed theoretical critics'[40] who dismissed authorial intentions and despised historicism: that is the certain reason why he subsequently took pains to patch in the 'background' to some of the key analyses on which critics challenged *Ambiguity*—though it does seem apparent too that at the time of writing the book he had been short of sufficient historical knowledge.[41] Thereafter he always attempted to recover or reconstruct a tenable interpretation of historical circumstance and creative intention: to plot both the local conditions and the likely aims of a literary work. He wrote in 1979:

Carey, in his Inaugural Lecture on becoming a Professor [in 1976], announced a rigorous policy; there must be no more paraphrase, no more reading in or spelling out, because all such tampering with a text was the work of Vandals. I came in for some of the rough stuff myself, and thought he could have found stronger examples in what I wrote fifty years ago, though I would never have intentionally gone beyond the intention of an author, either in his consciousness or his unconsciousness. But it struck me that the program as he announced it was actually incompatible with teaching, let alone his own style of written criticism; it became a question whether he would achieve a Houdini-like reappearance.[42]

Three years on, he felt genuinely pleased to find that John Carey was in fact 'deeply in sympathy with the author, knowing what he often wants to do . . . it is a welcome advance on [his] Inaugural.'[43]

'The modern classroom demands that the children need only read the words on the page before them,' Empson wrote in a letter (*c*.1973), 'and must never be expected to have any general information or knowledge of life (except of course the raw mass of prejudice which Teacher has to cater for): so I do feel mildly cheerful when I can speak as from outside this airless place.'[44] If 'bother-headed theoretical critics' confirmed him in his disinclination to venture a theory of criticism, the cheerful open air of human contextualism persuaded him never to underestimate a writer's intelligence. It was axiomatic, he believed, that any author would naturally question and probably dissent from conventional cultural doctrines. 'Contradiction is a powerful literary weapon,' he insisted in *Ambiguity* (p. 197); and again in the valuable preface to the second edition: 'When Mr James Smith objected [in *The Criterion* in 1931] to my dealing with "conflicts supposed to have raged within the author", I think he was overplaying his hand very seriously; he was striking at the roots of criticism, not at me.'[45] To strike at the roots of criticism was to deny that the critic could venture a valid interpretation: it denied him access both to the psychology of the poet and to the social and ideological context of the poetry.

As Empson interprets it, good poetry never makes glib syntheses but struggles to cope with the claims and counter-claims of the poet's culture; it certainly does not resolve the struggle by the grace of irony or paradox, which would mean saving faith and thought. By definition, the best authors always reserve their independence of judgement and outwit sub-servience. Art is at odds with orthodoxy. 'A society is always in develop-ment, and an artist has a function in it like that of the designer of fashions,' he was to write about Coleridge, taking his cue from Herbert Read's account, in *The True Voice of Feeling* (1953), of the claims of the Romantic artist—which Empson thought no novelty but a permanent condition of the creative mentality. 'The paradox of the artist is thus the opposite of the Christian one; he must say ruthlessly what he himself likes or wants, and only by this selfishness can he help his fellows.'[46] The paradox accords with the Benthamite ethic he had learned from I. A. Richards.[47] This abiding concern with rational resistance bridges the apparent gap between his supposedly exclusive and unjudging interests in the early books—first with technical analysis, then with linguistics—and the ethical declarations of *Milton's God* (1961) and related later essays.

Hugh Kenner once highlighted what he called the 'picaresque zest'[48] of *Ambiguity*; and more than twenty years later (in 1974) Empson himself tended to agree, though with firmly redeeming qualifications:

The term Ambiguity was a bad choice so far as it suggested that the author was being artful and tricky—he need only be conscious of the process, I suppose, enough to make him try for a different form of words if he has lit on a damaging ambiguity. Perhaps I liked the word because I was myself gleefully engaged in regarding the result of imagination as trick-work. But I think a willing reader soon got to ignore this harmful suggestion, which I certainly didn't want in serious cases.[49]

Certainly the two most serious cases had been his climactic analyses of Hopkins's 'The Windhover' and George Herbert's 'The Sacrifice', where he argued that the authors had felt obliged to confront rather than merely to accommodate themselves to the comforting but insidious pseudo-paradoxes of Christian doctrine. In other words, *Seven Types of Ambiguity* was already gathering the storm that was to break in *Milton's God*. It not only purveyed a new mode of submitting imaginative literature to the proof of cognitive analysis, it had also culminated—artfully and gleefully—with two analyses that specifically challenged Christian doctrine and history. While critics eventually caught up with Empson's heterodoxy, contemporary reviewers generally found themselves too stunned by his whole analytical approach to poetry to seize on his transgressiveness. But this is not to find fault with the perceptiveness of those readers who first

winced or wondered at the new criticism. At the time of writing, not even
Empson himself fully appreciated the more profound and enduring import
of his inflammatory insights, especially when (as he later came to think)
they had been distractingly infected by the equally new and ravishing
model of Freudian analysis. As Empson interpreted their poems, Hopkins
and Herbert had externalized in their poetry the sense of conflict between
the call of Christ and the resistant call of human intelligence and moral
independence. Even though he had partly couched his original analysis of
'The Sacrifice' (for instance) in Freudian terms, he insisted in later years,
his interpretation of the logical contradictions negotiated within the poem
was still absolutely correct. Readers should not neglect the true meaning
just because the youthful critic may have over-indulged himself in the way
he chose to explicate it. Herbert had faced up to a genuine 'mental
conflict', not a peculiar problem of a psychological order. 'I can claim,'
he was to write in 1947, 'that my last example of the last type of ambiguity
was not concerned with neurotic disunion but with a fully public theological poem.'[50] Still later, in 1963, he re-evaluated in 'Herbert's Quaintness':

I put 'The Sacrifice' last of the examples in my book, to stand for the most
extreme kind of ambiguity, because it presents Jesus as at the same time forgiving
his torturers and condemning them to eternal torture. It strikes me now that my
attitude was what I have come to call 'neo-Christian'; happy to find such an
extravagant specimen, I slapped the author on the back and egged him on to be
even nastier...Clearer now about what the light illuminates, I am keen to
stumble away from it.[51]

What Herbert confronted in his poetry, Empson insists, was the fundamental opposition between the demands of the Christian God and the
birthright of humanity: the responsibility to exercise individual judgement.
Those imperatives are traditionally incompatible, and the conflict in poets
who have felt compelled to tackle the subject stems from the effort not to
dissolve or resolve but to encompass such intolerable stresses. 'It was in the
air of Herbert's time that the paradoxes of Christianity were a moral
embarrassment,' he commented. 'The basic need of Metaphysical Wit,
though seldom its conscious purpose, was to keep these new qualms at
bay.'[52]

    In terms of Empson's career as a whole, therefore, his early pages on
'The Sacrifice' are a cardinal text; dating from 1929-30, they were to seed
the ferociously catechizing writings of his later years—notably *Milton's
God*.[53]

In 1941 John Crowe Ransom justly wrote of *Seven Types of Ambiguity*: 'I believe it is the most imaginative account of reading ever printed, and Empson the closest and most resourceful reader that poetry has yet publicly had.'[54] The book had succeeded in permanently changing the mode and function of literary criticism in English—reviewers and readers felt galvanized and disgruntled by turns, but never again could any serious critic merely 'appreciate' a poem without offering sustained verbal analysis—and yet the example it set took a decade or so to be accepted as first-rate sense, a model for the future. In the meantime, the mixed reception did little to improve his fortunes: he had no real job, and not even a working path to prospect. The reception of *Ambiguity* was invigorating, but he still wanted a career; otherwise, as he later confessed of this period in London (1930–1), he was beginning to behave in a 'hysterical' way in Bloomsbury.[55] Apart from falling down in his personal relations, he reckoned that money was in tight supply. In the summer of 1930 he had taken up private tutoring, as he told Richards: 'I am cramming some young men for the Civil Service English paper; it is rather good for me, as I have to bring them lists of dates and quotes to learn by heart; I have undertaken to do that till the beginning of August, but I shall be able to make some arrangement if I have to start before then.' Richards hoped to find him a 'start' in China, but no post seemed to be forthcoming as the months moved on. Accordingly, just as *Ambiguity* appeared in print (and with small sales being forecast), he checked with his brother Arthur as to the advisability of his depending on the modest income afforded him out of the family estate.

'Dear Bill,' his robustly realistic brother replied,

> There is nothing in the will about the rent charges being paid only when a certain amount of money comes in and you are presumably entitled to your money as long as the estate is a running concern . . .
>
> Generally speaking, however, the family situation about money is a little murky; no doubt it will buck up again but I should certainly not forgo any chance of earning an honest penny if I were you . . .
>
> Yours, Arthur[56]

Although Empson had begun to hanker to follow Richards to China, the only opportunity that turned up for him in 1931 was a post that had been prematurely renounced by Peter Quennell: a fixed-term (three-year) university appointment in Japan. With some misgiving, he took the job—though not before making a vain attempt to follow up an introduction by Eliot to Arthur Waley, the translator of Chinese and Japanese poetry (who never actually saw the Far East but who would be deemed to have established valuable contacts). He casually acknowledged Eliot's assistance:

Thanks for that introduction, which as it turned out I couldn't use, Waley being out. I have been offered a job in Tokyo, safer and more remunerative but (there seems no doubt) much less interesting: and shall be going there in August.
    Yours very sincerely, W. Empson[57]

It turned out to be exceptionally interesting, and ultimately rather dangerous.

11

The Trials of Tokyo

O N his first night in Tokyo, Empson caused a farcical incident that might have marred relations with his hosts. After booking into the Station Hotel, not far from the Imperial Palace, he gamely set off in search of food, drink, and tobacco. When he returned, it was so late that the hotel had already been locked up for the night. He was far from sober and set about trying to force an entrance through a ground-floor window—which happened to give access only to the redbrick station next to the hotel. 'Two guards on duty in the staff room of Tokyo Station were astonished to be woken by two long legs appearing at the window,' it was reported. 'They thought at once that a burglar had been trying to enter the building. So they seized the legs of the unknown intruder, pulling his body down. It happened to land in a bucket of water always kept ready for such emergencies as fire or earthquakes.' The situation was eventually sorted out when the hotel register confirmed the visitor's name.

Unhappily, the story of Empson's drunken blundering featured as an item of comic gossip in a newspaper, *Asahi*, the next day (1 September 1931), under the headline: 'Once caught, it was not a burglar but a university professor!'[1] He was wrongfooted from the start; and even though the kerfuffle was just as vexatious to himself as to anyone else, he could not afford to blot his copybook again. Empson was never strong on good or appropriate behaviour in general, and no one had adequately briefed him on the protocols of professional conduct in Tokyo.

His three-year contract as a professor of English Language and Literature at the University of Literature and Science (Tokyo Bunrika Daigaku, a newly established government institution for teacher training), beginning on 29 August 1931, would close with a more serious affair.

It was an inauspicious moment for a young teacher (not quite 25) to bring the tidings of English literature to the youth of Japan. Japan would set its course for confrontation with the West, and his students were to become possessed by the upsurge of ferocious nationalism that marked the beginning of what is properly acknowledged as the 'Fifteen Years' War'— truly it was the start of the Second World War—even within a month of his arrival in Tokyo. Six years later, in August 1937, he was to show up in Peking just as the Japanese army launched its full-scale offensive against mainland China. But it was in Tokyo that he heard of the so-called 'Mukden Incident' which signalled that on 18 September officers of the Kwantung Army, Japan's expeditionary forces in the Leased Territory of north China, had put into operation their plan to conquer Manchuria and so stem the perceived threats of Soviet Russia, Nationalist China, and Western imperialism. ('There seems to be no doubt,' Empson wrote to his mother, facetiously to reassure those at home, 'the Japanese don't want to *live* in Manchuria, which is cold and full of Chinese.')[2] In Tokyo a month earlier, Premier Hamaguchi Osachi, President of the Minseito party, who had been wounded by gunshot in 1930, had died of his injuries; he had bequeathed his lame-duck government to Wakatsuki Reijiro, whose cabinet lasted only until it resigned at the end of the year. His successor, Inukai Tsuyoshi, President of the Seiyukai party, survived less than five months: he was assassinated in the '15 May Incident' of 1932—a day when he was due to entertain Charlie Chaplin (who took himself off to see a Sumo tournament). Inouye Junnosuke, a former Minister of Finance, and the industrialist Baron Dan Takuma, director of the Mitsui holding company, both liberals, were murdered; and on 1 March the putatively independent state of Manchukuo was inaugurated, with the wretched ex-Emperor of China, Pu Yi, set up as puppet Chief Executive. Harried by economic problems and a crisis in foreign policy, both of the conservative political parties had failed to revive the country. Civilian and military bureaucracies seized power, at once stepping up military expenditure and war production and reflating the economy. Militarism had worsted parliamentary government.[3]

'The 15th May Incident had a significance for modern Chinese nationalism second only to that of the Manchurian Incident eight months earlier,' Richard Storry has written. 'After 15th May, 1932, liberalism, as a factor in official life, was a spent force. There could be no turning back from the path of overseas expansion, opened up by the seizure of Manchuria, or from the course of increasing authoritarian control at home.'[4]

Like every foreigner with little understanding of Japanese culture and sensibilities, Empson found it hard to come to terms with the country, especially in conditions of increasing regimentation. Peter Quennell, who had held the same contract post in 1930–1, recorded that 'every lecturer at a government school or university thinks of himself primarily as an official, and to succeed, must have the official point of view. Politically and socially, he must be irreproachable...'[5] The austere regard of his colleagues withered the Englishman's morale, and he was relieved to go home after a year. But then, a year after his return to London, and the year after Empson took himself off to Tokyo, Quennell capitalized on his wretched tour of duty by publishing in 1932 an elegant and remorselessly candid account of it, *A Superficial Journey through Tokyo and Peking*—which Empson thought 'a good book... though he oughtn't to have done it'.[6]

'I had pictured the Japanese as a sharp-witted, uncannily acute race, endowed by nature with every superficial gift,' wrote Quennell. 'At first acquaintance, the very opposite proved true; hesitating, tongue-tied and always nervous, they suggested a people of adolescents, alternately assertive and depreciatory, prone to sudden collapses and odd recoveries, to spurts of rudeness and long intervals of embarrassment, over-eager, over-calculating, over polite.'[7]

Empson had been forewarned in just such a vein, and in one of his first letters to I. A. Richards he broadly agreed, wavering between boisterous satire, second-thoughts, and shame for his self-pity:

Other people have been telling me what you said in your last letter, about the spiritual conditions being so pinched; I heard Quennell on that topic before I left London, anyway. It is quite true that the Japanese are uncomfortable bogus people who don't really enjoy anything in sight: the Christian converts who look at you with great liquid crucified eyes like spaniels with indigestion (a most embarrassing thing in a lecture room) seem anyway to have some emotional life: the others seem curiously toothy and bloodless, they hang on like lice to that state of life to which it has pleased the Emperor to call them. There is one teacher at the Bunrika who seems to enjoy what he reads: I think they are a good race, it is the immediate history of it makes them so frightful.

I have rather stupidly been talking about Pope and Donne (which they put up with so long as they are told it's the latest fashion) and such like: very little contact of any kind has occurred so far. The Japanese teachers don't know the students by name, anyway: everybody warns me whatever I do not to ask a student to lunch. That must surely be nonsense, but I am going in for listening to any advice. (A teacher warned me solemnly not to buy a bicycle, for my dignity's sake. But there I have kicked over the traces.) I haven't quarrelled with the teachers, anyway.

As for Quennell saying they are so ignorant, after all the English School at Cambridge isn't so amazing. If one could get them to be less antlike that wouldn't matter: but it is hard to believe they would ever really enjoy any literature, anyway.

But really, when people give me these very kind warnings about my nerves, I don't think I'm as tender as all that. Really with a large salary and a good cook and only eight hours work a week a young man ought to be able to keep a stiff upper lip . . . [8]

What worried him far more than the stiffness of personal relations was the sheer noise of Tokyo; it was a feature of the densely populated city he would never get used to. After lodging for a while in a cosy apartment house not far from the Imperial Palace, he lived for a few weeks with Austin William Medley (nephew of Augustine Birrell, and a well-liked old-style professor of English language at the Tokyo School of Foreign Languages), whom he called a 'Grand Old Man'. Then he rented a Japanese-style house, number 23 Fujimicho ('a pretty little house, very secluded, where I am rolling about on the correct mats [*tatami*]'),[9] at 5-chome, Kojimachi-ku, not far from both the British Embassy and the Yasukuni Jinja Shrine, and only about a mile by bicycle from the university. The rent was paid by the university. To keep a cook-housekeeper was the custom, and in his case less a luxury than a necessity, since he was unable to grasp enough of the language to go shopping. 'I got rather a horror of the infantilism of the language when I was trying to pick some up,' he would report; and he gave up the struggle at a very early stage.[10] As for the written word, it seemed beyond hope: 'a Japanese who wanted European script told me that Chinese writing had been the greatest curse China had given his country: which is all very well, but before Chinese writing came in (about 800 AD) they hadn't any writing at all. If they can hate China enough to give up Chinese writing it will do them a great deal of good, I should say. They are rather grand when they are moving, but give rather the effect of Tweedledum and Tweedledee when standing still.'[11] But obnoxious noises annoyed him above all else. 'The only thing Peter [Quennell] didn't complain of about Japan was the noise: that is the one thing at present that I can't get over,' he bewailed.[12] To his mother he lamented too: 'They are building a policeman's hospital near my house, which is very noisy: not more noisy than the wireless next door or my own cook, but still very noisy . . . The Japanese seem to have no feeling about noise, if it isn't interesting they don't listen.'[13] Quennell remarked that 'Japanese tongues patter as monotonously as Japanese clogs; the language is alive with slippery consonants.'[14] To his successor's tortured ears, the sound of squalling babies seemed not unlike the scarifying noises of the Japanese language. Empson even went so far as to rent a workplace in addition to his residence, first a room in an apartment house, and later still one 'beastly' hotel room after another, but there was no place to find Marvell's Fair Quiet.[15] Without question, his first year in Tokyo caused him a great deal of stress, including a 'fit of neurotic fear' (as he called it) that brought on a state of restless agitation; as he was to recollect five years later (in 1937), 'there was a period in Japan when I had two houses and three rooms in different hotels, and spent my time going from one to another searching for a moment when I could escape fear with my hands shaking too much to handle my chopsticks.'[16]

After a year, when his ears and nerves had been thoroughly battered, and at a time when Tokyo was 'crawling with sweat and beetles', he moved to 519 Shirokane Sankocho, a delightful and 'absurdly expensive' two-storey European-style house in Admiral Takarabe's compound in Taka-nawa (a high-class residential suburb), which suited him far better than his earlier billets.[17] Professor Fukuhara Rintaro, who had graduated from the Tokyo Higher Normal School and subsequently studied at London University,[18] and who was to become his closest colleague at the Bunrika, would recall: 'There was a main house looking over a pond quietly surrounded by numerous plum-trees and flower-gardens; two or three houses are seen standing by the same waterside. Mr Empson lived in one of such houses built in a villa-fashion.'[19] In the basement lived his housekeeper—'very clever in cooking'—who seemed so ancient, joked Empson, that she must have been rooted there 'since the Dutch settle-ment'. The ground floor consisted of two rooms: the first a sitting room, 'decorated with a bronze statue, book-cases and gramophone etc.', the other a spartan bedroom, with bedstead and cupboard, 'and on the wall Empson's mother's portrait-photograph'. Upstairs, as Fukuhara reported too, it 'looked rather like a chaos with bookcases, typewriter, bed, desk, bathing-tub, etc.' Empson was clearly in his unkempt element: it seems most likely that he would have let the lower floor look after itself, while he spread himself in the happy disarray of the bedsit life above. Yet in a quasi-testy letter written soon after the removal, though not ill-disposed towards the Japanese on every count, he said that he could never get away from the ubiquitous drawback of the rattling nuisance of noise.

Everybody finds something to grumble about in Japan, which is a pity in a way because the Japanese hate not to be loved (it is not simply that things are different, they really are 'quaint' on purpose, in that way: you remember the courtier in

Genji who had a genius for beating time— there is the same concentrated sense of style about dusting, which is done with a little flap on a stick—patter, patter, patter, smack, smack, smack—slow, ineffective, and done with an infantile air of charm which easily becomes loathsome) but I think the main thing that gets on people's nerves is the noise: the men selling bean cake in the street use a little flat whistle that makes you stop whatever you are doing and howl at the moon, it is a more Buddhist sound than one would have thought possible. I have just moved into a European house hoping to escape from it, and am very cross—indeed rather hopeless—at finding it as bad as ever. But I am now fairly out of earshot of Japanese babies and my cook, and the screech of the sliding screens [*fusuma*] of a Japanese house, which were holding up all mental life before.[20]

'The horn of the tofu seller is the most melancholy sound I have ever heard,' he told a student.[21] Tokyo afforded nothing but evil neighbourhoods of noise.

Yet the one really significant problem about the new lodging was that it lay quite a way to the south-west of the city centre, near Meguro Station, at a diagonal of some 5 or 6 miles from the university. Empson's answer was to get hold of a motorbike, which served him well for two years.[22] Tokyo was far from being as choked with traffic as it is today, though at rush hours, as Professor G. C. Allen (who lectured in Japan in the mid-1920s) was to recall, 'passengers could be seen clinging like flies to the outside of tramcars';[23] and in any case his push-bike had been stolen somewhere inside the university precincts.[24] All the same, he was once given a strict warning by a policeman for ignoring a traffic signal,[25] another time slightly hurt his nose in a minor accident, and on a third occasion lost the notebooks that were supposedly secured behind him.[26] His class would burst into applause when they heard his engine eructating into the university yard.[27] 'Sometimes one of his favourite students was seen on the bike with the poet,' one disciple recalls, 'and how we admired the poet-hero on the bike and how we envied the student who had the glory to accompany the poet on the bike!'[28]

Although Empson had been advised not to fraternize with the students, he eagerly spent time with them out of school and very quickly became a popular figure. He had arrived in Tokyo with little more than the warm suit he stood up to lecture in—according to one witness, his suitcase contained only a lemon and a pair of shoes[29]—and sweated profusely. When the students invited him to go for a swim in Shiba Park after his first class on 14 September, he readily agreed. Yes, he could swim, he snappily assured them, but he had no trunks; so they tied up his loins in the length of red cloth that is the traditional Japanese costume. It turned out that he could do little more than dog-paddle, however, whereas his pupils swam round him in circles. Not to be put down, he showed off his leg muscles, asserting that Westerners had much harder muscles than the soft-fleshed Japanese. But when Horii Kiyoshi, the best swimmer of all, got on to the diving board to demonstrate his skill, Empson jumped up and shoved him in; and he even managed to knock Horii's glasses into the water. 'What a stupid thing I've done!' Empson exclaimed; it was probably the only time he ever apologized to a Japanese student, one of their number wrote later.[30] The incident shows not just that Empson was afflicted with a fit of racial rivalry, he must also have felt jealous of these lithe youths who were of much the same generation as himself. But although he was immature, alienated, and competitive, he made every effort to get on better terms with his curiously opaque pupils: 'they resembled a murky and faded portrait group, which one must rub if separate figures are to emerge,' as Quennell had said; they also wore uniforms which helped only to blanch all personality. They looked like 'a congress of youthful tram conductors,' Quennell remarked; but there was more to them than that: 'The tunics and brass buttons which they wore gave them a look of decorous juvenility, but with very few exceptions they were all married and most the devoted fathers of several children.'[31] Still Empson would do his utmost to treat them as chums, often repairing with them to a coffee-house, or to the cinema. Despite his owlish looks, he was athletic and would play tennis too with anyone who felt game—'a tireless tennis, as I remember,' noted Fukuhara, 'as he was in his analytic reading of English.'[32] He drew the line, however, at the Japanese fanaticism for baseball, which he found altogether too American in its 'taste for quick precise movements and nervous excitement'.[33]

Most of his teaching took place at Tokyo Bunrika Daigaku, a dingy-looking place appended to the Higher Normal School in the Koishikawa district, but he was also down for a weekly class at the more prestigious Tokyo Imperial University (Teidai), which occupied a range of Georgian buildings on top of a hill closer to the Imperial Palace. The English Department at the Bunrika University was agreeably small, with just three professors and a couple of assistants; the Chairman was Professor Ishikawa Rinshiro (of whom Peter Quennell wrote: 'His policy of majestic laisser-faire was too thorough-going to be anything but deliberate; yet, on the other hand, my observations of his private character seemed to show him as a simple kindly soul');[34] Jimbo Kaku was Professor of Linguistics. At the far grander Teidai the Chairman of the English Faculty was Professor

Ichikawa Sanki (b. 1886), an austere philologist whom Edmund Blunden had found an all too depressingly serious colleague in 1925–6.[35] Empson, whom Ichikawa had personally appointed, after an interview in London, to the part-time lectureship at Tokyo Imperial University, had less need to cross his path and could usually salute him as a distant eminence.

His favourite teaching was Elizabethan drama and seventeenth-century poetry. He also taught a historical survey of English literature, including selected novelists like Woolf and Lawrence, and some modern poetry— using, for instance, the anthology *New Signatures* (edited by Michael Roberts) when it appeared in 1932.[36] John Morris, who went to Japan to teach English literature in 1938, discovered that 'T. S. Eliot is inextricably associated in the Japanese mind with my predecessor, William Empson, by whom they were introduced to the former's work.' In an introduction to a Japanese edition of Eliot's *Selected Essays* (1933), Empson would be concerned to emphasize how far Buddhism had anticipated the moral teachings of Christianity. Among other observations, he points out that Eliot's 'stress on society and tradition rather than the individual is [for the peoples of the Far East] not an argument for Christianity but for Buddhism'. Eliot's 'essential claim', he argues, 'is that man can somehow escape the valuelessness of mechanism, though Mr Eliot chooses to put it in Christian language ... but the claim is inherent, of course, in the very evasive Buddhist concept of Karma.' He wanted to make Eliot's thoughts on the Christian tradition accessible to the Japanese and to show that the same high ideals are already in place in Buddhism. His challenging conclusion follows: 'Either Mr Eliot's support of Christianity from tradition is a claim that the truth is national or racial or otherwise incidental, or the True Orthodoxy must not limit itself to the traditions of Christianity.'[37] Furthermore, Empson ventured in his classes many of the ideas later included in *Some Versions of Pastoral* (1935)—the intently self-disciplined students were treated to lectures on *Paradise Lost*, Marvell's 'The Garden', and Carroll's *Alice in Wonderland*, and even some essays that would find a final form nearly twenty years later in *The Structure of Complex Words*: he lectured even in 1932, for example, on the words 'honest' and 'sense' in Shakespeare. ('There is a great deal of *horror* of sensuality in Shakespeare, especially in the great tragedies,' he glumly advised one of his best pupils.)[38]

However, he soon realized that the Japanese could not follow the spoken word. Even a student like Ogawa Kazuo, who entered the Imperial University in April 1932 and attended Empson's classes for more than two years, and who would turn out to be a distinguished critic, found it 'incredibly difficult' to follow a lecture in English. The problem was not peculiar to Empson's airily rapid delivery; Lafcadio Hearn had dictated every lecture, including punctuation, and Quennell regretfully followed suit: 'A student may not understand what you are saying, but he takes it down and . . . feels that he has made a tangible acquisition. A page of notes is so wonderfully definite; it is knowledge. A mystic reverence for the written word lends it a value quite independent of its meaning.'[39] As a variation on this time-honoured practice, Empson compensated by writing the salient parts of his lectures on the blackboard, cleaning the surface as soon as he covered it, over and over again, till his head and shoulders were blanketed with chalk-dust. The satirical disdain for his students brusquely expressed in the following letter is thus less truly felt than flavoured for its recipient, the sardonic John Hayward: 'As for teaching, I quite like talking to myself in public. The thing is to look at the blackboard or anyway not at the assembled frogs. They can read what you write on the board though they can't understand what you say. If you write steadily on the board and keep up a spoken patter, *never* waiting for signs of intelligence or making jokes, the hour gets through all right.'[40] In fact, he issued a creditable apologia for the procedure in an article published first in Japanese in February 1934: 'The English lecturer, if too lazy to learn Japanese, should be expected to write all the remarks he thinks worth attention clearly on the blackboard, while keeping up a flow of talk partly to interest himself, partly to give his students practice in listening; the student should not then be expected to show embarrassment in asking questions afterwards with pen and paper, or in demanding them at a teaparty.'[41] Still, a year earlier, he had written rather more ambivalently to I. A. Richards:

I can't complain of boredom here because I wanted to subject myself to a firm course of boredom when I came: my nerves are a great deal better now than they were when I left Bloomsbury. And a year of talking cleverly at the blank air— throwing away 'brilliance'—has purged a lot of nonsense out of my mind. Whether two years more of it will amount to sheer self-destruction is another thing. (You might think this sounds hard on the pupils, but it seems true that they really like this process best: they take it from the tone of your voice, like dogs.—So long as you write some sentences on the blackboard afterwards.)[42]

Actually, as Professor Ishikawa Rinshiro reported, Empson was 'very earnest in his teaching' as well as 'kind to the students'[43]—though it seems likely that some of his classes were caviar to the general. In particular he would lecture at length and in unabashed detail on Donne and Marvell, seemingly unconcerned with any notion of covering the field of

English poetry. Ogawa Kazuo recalls that Empson never spoke about Tennyson or Browning, for example; and after discussing Wordsworth's 'Lucy' poems he was once heard to mutter: 'After that he only wrote bad, bad poetry.'[44]

'Public opinion dominates the mass, and no student wishes to stand out,' Peter Quennell lamented; 'uniformity, not singularity, is their aim, and a student when he speaks to you before the others is careful simply to voice the general view . . . I have spent hours trying to squeeze from my Japanese friends some authentic and highly-coloured personal prejudice.'[45] Nothing had changed in that respect by the time Empson took up his chalk; in fact, the problem was severely compounded by the massive dose of ultra-nationalism that was pumping through the student body. The students kept a rigid clamp on individual ideas in case they might be thought politically suspect. An instance of self-suppression occurred early on, with the result that Empson had to relay this sorry tale: 'I was reading *Mrs Dalloway* with some class and asked them at the end to write an essay about "how far is she ironical?", they came and said they didn't want to write about that because it might be connected with politics. They seem so much spied upon that it is mere nagging to try to extract thought from them: I just prate away at my appointed hours.'[46]

Since he was not himself sure whether or not *Mrs Dalloway* was an ironic political novel, it seems almost certain that the students' disinclination to address the question on account of its likely implications goaded him into writing his own essay on it. Thus in December 1932 he was to publish in *Eigo Seinen* ('The Rising Generation') a piece he would reprint in April 1933 under the provocative title '*Mrs Dalloway* as a Political Satire', for he had discovered that the novel not only hinged on a point of political conscience but also embodied a version of pastoral. The trick of 'putting the complex into the simple' is a device for assuming or preaching 'a proper or beautiful relation between rich and poor', he argued in *Some Versions of Pastoral*;[47] and in postulating such a harmony, in conveying the impression that society is integrated, the pastoral convention operates just like ambiguity against 'a background of conflict'. Dilys Powell, in a review of Empson's book, would correctly observe, 'Pastoral, as [Empson] understands it, while preserving the balance of sympathy between, let us say, peasant and aristocrat, is able, by its detachment, both to criticise and ennoble.'[48] In such terms, the pastoral convention functions as a critique, a mode of scepticism, independence of judgement, and even subversion, as much as it balances the conflicts within society. Society requires the pastoral hero at once to embody and to purge it of its own dissenting impulses: both insider

and outsider, he is the necessary and welcome token sacrifice, paradoxically the very model of a 'unifying social force'. Thus in his adroit article on
Mrs Dalloway Empson observed that the suicide of the shell-shocked Septi-
mus Warren Smith— the 'Christ and scapegoat'—has the function vis-à-
vis the vulnerable but brave heroine of both criticizing and ennobling her.
One paragraph needs to be quoted here because it demonstrates, in just
two vertiginous and poignantly cadenced sentences, the genuinely moving
effect of the pastoral moment as Empson was to frame it in *Pastoral*; it
draws together all the emotional, social, metaphysical, and existential
implications of the 'trick' of pastoral:

At the end, at the triumph of her party, her assertion of the same order of her
tribe, she hears of the suicide of the man who thought of himself as Christ and
scapegoat and feels that her sense that she might have done the same is a sort of
proof that she is genuine; she feels outside her snobbery because she can understand him; he becomes indeed to her for a moment what it was his madness to
think he was to everybody; he is the sacrificial hero and his tragedy reconciles her
to the world. The effect is to make Mrs Dalloway seem more real and deeply
rooted, because less dependent on shelter, to show the gulfs across which she can
reach her understanding, the uselessness of this power, even to herself, and its
dignity, the falsity and the truth of Smith's belief that he is an outcast, the intimacy
of the most distant human relationship, the dissolution of one of the most far-
reaching of human beliefs into one of the flickering and random illuminations
which go out immediately in her mind.[49]

Such reflections show a rare depth of moral insight, and truly comprehend
the waste of tragedy.

As for its distinct political implications, Empson notes, this novel, 'like
most post-war good writing, makes a blank statement of conflict; [Woolf]
shows that she can feel on both sides, knows both how to love and to hate
her aristocrats.' On the one hand, Virginia Woolf displays 'advanced
political notions' or radical insinuations; on the other, she seems to pet
the ruling class even while it gets on her nerves.[50] To write with such a
balance of judgement is a finer achievement, Empson argues, than to make
raw left- or right-wing assertions which stifle imaginative sympathy.

It was a brave lesson to give students who were being indoctrinated by
'fascism from above'. He was to remember as much with sorrow and scorn
a decade later, when he came to be writing propaganda for the BBC. In a
broadcast that was put out just a week after the bombing of Pearl Harbor
he would cite the students' collective recoil from the political ironies of *Mrs
Dalloway* as a frightful example of moral and intellectual tyranny. 'All these
boys, you see, were under rigid observation for any signs of Left-wing

political opinions. Once they were suspected of Dangerous Thoughts, they would never be able to get jobs, let alone the things that might happen to them in the Police Station. I think this general constraint and watchfulness in the students is the most striking thing about them. And, of course, no real education can go on at all when a growing mind is tied as tightly as that.'[51] He did not blame the students themselves, who could not help being the victims of a repressive state machine. The teachers, though, had a duty to show courage, to find ways of outwitting an apparatus that would set limits on educational freedom. In his Inaugural Lecture at Sheffield University in 1953, he was to stress this lesson: 'Of course, in such a case, it is very much not the business of a teacher to egg the students on to get into trouble, but on the other hand he must insist on showing the real climate of opinion which surrounded and nourished the literary writings he is set to teach.'[52]

In January 1932, when he had been teaching in Tokyo for just four months, hostilities broke out in Shanghai which brought the implications of a totalizing military-imperialistic ethos directly home to his classroom. The Japanese marines who had been detailed to 'protect' the Chinese borough of Chapei met a totally unexpected level of resistance from the Chinese 19th Route Army commanded by General Tsai Ting-kai, who declared that his force of 35,000 Cantonese would 'fight the Japanese to the last man if it has to dye the Whampo River red with its soldiers' blood'. The Japanese naval landing force was driven back to the barricades of the Japanese settlement. Thereupon Admiral Shiozawa pounded the Chinese soldiers and *franc-tireurs* with bombs and shell-fire, though without avail. The Japanese had no choice but to commit more and more troops to the engagement, until, after many days of fruitless fighting, they were pitting a force of some 70,000 against a body of Chinese that had been cut down to about 20,000. The Chinese Divisions were finally beaten, though not until some weeks after the fighting broke out; and on the Japanese side, army reinforcements had to relieve the beleaguered Imperial Navy. Japan won nothing from her victory. China, on the other hand, gained face over the inglorious Japanese: outmanned and outgunned, she had made a heroic stand before being defeated at the last.

Several members of Empson's class at the Bunrika were drafted during the course of the campaign, and one was in fact killed at Shanghai, so that the students' sense of a missionary patriotism was greatly inflamed. Empson was astonished to find how warfare had transfixed the minds of his students. He happened at the time to be talking to them about the poetry of A. E. Housman—only to discover they read it as a direct political message. Lines such as 'I wish one could know them . . . The lads that will die in their glory and never be old', were construed as a kind of gospel. 'We were reading Housman in one class, which I thought would suit them (suicide is the national sport, of course),' he reported home with black humour, 'but it was embarrassing to read a series of dull essays saying that Housman must be a good poet because he really did make them want to kill themselves, especially to go and die in Shanghai . . . I wonder if it would have made the old gentleman feel ashamed of himself?'[53] Although he reported it as a joke, he felt genuinely shocked by the students' response; and again he used it as an authentic piece of propaganda ten years later, in his BBC broadcast of 14 December 1941, when he argued that there really must be something maladjusted about young people who can respond to the poetry of Housman in this fashion: 'I think Housman is quite right. We will do no good to anyone by dying for our country, but we will be admired, and we all want to be admired, and anyway, we are better dead.'[54]

A measure of the moral chill his students cast over him in 1932 is supplied by the final paragraph of his BBC propaganda piece, directly following the Housman anecdote, in which he chose to depict the Japanese as so rootedly racist that they must be viewed with repugnance: they were unutterably alien, not puny pretenders at all.

I think an important difference has been developing between the young Japanese [his erstwhile students] and the older ones, whether for good or evil. The old ones can remember when they were not a dangerously great power, but just the funny little Japs, when the whites looked down on them. Now, the Japanese have been very careful not to let the rising generation know that anyone ever felt like that about Japan. The young ones are simply proud of being one of the great ruling races. The advantage of this is that it does make them much less touchy. Of course, when the Japanese say that they want racial equality for everyone—and that is one of their propaganda lines—they are quite consciously talking humbug. I must have read Shakespeare's *Othello* with Japanese students at least three times, and every time some honestly friendly and puzzled student would say to me, or write down, 'Why should you or I take any interest in a story about a negro?' They were quite sure that I would feel the same as they did; they weren't boasting, it was just the natural question, they felt, from one ruling race to another. Why should the English or the Japanese have to waste their time over the troubles of Othello?

His sojourn in Japan taught him, he said on the BBC, to feel 'very sorry' for his pupils and colleagues. 'It was already obvious then that they were caught up in this hideous machine and had no way out, hardly even for a breathing space.' He was far from adjusting his memories ten years after the event, since his immediate disgust with the military mind-control is evident in a letter dating from about March 1932:

The Japanese flag (a poached egg, or clot of blood on a bandage, which gives the insanely simple and self-centred effect of an amoeba when drugged) is very much in evidence: the theatre (as excellent as they say) has the deaths of heroes at Shanghai on display...The efforts of patriotism have made the whole country crawl with babies, dirty and noisy in themselves and sure to cause famine in the next generation.

    This is a squalid way to look at a country, though.[55]

    Whatever his distaste for ultra-nationalism, he went on teaching with enthusiasm, without taking cynical short-cuts or talking down to the students. It was a point of principle for him to stretch the best brains of a class. As the students were to recall, he was strict and even severe with their efforts. 'What do *you* think?' he urged them; and when they seemed to have nothing to say for themselves: 'You *must* have an opinion.' He spared no one his direct criticism. Probably the most useful service he gave was to write detailed comments on their essays. 'You've really got to define words, to distinguish between them,' he would insist. 'As for argument, you deal too narrowly with the problem.'[56]

    One particular essay—on Gray's 'Elegy in a Country Churchyard'—by Kyo Nogawa, so far rewarded Empson's attention that it provoked his own discussion of the poem in the opening pages of *Some Versions of Pastoral*. What troubled Empson about Gray is his comfortable condescension, his specious show of sympathy, since the 'Elegy' is assuredly 'an odd case of poetry with latent political ideas'. This gloss by Empson was unprecedented in the 1930s as a *tour de force* of critical deconstruction; and it remains an astonishing revelation:[57]

> Full many a gem of purest ray serene
> The dark, unfathomed caves of ocean bear;
> Full many a flower is born to blush unseen
> And waste its sweetness on the desert air.

What this means, as the context makes clear, is that eighteenth-century England had no scholarship system or *carrière ouverte aux talents*. This is stated as pathetic, but the reader is put into a mood in which one would not try to alter it ... By comparing the social arrangement to Nature he makes it seem inevitable, which it was not, and gives it a dignity which was undeserved. Furthermore, a gem does not mind being in a cave and a flower prefers not to be picked; we feel that the man is like the flower, as short-lived, natural, and valuable, and this tricks us into feeling that he is better off without opportunities. The sexual suggestion of *blush* brings in the Christian idea that virginity is good in itself, and so that any renunciation is good; this may trick us into feeling it lucky for the poor man that society keeps him unspotted from the World. The tone of melancholy claims that the poet understands the considerations opposed to aristocracy, though he judges against them; the truism of the reflections in the churchyard, the universality and impersonality this gives to the style, claim as if by comparison that we ought to accept the injustice of society as we do the inevitability of death.[58]

Such a shrewd analysis may well have been inspired by the fact that Empson found it necessary to gloss for Kyo Nogawa, in extensive notes written on his essay, the numerous points of diction and reference which would otherwise defeat a Japanese reader. For example, the epithet *jocund* ('which neither Gray nor the farmer would use of himself when actually cheerful')—in the line 'How jocund did they drive their team afield!'—Empson described for Kyo Nogawa as 'rather affectedly old-fashioned, so that you feel [Gray] is careful to put a distance between himself and his social inferiors'. Though not himself a Marxist, let alone a revolutionary, Empson suspected the conservatism of Gray's sentimentality, his covert acquiescence in social injustice. (While the American critic Kenneth Burke, who admired Empson's attention to sociological issues, hailed his analysis of Gray's poem as 'profoundly Marxist', one would have to say that it is 'Marxist' only in a rather superficial sense. Empson was more concerned with the ethics and suffering of the situation, with the truths of human experience, than with any specific political programme.) It is not surprising that when Kyo Nogawa in his essay called Gray 'genial, modest, reserved, and naturally sympathetic with obscure people', Empson smartly corrected him: 'No: a dismal old don; sympathetic only in theory.' Likewise when Kyo suggested that Gray suffered from his 'too fine susceptibility', while 'the human society is too coarse and rude for such a rare delicacy', Empson disputed his indulgence: 'Well, there are many such people but all people of very rare delicacy are not frustrated like Gray. It would be true probably to say that all people of fine susceptibility have to suffer very much, but many keep their vigour and achieve periods of great happiness.'[59] Since many of his students, as Empson was later to claim, were clandestine left-wingers, if not so-called *marukusu-boi* ('Marx boys'), they might not have needed him to deconstruct Gray's pastoral disguise. All in all, however, Empson deserves the compliment he bestowed on Virginia Woolf, for he showed not just a left-wing grouchiness of his own but a true balance of judgement when he came to write up, in *Pastoral*, the large-minded reflections that Gray's 'Elegy' inspired in him.

Two further sentences from Empson's analysis of the 'Elegy' express an intensity of emotional empathy which had not been widely apparent in his writings to date. For a man who had lost his own 'scholarship'—his bye-fellowship at Cambridge—who had cause to feel that a pitiless institutional morality had excluded him from the career in British academic life that his talents merited, and who was living in exile even while writing such reflections on English literature and society, it is understandable that he would have registered a sense of affinity with Gray's neglected soul.

Many people, without being communists, have been irritated by the complacence in the massive calm of the poem, and this seems partly because they feel there is a cheat in the implied politics; the 'bourgeois' themselves do not like literature to have too much 'bourgeois ideology'.

And yet what is said is one of the permanent truths; it is only in degree that any improvement of society could prevent wastage of human powers; the waste even in a fortunate life, the isolation even of a life rich in intimacy, cannot but be felt deeply, and is the central feeling of tragedy. And anything of value must accept this because it must not prostitute itself; its strength is to be prepared to waste itself, if it does not get its opportunity.[60]

Many other students benefited from his work on their essays. When Irie Yukio (a future professor) chose to write on Dickens for his graduation thesis at the Bunrika, he was enthused by Empson's warm response: 'That's splendid. I've been hoping to study more Dickens. Will you write a paper that's so interesting it will make me find more time to study Dickens?'[61] At the Imperial, Empson supervised a thesis on 'The Style of Virginia Woolf' by Kajiki Ryuichi, then an assistant in the Department of English Literature (later a professor), who was deeply influenced by his tutor's energy and intelligence.[62] So was Eitaro Sayama, another future professor, who received the Shakespeare Medal at the Bunrika for a first-year undergraduate paper on the poetry of Donne that Empson supervised and highly commended.[63] All the same, there is little doubt that the educational process was a big struggle on both sides; for every student who rose to Empson's methods there were several who never grasped how to examine a work of literature for themselves: they parroted the professor or some critical text. One student had the harrowing experience of being unable to understand a single question Empson asked during the oral examination of his dissertation on 'The Tragic Side in Joseph Conrad's Work'—he simply could not catch a word the Englishman was saying—but Empson passed him anyway. Another student was left with the distinct impression that Empson believed (though he never said as much) that the

Japanese could not understand the subtleties of English poetry, so that he pressed them to study the novelists instead—such as Fielding and Smollett. Certainly he encouraged them to read a good many novels of all kinds (in his very last lecture at the Imperial, in fact, he would recommend them to read both Ernest Hemingway and P. G. Wodehouse),[64] but it is almost impossible to imagine that he would have given up the effort to open their minds to poetry. He might have preferred to teach poetry alone, but he had to concede that the Japanese student would be better able to form a personal opinion about any good English prose. He willingly declared himself on this question in 'Teaching Literature', a pithy and beguiling manifesto that was first published in 1934, in a Japanese translation by one of his students, Narita Shigehisa,[65] in *Bungei* ('Literary Art'):

A lecturer is tempted to put most stress on verse because a concentrated medium is so convenient—one can give short striking examples and find plenty to say about them ... But though one can enjoy verse in a foreign language it is peculiarly hard to make an independent judgement of it ... the student has much more chance to become self-reliant about prose ...

What Japan had really to learn from Europe, the original reason why teachers like myself were imported, was the success of the sciences and of the habit of mind that produced them. The main signs of it in literature are control of logical structure, whose flower is rhetoric, and speed of judgement, whose flower is wit; they are important for poetry, but the source to learn them from is prose.[66]

The degree to which students rose to his rhetoric and his diligent example is far less certain. A fair idea of their level of attainment, and of his fondly patronizing attitude towards their efforts, may be gauged from this letter to John Hayward:

My students have to write an essay at the end of the year. (At both universities I am told they all have to pass. 'Mark them ABCD: D is failure, so mark them ABC': 'Under 60% fails them, so mark them up to 30 and add 60': are the instructions given to a friendly foreign professor). At the Imperial I sit in and they do it in two hours. At the end a young man came in and explained with great dignity and politeness that he was sorry he had been unable to attend my examination, as he was drunk last night and had only just woken up. He may have invented this merely to show there was no ill-feeling. At the Bunrika they are all going to be teachers so have to defend their dignity and write essays in their spare time. I gave a tea party (about fifteen, of a given year) nearly all of whom had chosen to write about D. H. Lawrence and Sex. The house was submerged in student life, all in a herd, rather stirring to me because I had a guilty feeling that my own student life was so similar—in which two young men sat down and wrote their essays about sex one on each side of the tea-table, in a war of Japanese speech with the gramophone playing. They are really rather sweet once you accept them as hopelessly silly.[67]

(When Empson entertained students at his home of an evening, he would serve them a simple dish such as tempura cooked up by his housekeeper; liquid refreshment took the form of a barrel of beer.)

He was heartened to find that at least at the Imperial 'Six people out of thirty spotted a quotation from Ben Jonson I hadn't used in lecturing—after all, blank as they are, the thing's not total farce.'[68] But for the most part his experience of the students closely rehearsed that of Peter Quennell the previous year: 'Always between the lecturer and his students hangs a curtain that may grow slighter but never dissolves. He knows nothing of their real tastes and private preferences; he continues to know nothing until the end.'[69]

Such optimism as Empson could salvage after his first year helped mostly to justify his activity as a teacher rather than the students' achievements. He wrote to I. A. Richards on 2 September 1932:

My pupils often ask me to explain about methodology, and I always tell them I have no idea what the word means . . . Fukuhara teases me by saying that my book (which you are so right in calling fluid) is full of methodology; so I am in need of a ruling on this point . . .

One reason I wanted to come East was to find out what teaching was like across so large a gulf, but most of the Bunrika students (having done some teaching already) are so anxious not to lose dignity that I am flung nervously into acting in sympathy with this object; after a year of it I know very little indeed even of what they know, still less what works for them in literature or what methods would make anything else work. When Peter [Quennell] says they none of them have any feeling for literature at all, though, he is probably complaining about the normal conditions of literature teaching: it is not necessarily useless because it is bluff at the time: I have some feeling for Virgil now though I had none when I was being taught it.[70]

Elsewhere he reiterated with despondency: 'the Japanese are always Jap-to-European, and always afraid of losing dignity.'[71]

'I . . . became seriously interested in the system when teaching English letters in Japan with no knowledge of Japanese,' Empson would write in 1935; 'it was sometimes the only thing that gave me a feeling that I was of any use.' He was referring to the system called Basic English, a simplified form of the English language, with a rudimentary grammar and a vocabulary of only 850 words, devised by C. K. Ogden (1889–1957) and passionately promoted by I. A. Richards. (At Richards's behest, Empson had met up with Ogden before leaving for Japan.) Although it was not strictly his business to teach the students the English language, powers of appreciation were never separable from analytical skill. His concern, he explained, 'was with young men of good powers and long knowledge of English, and for them the use of Basic was simply as a clearing in the mass of undergrowth of this great language; when their writing went out of sight in the undergrowth the only thing to do was to put down in Basic two or three of the possible senses.' Thus he found that Basic English was less vital as what Ogden hoped it would become—an international 'auxiliary' language, for the benefit of science and peace—than as a demonstrably practical 'first step in the direction of full English which gives the right feeling about the words'. His pupils splendidly proved this point in one class exercise: when he asked them to find other words for the adage 'Out of sight, out of mind', they came up with: 'Invisible, insane'.[72] Furthermore, as he discovered to the lasting benefit of his own work, the system was just as instructive 'as a test of a bit of writing for the Englishman himself, a way of separating statement from form and feeling (it may then be used at school for "paraphrases" . . .) For myself at least it has become a fixed process on reading something deeply true to see if it is still good sense in Basic.' His critical writings are deeply stamped with this technique; as he would keenly report to Ogden, 'in general . . . Basic is so analytic that it often seems gawky unless you expand a vague phrase depending on a key word: if you do that the result is usually better than the original.'[73]

Basic English began not as a teaching tool, he was to advise his audience during a later talk entitled 'Basic and Communication', but as an investigation into 'the root ideas needed for any language, or any clear thought. Dr Richards' book *Basic Rules of Reason* was made as a paper for the Aristotelian Society, a society of philosophers, and he made it in Basic because that seemed to him the only hope of getting the ideas of philosophers in order, or making a connection between the opinions of different philosophers.' Moreover, he again pointed to the togetherness of his theoretical and practical procedures when he argued that Basic naturally helps to develop intellectual clarity and critical sensibility:

Basic is not specially simple English; it keeps back the 'exceptions', the words with tricks that are of no value, but it makes necessary (if anything) more attention to 'grammar', to the general principles of word order and structure in English, than the language commonly used in talking; and to get a thing said fully in Basic may be a training in thought . . . The limited wordlist is not only the quickest way to give a man a working knowledge of English, of the sort that will be of most use; it is the best way to give him good taste, later on, in writing English or reading English books.

He therefore took a firm, though not unequivocal, stand in favour of Basic as probably the best medium for giving foreign learners a working access to the English language. 'I am not a fanatical Ogdenite,' he would admit, 'being a heretic about his verbs . . . ' While Ogden insisted that there were no verbs on the Basic list, but only 16 'operators' such as *give* and *take*, Empson could see no reason why nouns which can act as verbs, taking *-ing* and *-ed* forms, should not be classified as verbs.[74] Similarly, he did not think it helpful for Ogden to be so absolute in limiting the number of nouns (words for 'things') to 600. ' "Duty" is a hole in Basic, by the way,' he told Ogden in 1933, for example; 'it can only be strictly covered by two negatives—"what it would be *wrong not* to do in these conditions".'[75] For the very most part, however, he was solid in his support for Basic, for the good reason that he would recall in 1973: 'Any reasonable word-list would have been better than none, for both teachers and students, but Basic has several merits as a first landing-stage in the learning of English. For the student who is not going further, it allows a confident movement within what he has got, because he can rely on analogy without bumping into "irregular" grammatical forms.' Indeed, Empson could be waspishly witty in defending the system; when a reader complained to the *Japan Chronicle*, for example, that Basic was unsymbolic, artificial, not an introduction to literary English, and not suited to the Japanese, he retorted: 'No one denies that Basic is simple; it is as compact as a bomb; at worst it is only a part of English you have to learn anyway; and it is a valuable, as well as a convenient, thing to learn first.' Personally he feared what he finely called 'the despair of waste and the squalor of misunderstanding', so that one should welcome a system that dispelled irrationalism and incomprehension. 'That it is not suited to the Japanese I can believe; it is not suited to our mortal nature; it is a logical and analytical system which may prove too sharp a mental discipline, by itself, for people to use. But surely it would be a more cheerful first step in English than learning 20,000 words bang off.'[76]

'So I was glad to do a little campaigning for Basic in the Far East, too little I feel now,' he related in 1973; 'it was nearly all a matter of writing to local papers and exposing the lies told by the opponents. Such letters were hardly ever answered; the opponents just told the same lie again later on. I translated some of the essays of J. B. S. Haldane into Basic [*The Outlook of*

Science and *Science and Well-Being* (both 1935)], though I am afraid a good deal of correcting my verbal usages had to be done in the office. Still, this gave me a certain fluency in the dialect . . . '[77] In fact, he did more for Basic than he recalled in his modesty. Within just a few weeks of his arrival in Japan, on 16 October, for instance, he lectured on behalf of Basic to the 8th Annual Convention of the Institute for Research in English Teaching, positively pleading, as the *Japan Times* reported, that 'Basic did not depend on any tricks of language . . . Basic was not as some critics maintained nothing but a jargon or "pidgin".' More and more writers were appreciating the merits of 'a sober simple style,' he pointed out; the prose of Edward Garnett was 'very much like Basic English'; and even a poet such as Swinburne, whom we generally associate with a peculiar richness of language, when he wanted to create an effect of movement and energy, as in 'An Oblation', managed to use monosyllabic words and a simple sentence construction.[78]

And yet, as the *Japan Chronicle* indicated, there was an irony underlying this bright-eyed, bushy-tailed advocacy: 'for the present Professor Empson is by way of being a rebel, for the Institute has not yet officially approved of Basic English.'[79] The Institute for Research in English Teaching (IRET) had been set up with Japanese government blessing in 1923 by Harold E. Palmer (1877–1949), an Englishman of indubitable dynamism and resilience—'an iconoclast, a revolutionary, and an innovator,' as he has been called by his daughter[80]—who had been drafted into Japan only the year before as 'Linguistic Adviser to the Mombusho' (Department of Education). As Empson would report with a smirk, Palmer was therefore 'a very busy man in a remarkable position'—except for the fact that 'his advice has never been taken. He is very like Ogden, and unfortunately they met; there was some kind of explosion: it's still not clear what, though they have both given their versions of it in ample detail.'[81] Harold Palmer had apparently looked into Basic and killingly decreed that—according to a dissertation by Dr H. Bongers—'Basic English was indeed nothing other than its inventors had claimed for it: an artificial language not intended as an approach to Standard English.'[82] He had actually issued his own Standard English Readers, a five-year course, in 1925; so it is understandable, even in a far more disinterested educationalist, that he would not wish a pedagogue of another persuasion to poach on his patch. (In a revue staged by the Tokyo Amateur Dramatic Club, he had described himself in Gilbertian style: 'my mission, my ambition, is to be the living model of the perfect phonetician'.[83]) However, Palmer had been the first to affront vested interests in Tokyo, notably Professor Okakura Yoshisaburō

(1868–1936) of the Higher Normal School (precursor of the Bunrika University), doyen of teachers of English in Japan, who did not much like this linguist-come-lately-from-England.[84] On the other hand, Ishikawa Rinshiro, then a senior teacher at the Higher Normal School (later Empson's boss at the Bunrika), who must have thought Okakura an ageing reactionary, not only joined the board of the fledgling Institute but invited Palmer himself to become a regular lecturer at the school.[85] Perhaps not surprisingly, Okakura did favour the Basic system when it came along, and duly assumed the capacity of what Empson termed Ogden's 'O.C.' (Officer Commanding).[86]

Thus the cause of Basic, as Empson promptly became aware, served as a shuttlecock to be batted back and forth between Palmer and Ishikawa on one side and Okakura on the other. 'Okakura has a great deal of influence with his old pupils,' he related to Ogden in August 1932, 'though Ishikawa, who took his place at the Higher Normal and Bunrika, tends to influence the same people and is evasive but anti- . . . '.[87] There is no doubt at all that Palmer had been working for years (in fact, for longer than Ogden) on the principles of vocabulary selection, compiling his first word list in 1911. As early as 1915 he gave a lecture on limited vocabulary at University College London; in 1917 he had discussed Basic in *The Scientific Study and Teaching of Languages*; and the IRET *First Interim Report on Vocabulary Selection*, which appeared in 1930 (the same year as Ogden's *Basic English: A General Introduction with Rules and Grammar*), had been approved with a foreword by—of all people—I. A. Richards. He even issued his own 600-word vocabulary, principally for the retelling of simple stories at a beginners' level.[88] But he had not produced a system of the all-purpose sort that Basic English claimed to be, and which Okakura pronounced good.

Some years afterwards, Empson retailed what he could remember of the controversy to A. S. Hornby, Palmer's successor at the IRET:

it seemed to me that Palmer was cheating a great deal, particularly by bringing out schemes which were in fact clumsy copies of Ogden's methods but were presented as inventions of his own which he had been maturing for many years. The most obvious example was his 600-word limited vocabulary for beginners. I realise that my impressions might be wrong, and that accusations of dishonesty were made on both sides. What put the matter beyond all doubt, I thought, was a story told me in confidence by [H. Vere] Redman [who taught at Tokyo Commercial College, now Hitotsubashi University], who as you know has always been a loyal personal friend of Palmer [they co-wrote *This Language-Learning Business* in 1932]. He had been present at a meeting between Palmer and Professor Okakura, who had patiently detailed to Palmer, on and on, each of the cheats which Palmer had organised against Basic since it appeared. Palmer had no reply to make and eventually refused to listen any more. Redman's comment (made just after the meeting) was that he thought he had freed himself from racial prejudice, but he found it made him bitterly ashamed to hear a white man so totally exposed by a yellow one.[89]

Naturally Empson was not an impartial witness, since he had committed his energies to the advancement of Basic. But at least he was not adjusting his memory long after the events in question; even in June 1933 he had said, 'I don't feel the soul of Palmer is a great puzzle; he is a man with great powers of self-deception. But Okakura I don't understand, though I like him; it is much more clear that he is using Basic as a weapon against Palmer and others than that he really wants Basic to be a success.'[90] Whatever the case, Basic fell between two schools, and the upshot was an unhappy double irony: Palmer would not give his endorsement to a system that had been backed by Okakura; and but for Palmer's bias, Basic might have done well in Japan. Perhaps the best irony of all, as Empson remembered in 1973, was that the clash proved somewhat fruitful: 'The exasperating thing for us was that they kept on denouncing the whole Basic system as theoretically wrong and then, when their next year's textbooks came out, taking over whole chunks of it. The effect was of course to raise the standard of the teaching a great deal.'

Notwithstanding that partly constructive paradox, there were two other reasons why the Japanese chose to resist the Basic method. The first was a very natural anxiety: they dreaded sounding foolish when speaking English. 'This extraordinary terror of being ridiculous puts them against Basic,' wrote Empson to Ogden in 1932. His solution was astute though unavailing: 'the (my) answer is that nothing can obviously be laughed at in English unless it seems pretentious or arouses class-feeling, and Basic does neither; but that does not make them feel safe.' The other point of resistance was a matter of deep-seated academic dignity, as he again regretted: 'the immense literary stress of Japanese education, and the sense of safety they find in teasing themselves with difficulties (both so wholly destructive as far as the actual production of literature goes) make it a specially difficult field to introduce Basic.' At the Imperial University, for example, he observed that colleagues were 'so very literary' that they tended 'to content themselves with saying he [Okakura] is an old man amusing his leisure, which seems pretty true.'[91]

The laborious tactful pains that Empson took to try to coax his colleagues into accepting the good sense of Basic are evident in this letter to Richards:

When a man like Fukuhara holds out against it so adroitly I take it his feeling is that the literary attitude to language needs to be kept up (is important even in the intelligent use of language for mere statement) and yet can only be kept up by bluff, by the literary teachers keeping their stranglehold on education. All language teaching must be hooked on to literary language teaching. (So that to say they are trying to keep their jobs is ungenerous even when true.) 'We learn English for its moral qualities not for communication.' The only obvious answer would be insulting—that the Japanese student doesn't get any qualities out of the muddle he is left in, except in the rare cases who would have gone in for literary stuff anyway. The anti-literary feeling in Basic, the wish to push the language away when you don't want it, seems very like the Restoration wish to push Elizabethan poetic stock symbols away—in that case the movement obviously produced good writing (moved back to something very like Basic) and by now seems hallowed. But it is not much use saying that to Fukuhara, who needs rather to be told that one could pass very effectively from Basic to literary studies—which is true enough, but the artfulness required for both sides of the argument, even when disinterested, seems rather paralysing.[92]

He offered the same well-founded advice, tinged with exasperation, to Ogden the obstinate begetter of the system: 'The thing to stress in Japan is that Basic is only a very useful *first stage* in the portentous and now traditional business of collecting all stages of English, and Beowulf.'[93]

To John Hayward, his roguish old friend from Cambridge, on the other hand, he inevitably joked about Basic, 'in my heart I don't know whether it is a great invention or a simple rape on the gagged mouth of Britannia.'[94] However, even though he never quite carried the day, Empson probably derived much more satisfaction from the struggle to promote Basic than from dictating literary history and opinion to his pupils at the Bunrika and Imperial. As he roundly declared in a later letter, 'I am a Basic fan . . . [I]t is really my chief interest in the teaching business—the only thing that might do some good if they would use it.'[95]

Out of school, he liked travelling and soaking himself in local culture, especially the theatre and Buddhist art. When not restlessly on the move, he liked it equally well to lie naked in the summer sun, though always with a book on the go. He liked the sightseeing and sunbathing all the better if he could do them in the company of a young male friend. He both fancied and felt irritated by what he regarded as the infantilism of Japanese youth, its puppyish look and demeanour. One young man he met by chance was three years his senior, Nakano Yoshio (a teacher), a pupil of Edmund Blunden, who later became a critic and journalist, and a professor of

English Literature at Tokyo University. They made a date to see the Noh theatre, but when Nakano went to collect Empson at his home he found him naked, sunbathing in the porchway. As Nakano would tenderly recall after fifty years, Empson was utterly unconcerned about his appearance. 'We sat drinking a cup of tea for thirty minutes or so, with his sweet little uncircumcised treasure in full view ["unveiled"], staring me in the face.'[96] Then they shuffled off together to see the Noh play *Kakutagawa*, which Empson watched with absorption.

Empson went to the theatre once more with Nakano Yoshio, and at other times with other young men. He went with Eitaro Sayama to see a performance of *Nikudan sanyushi* ('Three heroes working as human bullets')—'a *Kabuki* play which is sensational in style and propagandistic in content, endorsing Japanese militarism in Manchuria'.[97] He recorded his first impressions for Sylvia Townsend Warner—'Funny to see Noh plays after reading Mr Waley [Arthur Waley's *The No Plays of Japan* (1921)]: they're not Celtic and hopeless as you might think because the dances are terrific South Sea Island affairs, all crowing and prating and stamping like buck rabbits'[98]—and very soon became an enthusiast for the Japanese style of theatre, its music and movement, not least because it provoked positive reflections on the differences in cultural disposition between East and West. He was captivated by the supra-personal beauty of the Noh.

After a fashion of loud and deathly slow ceremoniousness that came to delight him, the ethos of the Noh, he believed, chimed with the philosophical 'notion' informing much of his own poetry—that 'life involves maintaining oneself between contradictions'. He would substantially develop this crucial idea of balancing in a world-embracing essay entitled 'Ballet of the Far East' which he published in *The Listener* in 1937; it is worth quoting at some length, both for its nice analysis of a plausible correlation between kinds of dance and conceptions of divinity, and for the enthusiasm with which Empson declares himself in favour of the impersonality of the East over the individualism of the West.

In the West, the supreme God is a person, in the East He is not; their ideas about man follow from that . . . It is much the most fundamental line of division between the civilisations of the world, and we need to understand the people on the other side . . .

The Noh theatre is fantastically slow . . . The music has a direct effect on the nerves. It is based on eight slow beats, taken separately by different percussive instruments. Now the scientists seem to agree that we feel differently about rhythm according as it is slower or faster than a heart-beat, and nearly all European music goes faster than a heart-beat . . . All our instruments are meant to go bouncing along very frankly, like a nice well-intentioned dog; in their music you sit still and strengthen yourself like a cat ... A rhythm quicker than the heart-beat is one that you seem to control, or that seems controlled by some person; the apparently vast field of our music is always the frankness of the West, always the individual speaking up. Music based on rhythms slower than the heart-beat can carry a great weight of emotion and even of introspection, and of course inciden-tal runs will go quick, but it remains somehow impersonal. I only want to say here that you must take the music seriously as something that fits in with the whole story, and the story may well be the other half of the truth about the world ...

If you have got used to the Far Eastern stage it is very hard to take the Russian Ballet as seriously as all its audiences do. Beside dancing like this, the Russian Ballet is a glorified form of romping. In dancing of serious power, the dancer can stand still for several minutes and make you watch the imperceptible movements of his breathing like a cat watching a mouse. Now Western music cannot stand still; it is not built to give a dancer these opportunities. If we ever get what there is so little hope of at present, that is, a reasonable attempt to take the world as one place and use the best things in it, then it will be obvious that Far Eastern music is the normal kind of music for serious dancing. Sensible people who love the European ballet will tell you that the permanent thing about it is its eternal youth. This is quite true, but it is a limited kind of pleasure. In all the other arts the Far East has one thing and we have another, and it is stupid to say that either is better. But in dramatic dancing the Far East makes us ridiculous.

Breathless to escape the stifling heat of the capital in 1932, he was happy to be a guest lecturer at the Karuizawa Summer University—Karuizawa is a resort town about 90 miles north-west of Tokyo, close to the active volcano of Mount Asama, on the mild southern slopes of the so-called *Chubu* ('central part'), the principal alpine range of Japan—where he taught modern poetry.

In the autumn and winter, he would go skiing. At the end of 1932 he accepted an invitation from Doi Kochi, a professor of English Literature—author of the first Japanese essay on Joyce's *Ulysses*, published in the academic periodical *Kaizo* in 1927—at Tohoko Imperial University at Sendai (the capital of the north-eastern part of Japan), to accompany a party of students into the mountains where they kept a cabin. But he began to regret joining in the trip as soon as he saw the youngsters following their leader in a painfully precise fashion. 'All these little fishes of skiing students go up to the same nursery slope and come back from it together = the slopes a little further up are quite untrampled,' he sniffed in his notebook. The spectacle of this school of tame students put him into an ill temper; so did the wet snow and the large numbers of birch trees on the lower slopes. In fact, he thought, the many 'faults of Japan' conspired to make him go round 'all boiling and looking like an angry parrot'. (Never loath to coin a theory, he decided: 'one reason one keeps angry in a Japanese room is that there is no mirror—a very puncturing and therefore social object, though a bad one to live alone with.') Nevertheless, his dim view of this poorly endowed mountain paradoxically provoked him to celebrate the scene, albeit in purplish prose: 'The irritatingly frequent trees lower down were crusted with iced windblown snow so as to look like ghosts, in hopeless numbers, with a dusty effect about their cauliflower surfaces that gave them the strange eternal squalor which seems to hang about Japanese burial grounds. Also like cocoanut-icing cones on the tea-table, and . . . like the army of drummers that sent Alice and the noble warriors from the town.' But then, at the summit, he felt moved to find a Shinto shrine forming 'a wordless place to eat lunch, with Doi worshipping at it afterwards. Said it was "very old" and in reply to a further question (rather indignantly) that that meant nearer 500 than 50 years. It was so encrusted with winddriven snow as to look like the presents from Margate covered with shells. One is forced here to sympathise with Shinto for a moment: the bare smooth snow and frightening wind of the last slope—too steep to take with skis—had given me for a moment what one asks of the mountains. Lovely and deadly only because indifferent: a landscape simple as a pin.' Last of all, when they all bedded down at the end of the day, he found himself fairly much in favour of the accommodation: 'It is surprising but true that one can be comfortable in almost unheated rooms in that degree of cold: so long as one keeps under the futon, so that you must either write, talk, or sleep. It is only the sanitary arrangements that I have not yet learnt to face.' (Presently, when he and Doi moved into a *ryokan*, a traditional wood-and-paper inn, to greet the New Year 1933, he learned that there were two major sources of heat which were quite as efficacious: 'The hotel all slides open [it is built with walls of *shoji* rice paper] and is warmed only by charcoal kettle-boilers [*kotatsu*]: you sit under a rug with your feet on them: very comfortable. Japanese wine (like rice-pudding with a lot of cooking sherry in it) is a good drink so long as you are taking exercise.'[99])

Yet there was one last discovery in store for him in the university hut which brought back to mind just how foreign he found the young people he had to work with in Japan: the visitors' book for students included a remark that was chillingly reminiscent of the lesson his students at the Bunrika had taken from the poems of A. E. Housman. 'Some that had written in English, as a "literary" thing to do, had come to it in the summer,' Empson recorded in his notebook, 'and had to go on down the valley and come back with food for the night: tiring, and one might lose the way. But afterwards the accomplished student wrote in English "We must have no fear: if the death comes it will make us all handsome and beautiful." They are very brave when they have started, one must remember, but they start thinking about death when we would only be annoyed.' Apparently, Professor Doi 'blushed like a small boy' when Empson pointed out to him the unknown Japanese student's over-eager invocation of romantic death. 'So I couldn't go on to say the complimentary things I had thought up.'[100]

Very shrewdly he remarked upon the difference in his own disposition: 'How often I do things, timid as I am, which at any rate seem bold to me, out of mere irritation.'

Never put off by the sweltering hardships and inconveniences of travelling in the Far East, which he took in the spirit of junketing, he still found himself wondering in a witty letter of March 1933, 'Always rather embarrassing to wonder what one gets out of travel to make up for its privations; except that it requires so much imagination to stay at home'[101]—an apothegm that merits a place in any dictionary of quotations. He would later bring back to mind the fact that Dr Johnson had taken with him to the Western Isles of Scotland Crocker's *Arithmetic*, 'because (he said) you get tired of any work of literature, but a book of science is inexhaustible'.[102] He fully agreed with Johnson's point of view; as he would report during a later visit to India, 'I have bought a textbook of algebra to try and keep the soul alive on the boat.'[103] (During his period of refugeeing with the Chinese in 1937–9 he would prize 'a little book of school Problem Papers' for times of relaxation; but 'it was worth carrying the poems of Dylan Thomas as well because they were equally inexhaustible'.[104])

His most ambitious—and brave—excursions took him far afield in an unexpected direction, in search not of ski-slopes but of the faces of the Buddha. In a later year he would coyly claim that his nose had been 'rubbed very firmly in the Buddha' throughout his time in Japan and China.[105] The remarkable truth is that he sought out Buddha effigies with a learned amateur interest amounting to an obsession. 'The Buddhas are the only accessible art I find myself able to care about,' he said,[106] underplaying what had become a thoroughgoing involvement with the techniques and meaning of the innumerable images of the Buddha that he studied in Japan—and everywhere else he could reach in the Far East. In 1933, for instance, he spent his spring break from the university in travelling to China, with the specific purpose of visiting Yungang (to the northwest of Peking), where in the fifth century AD vast caves had been cut out of the rock, many with enormous Buddhas. He would write home from the Hotel du Nord in Peking:

I am sitting half drunk in this bar over a stupid book about Theories of Value, back today from the earliest Chinese Buddhist carvings in caves in a loop of the Great Wall (where there is no war), very lovely indeed, and being hacked to bits for American collectors (who like the faces only!!!) very fast. But the carvings by lasting just a millenium and a half have lasted till adequate photographs were taken (about a century before they will finally crumble away, unless elaborate and expensive steps are taken) which may be a reliable immortality. Many heads have been stolen since the 1924 collection of photos was made, and four of the thirty caves have fallen in altogether. It is really rather stirring that the photos were taken just in time—not that any photo is more than a souvenir, or one wouldn't take the trouble to go . . .

It seems obvious looking at the Peking altars and stuff that this universal-state sentiment, with or without emperor, will be revived: but I know nothing of it to claim feelings with. The disorder of the country seems much exaggerated: the horrid softness of the frowsy old men one gets as guides is the same in Japan as in China: not specially national.

I don't think I knew what the Chinese meant by those Ming dragons till I saw Chinese looking and moving like dragons—sleepy and while arrogant and dangerous in some way feminine—but a little work on portraits in the Museum would tell one that . . .

They could quite easily have become Michael Angelo in these early carvings—there are plenty of incidental floating angels with no Oriental introversion, at Yün-kang, with no Indian or other influence, but like the Han North-Chinese animal carvings: they just chose not to. I suppose most of our Great Traditions are only histories of refusals to follow up opportunities.[107]

Within Japan itself he scoured the ancient capital city of Nara, stuffed with icons, where he was excited to discover that the earliest Buddhas were 'really worth coming here to see. The later ones I can't like, though they are good sculpture (drapery and so on): the face rapidly becomes a slug-like affair with a pool of butter round the mouth. But the early ones feel as if everything was ready for an immense intellectual achievement which suddenly died.'[108] As for Kyoto, he thought like the true purist he had become, the late examples of the artistic expression first imported from Korea had been so comfortably assimilated by Japan as to be 'a sort of whimsical family joke'.[109] He even took lessons in drawing from Marjorie Nishiwaki, an English artist who was married to a Japanese and who lived in the old medieval capital of Kamakura, south of Tokyo—and apparently he showed talent above the average—primarily so that he could make skilful portraits of the Buddhas in their umpteen locations.

During another vacation, he struggled over to Korea, which was subject to the fierce colonial domination of Japan. He took detailed notes, only to lose most of them, but he was left with keen impressions of the art in Seoul:

The museums at the capital are very fine, but I only remember one large bronze Maitreya, the same type as the Koriuji one [in Kyoto] and I think better, of which I have no decent photographs. The fingers seem to be made by pushing smooth bronze tubes about with tweezers, and they are marvellous; you are held puzzling over them; they force you to imagine (if not to enter) an entirely strange state of being. I doubt whether I saw anything else in Korea that joins on to Nara and makes the historical connection plausible, except for details of drapery. Nearly all the good Korean stuff has been destroyed. The old palace had a fine site in the centre of town with a great avenue in front of it, and the Japanese have built an administrative barrack to usurp the view. A collection of statues in a cloister there is remarkable for maintaining the same cast-iron flatness in every face, lantern-jawed, sapless, not dead because never alive, and yet contriving to simper. They seem to be early.

For the passage back from Korea to Japan, he had to take a berth in steerage, which was chockfull and repulsive; so that he felt 'rather pleased at sleeping like a log on the bare boards of the deck'. But then he ran out of money in Kyoto, while still *en route* for Tokyo, and was somehow unable to cash a cheque. 'I discovered I had lost the notebook,' he wrote later, 'ran up a bill at a hotel, and spent about a week in a condition of complete failure, wandering about the streets. Some kind of disease was produced by despair, I forget what, probably a cold. In the end the hotel took my cheque and let me go home. I wish I could remember more about this odd gap in my life.' In all likelihood, he had simply drunk too much and slept the sleep of the sheerly exhausted.

Subsequently, when he finally quit his post in Tokyo, he stopped off during the long hot summer passage home in Burma, Ceylon, and India—again with the specific aim of seeking out Buddha images. His admiration for Buddhism over almost any other religion, including Hinduism, comes well to the fore in the notes he took in India, where he would write:

A revival of Buddhism no doubt can't be expected, but it would be fine; it was a vast relief to my feelings, at any rate, ill-informed as they may be, to see a few people in the yellow robe again when I got to the bo-tree of [the Buddha's] illumination at Bodh-Gaya. They have put up a very nice temple [the Mahabodhi temple] and rest-house there with curiously Anglican frescoes. Filthy and naked except for a loincloth and pendant asserting that he is the British Empire's official guide, the man who falls on you when you approach the ruins repeats incessantly in English that all statues belong to the Asoka period, from which no statues survive.

Bodh Gaya was the only place he visited in India which had seemed 'hardly worth the trouble,' he was to report to George Sansom (commercial counsellor at the British Embassy in Tokyo; one of the greatest savants of Japanese culture, who had himself researched temples, shrines, and museums throughout the length and breadth of Japan and Korea), but he had 'filled it out with a trot across country to the Barabar caves, empty and well polished', which he correctly guessed 'might be what Forster was thinking of [in his description of the Marabar caves] in *A Passage to India*, though they don't fit exactly.'[110]

The ethics of Buddhism struck him as altogether more humane than those of Christianity, and assuredly more generous in allowing the disciple to improve in moral worth through successive incarnations. However, it was not so much the morality of the faith which possessed him: it was the very meaning of the myriad faces of the Buddha that he had sought up and down the Far East. Two specific factors fascinated him about the earliest authentic representations of the Buddha: (i) the expressive enigma posed by the faces of the oldest statues, which managed at once to broadcast the essential meaning of the faith and to transcend national and racial boundaries; (ii) the process by which that image and its message had been dispersed all the way from India to the Pacific. To the casual Western tourist it can often seem that the inscrutable and even bland face of the Buddha is replicated throughout the Eastern world; Empson's assiduous eye enabled him to discriminate not only that the image varies from country to country, and indeed from one historical phase to another within each country, but also that the paradigm of the Buddha's expression manages to incorporate two apparently incompatible significations. He had early schooled himself in the ambiguities of literary expression for the book that brought him worldwide fame, *Seven Types of Ambiguity*; so, in the 1930s, he discerned that the secret of the Buddha's given expression likewise embodied a fundamental ambiguity. It should come as no surprise therefore to find that Dorothea Richards was to write in her journal late in 1934: 'Wm Empson is back & seems inclined to try his hand at an essay on the ambiguity of expression in Japanese sculpture, he seems to have been bowled over by Nara.'[111] On 5 February 1936 he published in *The Listener* a short article describing some of his observations, though he held in reserve the theoretical basis of his argument; and finally, at the very end of the Second World War, he sat down and completed his pet project, a monograph called *The Faces of the Buddha* (*Asymmetry in Buddha Faces* was an alternative, more augustly academic title), which he decked out with the numerous photographic illustrations he had gathered on his travels. Unhappily, through no fault of his own and to his lasting dismay, the finished work together with the photographs were lost in London soon after he returned to China in 1947. Among the draft papers he left heaped in his den, however, some few passages do survive—most fortunately this opening page which gives the key to his complete theory:

The experts have tended to avoid talking about the expressions of the great Buddha heads, partly because the whole subject of faces is so little understood by science that one can only assert a personal impression. Mr Langdon Warner of the Boston Museum gayly said 'that way madness lies' when I asked him about them. But the faces are magnificent; it is a strange confession of helplessness if we have to keep mum for fear of talking nonsense. I think there is a clear point to be made here which has been neglected by Western critics, a point that lets you understand and enjoy the statues better. It will be agreed that a good deal of the startling and compelling quality of these faces comes from their combining things that seem incompatible, especially a complete repose with an active power to help the worshipper. Now of course the two things must somehow be diffused through the whole face, or it would have no unity; the whole business is very subtle. But the normal way of getting the effect in the great periods is a reliable and simple one; the two incompatible things are largely separated onto the two sides of the face.

I had a chance when I was in Japan to suggest this theory to Mr Anesaki [Masaru, a great authority on religious art], which I did very timidly, expecting him to treat it as a fad. He treated it as something obvious and well-known, and told me to compare the masks of the Noh stage. These give something like historical evidence because the tradition of the craftsmen has not been lost (they are very much later than the Suiko statues); it is definitely known that their faces were constructed to wear two expressions.[112]

His observations closely tally with his arguments apropos literary ambiguity.

What had also been growing in his mind's eye was the recognition that the Buddha face represented something not necessarily, or even distinctively, national or racial (given its iconic origin in India), but that it perhaps linked cultural elements ranging geographically and historically from a point of contact with the Mediterranean world to the farthest reaches of the Eastern world. Having witnessed in Japan in the early 1930s the fiercely misplaced effects of nationalism, he became concerned to minimize the importance of national differences and to emphasize what different countries held in common through their religious myths and art, and through their mixtures of race. His article 'The Faces of Buddha' thus argues that it is a mistake to explain the Buddha expression as 'merely racial':

Græco-Roman artists in the North-West, about the first century A.D., seem to have broken the Indian convention that the Buddha must not be portrayed, and the calm of their Apollo made a conflict with the human and muscular earth-god tradition of Mathura . . . The merely racial difficulty in understanding the faces is indeed smaller than you would expect, and the artists at Angkor no less than Ajanta seem to have amused themselves by putting the same face on to all the races of mankind.

Even some three years earlier, while lamenting that he knew 'no decent book about faces later than Darwin's' (*The Expression of the Emotions in Man and the Animals*, 1873), he had stipulated: 'I am sure that the general rules about telling character from faces are the same for the whole human race—allowing for the type the individual varies from—but how much does the type mean? etc. etc.' He felt certain at the least that just as the Buddha image spans nations so it is a pernicious fallacy for any nation to assert itself as a fixed race. With reference to the imperialism of Japan, for example, he said in his capacity as BBC Chinese Editor during the Second World War:

Japanese anthropologists cheerfully admit a Chinese and a Mongol and a South Sea island wave of immigration. Then there's the Hairy Ainu in the north, who certainly intermarried with the Japanese, and the Hairy Ainu is supposed to be Caucasian like ourselves. The beautiful girl of the Utamaro woodcut has a long narrow face with a curled nose, a fine Jewish type, and she only really occurs among the Japanese aristocracy; and that element might come from Arab traders in the South Seas. In fact it's a very complete mixture of race.[113]

In October 1933, the start of the final year, he described for Sylvia Townsend Warner first the countryside and then the queerly fatalistic carry-on of the people—in terms of a mixture of sarcastic whimsy and contemptuous worry:

This is the best time of the year in Japan, a glittering sun in decently cool weather with a very high sky. You don't really get nothing but Autumn Tints as most trees are pines. It is perhaps better later on, though, when you are quite safe from them, and the rice fields have settled down as rather crisp looking stubble. It is only then that the country isn't irritatingly like Japanese prints.

Also the season for suicide, one of the national sports. There was a particularly sporting man who while throwing himself into the Oshima crater (on an island you go to for holidays—the most popular place for it) shouted out to all the trippers

'Come on—let's all do it'. The crater would in fact hold most of the nation. But the police take a graver view and put up little black-and-white notices—'Your country needs you'. 'Think again.' Most of my pupils are somehow sticky with a damp infantile gloom, even when giggling. If they were badly beaten after a long exhausting war—which they are asking for—they might really take to dying out like the people of the smaller islands further south. It is very much of a South Sea Island, though one mustn't tell them so—they are always in and out of the water, what with the baths and the swimming, their houses are obviously meant for warmer climates (it is most strange to ski past cottages with the snow piling up onto the rice-straw matting, whole walls open to the wind, and children lying teasing each other under quilts) and all the colours they use, even the clashing pinks, are somehow under-water colours, colours of jelly-fish, like the textures.[114]

He was not exaggerating when he suggested that many people had been emulating Empedocles on Etna by leaping into the crater of Mount Mihara. Edward Seidensticker has confirmed Empson's observation about the spate of suicides (many of which could be attributed to despondency, illness, and family difficulties, including the effects of the economic depression):

Early in 1933 a girl student from Tokyo jumped into a volcanic crater on Oshima, largest of the Izu Islands. Situated in and beyond Sagami Bay, south of Tokyo, the islands are a part of Tokyo Prefecture. The girl took along a friend to attest to the act and inform the world of it. A vogue for jumping into the same crater began. By the end of the year almost a thousand people, four-fifths of them young men, had jumped into it . . .
The year of all these suicides seems to have been a nervous and jumpy one in general. It was the year in which Japan, having rejected the Lytton Report, left the League of Nations [27 March]. The report demanded that Japan withdraw from Manchuria. Feelings of isolation and apprehension seem to have swept the land.[115]

The League of Nations formally adopted the Lytton Report on 17 February 1933. While it refused to recognize the phoney state of Manchukuo '*de jure* or *de facto*', however, it did nothing else to dislodge the Japanese; whereupon Japan withdrew from the League of Nations, thus proving that the League lacked teeth.

Empson felt no less isolated and alienated as the months wore on. On the campus, he reported with a startling directness in November 1932, 'one feels the popular jingoism and official militarism like a weight on the back of the neck; my Japanese colleagues more than I do.' As for the future of the war in China, he could only hazard a bad sanguine guess backed by ill-informed local opinion: 'no doubt it is a bad thing for the League to lose face so wholesale. But the immediate thing is that the game will rapidly send Japan bankrupt; there's no interference needed from outside for that.'[116] But as Professor G. C. Allen observed, the depression in Japan 'was comparatively short-lived. Recovery, which was well in train by 1933, was brought about largely by an expansionist monetary policy and improvements in industrial productivity.'

Empson's social contacts were limited. He knew certain individuals such as H. Vere Redman, as well as Sir George Sansom and his wife Catherine, both of whom he thought convivial. But that was about all. He enjoyed the odd expatriate louche spree, as when he teased John Hayward in October 1933: 'The Fleet is in, and I was taken drinking with some Able-Bodies: considered a charity to take them to the right beer-halls. One knew how blue-eyed and idealist and cultured they were, but it is stirring to an exile.'[117] Indeed it seems not unlikely that Empson enjoyed the cliché of a one-night stand with one of the ratings: when he visited his friend and contemporary Ronald Bottrall in Singapore *en route* for England in July 1934, he obliged Bottrall to put up with some bar-hopping. Bottrall would recall the benighted but epic quest in his dreadful doggerel for the Empson Festschrift in 1974 (Bottrall's verses, though bad, are sometimes reliable on matters of fact):

> In Singapore we lurched and searched
> Among the sailors in every sleazy den
> For Nobby Clark, but the man
> We found was not his Nobby
> Much to his chagrin.
> He didn't know, who chose words as his hobby,
> That in the Navy Clarks are all called Nobby.
>
> Cracked up to the skies by Margaret and me
> We had arranged next day
> For him to burgeon
> At a literary luncheon.
> The ladies, dressed in the most stylish way,
> Looked at him in awe.
> Before the food appeared the poet stood.
> An opening speech? Yes, short and quick:
> 'I'm going out to be sick.'
> And that was all the ladies heard or saw.[118]

At the other extreme, he was once asked to put in an appearance at the Japan-British Society, only to find himself conversing with Prince

Chichibu, the brother of the Emperor (Hirohito, later known by his reign name, Showa), who had studied briefly at Magdalen College, Oxford, and attended a period of instruction in the Department of Phonetics at University College, London. (Harold E. Palmer had at one time been his English tutor in Tokyo, as had Edmund Blunden.) His account of the meeting with royalty, featuring a heroic-absurd conversational gambit by Empson, merits quotation in full:

I went there after a bit of grumbling at the expense, because, though a professor is practically invisible, I didn't want to be out of any fun. A British minor diplomat yanked me by the collar and said, 'You talk to Chichibu'—because a diplomat could only address him in the very peculiar Japanese used only to royalty, where I would without breaking protocol address him in English, which of course he knew perfectly. It is like suddenly finding yourself on a lighted stage without knowing your lines. I shall always think better of myself because I thought at once of a tolerable thing to say to this friendly character. I said, 'Why don't you start a pack of hounds here in Japan?' and these were the only words I needed to say. Chichibu immediately said there was a fortune waiting for the first man who would start a pack of hounds in Japan, but the master would have to work in with the very peculiar fox-superstitions of the peasants. He must be both a fox god himself and a saviour of the fox god, but it wasn't hard to do, and Chichibu was going into great detail about this when suddenly I was yanked from the collar because a British diplomat had arrived who was prepared to address Chichibu in the very peculiar Japanese used only by royalty. Considering that after my first sentence I had expressed nothing except cries of pleasure, I hope I do not appear vain in reporting that I thought this interruption must have appeared tiresome to Chichibu; after all, he could not possibly have come to this peculiar club unless he had wanted to behave like he was doing to me. This incident . . . left stuck in my head that royalty wants to be addressed in an unfrightened manner, so long as the manner is not impudent or politically wrong.

Strange to say but somehow easy to believe, he took the prince's words quite seriously, and even suggested in a draft letter to his sister Molly that she and her husband Philip Kitching might consider emigrating to Japan to start a pack of hounds there. 'Foxes are at present an object of superstitious terror,' he truthfully reported; 'when you hire a horse and ride out into the country it is a toss-up whether the shrine at the cross-roads is a Buddha or a fox. A young woman from the country I know [probably Chiyoko Hatakeyama: see below] told me, when she was small, she told her young brother his mother was a fox (turned into a fox at night and barked at people): when the mother came back the small boy huddled in a corner and spat at her. You see how much hunting is needed. But you can't hunt in rice-country or you would trample the dykes (or would you?) anyway you can hunt in the north, which is pasture country . . . This seems a silly letter, but the heir to the Japanese throne agreed with me about it not ten days ago: only he said they had better take in bears as well as foxes. The English—especially things like hunting—have still a great influence in Japan—look at the way they all ski now; somebody has made a fortune out of that . . . You had much better be out here than me: they are good people from your angle, much less from mine.'[119] (So keen did he feel to persuade his sister and her husband to emigrate to Japan that he added to his letter, disingenuously: 'As for learning a little Japanese, which [Phil] would have to do, I know a man with a good system: you need only learn a thousand words, if so much, with a very simple grammar: nobody knows all Japanese.')

As for his encounters with all the tiny-pipe-puffing Japanese who were perhaps less worldly-wise than Chichibu (oddly enough, Japanese who had been schooled in England would sometimes refer to it as 'home'), they could be cramped by a prickly formality. Everyone knows it is difficult for the Japanese to be friendly with foreigners, Empson would assert in a BBC broadcast in 1942, and yet 'even between two Japanese, personal relations tend to be a bit blank. I remember the great linguist Okakura saying an odd thing, apropos of nothing, as Japanese confidences do come; he said to me "It's one of our great difficulties that we have no colloquial Japanese; we can't talk to each other as equals, as the English do; there is always a formal relationship implied in the grammar." So again I don't think the curious stiffness which the world has noticed in the Japanese can be regarded as a racial or inherent character; it's a very direct result of their recent history and their political set-up.'[120]

It is hardly surprising that whenever the weather was fine enough he would pass time at the Jingu swimming pool, near the Meiji Shrine, hoping to make acquaintances with whom he need have no formal dealings. One such friend was Sato Nobuo, a medical student, who noticed that the foreigner always brought to the pool a towel, a watch, and a different book for each visit, one day a volume on Buddhism, the next a new novel.[121] Indeed, Empson spent most of his time reading on the concrete apron, and swimming for only five or ten minutes in a two-hour period. He took Sato home for a drink, directing a taxi in poor Japanese. (With regard to the supposed stereotypical inability of the Japanese to arrive at a quick decision, Empson would mock during the Second World War: 'The taxi-drivers in Tokyo used to take another man around with them in the front seat to make up their minds with; the other man didn't know the way any more than the actual driver did, but as long as there were two of them they could think about it.'[122] The irony of such easy sarcasm would not have been lost on Empson, since in 1934 he was to come close to disaster because of travelling alone with a taxi-driver.) Empson's clothes were clean but scruffy, Sato noted; his hair was 'like a sparrow's nest', his house messy. Empson revealed that he was not a Christian, and explained the origin of the place-names 'Oxford' and 'Cambridge'. Thereafter they often met up at the pool, where Sato noted that Empson's swimming was just as bad as Sato's English. So Sato tried to teach him to swim properly, though without avail; but Empson kept up an air of not caring a jot about his lack of aquatic accomplishment.

One day they went hiking together, striking across the Miura Peninsula to the ancient city of Kamakura, where there is a huge concentration of Buddhist temples and Shinto shrines. As they walked, they talked. Sato knew nothing about English literature, so they chatted about botany, zoology, organic chemistry, and medicine. Sato was amazed by Empson's familiarity with such matters as carbon atoms, theories of probability, the structure of benzol and phenol, and even the relationship between vitamin D and ultra-violet light. (Another day, when a student took Empson to visit the cemetery where Lafcadio Hearn and the novelist Soseki are both buried, Empson showed off his mathematical skill by asking about the size of the graves and thereby calculating how many corpses were laid out in the entire cemetery.) When he and Sato got lost, Empson took out his penknife, stuck it in the ground, and lay down flat with his ear to it: he was listening to see if anyone was coming, he said. Once he had established that there was no one within earshot, they set off walking again at his furious pace. Reaching Kamakura in two hours, they went to a café and enjoyed a meal of eel and rice and watermelon. When a couple with a baby came in, Empson said he hated babies as much as he did snakes, so he and Sato left. In the poignantly lovely Hasedera Temple they beheld the 30-foot-high merciful Juchimen (eleven-faced Kannon), the largest carved wood statue in Japan, which— as Sato was again astonished to see—Empson knew all about. Then they went swimming in Sagami Bay, and wrestled on Yuigahama Beach. Empson buried his watch in the sand before they started swimming, and could not find it afterwards. 'Never mind, it was a cheap one,' he shrugged. (At times he seemed to have wanted to be loved for being so childish, so practically hopeless.) Next, according to Sato Nobuo's account, they left the beach— just as they were, naked and barefoot—and called at the house of Empson's art teacher, Marjorie Nishiwaki. Fortunately she was not at home. Later still, when searching for a tea-shop (presumably they had got dressed again by then), Empson stipulated it had to be 'one where they don't play records'. Back in Tokyo, they chose a Chinese restaurant, for Empson said he loved Chinese food—though inevitably he made a mix-up of 'flower' and 'flour' while doing his best to order the meal.

On another occasion they decided to go into the country to avoid the air-raid practice that day; and after equipping themselves with sandwiches they rode the train out past suburban Tokorozawa to the Murayama Reservoir. It was night by the time they arrived, and the blackout in force, so the lake looked pitch black. But Empson, a powerful walker, was not deterred. In town he would take a taxi for the shortest distances, Sato noted; but out in the country he walked so fast, it was hard to keep up with him. They got soaking wet with sweat and rain, and ate their picnic in darkness. It must have seemed at times as if Empson was playing the professional Englishman, since he would never rest until it was 'tea-time'. But in fact he was not making any sort of point at all: it was just his usual energetic way.

'What I liked most about him,' said Sato Nobuo, 'was his childlike naïveté, his forthrightness, his unwillingness to compromise on his opinions, and the way he would read a book at every possible spare moment.' Empson was generous towards Sato, lending him books, records, and even his typewriter. When he got back home to England, he told Sato, he would give up being a teacher.

Empson's only reference to his friendship with Sato Nobuo begins with a beautiful evocation of their jaunt to Kamakura which goes a long way to show the high level of his aesthetic sense; it ends by suggesting that his day-to-day life consisted of some spare-time fun but much professional sufferance:

I walked over the hills about six miles to Kamakura yesterday: pine and birch and bamboo, with little winding paths up and down. Very small steep dark green hills looking out over acid light green flat ricefields and the sea. Damp boiling electric sunlight, with wild tiger lilies and great velvet black butterflies. With such a nice young man I picked up at the Municipal Swimming Pool, who is preparing to be a doctor and attempting to teach me the crawl-stroke. It is time I left this country—I have always been afraid of the third year—but there is a very great deal of genuine lazy pleasure to be got out of doing nothing here. One can only like them much when they have nothing to do with literature, and can't like them much without being sorry for them, but indeed there is a great deal to be felt besides glum distaste and contempt.[123]

His affections were not confined to the young men he picked up at swimming pools. Early in 1933 he was writing to I. A. Richards as if

Japanese women were an unknown quantity: they were alien creatures who could never hold more than a theoretical interest for a Western male like himself. Indeed, when Richards floated the idea that Japanese women seemed strange to Westerners because their society had little or no tradition of romantic love, Empson mused upon his mentor's notion and came up with conclusions which were as disdainful as they were untested. To his credit, Empson himself thought these reflections 'rather squalid':

You say that romantic love is a novelty to the East: I don't know in what sense this can be true. All these lovers' suicides are traditional enough. Sansom tells me that what he would call romantic love poetry starts in Japan as soon as there is a leisured class not wholly occupied with military discipline. As for not being officially approved of, I don't know that Wertherism ever has been anywhere. And yet there seems a peculiar difference between Japanese and Western women which one can't explain by saying 'they haven't votes' or 'they are despised in practical matters': they are very different from South European women who seem to be legally placed much the same, and I'm told the wife does the accounts of these small shops and is as much in command as a Frenchwoman. You might make it Age rather than Sex War: the grandmothers are influential enough. The difference seems mainly in the idea of 'sitting at the head of the table'—'ruling the drawing-room'—what you miss is the sniff of the charlady which means she has summed the room up and means to show you what she thinks. No doubt it's all different in China: people sometimes say women are better off there. You can get Japanese to agree that there is much less pleasure to be got out of Japanese women (than they suppose from their reading is to be got from European women)—I always feel very sorry for the young men I like here on those grounds. But I can't see that is due [to] a shift in their use of words like 'love': it is chiefly that the conventions for women demand that they should be dull—and infantile, which is more hopeless.[124]

Things changed profoundly within a few months. During the summer of 1933, he began an affair with a young Japanese woman whose given name was Haru. Her family home was in Yokohama, and she was working as a nursemaid for the German ambassador in Tokyo. A pretty girl of slight build, she wore her hair in permanent waves: the latest fashion. She is mentioned only a few times in Empson's surviving papers, the first in a letter of 8 October 1933: ' "Too much rice" (the Chinese rickshaw boys' name for illness in general— I don't know whether they would use it for starvation) has been grown in Japan this year, and the farmers are badly off. My young woman was expecting to have to sell herself to a German business man to support her parents, but a brother-in-law has rallied and we are all right. I made no offers but bought her some clothes.'[125] If that reference seems crude or supercilious, it is almost certainly explained by the fact that in writing to John Hayward, Empson would invariably be flippant. (Were Haru's parents poor farmers, as the sequence of remarks might suggest, or landholders who had fallen on hard times? There is no written or personal evidence one way or the other.) But the relationship meant more to Empson—and to Haru—than an easy or exploitative sexual encounter. It inspired a poem, one of only a handful he wrote in Japan. 'Aubade' is also one of the few poems that is directly revealing about his private life. Thirty years later, in an interview, he glossed the poem in a way that suggests that at the time he nurtured honourable and well-intentioned hopes. 'When I was in Japan . . . it was usual for the old hand in the English colony to warn the young man: don't you go and marry a Japanese because we're going to be at war with Japan within ten years; you'll have awful trouble if you marry a Japanese, and this is what the poem is about.'[126]

This is the first half of the poem (in its final version):

> Hours before dawn we were woken by the quake.
> My house was on a cliff. The thing could take
> Bookloads off shelves, break bottles in a row.
> Then the long pause and then the bigger shake.
> It seemed the best thing to be up and go.
>
> And far too large for my feet to step by.
> I hoped that various buildings were brought low.
> The heart of standing is you cannot fly.
>
> It seemed quite safe till she got up and dressed.
> The guarded tourist makes the guide the test.
> Then I said The Garden? Laughing she said No.
> Taxi for her and for me healthy rest.
> It seemed the best thing to be up and go.
>
> The language problem but you have to try.
> Some solid ground for lying could she show?
> The heart of standing is you cannot fly.
>
> None of these deaths were her point at all.
> The thing was that being woken he would bawl
> And finding her not in earshot he would know.
> I tried saying Half an Hour to pay this call.
> It seemed the best thing to be up and go.[127]

While internal evidence, and the genre, might suggest that 'he' in the last stanza quoted could be the woman's husband or father, S. F. Bolt has revealed in a published letter: 'This person . . . was a small boy in the charge of the nursemaid who was the poet's companion—as Empson explained when I wrote something which assumed a husband was involved.'[128] Dr Bolt explained further for me: 'It occurred when I was poetry editor of *Delta*, and writing a series of articles on poetic devices. In the article on repetition I demonstrated how "The heart of standing etc." develops meaning, stanza by stanza. This involved interpretation, including taking "he" to be the husband. Ian MacKillop, another editor [and Empson's colleague at Sheffield University] showed it to Empson prior to publication, and wrote to me that Empson was indignant at the suggestion that the woman was another man's wife, affirming that she was a nursemaid employed by the German ambassador.'[129] It is likely that Ronald Bottrall was also mistaken, albeit about different details, when he remarked that Empson

> . . . rode to work on a whisky diet
> And had his love-play with the parlour-maid
> Of the somewhat sinister Swiss Minister.[130]

Empson had experienced his first earthquake, which killed thirteen people, just three weeks after his arrival in Tokyo, on 21 September 1931; and several minor tremors over the following two years. On the occasion related in this poem, as soon as the earth moves for the sleeping lovers, the woman's first imperative is not merely to seek safety by getting out of Empson's villa as fast as possible but to rush home by taxi. Although the affair was not adulterous, it might still be a scandal for her to be sleeping out with her lover.

The key to the poem is its oscillation between the resonant refrains, which point up the conflicting calls of duty and desire. 'It seemed the best thing to be up and go' gestures to the expatriate's patriotism. 'The heart of standing is you cannot fly' touches on love, the possibility of marriage, making a stand. Whether it would have been nobler for him to stand and marry the woman in Tokyo, or to heed the call of home and the deep honour of his political place: that question becomes the fulcrum of the remainder of the poem, and it closes by acceding to the large truth (reinforced by the generalization of the plural 'we' in the final line) that the new commitment must needs be surrendered to the long inalienable obligation. Neither choice would be satisfactory or less loaded with pain, but the principle of positive realism wins the contest.

> It is on contradiction that they grow.
> It seemed the best thing to be up and go.

> Up was the heartening and the strong reply.
> The heart of standing is we cannot fly.

Those last lines, Empson said, 'chiefly meant that you can't get away from this world war if it's going to happen'; their keynote is 'passive endurance. We have to put up with it, we can't avoid this situation of history.' Thus, with respect to the love affair with the Japanese girl dramatized in the poem, the lines say starkly: 'we can't marry, we must expect to separate.'

The next recorded reference to Haru occurs in January 1935, some months after they had separated. Empson says (in a letter to Catherine Sansom) that he had afforded the doleful Haru some financial assistance before he left Japan. 'I had a Christmas card from Haru in Tokyo in which she said she was keeping the money, very little, I gave her when I left and would send it back when I was seriously hard up, which she was sure I would be. She writes very cheerfully now. I wish there was some hopeful step that she could take.'[131] The phrasing suggests that he must have put a good deal of emotional distance between himself and her; and the last sentence, though kindly, does not suggest any wish that she might take a step in his direction.

The relationship did not end as bravely as it might have done after this brief cross-cultural encounter. Haru visited England in the summer of 1935, working as a nursemaid for the future poet and academic David Wevill, who was to recall many years later:

In autumn 1954 I had just started at Cambridge, coming from Canada. I wrote my parents a letter naming some of the poets I was reading, including Empson. My father, who knew nothing of writers or literature I think, wrote back asking if this was the William Empson he had confronted in our rented house in Croydon (I think) while we were on a visit to England [from Yokohama in 1935] . . . My parents had brought the young woman across as a baby-*amah* for me, and by law my father was responsible for her safe return to Japan, as a Japanese national. Empson knocked on the door asking to see her, telling what story I don't know, but I believe Empson tried several times to see her, by various means. I seem to recall my father might have appealed to the police to restrain Empson.[132]

Such uncertain recollections suggest that Wevill's father believed Empson had been harassing the woman, or was at least over-importunate (it is possible that Empson had treated himself to some alcoholic reinforcement before calling at the house). Empson did have a number of encounters with Haru—though it is not possible to determine who was the less willing. They even went out of town together—perhaps in a state of mounting awkwardness, regret, or recrimination—and probably visited his friend

Phyllis Chroustchoff at her family home in Devon. The evidence is this entry in a notebook he kept in 1942: 'I remember a Japanese girl walking into a Devonshire meadow with me, all roaring with its lush and careless summer; she looked at a hedge ten feet thick and fifteen feet high and said "In Japan we would eat all that" and otherwise was astounded and angry to find that everything hurt her legs: "Why do you let these things grow?" she could not understand, about the nettles and thistles. But I had thought of this as a form of the prettiness of Japan and the way farming there is gardening.'[133] On 11 October 1935 he notified Sansom: 'Haru leaves England today, quite cheerful after wangling a last meeting yesterday.'[134] Evidently he did not feel it incumbent upon him to see her off on the ship, which carried her to Canada.

His next bulletin to Sansom, on 13 November, conveys an unmistakable tone of relief that the responsibility for her well-being has passed away from him to others, perhaps even to Haru herself: 'Very cheerful letters from Haru in Canada, who has met friends there. The Wevilles mislaid their luggage and sent her on to fetch it back, and I do claim for Haru that she seems to have become a social figure as soon as let loose.'[135] Still, a hint as to his probable upset in the weeks after her departure is given in an aside in a letter from John Davenport to Julian Trevelyan: 'John Hayward heard from Bill, but as the letter had obviously been written under great emotional or alcoholic stress we were just as much in the dark as ever.'[136]

However, there is a further piece of evidence that has to be taken into account. As first published in *Life and Letters Today* (Winter 1937), 'Aubade' included eight lines, exactly halfway through the poem (following the opening stanzas quoted above), which suggest that the end of the affair was protracted, and probably hurtful—more so for the woman than for himself:

> This is unjust to her without a prose book.
> A lyric from a fact is bound to cook.
> It was more grinding; it was much more slow,
> But still the point's not how much time it took,
> It seemed the best thing to be up and go.
>
> I do not know what forces made it die.
> With what black life it may yet work below.
> The heart of standing is you cannot fly.

Perhaps he found that the initially beguiling liaison had turned with terrible swiftness into an irritating blank mistake, or a big lie he could not face down. (A few months after the appearance of the poem in its periodical form, he wrote to Robert Herring, editor of *Life & Letters Today*: 'The poem about a girl in Japan that you published left me entirely blank when I found it in the copy here. I feel only a vague embarrassment.'[137]) Perhaps he could not find it in himself to be firm enough to put an end to it. Or perhaps, when he begged to be released, she would not let it go. We cannot know for certain. All we do know is that he chose to cut out of future printings of the poem the lines last quoted, perhaps because the references to 'grinding' and 'black life' seemed to suggest that she had become bitter or simply, self-humiliatingly clinging.

The unhappy truth is that she probably did try to keep their love alive too long after its natural term, for Empson's last word on the relationship was written to Ronald Bottrall on 23 July 1940 (he had been to China and returned home again since last seeing 'poor Haru', as he now called her):

I found a grindingly sad letter from her when I got back to England, and then lost the address; but maybe after all that was the best thing to do.[138]

A further promising but not-entirely-satisfactory personal encounter was to take place in March 1934, when he briefly played host in Tokyo to a gifted woman from the north of Japan. They had been in contact by letter for some months. This was Chiyoko Hatakeyama, a 32-year-old poet and secondary-school English teacher who had been encouraged to send off to him a number of the poems she was writing in English.[139] Many years later, when he was questioned as to whether she had been a pupil of his in Tokyo, Empson had responded, candidly but rather breezily:

No, she was just a school teacher somewhere in the north of Japan who wrote and wanted to have the English of her poems polished up. I thought they were very good. I did see her once—she turned up in Tokyo after she'd done all these things—I mean after she'd sent me all these poems and I'd sent them back—and I was sort of very keen to keep up the connection. But she was very sort of shrinking. I never saw her again and she didn't leave an address. But there was no quarrel— she was just shrinking . . . I thought they were good poems.[140]

She was in fact four years senior to Empson. Born on 13 November 1902 in Takarae, Tome-gun, Miyagi-ken (a small village to the north of the northern regional capital of Sendai), Hatakeyama was the second daughter of the six children of a farmer—a breeder of silkworms whose business had collapsed in the wake of the Wall Street Crash. At the age of 8 she had suffered the terrible misfortune of dropping a heavy crate of mulberry leaves on her right arm; and although the limb was roughly splintered in a cedar-bark plaster, after a few days it was found to be irreparable and had to be amputated at the shoulder. This distressing early disability seems not to have impaired her progress—she could play tunes on the piano with her left hand, and even managed to ski—and she was fostered by enlightened teachers. In 1915 she entered Miyagi Girls' School in Sendai, a Christian foundation where she became a boarder, and from which she duly graduated in 1920: much of the instruction was given in English by missionary teachers, so that Chiyoko became quite well read in English, as well as competent at speaking the language. Between 1915 and 1920 she studied English Literature at the associated senior establishment, now known as Myagi Gakuin, a private women's university which had been set up by the missionaries in 1886. At university, among other activities, she acted in an uncut English-language production of *King Lear*; taking on the heavy leading role, she acquitted herself in dedicated style, being word-perfect from an early stage and constantly begging for more rehearsals. In April 1926 she took up employment as a teacher of English at a girls' school in Hirosaki in Aomori Prefecture (in the most northerly part of Honshu); but she took sick leave from the school some nine years later, in November 1935, when she contracted a severe bout of tuberculosis and endured a long convalescence—she was to quit the girls' school on grounds of ill health in March 1937.

Hatakeyama might have met Empson at an earlier date than March 1934. In 1932 he had taught the summer session at Karuizawa, and possibly he had been billed to teach there again the following year but for some reason could not manage to fulfil the engagement. She did attend another such summer seminar, possibly in 1933, and yet it is clear that she was not taught by Empson while studying there. It was a friend of hers, Hiroshi Hirai, a student of Empson's at Tokyo University, who acted as intermediary by arranging for her poems to be looked at by the visiting English professor in the summer of 1933.[141] Empson favoured her work, and was sufficiently interested in her progress to take the trouble to write her a series of letters about her trial verses, offering detailed suggestions for revision: he took care to amend all such matters as archaisms or antiquated poetical inversions, and any failures of idiom and other awkwardnesses. Above all, he paid her without condescension the compliment of pulling no punches at all in his thoroughgoing commentaries.

Categorically he informed her, even in his first letter (15 June 1933): 'To write verse in a foreign language is a very good way of digesting its literature, and to have digested a foreign literature is a great help for composing in one's own language: but the actual verse in the foreign language can hardly be more than an exercise. So if I criticize this verse harshly that is no reflection on your powers.'

In another letter he warns her against the temptation of taking up the seemingly easy option of presuming to think she can compose her poems in free verse: it is no good trying to bypass the very best kind of apprenticeship.

One's best poems are usually written fairly quickly: the better ones here I think are the easier: still one gets one's power to do it quickly from practice with slow ones. Your best way if you want to get a technique in English poetry is to write a regular ten-syllabled metre, say couplets: you needn't let this practice interfere with a genuine expression of feeling: try translating something you like well enough. The people who write good free verse in English have all trained themselves on regular metres—except Walt Whitman for instance, who isn't aiming at verse effect.[142]

Since the best free verse depends upon being keenly attuned to the rhythms of natural speech, he told her from the beginning: 'Free verse needs more directness, less variation from normal English, than verse in a strict form—it claims a special sincerity and has no excuse for forcing its language. So the inversion of *a child's look sere* [as she had written in a poem called 'Desire'] won't do.'[143] Likewise: 'Free verse is nearly always slight and shifty... [I]t is much harder, of course, to make the rhythm play round a strict metre: if you are not in the habit of *talking* English it may well not be possible.' And again:

You keep jumping from iambs to dactyls, which only seems like prose in free verse but in a strict form has a very strong effect on the reader: that I think is the chief reason why one can't write good English free verse without practice in the much more exacting rhythms of the strict forms (I don't mean harder to do well, but worse when they are a little wrong)...

Actually as a way of translating I should say that Arthur Waley's method with vers libre was much the best.

The thing is that we learn vers libre from metre.[144]

In another letter he encouraged her to reach beyond herself in her poems, to engage with intellectual reflection, or with the conflict of ideas or convictions in Japanese society, and not just to seek to express her feelings. In truth, he found a tactful way to suggest that her work was a touch too self-involved:

[The point] about life is to keep a wide variety of interests so that you can keep moving from one to another before they get stale, don't you think?... English poetry is getting into a sort of knot because so many things are said as well (and more likely to be read) in prose, and that makes it introspective: I don't know how it is with Japanese poetry. Of course in a foreign language it is hideously difficult to write verse with a variety of *sorts* of feeling in it: but in your Japanese verse it might be a good thing to try to show the clash of different philosophies and social comedy, and quote lines of poetry by people quite different from you that you have thought specially good,—in fact take to being 'clever' like the moderns. The intellect is an escape from emotion even when it doesn't have a good effect on the emotions afterwards, which it often does.

This may easily be bad advice.

Not that I think your poetry now is mere expression of emotion empty of thought: it isn't: but that writing about subjects far away from oneself is often more use in the end.

Yours sincerely

W. Empson.[145]

In April 1934, on a visit to Tokyo, she got her chance at last to meet Empson: he invited her to call at his house in Shirokane Sankocho. 'If I don't sleep tonight,' she noted in her diary on the eve of the appointment, 'I'll make a blathering exhibition of myself on our first meeting.' She had picked up the gossip that Empson had a reputation for absent-mindedness and was therefore quite capable of missing their date; so she added for her own amusement: 'For it is to be an interview between Mr Poet, who forgot his invitation to his pupil and went for a walk, and I who am casual about time.' On calling at the house, she was shown into a small sitting-room, whereupon Empson promptly appeared. 'At that moment, I sensed an inferiority like fear disappear from my heart. It was because he has a face which reminded me of a boyish Greek sculpture's—with a rather "shy" expression and, moreover, he returned my greeting with a gentle and calm voice.' Empson was well aware that she might be far more shy than he was—all but rigid with politeness and deference—and took pains to conduct himself as informally as possible. Ironically, his pointedly free-and-easy, anti-hierarchical manner was not an easy thing for her to cope with; nor was his spontaneous action in showing her a collection of photographs of images of the Buddha—he may not have been aware, or may have forgotten, that she was a devout Christian.

[W]hen I was offered cherries from a table, being a country person I felt a little embarrassed. By himself, he brought in a whole cake with a quarter cut, and offered it to me. Before we talked about anything, he took lots of Buddhist pictures from around his bookshelves and spread them out in front of me. I was confused about how to interpret this for a while, but I thought that 'maybe he might have associated them with my free and easy features, or connected me to them through the poems in English which I had sent him (even if they can't really be called poems in English).'

At all events, he didn't mention anything about poetry and literature. Being so fascinated by the pictures, I also forgot to express my gratitude for his courtesy. Then, after a few minutes, he suddenly said, 'How about having lunch together at Fuji-Ice in Ginza.' A country person, I was deeply impressed once again, but since the matter also concerned the dignity of Japanese women, I expressed my appreciation serenely and promised to meet him at 1 o'clock, and said goodbye.[146]

The next day, when she arrived at the Ice-cream Restaurant in good time, she was wryly amused when he turned up slightly late, since she was invariably the one who kept others waiting. A dish of lamb was ordered, and he expressed surprise when she asked him to cut up the meat on her plate—though even the unobservant Empson can hardly have failed to notice her prosthetic right arm. 'He took my plate and cut the lamb into pieces very carefully,' she noted in her diary, adding rather fulsomely that she 'could hardly anticipate such kindness'.[147] She was so 'excited' throughout the meal, she admitted to herself, that she could scarcely enjoy the food or their conversation. After lunch, they visited a shop in Marunouchi selling Egyptian ware and then a museum of Buddhist sculpture in Ueno. Not surprisingly, Hatakeyama felt at once flattered and self-conscious to quite a high degree: this was probably the first time she had walked out and about with an Englishman, or even with any male foreigner. 'As Mr E often talked to me about this and that, they must have taken me for his wife. But since we are of different races, perhaps they imagined I was his something else.' By the last phrase she clearly meant 'girlfriend' or even 'mistress'. She was beguiled—after all, he looked to her like 'a boyish Greek sculpture', and was 'shy' and gentle in his bearing towards her—and all in all pleased by the attentions of her 'Mr Poet'. 'When we parted, we promised to meet again in Sendai and shook hands! But in Sendai, I let it go completely. I'm sorry that happened. I really regret it.' In herself, she could be spirited, humorous, and outgoing; but her winsome and anxiously deferential posture towards the foreigner may have proved rather trying for Empson: he found her, as he said later, 'very sort of shrinking'. Equally, it seems clear, he had also found her quite fetching: 'I was sort of very keen to keep up the connection.' In a letter that appears to have been written subsequent to their sole meeting, he notes: 'Most of the poetry you have shown me is very introspective—more than you are in your own life, I should say.'[148] He felt sure she was possessed of a more fully engaging character than her demeanour had let on.

Ironically, in an exchange of letters shortly before he departed from Tokyo in the summer of 1934, she was to ask him—for reasons that may have been deeper than she could have said outright—whether her poetry conveyed enough of the characteristics of her gender: that is, if it seemed 'womanly' enough?

It seems certain [he replied] that women writers *don't* get good effects *only* by making themselves womanly—Emily Bronte was as 'unwomanly' as George Sand though in a different way. Jane Austen accepted the limitations of her life as a basis for art, but she depended on a strong 'catty' side that you could hardly call 'womanly'. I wouldn't worry about that if I were you.[149]

Presumably realizing on the instant that his words lacked gallantry, or that he had committed an unwanted ambiguity in the last sentence, he added in the margin: 'If anything I should say your art was too womanly rather than not enough.' Peter Robinson, who is responsible for the recovery of the Empson–Hatakeyama correspondence, comments on this: 'The likelihood of cultural differences here leading to misunderstandings is high. In Japanese terms, Hatakeyama may have been considered by no means womanly enough. She seems to have decided that marriage was not for her, and this in itself would have isolated her from some of the conventional behaviour patterns.'[150]

If their awkwardly conducted meeting did not lead to closer personal relations—each may have been drawn to the other, but it seems that neither had sufficient resolution to develop anything further—the encounter did serve to make Empson devote even more attention to her work. One poem that she drafted not long afterwards, on 16 April, and which she—the disciple to his *sensei*—duly submitted to him, is called 'A Lunatic Woman'; it is about a distracted woman who is falsely accused of having killed her son:

> From where your madness, young mother?
> 'I ate up the law that held my boy to smother.
> I stole a shawl to hide my darling,
> But the shawl with its spell hid my boy in the darkling.
>
> I saw him not in my prison home.
> He puffed away with the spell as it began to gloam.
> Ah, almighty judges, you declare I killed my boy?
> Oh, no, I loved him, loved him, my loveliest toy!'
>
> I see your madness whence, poor mother!
> But may there not be some heaven farther
> Than Heaven, where our darkness is light [,]
> Our blames are praises, the left is the right.

It is imbued with all the strengths and weaknesses characteristic of the verses she composed in English. Empson so liked the theme and mode of the poem—'To a Christian she can look for comfort in Heaven—the heaven farther than heaven is I suppose Buddhist?' he hopefully ventured in the comments he sent her; and he remarked very acutely too about the technique employed: 'The rhythm needs to be strong at the end to make the comfort seem serious. You make it run quickly and jingle'—that he presumed to start making it his own in a more deliberate way than ever before. Earlier, he had used a strictly editorial pen; now he went so far as to fashion his own version of her poem:

> Whence your madness, young mother?
> I ate the law my boy would smother.
> I stole a shawl to hide my dear.
> It was bewitched. He is not here,
>
> Was not in prison with me. Darkness fell
> And he puffed away like smoke, under a spell.
> He was my life, he was my joy—
> The judges say I killed my boy.

Fully aware that to appropriate her poem in that way could be hurtful, and was to say the least presumptuous—formerly he had edited her drafts, not used them as transliterations to be reconfigured wholesale—he sought to draw the sting by writing beside his version: 'My attempt is very nasty, now that I look at it later.' But he did not hold back from posting it off to her.

Perhaps the best way to appreciate this new phase of his proprietary dealings with her work is to credit the notion that he had come to feel more closely and sympathetically involved with it; that he was really concerned to 'professionalize' her productions, to make them fit for publication in English; also that he felt he was not stepping directly upon her toes since these recent offerings of hers were themselves draft translations. Notwithstanding, there is something insensitive and high-handed in such an act of appropriation, and it must be significant that it was only after he had returned home to England that he started treating her efforts to translate her own verses as if they were drafts for him to recompose. His distance from her, and from the context of their original association, must have helped him to feel detached enough to handle her work more robustly—as if her poems might readily become his. Yet his advance from editor into co-creator had not been discussed or agreed.

He was to go back to England in the summer of 1934. 'It seemed the best thing to be up and go,' he must have reflected.[151] Chiyoko Hatakeyama, who was not vouchsafed his home address before he left Japan, continued to write her own verses, including some in English as well as English versions of her Japanese poems, and she made efforts to reach him by post (one person of whom she enquired wrote back impudently, 'What is the relationship between you and Mr E? I am curious').[152] In her diary of this period she rather surprisingly recorded too: 'People that know Mr E, who is a misogynist, must think it unlikely for him to have a woman acquaintance in a far corner of the world.'[153] By 'misogynist' she could not have meant that she believed Empson hated women, but her use of the term assuredly implies that she had gathered the gossip about his liaisons with young men: she may have laboured under the misapprehension that to have homosexual feelings is to dislike women.

After some months back in England, he did receive a letter from her (now lost, or else thrown away) to which he chose not to reply. But towards the middle of 1935, he received a further communication from her. He responded on 9 July with a rather brusque, and even shocking, directness:

Dear Miss Hatakeyama,

I got your last letter and thought I would 'let the matter drop', which was rude and cowardly of me: then this letter sent such a good poem that I wrote one of my own from it which I enclose. I have sent it to a paper as yours *translated* by me, which I oughtn't to have done without your permission. I say 'one of my own' though the ideas are all yours, and that is really the trouble.

It is no use 'repairing' your teacher because in a way he was always a cheat. I wanted to see more translations of your Japanese poetry and thought the originals must be very good, but I never really believed (1) that you had a chance of writing good English poetry—good enough for you really to want to do it: you might have a kind of success but not with the best public. I know that medieval Europeans wrote fairly good Latin (and Japanese, Chinese) poems but both were using their normal medium, the only one they had been trained in. It is almost impossible to write good poetry in a foreign language, and you haven't even favourable conditions. And I never really believed (2) that my 'teaching' was anything but putting my sort of poetry into yours. Of course there were some mistakes of grammar but as poems they had better contain mistakes—the English reader must be made to see that Japanese ways of feeling must be guessed at, not English ones. If you were English and wrote as you do I should want to make many of the same 'corrections' and you would not let me do it, so that the personal reasons against 'correction' are as strong as the ones of national tradition.

What I would like to do is this—not out of goodnature or because I am sorry to have behaved badly, but because it would interest me and I think I might do it well—if you will send me 'corrected' versions of your poems, with some more English poems and direct ['simple' deleted] translations from your Japanese poems, I will try to do a small book of 'translations' and get it published in

England. Perhaps that is no use to you. But I shall think myself lucky to get such good material to work on if you will let me do it.

Yours very sincerely

W. Empson.

The letter was peremptory and uncompromising, though it was equally very impressive in its sincerity, its lack of pussyfooting or phoney temporizing.[154] The fundamental burden of it was indeed no different from what he had told her two years earlier, in his very first letter: 'the actual verse in the foreign language can hardly be more than an exercise.' Her translations were very promising, but they could never be good poems in English as they stood. He would enjoy the challenge of reworking them into English, but he would have to do so exclusively on his own terms. It could not be done by aspiring to negotiate some sort of mixed marriage between the cultures, or a crossover between her perception of what she had written and what he could make of it in English. He had always found himself, he said, 'putting my sort of poetry into yours'; he might as well have put it the other way round—that the best he could manage with her work, not having the Japanese, was to put her sort of poetry into his. The letter is remarkable for its candour; but it must have felt rather crushing for his correspondent, since she had always nurtured a desire to write poetry in English—her second and deeply loved language.

The poem she had enclosed with the letter which earned his sharply honest but disheartening response was her version in English of a poem she had entitled 'Baku' ('Fool'), which she had completed by 15 January 1935. Unfortunately, Hatakeyama's English version has not survived (there is no copy in the Empson Papers at Harvard, nor among her own papers in Japan); however, her original Japanese poem remains in existence, and this is a literal translation of it, made by Peter Robinson with Chikayo Saito and Eichi Hara:

> A great fool who cannot hate the others,
> look!
> He strides through the town.
>
> Eyes sagacious-looking
> Mouths distorted by common sense,
> the object of their ridicule
> is just his individual body.
>
> As if there were no vault of heaven,
> as if there were no world beyond the sight,
> people's eyes and mouths

demand an object to despise,
to set in the frame of their common sense.

Eyes swarming like maggots,
lips laughing like poison flowers,
look!
Notwithstanding these, among them
a great fool is strolling around.

For him, the eyes of people are bright stars,
to his ears which are unclean
the derisive laughter sounds like delicate music,
and he goes on in dream-visions
staring far away beyond the sky.

The fool who doesn't know how to hate others,
look!
He strides through the town.

> November 8, 1934

Empson felt so stimulated that he could not resist tinkering with it; he presently refashioned it as his own: tighter, more succinct, though scarcely less gnomic:

Describe the Fool who knows
All but his foes.
Wading through tears striding the covered sneers
And against tide, he goes.

Delighting in the freedom of those bounds
Your scorn and even your reason are his aid.
It is an absolute health that will not heal his wounds.
Wisdom's the charger mounts him above shade,

Hanged by suspense and eternally delayed.

'Your eyes are corpse-worms;
Your lips poison-flowers.'
They become stars, the eyes he thus transforms.
All the lips' whispers are cool summer showers.

Of the Fool's transfigurative percipience in the penultimate line, he explained in a note written by hand on the text he dispatched to Hatakeyama:

He gives them their dignity (extracts beauty from works of art made of his hatreds). I think you meant this but I'm not quite sure. You see how we stand—if you didn't mean it I don't mean to alter my translation. But for the book you would of course see the translations and stop me from misrepresenting you too seriously.

Perhaps the main difference I want to make in translating is to concentrate the ideas into fewer words—a thing present day English poetry is very anxious to do, perhaps too much.

The key thing to note in his remarks is the acknowledgement that he has now so far invested himself in rewriting the poem in his own fashion, it has become, as he claimed, less a translation than a work of his own. He would defend it, and he was not willing to countenance her corrections by return. She might have been forgiven for thinking that his generous efforts on her behalf had turned into something closer to a creative theft. Nevertheless, if there is a trace of impatience in the tone of his letter, a need to make her face the facts, his argument would have been hard to gainsay. The best of his letter came in his proposal that he was eager to put into English some of her poems in Japanese. But if that was flattering, the subtext was flattening. It was a paradox she would find hard to face: he could not work from her poems in Japanese, and was not happy enough with the poems she wrote in English. But she could not meet his wish to help her except by trying first of all to find for herself the best English equivalence for what she had written in Japanese. In a way, he was simply admitting to her, and to himself, that all the editorial suggestions and corrections he had put into her earlier poems had still not made them into good poems in English; in that sense, it was all a wasted effort, and one would be fooling oneself to think otherwise. Now, at a period when he was starting to run out of his own original poems, he may have felt he owed it to himself to make something more of Hatakeyama's work; but he could only do his utmost for her poems by overcoming the limitations of her efforts to translate them for herself—not by editorializing but by rewriting.

Peter Robinson keenly remarks that Empson is 'at pains to repudiate the implications of devotion and idealization in her treating him as a "teacher" or *sensei*'. He notes too of Hatakeyama's reception of the letter that she 'seems to have missed the implication in his phrase "with some more English poems". Despite the discouraging candour [of Empson's letter], he was also offering to revise work composed in English for publication. She received his letter on August 14, and noted in her diary the following day that he had written "very much against a foreigner's composing English poetry". She adds: "Although I can't help but agree that it is true, I am still not able to give up or alter my purpose so easily. I will wait for a chance. He praised the contents of my poetry very highly".' The steel in her character shows up well.

A draft passage of the reply she ultimately sent to Empson on 30 August has survived in her papers: dignified, modest, and yet still doughty:

Thank you very much for your answer which delighted me so much. I also feel it [an] honour to receive the proposal which has given worth to my poor poems. I understand well what you say because I always knew that I was stubborn about my English poetry. But I was too sorry to break my 'promise to myself'. I had planned... [155]

Indeed, she forthwith made efforts to rise to his expressed ambition to put together a volume of 'translations' of her poetry. The following year, she sent him three additional poems (despite succumbing to the tuberculosis in November), and two of them eventually found their way, along with 'The Fool', into Empson's *Complete Poems*, as written by 'C. Hatakeyama' and 'trans. W.E.' They included 'Echo' ('Hankyo'), composed in April 1936, which was to appear in Empson's version or 'translation' as 'The Shadow'. When writing to him soon after 30–1 May 1936 (when she was still ill), she seems to have been responding to a further prompt from him which has been lost:

I received your letter in the end of March and have been trying to send a few of my verses. But I could not do it although I have been much better since April...

I chose three of my verses which I think are comparatively like The Fool. 'A little bird's soliloquy' was written when I gave up my ambition of writing English verses.

With that last sentence she was signalling to her *sensei* that she was bowing to his frank and painful judgement of the verses she had written in English: the dignity of her obeisance might have caused him a pang of remorse.

A Japanese draft of the last of the few poems she was to send him in 1936 survives among her papers: it is 'Ko-tori no Dokuhaku' ('A little bird's soliloquy', as she was to translate the title), and it was written in August 1935, so that it coincided with the moment when she received his letter offering only a dispiriting estimate of her capacity for writing good poems in English. Her English version of the poem has not survived, but the draft in Japanese carries a note which reads in translation: 'Now that I am going to abandon writing poetry in English I would like to wish all the best for the bright future of my teacher W. E. I dedicate this to him.' This is a literal translation of her poem, by Peter Robinson with Chikayo Saito and Eichi Hara:

Fly high,
great hawk,
fly high, fly far and away
over mountains of night
into the eternal day.
From the sky it is your eye
views the world revealed by the sun's audacious light
and the secret the moon tells in whispers.

It is the very eye small birds cower before
When I hear the flutter of your wings above my head,
poor me, I fold my wings,
hide with a shudder behind a twig
and listen to the sound.

But, when
beyond doubtful smoke over mountains,
defying damp winds that ruffle skin and hair,
your wings magnificently wave,
from my eyes that push aside weakness and fear
flow tears of joy
and the sun shines over them.

Fly high, come, fly aloft,
great hawk,
my thought too will at least reach with your wings
to the place where you unlock the gates of Paradise
and pour light upon this shadowy globe.

It is possible Empson never realized that her poem may have been an allegory of her feelings about him—he is the big bird, the hawk, to her little one—nor that the poem stood as her valediction to the writing of poetry in English. The great hawk had indeed flown up and far away, never to be sighted by her again, but he represented for her an aspiration, as well as a measure of loss. Empson nevertheless admired this poem, and proceeded to recast it in the form of this compacted lyric first published in *The Listener* on 5 August 1936:

Fly up and away, large hawk,
To the eternal day of the abyss
Belittling the night about the mountains.
Your eyes that are our terror
Are well employed about the secrets of the moon
Or the larger betrayals of the noonday.

Do not stay just above
So that I must hide shuddering under inadequate twigs.
Sail through the dry smoke of volcanoes
Or the damp clouds if they will better encourage your feathers.
Then will I weep with joy seeing your splendour,
Forget my cowardice, forget my weakness,
Feel the whole sunlight fall upon my tears.
I shall believe you a key to Paradise.
I shall believe you the chief light upon this dark grey world.

C. HATAKEYAMA (transl. W. EMPSON)

'In September,' Robinson relates, 'Hatakeyama received a letter from [Empson's senior colleague] the Shakespeare scholar Rintaro Fukuhara of Bunrika University, Tokyo, enclosing a letter from Empson and page 252 of the *Listener* for August 5, 1936 ... Empson's not writing directly to her may mean that an address has gone astray, or circumstances prevent further contact, or he has again thought better of it.' The nature of Empson's letter is not known: whether it was matter-of-fact or yet more discouraging, or just a dry courtesy. But in answer to Robinson's surmises as to Empson's circumstances, it is unlikely that he would have written by way of Fukuhara unless he had genuinely lost Hatakeyama's address. He must have felt extremely pleased to have placed the poem in print, even though it was no longer exactly her poem. Equally, it is not known whether she ever wrote to him again, or felt badly put down by his strictures upon her poetry in English, or was more upset than she would admit by his brusque appropriation.

'Family memory has it,' writes Robinson, 'that Empson sent Hata-keyama a payment at about this time. Deriving from the publications in English magazines, this may have arrived in the form of two gold sover-eigns. They were used to buy a collar for a kimono, and flowers to put on graves.'[156] The money would have been welcome to the Hatakeyama household, but it must have meant less to her than the loss of the pupil–teacher relationship she had cherished and profited from. But Empson had made a smart shift in his ground: he was no longer to be her teacher, only the adaptor of her work—and as Robinson notes, 'Poet and "translator" were never in contact again.'

In *The Gathering Storm* Empson included 'The Fool', 'The Shadow', and 'The Small Bird to the Big', along with this endnote: 'I haven't been able to ask Miss Hatakeyama's permission to re-publish these "translations" of her work. My part was only to polish up her own English version, and I do not think I added a metaphor or a thought.' The tone is rather awkwardly self-defensive—it seems more disclaimer than simple explanation—so that behind the words he may have felt that he was taking some advantage of her work. Also, it was a redundant, and thus ironically provocative, point of scruple for him to have added to the same note: 'Maybe I ought to make clear that she has nothing to do with the Aubade poem.'

'In her diary entry for May 30, 1935,' Peter Robinson records, 'she notes that "The advertisement for a second-hand copy of Mr E's poetry book has been sent by Mr H. Though I want it, I feel sad that I don't have the money". The surviving written evidence and family memory suggest that Chiyoko Hatakeyama died without ever knowing about, let alone seeing, the various editions of Empson's verse which contain the translations of what he called her "very good poems".' That concluding note to Robinson's account of the matter is poignant, but without further evidence it perhaps makes his heroine seem more pathetic and abject than she was in life: as a self-responsible adult—a woman who could be manifestly plucky and vigorous and valiant, and was often light-hearted—she must have had opportunities to seek out editions of Empson's poetry if she so wanted. Peter Robinson helpfully summarizes her subsequent career: in the late 1930s she taught at Nakahara Girls' Senior High School in Kawasaki, Kanagawa Prefecture; in 1941 she taught for a while at Shoei Gakuin in Tokyo; during the Pacific War she worked to found an institute for the blind with Tadasu Yoshimoto, an Oxford graduate; and during the 1950s she taught at Sanuma Senior High in Hasama-cho, Miyagi Prefecture, retiring when she broke her hip. She was to die in the Hatakeyama family home on 26 January 1982, in her eightieth year.

Whatever the eventualities of history, it may indeed be true to say that as a consequence of having been so outspoken with her, Empson had cooked his own goose: the goose that might have laid the little set of translations he projected—though his versions of her poems in English were henceforth always to form part of the body of his work, in *The Gathering Storm* (1940) and *Collected Poems* (1955). Thus his own candour may well have ensured that he lost the chance for further collaboration. It is a sad story all round.

As late as 7 December 1932, shortly before the midpoint of his contract, though still some months before becoming involved with Haru, Empson had written home:

Life here is very comfortable if you are strong-minded (what I mean is, self-centred), enough: the Japanese are really very civilised people, one only grudges their being so miserable (and so like pre-war Russia in the attitude of the intelligentsia to politics, but that is part of it). You have to shut out the neurotic state of the country as best you can—I am sure I am living here like a worm in a pot—but Lord knows, you have to shut out a lot of England when you are there. People like [the poet Sherard] Vines who write nagging little books saying Japan isn't like Lafcadio Hearn seem to me fatuously unfair: who wants it to be like Lafcadio Hearn, anyway? Of course, I feel very much shut off from my own clique (and am grateful for letters, like the bedridden) but that was partly why I wanted to come.[157]

Lafcadio Hearn, who lived in Japan from 1890 and taught English Literature at the Tokyo Imperial University (1896–1903), wore Japanese dress; and he took both a Japanese wife and a Japanese name, Koizumo Yakumo. He 'went native', eagerly turning his back on his birthright and accommodating himself to his adopted culture. Empson was too much the Englishman ever to seek assimilation in Hearn's self-hating way, and in any case the quintessentially ceremonious culture that Hearn so successfully aped had already passed the way of the samurai, only to be invoked as a useful political myth. Instead, in the 1930s, Empson found a state that was torn by political stresses. His students seemed to be riven between a fascist-imperialistic government and a persecuted subculture; and they often nursed a soft-headed ideology of proletarian supremacy, which he considered a 'bogus concept'—at least when applied to literature. 'That there must be some kind of social conflict behind good writing is perhaps true,' he allowed in his essay 'Proletarian Literature' (the opening chapter of *Some Versions of Pastoral*), 'but this is no argument against communism as a political scheme . . . It is only an argument against the communist aesthetic.'[158]

However calm and well-balanced, 'strong-minded' and 'self-centred', he professed himself to be in December 1932, within a few months—probably coinciding with Japan's withdrawal from the League of Nations, when 'Japan became increasingly isolated from the West and reacted by rejecting Anglo-American influences in its political, social, and cultural life,' as Gordon M. Berger has written[159]—he set himself resolutely against his host nation's policies; and he took potentially perilous risks in making his position plain. Notably, according to an article, 'Japan Rampant', published in the Cambridge magazine *The Granta* on 10 May 1933 (it appeared above the initials 'C.-B.' but was actually written by Jacob Bronowski),[160] Empson had for some reason, presumably the pressure of his sense of public duty, penned a journal and 'privately circulated [it] to Europeans who have lived in Japan and continue to be interested in her problems.' Unfortunately, the journal is no longer in existence, but Bronowski's account of it goes quite far enough to show that Empson, whom Bronowski over-eggs as 'a scrupulous searcher and a profound judge', had been preparing in secret and sending overseas a document that the Japanese authorities would have regarded as patently seditious. In view of the admission that it was 'privately circulated', in fact, Bronowski's decision to publish its contents, however briefly and even in paraphrase, and without permission, amounted to an offensively irresponsible act which might have put the author in jeopardy. Empson 'describes the difficulties of teaching Japanese university students,' Bronowski wrote: 'the difficulties engendered by the family oligarchy, by the military dominance, above all by the excessive nationalist temper. He makes it clear that the Japanese students now play in Japan precisely the part of the Nazi students in Germany. Their lust is only for dominance and power, for ruling first the Pacific and then the world. With no culture of their own, they resent the cultures both of China and of the West.'[161] (Bronowski's paragraph carries on for a few more robust sentences, but after this point it looks as though he may be glossing the journal rather than simply putting it on record.)

The remarks about military dominance and excessive nationalist temper may very well stem directly from Empson. But one might suspect Bronowski of over-interpretation when he proceeds to insist that Empson tagged *all* of his students as chauvinists and megalomaniacs, Japanese counterparts of the Nazi youth: that does not sound likely, even in a sweepingly antagonistic mood. And yet it may still be the black fact that he was reluctant to admit even to himself in the last months of his contract. In truth, the government of Admiral Saito Makoto, which replaced the Seiyukai party administration of the assassinated Inukai Tsuyoshi, did determine during 1933 to pursue a policy of 'autonomous strength', which meant wiping out 'the influence of the Soviet Union, the Nationalist Government of China, and the Anglo-American nations by a diplomacy rooted in the efficacy of Japan's military force';[162] and Italy and Germany indirectly followed that cue for expansionism.[163]

On the other hand, Bronowski's epitome is contradicted by another piece of writing that Empson happily kept to himself. Pencilled into a skimpy notebook, it is a draft of a letter home which he probably forgot. It includes an observation that—had it fallen into the wrong hands—would have laid him open to possible criminal prosecution. 'The Communists I know in Japan (every bright young man is a Communist),' he wrote, 'tell me there isn't going to be a revolution...' The Japan Communist Party, formed in 1922 by socialists of various persuasions, was an illegal organisation. All Communists and fellow-travellers were being remorse-lessly hunted down—indeed, the Japan Communist Party was virtually eradicated by 1935, as a result of mass *tenko* (fewer than fifteen members survived by the end of the war). Those casual words could have cost him dear.[164]

Years later, he recalled of his time in Japan, 'I found that all my students held liberal or leftish views, very vague ones, and on the other hand were very afraid of letting them be known, chiefly because it would prevent them from getting jobs. The opinions were almost a necessary decency, like a pair of trousers, but the trousers mustn't be allowed to peep out. I do not mean to laugh: there was also some dangerous police witch-hunting going on . . .' The truly baleful prospect was the country's savage and increasingly ac-centuated nationalism. This much he proposed in a review of a book entitled *Japan in Crisis*, by H. E. Wildes, published in 1935 (after his return to England). '[T]o say that . . . "there is far more danger of a super-reac-tionary Fascism than of proletarianism in the Island Empire" is mislead-ing,' he argued from personal information, 'because they need not be very different. If Japan went proletarian it would remain extremely nationalist, and would very likely keep the Emperor who symbolises not a class-system but the nationalism. That is the point about the conversion of Communists in prison, though the torturing is true as well . . . Certainly the rulers at present are very much afraid of Communism, which they, unlike most local Communists, believe to be international. But Japan is one of the few countries which might have a more or less proletarian instead of bourgeois Fascism.'[165] (As Lenin had written, no working class could ever generate its own revolution: 'Since there can be no question of an independent ideology formulated by the working masses themselves in the process of their movement, the only choice is either bourgeois or socialist ideology.')[166]

At some possible risk to himself Empson went out of his way to include this provocative opinion in an essay (mentioned above) that was to be published first in Japanese translation in a journal called *Literary Art*, in February 1934. For the most part, or at least for most readers, 'Teaching Literature' is not contentious, let alone subversive: it is a fetching personal statement on the value of literary study. Empson proposes, for example, this liberal sentiment: 'If the process is not largely useless, the normal student gets from literature pleasure, cheap while he is in reach of libraries, fullness or breadth of emotional life, independence of mind and a sense of proportion.'[167] (Fukuhara Rintaro remembered, 'Empson had expressed a similar view in an extramural lecture 'Consequences of Literature' given in 1933 in the Bunrika University Hall.')[168] But the political censor was quick to catch a forbidden bit of implicit fleering in the middle of Empson's manifesto:

> It has been argued that the modern system of literary education, obviously so powerful an instrument for smothering independence of mind, was actually designed for that purpose by timid but artful minds hoping to escape political change. If this absurdity is the truth they made a mistake; it should be clear by now that the herd-mind is as easily herded into Communism as into Fascism; and it takes considerable independence of mind to keep a country at the same level as its neighbours.[169]

The censor was not embarrassed by the necessity to intervene here: without regard to preserving any sense in the passage, he cut out of the text as published in Japanese the phrases 'to escape political change' and 'easily herded into Communism'—even to mention such matters was evidently much too much.

Empson was no Communist, but he was acquainted with some academics who were well up with the movement; in particular, both Tokyo Imperial University and the First High School were hotbeds of Marxism. But there was nothing sinister about the fact that Empson came to know a 32-year-old New Zealander, William Maxwell Bickerton, who had been teaching in Tokyo since 1924, first at the Tokyo University of Commerce, then at the First High School, and most recently at the Furitsu (Prefectural) High School. Max Bickerton had a reputation as a translator into English of Japanese proletarian novels such as *The Cannery Boat*, by Kobayashi. On 13 March 1934, Bickerton was taken into police custody—where he was ill-treated or allegedly beaten—and charged with promoting Communist interests. The *Japan Advertiser* carried the story at the end of the month: 'Foreign Professor Held Two Weeks in Jail on Charge of Being Engaged in Red Activity'. At a preliminary examination held in the Tokyo District Court on 30 April, evidence was given that on four separate occasions since September 1933 he had made financial contributions to the Japan Communist party (he had not actually joined the party, but only because its leaders had already been arrested); he was charged under the Amendment made by Imperial Ordinance in 1928 to the Law relating to the Preservation of Peace and Order, and remanded for public trial. Mr Bickerton was 'well aware,' it was officially written, 'that the Japanese communist party was a secret organisation which aimed, as the Japan branch of the Comintern, at the transformation, by revolutionary means, of the national constitution of this country, at the negation of the system of private property, at the creation of a proletariat autocracy, and at the realisation of a socialistic state.'[170]

The British Consul in Tokyo acted energetically on Bickerton's behalf and in due course managed to get him released on bail. It was then that Empson became involved in the affair—not for ideological reasons but because he realized that imprisonment would be horrific in the terror state that Japan had become—in order to smuggle Bickerton out of the country. According to Ronald Bottrall (Empson himself must have told him the story), he took away Bickerton's clothes and provided him with an entirely different outfit, complete with dark glasses and a false moustache. Then he booked a passage for Bickerton, obviously in an assumed name, on a foreign freighter; and finally, keeping Bickerton out of sight as much as he could, he led him towards the ship. At this point, however, the story assumes what would seem to be a quality of apocryphal absurdity: as the pair approached the gangway, a member of the Secret Police appeared—only to present Bickerton with all of his old clothes cleaned and pressed. Yet that final detail of the furtive flight might not be so farcical as it would seem (Hetta Empson, whom Empson married in 1941, was also given to understand that Empson had somehow made a mistake in arranging delivery of the clothes). It just might have been the case that the Tokyo authorities preferred to turn a blind eye to Bickerton's escape—if not actually to assist him to abscond—than to have the matter blow up into anything more of an international incident. Whatever the truth of that detail, Bickerton certainly jumped bail and left Japan on the *Empress of India* on 8 June, bound for Victoria and Vancouver.

There is no suggestion that Empson alone arranged for Bickerton to get out of the country by subterfuge. In fact, we cannot even know if he was placed under suspicion for aiding and abetting the escape, or questioned about it. But there is evidence to indicate that he certainly knew the authorites had an eye on him by then. When Michael Roberts wrote early in 1934, asking about the possibility of getting a job in Japan, Empson replied categorically: 'My job isn't being revived. They are very frightened here of teachers with Dangerous Thoughts, political ideas however pale pink. The Imperial and Bunrika (my ones) mean to get elderly teachers who have been out here for some time and won't talk much to the students.'[171] It seems likely that he was simply advising Roberts, a former member of the British Communist party, that the Japanese would classify him as a teacher with 'Dangerous Thoughts...however pale pink'; but it is equally obvious that he was referring to himself. 'But for myself,' he went on, 'I feel sorry to be leaving (it is peaceful and often amusing and I am occupying myself with painting lessons [with Marjorie Nishiwaki])—

though of course one must: don't settle here.' The date of the letter is
28 March, two weeks after Max Bickerton had been taken into custody. It
is therefore reasonable to presume that he knew of the arrest, even though
it had not yet appeared in the newspapers, and was taking the lesson to
heart. Naturally, his letter does not betray the apprehension of any involvement with a plot to spring Bickerton, because it would be impossible
to devise such an expediency until after the New Zealander had been
committed for trial—at the end of the following month.

Empson seemed to be looking for trouble, as if he needed a periodic
crisis to relieve himself of nervous strain. Had he not been employed on a
fixed-term contract, it is likely that he would have got sacked anyway.
When the crunch came, the issue was not political but sexual—just as it
had been five years before at Cambridge. He got drunk in a bar and took a
taxi home, and then he made a pass at the taxi-driver. He told Bottrall with
absurd implausibility that 'the Japanese men and women look so alike that
I made a mistake'.[172] But it was a compromising mistake. The taxi-driver
seems to have reported the incident to the police, who in turn advised the
Rector of the Bunrika that it would be better if Empson left Japan. (Peter F.
Alexander, reporting an interview with Professor Ryuichi Kajiki, has
confirmed that Empson 'got into serious trouble with the authorities
because of his homosexual activity, and the Japanese police were involved'.[173]) Perhaps feeling more amused than deeply abashed by the
incident—he was not reluctant to admit to 'a diffused homosexual feeling'[174]—Empson introduced this scandal into some rough but beguiling
verses written the next year, 1935. Though seemingly about a woman
whose rare beauty he has lost, the piquant and wittily self-deprecating
epithalamion 'Letter VI: A Marriage' is in fact (as explained earlier)
addressed to his friend Desmond Lee, for whom he had yearned in his
final year as an undergraduate. As if suggesting that he is driven to seek out
this paragon in other forms, Empson reaches the third stanza:

> Envisioning however the same beauty in taxiboys
> And failing to recognise in one case
> What with drink and the infantilism of the Japanese type
> The fact that it had not yet attained puberty
> I was most rightly (because of another case
> Where the jealousy of the driver seemed the chief factor)
> —Not indeed technically, named only in vernacular newspapers,
> And who knows who knows—
> Deported from that virtuous and aesthetic country;
>   Life being as strange as this traditional theme.

On the other hand, it was well over a year before he brought himself to tell I. A. Richards about the incident, which may well suggest that he felt more shamefaced than he would willingly admit. 'I have told Richards, by the way, about my stupid behaviour in Japan, which I ought to have done before,' he wrote to Sansom in November 1935.[175] Indeed, it is possible that he confided in Richards at that time only because his trusty tutor was about to leave England for a visit to Japan, where he would be gravely disappointed to hear the sorry story at second hand.

Oddly enough, there is nothing in accounts of Empson's departure from Japan to suggest that he left under a cloud. On 22 June a farewell party was thrown in his honour at the Nanushinotaki Restaurant. Empson wore his customarily crumpled white linen suit. It was attended by Professor Ishikawa and Professor Fukuhara, together with more than two dozen of his crisply dressed students. A large group assembled with Fukuhara at Yokohama Station to see him off on the *Kashima maru*, which slipped away at three o'clock in the stifling afternoon of 8 July. Quite unexpectedly, just as the ship began to move, Empson took off his panama hat and threw it down amidst the group of friends and students.[176] As he cast off his hat, he fumbled and dropped his newspaper into the sea. The poet, thought Fukuhara, seemed 'now irretrievably high, a free man'. Empson had no plans—apart from a desire to see as many Buddha faces as he could find in Ceylon and India on the voyage home—only a vague hope that he could make his way in literary London.

Yet there is one other document, now lodged in the Public Record Office in London, which must be taken into account. If its substance is not an outright lie, it implies a background of blackmail or bribery. It suggests that Empson either sold his soul or took his Imperial Majesty's military for a splendid final ride—perhaps even both. On 4 December 1939 (two years before Japan attacked Pearl Harbor), the British Embassy in Tokyo conveyed to the Far Eastern Department of the Foreign Office some gossip gleaned by H. Vere Redman from one Major Kadamatsu of the Japanese Army General Staff. The burden of the letter was that the Japanese felt they had reason to regret having been generous in their dealings with British interests; and their complaints included this odd little item:

Continuing on the subject of publicity Major Kadamatsu mentioned the name of Mr. Empson, a former resident in Tokyo and subsequently professor in Peking University when it was at Yunnan. (He also visited Chungking.) Major Kadamatsu said that his department had employed him as a sort of publicity man at large with unlimited supplies of money—in the words of the Major, 'We kept him luxuriously for a year.'

The intention had been that he should influence foreign opinion in favour of the New Order. According to Major Kadamatsu, however, Mr. Empson's publicity activities were all too often detrimental to the prestige of the Japanese army. With all his brilliant intellectual gifts, he is a most erratic personality and quite unfitted to act in the capacity to which the military authorities appointed him. If Major Kadamatsu's account was true, the Japanese Army were guilty of a fantastic error of judgement.[177]

Empson would not have undertaken of his own free will to spread favourable propaganda for the putative 'New Order' in Japan, which he held in contempt. If it is true that he accepted an 'unlimited' sum of money from the Japanese military, we have first to consider whether he did so under duress. Perhaps they threatened him with physical abuse in consequence of his involvement in the Bickerton affair. They may have held out the prospect of a prison term as punishment for his homosexual importuning, promising to commute the sentence if he bowed to their demands; so that in the event he was only—as he says in the sarcastic terms of the verses quoted above—'most rightly... Deported from that virtuous and aesthetic country'. As he also indicates, he could only be 'technically' deported, since his time as a contract teacher was up in any case. In short, one remotely possible explanation is that they bullied him so severely that he agreed to do a deal, albeit disingenuously. But it is doubtful that he would have done anything at all if bullied: he was immensely stoical, and could tolerate a high level of pain.

Another possibility is that he somehow won their confidence and tricked them into awarding him a handsome remuneration for a hollow undertaking. In that event, the suggestion that he act as a 'double' would have been made by the Japanese. Empson, delighting in roguishness, would have loved every minute of it, knowing that the whole charade was to be undertaken at the expense of Japan. It would have gone far to relieve his boredom. Whatever the case, as the British Embassy said, they had badly mistaken their man.

When all is said and done, however, the whole affair still sounds like a foolish piece of disinformation. The fact that the Japanese military knew that Empson made a brief visit to Chungking during his two years in wartime China is surely intriguing, because it demonstrates that they had an excellent Intelligence organization—and why would they trouble to follow Empson's movements unless they had an interest in him?[178] Looking at that question from the opposite angle, however, one has to ask two better questions. Why would they pay their prisoner his own ransom in the first place? If they had a hold over him, why would they afford him an 'unlimited' sum of money? In sum, Major Kadamatsu's allegations would appear to be both bogus and pointless. If the claim had been made perhaps a year later, when Empson had started working for the BBC, it might have had a purpose—to damage his reputation—but in December 1939 he had no significant employment: he was struggling in the USA to raise enough money to get home to England.

In any event, if the allegation is true, Empson was both wise and witty; he acted deviously and got away with it (and a handsome profit). And even if he did make off with a Japanese remittance, he went on telling the truth as he saw it. There is no evidence, documentary or anecdotal, to suggest that he ever propagandized for Japan. Indeed, his right candour is fully apparent in a piece he wrote some two years after quitting the country. 'Living in Japan', published in *The Listener* in November 1936, is a review of two books: *Japan*, by Grace James, and *Living in Tokyo*, by his friend Lady Sansom; it is an honest *adieu*, totally true to his peculiar personal experience of the place:

There is a great difficulty in writing about Japan without either cloying praise or virulent attack, a difficulty that few such books escape; the country somehow imposes it. This has a bad effect (for one thing) on the many cultured Japanese who read them; one sort reinforces their complacence, the other makes them see the outside world as a bitter and unreasonable enemy. There are all sorts of Japanese, but very few can read the rude type of foreign book as mere amusing gossip. Besides, there is a serious need for better understanding, which the rude book does nothing to provide; these books are quite right to be amiable.

Both are by English ladies resident in Tokyo with a fair knowledge of the language. Mrs. James recently returned there, but remembers ten years of childhood in a different Tokyo; Lady Sansom has been a good while at the British Embassy and has many real Japanese friends. Neither attempts the business of defending Japanese policy, or writes the repulsive baby-talk of the official guides to foreign tourists, or praises Japan, as Lafcadio Hearn did, from a neurotic horror of Europeans. On the whole Lady Sansom is less concerned with the old-style charm, and more adroit at putting in criticisms while keeping her tone of praise, but there is the same impulse behind both. They feel that foreigners, and especially visitors, need to be told certain main points; that good manners are really the first thing in that country, that if you are friendly and willing there almost everything may be done for you, that once you can get used to continual small annoyances you will find the incidents of life in Japan continually human and delightful. It is true enough . . .

But an admirer of the purpose and execution of these books may feel a need to develop what they imply in their criticism. They cannot get away from the 'charm' of Japan, a thing that is really there, and that can give you a queer kind of revulsion. The Japanese have a power to seize on what is to us the least pleasant aspect of a thing as a source of charm; the willowtree outside the brothel where the girls had the last glimpse of their lovers, a great source of poetry, because the girls were permanently locked up; the rotten tooth which made the child emperor's face so 'piquant' in the *Tale of Genji*. It certainly does not come from cruelty or stupidity, and it is much older than the muddle of modernisation. It is connected perhaps with their being great manipulators rather than great thinkers; they have little desire to find the basic principles of anything. At any rate there is a kind of pervasive silliness, nothing to do with China, about this charm; delicious in somebody you love already, admirable as a preservative of beautiful small customs, and positively frightening as the stock outlook of an Imperial people. The gulf between the Japan of these books and that of (say) foreign policy corresponds to a gulf in the Japanese mind, and if you think, for instance, of modern Germany, where there is also a gulf, and the bad parts are quite as silly and dangerous, there seems much more hope that the German gulf will be bridged over. The more you like and admire the Japanese, the more you feel they are the last people who should have isolated themselves from the world.[179]

'There have been a lot of books written in English about how beastly Japan is,' he wrote elsewhere; 'they are all written by teachers: people like me.'[180] He never wrote one of his own.

12

Poems 1935

The advances of science in our time, though very likely to cause disaster, have been so magnificent that I could not wish to have been born earlier; and I estimate that most of the poets worth study who were in fact born earlier would have felt so if they were alive now

The Strengths of Shakespeare's Shrew, 146

D ESPITE winning an early reputation with the handful of poems that were included in *Cambridge Poetry 1929*, Empson had to wait a further six years before his publishers brought out a volume of his poetry. Coincidentally, in the very summer of 1929 when he at once gained his degree and lost his fellowship, he had written from Magdalene College to offer a collection of 'about twenty poems' for consideration by his friend Ian Parsons, who had recently joined the publishing house of Chatto & Windus. Parsons felt hesitant about the poems—'it is rather difficult to make a decision on so little work'[1]—but asked to see them in any case; he received the packet on 14 June, along with this modest and beguiling message:

Most of them you have seen already. There are twenty-three of them. I doubt if I have turned out enough even now (dear me; I mean turned out of the collection, of course, not 'output' in a professional sense) (though that would be true too); I should be glad of your advice.

Although Chatto initially rejected the poems, Parsons still took an informal lien on the poems: if *Seven Types of Ambiguity* performed well, it might help to float a volume of poetry. However, even though F. R. Leavis closed his review of *Ambiguity* (in the *Cambridge Review*, January 1931) with a helpful prompt—'And, immediately, there is that book of poems which he has given us a right to demand'[2]—it was not until February 1933 that Parsons thought to capitalize on the critical success of *Ambiguity*: 'it might be a good plan to follow up with some poetry soon.'[3] However, being a perennially loyal friend, he spoke of the matter once more on 24 May 1934: 'And how about poems?' In the meantime, Empson's reputation was helped forward by appearances in other publications, including the much-discussed anthology *New Signatures*, edited by Michael Roberts (London: Hogarth Press, 1932), which reprinted five of his poems: 'This Last Pain', 'Letter', 'Note on Local Flora', 'Camping Out', and 'Invitation to Juno'.

Poems, a collection of thirty poems with notes, bound in crimson cloth and priced at 6 shillings, appeared in an edition of 1,000 copies in May 1935—just a year after Dylan Thomas's debut volume, *18 Poems*.[4] The title-page was decorated with a hatched drawing of a feathered hat of fashion especially designed by Ian Parsons's wife, the artist Trekkie Ritchie (1902–95).[5] (Six hundred copies of *Poems* were sold by 1940, and the remaining warehouse stock was destroyed by German bombing raids in 1940 and 1941.[6] Empson received an advance on royalties of £10.) It was really the young Empson's book: even though he was nearly 30 by the time the volume came out, the majority of the works were the product of his early twenties. Twenty of the thirty poems in the volume had been published before 1930 (sixteen date from 1927 and 1928), though the book did contain most of those that Empson composed in the early 1930s, including the sceptical and stoical 'This Last Pain', the deistic 'Doctrinal Point', and his wonderful declaration of largesse, 'Homage to the British Museum'. (Nine others published by 1935, including 'Letter IV' and 'Travel Note'—subsequently retitled 'Four Legs, Two Legs, Three Legs'—were not included in this first collection.)

Critics exercised themselves to accommodate the strikingly individual poetic voice of *Poems*, tentatively praising their ingenious technique, their allusiveness, their intellectual precision, their wit. I. A. Richards alerted readers of the *Cambridge Review* (14 February 1936) to what he oddly called 'the extraordinary and inexplicable passion' of the poems; Michael Roberts helpfully pointed out Empson's sense of 'conflict between the scientific and the aesthetic approach to the world' (*London Mercury*, August 1935); and Edith Sitwell (*London Mercury*, February 1936) noted their intensity and depth of meaning.

What the first reviewers did not immediately discern beneath the stimulating and exacting tropes and the syntactical density of the poems

was the fact that—for all the Eliot-like appearance of the poetic materials
(and some of the mannerisms)—Empson had entered the lists of poetry
with a challenge to the predominant modernist mode set up by Eliot. He
would explain in 1974:

Most of the poets who were starting to write around 1930 hoped to learn methods
and techniques from the French Symbolists and also the seventeenth-century
English Metaphysicals; but Mallarmé would consider it vulgar to argue, if ever
confronted with argufying in poetry, whereas Donne did it all the time. The young
Eliot was large-minded and courageous, I still think, to write so much (in his prose)
recommending Donne, a poet so very remote from his own practice; and I
suppose he was merely being charitable or reassuring to his desciples when he
told them they needn't actually bother about the arguments. (*Contemporary Poets*,
third edition, London, 1980)

He was referring in that passage to Eliot's notorious later dictum (issued
in 1931), which he fiercely contested: 'Donne was, I insist, no sceptic'.[7]
Empson explained further, 'I imitated Donne only, which made me appear
pointlessly gawky or half undressed', and he went on to insist that 'argufying' was the heart and soul of his poetry. While he later acknowledged
that 'argufying' was 'perhaps a tiresomely playful word', nevertheless he
believed it served to convey the idea that poetry can properly and powerfully represent 'the kind of arguing we do in ordinary life ... a not specially
dignified sort of arguing'.[8] At any rate, the term validly differentiated his
own kind of poetry—conducting a debate, urging a position, driven by the
imperative of reason—from the Symbolist-Imagist axis: the modernist
doctrine of writing in pictures, of commending the visual above the
conceptual, image over verb.

Rosemond Tuve, in her magisterial study *Elizabethan and Jacobean Imagery*
(1947), was to dispute Empson's view that Donne's poetry embodies what
she called 'dissonant intention', the clash between tradition and new learning.[9] For her, the apparently novel complexity of Donne could best be
explained by reference to the rhetorical tradition and to strict Ramist logic.
In his vexed review of her book, 'Donne and the Rhetorical Tradition',
Empson would counter by claiming that such an interpretation diminishes
Donne's dissident genius by 'explaining away' the poems as traditional or
commonplace usage. Whether Tuve or Empson was in the right on that
question, one strong subsidiary argument of her book carried a rebuke to
the comparatively recent literary view that the representation of sensuous
experience is in any sense sufficient as a poetic. She takes issue with what is
essentially the modernist programme of poetry as percept, the portrayal of

states of feeling with sensuous particularity. Indeed, her rejoinder to the narrowly anti-rationalist aesthetic of symbolism-imagism is very much the same as Empson's. The philosopher and critic T. E. Hulme, whose theories lie behind much of the modernist aesthetic,[10] notably claimed that 'accurate description is a legitimate object for verse': the artist perceives just for the sake of perceiving. Hulme argued further that the 'felt visual sensation' and 'vivid impression' are the point of poetry; visual imagery provides 'the purely aesthetic emotion'.[11] Against Hulme's delimited doctrine, Empson and Tuve were at one in understanding that metaphysical poetry handles philosophical and ontological problems, being concerned with far more than the process of mind—the apotheosis of the individual sensorium—and striving beyond egoism to articulate general concepts and statements of meaning: concepts interpreted and evaluated with logical coherence.[12] As far as Empson was concerned, imagery is not an end in itself but has the office of serving a larger structure. That view of poetry is not reactionary, but it is radical; it has a proven pedigree. As early as 1927, when he started to publish his poems, Empson firmly stated: 'It is a fallacy that men of great abilities can produce what Mr. Eliot calls a "synthesis" simply by explaining their mental habits; they must do it by producing a work of art.'[13]

In a BBC broadcast, *The Poems of William Empson* (15 December 1952), he was to open with these remarks:

First all I want to say something about the whole idea of my sort of poetry—why anybody should want it. There was a general movement in the 1920s for the revival of what is called Metaphysical Poetry, mainly the style of John Donne, and mine I think was more direct imitation than anybody else's. This kind of poetry works by what are called 'conceits', following out a comparison ruthlessly or carrying an argument to an absurd extreme, without paying any attention to the demands of 'romantic' poetry, that the theme has to be exalted by the stock suggestions of the 'images' presented, or the words used, so that a general poetical tone is somehow in the atmosphere. I think many people found my verse difficult, when it first came out between the two wars, merely because they did not realise they were expected to hold on to the argument so firmly and with such indifference to other kinds of poetical effect.

However when I talk in this placid way about the technique it must seem a bit pointless. There is no reason after all why anyone should like the result. The object of the style, in my mind and I believe in Donne's mind, is to convey a mental state of great tension, in which conflicting impulses have no longer any barriers between them and therefore the strangeness of the world is felt very acutely.

In the typescript of that talk there followed a notable sentence, specifically adverting to Robert Graves's early theory of poetry as a mode of therapy, which was in due course omitted from the programme as broadcast: 'Some theories of poetry maintain that poetry ought first to state a conflict and then resolve it, but this kind of poetry seems to thrive on *un*-resolved and direct conflict, which is only resolved if at all by giving this sense of the strangeness of the world.' It is perhaps in that gap between conflict and resolution that both the strength and the difficulty of Empson's poetry lie, since the deeply contested problems he negotiates in the poems do not necessarily yield up limpid solutions.

Empson thus threw down the challenge of defiance to the Symbolist and Imagist programmes; he explained in an article written more than thirty years after starting to write his own poetry in a fashion modelled on the example of Donne:

> I can see now that I really liked [Donne] because he argued, whereas the others felt that this side of him needed handling tactfully, because it did not fit the symbolist theory... [T]he anti-intellectual movement, which has been one of the causes of symbolism, tells you that thinking is sordid or low-class... [T]he best poems written in English during this century are symbolist, and they are very good. But it has gone on long enough... [L]iterary theorists commonly talk as if no other kind of poetry is possible but symbolist poetry. The main rule is that a poet must never say what he wants to say directly; that would be what is called 'intellectualizing' it; he must invent a way of hinting at it by metaphors, which are then called images. I was pleased to see Mr Graham Hough, in a recent book, remark in passing that he could never set out to explain *The Waste Land* to students without feeling 'What a rude way to talk it is!'... The full doctrine says that all poetry consists only of a collage of logically unrelated images... It does harm, both in poetry and in prose, chiefly by fostering evasiveness and false suggestions ... [I]t is completely out of touch with another tradition, that of fair public debate... [T]he arguments one hears nowadays to support symbolism turn on the belief that all thinking is done by images. This was firmly expressed by the Imagist T. E. Hulme, who said shortly before the first world war that thought is prior to language and consists in the simultaneous presentment of two images ... [W]hat the literary people mean by an image seems to be nearly always a visual image, a picture in your head, but the psychologists recognize images of all sensations, and also of muscular activity... [A] visual image is hardly ever essential, I think... Yeats's 'Byzantium', though symbolist, is magnificently full of muscular images, but I think it is a story, a fascinating bit of science fiction.[14]

Empson's espousal of the metaphysical model of Donne's poetry caused some critics to do him a disservice. Hugh Kenner, for example, later found it enough to praise Empson's 'triumph of poise' and 'gay factitiousness';[15] and A. Alvarez was to argue that the poems represent 'acts of the most subtle critical reverence to the whole concept of style'.[16] Taking the argument a little further, however, critics gradually realized that Empson's poetry had such distinction that it could be compared only with Auden's, and indeed that its mode and meaning offered a challenging alternative to Auden's. F. W. Bateson later summed up the burden of that realization by describing Empson as the Rochester to Auden's Dryden. The best passages of Rochester and Empson, he suggested, have 'a more distinctly personal flavour than those of the humaner, but also more colourless, Dryden and Auden'.[17] Indeed, the arguments of his poems are intimately concerned, as Hilary Corke was to recognize in *The Listener* (6 October 1955), 'with human passions rather than metaphysical footnotes'.

Professor Denis Donoghue has written of Empson: 'The label "metaphysical" and the link-up with Donne, these are incidental. By nature and by inclination Empson is a didactic poet, heir to Pope rather than to Donne;'[18] but I believe his kinship with Donne is deep and real. He is a metaphysical poet not just in the sense of being witty and erudite but also in the sense of passionately enquiring into and arguing about the nature of existence and experience. On the authority of Sir Herbert Grierson we should understand:

Like Tennyson, Donne is much concerned with the progress of science, the revolution which was going on in men's knowledge of the universe, and its disintegrating effect on accepted beliefs. To him the new astronomy is as bewildering in its displacement of the earth and disturbance of a concentric universe as the new geology was to be to Tennyson. (*The Poems of John Donne*, ii (Oxford: Oxford University Press, 1905), p. xxviii)

Likewise, in his celebrated anthology *Metaphysical Lyrics and Poems of the Seventeenth Century* (1921), Grierson maintained that Donne's *Anniversaries* remains 'the fullest record in our literature of the disintegrating collision in a sensitive mind of the old tradition and new learning'.[19]

Just so, Empson undertook a closer reading of Donne's poems than T. S. Eliot ever pretended, and he affirmed Grierson's view. It is 'natural', he later wrote, 'to suppose that [Donne] believed what he says in the poems— that the unified worldpicture of Catholicism had broken up . . . into isolated individuals . . . ' He noted too that Donne 'read Kepler's book about a *nova* in 1606 and Galileo's about his discoveries through a telescope in 1610'.[20] Empson argues that the row about astronomy has profound theological and ethical consequences at any time of Christian culture, if you follow the logic of the discovery of a plurality of possible worlds beyond our own:

> In our time no less than in Donne's, to believe that there are rational creatures on other planets is very hard to reconcile with the belief that Salvation is only through Christ . . . The young Donne, to judge from his poems, believed that every planet could have its incarnation, and believed this with delight, because it automatically liberated an independent conscience from any earthly religious authority.[21]

Donne's repeated metaphor of the separate planet, he argued, stood both for freedom and for 'the awful isolation of the human creature'.[22] Empson registers for himself that same painful paradox in the context of modern scientific knowledge of the world. Of Donne's Holy Sonnet 'I am a little world made cunningly', he wrote for instance: 'I think the remorseful hope of atonement with God is crossed with a shrinking hunger for annihilation and escape from God.'[23] Likewise, in one of his own poems, 'Letter III', he hungers to be given again 'My undetailed order, the designer's sketches'; and the magnificent 'This Last Pain' argues for a harrowed and stoic agnosticism:

> All those large dreams by which men long live well
> Are magic-lanterned on the smoke of hell;
>   This then is real, I have implied,
>   A painted, small, transparent slide.

That stanza closely parallels his argument about how Donne dignifies the individual, and love between individuals, by comparison to the religious organization, the Church. Donne, he says, 'treats the institution as only a pallid imitation of the individual. All the imaginative structures which men have built to control themselves are only derived from these simple intimate basic relations . . .'[24] Empson explained in his notes to 'This Last Pain': 'The idea of the poem is that human nature can conceive divine states which it cannot attain';[25] so his conclusion is that man must needs live by his myths, however desperate:

> Feign then what's by a decent tact believed
> And act that state is only so conceived,
>   And build an edifice of form
>   For house where phantoms may keep warm.
>
> Imagine, then, by miracle, with me,
> (Ambiguous gifts, as what gods give must be)
>   What could not possibly be there,
>   And learn a style from a despair.

1. Famous forebear: Professor William Empson (1789–1852), Professor of Polity and the Laws of England at the East India College, Haileybury, editor of *The Edinburgh Review* and son-in-law of Francis Jeffrey

2. Mr and Mrs Arthur Reginald Empson of Yokefleet Hall, in the market square at Howden

3. William Empson's mother, Laura, the subject of the poem 'To An Old Lady': 'Stars how much further from me fill my night. | Strange that she too should be inaccessible.'

4. The family pile: Yokefleet Hall, Howden, Yorkshire, where William Empson spent his earliest years

5. William Empson (aged 3) with his sister Molly

6. William Empson: 'I am not a tough guy.'

7. The funeral procession for Jack Empson, May 1914. The patriarch Arthur Reginald Empson, who leads the cortège (flanked by his eldest sons and followed by Molly) was to die two years later

8. William the Wykehamist

9. The White House, Fulford, York, where Laura Empson retired after the death of her husband

10. 'The engines of love': Elizabeth Wiskemann

11. After swimming with his students from the Tokyo University of Literature and Science, 14 September 1933. Empson, Tamretsu Sai, Kiyoshi Horii, Yukio Irie

12. Enjoying an excursion to the Okutama district to the northwest of Tokyo, 7 October 1933. Standing: Yukio Irie, Hiroski Watanabe. Seated: Tamretsu Sai, Kiyoshi Horii, Kyo Nogawa, Empson

13. Haru, who inspired the poem 'Aubade'

14. Farewell Party at the Nanushinotaki Restaurant, Tokyo, 22 June 1934. Professor Rinshiro Ishikawa stands on Empson's right, Professor Rintaro Fukuhara on his left. Shigehisa Narita stands to the left of Professor Fukuhara; and Yukio Irie is on the extreme right of the photograph

15. The 'mud hut' classrooms of the Southwest Associated University in Kunming, Yunnan Province, China, where Empson taught during the Japanese invasion, 1938–39

16. The British and Foreign Bible Society, 78 Pei Men Kai, Kunming, China, where Empson lodged in 1938–39

In other words, man must suffer the agonizing strain of living by conceptions of absolute order which he knows to be only conceptions. Another poem, 'Doctrinal Point', rehearses this dilemma by dwelling with beautifully rapt envy on the insensate life of plants:

> Free by predestination in the blood,
> Saved by their own sap, shed for themselves,
> Their texture can impose their architecture;
> Their sapient matter is always already informed.

> Whether they burgeon, massed wax flames, or flare
> Plump spaced-out saints, in their gross prime, at prayer,
> Or leave the sooted branches bare
> To sag at tip from a sole blossom there
> They know no act that will not make them fair

—lines which readily, by deftly satirical puns, connote the idea that plants neither require nor look for a Redeemer.

Perhaps the most persistent difficulty of Empson's poetry, or primarily of the early poetry, is that the areas of learned reference he embraced lay outside the normal order for most readers. A product of the rational humanism favoured by Cambridge in the 1920s, he devoured the new science as much as literature: 'the crowning literature of our age is scientific,' he had declared in the debate on the subject of 'degeneration in the literature of today' at the Cambridge Union in October 1927.[26] The period between 1905 and 1930 witnessed revolutionary developments in our understanding of the nature of the physical world: the discoveries of Rutherford, Bohr, Einstein, Eddington—and Empson found his imaginative pabulum above all in Eddington's great studies: *The Nature of the Physical World* (1928), *Space Time and Gravitation*, and *Stars and Atoms* (1927). In 1928, for instance, Eddington recalled, in *The Nature of the Physical World*:

In 1911 Rutherford introduced the greatest change in our idea of matter since the time of Democritus . . . When we compare the universe as it is now supposed to be with the universe as we had ordinarily preconceived it, the most arresting change is not the rearrangement of space and time by Einstein but the dissolution of all that we regard as most solid into tiny specks floating in a void. That gives an abrupt jar to those who think that things are more or less what they seem. The revelation by modern physics of the void within the atom is more disturbing than the revelation by astronomy of the immense void of interstellar space.

The atom is as porous as the solar system. If we eliminated all the unfilled spaces in a man's body and collected his protons and electrons into one mass, the man would be reduced to a speck just visible with a magnifying glass.

After such knowledge, what poetry? The imaginative issues of Empson's early poetry were assuredly stirred by the human implications of modern science—not just astrophysics ('The World's End', 'Camping Out', 'Earth has Shrunk in the Wash', 'Letter I'), but also biology ('Invitation to Juno'), botany ('Value is in Activity' and 'China'), chemistry ('Villanelle', 'Bacchus', 'Missing Dates'), entomology ('The Ants'), geometry ('Letter V'), evolutionism ('Plenum and Vacuum'), anthropology ('Homage to the British Museum'), theories of time ('Dissatisfaction with Metaphysics'); the list could go on. In a letter to a Chinese acquaintance written in 1947 (at a time when he had virtually stopped writing poetry), Empson looked back with wonder:

The point where I most disagree with you is about science. I should have thought that the present age had very little to boast about in any form of imaginative work except the scientific one, and it is obvious that a physicist like Einstein or Eddington is making superb uses of the imagination. A critic who cuts himself off from the only fertile part of the contemporary mind is I think unlikely to understand what good work feels like when it is new, and as far as my own work is concerned anyway I am sure I have always found the world-picture of the scientists much more stimulating and useable than that of any 'literary influence'. In any case it seems to me trivial to say that scientific thought isn't real thought; it only suggests a quarrel between different faculties in a university about which should get more money and better buildings. For that matter all the good philosophy in the last fifty years has been influenced very strongly by modern physics, so by your own account poetry ought to be influenced too, but only as the lady's-maid who is not given the clothes till the fashion for them is out of date.[27]

But this is not to say that his poems are directly *about* science; as Professor Lewis Wolpert has insisted, for example, one of Empson's best-known and most frequently anthologized poems, 'Camping Out', is not really about astrophysics.[28] The peculiar strength of Empson's poetry derives from the scope and ingenuity of his analogizing imagination. Monroe K. Spears, in an essay on the subject of 'Cosmology and the Writer', has stated that 'The World's End' 'is one of the few successful poems about Relativity, contrasting its cosmos with the Miltonic and with extravagant Romantic imagery'—which is fair enough. Yet 'The World's End' is the only poem by Empson in which the science is both topic and trope, both tenor and vehicle. Spears also suggests: ' "To an Old Lady" may well be the only good poem based on astronomy (more or less modern in this case), and specifically on the possibility of space flight to another inhabited planet of the solar system (it would have to be specifically Mars).'[29] But that reflection only goes to show that Spears is not quite keeping his mind on the poem: whereas Empson is majestically figurative, positing his mother as out of this world, spiritually and socially at a far remove, Spears takes a literal view—even though he covers himself with the phrase 'based on'. But Mum is not a metaphor. (In an article on 'Science and Poetry' in 1961, T. R. Henn—who incidentally had been one of Empson's examiners for the English Tripos in 1929—specifically and mistakenly identified the 'old lady' as the moon.[30]) As for space flight, the real point is the very idea of it; and the idea of it is integrity and independence: it represents a bid for freedom from authority and institutionalization. The fundamental question that Empson confronts in his poetry is this: is the imagination equal to the challenge, the moral imposition, of the new science? His apprehension of the place of the sciences in the modern world charged his poetry (according to his friend Kathleen Raine) with distressing questions about the way in which man tries 'to impose order on fields of knowledge and experience so contradictory as to threaten the mind that contains them with disorder—the compulsion, as Empson writes, to "learn a style from a despair".'[31] The imagination he brought to the late 1920s 'had to adjust itself to a new scientific world-view at once alarming and inspiring,' Raine recalled. Empson wrote in an early article, for instance,

The scientific view of truth . . . is that the mind, otherwise passive, collects propositions about the external world; the application of scientific ideas to poetry is interesting because it reduces that idea of truth . . . to a self contradiction.
    And yet one must not accept such a contradiction as final . . .[32]

It is precisely for that reason that he disparaged the simple-mindedness of any writer who presumed to make up a synthesis out of radically opposed accounts of the world. His impatience with facile thinking is evident, for instance, in a review of C. E. Playne's *The Pre-War Mind in Britain* (1928): 'She has the "scientific" mind; she is fond, for instance, of repeating two opposite things earnestly, in the hope of implying a synthesis which combines them . . .'[33] It is small wonder that he later felt exasperated by certain critics who judged his own metaphysical poetry to be over-intellectualized. The big issue, in poetry as in life, was that science does not readily or even necessarily accommodate itself to human culture, ideas, or ethical structures.
    Several of his best poems convey the terrifying shock of modern physical science, the painful astonishment of conscience before the phenomenal

world. His poems are therefore metaphysical in the strict sense, based not
on what man's spirit might suppose about the world, but what the understanding of reality compels us to consider. 'Plenum and Vacuum', for
example, ends with this stanza:

> Matter includes what must matter enclose,
> Its consequent space, the glass firmament's air-holes.
> Heaven's but an attribute of her seven rainbows.
> It is Styx coerces and not Hell controls.

If the corpuscular theory of matter is exploded into the vacuum of quantum
theory, the poem argues, man's contractual conscience about sin and
punishment may well be no more than an ethical agreement projected
upon the literal unreality of existence.[34] If we now know that the universe is
more or less vacuous, we might conclude that ethical constraints, as well as
the divine designs we postulate, are assuredly little more than the metaphysical conceptions of mankind. The point here is that Empson is deploying science not as a fashionable property in poetry but in a spirit of painful
perplexity, finding himself badgered by ethical upsets. As he was to remark
in 1963—soon after he himself, in *Milton's God*, had vehemently condemned
the Christian God as a 'torture-monster'—'the highest event in ethics' is
'the moral discovery, which gets a man called a traitor by his own society'.[35]

Empson's wit and ingenuity are thus provoked by the excruciating
paradoxes or contradictions occasioned when science is placed in the
aesthetic or religious sphere of understanding. E. A. Burtt's famous book
The Metaphysical Foundations of Modern Science (1930), which came out just
when Empson was writing his earliest poems, argued that the first scientists
were forced into certain schemes because those schemes were the only
ones which would adequately order the facts they knew; in other words,
that their scientific conclusions were inevitably based on unrecognized
metaphysical assumptions. But, as Empson argued in his review of the
book, 'it is unsafe to explain discovery in terms of a man's intellectual
preconceptions, because the act of discovery is precisely that of stepping
outside preconceptions'.[36] Subtracting individual conscience from consen-
sus is not done without fear and awe, and the sort of piercing honesty
before turbulent implication which Empson offers in his poetry.

'The World's End' asks, abruptly, almost prescriptively, and yet also
wonderingly:

> Alas, how hope for freedom, no bars bind;
> Space is like earth, rounded, a padded cell;

Plumb the stars' depth, your lead bumps you behind;
Blind Satan's voice rattled the whole of Hell.

On cushioned air what is such metal worth
To pierce to the gulf that lies so snugly curled?
Each tangent plain touches one top of earth,
Each point in one direction ends the world.

Apple of knowledge and forgetful mere
From Tantalus too differential bend.
The shadow clings. The world's end is here.
This place's curvature precludes its end.

Like Marlowe's Mephistopheles, but without his supposed know-ledge, Empson questions whether this is hell. What can physical science tell us about man's destiny? Einstein's Special Theory of Relativity, presented in 1916, had defined the curvature of space-time, such that— as Professor James A. Coleman has more recently expressed the di-lemma—'there is no outside edge to the universe, for...continual travel in a space line brings you back to the starting-point. Our universe *closes on itself.'*[37]

We are dealing here with the four-dimensional world which has obsessed novelists in the last century (if not many poets) from H. G. Wells to Doris Lessing, Martin Amis, and Ian McEwan. The moral, if you like, is that we are imprisoned by our universe, which, as Empson's poem says, is then a 'padded cell', without bars—and the fact that it is 'snugly curled' (a startlingly ironic phrase) is as much a mortal threat as a comfort to man's spirit. A self-enclosing universe denies us the freedom to escape its claustrophobic system; the comprehension that there is literally no 'end' to space-time must stun our reckoning of spiritual aspirations.

Another poem which tries to escape Nature's frame of things, and which registers similar alarm at being unable to do so, is 'Camping Out'. This sonnet echoes Donne as much in its argument as in this disconcertingly dynamic opening:

And now she cleans her teeth into the lake:
Gives it (God's grace) for her own bounty's sake
What morning's pale and the crisp mist debars:
Its glass of the divine (that will could break)
Restores, beyond nature: or lets Heaven take
(Itself being dimmed) her pattern, who half awake
Milks between rocks a straddled sky of stars.

> Soap tension the star pattern magnifies.
> Smoothly Madonna through-assumes the skies
> Whose vaults are opened to achieve the Lord.

It is in essence an entirely realistic poem: in the morning mist which reflects nothing of the real sky the woman cleaning her teeth into the lake looks like the creator of a galaxy, dropping into the water flecks of toothpaste which fly apart because of water tension. In a microcosmic way she creates a world—'lets Heaven take . . . her pattern'—and like a Madonna or goddess she can then plunge into the universe she has created. (Of course Empson is here also satirizing the Christian doctrine of Christ's—and Mary's—bodily assumption into Heaven: in that sense, the sky would 'achieve the Lord', whereas Empson suggests that only a 'bullet boat' or spaceship would shoot off from earth in quite such a fashion.) The poem's fancy is that the woman can create and control and penetrate a separate world. That small account is then compared to doing it in the larger sphere, the universe beyond our world, which would actually be disastrous:

> No, it is we soaring explore galaxies,
> Our bullet boat light's speed by thousands flies,
> Who moves so among stars their frame unties;
> See where they blur, and die, and are outsoared.

Any material object which managed to exceed the highest possible velocity in the universe would destroy the universe. Einstein's Relativity leaves us one known absolute—'the velocity of light is the maximum possible velocity'—as James A. Coleman has explained:

the material objects with which we are familiar can never even travel as fast as light, because their mass would become infinite, which means that an *infinite* amount of energy would be required to get them up there. An infinite amount of energy means *all* the energy in the universe *plus a great deal more*.[38]

And yet the tone of the poem is confident, because it is also talking about the nature of ecstatic human love, which can allow itself the boldness of whimsy. The frame of the natural world threatens destruction but it can be escaped, 'outsoared', in the separate world of love.

Empson evidently yearned for the authority of knowledge, for an absolute knowable order which might finally explain us to ourselves. In one of his first published essays, 'Some Notes on Mr. Eliot' (November 1929), he quoted Eliot's lines about Donne from 'Whispers of Immortality'—

Donne, I suppose, was such another
Who found no substitute for sense,
To seize and clutch and penetrate;
Expert beyond experience,

He knew the anguish of the marrow
The ague of the skeleton;
No contact possible to flesh
Allayed the fever of the bone

—with the penetrating gloss that 'Value and a prior knowledge are not known through sense; and yet there is no other mode of knowledge. No human contact is possible to our isolation, and yet human contacts are known to be of absolute value.'[39] As it was, such contradictions compelled Empson to be a generous sceptic and humanist. The philosophy of his early poems—including 'The World's End' and 'This Last Pain', as well as the metaphysical conceit of 'Letter V'—accords with what he wrote in a prose piece dating from 1934: 'There seems no great need to be more sceptical than Hume, who decided that "the cause or causes of order in the universe probably have some remote analogy to human intelligence".'[40]

While teaching in Japan and China in the 1930s, Empson absorbed himself open-mindedly in codes of conduct and belief which challenged and contradicted what he thought the smugness of European Christianity, just as much as Copernicus and Galileo had challenged the view of the world that Donne inherited. 'In the West,' Empson was to explain in 1937, 'the supreme God is a person, in the East he is not; their ideas follow from that...It is much the most fundamental line of division between the civilisations of the world, and we need to understand the people on the other side.'[41] He determined that the deepest differences between nations are not racial but theological, and that in order to comprehend what unites and separates peoples it is necessary to search for the 'whole story'—'and the story may well be the other half of the truth about the world'.

Since he revelled also in *The Waste Land*, he followed Eliot's provisional lead in resorting to Buddhism (as well as T. H. Huxley's admiration for it), and so studied Buddhism at first hand; he profoundly desired to comprehend the different theological and philosophical systems of the world. He never actually espoused Buddhism (he inclined more towards a sort of pantheism, which he also discovered in his eager critical readings of Dylan Thomas), but his appreciation of the Buddhist code is the reason why his *Collected Poems* is prefaced by his own version of the famous Fire Sermon, not as an article of personal belief but as a challenge to any reader's parochial preconceptions.[42] In a way that is comparable to Donne's incitement about a possible plurality of worlds, Empson felt vexed by the contradictions represented by the alternative systems of belief on our planet. 'The man who made the supreme expression of the Far Eastern view of God and man was the Buddha,' he wrote, 'and he was an Aryan, the same race as ourselves...'[43] In yearning for an absolute upon which mankind could agree, Empson tormented himself in the effort to reconcile contradictions: the argument from those contradictions is the felt substance of all his poems.

Although his poetry shows him to have felt agonized and often desperate about man's inability to reconcile contradictory ideas and creeds, it is an index of his humane non-partisanship that he could write such a wonderfully magnanimous poem as 'Homage to the British Museum', offering respect to a god—the Australian Tangaroa, a sea god—which is portrayed as subsuming all deities:

> There is a Supreme God in the ethnological section;
> A hollow toad shape, faced with a blank shield.
> He needs his belly to include the Pantheon,
> Which is inserted through a hole behind.
> At the navel, at the points formally stressed, at the organs of sense,
> Lice glue themselves, dolls, local deities,
> His smooth wood creeps with all the creeds of the world.
>
> Attending there let us absorb the cultures of nations
> And dissolve into our judgement all their codes.
> Then, being clogged with a natural hesitation
> (People are continually asking one the way out),
> Let us stand here and admit that we have no road.
> Being everything, let us admit that is to be something,
> Or give ourselves the benefit of the doubt;
> Let us offer our pinch of dust all to this God,
> And grant his reign over the entire building.

That hendecasyllabic line 'His smooth wood creeps with all the creeds of the world' is a master-stroke in a poem which ambiguously expresses both a certain distaste and benign composure.

Empson was to follow T. S. Eliot's lead also in providing substantial notes to his own poems, though it was already—long before he published *Poems* in 1935—a deep conviction of his critical practice that the means and machinery of any and every poem ought to be explicable. He wrote to a friend as early as 1929:

Myself, of course, I am in favour of being chatty and explaining everything, but that is undergraduate of me. Once you begin to parley with the reasons for the impossibility of explanations you are whirled o'er the backside of the world far off.[44]

It was almost certainly in 1929 too that he put together an engaging essay on the subject, posthumously published as 'Obscurity and Annotation',[45] which urges the proposition that demanding contemporary authors really ought to write notes on their own poems:

Poets, on the face of it, have either got to be easier or to write their own notes; readers have either got to take more trouble over reading or cease to regard notes as pretentious and a sign of bad poetry...

Certainly some notes may be pedantic, and some impertinent, but the idea that all are likely to be (that one should look harshly on them at first sight) is unwise at all times, and particularly unwise just now. For it seems important that both parties should try to be tolerant on the matter; there is a genuine crux about notes giving information because the notion of general knowledge has changed...It really ought to be possible to write simple, goodhumoured, illuminating and long notes to one's own poems without annoying the reader. I quite see that no one had yet written notes to his own poems without looking a fool, but as knowledge becomes increasingly various it will eventually have to be done.

From the very beginning, when he first offered to Chatto & Windus his collection of 'about twenty poems', with the inducement (or perhaps it was meant as an ironic apology) that few of them would occupy more than a single page of text, he explained in a letter:

On the other hand I should want to print very full notes; at least as long as the text itself; explaining not only particular references, paraphrasing particularly con-densed grammar, and so on, but the point of a poem as a whole, and making any critical remarks that seemed interesting. And I should apologize for notes on such a scale, and say it was more of an impertinence to expect people to puzzle out my verses than to explain them at the end, and I should avoid the Eliot air of intellectual snobbery.[46]

Although a number of Eliot's notes to *The Waste Land* (1922) were, as the critic Grover Smith has argued, clearly meant for serious purposes[47]—and such crucial notes might seem even to be tendentious, formulating a critical reading of the point of Tiresias, for example, and of Saint Augus-tine and the Buddha, which students and other readers have been only too grateful to rehearse down the years—others have an air of arch learning or starchy antiquarianism.[48] Eliot came to think so too: in 'The Frontiers of Criticism' (1956) he spoke with feline regret of 'the remarkable exposition of bogus scholarship' he had found it necessary to fashion to meet the commercial expediency of bulking out the poem as a book: he felt 'penitent' because his notes had 'stimulated the wrong kind of interest'.[49]

While Eliot may therefore be taken to have provided his notes to *The Waste Land* in a mood of reluctant pedantry, Empson offered his as helpful exposition. 'It is impertinent,' he wrote in *Collected Poems*, 'to suggest that the reader ought to possess already any odd bit of information one may have picked up in a field where one is oneself ignorant'; and again in the sleeve notes to his record of *Selected Poems*: 'Notes are bound to be rather hit-or-miss, different people wanting different things, but may at least show that the author wants to be intelligible.' In at least one other place he construed Eliot's possible motives by his own generous lights: 'It is true that some of the Waste Land notes admit to private associations, but that makes one reason why the notes had to be written; the point of such a note is to prevent the reader from worrying and looking deeper' (*Criterion*, 15 (April 1936), 519). Empson's notes work to extend the area of 'public debate' of the poems; they do not betray self-congratulation.

He aimed from the start to go in for honest dealing, a kind of contract: he wanted his readers to have full access to the means and materials of his poetry. Though tricky, his poems were not intended to be tricksy: the poet did not propose to keep any cards up his sleeve. At best, a note was to serve as a function of the poem, and at the least it should be complementary—as well as showing that the poet desired to be positively communicative. The note should act as a 'prose bridge', as Empson was to put it in a 'Note on Notes' in his second volume, *The Gathering Storm* (1940). He had written to Parsons in 1929: 'When I am not actually faced with explaining them I feel notes aren't wanted; but I think people would be more easily tempted to read verse if there was plenty of critical writing thrown in, demanding less concentration of attention, and with more literary-critical magazine or novel-reading interest—I know *I* should. And there is a rather portentous air about compact verses without notes, like a seduction without conversation.'[50]

We might take that whimsical phrase 'seduction without conversation' as speaking to the fact that so many of Empson's poems are about the genuine desire for love and connectedness; it also serves to contest Denis Donoghue's assertion that Empson is basically a didactic poet. Despite their occasional abrupt assurances, their clipped precisions, Empson's poems are a function much more of uncertainty and anxious desire than of dogmatism; as he wrote in 1937, 'The first or only certain reason for writing verse is to clear your own mind and fix your own feelings'[51]—or again, ten years later, when in the course of analysing a poem by Dylan Thomas he made the sympathetic observation that 'obscurity in a writer may be due, not to concentration, but to a refusal to speak out'.[52]

Empson's beguiling decision to expound his own poems with a running commentary in prose is at odds with what literary historians like to think of as the rule of the Modernist-New Critical aesthetic, the doctrine of semantic autonomy and organic form, which denies that the author might originate and critically shape the meaning of a poem. If it is the special nature of many postmodernist texts to be self-commenting, so transgressing the sacred boundary between 'work' and 'commentary', as Steven Connor suggests, Empson was a postmodernist—in that sense only—*avant la lettre*: before anyone thought to pass the law.[53]

Reviewers have from time to time expressed outrage at Empson's notes, which they reckon to be either a pre-emptive strike, hijacking the reader's prerogative, or else merely impertinent. But a reasonable (albeit also appropriately riddling) way to look at the notes was to be provided by Hilary Corke in a review of *Collected Poems*: Empson 'is a critic of great distinction, and one whose poems are as much criticisms of his criticism as his criticisms are in another sense poems about his poems. Indeed, this poet's "unit of creation" is not the poem alone, but the poem *plus* the note upon it...What remains in the mind is not "a poem" in the old sense (a memorable and musical sequence of language), but an intellectual structure that, something like a sculptural "mobile", shifts its parts this way and that. The conservative are free to prefer the older sort of poem, but not to condemn Mr Empson's sort for not being what it does not set out to be.'[54] Although the critic Stanley Sultan has argued that Eliot's 'Notes' are really the notes *of*, and not *on*, *The Waste Land*, that useful distinction would be better applied—in the way Corke suggested—to Empson's 'Notes'.[55] His volumes of poetry are, in the best sense, double-voiced.

For all his reputation as the modern metaphysician, as the poet of witty riddling (or arid intellectualism—mentally fidgeting and scarcely truly feeling—as adverse critics would suggest), what mattered as much as anything to Empson was that his poetry was the vehicle of powerful emotion. In some books he is put down as 'the poet's poet'; and even his admirers among the poets, whether elders or contemporaries (in addition to T. S. Eliot, they ranged from W. H. Auden, Edith Sitwell, and John Betjeman to Roy Campbell and Dylan Thomas), have tended to salute him principally for his intellectual capacities—as did his mentor Richards. Robert Lowell was to write to Empson in 1958: 'it can't be denied that almost no praise would be too high for your poems. You have the stamina of Donne, yet a far more useful and empirical knowledge of modern science and English metrics. I think you are the most intelligent poet writing in our language and perhaps the best. I put you with Hardy and Graves and Auden and Philip Larkin.'[56] Elsewhere, Lowell hailed him as 'the king of the critics', and spoke with great enthusiasm of the 'intellect' in his poetry, though he also wrote on one occasion, 'Empson's best poems, half a dozen or more, though intellectual are forthright'—a statement that was presumably meant to imply that forthrightness is really the better part of poetry.[57] However, even if Lowell finally came to think of Empson-the-poet as more icon than inspiration, there is little doubt that much of Lowell's own early poetry, in the 1940s, took fire from Empson's.[58] Another great American poet, John Berryman, who also revelled in Empson the critic, noted with a manner that looks like surprise on the flyleaf of his copy of *Collected Poems* (1949): 'a poetry matter-of-fact, alert, spare; & yet *elegant*'.[59] Empson's friend Louis MacNeice put on record his opinion that 'surprisingly', Empson 'is generally a humane and quite often a moving poet'.[60] However, as far as Empson himself was concerned, the essence of his metaphysical poetry was emotional intensity. When A. Alvarez gently suspected to Empson in 1956 that he might have been playing to the gallery when reading his poems one day, he responded with this amicable but sharply candid declaration: 'They weren't meant to be at all esoteric. They came from more isolation and suffering than is suited to public performance, but that is well known to be true of most performances, including clowns.'[61]

Empson was alert to the fact that a number of poets in the 1950s took his work as a model, emulating what they considered to be (as the critic Anthony Hartley was to remark in a review) the nonconformist, cool, scientific, and analytical cast of his poems, the distrust of rhetoric and sentiment, and the attempt to convey complicated states of thought and moral meaning.[62] They also admired his skills as a technician: the fact, for example, that in his early poems he had brought the terza rima and villanelle, as well as ottava rima and rime royal, to such a high level of accomplishment in contemporary English poetry. In the knowledge that the poetry of his admirers was borrowing or mimicking the accidentals but not the driving emotion of his work—the 'isolation and suffering'—he was to observe in a BBC broadcast *Literary Opinion* in 1954:

Recently the magazine *Encounter* had a joke poem, with very funny notes, meaning that Empson is a bad influence on young poets. Do you know, I rather often said this myself to young poets, both in England and America, who have kindly shown me their stuff. It seems to me that Empson's own poetry, though it comes from a rather limited and narrow talent anyhow, isn't nearly as narrow as what turns up when somebody imitates it; that does feel very narrow, and I wouldn't be sensible if I didn't agree.[63]

Poetry is urged, he always maintained, by dissatisfaction, which the poetry itself might help to heal; the best a poet can do is to fight to discover and articulate meaning. Desperate persuasion is a long way from peda- gogical assurance, and it is a sorry matter that several critics have dis- cerned in Empson only cleverness—and not the truth that his poems speak from pain. Of 'Letter II', for example, he once notably remarked: 'I daresay the language is rather too violent for the subject matter, another unsatisfactory student love-affair, but they seemed to me upsetting enough at the time.' T. S. Eliot recognized as much when he came to look back on the work of the generation which came to maturity in the 1930s: Auden, Spender, MacNeice, Day-Lewis, and Empson. In a letter dating from 1939, Eliot notably saluted both the intelligence and the courage of Empson's poetry: 'damned if I don't think that Bill has more brain power, as well as more resistance to the ills that flesh is heir to...than the rest of 'em poets'.[64]

13

Scapegoat and Sacrifice:
Some Versions of Pastoral

'You suggest I am "waiting about" in a kind tone, and no doubt I shall start doing that in time,' Empson wrote to a friend in Tokyo on 13 January 1935. But he hastened to explain that he had not been idle over the past five months. 'Since getting [back] to England I have prepared three books for the press and am still busy.'[1] Actually, he underestimated his own productivity: in addition to readying for publication by Chatto & Windus both *Poems* (for publication in May 1935) and *Some Versions of Pastoral* (October 1935), he had prepared Basic English 'translations' of two little monographs by his old hero J. B. S. Haldane, *The Outlook of Science* and *Science and Well-Being* (both published as 'Psyche Miniatures' in 1935). He was also working hard on the monograph *The Faces of the Buddha*. It never crossed his mind that he ought to get a job on returning from Japan, he said in an interview years later; 'I needed to get some books out.'[2]

According to one authority, Empson's second prose volume, *Some Versions of Pastoral* (1935), represents 'the most important and the least helpful' attempt to analyse the complex mode of pastoral.[3] It is therefore necessary to consider from the start the question of whether or not Empson really had it in mind to talk about pastoral as a genre as such; whether the funny but unsatisfactory title he gave the volume actually did his work a disservice, even though the plural 'Versions' might have served to indicate to his readers a leap beyond any standard or normative mode. It is notable too that the subtitle eschews the term 'genre'—*A Study of the Pastoral Form in Literature*—probably because he was above such professionalizing terms.

He was slow to realize that the essays he produced during the early 1930s would eventually cohere in terms of theme and argument; the 'pastoral' focus of the essays only became fully clear in 1933–4.[4] He admitted in response to a quizzical review by John Middleton Murry, 'The fact was that I had written most of the essays before it struck me that they all bore on one topic, and had interested me for that reason; what I had to say on the topic I said, and then thought no harm in printing the essays as they grew.'[5] The modest, almost shrugging title he gave to this volume of essays might have done better to refer to 'variants' or 'diversions', or even 'mutations', 'metamorphoses' or simply 'shifts', since he largely ignores those works that are admitted to be classics of the pastoral genre, from Theocritus and Virgil to Spenser, Milton, Pope, Wordsworth and Hardy. Better still, his thesis might have been clearer to his first readers, and more widely appreciated, if he had identified 'mock-pastoral' in the title. His notion of the function of the traditional pastoral, which is the product of an urban-bourgeois culture, is that it transposes the complex into the simple. Humble shepherds, when given to enunciate the sentiments of (for example) courtiers, serve to place conflicting social and moral concerns into a different frame, both criticizing and ennobling—since the pastoral mode is a two-way mirror. The form works also to reconcile and harmonize potential class conflict. Pastoral, for all its superficial simplicity, therefore functions as a beautifully multilayered and sophisticated form. The bucolic situation, supposedly inheriting and preserving a moral and social affinity with the earthly paradise of Eden—since the symbolic shepherd is a priestlike and even Christlike figure dedicated to tending his flock—can be deployed both to flatter and to flout the ruling classes. However, what is so astonishing as to seem positively eccentric about *Some Versions of Pastoral* is the array of texts that Empson selects for discussion in terms of a generically modified definition of the form: they include a sonnet by Shakespeare, *The Faerie Queene*, *Troilus and Cressida*, Greene's *Friar Bacon and Friar Bungay*, Gray's 'Elegy in a Country Churchyard', Gay's *The Beggar's Opera*, and Carroll's *Alice* stories. At the culmination of the volume he remarks that Wordsworth's 'Resolution and Independence' is 'a genuine pastoral poem if ever there was one'; so it is absolutely important to reckon that what he lightly denotes the 'genuine' pastoral is not on the whole his game. 'Probably the cases I take are the surprising ones,' he admits in the first chapter, 'and once started on an example I follow it without regard to the unity of the book' (p. 25).[6]

In fact, at an early date he had come to the realization, though almost certainly without yet appreciating its full implications, that any investigation of the pastoral mode would have to revalue the 'tricks' of the old pastoral in innumerable variant forms, including the mock-heroic and the mock-pastoral. A remarkable number of modern instances could be understood to do duty for the shepherd's life and attitudes, usually as a mode of dramatic irony or as a covert intention or implication, occasionally as the unconscious underplot.[7]

In July 1930—four months before the appearance of *Seven Types of Ambiguity*—he reviewed a compilation of documents by A. V. Judges entitled *The Elizabethan Underworld*. This review marked a defining moment in his career as a critic, since it looked two ways: back to the still-forth-coming *Ambiguity* and forward to the as-yet-unconceived *Pastoral*. On the one hand, he made this specific reference to the semantic analyses he had been essaying for his first book: since the period of the Elizabethans, he wrote, 'our stress on the complexity of words in themselves has increased, so that a single word has come to be thought of as a complex molecule which must not be unpacked in ordinary use . . . ' On the other hand, he remarked with fascination, the so-called 'rogue pamphlets' of the Eliza-bethan era, by virtue of their imaginative sympathy, had an extraordinar-ily paradoxical power about them: the reader feels them to be at once a condemnation and a celebration of the villains they reported; they even work in accordance with Aristotelian tenets of tragedy:

> Perhaps the most striking thing about the pamphlets is a directness of feeling which could express warm sympathy with rogues while holding in mind both horror for their crimes as such, and full pity and terror for the consequences. Stories of successful cheats were 'merry', because the honest reader was to imagine himself both as the robber, so as to enjoy his courage, dexterity, triumph, and knowledge of human nature, and as the robbed, so as to feel that he is now stronger, and can beat this trick, since he is informed. A secret freedom kept these two from obstructing each other. (*SSS* 72–3)

Most notably, his attention was seized by some ballad verses entitled 'The Black Dog of Newgate', purportedly voiced by a chained, starving prisoner and so recorded by a real highwayman named Luke Hutton. One stanza in particular—because of its 'delicacy of grammatical pattern' and an 'intensity of analysis' that Empson believed would stand comparison with the sermons of Bishop Lancelot Andrewes—he would almost cer-tainly have discussed alongside Herbert's 'The Sacrifice' if only it had been known to him in time to be included in *Ambiguity*:[8]

> 'Woe's me,' thought I, 'for thee so bound in chains!
> Woe's me for them thou begs for to sustain!
> Woe's me for all whose want all woes contains!
> Woe's *me*, for me *that in our woes complain*! . . . '

Hutton's prisoner persona is evidently seeing himself as scapegoat and sacrifice; though a villain, he is equally the victim. He is both an individual and a representative figure; by speaking for the many he sets himself up as the one, both enduring and understanding his predicament, and offering himself as a propitiation. He is larger than the moment; his nobility makes him finer than the mass of prisoners for whom he protests. Empson was right therefore to single out this key factor in such rich verses: 'Hutton digs deeper with each isolated line, into something fundamental to the human situation; there is a latent comparison between the beggar and the Christ.' Just so, Empson determined as time moved on, any such mock-heroic or mock-pastoral figure could serve as an 'avatar' of Christ. Still more, the multiplicity of such exemplars, at once embodying and denying the heroic, could serve as an alternative to the singular revelation of Jesus Christ. Emerging out of the ordinary world of bourgeois humanism, they could yet rival the one Christ.

All the same, in 1930, Empson had not yet reached the moment for spelling out any such grand metaphysical and ethical statements. Until 1930 his major interest had been linguistics, since he was seeking to comprehend the cross-currents of statement and resistance in literature as revealed in passages of complex lexis and syntax. All the same, *conflict* had been his key word in *Ambiguity*, though he was to be criticized for having appeared to confine himself to the intraverbal tensions of the passages he had chosen for analysis, rather than to the larger socio-historical contexts that such passages expressed. It was a matter of grave regret to him that his first book should have invited the accusation of being decontextualized and even anti-historical. Accordingly, it was a wounded and wiser Empson who was to write, in the opening chapter of *Pastoral*: 'literature is a social process, and also an attempt to reconcile the conflicts of an individual in whom those of society will be mirrored.' We may infer that he had been quite badly stung by those critics who berated the narrowness of *Ambiguity*; and provoked into substituting in *Pastoral* a wide-angled view of society for the microscope that he had earlier used to peer at the 'complex molecule' of semantic and syntactic ambiguity. *Clash* is arguably the key word of *Pastoral*, since it is used as much as any other verb or noun in the seven essays of the book (though there is an equally high incidence of 'critic' and 'independent', the complementary positive terms). 'Conflict' might have done just as well, but 'clash' has more actual and consequential connotations than the more abstract term 'conflict'; it helped Empson to keep his attention focused outward towards social division rather than inward into linguistic signification.

In the early months of 1931, after the publication of *Ambiguity* and shortly before his departure for Japan, Empson spent part of his time at the British Museum copying out passages from the work of a scholar whose name had become, and still remains, a byword for wilful literal-mindedness, Dr Richard Bentley (1662–1742), the controversial and imperious Master of Trinity College, Cambridge.[9] Believing that Christianity was at once the root and the ruin of European culture, Empson had been exercised for some time by what he saw as an ambivalence in Milton's attitude in *Paradise Lost* toward the figure of Satan. So far from contriving a straight epic of the simple clash between good and evil, it seemed to him, Milton had so turned the story as to manifest a 'curious' and 'secret' parallel between Satan and Jesus Christ, as well as a clash between paganism and Christianity that was not unambiguously rigged in favour of the latter. For one thing, Milton's use of classical descriptions was not merely a form of allusive or intertextual filigree or a snobbish fidgeting: it gave evidence of a fundamental and deep-rooted conflict—within the author and within his society—of interests and ideologies: 'the fall from paganism is like the fall from paradise,' he observed.

An accomplished textual critic of Manilius, Horace, and Terence, Richard Bentley had been disturbed by what he considered the corrupt texts of Milton's epic as they had emerged in the sixty-five years since its publication in 1669. Successive editions had succeeded only in deforming a text which the blind Milton had obviously not been able to amend for himself—since he employed amanuenses. Bentley flattered himself that 'the Poet's own words' could be recovered '*by Sagacity, and happy Conjecture*', and therefore resolved as he approached the age of 70 that he would trust his own aesthetic sensibility to correct the supposedly degenerate text (even though his curious choice of copy-text was an edition of 1720 that had no authority whatever). Milton's great poem, which he adjudged to bristle with vile phraseology, poor sense coordination, and faulty metrics, should be brought into line with the criteria expected of classical epic; lucidity and logic should prevail over barbarous style. Bentley's *Milton's Paradise Lost: A New Edition* accordingly proposed over 800 emendations and about seventy deletions (with the biggest cut running to fifty-five lines: iii. 444–98). However, so far from offering his improvements according to strict philological principles, he ventured in many places to be a co-creator with Milton. His presumptuous editorial strategy and his misreadings were thereupon exposed in a 400-page indictment by Dr Zachary Pearce, *A Review of the Text of Milton's Paradise Lost* (1732), which re-established the authority of the first editions; and Bentley, who had already been mocked by Jonathan Swift, was also forthwith taken to task by Alexander Pope in the *Dunciad Variorum*.[10]

Empson was arguably the first critic for 200 years to pay respectful attention to Bentley's efforts (albeit he understood that Bentley's conjectural criticisms often misapprehended Milton's meaning, and that Bentley was infamously 'the Man who said the Tactless Thing'), but not—as it has been alleged against Empson—because he wanted simply to use him as a tool in the 'anti-Milton controversy'.[11] There is no question but that Empson had an enormous regard for *Paradise Lost*; and yet he found it all the more compelling because of its obvious antinomies. All the same, he felt every sympathy with Bentley's attempts to call to order Milton's sometimes pompous and evasive usages. Although his own purpose was by no means to cavil at the poem, he knew that Milton had left 'a grim posterity of shoddy thinking in blank verse'. But what he found especially beguiling was this observation: 'Milton's use of the pagan mythology seemed to [Bentley] to imply a doubt of the Christian mythology; and for myself I think, not only that he was right, but that the reverberations of this doubt are the real subject of the description of the Garden.' Ironically, in other words, when Milton describes the earthly paradise from which Adam and Eve are expelled, he renders it in terms of palpably pagan motifs (including an innocent sensuality which is the obverse of the sexual constraint begotten by the Fall). Eden is a world fit for 'sanctified pagans'. Faced with such an irony, Empson wrote with rueful eloquence: 'Surely Bentley was right to be surprised at finding Faunus haunting the bower, a ghost crying in the cold of paradise, and the lusts of Pan sacred even in comparison to Eden.' Milton may well have been seeking to justify God's dealings vis-à-vis man's first disobedience, but he could not help expressing in the poem his own wistful feelings for a more unlicensed world without sin.

Occasionally, Empson is quick to exploit certain apparent errors that were highlighted by Bentley's commentary. Both critics seize, for example, upon the moment in Book XI, line 102, when God warns the angel Michael to

> Take to thee from among the Cherubim
> Thy choice of flaming warriors, lest the fiend
> Or in behalf of man, or to invade
> Vacant possession some new trouble raise.

Bentley had felt wholly disconcerted by the notion that Satan might thus be said to give aid to Man—'Whence came this new Good-will to Man from the Arch-Enemy?'—and emended 'in behalf of' to 'in despite to us'. For Milton, however, 'in behalf of' would have carried the neutral sense of 'with regard to' or 'in respect of'. Knowing no better than Bentley in this instance, Empson hastened to take advantage of the anachronistic construction that had embarrassed the disambiguating Bentley. 'The view that there is a calculated progressive decay of Satan is not upheld by this passage...,' he claimed. Milton is allowing Satan a 'ruined generosity'. Similarly, Empson initially admits the evident irony in the following speech by Satan to Adam and Eve:

> League with you I seek
> And mutual amity so streight, so close,
> That I with you must dwell, or you with me
> Henceforth; my dwelling haply may not please
> Like this fair Paradise, your sense, yet such
> Accept your Maker's gift; he gave it me
> Which I as freely give; Hell shall unfold
> To entertain you two, her widest Gates,
> And send forth all her kings.

However, even while conceding that the passage almost certainly conveys a brutal or sarcastic irony on Satan's part (which is the accepted interpretation), Empson is simultaneously keen to turn the irony in Satan's favour: 'Satan may mean it as a real offer... [T]he irony is that of Milton's appalling God'—so anticipating by over twenty-five years the argument of his *Milton's God*.

Despite perpetrating mistaken readings with regard to some such passages of *Paradise Lost*, Empson still set out a strong and purposeful overall argument in his essay on the poem. If the ironic twist given to the pastoral genre results in an equation of paradise with paganism, the concomitant and equally ironic upshot is that Satan functions in this instance as the pastoral hero. At times, as Empson argues (and as later commentators have agreed), Milton knowingly makes use of an ironic parallel between Satan and Christ: for example, both are called Lucifer, the symbolic morning star—a point highlighted, for example, at v. 708–10, where it is said of Satan:[12]

> His countenance, as the morning star that guides
> The starry flock, allured them, and with lies
> Drew after him the third part of Heaven's host.

Satan can therefore be described as a fit alternative to Christ, at once a mock-heroic and a mock-pastoral figure, by a succinct paradoxical device; as Empson puts it, 'Satan is both the punisher of sin and the supreme sinner...; these are combined because... "it is hard to distinguish sin from independent judgement, the force needed for a full life", and I think because "the sinner becomes the judge".'[13] What appears on the face of it to be a contradiction in terms gains energy and purpose from performing as a paradox: the mock-hero of the mock-pastoral is celebrated by Empson as a positive counterpart, a genuine rival, to what he thought the cruel Christian schema. The religion of sacrificial redemption, according to which mankind bows to the intercession of a singular godhead, is challenged by the mock-hero of a secular humanism.

In two other early essays which eventually formed part of *Pastoral* Empson explored further aspects of the essential 'clash' that constitutes his ironical view of pastoral. 'They That Have Power' tackles Shakespeare's only political sonnet (number 94, 'They that have power to hurt, and will do none') in an attempt to interpret the complex relationship between the octet (which appears to extol powerful men who are inactive, idle, or perhaps dangerously passive, but who yet hold the power to 'move' others) and the sestet (which reflects on the beautiful, sweet-smelling, necessarily self-sufficient flower). Is the latter a metaphor for the former, and is the poem praising or blaming the stone-cold, reserved, and yet influential 'They' who 'husband' their powers? Are meanness and cool self-love being praised in this sonnet as not in others? Empson reads the poem as evincing an ironical praise for the Machiavellian, the careerist, the arriviste, the hypocrite (as it may be 'Mr W. H.' or Prince Hal): 'the young man must still be praised and loved, however he betrays his intimates, because we see him all shining with the virtues of success.'[14] Thus the essential 'clash' in this poem is that between 'admiration and contempt', which 'seems dependent on a clash of feeling about the classes', and which Shakespeare extraordinarily negotiates by comparing the qualities of the superior young man with those of the flower. While it seems virtually certain that the poem actually engages with even more complex levels of irony and ambivalence than Empson takes into account in his entertaining riff of paraphrases-with-commentaries (he jokily counted on '4,096 possible interpretations... with other possibilities'), nonetheless his exposition is a cogent one; it even allows the powerful and selfish patron to be interpreted as another version of the ironical hero of pastoral.[15] 'Full as they are of Christian echoes,' he remarks, 'the Sonnets are concerned with an idea strong enough to be balanced against Christianity; they state the opposite to the idea of self-sacrifice.' ('Balanced', a word borrowed from the work of his mentor I. A. Richards, is a large understatement in the context of *Pastoral* as a whole.)

Another form of the same kind of clash is the substance of 'Marvell's Garden', which Empson construes in a way that seeks to accommodate Richards's conviction that the truest poetry must balance and reconcile impulses. Moving on from his own finding in *Ambiguity* that utter, unresolvable conflict was of the essence of poetry, Empson now tries for a while to sustain Richards's credo that the truest poetry should be more than 'a vivid statement of a puzzle'. In the case of Marvell's great meditation on the metaphysics of the garden retreat, he decides: 'The chief point of the poem is to contrast and reconcile conscious and unconscious states, intuitive and intellectual modes of apprehension . . . This combines the idea of the conscious mind, including everything because understanding it, and that of the unconscious animal nature, including everything because in harmony with it . . . [T]he strength of the thing is to combine unusually intellectual with unusually primitive ideas; thought about the conditions of knowledge with a magical idea that the adept controls the external world by thought.' What is striking about Empson's formulation there is not only that it finds room for Richards's view of poetry as a reconciling good but also that it spells out a theory of poetry according to a binary principle.[16] According to this view, the pastoral hero is discovered to be at once the representative figure and the exceptional one (macrocosm and microcosm, complex and simple): he is at once the Many in so far as he embodies all and everything, and also the One as he comprehends all and everything: he is both insider and outsider, all-inclusive and emblematic: 'the pastoral figure is always ready to be the critic,' as Empson puts the paradox; 'he not only includes everything but may in some unexpected way know it.'

The factor that bulked larger and larger in Empson's thinking on this subject was therefore his awareness of a potently subversive correspondence between the heroes of post-Renaissance pastoral and the epiphany of Christ. He believed he had discovered in the secular order of literature a series of 'heroes' with the properties and functions of the one Saviour in the Christian myth. This mock-pastoral figure, being always an ironic homologue of the Redeemer, could serve to challenge the doctrinally singular Christian deity. In truth, his evolving theory of a pastoral 'formula' superseded the old-style view of the pastoral genre: it served to enforce his assault upon the received religion of the West. As an intellectually alert child of his time, Empson had been quick to study the most recent learning relating to anthropology, myth, and ritual that had revolutionized historical and cultural thinking since Darwin—notably the massive compilation of Sir James Frazer in *The Golden Bough* (1890) and related later pieces by critics including Aldous Huxley and Wyndham Lewis (1927), as well as R. E. Money-Kyrle's *The Development of the Sexual Impulses* (1932)—all of which went to inform his poetics and ethics of the modern pastoral.[17] In Frazer's compendium of comparative anthropology Empson delved especially into the fifth and sixth volumes (*Adonis, Attis, Osiris* and *Spirits of the Corn and of the Wild*), along with *The Scapegoat* (1913), which centred attention on the figure of the dying and reviving vegetative and fertility god, and on the connection between the sacrifice and the scapegoat. A majority of historical cultures, as Frazer so massively demonstrates, have placed faith in the concept of the *pharmakos* ('medicine'), a figure—in the beginning, he was literally a genuine criminal—who is appointed to assume the guilt and suffering of the community which is to be purged by his death. The paradox is that by taking upon himself the sins of his world, this oblation—the *pharmakos*—is empowered and deemed to be quasi-divine; he is invested with an aura and with *mana*. Thus the criminal turns out to be the cure: the ritual sacrifice of the paradigmatic victim begets rebirth. From being the locus of evil, the receptacle of blame, the scapegoat is transfigured into a beneficiary who regenerates the society by which he is sanctioned. René Girard was to formulate this process of conceptualization, this transvaluation of villain into deity, in these terms: 'There are two stages in myths, but interpreters have failed to distinguish them. The first is the act of accusing a scapegoat who is not yet sacred to whom all evil characteristics adhere. Then comes the second stage when he is made sacred by the community's reconciliation.'[18] The individual chosen as *pharmakos* acts for the majority; the One for the Many. However, as Girard also crucially remarks, Frazer—who (like Edward Gibbon before him) scorned Christianity—failed to appreciate the continuing force of the scapegoat phenomenon: 'He did not understand that there was something essential in this phenomenon for the understanding of the scapegoat; he did not see that it extended into our own time. He only saw an ignorant superstition that religious disbelief and positivism have served to remove.'[19]

Empson fully understood that for the Western world the concept and the characteristics of the scapegoat did not die with Christ. The phenomenon survived in numerous manifestations, crucially—as he was discovering—in what he called the literary 'trick' of the mock-pastoral. Furthermore, as a result of studying a critical monograph that is saturated with anthropological theory, *The Lion and the Fox: The Rôle of the Hero in the Plays of Shakespeare* (1927), by Wyndham Lewis, he learned that the tragic hero or dying king in Shakespeare can be understood as a prime exemplum of the scapegoat phenomenon. 'The function of the king is curiously bound up with the idea of sacrifice,' wrote Lewis. 'Overwhelming evidence to this effect is provided by Sir James Frazer . . . '[20] Since the scapegoat carries the burden of collective guilt and suffering, the primitive mind sees the death of the god-king as a form of expiation: his 'magical' death reconciles the tribe to itself. Moreover, Lewis's work may have helped Empson to frame his theory that other figures—specifically, the mock-heroes of the pastoral form—may take the place of the god; as Lewis maintained, 'another expression of the same notion of vicariousness is the choosing of a hero or champion who represents the people, and supports, like a shield in front of them, fortune's hardest blows' (p. 143). Nor is the connection between scapegoat-sacrifice and the pattern of pastoral merely structural, it is fundamental; as Empson remarked, the notion of the pastoral hero repeating or else impersonating the capacities of the scapegoat-god 'leads at once to a doubt either of the justice or the uniqueness of Christ'.

Taking his cue from what he called Lewis's 'excellent book', Empson opened his rather awkwardly distended essay on 'Double Plots' (subtitled 'Heroic and Pastoral in the Main Plot and Sub-Plot'), which was to become the second chapter of *Pastoral*, with these reflections on the wonderfully 'magical' implications of perceiving the tragic hero in anthropological and cultural terms: 'the tragic hero was a king on sacrificial as well as Aristotelian grounds; his death was somehow Christlike, somehow on his tribe's account, something like an atonement for his tribe that put it in harmony with God or nature.' Such a hero is not standing in for Christ, he is enacting in his own right all the functions which the Church has reserved only to the historical Jesus Christ, Son of God. In the first part of his essay Empson discusses a number of sixteenth- and seventeenth-century plays—Greene's *Friar Bacon and Friar Bungay*, Shakespeare's *Troilus and Cressida* and *1 Henry IV*, Dryden's *Marriage à la Mode*, and Middleton's *The Changeling*—with a view to elucidating the ways in which the subplot represents much more than light relief but is essentially intricated with the main plot. On the tragi-comic stage, he explains with persuasive evidence, there is 'a sort of marriage of the myths of heroic and pastoral'; and the comic characters are to be understood as performing as 'in a sense figures of pastoral myth . . .' But there is a further dimension to the topic which becomes fundamental. In *Troilus and Cressida* (on which Empson writes the most rewardingly of all), Shakespeare compares the sexual and the political standards of behaviour exposed in the two plots (with Thersites taking up the necessary role of 'the barking dog, the critic'):

The two parts make a mutual comparison that illuminates both parties ('love and war are alike') and their large-scale indefinite juxtaposition seems to encourage primitive ways of thought ('Cressida will bring Troy bad luck because she is bad'). This power of suggestion is the strength of the double plot; once you take the two parts to correspond, any character may take on *mana* because he seems to cause what he corresponds to or be Logos of what he symbolizes.

It is not by chance that Empson deploys in that context the Greek term *Logos* (*Word, Reason*), which the Church Fathers had used to designate Jesus Christ—the second person of the Trinity, true god and true man, sole and exclusive redeemer of mankind—because Empson's constant purpose in citing such examples was to challenge the prerogative of the historical Christ. '[T]he Logos,' as he explained, 'had been formulated as the underlying Reason of the universe and was also the Christ who had saved man by shedding his blood and sharing it in the Communion.' However, according to Empson's theory, Christ may have been an in-stance of the *pharmakos* but he was by no means incomparable. In short, Christ is relativized. 'Such an identification of one person with the whole moral, social, and at last physical order, was the standing device of the metaphysicals,' he remarks in passing, almost as if to suggest that such a tremendously dissentient notion is universally accepted.

The theory that any figure need not merely ape but can actually take on the role of the Logos, which is the nub of the later part of 'Double Plots', looks like a huge step beyond his theory of the latterday mock-pastoral as a form that accommodates the binaries of tragi-comedy, but in fact it was a direct extrapolation. Empson found reinforcement for his position on what he happily judged to be the blasphemous function of the mock-pastoral from an essay entitled 'On Metaphysical Poetry' (*Scrutiny*, 2/3, December 1933), by James Smith.[21] Smith ventured to define the obscure essence of metaphysical verse in these terms: 'verse properly called metaphysical is that to which the impulse is given by an overwhelming concern with metaphysical problems; with problems either deriving from, or closely resembling in the nature of their difficulty, the problem of the Many and the One.' As old as Plato, the problem of the Many and the One included these examples, he further noted: 'At times the individual has fought against, and depended upon, its fellow individual, much as multiplicity unity; or the individual has fought against the universal; or against the universe, or against God . . . [M]etaphysical problems rise out of pairs of opposites that behave almost exactly as do the elements of a metaphysical conceit. Take the multiplicity and unity of reality, for example . . . The two support and complete, and at the same time deny, each other.'[22] Empson thought Smith's piece 'excellent', and added by way of helpfully summarizing his own views:

The supreme example of the problem of the One and the Many was given by the Logos who was an individual man. In all those conceits where the general is given a sort of sacred local habitation in a particular . . . and the others are all dependent on it, there is an implied comparison to the sacrificial cult-hero, to Christ as the Son of Man . . . This at once leads to the dependence of the world upon the person or thing treated as a personification . . . If you choose an important member the result is heroic, if you choose an unimportant one it is pastoral.

Thus Empson's extended poetics and ethics of pastoral embrace the traditional 'magical' idea of the scapegoat and the sacrifice (the responsible representative being endowed with supernal qualities), the tragic hero, and a bid for 'a secret freedom'—a 'desire to make the individual more independent than Christianity allowed', which is to be achieved by apotheosizing in poetry a Logos other than the historical Christ. After all, the deification of Elizabeth I has an implicitly unchristian aspect to it; and Donne's glorification in his poetry of a loved woman has the same 'heretical' implication. As Empson adroitly stressed, 'to take the deity from [the Queen] and give it to someone without public importance is like the use of heroic language about the pastoral swain'. Of Donne's 'The First Anniversarie', he reasonably maintained too: 'The only way to make the poem sensible is to accept Elizabeth Drury as the Logos' (so that Ben Jonson had been astute to call the *Anniversaries* 'profane and full of Blasphemies').[23] Likewise, the tears of St Mary Magdalene in Crashaw's poem 'The Weeper' 'reconcile earth and heaven, they perform the function of the sacrificed god'.

But perhaps the most persuasive of the examples Empson puts forward in this chapter is his brief but thrilling discussion of Donne's sonnet 'I am a little world made cunningly'; it inaugurated a campaign that he was to prosecute with an almost obsessional fervour (some of his opponents would regard it as monomaniacal) for the rest of his life—especially in the postwar years when it appeared that there was nothing less than an institutionalized acceptance of T. S. Eliot's unsupported declaration that Donne was not a sceptic. According to Empson's spry interpretation, in lines such as—

> You which beyond that heaven which was most high
> Have found new sphears, and of new lands can write,
> Powre new seas in my eyes, that so I might
> Drowne my world with my weeping earnestly

—Donne 'takes the soul as isolated and independent; it is viewed as the world in the new astronomy, a small sphere, complete in itself, safe from interference...The idea that you can get right away to America, that human affairs are not organized round one certainly right authority (e.g. the Pope) is directly compared to the new idea that there are other worlds like this one, so that the inhabitants of each can live in their own way.' In truth, throughout the essay 'Double Plots', and indeed throughout *Pastoral* as a volume, Empson gently but persistently emphasizes his conviction that the ultimate rationale for the pastoral 'form' is a declaration of freedom and independence. The key expressions in this particular essay include 'a secret freedom' and 'an element of revolt'; there is also the idea that the pastoral hero and the hero of tragi-comedy, along with the sincere and deeply argued ideological conflicts expressed in the tropes of true metaphysical poetry, all coincide in standing 'for a set of ideas covertly opposed to Christianity'. This key idea is one that he was to reiterate in his notes for a class lecture in Peking in the late 1940s: 'Rhetorical trick of calling any person praised the Logos as he might carry the ideal without knowing it; puzzle how far this oblique blasphemy recognised.' It was only after he began to teach in England in the 1950s—when he realized that his 'heretical' arguments about Donne's poetry were being complacently set aside by critics such as Helen Gardner and Frank Kermode—that his language became more strident. In a preface to a paperback edition of *Pastoral* (1966), he was to insist: 'the love-poetry of Donne claims a defiant independence for the pair of lovers...'; later in the same piece, the word 'Independence' is capitalized in a kind of hortatory hypostatization. Thirty years earlier, he had felt no need to use loud and absolutist language.

The proclamation of intellectual independence and moral freedom is the keynote also of the last two essays in the volume, 'The Beggar's Opera: Mock-Pastoral as the Cult of Independence' and 'Alice in Wonderland: The Child as Swain'. Empson's thorough and engaging analysis of the role of Macheath in Gay's comic opera shows how mock-heroic and mock-pastoral are inseparable. A paradoxical hero, a pretender to pastoral, the highwayman Macheath is—as Empson describes him—like the 'rogue' in Luke Hutton's verses on 'Black Dog': he is at once scapegoat and irresistible hero, the One hailed and beloved by the Many, the criminal who is ironically best placed to be judge. Ideal and individual, he enacts the notion of 'a proper or beautiful relation between rich and poor'. He ameliorates class conflict by giving both sides a merry understanding of one another: they gain strength and sympathy from their comprehension of his career: knowing much more, feeling much better. As Empson observed, 'it is important for a nation with a strong class-system to have an art-form that not merely evades but breaks through it, that makes the classes feel part of a larger unity or simply at home with one another.' It is noticeable there how the terms of reference that define the quasi-magical functions of the *pharmakos* apply so precisely to Macheath. 'One of the traditional ideas at the back of the hero was that he was half outside morality, because he must be half outside his tribe in order to mediate between it and God, or it and Nature. (In the same way the swain of pastoral is half Man half "natural". The corresponding idea in religion is that Christ is the scapegoat.)' Macheath stands (so Empson suggests) between Cervantes and Shelley. In the one case, the 'cautiously implied comparisons' between Don Quixote and Christ make the knight of doleful countenance into 'the fool who becomes the judge'; on the other hand, the Romantic poet steals 'the dignities of the swain and the hero for himself ... It is clear that the view of the poet as outcast and unacknowledged legislator... puts him exactly in the position of the mythical tragic hero.' While literary criticism has usually reckoned with *The Beggar's Opera* as a satire on political institutions and machinations, loyalties and betrayals, Empson sees Macheath as possessing a far deeper significance: 'he is like the hero because he is strong enough to be independent of society (in some sense), and can therefore be the critic of it... Hence the "rogue become judge" formula, with its obscure Christian connexions. The interest of the Noble Savage (Dryden's phrase) was that he was another myth about the politically and intellectually free man.' There is no doubt that Gay's opera perfectly matches the pastoral paradigm as Empson reformulates it; to take the most staring example, the play includes evident references to the highwayman as a parody-Christ. Of Macheath's song 'At the tree I shall suffer with pleasure', Empson comments: 'The half-poetical, half-slang word "tree" applies both to the gibbet and the cross, where the supreme sacrificial hero suffered with ecstasy.' Macheath is the scapegoat as scallywag, the 'Christ' as charismatic and suffering cynosure, as well as the figure of honour and independent integrity.

If Macheath is the 'rogue become judge', Empson extends the same pastoral model to Lewis Carroll's Alice, whom he suitably dubs 'child become judge', and with witty and inventive results. Often reprinted since its first publication, his entertaining exegesis of *Alice* has become a modern *locus classicus* for the waggish but seriously telling application to literature of Darwinian and Freudian theories. What is immediately captivating is the bravado with which he applies to *Alice* the very latest analytical resources—'What fun! all the Freudian stuff!' as he had joked in *Ambiguity*—in a way that no literary critic before him had ever dared to venture.[24] '*Wonderland* is a dream, but the *Looking-Glass* is self-conscious-ness,' he unhesitatingly pronounces. 'But both are topical; whether you call the result allegory or "pure nonsense" it depends on ideas about progress and industrialization . . . ' He delights in blowing the gaff on Alice's mys-teriously silly, funny, and unnerving adventures, but his ideas do no harm to one's pleasure in Carroll's invention because his ingenious and provoca-tive findings seem altogether so appealing and true. 'The books are so frankly about growing up that there is no great discovery in translating them into Freudian terms,' he opens; but then, as if indulging in a kind of teasing foreplay, he holds off from supplying a prompt analytical explan-ation with this virtuoso excursus on evolutionism:

The only passage that I feel sure involves evolution comes at the beginning of *Wonderland* (the most spontaneous and 'subconscious' part of the books) when Alice gets out of the bath of tears that has magically released her from the underground chamber; it is made clear (for instance about watering-places) that the salt water is the sea from which life arose; as a bodily product it is also the amniotic fluid (there are other forces at work here); ontogeny then repeats phylogeny, and a whole Noah's Ark gets out of the sea with her. In Dodgson's own illustration as well as Tenniel's there is the disturbing head of a monkey and in the text there is an extinct bird. Our minds having thus been forced back onto the history of species there is a reading of history from the period when the Mouse 'came over' with the Conqueror; questions of race turn into questions of breeding in which Dodgson was more frankly interested, and there are obscure snubs for people who boast about their ancestors. We then have the Caucus Race . . . in which you begin running when you like and leave off when you like, and all win. The subtlety of this is that it supports Natural Selection (in the offensive way the nineteenth century did) to show the absurdity of democracy, and supports democracy (or at any rate liberty) to show the absurdity of Natural Selection. The race is not to the swift because idealism will not let it be to the swift, and because life, as we are told in the final poem, is at random and a dream. But there is no weakening of human values in this generosity; all the animals win, and Alice because she is Man has therefore to give them comfits, but though they demand this they do not fail to recognize that she is superior. They give her her own elegant thimble, the symbol of her labour, because she too has won, and because the highest among you shall be the servant of all. This is a solid piece of symbolism; the politically minded scientists preaching progress through 'selection' and *laissez-faire* are confronted with the full anarchy of Christ. And the pretence of infantilism allows it a certain grim honesty; Alice is a little ridiculous and discomfited, under cover of charm, and would prefer a more aristocratic system.

I have quoted a full paragraph both because it is so difficult to know *when* or even *if* to stop and because the manner and shape of the passage are so typical of Empson: apparently casual and freewheeling, full of fortuitous perceptions, hurriedly hitching one flourished idea to the next one. The paragraph is not short, but it comprises only ten sentences; though informal—the pace is fast, the pack of observations and explanations dealt out rapidly and seemingly simultaneously, 'it is...', 'it is...', 'there is...', 'there is...', 'This is...', 'Alice is...'—the quickfire action of analytical conceptualization is disarmingly impressive. The total effect is the exact opposite of mean: Empson hastens to explicate as many critical points as he can possibly balance in one paragraph. Sometimes, however, one feels he is running too far ahead, being scarcely patient enough to fill out a summary statement—as when he suddenly speaks of Alice as 'Man' and 'Christ' (one needs to have followed the full development of his mock-pastoral theme to take the force of that allusion, which of course is an argument for reading the book as a whole rather than as discrete essays). The style also conveys the occasional impression not of the orderly planning of an essay but of a randomness as between paragraphs, leaving the feeling that he is thinking on the hoof.[25] Over a dozen pages after the paragraph just quoted, for example, he picks up the notion of Alice's prenatal experience:

I said that the sea of tears she swims in was the amniotic fluid, which is much too simple. You may take it as Lethe in which the souls were bathed before re-birth (and it is their own tears; they forget, as we forget our childhood, through the repression of pain) or as the 'solution' of an intellectual contradiction through Intuition and a return to the Unconscious. Anyway it is a sordid image made pretty; one need not read Dodgson's satirical verses against babies to see how much he would dislike a child wallowing in its own tears in real life... The love for narcissists itself seems mainly based on a desire to keep oneself safely detached, which is the essential notion here.

From personal mythological association he leaps first to psychoanalysis and then to speculation on the psychology of Dodgson himself. Nevertheless, if the argument can feel improvised and occasionally hit-or-miss, it does seem admirable that he has the honesty to go back and pick a bone with himself.

Empson's zest for Freudian readings of Carroll's symbolism is given further free range in the following passage (which disingenuously concedes in the opening sentence that one can take or leave this sort of psychoanalytic chatter). Empson assumes the air of toying with such ideas, only to surprise us into assent. We need also to bear in mind here that at the beginning of the chapter, over a dozen pages earlier, he has casually mentioned as 'an obvious bit of interpretation' that 'the Queen of Hearts is a symbol of "uncontrolled animal passion" seen through the clear but blank eyes of sexlessness':

To make the dream-story from which *Wonderland* was elaborated seem Freudian one has only to tell it. A fall through a deep hole into the secrets of Mother Earth produces a new enclosed soul wondering who it is, what will be its position in the world, and how it can get out. It is in a long low hall, part of the palace of the Queen of Hearts (a neat touch), from which it can only get out to the fresh air and the fountains through a hole frighteningly too small. Strange changes, caused by the way it is nourished there, happen to it in this place, but always when it is big it cannot get out and when it is small it is not allowed to; for one thing, being a little girl, it has no key. The nightmare theme of the birth-trauma, that she grows too big for the room and is almost crushed by it, is not only used here but repeated more painfully after she seems to have got out; the rabbit sends her sternly into its house and some food there makes her grow again. In Dodgson's own drawing of Alice when cramped into the room with one foot up the chimney, kicking out the hateful thing that tries to come down (she takes away its pencil when it is a juror), she is much more obviously in the foetus position than in Tenniel's . . . Not that the clearness of the framework makes the interpretation simple; Alice peering through the hole into the garden may be wanting a return to the womb as well as an escape from it; she is fond, we are told, of taking both sides of an argument when talking to herself, and the whole book balances between the luscious nonsense-world of fantasy and the ironic nonsense-world of fact.

Or, to put it in his usual other terms, it shows a clash between fantasy and fact.

Whether one finds his 'scientific' readings of specific episodes critically compelling or merely capricious, there is little doubt that his major argument as to the role and function of Alice is brilliantly sustained.[26] Characterized as snobbish and stoical, and given to expressing herself with 'a tone of worldly goodness', Alice embodies a 'genuine sense of power'. She is 'a microcosm like Donne's world', and she inherits the Romantics' view of the child as being 'in the right relation to Nature'—that is, Wordsworth's belief that the child feels 'a unity with nature'—and having an intuitive right judgement. Yet the essence of Alice goes deeper still: 'she is the free and independent mind. Not that this is contradictory; because she is right about life she is independent from all the other characters who are wrong. But it is important to [Dodgson] because it enables him to clash the Wordsworth sentiments with the other main tradition about children derived from rogue-sentiment...Normally the idea of including all sorts of men in yourself brings in an idea of reconciling yourself with nature and therefore gaining power over it. The Alices are more self-protective...There is a real feeling of isolation and yet just that is taken as the source of power.' In sum, Alice is the independent intelligence; 'the child, though a means of imaginative escape, becomes the critic.' Empson's clever identification of Alice as an oblique but indubitable manifestation of the pastoral mode is arguably the masterstroke of the book.

Satan-pagan-arriviste-fool-rogue-criminal-child-critic: the pantheon of his pastoral parade features a series of outsiders or outcasts, each of which stands in one way or another for what he calls a 'hearty independence' from the conventions of religion and society. Each also demonstrates the capacity to embody the paradox of fulfilling the functions of the scapegoat (specifically as a way of challenging the Christian doctrine on redemption). They stand both for and against; they spell out or imply covert judgements. Moreover, as much as they take the place of the sacrificed Christ (as is clear from the kinds of evidence that Empson puts forward), they also represent the artist as critic.

The sub-genre that he resolutely casts out of his purview of pastoral is what he dubs the 'bogus' category of proletarian literature—a subject to which he assigns the opening chapter of the book. 'One might define proletarian art as the propaganda of a factory-working class which feels its interests opposed to the factory owners'; this narrow sense is perhaps what is usually meant but not very interesting. You couldn't have proletarian literature in this sense in a successful socialist state.' Accordingly, he argues—reproaching crude Marxist aesthetics—'the Worker, as used in proletarian propaganda', has to be seen as 'a mythical cult-figure'. The traditional pastoral may well be *about* humble folk such as the (mythical) swain, but it has never been written *by* or *for* such folk. The trick of it was to map bourgeois ideology onto the symbolic shepherd. More subtle and permanent ideas are at work in real (or mock) pastoral, so that one does best to take any good 'proletarian' art as 'Covert Pastoral'. Thus this later sentence goes to the heart of his aesthetics: 'To produce pure proletarian art the artist must be at one with the worker; this is impossible, not for political reasons, but because the artist never is at one with any public' (p. 19). It is therefore further arguable that the ultimate subtext of Empson's *Pastoral* is addressed to an allegorization of the artist's terribly solitary vocation as the 'detached intelligence'. The artist conjoins the functions of the scapegoat (a humanistic version of the sacrificial cult hero) and the free and independent critic of his society's values.

Perhaps ill-advisedly lacking a formal introduction in which Empson might have set out his revisionary terms of reference and explained that his essential business lay with an 'alternative' tradition of pastoral—the mock-pastoral, the mock-heroic—*Some Versions of Pastoral* met a mixed critical reception when published in October 1935.[27] To be sure, the large majority of reviewers were impressed by Empson's capacity for discriminating patterns of ideology and conflict in his chosen texts, as well as his persuasive accounts of their psychological implications, though many critics were both amazed and irked by his interpretative ingenuity and semiotic resourcefulness; still others admitted a difficulty in following his digressive or 'circumventory' style.[28] The American edition, published by W. W. Norton & Company in September 1937 with the even more harmfully misleading title, *English Pastoral Poetry* (which Empson, who had not been consulted about it, thought 'absurd'), received a similar bag of reviews. The poet and critic John Crowe Ransom (who was to become a devoted admirer of Empson after inviting him to lecture at the Kenyon College summer school in the late 1940s) judged that Empson indulged himself with 'extravagances'; and he encapsulated his final opinion in a single sentence of cruel wit: 'Mr Empson is a solipsistic critic, because he has much to say about anything, and not the strictest confidence about making what he says "correspond" with what the poet says.'[29] But most critics, in America as in Britain, found the local detail of Empson's analyses greatly illuminating—albeit seemingly adrift amidst alien vagaries of interpretation.

The most widespread (and enduring) criticism of the volume concerns the fact that Empson supplied innumerable hints about his reformulation of the pastoral mode but never the exact pith and marrow of it; as one critic put the question, the volume is studded with ideas or maxims, but what exactly was its thesis? Desmond Hawkins, writing in *The Spectator*, remarked: 'The archetypal characters of pastoral . . . are hastily drawn and continually sink under the weight of detail. The detail itself is admittedly excellent, but the central thesis might well have been salvaged from the jungle-growth of annotation.'[30] G. W. Stonier in the *New Statesman and Nation* lamented at rather more exasperated length: 'He only hints at a historical framework—the development from simple pastoral to ironic pastoral, the interaction of pastoral and heroic, for example—and I have read his book twice in an attempt to discover, or deduce, some sort of outline. The essays remain separate: facets chosen here and there, it would seem, for their unexpectedness, as though a piecemeal non-conformity were in itself more valuable than a general view . . . Mr Empson . . . tends to shy away from broad ideas . . . What links them together is not so much the vague conception of pastoralism as the uniformity of Mr Empson's method . . . *Some Versions of Pastoral* is a more brilliant and less academic book than the *Seven Types*—fascinating to read, impossible to epitomise.'[31] John Middleton Murry, in an anonymous review in the *Times Literary Supplement*, felt that Empson was 'determined to be impregnable' and not to specify or speak out his thesis; though it is 'an exciting and stimulating book run disappointingly to seed', *Pastoral* needs to discipline its 'intellectual gymnastics' with a 'normative influence of some kind'.[32] Empson was always eager in later years to bite back at obtuse or ill-informed reviewers—he relished a quarrel in public print—but on this occasion he chose only once to respond to his critics: he wrote a mild reply to Murry's review in the *TLS*: 'there is one thread running through [the] set of essays,' he maintained—though without retracing the clue for the sake of those who had missed it in the labyrinth of his book.[33]

Nearly forty years after its publication, however, the worth of the volume had come to look quite different to Professor Denis Donoghue, who estimated in a review of the Festschrift published to mark Empson's retirement: 'My own view is that the masterpiece is *Some Versions of Pastoral* . . . It is a greater book than *Seven Types of Ambiguity* or *Complex Words* or *Milton's God* because its concerns veto Empson's self-indulgence . . . *Some Versions of Pastoral* does not supply a method but classic examples of a mind's pliancy exercised in the best of causes.'[34]

Given that Empson takes pains to engage himself with the fundamental metaphysical problem of the One and the Many, together with the relations between pastoral hero and scapegoat, Christ and the sacrificial tragic hero, perhaps the most surprising criticism to be levelled at the book in later years was that enunciated by Professor Paul Alpers (a subtle authority on the pastoral genre who otherwise comprehends and compliments many of the aspects of pastoral that Empson seeks to explain). Empson's 'deepest assumptions about life and literature' are 'social and psychological,' Alpers alleged in 1978. 'He has very little sympathy with religious or metaphysical views of the human condition'; and conducts himself as though 'there are no metaphysical or existential plights. The human condition, to him, is always historical and social . . . '[35] It may be that Alpers finds fault with *Pastoral* for the fact that Empson does not avow a belief of his own in religious or visionary solutions;[36] but he shows himself to be remarkably blind to the scope of Empson's humane thinking on the subject when he fails to register the force of this passage (from the very opening pages of the volume) which sets out the way in which pastoral, through a series of ironies, embraces both social judgement and tragic heroism: 'The realistic sort of pastoral (the sort touched by mock-pastoral)...gives a natural expression for a sense of social injustice. So far as the person described is outside society because too poor for its benefits he is independent, as the artist claims to be, and can be a critic of society; so far as he is forced by this into crime he is the judge of the society that judges him. This is a source of irony both against him and against the society, and if he is a sympathetic criminal he can be made to suggest both Christ as the scapegoat (so invoking Christian charity) and the sacrificial tragic hero, who was normally above society rather than below it, which is a further source of irony.' *Pace* Stonier too, such a passage does epitomize *Pastoral*.

Empson must have felt a fair degree of personal involvement with the notion that the outcast may become the judge, the scapegoat the critic. For him, the lesson to be taken from Gray's 'Elegy' (discussed in the opening pages of the book) was that life requires great fortitude of the individual, and it has to be borne. '[T]he waste *even in a fortunate life*' must be met with stoicism, and if a man is denied his opportunity, his only stay against confusion is a dignified self-respect and not self-prostitution—and integrity invariably entails isolation. That the suffering begotten by wastage struck deep into Empson's heart is evident in the sheer emotionalism of one of his greatest poems of the mid-1930s, 'Missing Dates', which opens:

> Slowly the poison the whole blood stream fills.
> It is not the effort nor the failure tires.
> The waste remains, the waste remains and kills.
>
> It is not your system or clear sight that mills
> Down small to the consequence a life requires;
> Slowly the poison the whole blood stream fills.

With regard to his discussion in the final chapter of the elements of 'child-cult and snobbery' in *Alice*, he asks in passing whether Oscar Wilde can be regarded as an example of someone who bravely affirms values that are at odds with those of his society. The answer is that Wilde and his associates were not truly independent of their society. When they talked of 'sin', of course they really meant 'scandal'; their attempts to scandalize society were ironically an index of complicity—they bowed to the moral judgements of their contemporaries, though they believed otherwise. 'By their very hints that they deserved notice as sinners they pretended to accept all the moral ideas of society, because they wanted to succeed in it, and yet society only took them seriously because they were connected with an intellectual movement which refused to accept some of those ideas. The Byronic theme of the man unable to accept the moral ideas of his society and yet torn by his feelings about them is real and permanent, but to base it on intellectual dishonesty is to short-circuit it; and leads to a claim that the life of highest refinement must be allowed a certain avid infantile petulance.' That final, ringingly contemptuous phrase is unusually intense in Empson at this stage of his career; dismissive of disingenuousness, he also refers to Wilde's snobbish gestures toward rebelliousness as 'slavish'. Wilde, he believed, may have appeared to set himself apart, but actually he deeply coveted inclusion.

Empson's criticism thus conveys a good deal of his essential character and his heartfelt convictions. After all, it would have been difficult for him to dwell upon the functions of the pastoral hero in literature, and to insist throughout the volume on the necessity for the detached critical intelligence, for the outsider to be the judge, without simultaneously (and without self-pity) reflecting upon the fact that Magdalene College had made a sacrifice of him. Several passages of *Pastoral* have a loudly declarative and even a prescriptive air to them; and such passages accumulate in the final chapter to the point where they seem most like a statement of faith, a moral testimony. The very last sentence of the volume reads: 'The gentleman is not the slave of his conventions because at need he could destroy them; and yet, even if he did this, and all the more because he does not, he must adopt while despising it the attitude of the child.' The point of the remark about the gentleman being no 'slave' to convention is to make the obvious contrast with what he has said of Wilde; but the remainder of the sentence, with its limiting clauses and displaced phrases, is actually more difficult to disentangle than it might appear. The gentleman has the means, the intelligence, to cry out upon the conventions of his society, and yet he does not do so: his 'good manners' forbid it.[37] He must operate within his society even while standing morally outside it. But precisely because he has to put in question the moral values and religious codes of his society, he must suffer himself to be the 'child' as critic. To comprehend the full meaning of that ultimate sentence of the volume, one must turn back some fifteen pages to this definition: 'the child's independence is the important thing, and the theme behind that is the self-centred emotional life imposed by the detached intelligence.' Several times in this final chapter Empson harps on the necessity for the 'detached intelligence'— it is in fact the keynote—but in a way that outruns the evidence in Carroll's

Alice. He was obviously speaking from his own hard experience when he emphasized the supreme importance of the detached intelligence—the critic's integrity—along with the recognition that the price one pays for it is 'a painful isolation'.

14

◆═◆═◆

'Waiting for the end, boys': Politics, Poets, and Mass-Observation

HAVING finished off the typescript of *Pastoral*, Empson was keen to travel up to Cambridge to show it to his mentor I. A. Richards, whom he eventually went to see in November. Strangely enough, however, the piece he sent Richards in advance of his visit was not from *Pastoral*, it was apparently an early draft of one of the essays that would be published several years later in *The Structure of Complex Words*. 'William Empson . . . has just sent me the first draft of his new book—which I find intoxicatingly good,' Richards wrote to T. S. Eliot. 'A Dictionary article on the word *Honest*.'[1] Although Richards's phrasing allows for the possibility that Empson showed him *both* the book and a further article 'on the word *Honest*', there is no question but that the dutiful pupil shared with Richards primarily the piece that he knew he would relish, and which was in part inspired by Richards's work (as *Pastoral* was not). On 20–1 November he and Richards spent several hours in intense confabulation over what Richards called 'his "Honest" stuff and its technique. It really is astonishingly good. Just what I hoped someone would do when I wrote the Chapter on "Sense and Feeling" in *Practical Criticism*.'[2]

'He's behaved quite well so far,' he added for the benefit of his wife (who tended to find Empson unruly); ' . . . [and] is useful to me in lots of ways.' Still, the pupil rather tactlessly outstayed his welcome, as Richards suggested in a note to Dorothea five days later: 'W. Empson is being very charming but I hope he'll go soon as I want to get on w. my own stuff.

However he's going to do excellent work certainly in [illegible word] of my main endeavours. (Bless him).'³

Empson also went round to see F. R. Leavis at his home, 6 Chesterton Hall Crescent, primarily in the hope that Leavis would give a pre-publication airing in *Scrutiny* to one or more chapters from the forthcoming *Pastoral*. 'He's much changed,' Leavis reported:

Q [Sir Arthur Quiller-Couch] told him (having already emitted some damning implications about Richards) that he had become very like R. in looks, voice & manner. Altogether we [Leavis and his wife Queenie] didn't like him, & I imagine he gathered that. He came really to ask us to publish some of his next book in *Scrutiny*, I replied, guardedly, that we had to keep a close eye on sales—couldn't afford to drop any proportion of our public. That was the right move. He bounced out with, 'O, but I thought I was offering you a big draw,'—playful of course, but—. I made it plain that our printing anything depended on there being a good gap between the March *Scrutiny* [and] Chatto's bringing out the book (*Seven Types of Pastoral*). He brought round today a long piece of Freudian nagging about *Alice in Wonderland* which we shall *not* print with my consent, & a short (7 pages *circa*) article on Proletarian Literature which I decidedly want to have. Proletarian lit. as pastoral is quite a good idea, and he presents it sufficiently well.

Leavis was not alone in remarking that Empson had come to resemble Richards. The likeness would not have helped Empson to win favour with Leavis, who had come to regard himself as Richards's opponent, but Leavis found sufficient other grounds for disliking his young visitor. 'He seems no less the clever young man [than] when he went abroad,' he complained to Ronald Bottrall (who happened to admire Empson as both poet and critic), 'and I'm less patient. I'm earnest, of course, & *Scrutiny*'s earnest (no, I don't mean Empson said so). And *Scrutiny* couldn't have been kept going on the clever young man's interesting ideas, etc.' Nevertheless, he affirmed that he would publish 'Proletarian Literature' (a shorter version of the piece that eventually appeared in the book), though not his essay on *Alice*: 'We're printing in March quite a good thing of Empson's, on *Proletarian Literature*, from his next book (I'm afraid it won't be a book from his account of it). He badly wanted us to print his psycho-analytics about *Alice*. . . . Once you've seen the Freudian possibilities in Carroll, you can get some mild amusement in re-reading, but who wants the thing worked out?'⁴ Leavis was even less amused when, the next month, Empson gave a talk to the Cambridge University English Club at the Cosmopolitan Cinema, using 'Proletarian Literature' as his text, which in Leavis's opinion pre-empted the publication of the piece in the forthcoming *Scrutiny*. 'E's behaviour is unpardonable,' he wrote; and he was happy to report too that even a friend of Empson's agreed with him. 'I see William's behaving very meanly,' Edward Wilson is reported to have remarked to Leavis. Thus Leavis summed up his aversion to Empson in a further letter to Bottrall: 'Actually, I don't think Empson is very intelligent now, though he was once potentially. He was also dangerously clever, & I think that he's little else now: that terrible capacity for the intellectual game, for getting the ball back over the net, for never being at a loss—that's not thinking.'[5] (To his credit, Bottrall was outraged at the suggestion that Empson was at all stupid.)

One member of the audience at Empson's talk on proletarian literature at the English Club was Leo Salingar, who remembers an impressive performance—chaired by none other than Empson's friend Edward Wilson. Empson 'was very lively, very fluent, and probably a little drunk. Apart from the general subject, I can only recall his retort to a woman questioner—it might have been Margot Heinemann—who had disputed something he had said about some Japanese Communist intellectuals: "But great God, woman, they were brave men!" '[6]

Some while later, Leavis was astonished to learn that Richards, together with E. M. W. Tillyard, was manoeuvring to secure for Empson the part-time lectureship that ultimately went to Leavis himself in the summer of 1936.[7] But Richards not only failed to win Empson an academic appointment in Cambridge, he failed even to get him restored to the books at Magdalene. In mid-January Richards notified his wife that everything seemed to be going well: 'He [the Master] was also quite reasonable about Empson & is going to do his bit to get him back on the books (for his M.A.).'[8] Yet, within just a few days, Empson appears to have put his foot in it by dispatching a tactless letter of his own to the Master. 'Terrible about letter to Master though,' Richards lamented.[9] There was nothing for it but for the prize pupil to carry on as a freelance exile.

Empson had his £200 a year in trust from his father's will, and he had learned from experience at the start of the decade that he could live modestly but comfortably on £3 a week. He therefore headed back to London, though the metropolis was a distinctly unprepossessing place at this period: the streets and buildings were black with timeworn grime, and a faint smell of fish seemed to be all-pervasive. He rented a shabby, uncarpeted room with a truckle bed (and with use of a small kitchen in which he would add to the endemic smell by boiling up his favourite staple, kippers) on the first floor of No. 71 Marchmont Street, London—a squalid, rabbit-warren sort of building, as one visitor remembered it. ('Jonny' Back, his former landlady at number 65, had begun living with Edgell Rickword in February 1934.)[10] His new, blonde landlady, a Mrs Thompson, was the wife of a black musician who played in a nightclub. 'When I got back to Marchmont St,' Empson wrote to Catherine Sansom in Tokyo, 'it seemed full of babies, just like Japan, but I never see them now, so it must have been only a political feeling about the population problem. But my landlady undoubtedly did have a baby the day after I settled in the bed-sitting room, out of the blue, and bring me my breakfast next day: the baby is much older now...' Margaret Bottrall, who had recently married Ronald Bottrall, and who visited Empson at his Marchmont Street digs, was struck by the 'fearful mess' of which he seemed unaware; he was simply very hospitable and courteous, and not in the least concerned that the sink was overflowing with dirty dishes. 'In a way,' she recalled, 'he had very beautiful manners, because he had been brought up to have good manners. His mode of speech comes across in his writings—the incisive-ness, and a sense of the comic: there was a latent amusement in his voice, and very good articulation.'[11] All in all, he appeared at this period to be a combination of dignity and eccentricity.

In the equally sordid and even smaller room next to his lodged another intellectual in exile. Igor Vinogradoff was born in Moscow on 29 September 1901. His father, Paul Vinogradoff (1854–1925), who was eventually to be knighted by the British sovereign, was a distinguished professor of medieval history at Moscow University; a liberal academic who disagreed with the educational policies of the Czarist regime, he was invited to England and took up the Chair of Jurisprudence at Oxford in 1903. The son Igor was educated at the Dragon School in Oxford, and as a scholar at Winchester; then he won a scholarship to New College, Oxford, where he took a first in Modern History. After a period of further study in Rome which was cut short by the death of his father, he was for a while a lecturer in European and Medieval History at Edinburgh University before be-coming a leader writer for the *Manchester Guardian*. In 1927–8 he married Joy, daughter of the artist Algernon Newton and sister of the actor Robert Newton, but the marriage lasted only a short time, though they produced a daughter, Tanya (who was in due course to marry the writer and biblio-phile Anthony Hobson). In 1934, when Empson came to share with this charming young Russian his bleak, unsavoury digs in Marchmont Street, Vinogradoff was supporting himself through journalism and by working on BBC features, while endeavouring to realize his ambition to write a history of nineteenth-century Russia. Partly because he was already dissi-pating his generous talents with drinking—he has been described as 'the greatest wasted talent of his generation'—that major undertaking was never to be completed; but in the meantime he did manage to fill his fellow-lodger's head with copious ideas and information about Russian history which Empson would never forget.[12]

'The thing that struck me when I came back to England recently after three years,' Empson was to write in a 'London Letter' for the American periodical *Poetry* in 1937, 'was a queer kind of patience in every bus-driver; not fatalism or a conviction of doom, but a feeling that we have to keep quiet and watch our feet because any hopeful large change might make everything much worse.' It seemed symptomatic, he said, that there were 'comparatively large (and well deserved) sales in England of poems by Auden and Spender, who were viewed as young communist uplift. The bulk of that new public of buyers, which was mainly interested in the political feelings expressed, were not I think idealists in the sense of enjoying sentiments they did not mean to act on, nor yet definite sympathizers who wanted to get something like that done. In America they would have been one or the other; in England there was an obscure safety and bafflement in moving from the poem to consider what the country could possibly do.'[13] If the country in 1934–5 struck him as being wary, it was actually a period of willed calm: political instability, large-scale unemployment (official statistics recorded an unemployment figure of 2,389,068 in Great Britain in 1934), and the threatening rise of European fascism all soured the air, arousing anxiety and insecurity. By 1936 the country had certainly begun to apprehend the inevitability of a second world war. In March, German troops, defying the Treaty of Versailles, reoccupied the demilitarized Rhineland; in June the Emperor Haile Selassie was driven out of Abyssinia by Mussolini's Italian army; and the Spanish Civil War broke out in July. On 7 November, 2,000 hunger marchers converged on London. Symbolically too, 1936 was a turning point: King George V died in January; and his successor, Edward VIII, abdicated in December.

'The political poets of the early 1930s had good luck for poets,' Empson was to recall in 1954, 'in being able to recommend something practical (more socialism at home, a Popular Front against Hitler abroad) on which almost the whole country had come to agree with them by 1940.'[14] The next war had turned into a dead certainty, it was now only a question of predicting when it would occur, and in the meantime making what Empson called 'charming' jokes about it. 'A friend of mine,' he related at this time about Julian Trevelyan, 'paints in an old wharf on the Thames; he said it was sure to be mistaken for the Houses of Parliament, so he was going to paint Bomb Me on the roof.'[15]

His own best political joke of the period took the form of a satirical poem at the benign expense of W. H. Auden, whom he had no hesitation in regarding as one of the two greatest poets of the 1930s.[16] 'I very greatly admire the poet Auden: I think that he and Dylan Thomas, of the poets my age and younger, are the only ones you could call poets of genius,' he was to write of Auden's work in the Thirties.[17] (Empson first met Auden in the mid-1930s, possibly through T. S. Eliot, and they were to be surprised to meet one another again in Hong Kong in 1938.) By the mid-1930s the young virtuoso Auden was comprehensibly regarded as a left-wing prophet of doom. Auden's poems sang facetiously of the imminent collapse of traditional but defunctive English culture—the explosion of mania, the insurrection of neurotic dread—as much as they sounded the threat of an unidentified external assault. 'It is later than you think,' he famously admonished his large middle-class audience. Auden seems to have studied, and borrowed or assumed, Marxist ideas at the latest by 1932, when he wrote the poems 'A Communist to Others' and 'I have a handsome profile'; the following year, he produced a 'Marxist' play, *The Dance of Death*. Even though he wrote to his friend, the dancer and producer Rupert Doone, in the autumn of 1932, 'No. I am a bourgeois. I shall not joint the C.P.'—and indeed never did join the Communist party—it is clear that he was attracted to a pro-Marxist position in the mid-1930s. Louis MacNeice, for example, was to write to Anthony Blunt in January 1933: 'Auden turned up and talked a good deal of communism.'[18] In any event, Empson always held the conviction that Auden caught the age exactly on the raw. In his contribution in 1975 to a BBC television *Bookstand* programme on Auden, he firmly insisted that he had kept faith with the Auden of the 1930s:

It is very hard, you see, to write what years later people called pylon poetry—to write about how you ought to have the socialist state and how you'd like it—without sounding phoney. And Auden somehow made it sound perfectly sincere by making it sound as if he was jeering at you for not being more sensible, but you didn't quite know what he was laughing at, but you could hear this, this mysterious tone of fun going on. It seemed to be immensely impressive . . .

You see, the pylon poets, beginning with the great slump of 1929—you had tremendous numbers of people out of work, and the economic system was clearly badly out of order, and then you got Mussolini and Hitler coming up—what they were saying was that you ought to have more socialism at home, you want the Welfare State, and you ought to have the Popular Front against Hitler abroad, the line-up of the Allies. They went on saying that through the Thirties, and by 1942 the whole country agreed with them. Well, it's a very lucky thing for a poet, I'm very sorry I wasn't in on it.[19]

Empson's mocking ballad 'Just a Smack at Auden', first published in the autumn of 1937, not only reflects the style and substance of an Auden poem such as 'Danse Macabre' ('It's farewell to the drawing-room's civilised cry'), or of his verse plays, *The Dance of Death* (1933) and *On the Frontier* (1937), it turns Auden's own tone back on the 'boy' himself (and the joke about 'boys' in the poem is explained by the fact that Auden and his 'group' were often derided—most notably by Leavis and his colleagues in *Scrutiny*—as public schoolboys who were merely crying Marx, and by the knowledge that Auden and Empson were exactly the same age). Here are the first stanza, and the last two, of the full 10-stanza poem—in which the phrase 'Treason of the clerks' in the middle stanza aptly refers to Julien Benda's book *La Trahison des clercs* (Paris, 1928), which castigated a number of writers, from Barrès and Péguy to D'Annunzio, Kipling, and William James, for betraying their vocations as disinterested or 'pure' artists by electing to involve themselves in the politics of their day:[20]

> Waiting for the end, boys, waiting for the end.
> What is there to be or do?
> What's become of me or you?
> Are we kind or are we true?
> Sitting two and two, boys, waiting for the end.
>   .   .   .   .   .
>
> What was said by Marx, boys, what did he perpend?
> No good being sparks, boys, waiting for the end.
> Treason of the clerks, boys, curtains that descend,
> Lights becoming darks, boys, waiting for the end.
>
> Waiting for the end, boys, waiting for the end.
> Not a chance of blend, boys, things have got to tend.
> Think of those who vend, boys, think of how we wend,
> Waiting for the end, boys, waiting for the end.

Many readers have felt that Empson's poem, with its plangent and seemingly 'jeering' use of the rhetorical device of *epistrophe* on the word 'end', is actually quite antagonistic towards Auden's jaunty doom-mongering. But Empson always insisted that his poem was by way of being a political family joke—it was meant as a brotherly satire, less chiding than chaffing—and in a BBC programme *The Ambiguity of William Empson* in 1977, he commented:

The point about Auden's political poetry especially, and all his group, is their peculiar relation to [the] audience, you see, they're teasing the audience, they're telling them you're making fools of yourselves, you know perfectly well really what's going to happen and what you must do and you must face up to it, and this curious intimate relation to the audience is an extremely valuable one, of course. And when Leavis attacked it, saying that they're all talking like public schoolboys pretending to be workers, well, as a matter of fact it was all good propaganda; it wouldn't be now but it was then. The extent to which the country was prepared to resist Hitler in the end when the time [came] was very dependent on this immense amount of preparation . . . But I thought that the work of Auden in preparing the public mind for the war to come, which was coming, had been extremely important. I didn't mean [in this poem] to blame him for doing it, still less to say that the war wasn't coming, I too thought it was . . . I feel I ought to explain that, and Auden when I next saw him said he thought it was very funny. It was not a quarrel scene; however, it has all the appearance of one.[21]

Later still, just a few months before his death, he wrote to Andrew Motion (poet and biographer, and at that time poetry editor for Chatto & Windus): 'I entirely agreed with Auden, though I could not express the opinion nearly so well, that War II was coming, and that backing the People's Front was our only chance. I just thought that his hammering at it had become counter-productive, and by the time he read my joke he thought the hammering had become a boring duty.'[22] Indeed, he leant so far in favour of the politics and poetics of Auden in the 1930s that on several occasions in later years he even said he regretted not having been part of the 'gang'; that he had not been able to manage what he called the 'curl of the tongue' to write political poetry quite in Auden's fashion. Nonetheless, in a letter of 1975 he notably remarked: 'I suppose I look ridiculous when I claim to have been a political poet too, like Auden and Spender and all those geared-up propaganda boys in Oxford (whereas I was in Cambridge); and it is true that I never learned the technique so was never considered a political poet. But my second volume of verse *The Gathering Storm* [1940] means by the title just what Winston Churchill did when he stole it, the gradual sinister confusing approach to the Second World War. Of course the title was chosen after writing the poems, during the early years of the war, but nearly all the poems really are considering this prospect, with which I had been fairly closely confronted . . .' (His own political poems, which are indeed quite different in kind from Auden's, include 'Reflection from Rochester', 'China', and 'Autumn on Nan-Yueh'.) The only aspect of Auden's career as it developed that Empson thought lamentable was that Auden and his fellows had for some wrong-headed reason felt it necessary to revise, and even worse to renege on, their early political poems; 'surely,' Empson wrote, 'it was not essential to appear in a white sheet of shame, denouncing themselves for having said what everyone now agreed to (only Louis MacNeice kept out of this, I think, and obviously at severe nervous cost).'[23]

For his part, Auden reciprocated Empson's admiration, and later demonstrated he had taken no offence at Empson's incantatory lampoon—or 'gibing assault', as the critic Valentine Cunningham has unfairly characterized it—by honouring Empson with a piece of light verse entitled 'A Toast (To Professor William Empson on the occasion of his retirement in 1971)', written for the Festschrift edited by Roma Gill—though it first appeared in Auden's own collection *Epistle to a Godson* (London, 1972). Hailing Empson ('dear Bill, dear fellow mandarin'), Auden begins by recalling, thirty-five years on: 'As *quid pro quo* for your enchanting verses, | when approached by Sheffield, at first I wondered | if I could manage *Just a Smack at Empson*, | but nothing occurred.' Nevertheless, it is possible that Auden had initially felt the force of Empson's indulgent baying at the 'boys', for he was to write in the 'Prologue' to *The Double Man* (1941), ll. 17–19: 'For we know we're not boys | And never will be: part of us all hates life, | And some are completely against it.'

Janet Adam Smith, who worked in the early 1930s as assistant editor of *The Listener*, and who married the poet and anthologist Michael Roberts in 1935, was later to say of Empson that he and Michael Roberts 'shared something you could call maturity, or perhaps pessimism . . . I think they were more pessimistic and more realistic about politics than the younger writers; they perhaps had fewer illusions because they didn't ever expect quite so much, and they weren't particularly looking for a cause to hang their hats on.'[24] But that is not the way Empson would have seen himself in the mid-1930s: he felt a deep *causerie* with Auden, and he feared the gathering storm.

Waiting for the end, Empson worked very hard during his days at the British Library. After work, though not disposed to make intimate friends, he socialized with the best of them, and often with an abandon that rivalled the worst. Indeed, the urgency of his getting drunk speaks for a certain hysteria in the air. With or without the company of Igor Vinogradoff, Empson was to become a dedicated patron of the pubs of Bloomsbury and Fitzrovia, mixing with everyone from the novelist Arthur Calder-Marshall to John Davenport and Nina Hamnett, and not forgetting his old friend Boris de Chroustchoff and Boris's estranged wife Phyllis. 'I think Bill had life-long acquaintances,' remembered Calder-Marshall. 'He never struck me as being interested in people.'[25] Empson was not a great gossip like Isaiah Berlin; and even among those who claimed his friendship he would keep a certain distance by addressing them only by their surnames. At one quite typical party, Hubert Nicholson spotted him 'grinning, peering round through his thick glasses'—and presently 'Empson sang a hymn (*When I survey the wondrous Cross*), and a man with a lisp sang a lot of bawdy catches and folk-songs, army bugle-calls and shanties. "Somebody should write them down," said Empson, "they are the best things being produced".' On 4 February 1937 he was to dispatch a brand-new poem to his friend John Hayward, with this message: 'I thought you seemed irritated lately by my drunken triviality, so wanted to do you a carbon of this thing while I did a clean copy. The name of the thing had better be Villanelle but it is called Missing Dates.'[26] Hayward would ever after remember the day when Empson sent him 'an extremely good poem by way of apology for being very drunk and uproarious and destructive in B[ina] gardens [in Kensington, where Hayward lived.]'[27] On another occasion, he was drunk on arrival at the home of Julian Trevelyan and his wife Ursula—but he 'talked absolutely magnificently,' Trevelyan recalled. He was so animated that he broke a wine glass and cut himself badly; and yet he simply flicked the blood into the fire and carried on conversing.[28] Interviewed much later in life, Empson remarked, when asked what he got up to in the mid-1930s: 'from late in '34 to '37 . . . I really don't know what I was doing. I was busy and contented.'[29] Yet there is a good deal of evidence to say that he was often drinking to excess and so neglecting himself. David Gascoyne, who ran into him at the London Library one day in March 1937, found him an 'extraordinarily unprepossessing' sight: 'badly dressed; small face, small tight mouth, spectacles; slightly flushed; black fingernails.'[30] Thanks to a strong and resilient constitution, however, he could still get up every day and go to work at his typewriter or in the library.

   It was almost certainly in a pub, and possibly through John Davenport, that Empson first came face to face with the transfixing eyes, the pellucid skin, the pouting lip, and the charismatic personality and eloquence, of the slim young Dylan Thomas—the 'deboshed choirboy', as Desmond Hawkins was to dub him.[31] (Empson was to write, with considerable justification: 'of the people I come across and like, I doubt if anybody reads much modern verse who doesn't write it.')[32] Thomas must have spun him some fancy yarns about his life and times, because before long Empson was citing him (presumably disingenuously, and anyway not by name) as a figure of decidedly pastoral potential—as he wrote in his 'London Letter' for *Poetry*:

I was shocked recently by a Welsh poet who turned up in Kleinfeldt's saying he needed money and had had an offer as checker-in at a Welsh mine; this was very absurd, and he had a much more cozy plan to become a grocer. What with the Welsh nationalism, the vague and balanced but strong political interests of this man, the taste for violence in his writing, and the way he was already obviously exhausting his vein of poetry about events which involved the universe but happened inside his skin, it seemed to me that being a checker-in was just what he wanted; and I shouted at him for some time, against two talkers I should otherwise have been eager to hear, to tell him that he was wasting his opportunities as a Welshman and ought to make full use of a country in which he could nip across the classes. I still think that something like that ought to happen to him, but no doubt he was right in saying that that plan was no good. The English no less than the Americans cling to a touching belief that social distinctions in modern England are more bitter than elsewhere.[33]

In April 1936 Thomas was to write to his friend Vernon Watkins in Wales of having been living up to his reputation for 'promiscuity, booze, coloured shirts, too much talk, too little work', and also of 'Nights Out with those I always have Nights Out with'—mentioning Empson by name in that regard. He was delighted to report too that Empson was such a fan of his poetry that he had praised it in a notice of *The Faber Book of Modern Verse* (edited by Michael Roberts): 'Empson, by the way, has been very kind to me in print, in a review of the Faber anthology, saying, quite incorrectly, though than which etc. there could be nothing nicer for my momentary vanity, that little or nothing of importance, except for Owen and Eliot, comes between Eliot and ME. Ho! Ha!' Thomas reciprocated Empson's feeling of affectionate admiration, and when he came to devise his spoof whodunnit, *The Death of the King's Canary* (begun in the mid-1930s with Desmond Hawkins as his collaborator, and completed with John Davenport at the beginning of the 1940s), he delighted in composing a rather good parody of an Empson poem, this opening for a villanelle:

> Request to Leda
>   Homage to William Empson

> Not your winged lust but his must now change suit.
> The harp-winged Casanova rakes no range.
> The worm is (pin-point) rational in the fruit.

> Not girl for bird (gourd being man) breaks root.
> Taking no plume for index in love's change
> Not your winged lust but his must now change suit.

Thomas must have felt total confidence in Empson's sense of humour, for those lines were among the few passages from the secret spoof, *The Death of the King's Canary*, that were published in his lifetime (*Horizon*, 6 (July 1942)). Years later, in a review of some posthumous collections of work by Thomas, Empson was to urge: 'Surely it is high time to publish the detective story "The Death of the King's Canary" (the murder of the Poet Laureate), or at least to announce which elderly poet is threatening to sue for libel if it appears.'[34]

According to E. W. F. Tomlin, both Empson and Thomas were present, along with Geoffrey Faber, A. L. Rowse, and Babette Deutsch, at one of the occasional *Criterion* evenings that T. S. Eliot held at the offices of Faber & Faber at 24 Russell Square. 'Eliot, the most commanding figure there, dominated the assembly in the quietest way possible. He never seemed to raise his voice, whereas Empson, who rapidly got tight, would end every other sentence with a "whoop", accompanied by a lunge endangering the wine glasses of anyone who happened to be near. Dylan Thomas arrived drunk and, as I gathered, was particularly foul-mouthed.'[35] Yet there is no evidence at all that Eliot himself took such a condescending view of Empson. Despite forming a (friendly) view of Empson as too 'disreputable' to get a job, Eliot enjoyed his lively, clever company and accepted invitations to drink or dine with him on a number of occasions.[36] After one inebriated evening at John Hayward's flat in Bina Gardens, Eliot wrote the next day in joshing style:

Dear John

I would like you to understand that I would of left earlier as I had intended and would of been convenient to me having just arrived but I said to myself that would not be fair to John because Bill would certainly stay to All Hours in that case and if Bill is left to himself he will certainly stay until the whisky is gone and Bill wd. think nothing of walking all the way to Marchmont Street rather than miss any of the whisky Now dont think Im being malicious because I value Bill and am concerned about Him was he or was he not tight when he arrived I may be mistaken and hoping I am but my heart sunk it did when I saw the kind of stealthy sureptitious way he dived at the whisky without so much as having been introduced and then also if Bill had not been present I wd. not of drink so much whisky which is not good for me especially after being with my family so long and dishabituated to anything but Grade A milk and Chocolate ice cream but I could not stand the sight of Bill darting at that whisky and seeing that he was not appreciating the difference between 12. 6d. and 13. 9d. but to him it was just so much firewater you might say So I staid later and drunk more whisky than I intended . . . [37]

Empson took pains to arrange for Eliot to meet his friends the Sansoms when they were over from Japan, as well as his diplomat brother Charles and his wife from Palestine. Igor Vinogradoff observed that Eliot, though 'correct' in his demeanour, manifestly enjoyed frequenting the fringes of bohemia. Vinogradoff was present, for example, at the 'French' pub (in Dean Street, Soho) when Eliot enthusiastically played Russian billiards with Empson in an upstairs room.[38] Julian Trevelyan and his wife Ursula thought Empson 'rather thick' with Eliot; when they dined out together (at the Shanghai restaurant in Greek Street, Soho, in February 1936), Eliot was vivacious and loquacious.[39] For his part, Empson, who never claimed a friendship with Eliot (and almost certainly never got beyond addressing him as 'Mr Eliot'), regarded him with a mixture of affectionate respect and satirical scepticism. He was amused by Eliot's portentousness, his air of 'Johnsonian pessimism'.

There was a party...where Eliot broke into some chatter about a letter being misunderstood. 'Ah, letters,' he said, rather as if they were some rare kind of bird. 'I had to look into the question of letters at one time. I found that the mistake...that most people make...about letters, is that after writing their letters, carefully, they go out, and look for a pillar-box. I found that it is very much better, after giving one's attention to composing the letter, to...pop it into the fire.' This kind of thing was a little unnerving, because one did not know how tragically it ought to be taken; it was clearly not to be regarded as a flippancy.[40]

Another grave Eliot *mot* was triggered by a casual remark by Catherine Sansom—or perhaps by Empson's sister-in-law Monica (Charles's wife):

There was some dinner including a very charming diplomat's wife, who remarked that she too was fond of reading. She didn't get much time, but she was always reading in bed, biographies and things. 'With pen in hand?' inquired Mr Eliot, in a voice which contrived to form a question without leaving its lowest note of gloom. There was a rather fluttered disclaimer, and he went on, 'It is the chief penalty of becoming a professional literary man that one can no longer read anything with pleasure.' This went down very well, but it struck me that the Johnsonian manner requires more gusto as a contrast to the pessimism; perhaps, after all, looking back, a mistaken complaint, because if untruth is all that is required to justify this sort of quip it was surely quite untrue that he no longer read anything with pleasure.[41]

The sole thing Empson really held against Eliot was that he possessed, or was possessed by, a medieval mind: specifically, he believed in heaven and hell.[42]

In December 1936, he enjoyed an unambiguously happy holiday with the poet and critic Michael Roberts and his wife Janet Adam Smith, who had asked him to join them for a skiing trip in the French Alps.[43] The Robertses forewarned him that since they would be skiing across country, he should be prepared to travel light ('Just what I should enjoy about skiing,' he responded); but whereas they turned up at Victoria Station with bulging rucksacks and even an attaché case, he toted merely an almost empty rucksack, his spare clothes appearing to consist only of his Japanese ski-skins and a pair of rabbit-fur ear-muffs which he had bought from a newspaper boy in Tokyo. When they arrived at the Tarentaise, it turned out too that he was by far the better skier. It was not surprising: he had once passed a Ski Club of Great Britain test (second class), he revealed. Since there were almost no regular *pistes*, they had to get into practice for their cross-country adventure by clambering up to the passes and summits round the Lac de Tignes and skiing down again as best they could on powder snow, or windslab, or precariously icy gullies. Empson's trim figure—with the flaps of his ski cap flopping like the ears of the Buddha he would draw in a notebook at every spare moment—always took the lead, speeding down the slopes in high style.

Before they set off across the passes of the Grande Motte and the Grande Casse, Empson went out on a shopping expedition, thinking to get some toothpaste. He returned with a giant cake of pink soap. With firm dignity he had requested of the shopkeeper (as Janet Adam Smith, who overheard the exchange, reported to Roberts): 'savon pour les dents'. When the shopkeeper, failing to understand, produced a normal-sized cake of soap, Empson persisted, only with greater emphasis, 'Non, Monsieur, savon *pour les dents*', whereupon he was handed the vast pink cube which he felt obliged to purchase. It would surely come in handy, he insisted to the Robertses.

Their cross-country departure was delayed for a day or two after Michael Roberts suffered a twisted knee, but they beguiled the time by piecing together poems from memory. 'Ode to a Nightingale' gave little trouble, but they struggled with 'Ode on a Grecian Urn'; and Empson and Adam Smith managed between them to recover the whole of Yeats's 'Byzantium'. When Empson set himself one evening to remember the theorems connected with the Nine-Point Circle, he adamantly refused any assistance from Roberts (who taught mathematics at the Royal Grammar School in Newcastle): 'I want to work this out.' On another occasion Empson suddenly spoke about the preoccupations that would turn out to be the opening chapters of *The Structure of Complex Words*. 'Chatter about words,' Adam Smith recorded in her diary, 'honesty, sensibility etc'. (Empson was amused to hear a local explanation of the name of Les Dames Anglaises, a group of three pinnacles on the Peuterey ridge of Mont Blanc, as told to the Robertses by a guide: 'parce qu'elles restaient si longtemps vierges'.) Similarly, even as they warmed themselves by the stove in the first hut on their cross-country progress up and down the passes round the massif of the Grande Motte and the Grande Casse, Empson asked out of the blue: 'Do you know any propositions of the form A is B?'

'God is love, beauty is truth, might is right,' answered Michael promptly.

'Yes—I want to know what the verb "to be" means there. The Oxford Dictionary is interesting, but it misses the point. Love is God, truth is beauty, right is might, are quite different propositions. I want to analyse the A is B form. I think there's a book in it.'

'What about A is A?' asked Michael. 'Business is business, boys will be boys. The odd thing is, they aren't tautologies.'

'Yes, that's a new class,' said Bill, getting out his Bourg St Maurice notebook with the Buddhas in it.

He seemed quite undaunted by dangers; perils became for him no more than practical problems with which to tease his friends. While climbing the steep Col de la Leisse and traversing the long valley on the far side, they paused for a bite to eat on a bleak landscape where avalanches had split and buckled into fierce frozen shapes.

'What's puzzling me,' Empson mused aloud, 'is what you do if you have to spend the night out. Richards says that you can dig a hole with your skis and—'

'We're not going to spend the night out,' said Roberts.

'Or there's the igloo technique,' Empson went on.

'There's a man eating my dinner,' said Roberts. 'Come on.'

'Yes, to be sure,' Empson answered, fixing the bindings of his skis, 'you're the officer type. Now when the war comes, I shall rush for the ranks.'

Another day's journey, as Adam Smith has recalled, was the toughest: 'it involved skiing up a glacier, crossing the steep little Col de la Grande Casse, skiing down another glacier to the Champagny Valley.' They roped up to come down on the far side of the col, which inhibited steady progress, and the shadow of the mountain made it extremely cold—so much so that when they stopped to eat a snack, they found the water in their bottle frozen hard. Finally, towards the bottom of the valley they agreed to unrope themselves, but then Adam Smith went tumbling: 'my skis had slipped on a sideways traverse on hard snow and I shot down, a somersaulting tangle of limbs and skis and rucksack. As I picked myself up, wonderfully unhurt, Bill joined me; he had skied down properly almost as quickly as I had fallen: "I wanted to be in at the finish you know"—almost as if it had been the Derby!'

After further days of wonderfully companionable journeying, the weather turned bad, so they cut short the holiday and spent an extra day in Paris on the way home. Empson rejoiced that his command of French had improved almost to the level of his skill on skis; at a celebration dinner in the rue des Saints-Pères, he magnificently ordered, 'Garçon, un canard complet!'

At one of their mountain hostels, after Janet Adam Smith had gone straight off to bed after dinner, the men had whiled away the evening (as Roberts told his wife) by going 'over the list of their most promising contemporaries at Cambridge, counting up those who had gone off their heads, died, committed suicide, taken to drink, or dullness. Finally Bill and Michael had concluded that it was something for anyone of their generation to be alive, sane enough to be left at large, and sober enough to order another bottle.'

Though little detail survives to fill out the story of Empson's relations with women throughout the 1930s, it is evident that his friendship with Phyllis Chroustchoff in particular was deep and true and supportive.[44] He had got to know her first through her husband Boris, a larger-than-life and immensely erudite character who ran the Salamander Bookshop in Silver Street (now Bury Street), near the British Museum (the poet Roy Campbell occupied the flat below the shop), and with whom he would sometimes go drinking at the Plough. Boris (de) Chroustchoff was a clever, eccentric figure of White Russian descent, so naturally his bookshop specialized in books about Russia. His grandfather Alexander hailed from the Ukraine (as Empson was given to understand the situation, Boris's ancestors 'owned the lands on which the slave [Nikita] Kruschev was born'), and had lived for some while in a house in Munich, where he associated with the artist Kandinsky; he later settled in Lausanne.[45] Boris attended Harrow School and went on to Lincoln College, Oxford. A gifted linguist with a marvellous memory and a rich musical voice, he could speak Russian, Italian, French, German, and English; he even sang in German.[46] Among his avocations, he had a passion for collecting things; he collected African fetishes as fervently as he collected antiquarian books (it is said that D. H. Lawrence, who was friendly with Boris, first saw such fetishes at his bookshop). Though Boris himself did not drink much, he was nonetheless the complete hedonist: he invariably suited himself and behaved in an unfettered and often outrageous manner. He would even refuse to sell books to people he did not like. In addition, he loved cooking, but he expected people to be prompt to eat the food he took pains to prepare. Once when he was concocting a marvellous supper, his wife and their friends went off to a pub and left it only at closing time: when they arrived back at Bury Street, Boris opened the window and poured his lovingly prepared stew over them. But his wife was in her own fashion every bit as spirited as Boris was.

The daughter of a Cornish doctor, Phyllis Vipond-Crocker was more than six years older than Empson: she was born on 4 January 1900. Along with her two sisters, she was a great beauty, with black bobbed hair. The artist Laura Knight drew her portrait on a number of occasions (a particularly lovely study shows her at the age of 17), and the composer Philip Heseltine (alias Peter Warlock), who fell in love with her, wrote her many letters and poems. It was in fact Heseltine who introduced her to Boris Chroustchoff, and who was shattered when the couple married in 1920.[47] Though she bore a son, Igor, the following year, her diaries suggest that she soon became bored with the boy; as Igor himself was later to note, in one diary she had even written an entry along the lines of 'Novelty of baby worn off'. Deeply disliking the responsibility of being a mother, she neglected the child. Igor was carted off to a boarding school in Scotland, where—once safely deposited—nobody ever came to visit him; and he was subsequently adopted by a barrister (later judge) named Jellinek—who incidentally put up money for Chroustchoff's Salamander Bookshop. Sociable and feckless, Phyllis was yet a great reader; her son remembered that she once cited 'Haveth Childers Everywhere', from *Finnegans Wake*, when about to move house. She also liked to go walking in France and Switzerland. But above all she adored pubs and would often drink herself silly: she simply could not quit a pub. The current expression was 'to roar': everyone would have 'a roaring evening'—which meant having a tremendously uninhibited time without thought for the morrow. Phyllis 'was extremely witty,' her son recalled. 'If a joke was cruel but it would make people laugh, she wouldn't hesitate to make it.' But everyone also talked a good deal about their nerves. 'I think I'll have a Guinness,' Phyllis would say. 'It'll be good for my nerves.' That was evidently the dependable and humorous pub character whom Empson got to know; but it does seem highly likely that she also acted as Empson's friend and trusted confidante. Phyllis was '*fairly* promiscuous,' recalled Igor Vinogradoff in conversation, so it is even possible too that she went to bed with Empson—though her son doubted it.

Nevertheless, after a period of married life with Boris, Phyllis left him and went off to live with Dr Gilbert Back, another highly cultivated man (see Empson's poem 'Thanks for a Wedding Present', which quotes as an epigraph a charming poem that Dr Back wrote on the occasion of Empson's marriage to Hetta Crouse in 1941). This arrangement meant that Empson's friend Phyllis had ended up living with his former landlord and friend—a doctor who specialized in tuberculosis and who worked for the London County Council. Dr Back, a moustachioed figure who liked to go fishing in his spare time, was universally popular—even the young Igor Chroustchoff liked him, since Back once bought the child an axe as a birthday present! But not everything went well between Dr Back and Phyllis. Back would get upset, for example, when the slovenly Phyllis neglected their home and let things slip; her drinking and extravagant conduct must have been a strain for both of them. She was to take her own life on 17 March 1938—eight months after Empson had gone to China. Strangely enough, in the 1920s, everyone had constantly talked about suicide. The composer Van Dieren, who apparently suffered from a heart condition, used to carry around with him a little blue bottle: at any moment, he would announce, he might be overcome with agony; at any moment, he might drink the contents of the bottle. Phyllis became so fed up with this pose that she once snatched the bottle from him and drank it all down. Actually, she killed herself on Dr Back's birthday, at their home at 4 Henniker Mews in London, after some sort of domestic row. 'I'll give you a present!' she is said to have shouted at him, before flouncing off to bed, turning on the gas poker and inhaling it under the bedclothes. The death certificate records tersely, 'Carbon monoxide (coal gas) poisoning', while extending the ritual note of exonerating grace: 'Did kill herself while balance of her mind was disturbed.'

A dark and compelling riddle relating to Empson's largely unrecorded friendship with Phyllis is that the last twenty lines of his favourite poem— the wonderfully layered and allusively obscure ode to alcohol entitled 'Bacchus'—specifically refer to Phyllis. 'The end of the poem goes back to a personal situation,' Empson was to reveal in a post-war reading for the British Council, 'about a lady who was feeling the entire background to this thing'.[48] In addition, in 1940 he chose to dedicate to Phyllis's memory his second volume of poetry, *The Gathering Storm*, in which 'Bacchus' features as the major central piece. Although the biographical subtext is extremely difficult to get at, the crucial question is staringly irresistible: Is 'Bacchus', in some sense, or on some level, a coded elegy for Phyllis?

Here are the final lines of the poem:

> She whom the god had snatched into a cloud
> Came up my stair and called to me across
> The gulf she floated over of despair.
> Came roaring up as through triumphal arches
> Called I should warm my hands on her gold cope
> Called her despair the coping of her fire.
>
> The god in making fire from her despair
> Cast from the parabola of falling arches
> An arch that cast his focus to the skyline
>   Cold focus burning from the other's fire
>   Arachne sailing her own rope of cloud
>
>   A Tracer photon with a rocket's life-line
> And purged his path with a thin fan of fire
>
> Round steel behind the lights of the god's car
>
> A wheel of fire that span her head across
> Borne soaring forward through a crowd of cloud
> Robed in fire round as heaven's cope
> The god had lit up her despair to fire
> Fire behind grates of a part of her despair
> And rang like bells the vaults and the dark arches.

Professor J. H. Willis. Jr., in a commentary on Empson's poetry, notes that in those climactic lines Empson focuses on the mythological figure of Semele: 'He treats her despairing questioning of her divine lover, her courageous daring of fate, her flaming death, and her final apotheosis. She resembles a tragic heroine by the end of the poem... Her gold cope transformed into a fiery cloak combining qualities of both the cope of hell (compare *Paradise Lost*, I, 345) and of the empyrean, Semele's uneasy mastery of her despair has brought on her blazing destruction. Her ecstatic apotheosis occurs when Bacchus eventually delivers her from the "dark arches" of the underworld to the ringing vaults of the pantheon.'[49] The concluding twenty lines of this poem might therefore be construed, in one aspect, as an attempt by Empson to hymn a dithyramb for Phyllis, to absolve the ghastly manner of her death.

Nevertheless, the lines are not syntactically ordered—they are in fact the closest Empson ever came to writing a piece of surrealist verse—so they are extremely resistant to lucid interpretation. Empson in his notes says that the woman experiences 'tragic exultation', which might suggest that her close encounter with the fiery god, Jupiter/Zeus, as also with Bacchus (the god of alcohol), leads to her demise. Accordingly, one implication is that alcoholism was her doom. And yet—astonishingly—the whole of this last section of the poem, including portions subsequently cut from the full work, was written, and published, some months before Phyllis Chroustch-off's suicide in 1938.

To look at this problem from a different angle, then: it is strange that the one aspect of Bacchus/Dionysos that is not brought out in Empson's notes is the sexual one, especially since Empson always claimed to be fascinated by 'Freud and Frazer, in traces of the primitive', as he once put it.[50] In Frazerian terms, this god was a vegetation spirit, a fertility god, and his rites were certainly occasions for free (though holy) indulgence in sex as well as wine. Another way to regard the climax of the poem, therefore, is that the woman is enabled by drink to overcome her despair, cross the gulf it had created (l. 75), come up the 'stair' (l. 74), and initiate a successful sexual encounter, which the last line of the poem may celebrate. In terms of myth, Semele is snatched into a cloud by Jupiter, whereupon the god (perhaps it is now Bacchus, who is associated with fire from his birth as well as with sex and wine?) 'makes fire from her despair' (79) and 'lit up her despair to fire' (90).

But there is another aspect of the final section of the poem which complicates the picture in an extraordinary fashion. This fifth section of the poem was first published—in January 1937, that is more than a year before Phyllis's suicide—in *Poetry* (Chicago), in a version which included this passage immediately after the line 'Called her despair the coping of her fire':

> One cut as seizin from the turf the cross
> Whose arch of branches are the best for fire
> And made a fire enter their flue of cloud
> Who swallow into vaults a double cross
> And all the flounces of the trees made arches
> Whose offered branches were the first despair
> Whose rounded thought could hold a court for fire
> With which the raptured Adam could not cope
> And like a cow over the moon to fiddles
> We leapt in turn across the cope of fire.

As with the last twenty lines of the poem in their final form, this excised passage is not susceptible to paraphrase, but certain points of information and interpretation may be available. For one matter, *seizin*—Empson's spelling is anomalous—refers to the symbolical act known as *livery of seisin*, 'the delivery of corporeal possession of a land or tenement': the handing over of an object such as a turf as a token of possession. By offering such *seisin*, 'One' (presumably Phyllis) allows possession. The following lines seem to refer to the perhaps quasi-religious construction and burning of a bonfire, a holocaust or burnt offering. Without being too distracted by the possible female sexual connotations of 'flue' and 'vaults', it is next worth remarking that the fifth line of this excised passage borrows the final line of an earlier poem by Empson, 'Sleeping Out in a College Cloister': 'Drowned under flounces...of trees.' The fanciful accompaniment plays with the traditional idea that the form of Gothic architecture was suggested by trees, and also with the fact that 'groined vaulting' arises when two passages with Gothic ceilings meet. The word 'groin/groyne' is probably offstage here. Perhaps most notably of all, the final lines of the passage appear to bring together hints of Adam's happy fall in the Garden of Eden and a symbolical act of fertility. In 'Bacchus' as a whole, biblical imagery cuts across the classical, and the same thing happens in the excised passage. Probably, the 'offered branches' are the forbidden tree in Eden, and the 'rounded thought' is the apple, the fruit of the knowledge of good and evil. (In *Some Versions of Pastoral*, Empson wrote at length about the 'green thought' of Marvell's 'The Garden', l. 48; and 'rounded thought' may also be associated, since man's disobedience brought death to Eden, with Prospero's calm reflection on death in *The Tempest*, iv. i. 156–8: 'We are such stuff | As dreams are made on, and our little life | Is rounded with a sleep.') Accordingly, the phrase 'first despair' in line 6 of this passage may derive from a conjunction of the first words of Milton's *Paradise Lost* (i. 1–2)—'Of man's first disobedience, and the fruit | Of that forbidden tree'—and Belial's last-ditch counsel to the rebel angels in ii. 142–3—'our final hope | Is flat despair'. If such phrases are periphrastic, a manner of speaking of Adam's yielding to Eve's offer in Eden, then 'raptured Adam' in the following line may bring together Adam's access of passion at his first vision of Eve's pristine beauty—'transported I beheld, | Transported touch' (viii. 529–30)—and the sense that he 'could not cope' with the failure of obedience which issued in his fall. Whatever the interpretative significance of the allusion, in the penultimate line of this passage, to the nursery (or nonsense) rhyme, 'Hey diddle diddle, | The Cat and the Fiddle, | The Cow jump'd over the Moon...', there is no question but that Empson appeals in his final image of leaping across a fire to Sir James Frazer's concatenation of primitive rituals in *The Golden Bough*. As Frazer rehearses the topic (see, for example, Part I: *The Magic Art and The*

Evolution of Kings, vol. ii, and Part VI: *Balder the Beautiful*, vol. i), folk have been keen to jump over festive bonfires to promote generative effects, whether on the harvest or on human fecundity; bonfire-hurdling is otherwise good for purification. In sum, the 10-line passage that Empson finally cut from 'Bacchus' convokes pagan bonfires, the temptation and fall of Adam in Eden (forbidden knowledge and sexual experience?), and an exuberant primitive activity that is believed to promote fertility.

The import of the passage may therefore be a celebration of 'pagan' sexuality. Thus it seems feasible to suggest that Empson is celebrating in code his love for Phyllis, or even a love affair with her—it is the only point in the poem which speaks of an athletic activity being undertaken by the plural 'we'. But it is just as possible that it is in some sort a celebration of Phyllis Chroustchoff's love for Dr Back (whose very surname may be subsumed in 'Bacchus'). Whether or not a distinctly personal reading of that sort is tenable, these lines assuredly link ecstatic love, sexual consummation, and a suprahuman passion which eventuates in self-destruction. The key motifs of these final reverberant lines are despair and fire and divinity; the 'cope' or canopy of heaven is invoked alongside the 'arches' or 'vaults' of the tomb.

We can only speculate as to why Empson cut those ten lines from the conclusion of the poem. Maybe he felt that—in the face of Phyllis's actual fate, her ghastly (and possibly impulsive) suicide—their 'pagan' sexual exuberance was out of key. Maybe he came to dislike the style in which he had written them. Or maybe—most alarmingly of all—he recalled his own remark that poets often write about things and only then go on to experience them, so that he came to feel unnerved or even appalled that his images of ecstasy and consummation forecast so precisely the mode of Phyllis's death. Later in life, when he was asked why he had dedicated *The Gathering Storm* to one 'Phyllis Chroustchoff', he replied falteringly: 'I felt a large part of my life in which I'd been . . .'—and his voice trailed away, his feeling unspoken.[51]

Six years younger than Empson, Charles Madge followed him in winning a scholarship to Winchester; like Empson too, Madge won a scholarship to Magdalene College, Cambridge, where in 1931 he began reading science.[52] After a period of illness, he switched course and started to study (again like Empson) under I. A. Richards—who had just returned to Cambridge from his long absence in China. (At Cambridge, Madge read *Principles of Literary Criticism* and *Seven Types of Ambiguity*.) Unlike Empson, he left Cambridge without completing his degree. But also like Empson, he was well regarded for his youthful poetry, which attracted the interest of T. S. Eliot. In addition, Eliot was to recommend Madge for a job as a reporter on the *Daily Mirror*. At a party given by Hugh Sykes Davies, Madge met Davies's wife, the beautiful and talented young poet, Kathleen Raine—Empson's friend—with whom he presently ran away. By the time Empson got back in touch with Raine after his sojourn in Japan, she and Madge were living in Cornwall; but in any case Empson had recently read Madge's poetry and said he liked it, so he invited them to lunch with him. They did meet up for a lunch—Empson was all good cheer and kindness—but did not meet again for a while, since Madge and Raine went off to Sweden for a few months. Towards the close of 1936, when they got back together again, Madge and Raine were living in a beautiful eighteenth-century house, 6 Grotes Buildings, in Blackheath, south-east London, near the GPO Film Unit where another old friend, Humphrey Jennings, was at work; Jennings lived within walking distance.

Empson liked the modest but talented young Madge and cultivated him. He took him to have lunch with Edith Sitwell (an occasion on which Madge realized that Empson must have previously recommended his poetry to Sitwell);[53] they went to see a Disney film (though Empson did not much like whatever it was they saw—'The glory of the Disneys has departed,' he affectedly declared); and they went to the theatre to see *Showboat*: Empson enjoyed the song 'Old Man River' and was greatly taken with Paul Robeson. Madge—who very much liked Empson but considered him 'a strong and somewhat wilful personality'—was drafted along too to an evening at C. K. Ogden's home in Gordon Square, whereupon Ogden rather comically donned a mask and declaimed sprung verse and the *Odes* of Horace in order to prove a theory of the spoken word. 'Empson was rather indulgent to Ogden, as he was to Richards: the three were rather inseparable, I think,' Madge recalled for me. 'I have sometimes felt that a bit of Bill's eccentricity was derived from Richards and Ogden. Richards was not as eccentric as Ogden, and neither of them was as eccentric as Bill; but I think he was a bit encouraged in his eccentricity by their behaviour.' Madge would never forget the moment when he witnessed Empson walking along reading a book in the middle of London—and just wandering obliviously into the road at Cambridge Circus. 'It was frightening, in fact.'

Madge was a poet, a Communist, and a 'frustrated scientist-to-be' who was also deeply interested in surrealism. He was therefore captivated by the notion that the artist should seek not simply to express his own ideas and unconscious vision but to explore the psyche of society as a whole, the 'social unconscious'. Surrealism, he felt sure, could unite art and science. In November 1936 the awful conflagration of the Crystal Palace in London, followed in December by the Abdication Crisis, seemed to tap into very deep wellsprings of the popular mind in a way which Madge felt necessitated much closer investigation.[54] At the *Daily Mirror*, where he acted from time to time as a sub-editor with responsibility for laying out the photo-spread on the centre-pages, he was fascinated by the way that experienced lay-out men seemed so intuitive, so responsive, so much in tune with what he called the 'mass-wish'; they shaped the pattern of photographs so skilfully as to create a form of collage, a 'visual poem'—an expression both of the general national consciousness and, more remarkably, of 'the unconscious fears and wishes of the mass'.[55] Such ideas and influences helped to determine his conviction that he could undertake an anthropology of Britain—a true ethnography—with masses of volunteer observers recording the routines and rituals, the paraphernalia and symbols, of 'unremarkable' everyday life. In the words of Kathleen Raine, Madge envisaged his project 'as a technique for recording the subliminal stirrings of the collective mind of the nation; through the images thrown up in such things as advertisements, popular songs, themes in the press, the objects with which people surrounded themselves . . . This idea was akin to (perhaps in part determined by) the surrealist *'objet trouvé'* (objects functioning symbolically) . . . '. The outcome, combining 'a surrealist conception of the irrational with a new kind of sociology', was 'Mass-Observation'.[56]

Brainstorming sessions to get the project organized were held at Madge's and Raine's home. The gifted and articulate Humphrey Jennings, who had recently served on the committee organizing the spectacular international surrealist exhibition in London, took part; so did other friends including David Gascoyne, Stuart Legg, Ruthven Todd, and Julian Trevelyan. So too did Empson, who several times made the train journey down to south-west London. (Gascoyne was irked by Madge's and Raine's great admiration for Empson, and by their inclination to 'quote all his opinions'.)[57]

However, in conversations about Mass-Observation—as Empson would recall in a memoir—it was the voluble and inventive artist and film-maker Humphrey Jennings who most captured the imaginative attention:

Humphrey became enthralled by the secret messages in the juxtaposition of the headlines of the Sunday papers. It was not a set performance; he was discovering with astonishment that there was something to decode on every page. Some of them might express the aspirations of popular religion, for example space-flight or being reborn as a racehorse, but most were simple old New Statesman jibes against the plutocracy. The technique was necessarily a kind of Imagism, but no messages were 'aesthetic' in the usual sense of the term. All could be translated into short sentences, though to do so robbed them of their sparkle. 'Could the sub-editors and make-up men realise what they were doing?' we asked one another; admiring them, of course, just as much whether they did or not. The problem was already familiar about the translators of the Bible, and in a lesser degree about most of the dead authors we found ourselves able to revere. At that time most journalists working for Tory papers actually had become very pink, though they were not likely to struggle to express it by this means; but they probably did try to get an effect of variety onto the page, to abate its dullness. Of course, the fancy was not at all trivial for Humphrey, who by that time was making films, and considered that any material could be given aesthetic interest by pace and contrast on the cutting-floor. But he would not choose dull material merely to show his artistry, nor even rely on Imagist technique to put over a general idea—the people who praise this side of his programme seem to me liable to do him an injustice. He swung away from academic literary criticism, but not away from open debate and plain reasons; and he knew he was capable as a writer—he got a First with a Star.[58]

Charles Madge was to remember their conversations about Mass-Observation with a slightly different emphasis: 'There were quite a few occasions when Bill and Humphrey Jennings both talked in their particular ways, and I was unable to get a word in edgeways. Two of the most interesting people one could possibly talk to, but they talked *past* each other. Total monologuists. The most brilliant and suggestive talker was Humphrey Jennings. Bill had a much less imaginatively extended way of talking but evinced a much more solid set of judgements. Humphrey was *so* imaginative that he would imagine himself out of reality in what he was saying. Undoubtedly they were the two most remarkable people that I met in my younger days.'[59]

The inaugural production of their aesthetic deliberations and strategic planning was a volume entitled *May the Twelfth: Mass-Observation Day-Survey 1937* (London: Faber & Faber, 1937), which was officially edited by Jennings and Madge, but which also sported the name of William Empson on the title-page as one of a group of five subsidiary editors (including Kathleen Raine). This monumental work is an edited compilation of hundreds of reports on the Coronation of King George VI: responses to the weeks of preparation, and reactions to the progress of the day's ceremonials—'floating opinions and counter-opinions . . . and the inter-actions of opinion'—both in London and from around the country.

Although the vast bulk of the book purports to represent the testimonies of its multitude of witnesses in an impartial and supposedly 'scientific' manner— 'mainly arranged in a simple documentary way,' as the editors believed—the volume has been shown to be actually rather polemical in its editorial 'design'.[60] While the numerous quotations extracted from the reports were supposed to speak for themselves, the volume amounts in fact to a socialist document as much as it professes to be straightforward sociological documentation. In a later interview, Madge recalled *May the Twelfth* as 'a reflection of the tangle of life, unedited reality', which perhaps leaves open the possibility that the ulterior or deeper motives of the editors themselves were, ironically, at least partly unconscious. Nonetheless, as Jeremy MacClancy has argued, even their opening chapter, despite being put together entirely out of newspaper cuttings, is in fact by no means disinterested: 'by repeatedly juxtaposing accounts of official preparations with reports of strikes, riots, and the miserable conditions of workers involved in the run-up to the big day, Madge and Jennings lend a deeply ironical dimension to the uplifting rhetoric of obsequious newspaper editors, and lay bare the tensions of organizing a nationwide celebration of unity in a country where equality is not the rule.'[61] The volume works to undermine the official line, since it deflates nationalistic pride and pomp; it is also self-consciously literary, with direct citations from works such as *Henry V*, and with some of the supposedly authentic conversations being rendered in 'their own rhythms and expressive styles'. Furthermore, there is an aspect to it which may owe a fair deal to Empson's contributions to its planning: whereas Samuel Hynes has suggested that the volume reads like a proletarian novel of urban life as composed by an avant-garde writer, MacClancy notes:

Jennings and Madge took pains, however, to affirm that they were *not* writing a novel. They claimed that even the most sensitive of realistic novelists . . . found it difficult 'if not impossible' to describe the texture of the proletarian world. In sharp contrast to these educated failures, observers, both working-and middle-class . . . , were said to be 'actually speaking in a language natural to them (Jennings & Madge 1937: 37). . . . In this sense Madge and Jennings were not just promoting a democratic surrealism, but a demotic one as well. They were giving voice to the people, in the people's own tongue.[62]

That being the case, Jennings and Madge were evidently heeding Empson's critique of proletarian literature—that it cannot be said to exist in a true sense—and indeed attempting to overcome his warnings against the factitiousness of the proletarian aesthetic by making out that the speeches and speech acts they represent in their volume were not artificial but actual. Moreover, there is one passage of editorial commentary in the book which borrows Empson's terms of reference in respect of kingship—except that in the case of this new king, George VI, Madge and Jennings subversively suggest that he is clearly not capable of functioning as a representative and unifying social hero: 'so far as the King himself becomes an object of emotion he is conceived in family or "Freudian" relations, not as a person who might do anything and hardly even as representing a country or a class. The performance in fact was viewed very largely in an aesthetic way, and this was the way which involved least strain and was for the majority the best social adaptation to the circumstances.'[63] In any event, such a comment, figuring as it does in a volume that pretends to scientific impartiality, clearly speaks for a stroke of editorial tendentiousness; the book has a definite bias. As MacClancy concludes: 'a key aim of their book was to provide a pointed contrast with the unifying purpose underlying much of the official rhetoric, and they pursued this aim by proffering a subversive variety of alternatives: alternative events and interpretations, and alternative ways to read these. To Madge and Jennings, *May 12th* was not singular, but plural.'[64] It is anyway quite certain that Madge did take stock of Empson's strictures on proletarian literature, because he and Tom Harrisson were to quote from Empson in a book entitled *Britain by Mass-Observation* (published as a Penguin Special in January 1939), in which a section on the song-and-dance number 'The Lambeth Walk' cites Empson as its principal authority. Writing of *Me and My Girl* (1937), the musical show which features the Lambeth Walk, the authors maintained (p. 157):

The point of the show is essentially the contrast between the *natural* behaviour of the Lambethians and the affectation of the upper class. In a difficultly academic book of criticism called *Some Versions of Pastoral*, William Empson has pointed out how important this sort of contrast has been in literature, and it is worth quoting what he has to say at this stage, because it is this contrast which gives its basic appeal to the 'Lambeth Walk' song and dance. 'The essential trick of the old pastoral, which was felt to imply a beautiful relation between rich and poor, was to make simple people express strong feelings . . . [I]t was much parodied, especially to make the poor man worthy but ridiculous, as often in Shakespeare; nor is this merely snobbish when in its full form. The simple man becomes a clumsy fool who yet has better 'sense' than his betters and can say things more fundamentally true; he is 'in contact with nature,' which the complex man needs to be, so that Bottom is not afraid of the fairies; he is in contact with the mysterious forces of his own nature, so that the clown has the wit of the Unconscious; he can speak the truth because he has nothing to lose.'[65]

They also gave some quotations from the script of *Me and My Girl* which—as Madge later related their understanding of it—'amply bear out Bill's point'.[66] Not surprisingly, their exploitation of Empson's 'Proletarian Literature' was more pointedly left-wing in tendency than his words warranted in context.

Drinking beer in a local pub, Empson was happy to discuss the nature of *May the Twelfth* with Jennings and others. However, apart from the fact that he shared with them his ideas on proletarian literature—Jennings was just as keen as Madge on a socialist refashioning of society—it is not possible to identify any specific contribution that Empson made to the volume, though he may well have helped to collate the innumerable reports submitted from around the country—'with the aim in view not only of presenting, but of classifying and analysing, the immediate human world,' as the editors wrote on the very last page of all—or else to pen or edit the introductory notes. But he was valued for his good opinion; as Madge later said, 'I wouldn't like to say that he was responsible for anything in that book; we were fortified by the fact that in this instance he didn't think the whole thing was total rubbish.'[67] (Despite the fact that *May the Twelfth* may have lasting value less as scientific documentary than as an artistic product, it has been favourably compared with its more famous American counterpart, *Let Us Now Praise Famous Men*, edited by James Agee and Walker Evans, which came out four years later.)[68]

All the same, Tom Harrisson, who joined the Mass-Observation movement early in 1937, but who was not directly involved in compiling *May the Twelfth*, mocked the book in a rude way that may well be taken to extend to Empson and his marginal part in the venture. 'It was a crazy idea to have it edited by a whole bunch of intellectual poets,' he wrote.[69] Five years younger than Empson, the buccaneering Harrisson—who had made friends at Cambridge with Malcolm Lowry—was, at the age of 25, a highly experienced traveller, explorer, and scholar. He was also a self-taught ornithologist and a (self-styled) anthropologist: he had been on Oxford University expeditions to the Arctic, to Borneo, and to the New Hebrides where he had gained a certain notoriety through his zeal for 'going native'—supposedly living the life of the Malekulan tribes even to the extent of eating human meat: 'the taste is like that of tender pork, rather sweet,' he reported. Even before coming together with Madge and Jennings early in 1937, he had determined to study 'the cannibals of Britain' and set himself up in a little back-street house, and with a job in a cotton mill, in the Lancashire town of Bolton, which he renamed 'Worktown'. A supposedly self-abnegating anthropologist, he had thus resolved to take total local colouring. However, when he visited his fellow anthropologists in Blackheath, it turned out that this lean, handsome, serious young man, who spoke in a deadpan voice but was also tremendously funny, was every bit as forcefully articulate as Humphrey Jennings. 'What I chiefly remember of the evening,' wrote David Gascoyne, 'is the picture of Humphrey, with his elbow on one end of the mantlepiece, and Harrisson, with *his* elbow on the other end of the mantlepiece, both talking loudly and simultaneously to those present in general, without either of them paying the slightest attention to what the other was saying.'[70] Harrisson and Jennings took against one another from the start; and Jennings, the poet, artist, and film-maker of genius, was presently overborne by the 'scientific' rigour of Harrisson's approach. Berating Harrisson, the stubbornly naive empiricist, as banal, Jennings left the movement soon after the production of *May the Twelfth*. However, if some people were put off by Harrisson's organizational pushiness, his man-of-action pose, and his gift for publicity and self-promotion, others responded well to, or were tolerant of, his exhausting enthusiasm and quirky humour. 'Oh, I don't know,' said Empson, 'Tom may be a rat, but he's a nice rat.'[71]

On 16 June, Julian Trevelyan was to drive Harrisson, with Empson in the back of the car, from London to Bolton. They set off at 10 o'clock at night:

Along the great trunk road we drove, past the streams of lorries, their lights flashing and dipping in the secret language known only to their drivers. At last, about five in the morning, Bill became restless, and we had to stop in a café, so that he should not see the dawn that upset him strangely. We slept for a few hours on the greasy benches and then pounded on in the daylight, arriving at Davenport Street for breakfast. A house like any other in Bolton, it contained a few beds and office desks, and an old crone who cooked us bacon and eggs and tea on a smoky grate.[72]

The ever-changing but ever-game troop of volunteers temporarily lodging at 85 Davenport Street (they included what Harrisson styled a 'Harpo Marxist') were assigned their observational tasks according to the caprice of Harrisson. While Trevelyan was told to paint the town, especially the Bolton chimneys—they were, declared Harrisson, 'like saltmines without the savour'[73]—Empson was sent off to make a report on the contents of a sweet-shop window. He enjoyed a curious success, as Trevelyan discovered when he returned from his first day of attempting to create a collage of cotton mills and cobblestones: 'I found everyone admiring a rich Freudian trophy that Bill had brought back from the sweet-shop, a silver cardboard ladder leading up to a golden key from which hung a ring.'[74] At another time during his brief visit to Bolton, Empson was apparently set to observe the rate at which a blind man drank his beer in a pub; it turned out, rather to Empson's surprise, that the blind man knocked back his drink at the same pace as the sighted folk around him.

'I went once to Bolton and very entertaining and fascinating it was, but hardly more than a weekend,' said Empson in a later year. 'I can't pretend to have been busy about that.'[75] Indeed, his casual association with Mass-Observation lasted for no more than a few weeks; within two months of the visit to Bolton he was to turn into an alert, and increasingly partisan, witness to the Sino-Japanese War. Never one of the principals in the Mass-Observation project (which was to continue to develop for several years), he was primarily an interested lay party, and an occasional participant in the *conversazione*. In any case, the modest level of his practical involvement has almost all gone undocumented. To be sure, he would have brought suggestions and counter-suggestions, for he was not shy of questioning the opinions and assumptions of others. But above all, he was a sound, supportive friend to the ringleaders Madge, Jennings, and Harrisson. It is a sure index of Empson's affection that he liked to tease his real friends, as is apparent in this wartime letter to C. K. Ogden which makes indulgent fun of Madge's penchant for generating big social-psychological theories out of every little symptom: 'I passed on to Madge your desire for information about coldcatching, and he proposes to do it, naturally after transforming it in his own mind into a general psychological inquiry into the nervous effects of the war. It is a very totalitarian or fashionplate outlook; you wouldn't get them to separate a cold from the war. It seems to me a healthy literary movement.'[76] Equally, in the same letter, he desired to place on record his praise for what he thought truly valuable in the findings of Mass-Observation: 'The new Mass Observation book, *War Begins at Home*, seemed to me much better than what they have produced before. I agree that a competent publicist would know that sort of thing already, but the present government people don't and can be got at by the sort of evidence that Harrisson collects, so it seems a genuinely useful branch of Information. No doubt that's a different thing from Science.' He was right about all that.[77]

Yet perhaps the best thing Empson ever did for Madge (and maybe through Madge for the Mass-Observation movement and its subsequent publications as a whole) was to give him a severe lesson in the importance of lucid, plain, effective communication: the utter importance of finding exactly what you want to say and of holding in mind the audience whom

you are addressing. Early in 1936 Madge believed he had completed what
he would later describe as a 'long and probably half-baked and undigested
manuscript' about Chaucer, Spenser, and Milton. T. S. Eliot told Madge
he liked what Madge himself would later reckon his 'extraordinary' work,
and indicated he wanted to publish it. Nonetheless, Madge showed it also
to Empson for his honest opinion. In a three-page letter of 16 March 1936,
Empson began in the time-honoured and best pedagogical way, by high-
lighting what he thought the strengths of the work: 'I have turned over all
the pages and read many of them; there's a lot of very interesting material
of course. About lions being magnanimous—Wycherley's Plain Dealer
says [that] instead of being like a crocodile it is better to tear your friends
in pieces honestly like generous lions and tigers;[78] this is just when the
modern sense of generous was coming in, and I thought he meant what we
would—your stuff on m[agnanimity] makes it more likely. Interesting
because I too feel that the mammals are generous in some obscure way
and don't know why...' But after a few more such comments on various
good features of the text, he moved on to criticize what he considered the
profoundly serious weakness of Madge's approach—not in a destructive
spirit, more by way of a hearty exhortation which merits quotation at
length:

The shape of the book I think is bloody insolent. This idea that one must write
very esoteric stuff because nobody will read [it] anyway seems to me nonsense—
you get plenty of readers if you give anybody a chance. Surely even a communist
can have a reasonable amount of democratic feeling; the point about writing as
plainly as you can is that you are testing your ideas against somebody who is not a
specialist and just knows about life in general. Really subjective writing seems to
me nasty to touch, gluey on the outside like David Gascoyne. I feel I have some
right to be rude about this because [I am] so much open to the same faults. You
had much better imagine before you write anything that England has long been a
settled communist state, and that the only difficulties before you are (a) making the
comrades hear what you want to say (b) convincing them that you are not talking
nonsense; assuming the future to have arrived is a piece of symbolism quite in
your manner; you will find it works much better both as making you write better
and making people buy your books. Actual chapters of quotation without confessing what you quote for, actual articles in quotation without confessing who
they are quoted from, all that kind of thing, is merely indulging yourself in
madness without the excuse of being mad. Of course there isn't much money in
the kind of criticism we write anyway, but the kind of thing one needs in the way of
sales and success, enough recognition and criticism to go on doing one's stuff
without the insanity of isolation, you can get in presentday England at once, but
only if you don't pretend to be mad. You must expect me to take you seriously if

you left the MS to ask my view of it, and I advise you very heartily not to publish this as it stands. Better make it several books and put in a great deal of your political opinions; I don't see that you lose anything by putting them in, it will make the thing far more human, and you may become sufficiently interested to find the main things you wanted to say. I myself generally find what I was trying to talk about while I am re-writing so as to try to be intelligible, and one reason why I haven't even read many of your pages of quotation is that I very much doubt whether you have even yet discovered, what I am sure is genuine when found, the reasons why you think them interesting.

I smack this out in a state of moderate beer assuming that you are not appallingly sensitive. The difficult thing would be to say it tactfully, but I don't believe you are as neurotic as your piece of writing. As to a public, of course there is a real muddle; the recent events have kept on showing a public opinion which I find I agree with, its muddle is my own, and I feel I can write decent (of course unselling) books with a notion that it is part of the country that provides the language. A man who doesn't feel that at all has of course a different situation, and I should have thought the straight way out was to bring in the politics firm and clear. Surely you haven't Magdalene [College] on your mind as a source of isolation? When I meet any of those old parties I am eagerly friendly out of gratitude to them for sending me away. Anyway, just as a point of theory, literary symbolism demands a public for symbolism; by all means imagine a public, and as a matter of fact you will imagine a real one; but those who write for no public are even unconscious of their asylum.

  Love to you and Kathleen
        Bill Empson[79]

Madge took the lesson well, and did not publish his typescript. He valued Empson's robust words so highly that he kept the letter by him till he died.

15

Camping Out: China, 1937–1938

Verse has been lectured to a treat
Against Escape and being blah.
It struck me trying not to fly
Let them escape a bit too far.
It is an aeronautic feat
Called soaring, makes you quite a star

'Autumn on Nan-Yüch'

'WHAT an ass I would have been if I had refused to leave England,'
Empson wrote with considerable self-surprise in March 1938, after
spending more than six months in war-torn China.[1] In the event, he would
work there—the only European to endure what he justifiably called 'the
horrors of native life'[2]—for just over two full years ending in August 1939.
But in August 1937 his decision to leave for China was touch and go.

He had been notified of his three-year appointment at the National
Peking University (the oldest and the first government-sponsored modern
university in China) early in 1937, and he found it an immense relief. For
the past two years he had lived in London on a small but sufficient private
income eked out with giving private tuitions and publishing occasional
essays and reviews; and he had suffered an almost irresistible 'drag to
Fitzrovia'[3]—by which he meant parties and pubs, the stub-end of Bloomsbury. Earlier still he had considered applying for an academic appointment in Singapore, but he let the opportunity slip. On another occasion he
asked T. S. Eliot to supply him with a testimonial for a professorial position
at the Egyptian University in Cairo. 'I really am an interested and indus-
trious lecturer, but can hardly expect you to know it,' he told Eliot; and he
was evidently keen to get the job, or indeed any job, for Geoffrey Faber's

secretary Erica Wright sometime scribbled on Empson's letter this note for Mr Eliot: 'Mr Empson rang up anxiously about this.'[4] His appointment in Peking therefore combined 'the advantages of both worlds,' he wrote, 'knowing I had a job and running about London'.

In mid-year he went home to York, to collect everything he needed for the journey and to say farewell to his mother. His brother Arthur, who drove him south after they had paid a visit to Edith Sitwell at Renishaw Hall near Sheffield, dropped him at the station at Welwyn Garden City. There on the station platform they saw the first newspaper reports of a Japanese invasion of China after a so-called 'incident' on 7 July at the Marco Polo Bridge in Peking—or Peiping, as it was optimistically denominated at the time (*Peking* means merely 'North Capital', *Peiping* 'Peace in the North'). 'The only fear then was being stopped,' wrote Empson later.[5] He sought further information from C. K. Ogden, who told him on 9 August:

I had a cable on Friday from Peking . . . with the implication that all was as well as could be expected—'surviving'.

I gather that it is anyhow difficult . . . or impossible to get away, and that the inhabitants hear the sounds of war and carry on—hoping that there will be no bombing without due warning, or reprisals, or riots.[6]

As Empson remarked with unusual redundancy, it seemed clear to him that Richards 'was on the spot'. Ogden advised him to wait for further news, but he dispatched two cables in succession, worded 'Coming unless told not to' and giving a different deadline for each—the second on 12 August.

Ivor and Dorothea Richards were in fact unable to cable back from Peking, since telegraphic communications had been cut and letters were censored. But Dorothea Richards had written a letter, which Empson never received:

Not v. tempting at the moment. Situation rather alarming. We have no idea of what is really happening & can hear fighting just outside the city all round. The trains have been stopped. There are any number of C[hinese] troops but without any equipment or organization & its likely to become another Abysynia if it comes to fighting more than these minor skirmishes. Probably P[eking] will pass into J[apanese] hands in a few days. Nastily hot. Naturally it puts all our B[asic] E[nglish] . . . plans into uncertainty. Hope you are not worrying . . . Its all terribly depressing and hopeless. As for ourselves, we are unlikely to see very much here in the city. Its keeping extremely calm, the gates are opened at 6 am and closed at 8 pm. There is a curfew at 9 pm after which everyone but a few foreigners stays at home . . . [W]hen you'll get this I don't know. Getting hot.[7]

The Richardses were 'virtually prisoners in Peking,' as Dorothea Richards wrote to another correspondent. Uncertain as to whether the incident would blow up into a full-scale Sino-Japanese war, they at first took the view that the Chinese, who wielded obsolescent equipment unequal to the Japanese, ought to make any sort of peace terms—however humiliating—rather than risk a massacre.[8] In any event, the Japanese clearly hoped to force the local defence to retreat to the south without significant resistance. Aeroplanes flew 30 feet overhead, and street fighting could be heard just a few blocks away. On Saturday, 28 July, Dorothea recorded in her journal: 'Sat up till 2 am hearing the propaganda of the world. Japanese ridiculous contradictions... London all Wimbledon tennis, negligible far Eastern news except ultimatum—v. complaisent.' Trenches were dug at the end of every *hutung* (lane) in the city; and on 28 July all foreign embassies instructed their nationals to seek shelter in the Legation Quarter. After four days everyone went back to their own homes. Though still isolated—even journalists were allowed to send only 300-word dispatches over the radio at the British Embassy—Peking had fallen quiet again: the Japanese had taken the city, and would remain in command for the next eight years. 'P[eking] is v. tranquil & normal in appearance under its new rulers & work proceeds as usual,' wrote Dorothea Richards. 'We get very little news & can get no real idea of what is happening partly because the wireless is jammed & partly because our news is mostly propaganda... The great universities will be shut & moved s[outh]...'[9]

'Bill Empson is with us,' she added to the same entry on 1 September; 'he arrived 3 days ago on the Trans. Sib with no job to go to. A maddening situation.' Empson had actually departed from London on 12 August, and later wished he had left earlier still. He had no naive expectations of finding himself in an area of glamorous excitement, but he foresaw the global significance of a war in the Far East; and when boarding the Trans-Siberian Express he set himself to give an honest account of everything he witnessed.

Dismissing Germany as 'an impoverished and painful place', he felt eager to reach Russia. He had taken an interest in Marxism during the early 1930s and had learned much about Russian history from conversations with his flatmate Igor Vinogradoff. At the frontier he watched as two German women produced jewel cases which the customs officers attempted to value by 'a process of divination'. The only treasure he could put before them was a pocketful of unwanted half-crowns. Station walls carried the legend 'Workers of the world, Unite', written in most

European languages. Seated next to a businessman from ICI, Empson attempted to help the German women resolve the question of whether they should return home before reaching the Chinese border or proceed to their destination, Shanghai. As soon as the party reached Moscow he felt happy to abandon the more decisive of the couple—who had a taste for vodka ('which made talk easier because nobody acquainted with beer can swallow Russian beer')—to her nostalgic musings on the aristocracy, while he took the tram to visit the Museum of Modern Western Art. He left no record of exactly which paintings he saw, but he must have been thinking of *Gathering Fruit* when he noted that Gauguin 'has the sky a gamboge yellow (just yellow, but he can't help the gamboge) and his characters burst out of it in what you may call a vulgar and poster effect but I confess I think an astounding beauty'. Gauguin was not a romantic, he remarked, only an exact reporter—and from that observation he drew a lesson that would stand him in good stead throughout his two years in China: 'decent reporting,' he judged, had the crucial power 'to tell one race how to respect another'.

He had made the journey once before, on his way to Japan in 1931, and on that occasion he had been fortunate to encounter in his carriage a number of Russians who could speak French. This time he felt estranged and apprehensive, and glad only that he could not understand the wireless that broadcast continuous political messages. At various small halts, as he later recorded in his travel notes, he observed that the Russian woman 'is the beast of burden as she is not in China', and saw 'beggars making monuments of the platforms'. The railway stations presented a 'scene of as harsh a distinction of classes as ever, and the new gain is this queer weight of fear'.

'I am not talking about the theory of Communism, an important thing that the civilised parts of the world need and have to digest,' he added, 'but about that terrible country whose history has driven it downwards ever since the sixteenth century when Europe invented progress.' Russian history seemed 'as real as a burn':

Nobody with any sense of history is going to be surprised at the orgy of killing bureaucrats in modern Russia. I should fancy the country needs three centuries, and nobody could feel more excitement about a race than I did, trotting up and down the platforms and peeping at the cheekbones of the exhausted; I think them a tremendous people; and even this awful present day despair I think is only a thing lanced and let to the surface. But goodness me, tell a Durham miner that Marx has something to tell him, and so he may, but don't pretend Stalin has.

At one morning halt where several tracks converged alongside nothing more than a few huts and a statue of Stalin, five or six engines continually hooted at each other through the chill mist; Empson felt he had entered a school of whales straight out of *Moby-Dick*, or 'like little Toomai seeing the dance of the elephants'. Often the train had to give place to other trains carrying troops towards the East, so he felt it an extraordinary relief to see the last of Siberia and to enter Manchuria on a clean Japanese train equipped with pretty attendants, fresh bread, and beer. Even the frontier officials seemed to offer an ironic welcome with their eager questions about troop movements. After the stodgy and endlessly shunting progress across Russia, he found the unbroken night-time rhythm of the sprucely furnished Japanese train 'so light and brilliant and reliable' that he put the light on above his bunk and jotted some verses that later turned into a poem, 'The Beautiful Train', ending with the syncopated line 'So firm, so burdened, on such light gay feet.' On the other hand, he had to admit that it discomfited him to derive such pleasure from the train, when its Japanese proprietors were now assaulting the very country he had chosen to serve. The ambivalent sentiments he experienced at that very moment are honestly encompassed in the penultimate line of the same poem: 'And I a twister love what I abhor.'

Within a day he was looking again with deeply mixed feelings at the Japanese faces he had last seen in any number in 1934. A German hotel keeper in Harbin gave him the anxious news that the universities of northern China had all closed down, mainly because the Japanese regarded Chinese teachers with suspicion. Furthermore, the threat of Chinese 'bandits'—the Communist resistance—prevented any movements out of town. The next day, he had to board a Japanese troop-train and found himself seated in the corner of a plush carriage being utilized as an office by some Japanese commanding officers. In the restaurant car, when he tried to make use of his small Japanese by ordering *domburi*, he was surprised to find that the attendants were providing only one elaborate dish of fish and meat, which the Japanese soldiers—even the Buddhists among them—had to force themselves to eat. On returning to his carriage he discovered that the officers had been bullied out by an officious platoon of European women and children. He dozed where he sat, watching the sun rise over the flooded rice-fields; and after changing trains at Tientsin, the final leg of the journey across the dusty plain to Peking was delayed again and again as Japanese military personnel inspected the Chinese passengers.

In 1933, on his first visit to China, he had felt 'bowled over' by Peking. Surveying the Forbidden City from the white dagoba to the north-west, he had felt that it looked 'like an Armada anchored at random in an invincible harbour'. It impressed him as being the only city he had yet seen that was 'an instrument of government and not the tomb of one man's vanity'. In the museum rooms of the Imperial Palace he had been struck by the tender sight of Chinese soldiers holding hands and staring at the ancient treasures as they shuffled round in rope sandals: troops without boots looked oddly unformidable. To the west of the city, he had crossed the Great Wall in search of the ancient Buddhist caves of Yun-kang, and he spent the final stage of that journey squatting on straw matting in a covered wagon drawn by bullocks. Goats and cows had been put to shelter in the carved caves, and the colossal statues vandalized: their hands had been lopped off for sale by profiteers. At that time, Chinese and Japanese forces were already fighting along the line of the Great Wall, so in the expectation that most of the bullock carts would be commandeered he had retained a guide—'otherwise I hope I should have had enough bounce to buy a phrase book and rely on the public'. He had lost all his introductions and 'hardly met anybody', he recalled in a notebook.

Now, in the final week of August 1937, the Japanese had just completed their brutal offensive and were occupying the city, after slaughtering some 2,000 troops (out of 10,000) of the 29th Army under General Sung. Still, in the midst of a swarming evacuation at the railway station, an incongruous reception took place. Empson was met and conducted through the old Water Gate of the Tartar City by an august committee of four professors from the Orthological (Basic English) Institute of China (officially founded in 1933), including its enthusiastic and good-humoured American director, R. D. ('Jim') Jameson—'a man with a funny goatee and glasses, an enormous grin and charming manners,' as the young sinologist John King Fairbank described him in the 1930s—who had been teaching English literature at the National Tsinghua (Qinghua) University in Peking since 1925. Jameson had been inspired by I. A. Richards to devote himself to the cause of Basic English in China.[10] Empson felt disappointed only that Richards himself, who happened to be dining out that evening, was not among the reception party. Professor Wu Fu-heng (future President of Shandong University in Jinan) remembers that after a few courteous words Empson remarked, curiously: 'I am coming to China like a ghost.'[11]

At 5 Sui An Po Hutung, the spacious headquarters of the Orthological Institute, hurried consultations took place about the prospects for establishing Basic English on the curriculum of the Chinese Middle Schools. Stimulated and distracted, Empson would periodically jump up from his chair to search for his cigarette-holder: his carry-on made another member of the committee, Shui Tien-tung—who was only four years his junior, but already a mainstay of Basic—feel that he was the very model of the absent-minded professor.[12]

But there was every sort of reason for agitation. Foreign nationals could not remain in safety for long, even in the Legation Quarter—Dorothea Richards much later recalled sitting in a compound with Empson and hearing bullets whine just outside the walls—so Empson soon took refuge with the Richardses in the Grand Hotel des Wagon-lits, which was managed by Germans. Apart from welcoming the company of the Richardses for themselves, Empson had another crucial reason for clinging to them: no university money could reach him from the Nationalist capital at Nanking.

'The holy city is wonderfully beautiful and quite silent, because the Chinese are depressed; very eerie,' he wrote home in a hand that betrayed his tension—or perhaps it was the blurring of alcohol. 'No news gets in and we swap rumours all the time, very repulsive.'[13]

Presently they travelled back to Tientsin—it was a dangerous journey, for snipers in the fields of tall millet would shoot at everything that moved, regardless of friend or foe—where they hoped to take ship via Shanghai for Hong Kong; and they spent some hours drinking good German beer with the gregarious American journalist Edgar Snow.[14] In 1936 Snow had managed the extraordinary feat of penetrating the northern Shansi revolutionary base area and interviewing the Communist leaders including Mao Tse-tung and Chou En-lai: his pioneering report, *Red Star over China*, had only just appeared, in July 1937. Snow cherished one special memory from encountering the transient British scholars, as he noted in *The Battle for Asia* (1941), 'because either Richards or Empson coined a new and now widely popular cognomen for Nipponese, the diminutive "Nip"—which somehow seemed peculiarly appropriate for the Japanese in China as distinguished from those at home.'[15] (Empson should almost certainly be given that little credit, for he had a habit of coining or shortening proper names.)

Richards exhibited all his impressive natural authority in wangling their passage by sea. They discovered just one available steamboat, but they also learned that the authorities had forbidden any women to enter Shanghai. Richards promptly interviewed the consul and the shipping agent, whereupon permission was given for Dorothea to travel with her husband. At Tsingtao they sighted another vessel, a Blue Funnel boat, which turned out to be already full; but Richards produced a sovereign remedy—some Magdalene College notepaper—and wrote magic words like 'Rockefeller' on it. The agent, Empson recorded, happened to be 'an old Magdalene boy (beastly little rabbit)', with the result that beds were promptly made up for them to camp in the officers' smoking room (at the full first-class fare of £11 each), and 'the English lady' Dorothea was again 'saved'.[16] They landed at Hong Kong in the second week of September, and Empson lodged at the Hong Kong Club while plans were laid to move inland.

The object of the trip was to establish a Committee for Basic English in southern China, and the city of Changsha in Hunan province was to be the point of rendezvous with delegates from the Chinese Ministry of Education. 'We hope to find opportunities for B. E. South of the firing line, leaving the Institute in P[eking] to handle the situation N[orth],' Dorothea had written in the Richards journal on 1 September:

Its mostly a matter of writing books in B. suitable for t[eaching] Chinese schools. At present all teaching is in great confusion. The J[apanese] are making a dead set at the U[niversities], which they consider hot beds of dangerous thought, that is anything that leads anyone to question anything they are told. The whole thing is simply damnable & the official attitude to it shows a surprising weakness—only the Ambassadorial wound has invoked anything better than a grovel—though ten[s] of thousands of other non combatants have been blown to pieces without any protest being made.

Among other contacts in Hong Kong, Empson had his first meeting with the Dean of Peking University—'the great Hu Shih', he called him— who was on his way to propagandize for China as Ambassador in Washington. One of the leading figures in the Sino-foreign liberal academic community, Hu Shih was described by John King Fairbank (who met him five years earlier) as 'the modern Voltaire'. Born in 1891, he had studied at Cornell and Columbia, had acted as a translator for the philosopher John Dewey during his lecture tour of China in 1919–21, and later edited the journal *Tu-li p'ing-lun* ('The Independent Critic'). At the University of Chicago he had lectured on *The Chinese Renaissance*, and he had even published a memoir, *Ssu-shih tzu-shu* ('Autobiography at Forty'). 'Peking will be settled under China again next year,' Hu Shih told Empson, who amicably judged him to be 'not a believable man, but a very good talker'.[17]

Another new acquaintance was Victor Purcell, a British civil servant who had worked since 1924 in the Chinese secretariat of the Malayan Civil Service at Penang—becoming Assistant Director of the Education Department for the Straits Settlements—and who would spend the next month travelling with Empson and the Richardses through southern

China. He had been awarded a Commonwealth Service Research Fellowship to work with Basic English. 'I think he is a remarkable man,' wrote Richards of Purcell at the time. 'Everything here is in the hands of the Colonial Service people and a keen and discerning Basic enthusiast, who belongs to the Service like Purcell, is invaluable. I am learning a lot from him. He seems to me to see the general Chinese educational problem very clearly too.'[18] More notably (for our purposes), Purcell would publish in 1938 a sizeable and highly readable book commemorating his few weeks in their company. *Chinese Evergreen* is in fact a thoroughly authentic account of their travels, since Purcell tampered little with the facts except for purporting to disguise the identities of his highly eccentric companions. I. A. Richards figures as 'Edwards', Empson naturally as 'Dudley'— after the infamous Empson and Dudley (it was the same pseudonym that Dylan Thomas would later pin on him in his spoof *The Death of the King's Canary*).

Getting out of Hong Kong proved to be just as difficult as getting in. The Canton–Kowloon railway was constantly subjected to Japanese bombing raids, and ships had been sunk in the West River to prevent a naval attack on Canton. Accordingly, on 21 September, a party of thirteen intrepid travellers assembled at Kai Tek Aerodrome in order to board a small plane, a three-engined Junker, under the command of a German pilot. That very morning, as the radio informed them, twenty-one Japanese aircraft had bombed Canton, less than 80 miles from Hong Kong, and there seemed to be every danger that their route back to Formosa would cut across the Junker's northerly flight path to Changsha. The slight but all-too-conspicuous Junker, which looked like corrugated iron painted in aluminium, bore Chinese identification marks.[19] Dorothea Richards, who felt queasy as the plane corkscrewed up out of Hong Kong harbour to the height of the Peak, looked on in amazement as Empson quietly took his seat and doodled algebraic exercises in seemingly complete composure. But the flight happily passed without incident.[20] Following the course of the North River, they flew through the Cheling Pass across the Nanling Mountains, and then over numerous rivers that were silted with 'all colours from blue and green to coffee and tomato soup,' as Mrs Richards described them. 'The rice cultivation was like sufficiently bad stained glass,' she remarked, 'and the railway from 3000 ft or so is almost invisible which explains the strange failure of bombers to cut what is almost the life line of Ch[ina].' After a flight that went on for several hours at a speed of about 100 miles an hour, they descended upon the varicoloured and humid landscape of Hunan Province.

Squatting astride the Siang (Xiang) River, Changsha was a city of solid grey, with narrow stone-flagged streets twisting between thick-walled houses. To the north-east of the city, a large American Bible Institute pretentiously styled 'Yale in China' and run by a President and Mrs Hutchins, acted as host to the Conference on the teaching of English. 'Yale in China,' wrote Richards, 'is like a little patch of Ann Arbor annexed to a large, sprawling and rather ugly town with a horrid damp climate.' The compound of the Institute lay all too unnerv-ingly close to the railway—a key target for bombers, as Mrs Richards said—though the Americans thought to spread Red Cross flags on the grass in front of the local hospital in a vain attempt to caution the Japanese against bombing neutral property.[21] Empson and Purcell decided to move out of the institute as soon as possible: they were not unduly concerned about air raids, but the continual hymn-singing at the mission really did get on their nerves. As Richards noted in the journal that he and his wife kept in common, 'Purcell & Empson came in to announce that they had fixed themselves up at a low German dive with lots of drinks.'[22]

The thirteen official representatives at the Basic English conference included Dr Tseng Po Sun, descendant of an old Hunanese landlord family (his great-grandfather had been Tseng Kuo-fen, conqueror of the Taipings). A small man who affected the classical grey gown of the Chinese scholar, Tseng Po Sun was a practising Quaker; he had long practical experience of the problems of education in China and wielded an excep-tionally subtle intelligence. Victor Purcell described him as a person who 'spoke laconically with a simple answer to your questions, terminated each time by a sharp closing of his lips which brought them further into a pout. But if he once started on a theme that interested him, he was one of the most fluent and voluble men I have ever met. There was never a falter in his argument; he found in the most casual interjection a point to seize on that would carry his argument forward, and he never gave the sense of monopolizing the conversation.'[23] Another key participant was Professor George Yeh (Yeh Kung-chao or Ye Gongchao), a free-natured, jovial, talkative educationalist. The son of a cultivated Cantonese family (and just three years older than Empson), Yeh had gained an MA in Indo-European linguistics at Cambridge University, after taking a first degree in English Literature *magna cum laude* at Amherst College, Massachusetts (where his gifts brought him to the attention of Robert Frost); and since 1935 he had been teaching in the Department of Western Languages and Literature at Peking University.[24] He was also presently lauded as 'the Dr

Johnson of China'. Taking his cue from Richards, Yeh had been instrumental in arranging Empson's appointment to Peking University.

Although Empson was not an official delegate at the Conference, his experience of making use of Basic English during his years in Japan, and his proven literary skills, were genuine assets, and he was accordingly co-opted into the discussions. 'He is quite one of the best Basic experts there are and has already learnt enough Chinese to be very useful,' Richards informed the Rockefeller Foundation. (The diplomatic exaggeration of the latter part of his statement need not lead us to doubt the veracity of the opening gambit.[25]) 'The future of education in a country of 480,000,000 is no bagatelle,' as Purcell properly commented.[26]

Empson wrote later, 'The fact that teachers were liable to spend an entire year on dogZ and catS was generally recognized by the committee as a disaster; in fact this particular point became a kind of slogan. For that matter, I have also known students, both Chinese and Japanese, speak with bitter anger about their first teachers of the English language, because they had made it almost impossible to learn precisely by insisting on this kind of point.'[27] On the question of pronunciation, he felt it urgent for students to be encouraged 'to speak with tolerable ease' by the most practical means possible. 'The ideal of teaching upperclass southern English pronunciation seems a typical case of the best being the enemy of the good, even supposing that this pronunciation is the best.' Questions of vocabulary and grammar absorbed the committee for days—according to Purcell, the discussion groups became 'saturnalias of talking'[28]—but certain resolutions were duly agreed. As Empson recalled some years later, the main recommendations were that a limited vocabulary method on the lines of Basic English 'was needed in the Middle Schools, with careful grading of the words to be introduced at each stage, that problems and irregularities of grammar should be kept to a minimum, and that the aim should be to give the student at an early stage a sense of assurance and freedom in the use of this limited vocabulary and grammatical scheme, which he would have time to practise thoroughly.' Such a programme sounded straightforward enough; but as Empson soon came to realize, it was another matter entirely to put the scheme into practice in a theatre of war, especially in the face of Nationalist bureaucracy and regional factionalism. Many years later, even after the liberation of Peking brought an end to the Civil War, he had good cause to lament that the official recommendations of the committee had never been enacted in the intervening years—'and indeed there has been a great deal to prevent it,' as he was to comment (staunchly and without too-obvious irony) to the Communist authorities of the New China in 1950.[29]

Ivor and Dorothea Richards next decided to travel towards south-west China in order to have a holiday and climb some mountains. Students of Peking University (Empson's putative employer, commonly known by the abbreviation 'Peita'), as well as of Tsinghua University (also Peking) and Nankai University from Tientsin—all of whom were on vacation at the time of the Japanese invasion—had been instructed to convene for the following term in Changsha (where Mao Tse-tung had once taught at the Normal School number 1). Since the combined universities had not yet assembled, Empson opted to use the time available for sightseeing and to go along for the ride with the Richardses, who shared his indifference to possible dangers.

The group made contact with a chubby, thick-necked, crop-headed and well-disposed man named Wang Fan-sen, the Nationalist Vice-Minister of Communications, who happened to be travelling on duty through the south. 'The Minister is a jovial and imperturbable man, more the war lord than the mandarin,' Empson reported. 'When one of his subordinates lit two of our cigarettes and then prepared to light his own—this, of course, was infringing a European superstitition—the Minister dashed the match from his hand, and apologized for the subordinate. "He does not know the customs," he said, "but he is faithful." '[30] Mr Wang Fan-sen kindly agreed to arrange transportation for a most curiously mixed party—which eventually included a representative of the army named General Li with his wife and sickly son, a Turk who taught a Chinese dialect in China, and a handful of other Chinese men and women—and after a delay of several days he laid on a convoy of seven cars and two lorries, together with an escort of armed soldiers. 'The point of the convoy is not so much brigands, though they are in question,' Empson wrote, 'as that nearly all cars and buses are needed by the military, so the trip takes a special arrangement.'[31] Two of the cars were painted with a camouflage of green, brown, and black, and the British visitors were bidden to travel in a 1937 Ford V Eight supplied by the Governor of Hunan—who also providentially afforded them an invaluable letter of introduction to the Governor of Yunnan ('N.B. Chinese visas insufficient,' Dorothea Richards took care to note in her journal on 13 October; 'must have provincial letters').

The 'British' car began by taking the lead—'Purcell v. disagreeable,' wrote Mrs Richards (30 September), 'wouldn't wait for the Minister who got a long way behind'—but Vice-Minister Wang presently got his own back by requesting that his visitors assume the middle station behind the bus of soldiers. He was afraid of encountering bandits, he courteously and responsibly explained, as well as 'Trotskyites'—by which he evidently meant members of the Red Army rather than regular highwaymen. The change of order meant that the overseas visitors were subjected not only to the intense heat of the highway but also the glutinous red dust thrown up by the vehicles in front, which made 'the hands feel as if they were encased in rough-dried wash-leather gloves,' as Purcell related the harsh experience.[32] The roads were primitive, gritty, and pot-holed, the scenery monotonously baked and barren, and every river had to be crossed by means of a motorized pontoon. Moreover at every stopping-place they were mobbed by urchins—'a cake of humanity as thick as caviar,' Purcell called them—who all too often suffered from severe trachoma. But they were offered good food which they washed down with a supposedly refreshing tea—though the tea, by Purcell's account, invariably tasted like 'a sickly tisane' or else dirty hot water.[33]

The Vice-Minister travelled in an undress uniform of singlet and baggy trousers; I. A. Richards wore shorts and heavy shoes, together with a collar and tie—which Purcell regarded as 'a very nice compromise—lower half explorer; top half diplomat and scholar'—and Dorothea Richards 'a sturdy utilitarian outfit, a tweed hiking dress and double *terai*'. Ivor and Dorothea Richards were in fact rarely separated, Purcell observed too. 'They made a unit together, furnishing their own commissariat, and acting always with perfect mutuality.'[34] (The Richardses had actually arranged for all their climbing gear, including tents and ice picks, to be delivered by rail from Canton. Empson likewise included a set of skis among his travelling accessories; but he never found a use for them, and they were stolen some six months later.) Purcell went on, 'It made [Empson] and myself feel improvident to see the way the [Richards'] *ménage* arranged to be self-sufficient and self-supporting—at least it made *me* feel like that, but I don't think [Empson] thought of it one way or the other. He always wandered off on his own and smoked a pipe. He was never worried or concerned. I have read [Empson's] poetry since and it is first-rate stuff, but he was the most unvocal poet imaginable except under the influence of hot beer.'[35]

Progress was so slow that it took a full day to travel the distance of less than a hundred miles to the town of Hengyang, where Empson and Purcell shared a bug-ridden bed in a rickety wooden yamen patched with fishy-smelling paint (it accommodated seventy men and women, with only one W.C. for the entire body). Purcell felt doubly irritated to discover that the nightly discomforts of the journey—stinks, creepy-crawlies, fleas, mosquitoes—seemed to have no effect whatever on Empson's sound slumbers.[36] He was clearly not exaggerating the squalor they experienced on the road to the south-west; even Dorothea Richards, who was more or less inured to the horrors and deprivations of rough travel, would admit, 'this was really disgustingly sordid... [W]e were stopping at small town ambitious hotels where the filth is indescribable.'[37]

Over the evening meal, Mrs Richards, always an energetic and self-determined person, had urged the Vice-Minister to delay their departure the next day so that they could climb the local Sacred Mountain, called Hengshan or Nanyueh (Nanyu). Victor Purcell recorded samples of their conversation:

'It would have been lovely to have visited the Sacred Mountain, Mr [Wang]. I did so look forward to visiting the Sacred Mountain. I have been up two others of the Sacred Five and I do so want to go up all of them.'
'She collects Sacred Mountains—like postage stamps,' murmured [Empson] aside to me as he played havoc with a dish of pork garnished with mushrooms...
'I hope we get to Kweilin [Guilin] to-morrow,' the Vice-Minister said. 'Kweilin is a very famous place. Chinese artists think Kweilin best place in the world. Wonderful rocks—caves—like Sung Dynasty paintings.'
'Very few people have climbed all five of the Sacred Mountains,' Mrs [Richards] insisted. 'It seems stupid coming so near and not going up this one. I would so have liked—but of course—'[38]

Of course, the irresistible Mrs Richards had her way and the party duly climbed the mountain, in company with a sedan chair that the Vice-Minister pressed upon them. (Dorothea Richards's own account of this passage of wills, written some days later, thus incorporates an ironic turn of phrase of which she may not have been at all aware: 'the first day we ran past Yoloshan [Hengshan] one of the famous five sacred mountains of China and when I expressed a regret that we had not stopped to go up it— the Minister at once flamed with enthusiasm and turned the caravan back a whole 70 miles— much against its will—so we slept up at the summit one night, running down to resume our progress at dawn next day.'[39]) It was not an exacting ascent, though the views were utterly delightful, and in Purcell's opinion—Empson and the Richardses strongly disagreed with him—the Buddhist monastery they aimed at was hardly worth the moderate effort: 'In the central hall there was a huge stone figure of Buddha. It had a smug, simpering expression.'[40] Although the monastery afforded a courteous welcome and an exemplary vegetarian dinner, its guest quarters fell short of any corresponding luxury: Purcell had to bed down in a room that ran with rats. Empson occasioned the one real drama of the expedition, though fortunately it turned out to be a minor one. Always keen to move on quickly, he had gone ahead up the mountain just too fast and lost his companions. After reaching the summit in good time he had sensibly returned to the town rather than hang about until nightfall. He missed the Buddhist feast, but on the way back a charitable farmer fed the 'foreign devil' with monkey-nuts.[41]

At the border of Kwangsi province the convoy was met by a military deputation to the Vice-Minister carrying lanterns on which 'Welcome' was written in Chinese characters.[42] At one point on the road, Empson observed, a 'Hamlet-like cloaked figure' wearing what looked like a Welshwoman's hat 'levelled its wand at us in a snap which no muscle seemed to move to cause'; as far as Empson could make out, the convoy had been 'cursed by a Taoist'. Pressing on late into the night, through floods that had in many places washed out the road, they arrived at Kweilin, the fortified capital city of Kwangsi, which seemed to be completely dominated by the Nationalist army. 'The young of both sexes go about looking dapper in uniforms,' Empson wrote in his 'Letter from China' published in the glossy London magazine *Night and Day* some six weeks later, 'and all officials except the very top ones wear little tabs on the chest stating their name and rank, like Rotarians. Students of course wear them too; their living arrangements are run by the army in the barrack style, and they have five hours' military training a week . . . I just put these bits of information down; I don't know what fascism amounts to here. The communist risings did not get so far south, and there is no feeling of repression, as in Germany, that I can smell out.'[43]

In the opening paragraph of the same published letter he carelessly revealed, 'We now plan to set off tomorrow for French Indo-China, but there is some doubt what certificates of inoculation for the prevalent cholera are going to be needed at the frontier, so it isn't a very reliable way to Yunnan.' Further delays inevitably ensued and kept them in Kweilin for ten days more. They were lodged in an uncomfortable, jerry-built inn with the unmerited name of 'Unicorn Palace'. But there were entertainments and excursions to beguile the restless foreigners. When General Li left to take up a command in northern China, they enjoyed a banquet accompanied by theatrical entertainments. 'The only moral I could extract from the plays would be that women make better soldiers than men,' Empson surmised.[44] On another night they watched military manoeuvres at the local airfield.

Kweilin is famous for its landscape of astonishingly towering limestone hills, and Empson found its karst bastions as enthralling as the Vice-Minister had predicted: 'A collection of ant-like hills about two hundred feet high, or like the ruined stupas in Ceylon if you've seen them . . . I think it was Ruskin who said that Chinese landscape was no good because it never painted the bones of a hill, but these hills really haven't any bones. Still they don't look positively slimy to touch as they do in the paintings . . . There is one in the middle of the town, about twenty yards across and sixty high, popping out of a small flat park, and looking like a mountain . . . It is rumoured to hold unbombable caves which could hold the entire Chinese Government and War Office.'[45]

The most memorable outing had a remarkably Forsterian character about it, for it led them to what Empson called simply 'a noise' and inspired him to sketch this celebration of the haunting power of Buddhist song:

Most of the Vice-Minister's party were being taken out in the grand cars to look at local beauty-spots, which appeared to be all within ten minutes' walk; kind pretty Mrs Wong was full of comforting information, but had no idea what the party was going to do, whether the party was deciding anything for itself or being herded by the chauffeurs, how long the party would want to dawdle and fidget on the present spot—a thing it could do for any length of time with that noble inability even to conceive of boredom that you expect only in the lower animals, and that made Keats treat the nightingale as immortal. (Like any other petulant remark I may make about China, this is also true of the Japanese.) We had an idea that the Fascist state [of Kwangsi] wouldn't like us to wander about much alone, which was more timid or polite than we need have been. I am perhaps rather neurotic about walking, anyway get badly fidgetted if it can't be done in a sturdy and consecutive manner—sitting and doing nothing in one place doesn't seem so bad. However, we got to one of the little melodramatic hills full of tunnels which had a temple at the mouth of one, and some of us clambered along a rock path round the bottom, which turned out difficult enough to be fun. You went through bits of cave or passed mouths of tunnel where the farmers (it seemed) occasionally camped and usually kept a lot of stuff, and one of these looked purposive and inviting. I paddled through the dirt till it got quite dark, and then matches thrown ahead showed it was twisting and going steep down, very slippery rock, a thing it would be stupid to follow without a torch. Then far down out of the depths of this tunnel I heard the deep and splendid chanting of the Buddhist ritual. A certain amount of irreverent hollooing when the others came up failed to get any answer, but perhaps we were merely ignored. Probably it came through from a temple in daylight on the other side; nobody seemed to care to find out. Never-to-be-forgotten, that pretty flower-name of the newspapers, was what I thought about the thing; all the legends of the religion (those that I know) turned over together in my heart where they lie forgotten; and when Maitreya has arisen and superseded the Blessed One so that his cult is entirely abandoned by men I should wish my spirit to revisit that small tunnel and hear the great rhythms still pulse unweakened in the black heart of the mountain.

Victor Purcell felt alarmed by their expedition into the black cavern, but his own account otherwise concurs with Empson's estimate of its sounds and sweet airs: 'Thinking of it now in the daylight with terra firma under my feet the solemn chanting and intoning echoing through the infinite galleries and reticulations of this Stygian labyrinth was mystic and beautiful, but at the time it gave me the jimjams.'[46]

In a spiritual or intellectual sense at least, Empson's passionate interest in Buddhism and its iconography gave him a large part of the authority for his very presence in China. He had as yet no brief as a teacher, and there was still no certainty that he would ever be employed at the university. Rather than lapse into aimless tourism, however, he had already begun to consider writing a travel book about his observations in wartime China,[47] in addition to completing the monograph on Buddhist art to which he had committed himself in Japan. In the event, although he sketched a number of pages of what he called 'chat' about his travels, that proposal was never to be fulfilled, largely for the creditable reason that he lacked the egoism to perceive himself as a principal subject in any drama. 'The real autobiography there seems no great need to record,' he would write to his publisher on 16 May 1939.[48] The largest part of his interests and concerns always drew him beyond himself; and while in China it seemed 'intolerably footling,' he reflected, 'to write chatty personal impressions as the world stands at present'.[49] (Almost a year later, when he heard that Victor Purcell had brought out his book about their travels together, he remarked, 'How I enjoyed all that, and what good material for a book it is, but poor old Purcell of course can't tell the story; he was just one of the characters. Nothing but bitter poverty would make me write it, either; how can your friends trust you if you gossip in public like that; I am all for other authors being cads, but not me.')[50]

But the magical surprise of the cave at Kweilin redoubled his determination to seek out and study all the Buddhist sites he could possibly reach; and in April 1938, even after six months of slogging for thousands of miles back and forth across southern China, he would still find the energy to go and visit Angkor Vat in Cambodia.

With every day that passed in Kweilin, the Europeans of the party became more and more restless and irritable, even though the Vice-Minister regularly advertised that they would be leaving on the morrow; they came to scorn his bulletins as little better than pawky procrastinations.

Although they were his guests in the convoy, they tended to behave as if he should meet their priorities forthwith. Still he kept his word and finally delivered them to French Indo-China. At Nanning he had to take leave of them, and the depleted party was crushed together with luggage and soldiers into a single bus which jounced them on to Lungchau, from where they proposed to catch the train for Hanoi. 'The driver drove like a rabbit shot through the brain,' Purcell recorded. At one point, in fact, the driver only just recovered the bus as it whipped over the edge of an embankment, and later on he fatalistically yelled his head off while careering under a bridge: it seems he had judged that it would be too low for his vehicle and might rip off the roof.[51]

Yet another jolt lay in store. When they stopped for tea at a bus administration station they discovered a map which put the railhead at Longsan, some 60 miles beyond the frontier, and not at Lungchau as shown on the *Tourist's Road Map of China* issued by the National Highways Traffic Commission as recently as June 1937.[52] Exploding with accumulated frustrations, the British contingent attempted to prevail on the driver to take the fork for Longsan; but despite their furious protestations he still insisted on conveying them first to Lungchau. It was 10 October, the Chinese 'Double Tenth'—the twenty-sixth anniversary of the inauguration of the Republic of China—and none of them could cross the border until their passports had been properly inspected. But luckily they managed to catch the French consul just as he was leaving for a celebratory dinner with the local Prefect.

'The night before reaching the frontier,' Empson was to recall over thirty years later, 'we were all issued with bogus certificates for the injections demanded by the French, so it really did feel grand.' It made a story to dine out on.

After all the vicissitudes of the Chinese part of the journey, it seemed an immense relief to cross into Indo-China (the future Vietnam), as Empson was to write in his piece for *Night and Day*: 'There with the proper jerk was an entirely different population, the delicious smoky kitten-savage softness of Malaya and Burma, rich rust brown gowns, scarlet and emerald scarves, a serious attention to Buddhism and, as the contribution of the ruling race, the intense and successful narrowness of provincial France.'[53] (The appearances that Empson reported, as history was soon to demonstrate when Indo-China erupted into its war of independence, were in this case terribly deceptive.) In the second week of October the travellers arrived in the steaming city of Hanoi, which Dorothea Richards described in her diary for 11 October as a 'well planned, spacious capital—with broad avenues with trees & shops round a lake. Hotel de France excellent in a simple, inexpensive way... but still at 5. 30 pm dripping hot & life without a fan would be hard.'

The party began to split up. Purcell caught a boat home from Haiphong, while Empson travelled back up into China to spend a few more days with the Richardses in the city of Kunming (Yunnan-fu), where they met up with the anthropologist Joseph F. Rock. The robust Rock, who was studying the people of the ancient Na-khi (Naxi) kingdom in the high hinterland of Yunnan, was a man to speak his mind; but sadly only one significant story survives of his dealings with the young Empson, as Richards was later to relate it (Richards was not a man to tell tales out of school, so this anecdote must have struck him as harmlessly but memorably amusing): 'When Empson smoked a pipe, Rock said like a sultan "Put that dirty thing away," as he pointed to Empson's pipe. Empson was so affable that he just did so without any ado.'[54]

On 19 October Empson left the Richardses in Yunnan and set off to return to Changsha.[55] After flying to the the city of Chengtu, capital of Szechwan province, he took a bus to Chungking on a peninsula of the high Yangtze—where he had to sit out what he called 'two fancy air raids' ('If you see a man asleep in the Far East,' he sarcastically noted from hard experience, 'it is the polite thing to wake him up and ask if he is comfortable')—and finally a steamer downriver to Changsha.

The explosive confrontation with the newfound map had marked the lowest point in the relations of the travellers: to most of them it had seemed the last straw in a succession of setbacks and discomforts, and they blamed the Vice-Minister for having delayed their progress with what they regarded as unnecessary difficulties and infuriatingly temporizing reassurances.

Victor Purcell, who readily admitted to his own exasperation, later felt he had never really got through to his companions. Whilst he admired Dorothea Richards's cheerful determination in the face of all odds, he found her husband too aloof for any comfortable communication to take place between them. Richards seemed 'as elusive and remote as a will-o'-the-wisp,' he wrote. But Empson he considered both congenial and almost nervelessly self-contained, as he testified in *Chinese Evergreen*: 'I wouldn't mind going on a really difficult journey with [Empson]—to Kashgar on a dromedary, say—he would not get on my nerves. He is purely impersonal.'[56]

Purcell marvelled at his ability to absorb himself in working out a problem in algebra:

It was always the same problem. I saw the diagram of it on at least two hundred different bits of paper, accompanied in some cases with a page and a half of algebraic signs, but I never ascertained exactly what the problem was. It had something to do with proving that a certain circle touches a triangle at nine points—which sounds nonsense so I must have got it wrong. [Empson] said that he could prove it easily enough by algebra, but that there ought to be a simple geometrical proof if he could only find it. He was not aware whether anyone else had ever found it, so he could not say whether he was searching for the lost tribes of Israel or, on the other hand, for another planet. In any case he found it a never failing source of consolation. In times of trial and tribulation when delays or diplomatic negotiations were more than usually exasperating or when we were forgotten on the roadside like umbrellas in taxis, [Richards] would fume mildly in his remote way, Mrs. [Richards] would express her annoyance in modulations on a single theme, I would sit with murder in my heart, and [Empson] would bring out his cigarette holder and the paper with his problem on it. He usually sat on a stone or something at a distance from us and our little troubles and would refuse to be associated with the business in any way. I did see him on one occasion stirred, at least, but the utmost condemnation he would commit himself to at ordinary times was: 'How like the Japanese!' He was incapable of animus, I thought.[57]

But Empson was by no means as abstracted and unobservant as he seemed to his companions. He judged that the Vice-Minister had been altogether 'generous jovial and efficient' in taking the trouble to explain to the best of his ability their protracted detention in Kweilin. Furthermore, he presently extrapolated from Wang's conduct in order to sketch a brief analysis of the peculiarities of 'Chinese Politeness' (which he felt to be quite interestingly different from 'the nervous embarrassment and the self-assertion' that was characteristic of the Japanese):

One of the ideas knocking about in England, when people think of the Chinese, is that the Chinese are all grotesquely overcivil to each other and speak with a sinister false humility. This 'Wallet of Kai Lung' stuff is connected in English people's minds with arty tittering about the torture-chambers held ready in the background; politeness is held to go with cruelty. It is a very dislikeable picture.

These popular legends are seldom altogether false, and at worst they have lasted longer than the official propaganda line of the moment; they have deeper roots; they are worth considering. It looks as if the Europeans invented or realised this stock type of Chinaman [Empson had not yet learned that it is offensive to a Chinese to be so designated] out of a strand of European (and especially English) character and aesthetic fashion—nobody heard of this Kai Lung Chinaman till we were defending ourselves against accusations about the Opium Wars, to start with, and he fitted in with the English literary 'decadents'. But never mind; that doesn't prove we weren't right; our own sins may have taught us to understand the typical sins of a Chinese. It would be stupid to argue that there never was such a Chinese or such an Englishman as Kai Lung; of course there was; the point where you need a breath of fact is in considering whether the type crops up much at present or is being bred for the near future.

Who *is* the Kai Lung Chinese? The government and semigovernment official, of course. Is he really more Chinese than English? Yes, because we took over from the Chinese the whole idea of the Civil Service chosen by examination, and it was the best thing they have given us (better than tea or silk, and probably they didn't give us printing—of course Gladstone didn't admit where his Civil Service plans came from, but the connection of thought can be traced tidily). Are the Chinese ruling classes now sold to keeping themselves like that? Well, not at all dangerously, not as much as the English are.

The rigid rules of Chinese highgrade politeness are no longer taught to the Chinese young, nor for that matter to the Japanese young, and both of them are often rather more abrupt than they need to be. However most Chinese still take more care about the other man's feelings than most Englishmen up to the point where an ugly truth becomes necessary, or anyway observers agree on saying so. This was described by Englishmen in Pidgin English as care for 'face'. It seems now to be agreed that 'facesaving' is a useful English word, that is, not only useful for describing a peculiarity of the Chinese. My own experience has been a very limited one but from my own small contacts I would agree with what broader men have told me, that there is more Kai Lung here [in England] than there.

Let us get clear that the brutal use of politeness does exist in China, and will continue. I was one of a party being carried in a fleet of cars from Changsha to Indochina under convoy of the then Chinese Vice-Minister of Communications, whose purpose on this journey was not told us but was evidently to check up on possible political confusions of various types on what was then an important highway. Meanwhile he was ready to trail a convoy of Europeans etc. on their way out of China. It became clear before the end of our trip that these possible confusions and also the countering Chinese spymania near the frontier were so large that without his help we wouldn't have got through at all. Meanwhile of course he had his jobs to do in various towns, and it was in no way his business to tell us why he had to stop anywhere. I took perhaps an unduly pro-Chinese view of the pauses because I was pleased to have a look round, whereas my companions were aiming at sailing times or other dates. They were therefore thrown into fits of (to me) ludicrous irritation by the official formula...I want you to see the gathering madness of the important Europeans when every day for ten days in Kweilin the Vice-Minister appeared briefly in the mornings (we knew he was in an office with the telephone working all day) and said 'It is all right. We leave tomorrow'. After about five days he was received with growling and he said it with the patient kindly manner of a man who hardly expected to be understood by children, but who would none the less always explain things to them and treat them kindly. It was tedious, he implied, to hear people who were determined to misunderstand, but he would find a little time to listen. Now this was an elderly Chinese, and a younger one would have been much franker; indeed a younger one would probably not have exposed himself to unnecessary insult by helping us at all. Remember that a man in his position could not with any patriotism have told an audience of potential spies *why* we were being held up. He could not have said 'You are held up indefinitely' without receiving a storm of undeserved complaints. He was rightly confident than he was going to satisfy our ridiculous demands about time. He was determined to show himself daily as a host to reassure his guests and check up on their complaints. He then did it on formula in a strikingly unflinching manner.

Empson's essay reflects very well indeed on his capacity for imaginative sympathy. He generously conceded, 'The others had to arrive on time, and I had only to look about me, without care for time or place, so I had a source of inner calm that couldn't decently be flaunted.' Even though he was a passenger without portfolio, however, his tolerant bearing can be explained only in part by the fact he was not pressed for time. In the main he was temperamentally disposed to endure with all the patience of a Taoist monk the multitudinous and gross stresses that would leave perhaps most other individuals weeping with frustration and self-pity. While he was by no means impervious to what he called 'the insane irritations of Chinese travel', he could also write, without a trace of complacence: 'I do not find that mere discomfort catches the memory or even makes a good thing to describe . . . '[58]

'But a touch of drama is the proper thing about travel, until you have been travelling off and on for two or three months,' Empson conceded in 1937.[59] He felt proud of making it back to Changsha alone, for he quite justifiably sensed that I. A. Richards had begun to regard him as 'a dreamy and incompetent traveller'.[60] In fact, he had taken good note of all the snags and opportunities of their trip together, and he was just as alert to the interpersonal and international tensions of the party. Though always loath to make a fuss about his own well-being, he was to observe with winsome self-awareness later in the year that 'anybody begins to attend to the external world when things get noticeably difficult'.[61]

The move back to Changsha brought him much closer to the havoc wrought by the Japanese invasion of northern China and its brutally expert thrust through the eastern seaboard. In the weeks immediately after 7 July the Japanese had worked with almost textbook efficiency, encountering only a poorly organized resistance as its land forces attained their military objectives and won control of towns, railways, and highways; and their aircraft held sway in the sky. Nonetheless, on 13 August, just over a month after the outbreak of hostilities, Chiang Kai-shek had determined to hold Shanghai and the valley of the lower Yangtze, though the bloody effort was ultimately in vain. As Theodore H. White and Annalee Jacoby reported in *Thunder out of China* (1946), 'The resistance at Shanghai was futile in a military sense; in a political sense it was one of the great demonstrations of the war. It astounded the most world-weary of old China hands, and it proved beyond further question in the record of history how much suffering and heroism the Chinese people could display in the face of hopeless odds. The demonstration at Shanghai was even more valuable internally. The tale of the battle, carried into the interior by word of mouth, kindled a spreading bonfire of patriotic fervor. The line at the Yangtze gave time to mobilize the nation.'[62]

Throughout the following weeks vast numbers of people from the eastern seaboard hastily abandoned their occupied homelands and migrated inland. Wherever possible, factories and industrial plants were transported in what became one of the most amazing evacuations of modern times. Empson recalled seeing 'a twenty ton boiler as big as two cottages being pulled along an unmetalled dusty road by hand with a winch. They fix the winch fifty yards ahead and twenty coolies pull with ropes on the purchase they get from that. And they sing all the time mind you for the rhythm to pull together. And that boiler's going 500 miles. And when you come back maybe three days later in your car after fixing up your bit of business hundreds of miles off there the beastly thing still is, and they're still singing, only to be sure when you come to think of it, it's done six miles or so. Well, that's all right, it's working to time, two miles a day; it'll be ready for production well within a year. Nothing's impossible if you keep on at it. This boiler I'm thinking about has been in full operation for six months now.' All the same, as White and Jacoby reported, 'China salvaged less than 10 per cent of her textile capacity, with perhaps 40 per cent of her machine shops and heavy industry, but she saved more than 80 per cent of her eleven obsolescent arsenals. This meant that the Chinese would be threadbare during the following years, but that the army's minimum needs might be met.'[63] And for all the hundreds of thousands of people who managed to slip the net and join the exodus, millions more were doomed to spend the next eight years contained by the occupation.

The Japanese nurtured a particular loathing for the great universities of northern China, which had long and actively denounced their territorial annexations and corrupt dominance; and in the first fierce wave of the war the invaders took their revenge, especially against Tsinghua University (Peking), which had been heavily financed by the Americans. 'They smashed its laboratories or removed its equipment to Japan and used the student gymnasium to stable Japanese horses,' White and Jacoby noted.[64] During the course of the war, in fact, Tsinghua's buildings were used variously as hospital, bar, and brothel.[65] At the end of July 1937, the first month of the war, Nankai University in Tientsin was almost completely destroyed by targeted bombing followed by point-blank artillery fire. 'In the basement of Peking University, the seat of China's intellectual resistance, Japanese special police set up examination headquarters for their political and military inquisition.' Altogether, ninety-one colleges and universities were either destroyed or forced to shut down by the end of the first year of the war. While the Japanese swiftly overran or smashed the fabric and facilities of the universities, however, they could not contain their human resources; and in a very short while considerable numbers of staff and students joined the hegira out of the occupied territories. In all, no fewer than fifty-two educational institutions fled to the interior; twenty-five others took refuge in the foreign concessions or Hong Kong. 'The enemy can destroy the body of my Nankai,' said Chancellor Chang Po-ling; 'he cannot destroy its soul.'

'No aspect of this western trek has been more significant and indeed epic than the reconstitution, under extremely difficult conditions, in Szechwan and Yunnan of the Universities which the Japanese had deliberately destroyed in the East,' wrote Professor P. M. Roxby (an authority on the Far East) in 1942. 'They were a principal target of enemy attack because they were centres of the intellectual leadership and cultural movements which had played so notable a part in the renascence of China.'[66]

Peking National University and Tsinghua University, together with Nankai University, reconvened for the start of the autumn term on 1 November; once in Changsha, they were amalgamated under the title of the Temporary University (*Chang-sha lin-shih ta-hsueh*, or *Linta* for short). As Empson reported, 'people got there across the vague Japanese lines with the clothes they stood up in and maybe some lecture notes; a fairly dangerous business, and you certainly couldn't take a library. It is curious to think of Oxford and Cambridge arriving together in Barrow under those conditions, and not quarrelling too much to combine.'[67]

But a drastic shortage of living space in the city necessitated a dispersal of the assembled body. Members of the School of Arts were taken by bus on a one-day journey south to the market town of Hengshan at the foot of the Heng Mountains, which make up an unbroken chain of seventy-two

peaks. A few miles beyond Hengshan, they arrived at the simple village of
Nan-Yueh (Nanyu), on the beautiful lower slopes of the Sacred Mountain
called Tu Yun Feng: it was in fact the very mountain that Empson had
climbed with the Richardses just a few weeks earlier. (Chinese names are
so confusing that Empson never quite learned to distinguish between town
and mountain: his celebratory poem 'Autumn on Nan-Yueh' should
strictly speaking be entitled 'Autumn at Nan-Yueh' or 'Autumn on Tu
Yun Feng'.)

Rosalie Chou—better known as the writer and novelist Han Suyin—
who had to fall in with another wave of refugees that came to lodge for a
while at Nan-Yueh just a year later, wrote in a letter on 28 October 1938
that the countryside was 'wonderful'; and in *Birdless Summer*, the third
volume of her wonderful autobiography, she evoked the village in these
terms:

The great north-to-south Imperial highway paved with enormous blocks of
limestone runs through it, for Nanyu was a fair centre on the road from Canton
in the south to the Yangtze River cities—a road used by cavalrymen of the
dynasties and the chariots of officials for centuries—and a place of pilgrimage.
The beautiful Sung dynasty bridge which spanned the lovely river, with its
tributary torrents leaping from the mountains, had seen the tribute of salt and
grain pass over it, and silk for the Imperial Courts in Peking from the fertile
provinces of central China, and fighting men and refugees had walked it many
times. It had served the cohorts of the peasant uprisings in Taiping days, those
peasant fighters marching up the road through Nanyu to Changsha and onwards
to take Wuhan, a century ago.[68]

In November 1937 the School of Arts of the Temporary University took
up its temporary residence in the simple buildings of a missionary Bible
School, which Empson aptly described as a kind of 'fundamentalist
Simla'.[69] If the quarters were cramped and unsophisticated, the mountain
scenery provided a spectacularly picturesque compensation. Nearby was
Bai Long Tan ('White Dragon Pool'), a lake with an attractive waterfall,
and another beauty spot called Shui Lian Tong ('Water-Curtained Cave');
and for more strenuous exercise the Zen Buddhist temple at the summit of
the sacred mountain could be reached over a distance of about 12 miles.
Empson observed, 'The rule for a sacred mountain is that (first) it must be
isolated so that people from all round can see the home town (second) that
it must do the queer trick of seeming much bigger than it is...Sure
enough, it gave me real delight, when I first trotted over this mountain,
to find that I could get almost immediately over the shoulder into the next

of the enormous gorges. The heart of magic is the sense of power; and any tolerable walker gets a sense of power here . . . ' He found the landscape entrancing, 'airy and cosy, and the country . . . more beautiful every time you looked out of the window. The fog which envelops Hunan in the winter was to us merely a change in the view, and sometimes it was like the more improbable effects of Chinese painting, for instance the fog which is a mere flat white band with a round end, in the middle distance . . . '.[70]

Every year thousands of pilgrims climbed the Holy Mountain, but many of them were so distressingly deformed that they needed to be carried up in baskets. If healthy walkers declined to give them alms, they would yell lusty criticisms from one basket to another: 'the impossible corpses are bursting with vitality,' Empson candidly observed,[71] 'with the entire and indestructible gaiety of the Chinese people.' 'The holy mountain where I live,' he wrote in 'Autumn on Nan-Yueh',

> . . . has deformities to give
> You dreams by all its paths and gates.
> They may be dreamless. It is odd
> To hear them yell out jokes and hates
> And pass the pilgrims through a sieve,
> Brought there in baskets or in crates.
> The pilgrims fly because they plod.

'I have flown here, part of the way,' he appropriately remarks earlier in the poem, meaning that he has flown by aeroplane part of the way from Kunming to Changsha; now, along with millions of the Chinese, he was flying—fleeing—from the Japanese enemy, though pausing to reflect that the pilgrims on the holy mountain intimated a different kind of mortal refuge:

> We do not fly when we are clay.
> We hope to fly when we are dust.

Even old women with bound feet and with babies on their backs somehow got up the mountain in a single day. Empson felt sick at the sight of their tortured feet, and totally amazed at their energy and determination. Yet fashions that abused women were not confined to the Far East, he soberly reminded himself: his own mother in her stays could never have managed the mountain. But in spite of coming across so many disturbing sights he considered the trek to the head of the holy path amply rewarded by the 'genuine civilisation' of the Buddhist monastery, where he fancied that the splendidly eloquent 'topmost abbot' (as he calls him in the poem) might well have 'passed Greats'. Han Suyin was to share Empson's sense of exaltation on the mountain, as she recalled in *Birdless Summer*. 'Large Buddhist temples, red-walled, golden-roofed, of graceful proportions, surrounded by centennial trees, glowed purple and amber, and their magnificence compared to the diminutive and poor village of Nanyu was a perpetual astonishment.'

Many of Empson's colleagues, often educated overseas, were so accustomed to urban amenities that their first real experience of rural life hit them with all the shock of the new. Empson regarded their unwonted and assuredly arduous contact with the countryside as 'an obviously healthy change.' 'I remember,' he was to write more than two years later, 'when . . . the bus was waiting for the petrol ferry to come chugging slowly over one of the broad rivers, one of the colleagues said, "fancy finding this in the Interior." That was early in the great trek; he was not yet used to the idea that there were petrol ferries for another thousand miles westward.'[72] Empson made such a comment without feeling any sense of superiority towards his colleagues, for he experienced just as many difficulties in adjusting to the brave new world. Indeed, as the only European on the mountain, he had to cope with enormous cultural challenges, not the least being his inability to communicate with anybody who could not speak English.

Happily he shared a room with one of China's foremost philosophers, Chin Yue Lin (Jin Yuelin), who, like the large majority of the faculty, had sometime studied in America and England: they enjoyed sitting together on the college balcony and swapping anecdotes about Wittgenstein.[73] But even the pet name of 'Lao Chin' ('Old Chin') goaded Empson with the knowledge that he could not come to terms with learning the Chinese language. 'The evil genius of the Wade system is a fantastic extra barrier between China and Europe,' he lamented. ' "Ao" is pronounced OW, and Taoism is pronounced DOWISM, but it is no use my writing any English letters to give the sound of "loud" without "d", because there are none. The second name is pronounced GIN, but people with better ears than mine can hear an obscure difference from gin, and you are contemptible if you can't.'[74] On another page of his typewritten notes he drew this fragile lesson from the problem: 'To be sure my ignorance of Chinese (which I have studied, so like a deaf old lady I have embarrassing gaps of intelligence and am not the fool I choose to look) is a means of protection. But I hope I am not yet so frightened as to put down mere laziness (a proud thing) to fear.' And almost a year later he reiterated, 'I think I am an awful fool not to learn a usable amount of Chinese, but the truth is that I can't get interested in the language; it seems such a bad one.'[75] Likewise, since he claimed never to form visual images when reading or thinking, the Chinese written character must have struck him as just as much of a dead-letter deterrent.

For his part, Professor Chin was perhaps equally perturbed by Empson's shameless but seemingly comfortable indifference to washing either himself or his clothing. 'We had to force him to wash,' he recalled for me. He thought Empson otherwise a delightful companion, with 'very good spirit', but preoccupied to the point of eccentricity. For instance, one day on arriving in the dining-room Empson suddenly noticed an asymmetry about his person: he found that he was wearing only one slipper, and yet rather than go and fetch the other from the dormitory he simply discarded the one he had put on.[76]

Food seemed to pose another small problem, at least in the beginning. Like many foreigners Empson claimed that he liked Chinese food, but he soon learned to express himself more cautiously. His colleagues could not help laughing at him when the college cook produced virtually inedible food, whereupon he resolved to say that he always enjoyed *good* Chinese food (though he would later boast about being 'the only man on the Peita staff who enjoyed low-class Chinese food').[77] His first experience of attending a university feast was just as disconcerting. Oddly enough, he was in any case late for the meal, because at the last minute he had decided to chance his first bath on the mountain. His own notes take up the story: 'The start was depressing to a hungry man, as would hors d'oeuvres if you had no security about what was coming; four dishes all fine and fantastic flavours, but none eatable in bulk; however as the food kept rolling in and [I] got down the Tiger Bone it became clear that this feast was all right. It was very fine indeed; I hope it goes on the messbill and isn't somebody's ruinous and unthanked gift.' (In the notes to 'Autumn on Nan-Yueh' he explained that he found Tiger Bone 'a good drink to sit over when drowned in hot water. The tiger bones in it are supposed to make you brave.' The ambiguity in that phrasing allows for the possibility that he had drunk too much of the wine—drowned in his own hot bath—even before appearing for the meal.) At a certain point he felt he had eaten quite enough and looked forward to some kind of savoury or cheese; but 'an incalculable succession of things [kept] rolling in at random times'. The courses included scrambled eggs with cress ('more or less'), and then a chicken, followed by 'a fantastic soup which they say is from a sea medusa, however it got up the mountain, which George [Yeh] praises for its rarity'. Later still came stewed cabbage. ' "That's much better," says George, meaning better than the medusa, and sets to firmly on the cabbage. This baffles me entirely, because I could understand a complete indifference to order of dishes, but he obviously means the cabbages are better at this stage of the meal.' Unlike the Imperial Palace in Peking, he judged, the meal seemed deficient in architecture.

All the same, as he remembered many years later, he had already learned what he called an 'important fact about Chinese food' while travelling in the Vice-Minister's motorcade through south-west China:

> They have a delicious citron fruit there called pumelo, a parent of the grape-fruit I was told, like an orange but with a very thick pulpy white rind just under the skin. We were enjoying these in the heat and throwing the skin onto the road from the motor-cars, and I noticed a wrinkled old hag who was picking it all up. What a horrible thing it is, I felt for a moment, to close one's eyes to such desperate misery as must be going on all around us. But that same evening, when we were feasted as usual at a sprawling ramshackle hotel, the rind of the pumelo was served, reduced to human food in some magical way with a thick encouraging sauce, and it was agreed to be one of the best things we were given. The old woman did not collect this stuff because she was starving, but because it was a delicacy which somebody in her house knew how to cook. The peasantry in China expect to eat well, when things are normal, and hold varying opinions about how to do it. I must not be ignorantly cheerful; someone wrote that there has been a famine in one province or another of China every ten years since the time of Confucius; but in your own province this would only work out as once in every two or three generations. In between whiles there has long been a broad-based satisfaction about food, not easy to match elsewhere in Asia, or indeed in the whole human story.[78]

(Empson would experience something a bit closer to famine at first hand over a decade later, in the year after the Communist Liberation of Peking.)

While in Nan-Yueh he also found himself disagreeing with his colleagues on the question of how to make good tea. 'Very odd that the Chinese don't understand tea; they tell me I don't. Red tea has to have boiling water, but ordinary green tea doesn't need it; in fact some of the Japanese green teas are spoiled if you make them with boiling water. But my colleagues will make red tea out of Thermos flasks, which is beastly, and don't like green tea at all.' Their mistake, he concluded with a good-humoured lack of conviction, 'is the perpetual one of idealism: they allow the notion of a very perfect flavour of green tea to force on them a very actively nasty flavour of dark red tea. But you may prefer to believe they are right in telling me I have no taste for tea.'

Autumn and winter brought on cold, wet weather for which the Bible School had not been designed: the buildings had no fireplaces or chimneys—'a curious thing,' as Empson remarked. Staff and students tried to keep warm by burning charcoal on iron plates, an activity so perilous that at least four students suffered from carbon monoxide poisoning—'it turns the blood cherry pink,' Empson observed with wincingly scientific detachment[79]—and had to be revived with artificial respiration. At the very end of his stay on the mountain Empson acquired the luxury of a single room, but it made him all the more apprehensive about the very real danger of asphyxiating himself with no one at hand to pump his chest. He adopted Chinese padded clothing but found that it made him sweat heavily during any sort of exercise, even typing or eager talking. The weight of clothing slowed him down, and the overall effect led him to think that he had discovered a partial if still puzzling insight into the Chinese mentality:

Life inside a bundle, cuddling the fingers, has to be conducted below what I consider par; you aim at keeping passive; the well-known inscrutable calm of the East begins to crop up. The wisdom of making few the desires becomes particularly obvious; you eat less, sleep less, and get less done. One might count it as one of the forces against individualism, because no man feels unique while he is just ticking over. The only thing that doesn't seem to fit this theory is the word 'bombast', which is easy here to explain on the blackboard; the Elizabethans called padded blank verse lines after their padded clothes, such as we all wear here, and the Elizabethans were about as rowdy, individualistic, and above par as any people you could name.

With an eye on the tormented politics of the country, and its unprecedented uprush of nationalistic sentiment, he judged too that even Ralph Waldo Emerson's message to New England offered a real parallel to the Chinese experience, since it paradoxically spoke of self-denial: 'the Boston Brahmins were really brahmin and (as they kept saying) transcendental in the sense that they felt a strong pull towards All is One, the kind of mysticism that breaks down the individual; you get it in all the new countries that felt they needed a natural unity, Germany Italy and America.'

About 1,500 students had arrived in Changsha at the start of the academic year, but nearly 500 of them subsequently left, the majority to join the forces of Mao Tse-tung or to attend a course in wartime education and Marxist ideology at the Communist Resistance University in Yenan, and the remainder to enlist in the war area service corps attached to the Nationalist Army. Since the northern universities had a long tradition of anti-Japanese agitation, the students enrolled at the Temporary University naturally found themselves grimly divided between manifesting

their patriotism and taking a pride in their studies. General Chang Chih-
chung, Governor of Hunan, upbraided the students in a visiting lecture:
'During this national crisis what the hell are you young people doing lying
around here instead of going to the front?'[80] As Empson reported, groups
of students would periodically solicit a few Shanghai dollars from their
professors in order to finance the trip to the Communist base in Yenan. At
least one specialist teacher, a neurologist, likewise set off to join the Red
Army, but he apparently failed to get there and returned to the university
looking depressed though still determined. On the other hand, another
local general, Chen Cheng, successfully exhorted the students to go on
with their studies; they were national treasures, he argued, and their
destiny was to become the leaders of a recovered China.

Nonetheless, for the large number of students who did stay with the
university, life was by no means easy. Perhaps the most crucial difficulty
was that the School of Arts had practically no books for them to study.
'The lectures went on sturdily from memory,' as Empson recorded with
frank pride.[81] 'And it is a good joke, as far as it goes, to see the professors
lecturing from memory. I know enough verse by heart, but I can't do
prose.' These verses from 'Autumn on Nan-Yueh', which begin by pun-
ning on an epigraph taken from Yeats, gaily celebrate the trials of the
teaching:

> 'The soul remembering' is just
> What we professors have to do.
>
> .   .   .   .   .
>
> The abandoned libraries entomb
> What all the lectures still go through.
>
> .   .   .   .   .
>
> And men get curiously non-plussed
> Searching the memory for a clue.
>
> .   .   .   .   .
>
> Let textual variants be discussed;
> We teach a poem as it grew.
>
> Remembering prose is quite a trouble
>   But of Mrs. Woolf one tatter
> Many years have failed to smother.
>   As a piece of classroom patter
> It would not repay me double.

The students were in fact staggered by his ability to reproduce on his
typewriter enormous quantities of poetry, including Shakespeare and

Milton, and it is certainly true that he had an extraordinary facility for remembering lyric poetry in particular. His feats of memorial reconstruction are themselves remembered to this day; they have become part of the folklore of the refugee universities. Empson modestly recalled in his Inaugural Lecture at Sheffield University in 1953, 'It didn't upset the Chinese lecturer as much as it would most, because they have a long tradition of knowing a standard text by heart. I was well thought of because I could type out from memory a course of reading in English poetry, but this was praised more because it was good going for a foreigner than because it would have been remarkable for a Chinese. Actually we did have an anthology of prose essays which could be typed out for them to do their Composition Class with [the anthology included essays by Lytton Strachey, Aldous Huxley, Virginia Woolf, and T. S. Eliot] . . . but apart from that there were really hardly any books.'[82] And in the same lecture he graciously turned his own high capacity into a tribute to his students and colleagues: 'I thought the results we were getting by this method were strikingly good. No doubt the chief reason was that the standard of the students was very high; I was seeing the last of the great days of the effort of China to digest the achievements of Europe, when a well educated Chinese was about the best educated man in Europe. My colleagues habitually talked to each other in a jumble of three or four languages, without affectation, merely for convenience, using rather more English if they remembered I was listening; and of course a thorough grounding in Chinese literature would be taken for granted.'[83]

So much is true; but as so often the legend has tended to outrun even the remarkable facts, though it should also be said that nobody has been guilty of deliberate exaggeration. Some of his former students (many of whom would become distinguished professors in their own right) recalled for example that Empson typed out the whole of *Othello* from memory;[84] whereas his own contemporary jottings honestly disclose the truth of the matter: 'A charitable man lent me a blinding 1850 complete Shakespeare, which makes me safe for one course. It turned out to have a loose flyleaf in it with autographs of both Swift and Pope, rather stirring on the sacred mountain.'[85] To cite such an admission is not to minimize his achievement, only to keep it in proportion; and it is certain that Empson never claimed for himself any more than he achieved. (He felt a warm sense of sympathy and relief when George Yeh, who had lectured on the History of Criticism for many years, anxiously asked him what Aristotle could have meant by *mimesis*. 'I only knew he said music was an imitation of nature, and that nobody knew what Greek music was; but we agreed that, if Greek music was anything like either Chinese or European music, then Aristotle couldn't have meant anything sensible by imitation of nature. And there the matter rests.')

Being obliged to reconstruct a work of literature from memory has 'a great effect,' Empson believed, 'in forcing you to consider what really matters, or what you already do know if you think, or what you want to get to know when you can.' It is well known too that he customarily quoted poetry from memory when writing his criticism, a procedure which might suggest either that he felt indifferent to details of phraseology and syntax or—what is much more likely—that in every sense he had taken the poetry to heart. All the available evidence points to the latter case. On Christmas Eve, for example, when Professor Chin Yue Lin spontaneously sang a lovely German carol, Empson felt genuinely annoyed with himself for not being able to reproduce all the words of 'Venite Adoramus'. 'We ought to be taught things by heart as children much more than we are,' he wrote the very next day (Christmas Day, which was not celebrated on the Sacred Mountain); 'the craving for quantity misleads all educators paid by result, and if you can select the right poem the other poems in the same style will be picked up as obvious; but then maybe nobody can do the selection.'[86]

In class, as he recorded soon afterwards, he decided to introduce his students to the poetry of A. E. Housman, 'because the music and structure are obviously good, and the meaning looks so plain, and is really so subtle, that people cheerfully read into it what they feel themselves. Besides, I knew a good deal of him by heart.' However, unlike in Japan, where his students had responded with awful eagerness to Housman's fatalistic sentiments, the Chinese students disdained them. Their country was fighting for its life, not indulging in any sort of death wish, and the students desired nothing so much as national liberation and peace:

the damp gush of Eastern quietism that he evoked from his sympathisers in essays began to tease my nerves, and I moved over to a glum and theoretical assault on the Metaphysicals, which lightened the weight of typing by removing most of the class. Housman's taste for war as the most dignified form of suicide, with which Japan had been so perfectly at home, was received in China with really surprising blankness; I knew they wouldn't agree with it, but no amount of explaining could make them mention it in essays without being absurd. A very fine puzzle occurred over

> Far the calling bugles hollo;
> High the screaming fife replies;
> Gay the files of scarlet follow;
> Woman bore me, I will rise.

A textual emendation, 'Woman bores me' (or 'Women bore me') was felt to be the only rational way to explain how the line occurred.

Time and time again, in fact, he realized that any conclusions he may have drawn about the Japanese mentality would not apply easily in China. Among his most startling discoveries was what he described as the students'

taste for solemn moralising on what seems to us a wholly immoral basis. The best case of this was a man writing about the character of Desdemona, who I thought smashed, quite involuntarily, the whole line of moral reflection into which the great [A. C.] Bradley was too often tempted. 'Her too mild temper is the reason for her death, and her openmindedness, frankness, and too great generosity are the things inviting criticism, especially for Iago.' This is no accident; a page or two later: 'And her treatment of Cassio is too generous to escape the critical eye of Iago'. Almost thou persuadest me to be a Christian; it is not at all silly (you don't, of course, know how to run your life competently unless you know how to shield yourself from Iago), and it belongs to a civilisation quite separate from our own.[87]

It is characteristic of Empson's breadth of mind that he regarded his student's apparent impatience with Desdemona, his lack of sympathetic imagination, not as an untenable position but as a valid interpretation drawn on a different cultural bank. 'It is what the missionaries used to call the eerie absence of the sense of sin,' he commented elsewhere.[88]

The same baffling spirit [he went on in the same place] appears in the man who said that A. E. Housman 'is neither optimistic nor pessimistic, but rather self-complacent', and went on to explain that all the best poets of China had been self-complacent. It is very queer to think of all that hideous self-contempt and self-mortification [in Housman's poetry] working round to the same literary effect as a Chinese poet who had learned how to be self-complacent. Heaven knows a mere howler is a bore; I only quote him because I think he said something true; it is neither a mistake in language nor a failure in criticism.[89]

As a matter of principle, Empson worked even in his language teaching not simply to correct the grammatical errors of his students but to reflect upon their modes of expression, in case they spoke for unacknowledged assumptions—for possibly unconscious but nonetheless real attitudes. A consequential practice is fully evident in his investigations into the ambiguities of the language of literature, as in this summary explanation of what he called 'the moral' behind his theory of complex words: 'a developing society decides practical questions more by the way it interprets words it thinks obvious and traditional than by its official statements of

current dogma.' After a class on ballads, for example, one student wrote in
an essay that 'The ballad should be as simple and vulgar as possible', a
statement which caused Empson to reflect: 'Heaven knows what these
snob words mean when picked up, but I believe that purely verbal errors
masquerading as errors of taste are much rarer than you think.' That
vexed but decisive comment from his contemporary notes in fact holds the
key to the burden of *The Structure of Complex Words* (1951). Two years later, in
a lecture on 'Basic and Communication', he cited the student's sentence as
an apt example of the kind of linguistic 'trick' that yields dividends to close
analysis:

Should here gives an idea that all ballads have to be the same sort of thing—
because it is bad not to be normal. But a thing may be good verse though it is not
quite a ballad: a man writing a ballad is not attempting to do The Normal Ballad.
The language of right and wrong has no place here; in fact there is not even any
question of attempting a ballad (in the chief sense of the word) because the true
ballads are part of history and come from a society very different from ours. But
that is not very important; the humour of this statement is in 'vulgar'. It is a talking
word. It says that poor men who have no education have low tastes. Now this may
be true in general, but poor men certainly kept the beautiful ballads in existence
and very possibly made them. The effect of the word here is to say that the writer
is very much disgusted by ballads, but not ready to say so clearly. This was
probably part of the man's feeling, but he had no idea that he was letting it out
so violently. I take this example because there is a word in the [Basic English] list
with the same trick, nearly the only word in it that is a loud talker. 'Common' is
'frequent or general' and 'of low taste', and would give the same effect here as
'vulgar'. So it is not a completely safe word, though one of very wide use. What the
writer here had in mind was 'good ballads have an attraction for men without
special education' or 'education in other sorts of verse'. But he had other things in
mind as well, and one was that ballads are not a very high sort of verse. It was
because of a good knowledge of the word 'vulgar', or at least a bit of knowledge
about it that would be a help in his reading, that he had a feeling that it would do
well here. He was only a bad judge of the forces at work; the force here is strong
enough for the complete destruction of the quiet approval he was giving to ballads
in the rest of his paper.[90]

While in Japan he had observed from the responses of his students that
the word 'quite' (which figures in the 'operative' group of the Basic English
list of 850 words) can play similar tricks of implication. '*Quite* is "completely, but without interest", so that it goes wrong if you are talking
warmly; "the death of King Lear is quite tragic" says you are not much
interested in the play.'

All unknowingly, therefore, his students both in Japan and in China continually helped him to question his own moral preconceptions, which ultimately derived from the received wisdom of Western liberalism, as well as his critical perceptions; and they crucially helped to validate his analysis of what he called 'compacted doctrines' in *The Structure of Complex Words*— since many of the essays incorporated in that book, including 'Sense in Measure for Measure' and 'Sense in the Prelude', were first drafted in China. In 'Feelings in Words' (1936), for instance, he was directly prompted by the essays of his Japanese students to take the example of 'quite' as a fascinating example of 'some words which are concerned to fix (and if possible transmit) a mere state of feeling, without directly naming it, and without connecting this Feeling to their Sense; nor are they unstable words.' Quite obviously, he believed, the word 'quite' offered 'a real case . . . for talking about the Emotive part of a word as something flatly detached from its sense'; and after exploring the emotive shifts of the word he drew the conclusion 'that to explain the word you want a Sense and an Emotion, only one, and that these are the basis for its whole performance of moods. I do not pretend to explain why partial contradiction of the emotion did in fact, at a certain date, resolve itself so firmly into the cosy mood, or (probably the same question) what keeps an unsupported emotion alive in this charming and very English word.'[91] Whilst he invariably discouraged his students from reading his own published criticism—he modestly thought his books 'would only worry and distract them'—he readily acknowledged that '*They* have sometimes taught *me* something theoretical, or so I thought, when I had to consider why they found something difficult to learn . . .'.

The sojourn at Nan-Yueh lasted just over two months, from November 1937 till February the following year. Although some of the faculty had found it far too exacting to teach from memory, Empson believed he had gained enormously from the experience—his students felt stimulated by his professionalism, his mental alertness, and his gift for treating them as intellectual equals—as well as in developing a sense of solidarity with his colleagues; and he would always think of the mountain as his ideal of the academic community. Terribly isolated and poorly supplied with resources, the whole faculty of scholar-gypsies had developed an extraordinary sense of purpose. Though refugees in status, they had been able to define their wartime role as maintaining an intellectual and civil leadership. As the philosopher Feng Youlan (1895–1990) was later to write,

We were sufferers of the same fate met by the Southern Song dynasty, that of being driven southward by a foreign army. Yet we lived in a wonderful society of philosophers, writers, and scholars, all in one building. It was this combination of the historical moment, the geographical location, and the human gathering that made the occasion so exceptionally stimulating and inspiring.[92]

'So far I seem to have forgot | About the men who really soar,' Empson wrote about the Chinese politicians and generals in 'Autumn on Nan-Yueh'; and yet, he protested,

> We think about them quite a bit;
>   Elsewhere there's reason to think more.
> With Ministers upon the spot
>   (Driven a long way from the War)
> And training camps, the place is fit
>   For bombs . . .
>
> Politics are what verse should
>   Not fly from, or it goes all wrong.
> I feel the force of that all right,
>   And I had speeches they were song.
> But really, does it do much good
>   To put into verse however strong
> The welter of a doubt at night
>   At home, in which I too belong? . . .
>
> What are these things I do not face,
>   The reasons for entire despair,
> Trenching the map into the lines
>   That prove no building can be square?
> Not nationalism nor yet race
>   Poisons the mind, poisons the air,
> Excuses, consequences, signs,
>   But not the large thing that is there.

Shanghai fell in November, with barbaric slaughter and molestation; and then on 13 December, Nanjing, so that Chiang Kai-shek had to retreat deep inland and eventually re-establish his government at Chungking on the sheer cliffs of the upper Yangtze. On the Sacred Mountain, the refugee university anxiously followed the progress of events in the major arena; fears and tensions were inescapable, despite the serenity of the locale.

In the evening of Christmas Day 1937, after giving a very good lecture on *Othello* ('Othello was an intolerable fool,' he mused to himself in his notes; and again, 'Othello is the only man in Shakespeare who talks like Milton, and Iago the only man who talks like Pope, and real people have no business to do either')—a lecture that appeared to be well received[93]—Empson suffered what he called 'an attack of neurotic fear'. He had experienced nothing quite so dreadful since his first year in Tokyo in 1931–2. 'Really it is only the art of writing that makes me think at all,' he wrote in another context;[94] and even on this occasion he tried to cope with his sudden and uncontrollable bout of gross anxiety by writing down a possible explanation. 'Unlike any fixed university lecturer, who has the same kind of attitude to students as the American of the South to negroes, the recently imported lecturer has a desire to please; an indecent thing, which he must avoid confessing at random. I am much more vain of my powers as a lecturer than of my printed stuff, criticism and poetry; of course I would be appalled at having the lecture printed, and make much more work about anything printed, and all that; but still there was nothing to excite anxiety neurosis about the success of the morning's lecture.' Fundamentally a nervous if stubborn man, he found he could usually quell his inhibitions either in writing (where intensity of interest overrode nervous anxiety) or by means of alcohol. On this occasion he downed a good deal of Tiger Bone, but found it 'curiously bad at melting' the nerves. In fact, the most probable cause of his anxiety attack was not the inadequacy of his teaching but a deep sense of insecurity about his personal circumstances—which he would normally overcome by working hard and by hectic conviviality— compounded by the menace of the war. In his self-exploratory notes he wrote, 'the whole trouble with neurotic fear is that it isn't fear of anything you can tell yourself about. In myself it seems to appear in a reasonable manner, when I have a long prospect before me of a poor kind of life, but you can't make it into straightforward fear of that, or you would give yourself promises to take care about that, and feel better.' Whatever the cause this time, however, he could not solve it in terms of 'taking care' of his prospects, for he was in no position to control his future in wartime China.

In any event, the Japanese forward line had encroached upon Hunan, and bombs started to fall on Changsha. The university had to evacuate the area and move even further south, to somewhere in the province of Yunnan, which Empson had visited the year before with the Richardses. 'The whole thing is on a hearty scale,' Empson wrote in a draft 'Letter from China', 'and comes just as the Japanese give one of their chivalrous announcements that they mean to give the railway a thorough bombing. I live very much out of the world here, and haven't seen the chancellor since his interview with Chiang Kai Shek about the move, and have very little gossip. It is a striking thing that the government would sooner pay for the journey round by sea than lend lorries for it across China, but we would certainly need a lot of lorries, or call them buses.'

If at that moment he considered any alternative course of action for himself, such as the chance of catching a boat straight home from Hong Kong, he never mentioned it. He had decided to commit himself to the fortunes of the university for at least another year; and there can be no doubt that in doing so he showed a lot of pluck—a jolly term he himself often used about other people and even places (he later used it ironically when referring to the 'Plucky Little Japs'). His pluck is manifest in these lines from 'Autumn on Nan-Yueh':

> The 'News', the conferences that leer,
> The creeping fog, the civil traps,
>   These are what force you into fear.
> Besides, you aren't quite good for nowt
>   Or clinging wholly as a burr
> Replacing men who must get out,
>   Nor is it shameful to aver
> A vague desire to be about
>   Where the important things occur...

The final stanza of the poem is an equally brave and poignant elegy on the sadly forsaken life of the Sacred Mountain:

> I said I wouldn't fly again
>   For quite a bit. I did not know.
> Even in breathing tempest-tossed,
>   Scattering to winnow and to sow,
> With convolutions for a brain,
>   Man moves, and we have got to go.
> Claiming no heavy personal cost
>   I feel the poem would be slow
> Furtively finished on the plain.
>   We have had the autumn here. But oh
> That lovely balcony is lost
>   Just as the mountains take the snow.
> The soldiers will come here and train.
>   The streams will chatter as they flow.

He set off southward by the beginning of March, proposing to stay for a while with a friend named Norman France ('very good company') whom he must have known at Cambridge and who lectured at Hong Kong University. His own university forwarding address was yet unknown.

As he was leaving the sacred mountain he noticed that some workmen were constructing a metalled road up to the Bible College. People whispered that the Generalissimo himself was coming to Nan-Yueh. It was not in fact until eight months later, in October 1938, that Chiang Kai-shek abandoned Wuhan to the Japanese and did indeed assemble his ministers and generals for a conference at Nan-Yueh. There, after days of deliberation, he devised his infamous 'scorched earth' policy, with the slogan of trading space for time: it meant that the Chinese Communist forces, his nominal allies, would have to fight the war of resistance by themselves. From the end of 1938 until 1945 Chiang would wage a largely phoney war against the declared enemy while actively assailing what he perceived as the internal curse of the Red menace.

On 12 November, Chiang burned the city of Changsha, supposedly as part of his 'scorched earth' policy but more probably, as Han Suyin observed,

because there was an active communist underground in the city; it was also rumoured that the secret police wanted to kill Chou Enlai, who was there at the time. The whole area was alive with clandestine guerrillas; Changsha had been the headquarters of the underground Communist Party for some years. And Mao Tsetung had trained a good many people there . . .

On November 13th, Chiang and his wife flew to the new bastion, Chungking, 'capital of Free China', together with the higher officials . . . [95]

Thus it followed, as Han Suyin further remarked, that by the end of 1938 'Yenan, the great Red Base' came to stand out as 'a shining beacon of fervour and patriotism, attracting students and intellectuals from all over China . . . If Chiang gave in to the Japanese, the prestige of Yenan would sweep the whole of China irresistibly.'[96]

The Japanese seized Nan-Yueh, the humble village that had become a towering symbol of Chinese intellectual resistance, in 1944.

'A fashion has already got about of saying that no work was done on Nanyueh,' Empson was to write in 1939. 'We just ticked over. I resent this very much.'[97] Certainly he and his colleagues had kept up their teaching to the very best of their abilities; and somehow they were able to produce a remarkable amount of scholarly writing. Empson continued to draft the essays that would eventually become *The Structure of Complex Words*; Chin Yue Lin completed his book *On the Tao*; Feng Youlan, China's most celebrated neo-Confucian scholar, finished the *Xin Li Xue* ('The New Neo-Confucianism'); Tang Yongtong completed the first part of his *History of Chinese Buddhism*.[98] Other faculty members included the historian Wu Han, the poet Bian Zhilin, the legendary poet, artist, scholar, and political activist Wen Yiduo, who was to be murdered by the KMT in 1946, and the logical positivist Hong Qian (1909–92), who had studied at Berlin and Jena, and who had recently returned from eight years of graduate work at Vienna University, where he attended meetings of the Vienna Circle (in later years he would become China's most distinguished contemporary philosopher, directing the study of Western philosophy at Peking University, 1952–86, and the recipient of visiting fellowships at Oxford).[99]

Empson even managed while on the mountain to write a substantial amount of a novel, the title-piece of the posthumous collection *The Royal Beasts and Other Works* (1986).[100] Strictly speaking a fable, 'The Royal Beasts' actually supplies the imaginative link between his early interest in biological and anthropological science (including Darwinian evolutionism), as well as in versions of pastoral, and the challenges to Christian dogma he enunciated at length in *Milton's God* (1961). Begun in a provocative 'holiday' humour and drawing on many of Empson's religious and cultural preoccupations while in China, it tells how a group of newly discovered African mutants—rational creatures with the character of subhuman primates—cannily refuse to be classified as human beings. Empson's sympathetic and clever hero 'Wuzzoo' sets off a series of comic reactions which embarrass the cultural presuppositions of Western man. Firmly locating itself in the tradition of Jonathan Swift, Samuel Butler, Aldous Huxley, and T. F. Powys, the tale is rich in theological and sociological implication, and generously satirical.

It is not possible to determine exactly how long Empson worked on his only exercise in prose fiction, but the starting date is clear: he began it just a few days after arriving in China. Dorothea Richards wrote in her journal on 8 September 1937, under the heading 'SHANGHAI 50 MILES OUT' (that is, during their passage from Tientsin to Hong Kong): 'Bill started his Wuzzoo animal novel. Several amusing episodes—a love scene & an Archbishop's speech.'[101] (Sadly, the love scene has not survived.) On another page Mrs Richards even referred to Empson himself as 'Wuzzoo' (10 September). But he sketched the bulk of it on the sacred mountain; one of the manuscript pages is written on the back of a typescript draft of two stanzas of the poem 'Autumn on Nan-Yueh'.

'The Royal Beasts' is best described in the following undated and unposted letter that Empson addressed at the time to Solly (the future Lord) Zuckerman, who had recently published two authoritative studies of mammalian physiology and sociology, *The Social Life of Monkeys and Apes* (1932) and *Functional Affinities of Man, Monkeys, and Apes* (1933). (In view of the fact that Empson mistakes the spelling of the name Zuckerman, it is unlikely that he was writing with those books to hand, and in that event it is remarkable how closely he recalls the complex morphological problems he had to face in postulating his imagined race of Wurroos.)

Dear Dr Zuckermann,

I am starting to write a fantasy novel, about a Central African tribe which is not of human stock. It would be giving too much trouble to ask your advice, but I propose to put down the main points of the novel in a letter, and would be grateful if you feel interested enough to answer. Various Peking universities have had their arts departments moved onto a sacred mountain in Hunan, a rather isolated place, and it seems best to have a novel to write, now I have got there.

The boundary between a separatist Dominion and a British Crown Colony, in an inaccessible and mountainous part, has been taken over from a previous treaty with an African chief, and is therefore defined in terms of tribal areas not of territory. All land up to the last tribes south of the mountains belongs to the Dominion. Then a gold mine is discovered at the foot of the mountains in the territory of this new tribe. Britain has reached a condition where there is an urgent need for gold. The governor of the colony takes up the claim that these men do not constitute a tribe, and the case goes to the Lords. Britain I think wins the case, and then in a second case it is decided that the creatures are persons in the same sense as Joint Stock Companies, so that British Law applies to them. All the Christian sects demand to send missionaries, and the Japanese for purposes of cultural penetration claim that Buddhism is the only religion open to non-human species. The difficulty is to stop the novel with a good enough bang. I am rather afraid that they will all have to die of a plague of colds. A great deal of the stuff needs technical knowledge that I can't scratch together here.

About the creatures themselves. I want them attractive enough to excite sympathy and clever enough to stick to their case. They are well informed about the Dominion treatment of negroes and determined to keep out of it; they swear by their gods they are not men. (Rather tempting to make them swear they are parrots on totemistic grounds; business of hushing this up). They are covered with valuable fur, and to keep this off the market they demand the status of Royal Beasts, like sturgeon. They have a rigid breeding season with some kind of bodily change; a sexual skin is hardly pretty enough and apparently does not go with a breeding season. One could say they are a Lemuroid stock, but they have a broad nose and muzzle; all the lemuroids seem to have a rat expression which I don't want. Having a breeding season means that they have become rational without using Freudian machinery, interesting to try and work out. They rebuke mankind a good deal on this point. But they pick fur all the year round, have a craving for it. The hero is presented with a Persian cat and throws it out of the window, much shocked at being incited to an obscene perversion. They are incapable of interbreeding with man, at least such evidence as is timidly brought into court leads to that view, because it was acquired in a criminal manner, so it cannot be a strong argument. However their blood can't be transfused with any human group, and they have long furry tails. I don't think there would be much difficulty in getting a united front of scientific experts in court to say they weren't men, though some experts would say they were a closely allied species. You might easily get the law refusing to concern itself with the scientific definition, though, and saying that a man in law is a rational creature capable of observing contracts or what not. The Catholic Church would I think undoubtedly claim that they were men, on such grounds as were used in its great sixteenth century decision that the Terra del Fuegans were; but I need to find out what grounds were given then.

It seems possible to make them a very recent mutation, all descended from one ancestor three or four generations ago. Hence all their customs are in a state of flux, they need a new language and so on. There was a 'language' before but with no object-nouns as it was entirely concerned with distinguishing social situations. In that case the Catholics might claim that they have only had souls since the mutation, a clear example of the divine purpose. But this would only make the story rather more unplausible, I suppose.

Apart from fun with politics and theology the interesting question is whether an intelligent race with a breeding season could develop at all, and whether it would be very unlike ourselves mentally. They get no social training from family life and no source of mental energy from repressed sex; most of the year they are a herd like wolves and sheep. One must suppose a period of very hard conditions in which they survive by learning to make concerted plans under a leader. I was tempted to make them vegetarians with a strong head for alcohol, but it is only in hunting that you get much scope for concerted plans. If they were water animals they might make plans like beavers, but there seem to be no water monkeys. Possible reasons are that the primate body does not swim fast and catches cold easily. A water animal with the use of fire might have entertaining customs, but does not seem plausible. I take it they can't with decent plausibility be made grazing animals, with hay being demanded at the big political dinner, because no monkey digests cellulose. (It is no good making them an entirely new kind of creature because there must be serious doubt whether they are men or not). They have retreated to a single mountain area which they defend against negro attacks; the negroes are afraid of them, don't talk much about them, and when they do say things that sound like romancing. This makes it reasonable enough that they haven't been discovered. But it is not clear what large animals they can hunt up in the mountains. They must have an elaborate social structure of personal domin-ance, I think, reflected in the old language; because otherwise their lives seem too blank to develop intelligence. Rice-growing, come to think of it, would be a very neat employment for them; once they had taken to the mountain they would have to do a great deal of centralised waterwork to make the stuff grow, and the planning would require dominant leaders. Or some plant like rice; rice could hardly be got to them. The dominating situation arises during the breeding season only, when the herd originally split up into pairs for a short period. It is not clear how this could spread over into the placid herd situations between breeding seasons. The sexes are then hardly distinguished, but you discriminate a good deal about your furpicking partner. The hunting cooperation seems an easier thing to invent, partly because somebody is already dominant over the animal hunted, partly because the object is more in view. An intelligent race without either domination or pervasive sex I find too hard to imagine. To be sure one could run the novel on making them simply a tribe with evidence it wasn't human stock, but this seems hardly interesting enough.

You see the kind of topic. Grateful if you care to send comments.

Lord Zuckerman had no specific recollection of being consulted by Empson, then or later, but he did read the transcript I sent him and commented that he found it 'fascinating. Nothing in [Empson's] text is an affront to biological wisdom, and the Wuzzoo and all the others like him are beautiful, fantastic creatures. I particularly liked the way he brought in the breeding season.'[102]

As soon as he appears, Wuzzoo (the confusingly named chief representative of the Wurroos) is seen to be covered with thick black fur, and he has a long tail and floppy ears. Accordingly, in spite of observing the evident fact that this creature is rational, articulate, and perspicacious, the liberal but puzzled colonial administrator George Bickersteth provisionally decides that he must be put upon the footing of 'the family dog'. Although considerations of primate taxonomy and phylogeny are not seriously in question on the creature's first encounter with a human being, his initial status as a precociously intelligent pet cannot rest for long.

Empson's intention in describing the creature so exactly is to invite the human race to puzzle over a cultural and philosophical dilemma: what social and spiritual value would we accord to a newly discovered lower mammal that is yet capable of reason? This quick issue is signalled when Mrs Bickersteth (a character who surely owes quite a deal to Lorelei Lee and her friend Dorothy in Anita Loos's *Gentlemen Prefer Blondes*) discovers that the Wurroos have a demarcated breeding season. Although Empson did not particularly favour the looks of the genus *Lemur*, he had (as he told Zuckerman) considered the idea that the Wurroo might be of 'lemuroid stock'—principally because of this peculiarity of breeding habit, which virtually requires it to be taken as a sub-order of primate. Monkeys and apes are 'like man' in experiencing 'a smooth and uninterrupted sexual and reproductive life' (as Zuckerman points out in a phrase suggestive of unalloyed happiness).[103] The Wurroos' yearly season of anoestrus is 'unknown even among the great apes': so argues the advocate before the

House of Lords on behalf of the Wurroos' claim that they are non-primate mammals. His presentation of the evidence thus follows the facts set out in Zuckerman's published studies, in particular that an intermittent breeding habit has the phyletic significance of putting such creatures at a remove even from the subhuman primates: 'For the purpose of sociological analysis, mammals can be divided into three main groups, the first of which comprises the monkeys and apes (Order *Primates*). The members of the second group are those of the non-primate or lower mammals that have an anoestrus and a demarcated breeding season.'[104]

The lawyer for the Wurroos brings forward the further crucial evidence that they are unable to cross-breed with man: inter-specific barriers of that kind obey the implication of the Linnaean concept that 'a species should be unable to cross successfully with a neighbouring but different one'.[105] Accordingly, if the Wurroos have no apparent physiological affinity with mankind, they must have a different morphological status. In sum, if there is no possibility of a Wurroo–human hybrid, and whatever their level of intelligence, the law sets these creatures outside the race of man—which is ironically just what they desire: they have somehow heard the bad news about racial oppression, and would prefer to be treated not as a 'tribe . . . a lot of black men' but as a protected species.

Another point at which Empson hints is that, like apes and monkeys, the Wurroos are normally polygynous: in one of the fragments of Empson's text Wuzzoo mentions that he has had three children. 'I suppose you could call it favouritism rather . . . they were all by the same female. People thought it rather pretty, you know, evidently we liked each other a lot and so on.' It is 'rather eccentric' behaviour, he tellingly observes. 'The idea of permanent sexual relationships,' Zuckerman states,

conflicts with the annual transition of a sexual animal with functional reproductive organs, into an asexual animal with non-functioning sexual organs. This seasonal alteration from sexual to completely asexual behaviour is outside the range of human experience. It is as if an animal were periodically castrated and then, after an interval, subjected to the operation of implanting a functional gonad . . . [S]exual selection, as defined by Darwin, has no important place in the social mechanisms of those sub-human primates whose behaviour is known. Affective sentiments . . . are not necessarily linked with sexual relationships.[106]

It is therefore a bit odd for Wuzzoo to have confined his sexual relations to one female for three years running, even though the pair felt affection for one another (which is peculiar in itself). The Wurroos are in addition furpicking mammals, which according to Zuckerman is a fundamental factor in the social behaviour of subhuman primates.[107]

However, if science and the law must needs determine that the Wurroo is a subhuman species, does the creature's obvious intelligence nonetheless suggest a spiritual capability? 'Anybody can see that we are like animals,' Empson wrote in a book review the year before beginning his fable, 'but the theological issue comes with the question whether the dividing line is sharp or blurred.'[108]

This is the crux of the story for Empson, and explains why he took such care to fashion his exotic creature as an authentic biological possibility: it is his mode of bringing a creature from outer space literally down to earth, with the fabulous Wurroo being analogous to a fantastic Martian. From his early years Empson thought it impudent and parochial for Christians to believe that they bore witness to the one true God and had been offered the salvation of souls through the redemption of Christ's sacrifice on the cross. His direct onslaught against the Christian God became widely known only with the publication of *Milton's God*, but for many years he had felt distressed by the nature of the Christian atonement. However, even though he deplored the Christian God, he did not glibly dismiss the possibilities of religious faith. As a metaphysician from his earliest years he agonized over the meaning and purpose of human life. Even in 1927 he had taken sober heed of Wyndham Lewis's rehearsal in *Time and Western Man* of the fact that recent cultural developments had permanently damaged some of the 'main props of our faith in Western common-sense'—chief among them being (in Empson's words) 'private integrity of thought, by the removal of a fixed God, which has fostered the idea of an unknowable, ever-changing organic flux, and referred all belief to contemporary shifting needs.'[109]

Consequently, there is a good case for identifying Empson with Wuz-zoo. Whether or not Empson perceived his protagonist as himself is not known, but certainly the character very often speaks for the author. If Empson felt like something of an alien being in China, estranged by cultural tradition as much as by language, he felt even more deeply alienated from the dominant religious dispensation of the Western world. In that respect, then, 'The Royal Beasts' is also an allegory of the religious differences between East and West; and in writing it Empson firmly decided his own preference. He was to insist in one of the unpublished open letters he drafted in 1938, 'in China the only one of the four great religions likely to do rapid good is Buddhism'.

In his article 'Donne the Space Man' (1957), which has a direct bearing on the central issue of 'The Royal Beasts' dating from twenty years earlier,

Empson was to argue that astronomical discoveries have profound theological and ethical consequences at any time of Christian culture, if you follow the logic of the discovery of a plurality of possible worlds beyond our own:

One might suppose, to preserve God's justice, that Christ repeats his sacrifice on all worlds ... but this already denies uniqueness to Jesus, and must in some way qualify the identity of the man with the divine person. It becomes natural to envisage frequent partial or occasional Incarnations on this earth ...[110]

'The Royal Beasts' features not a spaceman but a version of an apeman, but the issues Empson raises about his particular creature apply either way. This observation from 'Donne the Space Man' has an equally obvious applicability to the puzzle of the Wurroos: 'The present state of scientific enquiry ... almost forces us to believe in life on other planets ... [I]t makes the mind revolt at any doctrine which positively requires our earth to have the only rational inhabitants ... [T]he European maritime expansion made it hit the attention of Christians much more; the number and variety of people found to be living out of reach of the Gospel, many of them not noticeably worse than Christians, came as a shock.'[111] (The analogous political dimension of the novel, which satirizes the colonialist designs of the human beings upon the non-primate Wurroos, is clearly levelled at the West's traditional treatment of the Far East as much as other non-European countries.)

This crucial religious issue is raised at the end of section III of the novel, when the character Mr Thompson adroitly questions the theological consequence of excluding the creatures from the race of man—'Are these Wurroos for ever, by one act of this court, to be shut out from heaven?'—and it is developed in sections IV and V. 'Of course, I ought to have said before,' remarks an unnamed speaker in the novel, 'it was an essential claim for Christianity as a powerful centralised religion that you couldn't possibly get to heaven without it':

The justice of God was under a great strain anyway, because the vast majority of men hadn't been given a chance. There were all the great classical pagans before Christ appeared at all, and even the Chinese didn't hear of him for a thousand years. I daresay it seems easier now that the missionaries have got about a good deal, but Dante felt it all right; how God can be just at all had to be made a supreme mystery with a whole crowd of interlocking allegories.

The Chinese had never heard of Christianity before European missionaries thrust the religion upon them: were they therefore damned, along with the Wurroos and other worlds, until that time? This line of thought became central for Empson not only for its speculative and sceptical value but because the historical Church had made it a life-and-death issue. At the turn of the seventeenth century the Inquisition had indicted Giordano Bruno for his belief in a possible plurality of worlds, and it is justifiably believed that the heresy he thus professed was brought up as one of the charges which led to his execution. 'They wanted the earth to be the only habitable planet so that Christ could be unique,' Empson's spokesman comments in 'The Royal Beasts'. Furthermore, as Empson pointed out in his essay 'Literary Criticism and the Christian Revival' (1966),

Melanchthon, as soon as Copernicus published, had denounced him for implying an argument against Christianity: 'Does Jesus Christ get crucified on each of the planets in turn? Or is the Father totally unjust to the Martians?' . . . Professor Marjorie Nicolson was still saying in 1935 (*Studies in Philology*), 'The idea of a plurality of worlds, which Donne had suggested in his earlier poetry, was indeed for churchmen a dangerous tenet, even, as it came to be called, the "new heresy".'[112]

Once possessed by what he regarded as the absolute imperative of defying the Christian God, a passion which can be dated even as far back as his reading of J. B. S. Haldane's *Possible Worlds* in 1929, Empson took every opportunity to reiterate it. He was to enlist to his camp another literary giant some thirty years after writing 'The Royal Beasts', when he protested (or provocatively conjectured against the Christian orthodoxy of Professor Northrop Frye) that Milton's 'theological position made him want to have man-like creatures on other planets because that would be a decisive blow against the claim of any Church to be the only source of salvation'.[113] Empson's voice of reason in 'The Royal Beasts' argues that 'once there were any number of possible worlds that Christ hadn't died on and where people couldn't possibly hear the gospel the injustice of the thing would become intolerable.' His humane solution follows: 'The only way out is to say that Christ does it on all the different worlds . . . and that gives you quite a different idea of the historical Jesus; for one thing, Christ may just as well have other incarnations as a man.' As he explained in a later article (on Dylan Thomas), 'The idea that any man can become Christ, who is a universal, was a major sixteenth-century heresy and has been kept up among the poets.'[114] It would be no less a heresy today, of course, but Empson was at once begging the question and trailing his coat.

The religion and morality he adumbrates in 'The Royal Beasts'—which postulates a position (as the text has it) 'ambiguous between pantheism and

Arianism, in which the historical importance of the events related in the gospels is reduced to a reassuring unimportance'—owes much to his understanding of Mahayana Buddhism. At some time during the 1930s, for instance, he had made these precise and interested notes on the concept of 'Suchness':

> The Bodhisattva becomes not merely a Buddha, but Buddha, the ultimate undifferentiated reality, suchness...
>
> Between Asoka and AD 1 [there were] important changes in the idea of the nature of a Buddha...Everyone might now aim at becoming a Buddha. The term bodhisattva occurs in the sutras, where it means the state of a Buddha before his enlightenment.

Likewise, his defiance of the doctrine of the uniqueness of Christ anticipates his applause for Aldous Huxley's formulation in *The Perennial Philosophy* (1946) of the concept that everyone participates in the 'Divine Ground'.[115] The need to bypass Christian doctrine became a moral passion for Empson. A religious position which might somehow conjoin pantheism and the Buddhist doctrine of Karma seemed to him at once more generous and just than the options of heaven or hell: 'the universalizing of the idea of Christ,' he suggested in 'Donne the Space Man' (and earlier still, in sections IV and V of 'The Royal Beasts'), makes 'individuality less important'.[116]

The entirety of 'The Royal Beasts' is first-draft work; but even without any finish of style or structure it raises all the crucial aspects of Empson's ethical concerns and researches during the 1930s, and it gestures forward to the indictment of Christianity that is central to *Milton's God*. The primary function of imaginative literature, he believed, 'is to make you realize that other people act on moral convictions different from your own...What is more, it has been thought from Aeschylus to Ibsen that a literary work may present a current moral problem, and to some extent alter the judgement of those who appreciate it by making them see the case as a whole.'[117] Equally, 'The Royal Beasts' stands on the brink of the imaginative act of cultural and moral equity that he would try to compose between East and West in a plan for a ballet, entitled 'The Elephant and the Birds', five years later. Despite the forceful thematic burden of his fable, however, there is no doubt that Empson felt about 'The Royal Beasts' what he wrote about the contemporary poem 'Autumn on Nan-Yueh': 'I hope the gaiety of the thing comes through.'[118]

Since Empson in China was kept so busy with his teaching in extremely difficult conditions, which included the constant threat of Japanese bombing raids, it is surprising not that he failed to finish 'The Royal Beasts' but that he wrote quite so much of it. We cannot assume that he tired of his novel or thought it an unsuccessful venture, only that he was overtaken by circumstances. Suffice it to say that he still had the manuscript with him during the Communist Liberation of Peking at the end of the 1940s, and that he certainly felt grateful when a Burmese friend (who happened also to be a Buddhist) later rescued his well-worn papers: 'When I left Communist Peking he smuggled out for me a small suitcase containing unfinished plays, an unfinished novel about Africa, none of it to do with China; I have never looked at them since but revere Myat Tun [U Myint Thein][119] for saving them with such firm instructions and energetic adroitness.'

16

'The savage life and the fleas and the bombs': China, 1938–1939

That seems a fair dollop of gossip.

Empson to Michael Roberts, 12 January 1939

Tra la la. It all looks fairly black, but at last the wireless has broken here, so we aren't forced to hear the news.

Empson to Ian Parsons, 16 May 1939

THE journey by rail from Changsha to Hong Kong took three days and three nights, with no sleeping berth. After sitting up for so long, Empson and George Yeh (who had travelled with him from Changsha) felt utterly downcast to find the city overflowing with Chinese exiles and foreign journalists. Empson pondered the possibility of seeking out a policeman, but just after midnight Yeh found some friends who were willing for them to sleep on the floor of their apartment, along with a huddle of other refugees and their babies. (As Empson recalled with some exasperation, 'the normal Chinese method [of organization] is to give no information at all till a plan is known, then a gradual crescendo of worse and worse information, ending on the station platform with "I suppose you know you've nowhere to sleep tonight? Or have you arranged to stay with somebody?" '[1]) Presently Empson moved into Norman France's beautiful house on the east side of the colony, where he could look out at the smaller islands that looked velvet in texture and wallowed like whales in the moonlight.

He raced about the island, eager to pick up hard news rather than the colony's copious and overworked gossip, and promptly ran into W. H.

Auden and Christopher Isherwood, who had just arrived in Hong Kong on their journey to the war. 'Isherwood was the one who was worrying about politics I thought,' Empson noted;[2] Auden he found grand and amusing, 'thick-necked and smoking big cigars' and with 'the glamour of Oscar Wilde'. The two correspondents had been invited to visit the Hong Kong-Shanghai Bank, they told him, and naturally took the opportunity to ask the Governor—'the Governor of the Governor of Hong Kong,' as Empson aptly dubbed him—for his opinion on the war. 'Well, it's just the natives fighting,' the Governor had commented.[3] (Isherwood's corroborative version of the same tale figures not in *Journey to a War* (1939) but in *Christopher and His Kind* (1977): 'Speaking of the invasion of China, a businessman said to Christopher: "Of course, from our point of view, both sides are just natives." '[4])

The newspapers in Hong Kong were alarmist, reporting among other things that Canton had been placed under martial law after suppressing a pro-Japanese coup; but Empson went there and found it 'a very carefree and glittering city, the streets and shops crowded'. There was no evidence of 'the fever of suspicion and anxiety' he had read about in Hong Kong.[5] On another trip, 40 miles across the Pearl River Estuary to the poor and raffish Portuguese colony of Macao (Europe's oldest Asian colony, with an area of 7 square miles), he stayed first with an English lecturer named George Rainer ('who eats and dresses Chinese'), then with a couple named Tyrrell (the wife 'a great tough American girl, once let loose, from the South') from the British consulate who lived in more or less voluntary isolation and shunned contact with the natives. 'Macao has a legend of wickedness,' Empson told his mother, 'very trying to the Macinese, who wouldn't let their daughters come to your Fulford cocktail parties.' During Carnival Week he attended a grand fancy dress ball, where guests of every available nationality contrived to look unmistakably like themselves. The Indians wore turbans, and 'White Russians, all mild as milk, came dressed as white russians'; though he also saw 'heavy disillusioned old half-black mommas' chaperoning 'daughters who were heartbreaking half-Chinese half-European girls'. A short man in a dusty frock-coat turned out to be a 'Fallen Statesman'—a former senator—who had gambled away a huge fortune; he maintained a glazed and beaming expression when someone playfully dressed him up with a red silk sash. Aside from that proud revenant, Empson found it hard to spot any pure Portuguese. He admired them—for one thing, the early colonists had readily intermarried with the local people—and wrote with approval that the Portuguese had 'failed at empire while the British have up to now succeeded'. When he returned to Hong Kong he felt only that he had left 'the real thing for the pathetic failure'.[6] One typical example of colonial offensiveness was that the rules of the Hong Kong Club forbade him to entertain George Yeh to lunch.

Days became weeks as he ached to get away from 'the roar of the great rumour factories';[7] and eventually Yeh gave him official leave of absence for a short trip to Cambodia, where he headed straight for the great Buddhist site of Angkor Vat.[8] Late in April he returned to China by way of the gulf of Tonking into French Indo-China, for he had been advised at last that his university department was to be reopened at the small town of Mengtzu (Mengzi) in the highlands of Yunnan, the most south-westerly province of China. University scouts had prevailed upon the provincial governor to let the three universities-in-exile, now reconstituted as the National South-West Associated University (*Hsi-na lien-ho ta-hsueh (Xinan Lianhe Daxue)*), commonly abbreviated to the acronym *Lienta (Lianda)*), establish themselves in the capital, Kunming.[9] But dire shortage of space again required both the College of Arts and Letters and the College of Law to shift out of town, at least for the summer semester.

The passage from Hanoi to Mengtzu involved a wearisome train journey of more than 200 miles up the valley of the Red River (the full ride to Kunming took three days), from the tropical paddy fields of the delta, through the sodden humidity of the rainforests, and across the Chinese frontier at the chill town of Lao-Kai [Lao Kay] ('cultivated town with paved streets & electric light in the middle of a jungle,' Dorothea Richards had noted the previous year). The last stage involved a laborious, queasily twisting ascent to the Central Asian plateau at a salubrious height of about 7,000 feet above sea level.

'Meng-Tzu is an old-fashioned joke, like the horse-marines,' one contemporary traveller reported.[10] Situated about a hundred miles south of Kunming, and a few hours' journey north of the Tonking–Yunnan border, the town was a ghost of recent history. Mengtzu 'is just departed greatness,' Empson observed.[11] 'The accommodations...found in Mengzi were a legacy of modern China's encounter with western imperialism,' John Israel explains in his history of the South-west Associated University. 'In 1899, as a result of the defeat in the Sino-French war, China had agreed to declare Mengzi a treaty port, open to trade under conditions established by foreign powers. A customs house and French consulate had been erected outside the city wall.'[12] By 1938, however, the town's grand function had fallen into disuse; the population of what had once bidden fair to be a sizeable trading city now amounted to only 10,000. 'Within the city walls life centered on a single unpaved street that had a bank, a post office, and some shops constructed of wood or adobe,' Israel writes.[13] Empson could scarcely believe he had reached the city as he crossed the great flat plain and spotted only what looked like a clump of trees; but it proved to be a pretty place despite its semi-dereliction.

As a so-called 'treaty port', Mengtzu was in any event a weird anomaly. No river or navigable sea ran near it, and yet a half-pay officer of the maritime customs still held his post so as 'to pass the ships' manifests of muleteers and to give *pratique*,' as Gerald Reitlinger observed at the time.[14] Nor did the French railway ever reach it, since the local people had aways debarred it (apparently on religious grounds); instead, a spur called the Ge-Bi-Shi Railroad, using a small gauge that was unsuitable for French engines, passed nearby in order to reach the notorious tin mines of the vicinity. Of the roughly 200 Europeans who had traded in Mengtzu just fifteen years earlier, only the customs officer and a Greek merchant remained.

Empson was billeted in one of the rooms of the dishevelled but extensive customs compound, which stood close to the wall on the east side of the town. Built as a long series of single rooms laid out in courts, and supposedly modelled on the Forbidden City in Peking, the half-ruined compound still provided enough space even for classroom accommodation; Empson had to walk just 10 yards to his lectures. (Although the French were at first unwilling to allow any 'Natives' to occupy the consulate itself, the embassy in Shanghai eventually gave permission for their offices to be made available—but only for 'public occasions', not as working or sleeping quarters.) 'I have a kind of loosebox with centipedes and things,' Empson reported, 'and eat with the professors for twelve shillings a month.'[15] The walls of his cell were made of ill-fitting matchboard through which he could see and unescapably hear his immediate neighbours: they were military instructors, and their piercing chatter at all hours of the day and night bothered him far more than the bugs of his own box.[16] 'No Chinese hears noise,' he exclaimed with witty irritation. 'The school servants quite innocently stand outside the door and yell to each other at the tops of their voices at any hour of night. A Chinese yawn can be heard a hundred yards away. They clear their throats (nearly all the time) like a rhinoceros about to charge. Ordinary talk is a piercing squawl and yowl. You are never out of earshot. This being true of Japan as well as China, and I myself being rather too easily bothered by noise, it is really very stupid of me to try and live in these parts. I am rather afraid of next year, when we will be in really cramped quarters, but on the other hand it might be seriously interesting.'[17] Later he was to realize that the cultivated

Chinese he worked alongside could certainly keep quiet when necessary; 'One of the things that really deserve respect about the university people, when you compare them to others, is their capacity for a decent and unembarrassing silence.'

His first proper meal in Mengtzu held out no promise of an appetizing local cuisine to console him for his domestic disquiet. The cooks brought him a breakfast of painfully thin gruel laced with a raw egg and trimmed with a handful of salted peanuts. Then there occurred what he regarded as a positively Kafkaesque incident. Noticing that a fellow patron was enjoying a boiled egg, Empson tried to indicate that he would like to order one too, whereupon his well-satisfied neighbour, who helped to translate his signals, remarked that the kitchen staff would have to make up a fire before they could meet such a request. When Empson saw that the cooks were indeed collecting sticks in the yard, he abandoned all hope and went off to take his class.[18] Much later he negotiated for better quarters—'one room still standing in a ruin with a family camping in it who would cook dinners'[19]—but the university pulled out of Mengtzu before he could make his own move.

If living conditions allowed him little in the way of creature comforts, the colonial customs compound yet retained fine evidence of its 'departed wealth'. Its gardens, which had been partly laid out by Stella Benson, included a large lawn and a delightful arboretum of mature eucalyptus, mango, and papaya. (Benson's ex-husband had recently visited the place, the customs officer told Empson, and kept bursting into tears as he walked round the garden.)[20] Close to the compound and edged with eucalyptus and willow was a lake called Nan Hu ('South Lake') which the hot season (the climate is subtropical) had caked to a bed that was firm enough to walk on, but by June the wet season rapidly transformed it from 'a field of muck' to a murky liquid; and alone among the faculty Empson delighted in cooling the blood with a daily plunge.[21]

'This place is a backwater, not romance like Changsha,' Empson wrote, 'but I expect to stick to my undertakings, that is, stay another year.'[22] Just as in Changsha, in fact, he calmly carried on with his heavy stint of teaching: lecturing in the mornings, and adjourning in the afternoon to a Vietnamese coffee-house where he drank cup after cup of strong black coffee and chainsmoked Turkish cigarettes while assiduously correcting student essays.[23] At night he would drink large quantities of Greek wine. (The local shopkeeper, a black-clothed Jewish-Greek merchant whose name, Kalos, was transliterated into Chinese as 'Geluoshi'—the 'mad Greek', as Empson called him—refused to order French wine from

Hanoi; he disliked the French and alleged that they adulterated their wine.)[24] After one drinking session Empson (who anyway suffered from myopia) fell over, cut himself, and broke his glasses, which had to be patched together with sticking plaster. But his students noted that in any case he felt no self-consciousness at all about his constantly bedraggled appearance and the almost studied informality—the waywardness—of his manners. When a student called on him at his room, Empson offered him tea in a mug he had just utilized for shaving.[25] Nor did a hangover or any other badge of boozing ever keep him from his duties. He was in fact so conscientious as a teacher, recalls Li Fu-ning (a senior student of the time), that he took his class even when looking terribly ill, with a fever that would have prostrated anyone else (unusually for Empson, he even admitted to feeling weak, so he must have been truly unwell).[26] When he grumbled aloud, he did so not on his own behalf but for the sake of his students. 'I wish [the authorities] wouldn't show respect for War conditions . . . by not allowing the students decent lighting or a doctor,' he complained home. 'One of the great Sung family [Hu Shih] was heard saying in Hongkong that an army marches on its Red Cross, and if the Chinese have learned this from the war it is a real set-off to learning militarism.'[27]

A sizeable minority of the students, together with a few of the faculty—257 students and eleven teachers—had 'learned militarism' as a result of having walked overland from Changsha to Kunming. (The male students were not in fact 'instructed to walk from Changsha to Kunming,' as Jonathan Spence writes in his splendid saga *The Gate of Heavenly Peace: The Chinese and their Revolution, 1895–1980*, though some 300 students did so.[28] All the same, as Empson noted, 'at least one able student was refused an extra year's scholarship because he did not choose to join the symbolic party.') The physical difficulties that the walkers endured on the unavoidably indirect journey—covering more than a thousand miles in a period of about forty days—evidently hardened their sense of wartime *causerie*; and they tended to scorn their fellows—some 800 students and faculty—who had taken the soft option of the rail route via Canton to Hong Kong and thence by sea to Haiphong. The arduous trek had given them the cachet of being a 'marching brigade', whereas those who had taken the safer and quicker way by public transport could not equal their sense of a common resolve: some of the latter had even treated themselves with visits to restaurants and theatres, and (clearly far worse) they had wasted both their money and their national pride by buying Japanese goods in Hong Kong. The trekkers thus felt justified in deriding the rail-sea party for their shameless self-indulgence: 'This world has really reached the point when a sweeping reform is in order! When the nation is in such economic straits, what is the point in wasting huge sums of money to send these things to the rear? To manufacture high-class refugee traitors?'[29]

Empson himself felt a certain misgiving about taking the rail-sea route, and remarked while in Hong Kong, 'Some of us professors ought to be doing the walk, I feel, but how many reasons there are why each of us finds it urgent to pass through Hongkong.' Once established in Yunnan, however, the rail-sea refugees evidently retaliated for a while against the scornful pride of the walkers, though Empson continued to respect the value of the heroic gesture: 'it was a fair symbol of the willingness and enthusiasm of the student body,' he judged.[30] The foot-slogging retreat had instilled in the students a deep sense both of anti-Japanese solidarity and of emulating the legendary and more harrowing Communist Long March four years earlier. 'You hear gossip against the march of students to Yunnan,' Empson noted, 'though there is no real joke against it, because it was organised with a sense of the dramatic position; it was partly propaganda.'

Far more disturbing was the fact that his students began by either patronizing or shunning the non-Chinese tribes of the region. 'Mengtzu means the Dull Place, and the Chinese despise it and the tribes bitterly,' he reported in a letter of 23 May.[31] Twice each month the many unassimilated aboriginal peoples, who spoke in tribal dialects, came to market in Mengtzu and had to use sign language to do business with the Han Chinese (about a third of Yunnan's total population of 11 million consisted of some fifty different tribes). They seemed to be poles apart from the sophisticated female students of Lianda who would often wear cosmetics along with a high-slit cheongsam and flesh-coloured stockings, and who accordingly disdained the natives as 'primitive'.[32] Whilst Empson admired the manners of the predominant Miao tribespeople, as well as the women's costume of embroidered 'kilts' with silver bracelets and necklaces, his students seemed to think that 'a wild Miao would eat them,' he reported.[33] The students had grown up in modernized coastal cities and were used to Western amenities, and they had jumped to the conclusion that the tribespeople of Yunnan (along with the Annamites of French Indo-China, which Chinese nationalists regarded as 'stolen property') must be yearning for nothing more than to become part of the true China. Empson believed quite otherwise, and he valued the political independence and the customs of the south-west. He presciently feared for the day when the Chinese would 'try to do an Anschluss', and found from his personal experience in China that 'you get far more easy friendliness from the casual native than in any British colony'.[34]

The same situation did not apply in Indo-China, though Empson certainly thought it did. Hanoi appeared to be ably administered by the French, who provided well for the majority population of Annamites—or so he had badly judged during his too brief visit. More importantly, he believed, the Annamites themselves, who were assuredly not Chinese by origin (though often Sinified in custom), did not look kindly on the idea of being overtaken by the Chinese. An alpaca-clad, topee-toting Annamite on a bus had pointed out to him that the bus company was run by the Chinese, and immediately followed up that information with a sorry question, 'I suppose even in London most of the business is done by Chinese?'[35] But Empson was foolish to generalize from that chance encounter: in 1938 the Vietnamese were in fact struggling hard for liberation from the French, and by the spring of 1939 their colonial masters entered into a brutal collaboration with Japanese infiltrators in an effort to suppress the independence movement. Empson always felt ashamed of himself for having misjudged the situation in Indo-China (later Vietnam). Even as late as March 1980 he lamented in a letter to Professor Jin Di (who had been one of his post-war students): 'My worst political prophecy was about Indochina, to which I would retire during 1939 for luxury during the vacations at Mengtzu or Kunming. I thought the Annamites very happy, and the French much more at home and friendly among them than the British were among their colonial subjects, and I thought: Thank God, though all the rest of the world will soon be at war, these people are certain to remain peaceful. I was uncertain whether to despise them for it, but on the whole I did not. They have continued fighting ever since, for forty years, with extreme heroism, and by now you could almost call it a hysterical fixation. So don't ever tell me my political prophecies are wise.'[36]

If in 1938 his students felt at first a little leery of the natives of Yunnan, Empson yet despised all rumours of banditry and other perils and insisted on looking into things for himself—not so much because he was brave to the point of foolhardiness as because he hated hearsay and was incorrigibly inquisitive. Mengtzu was situated in an enormous saucer-shaped plain with hills at the rim, and he felt oppressed by that taunting horizon; being an energetic sightseer, he aimed to see what lay beyond the hills. 'It is a very large uninterrupted plain, and so flat that the contours of the paddy fields are plain rectangles,' he wrote soon after his arrival in Mengtzu. 'When you walk outside the town you find that there is no reason to walk one way rather than another, and the hills though deceptively near are all out of reach.' One of his first walks brought him to one of the local open-cast tin mines, which the League of Nations had long since indicted for their inhuman practices. They were often worked by small boys who had been sold by penurious parents or else kidnapped; sleeping in the open throughout the year, the children soon contracted tuberculosis and other diseases, and after starting work in the mines had an average life expectancy of three years. But Empson had come across a modernized mine that took better care of its labourers. 'I seem to have no eye for bad conditions,' he wrote, doubting the evidence before him and feeling that he ought to be able to report the savage conditions he had heard about. 'The men looked cross and dirty but quite healthy and plump. It is lovely country, fearfully bare, and much bigger than you expect; especially after the sacred mountain . . . ' In another letter he described how he had at last managed to venture a good way out of town, with this pleasantly surprising result:

when I got just over this bare rocky series of fatuous rolling hills there turned out to be a little valley over the top, rich with trees, a whole village snug inside them, a lake or large pond with a sturdy temple at the far side . . . and coming down to the side into the lake the real hanging gardens of the mountain paddy fields, curved like the lines of bees' wings under the microscope, high thin standing rice at each stage that you could see down to the water through, a delicate pale acid green, and that strange effect of massive engineering or 'structural' palatial architecture (the terraces are very deep)—all in a little hollow just hidden from us that happens to have water, only a dimple if we could see it on our Siberian view of hills. It felt like coming home, I mean it gave me a nostalgia for the attractive parts of China and started me remembering my travels instead of daydreaming.[37]

His delight in this freshly discovered landscape even prompted a stanza in his poem 'China'—

> The paddy-fields are wings of bees
>   (The Great Wall as a dragon crawls—)
> To one who flies or one who sees
>   (—the twisted contour of their walls)

—which he glossed with this note: 'The paddy fields in hill country . . . are extremely beautiful . . . and seem never to have been treated by all the long and great tradition of Far Eastern landscape painters. And yet they have the same surprising jerking texture as the Great Wall making its way round precipitous hills, and the familiar dragon of the tea-cups (and by this identity the real line of military or magical defence is the country itself). The whole business of what a culture can become unconscious of and still use is an important and strange one.' But it must be said again that he was too quick to construct his general thesis before he had looked thoroughly into the subject. The terraced paddy fields would actually have been introduced into such a landscape only when the population outgrew flat arable lands; and moreover, as Professor Yang Zhouhan (one of Empson's former pupils) remarked to me, 'Even if they existed when painters of later dynasties were active, they would not have painted them because they were not part of Nature and smacked of "this-worldliness".'[38]

Empson was often warned that the countryside was as dangerous as it was unexpectedly beautiful. But as far as he was concerned the 'bandit situation had very intelligible causes', chief among them being the obvious fact that Mengtzu 'had hardly any other function in human affairs but to be a smugglers' town . . . Also the suppression of opium-growing and the wartime rise of taxes was believed to have made a number of simple farmers take to the road; though contrariwise many of these losers had been conscripted.' All the same, he drew so much pleasure from his careless forays into the countryside that he must have begun to think that all stories about bandits were simply fantastical. (Altogether more dangerous, he must have felt, was the large bear at the ghastly local zoo which bit him when he tried to give it a drink.)[39]

However, his luck could not last forever, and he did encounter some bandits during a hike to one of the tin mines:

By the time I got onto the main slope [of a hill] I found my legs actually wouldn't push me up, and there was all the way to get back. I can't tell you what a beautiful lost hope that ghastly tinmine seemed in the evening, with the singing and the mulebells; it is lovely country. Then on the way back after the allday solitude and drought and heat the cramps began, and I would count a hundred paces and then drop and count a hundred and then go on. Luckily there was a moon, and I thought I can sleep on the road if this gets worse, but I will behave normally and meet my class at ten tomorrow. I remembered other walks a good deal. I was in severe pain. Thus the holdup seemed very incidental; it came when I was having the last rest with the light on the gates of Mengtzu looking reasonably near. In rubbing the back of one leg to remove cramp one was always being caught by the other leg suddenly going wrong owing to taking a strained position, and it was very exhausting to deal with both at once. Seeing someone pass in the moonlight I felt it polite to express mild complaints because I might otherwise appear crazy. The figure slouched on without reply, and then three suddenly converged, with daggers, I assure you, flashing in the moonlight. Maybe if I had been more frightened or more angry the cramp might have solved itself, but as it was I had to go on rubbing my left calf. Two men held me with what seemed scientific efficiency while a third went through the pockets. Scientific efficiency however interfered with rubbing the left leg and threatened to bring on cramp in the right leg; I had to object, and a compromise was reached. The wristwatch was taken without comment, the very small amount of money carried was a matter of course; the spectacles were taken, and I stopped rubbing my legs to represent the absurd injustice of this step—there was a fateful pause, and they were put back on my nose. I suppose it would have meant being led down to Indochina for new ones. Then the important thing happened; the searcher found the cigarettes and the matches. All three gasped with pleasure. I think it says a good deal for the local police that the boys couldn't slip into the town and buy cigarettes. The sinister figures then melted into the night and I went on rubbing both legs. After a pause one sinister figure came back and asked if I wanted help up to the gate; he was sorry he couldn't take me in. I assured him I would be all right in a minute or two, so he melted back again. All this sounds as if I talk fluent Chinese, which I don't, but there was no language problem.[40]

He reported the incident to his mother, and—predictably enough—felt obliged to comfort her with a little self-deprecation in his very next letter: 'As to the robbers, who you say dismay you, they are no trouble at all at present, unless you are mad enough to become ill after dark outside the town, and then only take what you carry, and don't hurt you. But they are an interesting topic.'[41] Despite the casual character of his account, there is no reason at all to doubt the authenticity of his encounter with petty robbers: and it was widely reported round town. If he took the incident lightly, however, the university authorities were in no mind to neglect the continuous danger. 'The library in the customs compound was open after dark,' Professor Israel records, 'but every hour a bell rang to alert students who had finished their studies that an armed escort was ready to accompany them to their dormitories.'[42]

Nonetheless, even if it could be demonstrated that Empson had simply reverted to type and stiffened his British upper lip when describing his own mugging, he continued quite rightly to believe that bandits were not always just wild men of the mountains, dropouts from the Long March, or sundry privateers. The very term 'bandit' covered a multitude of manifestations, including smugglers who would otherwise profess loyalty to the governor of Yunnan (if not to the Nationalist government) as well as members of what he termed 'the mysterious Mengtzu gentry'.[43]

The 'landed gentry'—'a kind of bandit Trades Union'[44]—certainly made their authority known to the university when they forbade girl students from swimming in the lake ('naturally in smart Shanghai swimming suits,' as Empson noted), and they likewise made a formal protest against 'Mixed Walking'. Then the same 'landed gentry' issued a frightful ultimatum, since the influx of teachers and students had caused rents to rise to an uneconomic level which had the inevitable effect of deterring traders (and presumably smugglers) from distant parts. If the university took any more rooms in the town, the bandits threatened, they would shoot two students, one male and one female, to show that they meant to uphold their business. The university ('with a pretence of indifference,' Empson observed) felt powerless to call their bluff, and apparently took no more rooms.[45] 'In its way it was quite a rational bit of County Council work,' Empson commented; 'and the same type of unofficial council further east would be equally ready to stand up against Japanese occupying forces.'

Whilst Empson acknowledged that in more remote and mountainous regions the prevalent banditry had until very recently taken the form of a murderous tyranny (even a year or so earlier no caravans had dared to venture into the highlands without a military detachment in train), he certainly understood the rationale behind the bandits' threats in the town. Still a number of his students construed their intimidating memoranda as further proof (if proof were needed) of the barbarity of the unassimilated province to which they had been exiled. 'The presence of non-Chinese tribesmen in the hills rather complicated the problem for us,' Empson wrote; 'some students believed that these people needed a severed head for the autumn sowing, which was very unjust.' Those students—and even the far greater number who held no such adverse superstitions—believed that it was their mission to lead the provincial tribes out of their backwardness; and yet at the same time they were sincerely troubled by the contradictions inherent in their appointed task. In particular (quite apart from their first awkward encounters with the local tribespeople), the students were deeply sensible of a fundamental dilemma arising out of their privileged status as an educated elite.

Empson sympathetically highlighted their problem in a propaganda piece he wrote four years later, while working for the Far Eastern section of the BBC. As broadcast on the Home Service on 27 April 1942, 'China on the March' was a severely cut version of Empson's original script and ran for just half an hour. The first draft version, which fills eighteen pages of single-spaced typescript, is far more revealing of Empson's personal attitudes, and I shall quote from it here. Drawing almost entirely on his own experiences and observations, it takes the form of a supposedly fictional round-table discussion about China's political prospects, with contributions from five speakers: an announcer, 'A', who is described as 'romantic' and who 'hasn't been to China'; 'B', a businessman with socialist sympathies employed by a British firm in China; 'C', a good-tempered upper-class figure; and 'D', an elderly Protestant missionary. The final member of the group, opportunely 'E'—a 'Teacher from refugee Government university; pro-modern China but less Left-Wing than B'—speaks more or less directly for Empson himself, and comments among other matters on the ambitions of his students:

Of course they all talk about democracy. It's the smart thing. They would disapprove of a poem if it wasn't a proletarian poem. But would they put on a coolie's pyjama suit? They'd be so shocked at the idea that they wouldn't know how to forgive you, if you suggested it. What they wear, of course, are things like tramdriver's uniforms; the idea of a uniform for students came from Germany, and it has been very convenient for both China and Japan. It's a bold student who wears an ordinary Chinese gown; that means he's very Right Wing. If you're a very Left Wing student, both in China and Japan, you have your tramdriver's uniform very old, tattered and dirty. But however communist you are you never dream of dressing like a coolie…[The Chinese student] despises the coolie probably much more than you do…because it kind of makes public the false position he feels he's in…Don't talk to me about the corruption of officials and the closed ring of the KuoMinTang; all officials are corrupt unless they are stopped by public opinion, and they are right, because if the public opinion doesn't exist, if there is nothing between—rule from the top or anarchy, then it is better to have rule from the top. And in fact all my boys feel the contrast so sharply that they're bound to feel they want to rule from the top. Don't think they're corrupt. Not a bit.

Empson assumed a stout tone in such remarks, not in order to discredit the putatively democratic aspirations of the Chinese but to confront his listeners with the fact that the country still suffered from its legacy of radical social imbalance. Between the intellectual leader and the agricultural labourer there existed a historical and educational gulf that any progressive ruler could hope to bridge only after many years of cultural reconstruction. A socialist himself, Empson weighed up what he subsequently learned about the Communist political programme for China, and intelligently baulked at the concept of a 'proletarian dictatorship' and at a land policy of enforced collectivization. John Israel, in an article entitled 'Southwest Associated University: Preservation as an Ultimate Value', fully confirms Empson's assessment of the students' situation and expectations: 'Being reduced to a working class standard of living did not endow students with a working class world view any more than raising their own vegetables, as many did, caused them to think like peasants. The proletarianization of living standards seemed, in fact, to reinforce their dogged determination to get an education. They remained an intellectual elite...'[46] If genuine democracy seemed a long way off, the best that China might achieve in the short term would be a genuinely enlightened oligarchy, Empson believed; but meanwhile his students felt 'deeply embarrassed', as he acknowledged in his BBC script, 'because they have committed themselves to shoving a modern democracy onto a society based on coolie labour'.

With hindsight it can be seen that he took too optimistic a view of the inclinations of the Nationalist government, at least until late in 1939, largely because (just like Han Suyin as well as the large majority of Sino-liberal academics at the same time) he heeded Chiang Kai-shek's declarations more than his deeds, and trusted that Chiang would uphold the spirit of the prime movers of the Republic. In 1924, Sun Yat-sen had issued a manifesto to the effect that the new Chinese government should evolve through three stages: (1) a period of military operations; (2) a period of political tutelage; leading to (3) constitutional government. And for a long time Chiang Kai-shek appeared (to the outside world at least) to insist on adhering to the same resolution, for he declared even at the closing session of the People's Political Council in 1941 that he sought to establish a democratic form of government in China; and to that end he appealed to other parties not to obstruct the Kuomintang's 'historic mission of one-party rule during the period of political tutelage prescribed by Sun Yat-sen'. But his remarks actually amounted to an assumption of demagogism, not to the prospect of a free democracy; and his energies were increasingly directed far more towards the violent suppression of Chinese Communists than to the defeat of their common enemy. Empson's hopeful and in the event mistaken impression throughout his two years in China was that the Nationalists might in the long run represent a force for good. Whilst he never underestimated Mao Tse-tung's highly cultivated intelligence and his indisputable popular support, he did feel that many of his students at Lianda automatically dismissed Chiang Kai-shek's accomplishments—in particular the way in which he seemed to have gathered the country together.[47]

'It is the common gossip of foreigners that China lives in a state of nervous and perpetual intrigue,' Empson protested in the draft of an unpublished open letter. As far as he could see from the 'backwater' of Yunnan in 1938, the Chinese were less intriguing than combining—to such an extent, in fact, that he feared for the survival of regional integrity and tribal traditions. Even from the point of view of its geographical scale, which approximated to the size of Europe (with most of its more than twenty constituent provinces being bigger than England), China knew that any previous effort to unify itself as a nation had failed in the face of regional jealousies and the distinct nationalities of its remoter provinces. Indeed, the Japanese banked on the belief that the cultural amorphousness of China, and its lack of centralized organization, would yield them a swift and easy victory. As Empson wrote home from Hong Kong in March 1938, 'The Japanese of course didn't expect to find any serious national feeling, a thing that has only grown up recently, but even in spite of that I think they might win, and the process of winning, if they do, and quite apart from the actual fighting, will be a real hideous one.'[48]

Given the common understanding that China represented at best an unstable confederacy rather than a single nation, it had stunned Empson just as much as any 'Old China Hand' that the country promptly pulled itself together in order to fight off the invaders. Instances of this unprecedented spirit of nationalism sprang up everywhere—'and the most Proustian brutalities of the hostage system in the towns cannot hold that country against that,' Empson wrote.[49] In the first wave of the war, for example, the fiercely independent governor of Yunnan dispatched 20,000 troops to the defence of Shanghai. Even the exuberant customs officer in Mengtzu (a Murphy by name) expressed total astonishment and distaste when his Lolo wife—who had long resented the Chinese for their dreadful treatment of her tribe and never in his experience expressed any interest in national news—started to speak in terms of 'Our Troops' and 'Our Victories'.[50]

The flashfire of nationalism spread right to the Szechwan-Tibet border, as Empson presently discovered. During the hot summer recess of August, when the College of Arts finally quit Mengtzu, he travelled up to the watershed mountain ranges of Tali (Dali), about 300 miles west of Kunming, in order to stay with the anthropologist C. P. Fitzgerald.[51] In that remote and wutheringly beautiful region—where the small walled town, which had been virtually destroyed by an earthquake in 1928, lay between the sheer blue waterway of Erh Hai ('Ear Lake') and the soaring 14,000-foot mountain of Ts'ang Shan with its vast blanket of magnolia and rhododendron trees, dwarf bamboos, and giant pines—Empson visited a newly mechanized salt mine and unexpectedly found its manager dressed as a military officer and wearing a Sam Browne belt, though he was not in fact a soldier. The mine had been commandeered by a division of the Yunnan army. However, so far from being put out by this development, the manager said that he felt utterly delighted about the changeover. But for the war, he explained, the mine would not have been mechanized for at least another twenty years.

And Empson travelled even farther afield over the bright red landscape of south-west China—on muleback—making a 90-mile journey in five or six days to visit the lovely far-flung trading town of Li-Chiang (Lijiang)—famous among other things for its sumptuous rhododendrons, and for the 10,000-foot wall of its gorge slicing through the dazzling mass of the Snow Mountain range, the eastward extension of the Himalayas—which Gerald Reitlinger described at the time as 'the last city within the country subject to Chinese government before the high forest valleys of the Tibetan border states.' Its citizens—the Nashi (Naxi) people—are Tibeto-Burman by race and for many centuries (till the eighteenth century) boasted their own king.[52] The 'chief peculiarity' of the Nashi, as it was reported in 1938, was that 'the women do everything while the men stay at home and mind the children.'[53] The big women did business in the market; their men kept house and went in for fine sewing. (Fifty-five years later, Li-Chiang was to be the ravishing location for a Channel 4 television series focusing on the lives of selected figures in the community: *Beyond the Clouds* was first broadcast in 1994.) Late on a dark night in 1938, Empson and his companions drew near to an outlying village and suddenly heard what sounded like 'a wild howling'. Just what this terrible noise really meant he found so memorable that he incorporated the tale into his BBC radio feature 'China on the March' four years later:

Now this was the Nashi district, and they are rather famous among missionaries who know about them for orgies, so I really began to think we were walking into the middle of a Nashi orgy. And we had a young American Baptist with us, and he said 'Ah doant seem to reckernise that toon'. I thought that was very good, I kind of saved that up as the most absurd thing he'd said so far. But when we came up to this village it turned out that he was perfectly right. What we found was a lot of schoolchildren singing one of the big soldiers' songs that have gone right across China. As a rule in travellers' stories the native village pays a lot of attention to the European travellers. These children just went straight on singing. We tried to bribe a man to take us to our right village but he said he was afraid to do it even for kindness and went back to bed. So we stood and sang with them for a minute or two and then limped on after the mules. We did find the place in the end, more by luck than anything else, and then my colleague unrolled a large poster of Chiang Kai Shek and gave it to the head man. It was a curious scene because the head man, who was wearing a rather smart Norfolk shooting jacket given him by the anthropologist, felt embarrassed and a bit offended. He said he was glad to have another, but he'd got one up in the village school already; and he soon found occasion to point out that fifty of his men, out of a hundred or a hundred and fifty houses, had already left for the Chinese army. Now you must remember that the history of Chinese relations with these tribes is pretty bad. The idea that these people, who wear fantastic clothes and don't talk or write Chinese at all, are quite placidly and solidly determined to defeat the Japanese invader some two thousand miles away, is an entirely new thing in Chinese history. Ten years before those people were positively hating the Chinese. That was what convinced me that the Chinese Empire is now united. If it doesn't convince you I don't know what would.

Stanzas 4 and 5 of his poem 'China', which dates from a few months earlier in 1938, make the political point that Japan and China are like 'two peas' from the same pod, at least partly for the reason that both countries have traditionally ruled 'by music and by rites'. Confucius had said that the Chinese Empire was ruled by music and by ceremony, meaning that the established leaders constrained themselves to give service and obedi-ence. The result has been that the educated Chinese, as Empson remarked in his BBC script, 'have always despised the coolie singing'—which has the less stressful and (to Western ears) more natural function of accompanying and cheering on manual labour. Empson concluded that 'the real problem for the educated Chinese is not joining onto Western culture but joining onto their own coolie singing': in other words, that the governing classes had never yet found common cause with the peasants and really needed to do so if they hoped to build a new China. 'Lin Yutang said a good thing there; he said that before the Chinese had suffered together they couldn't sing together.' Thus Empson's discovery that the non-Chinese tribes of the western frontier had assumed the songs of the frontline fighters convinced him that China had made a great leap forward as a nation state.

However, there is a strong element of implied political mysticism in stanzas 4 and 5 of 'China', and it seems to be contradicted by the other main political argument put forward in the poem—an argument derived from a selective interpretation of the classic treatise known as the *Tao Te Ching* (which Empson had studied in Arthur Waley's translation). Like many visitors to China, Empson admitted to what he called an 'ignorant glee' about the beautiful vitality of its people and accordingly persuaded himself that the suppleness and pliancy of the Chinese temperament—or its trained character, as partly informed by Taoist philosophy—would 'absorb the Japanese however completely they over-run her'. That fragile trust or supposition is underscored in the final stanza of the poem, which features a metaphor taken from the life-cycle of the liver-fluke—

> A liver fluke of sheep agrees
> > Most rightly proud of her complacencies
> With snail so well they make one piece
> > Most wrecked and longest of all histories.

Empson explained in his contemporary notes to the poem that the lines refer to the fact that a liver-fluke when fully inside a snail 'cannot...be distinguished anywhere from the body of the snail'. The suggestion is that however much the Japanese parasite might infest the host, China could digest the intruder and still reconstitute and sustain itself much as before. (As Philip and Averil Gardner helpfully point out in *The God Approached: A Commentary on the Poems of William Empson*, Empson actually misremembers both the source of his information and the specific kind of liver-fluke in question. *Distomum macrostomum* does not invade sheep but gets itself repulsively transferred from snail to bird and back again to snail—where it develops into 'a shapeless radiating web of living tissue...which becomes so mixed up with [the snail's] tissues that it is difficult or impossible for a dissector to separate it complete away'.[54] But Empson's forgetfulness does no real damage to the idea of the stanza.) The argument 'buried' in the poem therefore relies on the axiom that the meek gain all the more strength from their submissiveness, and that in the longer term the Chinese would be the victors even if ostensibly overcome by the Japanese. As Empson added in his notes to 'China', 'The ideas of learning wisdom by not worrying and of getting your way by yielding, as in water, of course go a long way back into Chinese thought.' But it should be recognized that such a concept refers back only to Taoism, whereas Confucianism had always been the dominant ideology in Chinese moral philosophy. Empson debated his view of Taoism in 1947 in correspondence with Professor Chien Hsueh-hsi, who persuasively argued that Arthur Waley's mystical and quietistic version of the *Lao Tzu* had in fact travestied the essential realism of its philosophy. The Taoistic teaching of peace or union with all 'is far from "mystical",' Professor Chien stressed; 'it can be reached by simple reasoning upon commonly-accessible experience.' Waley's version had simply grafted on to Taoism two inapplicable motifs: a yoga-quietism and a definite antagonism towards 'realists'. Suffice it to say that the poem 'China', in appealing to such a dubious version of the *Lao Tzu*, borrowed its argumentative burden from Waley; but in doing so Empson certainly relied more on his moral faith in the Chinese he knew in person than on any sincere argument for quietism or pacifism, which he never actually credited. As he conceded in his notes to the poem, the 'common forecast' that China would absorb a successful invader 'might work out, grindingly, after a few centuries, but does not make her need for victory now less urgent'. In any event, the fact that during the course of its long history the Chinese Empire had indeed absorbed successive conquering nations was clearly due to a variety of causes other than merely yielding; and as

Empson himself later recognized, his understanding of China at the time of writing the poem was faulty. Indeed, the argument of the poem, written in the early part of 1938, was fundamentally put in question by the events of that summer, when Empson personally witnessed China's unprecedented upsurge of nationalist feeling—its collective if uncoordinated determination not to yield but to fight.

'What created the mass resistance to the Japanese was the news that swept over the country that the Japanese were not fighting like the old war lords,' Empson wrote later. 'It wasn't merely the raping and the bombing of open cities. The Japanese did a thing which seems to have struck the peasant mind much more sharply than that. They were known to have turned their horses into standing ricefields. Now that meant real barbarism.' His convoluted poem 'Bacchus', begun in Japan and finished in China in 1938, makes unexpected, baleful and yet ironically very beautiful—lyrical—reference to this horror, this evidence of the invaders' inhumanity:

> The plains around him flood with the destroyers
> Pasturing the stallions in the standing corn.

Empson distrusted nationalism as 'an infectious and invincible disease'—'a senseless thing'—'but empirically,' he believed, 'it is the strongest thing in international politics'.[55] And he immediately saw it as China's most potent weapon: it left him in no doubt at all that China would eventually win the war. 'If the Chinese can nurse up a nationalism they are all right,' he wrote in mid-1938; 'after all we [the British] can't rule Ireland or Palestine against nationalism.'[56] But his sudden certainty on that question provoked newly pressing questions. How would China handle its victory in the short or the long term? Would a sudden demobilization of peasant conscripts simply exacerbate the problem of banditry? Would it be at least politically expedient if the Japanese retained a foothold in northern China, so that soldiers would be needed to harry them? But two questions above all struck him with immense force. Would China's pride in its newfound nationalism—which might be taken to vindicate a hardline ideology—cause the country to limit free trade and close the door to international influence in general? Or would China turn on itself in a civil war? 'The only people I despair of in this war are the Japanese,' he wrote; 'they may succeed in splitting China into a Communist north and a capitalist south.' And he was not reluctant to declare his own political preference: 'What I fear the Japanese may succeed in doing (with disaster to themselves) is to make a communist north.'[57] Whether or not a quick victory for the Chinese would have disastrous consequences, he still regretted that the British government would not give more immediate financial support to the Chinese, if only with a view to the eventual gain of trading advantages. 'But it may well be, as I tell my chaps, that [Neville] Chamberlain no more wants a proud China than a proud Japan; both are worth fearing and neither is going to win too quickly.'[58]

His fullest statement of the political case, dating from June 1938, is worth quoting at length, both for its adroit analysis and as a fair argument against the eventual outcome:

It is very hard to see any end to this war, and I have a sneaking sympathy for the British attitude 'let 'em weaken each other', or in this case 'let the Japs use themselves up'. I can't see Peking coming back to the central government on a rapid peace, within a year; and then again, the way the money has all gone to the ports (instead of the successful man ending his life by being grand and a patron in his own village) has been doing great harm to China for fifty years—you can imagine good political effects from a slow and horrible war. It would tie up the Chinese Communists with the existing system, probably (unless they are holding their hand to appear as saviours in the end, but I don't believe that) and I can't see that doctrinaire Communism would be good in a rice-farming (or rice gardening) country—energy and a definite plan is badly wanted, but they are so little accustomed to centralised government anyhow.[59]

From the viewpoint of 1938 no one could really have looked a decade ahead to the time when the Communists would indeed appear as saviours; but in all other respects Empson's analysis was remarkably far-sighted.

The weeks of physical hardship and moral belittlement took their toll of Empson. In an undated letter written towards the end of the term in Mengtzu he half-heartedly resolved, 'though I have almost promised to stay next year I don't feel sure I will'. Nevertheless, both George Yeh and Chiang Monlin (Jiang Menglin), the Chancellor of the National Peking University,[60] made personal requests for him to stay: they needed teachers of his calibre. 'But it's nobody's life's work to help these people save their faces with the Chinese Ministry of Education,' Empson commented.[61] His sourness obviously stemmed from extreme tiredness and demoralization. On 14 July he reported, 'Anyway a lot of good is being done (which would have been done more slowly anyhow of course) by cutting out some lazy swine and more important by moving a lot of rich or educated Chinese into what they call "the interior"; the country gent. system was running in China till the foreign ports got strong, quite recently, and the drag of all money and ability to the ports has made the villages frightfully poorer. My impulses are all poisoned by a sense that "*we*" want both parties to weaken each other; the British patriot would be insane to back the Japanese, but he could also fairly be frightened of a rapidly victorious China.'[62] Yet it heartened him to learn that even after many weeks of bombing, the Japanese had so far failed to cut the Canton–Kowloon railway. Some officers of the Royal Air Force consequently remarked to him about the Japanese fighters, 'It's disgusting. They're letting the whole show down'[63]—comments which certainly refreshed his own sense of professional pride (though Canton eventually fell to the Japanese in October).

Notwithstanding such momentary moral fillips, a key question about his career is: why did he in fact resolve to remain in China at a point when the war seemed set to drag on without any prospect of a decisive conclusion? The answer was partly academic. He knew that the Japanese had bitten off more than they could chew when they proclaimed to the world that they would conquer the whole of the Yangtze valley, a commitment which every passing week proved them less likely to fulfil.[64] Empson admitted, 'I have an ill-natured greed to see a defeat of that brave and silly people, because I am so curious to know what they could possibly do.'[65] In contrast to his theory that in the long run the Chinese could win out of weakness, the Japanese had schooled themselves to feel utterly crushed when conquered.

On 11 August he set out the full schedule of his mixed personal feelings in this remarkably candid letter:

I cannot pretend all these passions about backing freedom against fascism, and all that, which make most of my friends think it dignified to be in China . . . I am proud to say that all these beastly little Lovers of the Far East have slunk off leaving only one man namely me . . . But still I like quite enough people here to make it seem worth staying . . . As to Love of the Far East as such, I feel nearly as bleak as Chamberlain; the great reason for backing China heartily, and that I really do, is only that Japan must not be too strong. A strong China under Chiang Kai Shek might be the same kind of thing, but before that there is time to look round. Meanwhile I am in a false position with all my communist friends, who were beginning to gather that I was shaky in the faith but now seem to imagine that I am practically in the front line. A reasonable show of not deserting the Chinese intellectuals entirely, and there have been a massive pot of desertions, is a thing that some Englishman ought to be on the spot to do, not expecting gratitude, what for, not on some absurd political ground, but merely to keep the old thing ticking over . . . All the German business men here do business in English, and so on; and it hangs to a certain extent on the prestige of English teaching . . . I like it well enough, and have no other job in sight at present, so there is no reason to talk grandly. It doesn't matter whether I go or stay. But I want to stick to my undertaking more than We Who Love China.[66]

The letter is extraordinarily impressive, particularly in its refusal to pretend to any convenient but sentimental untruth. He was not yet ready to adopt the reflexive enthusiasm of the growing number of his students who put all their faith for the future in the Camelot of the Communist party. If the Reds of Yenan were to win his vote, they would have to prove themselves fit to govern with handsome and genuinely progressive deeds, and do it with more honour than the Nationalists. In any case, the people's choice was not Empson's to make: the internal politics of China were not his direct business except as they impinged on his own trade of teaching.

His declaration also contains strong elements of both self-pity and resentment at being abandoned by his British colleagues. Both of those reactions were understandable, not only because he felt temporarily jaded and trapped by circumstance, nor even because in comparison with his students he felt like something of a political reactionary. He had gone to China not with an especially virtuous purpose but simply to fill a paid post, whereas those educators who set themselves up as cultural missionaries— he had Dorothea Richards in mind as one of a number who spoke in terms of 'We Who Love China'[67]—had withdrawn from the field of action. Supposedly those good people continued to care for China from a distance and did not care to provide moral support in person. He therefore found it a necessary psychological release to turn his embarrassment into resentment.

The fundamental honesty of the letter lies in the fact that he admits to feeling at once disaffected with his personal and professional position and yet committed to carrying on with the job. Whatever misgivings he felt about his role, he had discovered a large truth when he realized that cussedness could see him through as well as courage. Not unlike the Japanese, as he wryly perceived, his pride was now at stake: 'Personally I am like the Japanese, who are now so painfully trapped by their own point of honour here . . . by the time I have said I am going to do something the reasons against are only alarming to hear, not a decent ground for stopping.'[68]

It was not just a matter of personal pride or grudging. Above all else, he believed, educational reform in China had been severely set back by the departure or 'desertion' (to use his own word) of I. A. Richards, who had at first undertaken to direct the teaching of Basic English and straightaway gone off to a new job in Cambridge, Massachusetts. Even ten years later, when requesting that Richards should return to China and pursue the essential work, Empson wrote to his mentor in these most forceful terms: 'Of course I think you have a positive duty to come . . . and clear up the business . . . I have always felt, since George Yeh and I sat in Hongkong waiting for you in 1938 and you did not come, that you had let the Chinese down; foolishly at the moment as it turned out, but in the long run I was not foolish if you do not come back some time and make good the promise . . . no enormous piece of effort is being asked of you but merely to complete one of the important parts of your achievement which unless placidly completed would show as a total loss.'[69]

If Empson was severe in evaluating his own seemingly false position in the late summer of 1938, he insisted just as firmly that he had derived an extraordinary amount of pleasure from travelling and working with his exceptionally capable and resilient friends in the university. Time and again in his journalistic jottings, he gave such generous praise to his colleagues:

Camp life was fun; I was in very good company; the lectures seemed to go off all right. I hoped I wasn't making too much noise typing about the use of *sense* in *Measure for Measure*. It is an extremely shortsighted mind. But I know the quality of the men I have to eat with. I suppose there is no other country in the world where that type of man would take the migration and its startling hardships, not merely without false heroics, but as a trip that leaves you both waiting to collect news about your special branch of learning and also interested in the local scenery and food.[70] . . .

Imagine camping out with a set of dons. Keep in mind what dons are. See if your conversation at High Table would be still conversation around the campfire with all the insects. My own feeling is probably merely a product of escape; it is as wrong to be in the place as to dream of it. Maybe. But the beauty of the thing, the mere healing of the thing . . . comes over me like diving on a hot day whenever one of my Chinese friends is kind enough to ask me to dinner.[71]

Even so, in a less sentimental mood, he would write to his friend in Tokyo, Catherine (Lady) Sansom, during a thankful vacation in Hanoi: 'I am glad to be out of Mengtzu, the dead city, but it is a place to have lived in.'[72]

After his summer excursion to the mountains of the Tibetan frontier, Empson tripped south again in order to visit the academic and critic Graham Hough, who was then teaching at Raffles College in Singapore. Almost fifty years later, following Empson's death in 1984, Hough was to recall of his occasional encounters with Empson in the Far East:

I was rather frightened of him. Only about my own age, he was a great deal more sophisticated and infinitely more intelligent. It was plain that he didn't suffer fools gladly, and in his presence I often felt rather a fool. He had an impatient way of being always two steps ahead of you in any discussion. The best response to that was to slow the pace and insist that the steps of the argument should be trodden one by one. This he would not resist; if pulled up, he would always make things plain. But I often got shy of these delaying tactics, and so was left stumbling in the rear . . .

I was never really long enough in his company to sort out all the strands. We met at intervals in different places—in Singapore, in Yunnan, in Hanoi . . . [M]y impression of Empson abroad is always of an uncompromisingly English figure— speech, manners and bearing quite unmodified, and somehow sailing through everything with an unconquerable air of slightly arrogant courtesy and extreme intelligence. I suspect this apparent self-possession was often hard-won. His lot was a lonely one. His power of abstract concentration was legendary, but in the right company he could be gregarious and convivial. His life in China did not give him all that much of a chance. I was often acutely aware that I was ensconced in a prosperous corner of the British Raj, with a fair sprinkling of people of my own sort, while he was going back to a refugee university, in a China being rapidly overrun, to write up what English literature he could remember on the black-board because there were no books.

It is not pointless to recall all this, for I think it helps to account for the elusive, elliptical nature of his conversation and of much of his writing. His natural form of expression was conversation; he liked its informality and its give-and-take. But for long stretches of his life the necessary companions weren't there, and the conversation went on only in his own head. What came out when you met him, or often when he sat down to write, was a brusque summary; or the conclusion of the discourse; or one side of an argument, the part of the imaginary opponent being omitted; or the concealed meaning, the obvious one having been long ago brushed aside. So that the exhilaration of his discourse—I seem to have been emphasizing its difficulties, but the charm, too, was overwhelming—was that of an obstacle-race or a treasure hunt.[73]

Empson would not have agreed with Hough's estimate that he lacked the 'necessary companions' while in China; he believed his sharp, sage col-leagues in the refugee university were up to the intellectual demands of any conversation.

He returned from Singapore to the National South-west Associated University at the beginning of December 1938, just in time for the opening of the new term in a new place—the walled city of Kunming, capital of Yunnan province. (George Yeh, who had become his closest friend during the year of 'camping out', had meanwhile travelled to Peking in order to visit his wife and family; passing himself off under a false name as the manager of a radio firm, he had apparently stood up to cross-examination by the Japanese and returned south to tell the tale.)[74]

Appropriately styled 'The Spring City and the Flower Kingdom', Kunming is located on an enormous plateau about a mile (1,900 metres) above sea level. To the south the French railway connects it with Indo-China and the sea; to the west runs the Burma Road, running all the way to Rangoon; to the east, a highway to central China (via Guizhou to Chongqing). Such is its position as a crossroads city that it has been an important metropolis for hundreds of years. Marco Polo, who visited it in 1280, found it a 'large and splendid city' with numerous traders and craftsmen. (Among the local tribesmen he reported the first known instance of couvade; and he was just as astonished to discover that the Chinese heated themselves by burning 'black stones'.) Enjoying semi-tropical conditions, with an average annual temperature of 15°C, and without the enervating humidity of lower latitudes, it is a paradise of flowers: its 15,000 varieties of flora include azaleas, magnolias, orchids, and cherry trees, and more than a hundred varieties of camellia and primrose. Just a few miles to the south-west of the city is Dianchi Lake (also known as Kunming Lake, Kunming Pool, and Lake Diannan), lapping the foot of the Xishan Hills. Formed by a fault in the central Yunnan–Guizhou Plateau, at an elevation twice as high as Mount Snowdon in Wales, it is the sixth largest freshwater lake in China: some local inhabitants call it a 'sea'. It is 95 miles in circumference, covering 130 square miles, and it is surrounded by hills and a highly fertile basin which in 1938 supported crops of rice, wheat, oats, and peanuts, as well as the finest opium in China. The 'Great River' of the Yunnanese opium trade gushed out through Indo-China.

But urban life fell far short of the promise of Yunnan's salubrious natural conditions. Within the old walled city ran a few broad thoroughfares, cobbled or flagstoned avenues flanked by colonial buildings in so-called *Yanglo* style, with stone-clad ground floors and an upper storey made of intricately ornamented and green-painted wood. (Perhaps it was this kind of architecture which prompted Empson to remark to a student one day that Kunming reminded him of Florence, the buildings and the surrounding hills.)[75] Off those highways lay the very much larger number of mean streets and lanes of dirt, brick, or shingle, lined with ill-constructed dwellings of mud-and-wattle washed in white or pastel colours, with beaten earth floors and generally devoid of amenities and hygiene: charming, quaint, or picturesque they may have appeared, but most of them were no more than slum accommodations for the masses of native peasants, tradesmen, and artisans. (When it rained, the unpaved lanes turned quickly glutinous; Empson, who always loved walking—there was little alternative—would appear to be totally swathed in mud.)

Blue-garbed Han Chinese mixed with some twenty-four ethnic minorities dressed in more colourful costumes, most predominantly the peoples of Yi, Hui, Bai, Dai, Hani, Lahu, Naxi, Jingpo, Bulang, Achang, Nu, De'ang, Jinuo, and Dulong, as well as numbers of Moslems and Vietnamese immigrants. Just three years after the arrival of the university, the American General Clair L. Chennault, commander of the famous Flying Tigers, witnessed very much the same Kunming that Empson had first visited with Ivor and Dorothea Richards in 1937:

> Squat brown tribesmen crowned with fading blue turbans carried on the provincial commerce, driving packmule caravans laden with salt, tin, and opium over narrow mountain trails. Creaking, ungreased pony carts rattled and groaned over Kunming's cobbled streets. Water buffalo, cattle, and herds of fat pigs were not uncommon sights between the pepper trees lining the main thoroughfare. Here and there the alien lines of a French villa loomed incongruously out of a welter of sooty tiled roofs and lofty olive-green eucalyptus trees.[76]

The population numbered only 150,000, but the city had already outgrown itself, and an ugly gravel boulevard (or ring road) encircled the walls and linked old and more recently developed districts. Foreign consulates hugged themselves close to the north gate. For the working-class population life remained base when not squalid, whilst the elite—merchants, landlords, compradores, bankers—earned their wealth from the crippling physical labours of the underdog majority. The ruling few, who secured themselves behind walled compounds, had long maintained China's age-old feudal system and cared little for the economic or educational interests of the peasant. 'Before the war,' according to White and Jacoby in *Thunder out of China*, 'Kunming had been even more backward than Chungking'—which became the Nationalist capital late in 1938. 'Its streets were narrow, its alleyways filthy; it was one of the national strongholds of the opium merchants. Almost up to the outbreak of war its prostitutes were penned in a street chained off at both ends; rich families bought girl slaves to serve in the household.'[77] With only three higher middle schools and one recently established university (founded in 1922 and predominantly staffed by French-educated academics, Yunnan University was turned into a national university only in July 1938), Kunming had long been regarded as a cultural backwater—as 'sleepy' or 'primitive' depending on the point of view of the observer—and the Yunnanese themselves suffered from a self-acknowledged and devastating inferiority complex.[78]

'The war had dumped into this medieval cesspool,' wrote White and Jacoby, 'two elements out of the twentieth century in the shape of the finest universities in China and the shrewdest banking and commercial speculators in the land. Both these elements were sheltered by the governor, the refugee universities because their liberal professors formed a front of restrained but vociferous opposition to Chiang's dictatorship, the speculators because their completely unscrupulous black-marketeering added daily to the wealth of the city he ruled.'[79] Yet the cynical tone of that report needs to be tempered with hindsight.

To begin with, Governor Long Yun had feared that the influx of Lianda's staff and students, on top of tens of thousands of other refugees, would destabilize the power he guarded with fierce jealousy. The Sino-liberal and critical mind of the East, when confronted in the Kunming cockpit with the tribal xenophobia of Yunnan, might too easily topple the delicate balance of his internal control. But as John Israel comments, Long was quickly persuaded that 'the presence of Lianda's academics could bolster local culture and education as well as augment Long's own prestige'.[80] Once the Nationalist Government gave its approval to the relocation of the universities, the Governor reversed his originally defensive posture: 'resistance would mean direct confrontation with Chiang Kai-shek, something that Long was determined to avoid.'[81] He would thenceforward use the universities as both a shield and a sanction for his own activities, and in turn he would protect the universities as best he could.

The university opened its doors on 1 December, with term commencing on the 8th; and the authorities decided that the first full academic year would run without a break until the end of June 1939. There were 2,100 new and returning students. Lianda was lodged in various quarters throughout the city, among them a number of abandoned schools and even disused temples, but the centrepiece of the university became the comparatively grand three-storeyed building of the Kunhua Agricultural School, the occupants of which had evacuated the town for fear of bombs. Located just outside the West Gate, its campus included a two-storeyed barnlike structure (with unglazed apertures for windows) that served as a cramped and fetid dormitory. Empson was provisionally detailed to share a room—a 'cubicle' or 'hutch', he called it—with seven other teachers. For want of a proper bed he uncomplainingly slept on a blackboard laid across trestles; as much as any other of the rigours he endured in China, his readiness to sleep rough convinced him of his own professional dedication: 'it wasn't any hardship,' he recalled some fifteen years later, 'but I felt it made me a serious teacher somehow.' (His mother dispatched two hot-water bottles, which duly arrived.)[82] Professors were later afforded rooms in pairs. The students were even more close-quartered, for they slept in tiers of more than twenty to each dormitory. The place was poorly lit; and the airless conditions in those and other quarters later produced several cases of tuberculosis. Other common complaints, already much in evidence by 1939, included trachoma, typhoid (rats ranged freely), smallpox, scarlet fever, and malaria, and various internal disorders resulting from inadequate nutrition.[83] (When a smallpox epidemic broke out in town, certain local children believed the sickness came from God and called it 'flowers from the sky' because of the spots appearing on their faces; some of them refused medicine because of this belief.)[84] 'The overcrowding is so bad', Empson reported, 'that they can't get library room for what books they have.'[85] During the year the university started to build new classrooms in the form of what he called 'expensive mud huts' with thatched roofs:[86] they had a 'whimsical look,' he accurately reported, 'the mud painted black with the patchy effect of soaked blottingpaper, the thatch like pale cowcake a little crumbled.'[87] (The point of all this slapdash paintwork was for it to serve as camouflage.) A student named Hsu Kai-yu would describe life in the huts, which each accommodated about forty students sleeping in crude bunk beds, in these doggerel verses:

> When it pours outside
> It drizzles inside;
> When it stops raining outside
> It still drips inside.[88]

(One of the huts is still preserved as a memorial to Lianda, though now with corrugated iron instead of thatch on top.)

If Empson felt he had reached a safe if stuffily cabined haven, he was disabused on his first night when he walked over to the dining hall only to discover by moonlight that it had been bombed to pieces.[89] Undismayed, he dined on tinned salmon and water-beetles, with hot water from a Thermos flask and some French brandy to wash the lot down. (The first air raid had taken place on 28 September, when the buildings of the Normal School, part of which had been rented by Tsinghua University as dormitories for professors and students, were severely damaged; a number of students and servants, and local people, were killed or wounded.) Thereafter Empson enjoyed an occasional meal at a restaurant called Haitang Chun ('Crabapple Spring'), and for sociable drinking he went to the 'insanely costly' Hotel du Commerce near the railway station to the south of the city, where he would get quite drunk enough to have real need of the 'man-strength-vehicle' (rickshaw) that took him back to the dormitory; and he was robbed at least once.[90] It came as no surprise to anyone, as it was reported, that when a student or servant (or perhaps his colleague George Yeh) called at Empson's room one day he found him lying *under* his bed.[91] But his bouts of heavy drinking did nothing to diminish his standing with the students; on the contrary, they served all the better to secure his high-mettled status in the Chinese classical tradition of venerably inebriated poets.

Air raid alarms sounded virtually all the time, but presently everyone realized that the Japanese would strike only at certain times around the middle of the day (since the bombers needed to return to their bases by nightfall), so classes were held between 7 and 10 in the morning, dispersing into the surrounding countryside after having lunch before noon, and resumed from 3 to 6 p.m. The bombers flew so low that people on the ground could make out their faces. 'The bomb situation is complex but mild,' Empson remarked with characteristic insouciance. 'Last false alarm three people were crushed to death leaving the town, in the gates; getting caught in the town while shopping might be bad.'[92] But as John Israel notes, 'there was a grim reality to the air raids. On several occasions bombs wrecked classrooms, laboratories, dormitories, and faculty housing. Though human casualties were rare, the bombers' wanton destructiveness reinforced the consciousness of mission in the Lienta community... Putative evidence that China's cultural institutions were primary targets of Japanese aggression nourished the belief that preservations of these institutions constituted an act of patriotic defiance.'[93] Unbelievably, Kunming had no fire engine, and the city's high water-table made it impossible to construct air raid shelters. But the authorities had dug up the graveyard on the high ground to the north of the city—'replanting' the bones, as Empson noted, 'in large pies [*sic*] on the hills'—so as to provide slit trenches for anyone who could reach them. 'It was nice when we had an air raid alarm at the beginning of this term, when one walks out among the graves outside the town,' Empson observed, 'and we saw some men digging a hole, and when asked why they were digging the hole they said This is the Burma Railway. The embankments round here are made now but may melt in the rains.'[94] He became so accustomed to the routine evacuations that by 11 February he felt almost game for the danger: 'We haven't been bombed for a long while, which rather offends us, but presumably they will get here before the rains.'[95] Fortunately most of the intensive bombing slacked off in the first months of 1939, only to be resumed (after Empson had returned to England) in 1940.

As Governor Long had feared, relations between the newcomers and the Yunnanese were strained when not openly hostile. The locals resented the *waishengren* (people from 'outside provinces'), who were indeed utterly foreign to them, and sometimes beat up students and even professors. 'The local slang for assaulting non-Yunnanese was "beating Shanghaiese" [*Da Shangairen*], a generic term used for outsiders regardless of their province,' writes John Israel. 'It was no accident that "Shanghaiese" became a pejorative, for the stereotype of the "Shanghai sharpie" fit some of the financiers, businessmen, and government officials who moved into south-west China to compete with the local élite.'[96] As for the intrusive academics, they were proud outsiders who not only scorned the illiterate masses as ignorant, lazy and opium-sotted but even snubbed the Yunnanese elite as a 'feudal' ruling class.[97]

In view of the widespread tensions between the university body and the Yunnanese, and between the provincial and national governments, issues of local politics came to dominate Empson's travel notes and letters throughout the academic year. 'The question ... is whether the governor and his wealthy allies are to retain power or whether the central government is to obtain full control. The prejudice of the present writer is all for the present governor,' Empson stressed—along with this important qualification: 'though to be sure they might behave better ...'[98] Most European visitors, deeply distrusting Long Yun's aims and tactics, judged that the backwardness of the province could be remedied only by way of quick and complete central government control. Sentimentalists, on the other hand, overlooking the poverty, debt, and disease that constantly beset the natives, cried out against the day when Yunnan would be 'spoilt' by modernization. As one of the world's richest storehouses of unexploited minerals, with particularly large deposits of tin, it offered high promise for what Empson hoped would be 'decent' development. The key problem was how 'to get this supply of wealth used for the people'.[99] Provincial landlords and other businessmen had earned for themselves an age-old reputation for being nefarious profiteers; but Empson considered it 'stupid to say both that the province needs capital (as it does) and that these men are cormorants refusing to let capital in. They are in fact getting into the province, sometimes by rather fabulous means, the capital that it requires.' If the central government took over the running of Yunnan, it would almost certainly siphon away its industrial profits: 'there really is such an entity as the Yunnanese ... a hearty identity with China would mean intense injustice to the tribespeople,' Empson insisted. On the other hand, even if the governor and his allies were given to chicanery, their policy of self-interest would at least be more likely to benefit the local populace as a whole. 'It is quite true to say that the governor though well intentioned is bound up with a group of rich Yunnanese. All that is asked of these men, as a business matter, is to allow themselves to get richer. The economist will naturally be disturbed at hearing any refusal on this point, and indeed some of the refusals are simply bad, and if so mistaken. But the idea of economic independence in Yunnan is not contemptible at all.'

He thus felt cautiously optimistic about the separatist policy of the province. So long as the local government was moderate enough for the Yunannese to remain 'allies of China', it had best be left to determine matters of economic and local planning for itself. Economic independence would not otherwise effect the patriotism of the province. Although Empson was as yet reluctant to admit the fact, even in Yunnan that local patriotism most resolutely backed the Communists in their fight against the Japanese, not Chiang Kai-shek's squalidly effected (or enforced) policy of withdrawing and retreating or the right-wing paranoia of his determination to eviscerate the Communist body. The spirit of Chinese patriotism could and did flourish locally in the absence of nationalism, without any contradiction; it was only after the war that Empson conceded (as he wrote in *Milton's God* in 1961) that 'a certain amount of democratic sentiment is inherently part of the cost of enjoying a nationalist sentiment'.[100]

The Governor's chief adviser Miao Yuntai, who controlled the provincial bank and other commercial interests, had already decreed that a minimum of 51 per cent of the capital in industrial enterprises had to come from a Yunnanese (that is, a non-Chinese) source, a ruling which would obviously antagonize outsiders. Such was the Yunnanese leaders' reputation for deviousness, however, that a well-travelled authority on China could allege as late as 1946, 'Yunnanese politics reeked with corruption and graft, and it was believed by many that Mr. Miao was ready to sell his province to the highest bidder. He was in full control of all the tin which passed out of China.'[101] Empson in 1938 took a more sanguine view, even while conceding that Miao probably did engage in a certain amount of financial sequestration: 'It seems not to be denied that even the great Miao himself (naturally a man like that wants a nest-egg abroad) puts most of his money into the province.'

Long Yun, the classic warlord, was not a Chinese, he was a member of the Li nationality; though a Buddhist, Empson was given to understand, he sent his children to Christian schools.[102] Empson liked him for giving the lie to the stereotype of the feudal warlord as an autocratic and unspeakably remote figure. 'Often cheated by his subordinates, the governor is not merely pleased by, but immediately ready to put trust in, the type of European who blankly and at once tells him of something gone wrong. The type of European who approaches the governor with earnest politeness tends to go away saying that the governor smokes opium.' The Governor did indeed smoke opium—as did enormous numbers of other people, high and low (Lianda students 'were shocked to find opium offered to guests as a matter of course, even in government offices,' John Israel notes)[103]—a fact which Long's opponents often cited to traduce his integrity. (It was even alleged against Long that he was China's chief opium exporter.) Yet Empson so far favoured the Governor that he was prepared to venture an ill-informed opinion about the relative harmlessness of smoking opium: 'The present writer drinks alcohol and thinks from observing available addicts that alcohol is rather the more dangerous drug... The Empress Dowager led a very active and harmful life to a great age smoking every day. Opium perhaps is about as dangerous as gin; so far as you can control it by price, it ought to be a Saturday night thing for working people. It has a more dangerous quality than alcohol because it imposes more grimly the habit once formed. Apart from that it works just the same, and any pretence of horror about it is hypocrisy. It has the immense claim as against alcohol of making people talk freely without making them fight. It is high time that opium was distinguished from real terror drugs like heroin, just as they have distinguished tea from gin from beer. The governor is not dying of opium, and it is useless to sit hoping for this incident.'[104] Empson himself tried opium, though probably no more than once, and must have found that it roused him to a genial loquaciousness; but in offering his specious recommendation he had failed to observe that its toxicity is less acute when the smoker is otherwise healthy and well fed. For those who gave up everything to feed the habit, so starving themselves of any proper nourishment, the effects could be lethal. Han Suyin described the symptoms which she observed more closely, also in 1938: 'The glazed yellow skins, the bleared hooded eyes, the set of the gaunt bodies showed it; the wealthy smoked too, but they also ate well, and opium did not leave its traces upon them, but it quickly destroyed those who relied upon opium for strength, for "breath" as they called it, and those were the toilers, the load-carriers, the huakan men, the pullers of junks, who had not enough to eat.'[105] It is fortunate that Empson found no occasion at the time for publishing his misguided opinion; yet the context of his remarks shows that he was far less concerned to advocate the legitimization of opium than to set aside relatively minor objections to the Governor's conduct, since Long's enemies would attack his personal life and morality when they could find no good grounds for assailing his public administration.

But Empson's specious view of opium addiction by no means discredited his apologia for Long Yun. The new Burma Road, which opened in December 1938, covered 715 miles and enabled travellers and supply convoys to cross the old flagstone Marco Polo route from Kunming to Lashio in just six days (a stage that used to take a day could now be covered in about an hour).[106] Empson justifiably judged the road to be the best possible symbol of the Governor's real authority and resolve. 'It was a miracle that the Chinese could make the Burma Road,' Empson's spokesman was to proclaim in his BBC feature 'China on the March' (April 1942). The construction of the Burma Road signified more than anything else not merely (and amazingly) that the Governor had facilitated the material organization for such a vast engineering project but that he had imposed quite enough order on refractory tribes and bandits for it to be completed at all: 'Six hundred miles over some of the hardest country in the world, gorges eight thousand feet high, practically sheer, and built in three months, and built on time, and built very largely with bare hands.' Only in the early 1930s had the first 'vapour-chariot' or motor vehicle (a bus) penetrated the Tali plain, where Empson had foot-slogged with a mule to visit C. P. Fitzgerald; and until very recent months no travellers could pass through the mountains without running the risk of being ravaged by bandits. (All the same, C. P. Fitzgerald, in a letter to Dorothea Richards the previous year, had advised mainly, 'If you have one, bring a gun or revolver, for the wolves are very numerous on the mountain. No bandits here, quite peaceful on the road. No escort needed.'[107]) Even late in 1938 rumour had it that a group of 2,000 bandits was operating about 50 miles south-west of Kunming, near the refugee Sun Yat Sen University.[108] (In any event, taking the Burma Road was a highly perilous business, subject to landslides and torrential rains: in the summer of 1939, Empson was to ascertain from the American consul, the 'average daily casualties' were 'two lorries and three men; the lorries rolling off the track and [being] destroyed, the men killed'.[109]) The central government had a long record of stupidity and treachery in dealing with remote tribes—it had murdered the last Muly king after inviting him to dinner—which the provincial minorities would not easily forget. Also, given the rapidly rising price and short supply of petrol, perhaps a majority of the goods over the Burma Road would have to be carried by mule-train, taking about thirty days; and many of the muleteers were proud Muslims, whom the Chinese had slaughtered in large numbers after a revolt in 1870.

In Empson's mind it all added up to a thesis amply proven by results, as he wrote in another unpublished open letter: 'the present governor is important because he can keep order, to a remarkable extent. It is not clear that a new man appointed from Chungking could. And one must not think that these conditions simply mean a chaos that needs cleaning up. For one thing, the province believes that it only just escaped being ruled by the French, and escaped chiefly by continual petty obstruction. It puts a value on that kind of local freedom.' It also prompted from him an ambivalent argument for anticipating a prosperous future for Yunnan, whether as a productive but unilateralist province or as Britain's doorway to the whole of China: 'The question is of some importance now that British capital is being put into the Burma railway; if all that engineering only ended in a separatist Yunnan instead of a gateway to China it might seem a disappointment. But for that matter once the enormous mineral reserves of Yunnan were developed it might turn out a commercial convenience to have a separatist Yunnan and a British railway to it. Though a great diplomatic loss.'

At the time, in 1938 and 1939, very few observers shared Empson's positive view of the Governor: 'the intelligent visitor never seems to realise what chaos he got the country out of,' he wrote in a letter.[110] After one particularly incompetent air raid on Kunming, for example, a rumour spread round town that the Governor must have made a private deal with the Japanese in order to spare his interests.[111] (In that particular case the story was probably as silly as it sounded, but other Nationalist leaders—most notably Chiang Kai-shek himself—certainly trafficked with the enemy.)

But Empson was by no means sanguine about every aspect of provincial organization. The almost complete lack of social and medical services distressed him beyond measure. Goitre, for example, was a common complaint in Kunming, with many people suffering from elephantine necks or Adam's-apples swelling as far as their noses (during the academic year there were no fewer than ten cases of goitre among the university students); but the provincial government not only levied a salt-gabelle to help pay for foreign loans but declined to tincture the salt with iodine, which would have cost it some 20,000 dollars a year.[112] 'It seemed to me in 1937 that the Chinese [armies] were certain to break on the doctoring,' Empson commented in his BBC script.

Yet he was staggered one day by the local government's efficiency in dealing with a 'cholera scare' in Kunming. At regular intervals of a hundred yards the authorities hung across every major street 'a flaring red and blue poster' depicting 'a man having cholera, squatting on a tub and filling it with blood, till it ran over. And at every street corner there were men out talking to a crowd about what cholera was and giving free injections... I must say frankly that by the time I had walked across this town to the doctor I had begun to get very frightened of cholera. It had become a thing that might happen to me, not just an impossible thing that you ought to go through formalities about. And by the way this savage technique was completely successful. What the local government was worrying about were *two* rather doubtful cases of cholera, and these did not spread at all.' The drastic obscenity of such a public information campaign, conceived at the shortest notice, so impressed Empson that he exploited it as a significant piece of propaganda for his BBC audience: 'that I think is the kind of thing *democracy* means. It means that the local town authorities were trusted in the town, and they had to do something very fast, and they weren't talking in a BBC voice or frightened of offending somebody...' Yet the government's swiftness in preserving the city from that particular epidemic, while useful as wartime propaganda on behalf of China, by no means typified the country's medical or social practices in general. It insisted in 1938 on the training of more and more top doctors, Empson lamented, but it had failed to make provision for village clinics which could readily treat the widespread incidence of infantile dysentery, trachoma, and belly worms.

In the main, however, and quite contrary to the prejudices of visitors and newcomers to Kunming, Empson's defence of the Governor was justified and far-sighted. As John Israel writes in his history of Lianda,

Governor Long Yun had risen to power as an old-style warlord with new-style weapons but he had added to his entourage a number of modern advisers. The province he had seized in 1927 had been in continual turmoil because its military power had been based upon the decentralized personalized leadership of army garrisons and its economic power upon the production and taxation of opium. Governor Long abolished the garrison system and sought alternatives to opium as a cash crop. Following the counsel of his American-trained adviser, Miao Yuntai, he developed Yunnan's tin resources and took the first steps toward industrialization under a system of state capitalism. Hence, the notion of Long as a benighted warlord—an impression held by most Lianda modernists—was somewhat out of date. He was actually one of a group of reformist military governors... who considered their power inseparable from the political and economic development of their realms.[113]

As a militarist, Long Yun gave redoubtable support to the Nationalist Government's ostensibly active campaign against the Japanese, and he did much to develop China's internal resources. In the two years ending in

1940, for example, he established in Kunming four arsenals for the production of small arms. During the same period more than twenty new factories came into operation in his capital, including power plants and cotton mills (with 18,000 spindles); although in 1940 the then principal supply-line for requisite materials, the Haiphong–Kunming railway, was cut when the Vichy French government of Indo-China gave way to Japan.[114] In addition he harboured the outspokenly liberal body of the National South-west Associated University, curtailing press censorship and limiting the surveillance and harassment carried out by Chiang Kai-shek's secret police. (Early in 1939 Empson could afford to joke, 'As to censorship . . . the only case heard of was when an exile from the east wrote how he loathed Yunnan and the censor passed the letter with NOT TRUE NOT TRUE written all down the margin,' but he could not foresee just how bad things would become before very long.[115]) As a result of Long's patronage, writes John King Fairbank in *The Great Chinese Revolution 1800–1985*, 'the Nationalist police were unable to suppress the student and faculty movement for a coalition government and against civil war at the Southwest Associated University in Kunming until the end of 1945. When a leading and patriotic faculty member, Wen I-to (Wen Yidus), was assassinated in mid-1946, the event confirmed the general alienation of Sino-liberal intellectuals from the fascist-minded KMT regime.'[116] By 1944 Long Yun was so disaffected by the policies of the central government that, together with other provincial militarists from Shansi and Szechwan, he entered into an otherwise unlikely conspiracy with leaders of the Federation of Democratic Parties in order to overthrow the Chungking government and institute a Government of National Defence. Long Yun's plot came to nothing, however, when in October 1945 Chiang Kai-shek staged a coup in Kunming and carried Long into custody.[117]

Empson was thus remarkably perceptive and indeed prescient in speaking up for the Governor against the prevailing trend of opinion in 1938. His one grave mistake lay in supposing that the Nationalist Government had acknowledged Governor Long's arrangements and more or less readily granted his prerogative of independent development. 'The process of keeping the [Burma] road open is likely to be an elaborate one of arrangement between important local figures, some of whom Chungking might call bandits,' Empson wrote at the time; 'and if the central government excited enough resentment (which it is not likely to do) the bandits would soon have to be re-named as guerrillas.' The parenthetical supposition that the central government was 'not likely' to excite resentment in Yunnan provides an index of Empson's over-optimistic view of the situation and his lack of wider knowledge. In other places he suggested that the centralist policy was variously 'tactful and well-informed'[118] and 'unswervingly intelligent'; though it is certainly possible that by praising the Nationalists in such terms—all of which are taken from drafts of open letters intended for publication—he hoped to woo them towards better behaviour.

With regard to the management of local (non-university) business, he tended likewise to put a hopeful gloss on eventualities. Lloyd E. Eastman has described how entrepreneurial refugees from the east attempted 'to monopolize the major functions of government and to seize control of banking, trade and the economy generally. The most desirable jobs in government offices and factories were denied the natives, whom the down-river people [*hsia-chiang jen*] regarded as lazy and unskilled... [T]he natives' resentment against discrimination in jobs and social status never wholly dissipated as long as the war lasted.'[119] By comparison with that authoritative account, and even allowing for the possibility that in 1938 the process may have been less marked in Yunnan than in other western provinces, Empson's contemporary report of the same trend sounds almost blithely innocent and all too accommodating: 'What is happening is a steady infiltration of Eastern Chinese to minor positions, on the honest ground of superior competence, and meanwhile a gradual healing of separatist feelings at the top, a growing belief of important figures in the province that modernisation will work, and a rapid growth of patriotism towards China, and trust in China, from below.'[120] If meant as propaganda, Empson's words were smokably apprentice work.

Thus the unavoidable question is whether Empson in 1938–9 was more credulous than cunning in his assessment of the policies and activities of the Nationalist Government. 'The newsy titbits I put into letters generally turn out to be wrong (and unfair) within the week,' he readily admitted in an unpublished 'Letter from Yunnan'. Yet throughout a number of the open letters that he mostly drafted late in 1938 he insisted on taking an optimistic view of the relations between the provincial and central governments. Partly his response was a matter of temperament, a habit of what he called seeking out 'the cheerful prospect' and an unwillingness to attribute bad motives; partly a tendency to react sceptically against the fervour with which many of his students increasingly swung towards the Communist camp. As Han Suyin has attested, the Chinese Red Army alone had come to represent 'the growing symbol of patriotic unity, resistance to Japan, and social change.' Reports of the grotesquely right-wing activities of the Kuomintang, even if they had filtered through to the far south-west, would have seemed impossibly hard to credit in

1938—especially when Chiang Kai-shek had so recently, on 22 September 1937, ratified the formation of a United Front with the Communist forces of the Eighth Route Army, with Chou Enlai as the latter's (increasingly impotent) representative in Chungking. Empson's trust that the Nationalists would provide honest and intelligent leadership had undoubtedly been shaken in the spring of 1938 by the news that Chiang Kai-shek's commanders had breached the dykes of the Yellow River, hoping to flush out the Japanese and succeeding principally in drowning tens of thousands of native Chinese in the northern Chinese plain.[121] But for Empson, as for many Chinese patriots, most of the immediately adverse reflections on the Generalissimo's gross folly in that instance were overwhelmed by reports of the atrocities perpetrated by the Japanese. Furthermore, and perhaps most significantly, the political and cultural situation in Yunnan was (at least in the first years of the war) so peculiar that no local report could even pretend to speak for the larger part of so-called 'Free China'. Empson perhaps too complacently conceded the case when he wrote, 'As to China, she seems to be doing well; we live in Yunnan.'[122]

Ironically, the special and comparatively sheltered view Empson formed in Yunnan had been acquired as a direct result of the staunchly defensive tactics of the very governor whom he praised for his progressive and conciliatory dealings both with the 'national minorities' and with the Nationalist (KMT) Government;[123] praised too for his separatist stance— as when he wrote that the happiest post-war outlook for Yunnan would be for it to achieve 'Dominion Status'. (When the price of rice shot up in the spring of 1939, Empson was given a clue which he apparently failed to follow up: 'The story is that the central government wanted to send some of its own troops as garrison here and this is the curious retort of the local governor.')[124]

In 'A Chinese University', a short and self-conscious propagandist article he published in London in 1940 after returning home from China, Empson seemed to extol the Nationalists' supposedly sensible decision to discourage students from playing any full part in the war:

for one thing, I gather, [the students] got a name for complaining about the inefficiency of their superior officers, so that one of the colleagues [actually a student] said gravely to me, 'it is considered that, at the front, students do more harm than soldiers.' A student wrote me an essay on this subject . . . and told an appalling story of a Students' Brigade in the defence of Shanghai, which insisted on being allowed to hold a particularly dangerous position, and then broke and ran and was shot down almost to a man by the regulars behind it. This showed, he wrote, with that Chinese phlegm which has so much more morgue than even the

Englishman of legend ever achieved, that the student type is not really well suited to soldiering.[125]

A crucial piece of evidence about his unhappily trusting view of the Nationalist programme stems from his over-interpretation of a conversation that he had with some students. On the final day of May 1939, partly in order to entertain and inform a friend named George Reicher (a Cantonese speaker) who was visiting Kunming from Hong Kong, he gathered together what he called a 'party of grim young patriots', all of whom had been sent back to the university after a period of fighting as guerrillas, principally as liaison officers. They were not students of English and could not speak any foreign language, so that Empson had to rely on a third-party translation.

They seemed rather stupid about the foreign visitors' questions [he commented in his BBC script]. When asked 'Don't the peasants all hate you?' they said angrily 'they love us. They give us meat. We give it back.' A typical propaganda answer. But you can only judge these things by looking at the witnesses. These boys were so honestly surprised at the way the questions were going that it took a bit of tact not to break up the dinner-party. 'We're friends here' we said, 'we know these things are bound to be a bit hard to handle. We want to know just how hard it was for the peasants.' Well, no Chinese is too fanatical to see the point of that, and they at once said that the peasants were doing rather better than before, as well as being heartily patriotic. The Central Government had given up normal taxation inside the conquered territories in exchange for the agreement that the peasants would support guerrillas... What these boys were rather noisy about saying was that 'We don't deserve to have these quite surprising insults thrown at us,' and these were insults only thrown by me and my friend at this dinner-party. Their main function was to see that the guerrillas didn't cause famine in one village while there was enough food ten miles away across the mountains, and that they believed they had done. Naturally I didn't ask them whether they could keep alive on coolie food, because they had patiently kept alive on it for a year.

(Professors at Lianda, including Empson, lived on 12 Shanghai dollars a month—equivalent to approximately 7 shillings—students on 8; incredibly, the fighting coolie had to survive on little more than a dollar. Empson actually gave up half his contracted salary so as to share in the cuts made in the incomes of his Chinese colleagues.)[126]

In his BBC piece, the speaker 'E' (Empson) proceeds to claim from such testimony, without offering further supporting evidence, that the guerrilla movement in occupied territories was 'a very surprisingly smooth piece of Central Government organisation... [These boys] had been picked out of their guerrilla unit thirty miles outside Peking or whatever it was and sent two thousand miles across China to Kunming to read Baudelaire or engineering or whatever it was, and they were patiently doing their work, they didn't think it was at all surprising. It's no good telling me they must have been communists; they weren't; they weren't at all shy about expressing their opinions...' The only people who publish anything in England or America about the guerrilla movement, 'E' goes on to argue, 'are those good Left-Wing writers, and the way they talk you'd think it only happened in the far north of China under the communists. Actually the strongest centre of the cooperatives is in Hunan, the next province north of Canton, thoroughly under the Central Government.'

Presumably it did not occur to Empson that—if the students were telling the truth when they said they were not Communists—they might have been innocent of the devious intentions behind the Nationalist Government's insistence that they retire from the front line to the university; or else that they themselves might well have been members of the Youth Corps, an organization set up to counter the powerful popular appeal of the Communist front.

From 1938 Chiang Kai-shek's Minister of Education had been Ch'en Li-fu, a man who had studied mining engineering at the University of Pittsburgh but who occupied the extreme right wing in political philosophy; a Confucian reactionary, he was also a member of the notorious secret societies known as the Triads. As Professor E-tu Zen Sun writes, Ch'en Li-fu 'aspired to expand Free China's student body and organize its ideological adherence to Sun Yat-sen's Three Principles of the People, hoping thereby to prevent disaffected youths turning toward the CCP [Chinese Communist Party].'[127] Established on 16 June 1938, the Three Principles Youth Corps (*San-min chu-i ching-nien tuan*) served to train students in the fascistic 'principles' and methods of the Kuomintang. The government paid for its members—who numbered 50,000 by the summer of 1939 (when Empson interviewed the students at his party)—to attend university, where they were given full government licence to bully liberals and radicals. White and Jacoby reported, 'Professors wailed that colleges were being ruined because, although Corps members pulled down the scholarship level, they could not be flunked.'[128] As Han Suyin confirms, when the Ministry of Education proclaimed that students should 'reserve themselves for national reconstruction' its real intent was to mobilize the young as a direct counteraction to Communist influence.

In addition to conscripting the minds of the young by that means, Ch'en worked intensively to stifle freedom of thought within the universities. He established 'an intellectual reign of terror in political subjects such as history, economics, and sociology';[129] he shifted the emphasis of the curriculum from Humanities to 'utilitarian' subjects; and he blackmailed the universities by controlling government rations. In March 1938 an emergency congress of the Kuomintang decreed: 'A program of wartime education shall be instituted with emphasis on the cultivation of people's morals, and the enhancement of scientific research, and the expansion of necessary facilities shall be effected.' Many professors, in scientific disciplines as much as in Humanities, contested the very concept of 'wartime education': they perceived the spuriousness of the so-called 'moral cultivation' proposed by the Kuomintang and believed that a wholesale shift of emphasis towards practical or utilitarian teaching undermined China's highly valued tradition of educational liberalism (which Chiang Kai-shek increasingly scorned). Those who spoke out against the government ordinance included Empson's friend the philosopher Chin Yue Lin (Jin Yuelin), who cannily observed that 'we can easily see that too much ... diversion of young men into one or two even admittedly useful lines will not give us the kind of citizens that some of us want'.[130]

'Ch'en Li-fu said he believed in academic freedom,' wrote White and Jacoby, 'but professors who disagreed with him grew thin and hungry as inflation took its course.'[131] Inflation hit Kunming far more severely than other places, and by April 1939 Empson reported with a sense of bafflement that the price of rice had 'gone up suddenly from fifteen to forty (of what I forget), apparently only in this one town ... My school, after undertaking to feed students for eight dollars a month, now tells them that they must find their own rice.'[132] The value of the natal (Chinese National) dollar plummeted between March and August 1939; in March CN$700 could buy US$100, but by August the purchase price was CN$2,000. However, if prices merely tripled that summer (when the Chinese dollar was worth about eight pence), thereafter inflation became a nightmare, and by November 1943 the cost of living index was 410 times the manageable level it had held in July 1937.[133]

As the final measure of his intellectual tyranny, Ch'en Li-fu flooded the university with students in an obvious attempt to exhaust the dissident energies of liberal academics through the combination of overwork and personal privation.

In all the muddle and difficulty of the academic year ending in 1939 Empson had misread the political situation. Characteristically attempting to put a generous construction on every eventuality, he would have found it almost impossible to believe the common charge that the Nationalist Government was rife with corruption and perfidy. Disbelieving his students' salutations to the Red Army, he trusted that the established leadership would honour its military commitments and that, in the absence of hard evidence to the contrary, it should be supported in its putatively patriotic efforts. Accordingly he addressed himself to believing that its policy towards Lianda reflected good counsel taken in exigent circumstances. In 'A Chinese University' he included these remarks:

> The government view seems to be, firstly no doubt that China urgently needs skilled men, secondly that you don't want a mass of students wandering about the country looking for the Red Army... It is partly perhaps to prevent that that the Central Government has been insisting that we must take a great increase of students for this year; hard on the university, because it means lowering the standards.[134]

It could be suggested that Empson wrote his article with knowing intelligence, as a piece of propaganda ('The hearty sympathiser with China is tempted to suppress the truths likely to be misunderstood, or still better to keep quiet altogether,' he wrote in some other notes), for he goes on immediately to remark that 'I don't tell this as any kind of scandal' and yet ends up with this surely ironic praise of the Kuomintang: 'The guerrillas in Japanese conquered territory were simply and steadily under the control of the Central Government, and after a year of this work the boys had been ordered to come back and do a bit more schooling. It struck me as an important point because it argues a sturdy amount of organization' (p. 194). But, as the draft of his BBC script 'China on the March' makes clear, the fact is that his kindly effort to justify the Nationalists was not the work of a disinterested reporter but had run ahead of the evidence the students presented: 'Of course these boys didn't say that; it wouldn't occur to them to say it; it was simply what happened to them.' Likewise, in his very first report of the student conversation—in a letter to his mother written on 2 June 1939—he had unfortunately assumed a rather self-congratulatory tone upon perceiving evidence of what he took to be the Nationalists' good conduct of the war:

> The striking thing is that these boys while fighting as guerrillas behind the Japanese lines were well under central government control, and these particular ones came back to finish their university training because they were told to from above... People always say that the Chinese can't organise anything, but they may be the first people ever to organise a guerrilla war from the top; the striking thing from the artless confessions was how much central organisation is going on, and we had three provinces represented going from west to east.[135]

In truth, Empson himself had been somewhat naive or 'artless' in that interpretation, for the government policy on education was actually motivated more by punitive craftiness than by care or constructive planning. He had swallowed a line of propaganda, which he in turn exploited in his own BBC propaganda (as well as in 'A Chinese University', 245), with some selective heightening to enforce the validity of the point: he bulked up his first authentic report of 'three provinces represented' to 'five boys from five provinces in line'.

But Empson cannot be blamed for his misinterpretation of the activities and ruses of the Kuomintang. He had left China by the autumn of 1939; and before that time even Chiang Kai-shek's most dedicated antagonists could have apprehended only a small portion of the full phantasmagoria of his dealings, as Han Suyin has testified. 'I did not know,' she wrote in *Birdless Summer*, that Chiang's policy of retreat and inaction 'was not heroic defiance, but a series of careful calculations, well ordered perfidies . . . The joy that was mine was an illusion; it was an illusion shared by a good many, who honestly believed that Chiang meant to fight.' It was only after Empson had left China that the Kuomintang and the Ministry of Education really started doing everything in their power to dominate the university; only during the 1940s did they choke Lianda with students and curtail its resources in a determined effort to inhibit its political liberalism and to snaffle those students who desired to serve China under the Communist flag. As White and Jacoby recorded in 1946, 'The government, always suspicious of the advanced political views of the northern universities, watched these refugee institutions like a hawk, tightening the net of surveillance closer about them with each passing year.'[136]

In any event, Empson's 1940 article, 'A Chinese University', would have done no damage. On the contrary, it served its purpose as very good propaganda for China, since its central burden is to praise Chinese worth and to encourage the Western Allies to support its stand against the Japanese. It gives what credit it can to Chiang Kai-shek and his regime for their supposedly enlightened policy on education—'The government view seems to be, firstly no doubt that China urgently needs skilled men'— but it reserves highest praise for the university itself: its resourcefulness and integrity, as well as its determination to survive. Chiang Kai-shek at least had an authority recognized by the international community, if not a popular mandate. Mao Tse-tung and the Red Army looked like insurgents, and even calling them 'guerrillas' could seem like a double-edged designation. It would not do for Empson in 1940 to subvert Anglo-Chinese relations by exposing Nationalist misrule or internal conflict. Chiang demonstrated that he held the initiative, as Empson truly suggested in 'A Chinese University', when he increased university enrolment in order to try to counteract communist enlistment. But Empson stipulated the necessary limits to that strategy in a loaded aside: 'it is important by any reasonable method to lessen the danger of a north-*v.*-south civil war' (p. 244).

It is also necessary to realize that whereas a number of the university students embraced the Communist camp, the vast majority of the faculty stood with Empson in supporting the Nationalists. 'Chinese intellectuals were nationalists first, liberals second,' John Israel observes. 'Faced with a state authority that demonstrated even a modest capacity to give China stability at home and respect abroad, most Chinese intellectuals were more than ready to bury their liberal scruples. Hence they backed the Guomindang [KMT] in the 1930s and the Communists in the 1950s . . . At no time prior to 1949 did the majority of liberal intellectuals become pro-Communist. They simply became more and more anti-Guomindang.'[137]

There is in any event solid evidence that by the time Empson left China he had seen quite enough to start changing his mind about Chiang Kaishek and his government. He was too honest not to say in 'A Chinese University' what he believed to be for the best, and certainly not stupid enough to suggest any sharp criticism of China's prosecution of the war—which would have undermined the article's very value as a piece of propaganda authenticated by buoyant personal witness—but it is surely significant that his argument on behalf of the government is couched in phrases such as 'no doubt' and 'partly perhaps'. In contrast to the conservative caution of his published article, moreover, the notes he took for himself as early as 1938 categorically insist that the central government's ploy in restraining the students 'is one of the many failures of detailed administration':

There is certainly a great mass of dull office work that needs doing efficiently and is at present lacking behind the Chinese lines, and the students could do it. You hear it said that when they get there they are too vain and restless to be useful. This is merely because they realise that the work given them is pointless. Let it be much duller, only organised from the top and with a solid claim to be needed, and the critical powers of the educated would not take this painful form; there are certainly many students with ability and devotion enough to give the country great help . . . But it must be patriotic work, and recognised as such by the government in some form that they can keep and show afterwards, because otherwise they may lose the very important position of dignity gained by the university education.

Furthermore, in one of the very last letters he wrote from China (dated 8 August 1939), he finally acknowledged, though still reluctantly, that a Communist dispensation could well turn out to be right for China; and in view of John Israel's evidence cited earlier, Empson must have been one of the very first of Lianda's professors to do so:

It seems clear that some kind of communism would be the only working arrangement that could give hope of a stable state (if that is wanted) other than a simple agricultural one ... [P]eople keep saying now that Russia is like Germany, and morally it may be, but one claims to escape slumps and the other can't. I am not convinced of the claim anyhow, but it seems the main subject about the future of the world.[138]

'Until very late in the war...,' writes John Israel, 'there were no Marxists among the 200 full and associate professors on the faculty. Furthermore, the variety of Marxism that eventually gained an audience (more among students than among their teachers) was the moderate united front known as "The New Democracy." Though Yan'an [Yenan] became a Mecca for the faithful, the Communist leader with the greatest magnetism for Kunming's leftists was not the earthy populist Mao but the urbane aristocrat, Zhou Enlai.'

Early in 1940 Madame Chiang Kai-shek published a collection of her propaganda articles under the title *China in Peace and War*, with a jacket photograph that showed her as usual—'very charmingly,' observed Empson (keeping his own face straight)—as a deeply painted lady. (Once, when a 'very intelligent Chinese' expressed to Empson his misgivings about Madame Chiang's elaborate make-up, Empson had very pointedly and aptly remarked that she looked like the Empress Dowager.) Empson's review of the book, published in *The Spectator*, reveals just how very far he had progressed both in terms of foreseeing a Communist destiny for China and in general political shrewdness. Madame Chiang had produced 'rather a dull book,' he wrote, even while she managed somehow to be 'very rousing and trustworthy'—except on this key issue:

What may turn out too narrow in her influence is her rigid resistance to the Chinese Communists (referred to here casually as 'bandits'). It is very hard to see one's way through that. But the Chinese have very little respect for foreigners' theories; the present Chinese Communist policy seems mainly a good agrarian one; a great deal of Government control of business is anyway normal to China outside the ports; and altogether there seems room to absorb a Chinese brand of Communism under the name of Sun Yat Sen. The chief thing as time drags on will be to avoid a civil war between north and south, which would force the north under control of Moscow.

'The story goes,' Empson remarked with sharp disingenuousness, 'that Chiang feels that more than his wife does.'[139]

In one of the unfinished open letters that Empson wrote while still living in Yunnan, he determined that 'local, even sub-provincial, politics, is the strength of China, and . . . the chief and unsolved problem (both for running the war and for the aftermath) is to gear that life onto the ample products of the higher education.'

Throughout the academic year, he thought, the university carried on its work in a wonderfully impressive fashion. A large number of first-year students of Chemistry were still being given practical classes, even though the material resources they required were virtually non-existent. 'Burning methylated spirits under retorts was a particularly desperate academic extravagance,' he observed, 'but I hear we have now thrown dignity to the winds and taken to using the local rice wine; it gives a very hot flame.'[140] Botanists did experimental research on a vast range of wheats collected from the upland countryside; other scientists developed a commercial scheme for turning castor-beans, 'which they are given free as weeds,' into aeroplane oil, vaseline, and candles.[141]

Being always eager to keep up with new scientific discoveries, Empson in September 1938 sniffed out a rumour that Sir Arthur Eddington had calculated the exact number of protons in the universe, but felt dashed not to be able to gather anything about the question from the physicists of Raffles College at Singapore during his visit to Graham Hough. However, once he got to Kunming, he happened to mention it to a colleague at Lianda, 'a man who had had to leave all his own books two years before, who was now living two or three to a cubicle, and who had spent the intervening time in the interior of China, where you are lucky if the post works even if you know what to write for. But to him none of this was the point at all . . . He said with a cry of sympathy, "Oh, *why* didn't you tell us before you went? Of course we've got all that stuff here. I'll show it to you tomorrow." And they had. It is, you see, a university, not a bad place for an inquisitive mind to live . . .'[142]

'If you want to know about Thibetan iconography or whether there have been any recent diggings in Mexico you simply ask who is our man on that,' he reiterated on another page of his notes; 'you may find he is below par, but we have got one.'[143] He was by no means exaggerating the situation: as if to exemplify his extolment of the university, he revelled during a coffee-break one day in a long spontaneous conversation on the subject of Chinese goldfish with a well-informed professor of German.[144]

'Getting horribly lazy,' he undeservedly wrote about himself in his very first week in Kunming.[145] He taught courses on Shakespeare and on contemporary British and American poetry (still dictating and improvising while texts remained scarce), which the students very much admired; and when not teaching or painstakingly correcting student essays he contrived to keep on typing drafts of his own critical essays. But in the middle of the academic year, during a fortifying spree in what he termed 'the fleshpots of Annam',[146] he somehow managed to dislocate his right arm, which baulked his usual procedure of writing out the whole of each lecture on the blackboard. (For a short while, in March 1939, he taught too at a private school run by a Franco-Chinese gentleman, a 'strange little man' who liked to tell endless stories about his long-lost wealth and high connections. 'My first lecture there he kept running in and out like a butler bringing brandy and cigarettes, a great nuisance, and he is supposed not to be able to afford it . . . He goes back before the railway.'[147])

But his university students had become subdued, he remarked. 'It was the most difficult period of the war for us Chinese,' recalled Professor Li Fu-ning. 'The enemy had occupied a large part of our territory, laying waste our land and slaughtering our people. We despaired of support from other nations in our defensive war of national salvation.'[148] The enthusiasm that the students had displayed during the first year of the war had 'noticeably cooled', Empson observed;[149] and ironically they suffered from 'a healthy boredom about the arguments in favour of doing things that the government does not want them to do . . . Certainly the patriotism is still there, but the old dramatic importance of the Peking student is not.'[150]

'One must remember,' he correctly explained in a draft essay entitled 'Students in China', 'that these figures, or their predecessors in the universities, were effective figures in the evasive politics of their day; not only in forcing the government's hand by demonstrations [but] also in fraternising with the troops of various armies and spreading high political ideals. Now they have been tucked away in Yunnan among an unfriendly local population . . .' The result, he noted elsewhere, was an 'unwilling impotence'—though their patriotism ran just as high as ever.

Increasingly, Empson felt just as cast down as his students, for many reasons including the fact that he could make too little progress with writing his own critical essays. Bamboozled by bombs, bureaucracy, and local politics, he found it hard enough just to live and teach in Kunming, let alone sit down and write for any sustained length of time. Unlike many Chinese, he was acutely sensitive to human hubbub—the constant clamour of life in a Chinese city—and longed for some peace and quiet. 'I wish to God I could get on with my mad little literary book,' he complained in May, 'the Sibylline leaves are gradually being thrown away by the servant.'[151] (The servant had in fact thrown away one whole chapter.)[152] The projected book, which turned out a decade later to be *The Structure of Complex Words*, had 'no shape,' he lamented;[153] it seemed 'confused', with 'an unpleasant way of seeming either trivial or crazy.'[154] But it was not so much the book that got him down, it was dealing with the trivia and craziness of everyday life and officialdom. As late as February 1939 he believed that the academic year in Kunming was turning out to be 'a useful burial to get my beastly little linguistic book pulled into order',[155] but things turned out quite differently.

After the first days of sleeping on his blackboard, he moved into a house owned by the British and Foreign Bible Society (there were in fact two separate societies with an uneasy working relationship). First in Changsha, then in Nan Yueh, and finally in Kunming, Empson the anti-Christian had developed a knack for putting up with Christian dwellings. Oddly enough, the British interest in the Bible Society was represented by a smoking and drinking Dane named Molgard—'a competent business man' who managed a good trade in peddling bibles—the Foreign (American) side by a 'wicked Dr Huong'.[156] 'Molgard is a very queer chap who likes to play between two worlds,' Empson reported; 'if you are not a missionary he offers you beer, with an obscene leer.'[157] Located in a simple but pleasant two-storeyed, timbered and terraced house on high ground in the northern part of Kunming, the mission at number 78 Pei Men Kai (Beimen Street) had a balcony running the width of the building front and back, as well as a garden. Empson at last had a room to himself, and delighted in his partial vista of the town. 'It is almost the boarding house life which I thought vainly I should never lead,' he wrote.[158] 'The missionaries are really very queer. The previous British Consul asked all British subjects to a garden party on the King's birthday, and received a series of letters of real flaming anger because this meant that they would be asked to drink alcohol to the health of the king. None of them came. Now it is very sensible to say that alcohol does harm...but surely if you are a missionary into wild paganism it is not sensible to be afraid of being contaminated.'[159]

Close at hand, to the north of the lotus-laden Cui Hu (Green Lake) Park at the centre of the city, was the British consulate. (Japanese bombers had no trouble in locating the city, day or night, because the lake shone like a mirror. When a bomb struck the lake, mud and slime cascaded upon the consulate, making the white one brown. 'I'm glad this has happened,' said the British consul, 'I wanted to paint the house this colour anyway.'[160]) And yet the consul, who put on a 'blank and glum style', Empson considered in general 'a pity': 'He is famous for getting an injunction from Shanghai (under extraterritorial rights, this year) to suppress a dog in the next house which he said barked. He gets £100 entertainment allowance and doesn't entertain at all. His wife is fond of saying she liked Japan and the Chinese say he is a Japanese spy... He told [a friend] the Burma road was closed two days before an arranged visit of Burma government people came up the road with fifty tons of machine guns to discuss prospects with him. A disappointed man.' On the other hand, the American Consul and his wife, the Meyers, threw many a splendid do. 'Touchingly generous, there was a big party which went on flowing with champagne because, they said, they had run out of everything else.'[161] They aspired to 'pursue culture', but still Empson enjoyed their company and their parties, though all too often with sorry consequences. 'As I get older,' he confessed (at the ripe old age of 32) to his friend John Hayward, 'I find I still act the same way at parties but get alcoholic remorse the next and even subsequent days more heavily.'[162]

Molgard and Huong presently went on long leave, and a short-statured, blue-eyed, energetic Scotsman named Arthur Pollard-Urquhart (who had taught English for many years in the Western Languages Department at Tsinghua University) rented their premises at 78 Pei Men Kai in order to run a branch of the Basic English Institute, with considerable support from the Rockefeller Foundation, on behalf of R. D. Jameson and I. A. Richards.[163] It was Pollard-Urquhart who had invited Richards to make his first trip to China in 1929. (Richards had recently completed, and published in Peking in October, a first-year primer of Basic English running to 427 pages, *A First Book of English for Chinese Learners*, which Empson considered 'very good if rather metaphysical'.)[164] Pollard-Urquhart arrived in Kunming on 25 August, three months after Richards's return to the United States. According to Empson, who liked his company, Pollard-Urquhart was at root a 'Peking art-and-sin fan', but he exercised very good diplomatic skills in forwarding the cause and purveying the texts of Basic English against enormous odds. Distressed by the hardships he discovered in Kunming, 'Polly' (as Empson liked to call him) also turned out to be 'nature's landlady though furious at being made one': he liked to fill the house with temporary lodgers including a Shanghai bible salesman and his wife and 'a depressed refugee Jew who teaches German'. Uncharacteristically, Empson found the constant noise and bustle of the Institute a matter for good-humoured regret:

from the Spartan sleeping on the blackboard, the high ideals, the companionable silence throughout the Chinese meal, I now go down from my charming bedroom and balcony to a perpetual squeal of complaint and attack on China throughout the excellent European meal. I was puzzled to know why [Polly] contradicted himself till I realised it was because virtue is a mean; there are therefore always two possible complaints on every topic, and he says both. Happy talk about birds is going safely on with the Bible salesman. Polly: Of course the Chinese catch birds and sell them *alive*, something for nothing, irresistible to a Chinese, of course that's all they care about birds. After a pause the Bible salesman says Of course some Chinese are very fond of birds, they *buy* birds. I KNOW says Polly leaping on him, they give far too much, ridiculous extravagance. It is a great change after last year.[165]

Streams of other visitors included lots of students as well as 'odd Chinese professors' who would ask to lie down between meals, as well as Norman France from Hong Kong: 'it gets to seem awful hard work always pushing people into the right eating-house at the right time,' sighed Empson.[166]

During the winter he participated too in a short 'training course' in Basic English for Chinese Middle School teachers (though only 15 attended). He later thought it had been a waste of time to lecture at them, especially when they had obvious difficulty understanding what he wrote on the blackboard, rather than make them talk about their problems: 'once the teachers can be got to discuss and take an interest they can be wooed round to see what is wrong with the present textbooks,' he unconvincingly reassured Richards.[167] Nevertheless, the prospects for promoting Basic English in Yunnan still looked good. By the spring, however, the Rockefeller Foundation threatened to withdraw its grant. 'They are always chopping and changing,' Empson protested.[168] Good results were not appearing fast enough, they complained, and anyway the Chinese did not really appreciate their assistance.

Other political problems threatening the future of Basic English stemmed from the intense rivalry between local and national governments. Since both the universities, Lianda and Yunda, were under the control of the central government, the provincial Commissioner for Education had taken pride in having what Empson called 'a show of his own backed by Rockefeller' (the Basic English Institute remained adamantly independent of the central government) and had refused to allow any of the University Chinese to teach at the winter 'holiday course'.[169] Presumably in direct retaliation to that snub, the central government decided to organize its own big summer school and threatened to exclude from it any lecturers from the Basic English Institute. At the end of March, Pollard-Urquhart

left for a two-month trip in England (his mother had died, and he had to
settle family affairs), so Empson was left to 'try to push Richards' scheme a
bit'[170] (as he saw it)—though he was not officially attached to the Institute
but employed by Lianda. I. A. Richards had sensibly delegated two
Chinese colleagues, Wu Fu-heng (who was subsequently granted a fellowship to study under Richards at Harvard) and Chao Chao-Hsiung, to help
run the Basic English interest; but the 'very wicked' Chao embarrassed the
Institute by taking a job at the National Yunnan University as soon as he
arrived in Kunming.[171]

Empson claimed to find such crises 'amusing', but the efforts he put into
resolving them were manifestly time-consuming and deeply frustrating:
'who decides on the course?' he protested,

> the commissioner now says he is wholly loyal to the government so naturally he
> waits for orders and can only act as business manager. The only statement so far
> from the other side is the demand of the Chancellor of my university that the
> universities must do the work not men from Pollard's local office. But as none of
> the university people want to do it, and as all three of Pollard's office can be
> technically wangled in to one or the other university for this purpose, it looks as if
> we may end up by being able to plan a coherent course.[172]

'You understand,' he emphasized in the same letter to his mother, 'all this
muddling refers back to the slow big fight between the central government
and the provinces.' Whether or not his mother did understand the complex infighting of Chinese politics, Empson found his very worst enemy to
be 'blank indecision'.[173] Eventually, after long struggles to save face, the
two parties to the quarrel did reach an unwilling reconciliation and
the summer school went ahead at the end of the university year in July,
with official participation from the Basic English Institute. (The Hanoi–
Kunming railway had lately become so congested that only French supplies were being allowed through from Indo-China, but the French Consul
assisted the cause of Basic English by arranging for parcels of the Richards
textbook to be addressed to him at the Consulate.)

Empson contributed three lectures to the school for Middle School
teachers, including one he entitled simply 'Basic and Communication'.
Basic English began not as a teaching tool, he advised his audience, but as
an investigation into 'the root ideas needed for any language, or any clear
thought. Dr Richards's book *Basic Rules of Reason* was made as a paper for
the Aristotelian Society, a society of philosophers, and he made it in Basic
because that seemed to him the only hope of getting the ideas of philosophers in order, or making a connection between the ideas of different

philosophers.' He also pointed to the coincidence of his own theoretical and practical procedures later in the same talk, when he argued that Basic English naturally develops intellectual clarity and critical sensibility:

Basic is not specially simple English; it keeps back the 'exceptions', the words with tricks that are of no value, but it makes necessary (if anything) more attention to 'grammar', to the general principles of word order and structure in English, than the language commonly used in talking; and to get a thing said fully in Basic may be a training in thought . . . The limited word list is not only the quickest way to give a man a working knowledge of English, of the sort that will be of most use; it is the best way to give him good taste, later on, in writing English or reading English books.[174]

Despite the straightforward appeal of his talk, Empson clearly felt discouraged by the response he encountered. In a lecture given to a different kind of audience later the same year, he explained why it had been so urgently necessary to inculcate the teaching of Basic English in Chinese Middle Schools: 'the students tied themselves in knots with English sentences all composed of complex words. You could always clear up the ambiguities by writing alternate sentences largely in Basic, and this is a great help because it gives you solid ground to go back to . . . But I have rarely been able to get Far Eastern students to use Basic for themselves, because they are too proud; they say they know more English than that already. Of course it ought to be introduced earlier, not at the university level.' In August 1939, then, he felt he could pass on only this much watery encouragement in a letter to I. A. Richards: 'Basic news generally good except that the local Middle School teachers are too ignorant to learn a method and the graduates who get forced into the job are too vain.'

Domestic problems compounded the exacerbation of his professional life. By the summer, the British and Foreign interests in the Bible Society had decided to amalgamate, but for some reason a 'Bible War' broke out and the two partners tried to evict one other from the premises at 78 Pei Men Kai. In any event, Molgard the Dane came back to Kunming at the end of July and Empson had to find other accommodation at short notice. He and Pollard-Urquhart, who had just returned from England, ended up 'camping in a large Tomb' which George Yeh had hired with a view to accommodating his wife and family (who had managed to get out of Peking). The tomb was Empson's last lodging-place in Kunming, though it was not actually as grim as it sounded. He explained in a letter to Michael Roberts, 'I am living in a holy summerhouse in a large tomb, very quiet and pleasant; stewards of the great house come and peer in to see if I am desecrating it; the chief article of furniture is a full size pingpong table.'[175] Despite being blessed with such a luxury, it lacked water, electric light, and drainage.

Then the central government issued a direct order to the university to evacuate the town. The university refused to do so: any further upheavals would mean complete disruption, they argued, and in any case they were already planning to move to new premises outside the city walls (about 50 yards outside, to be precise)—the expensive mud huts of the so-called 'New Campus'.[176] The university won that particular battle, and remained in Kunming for the rest of the war. But Empson had left Lianda long before the quarrel had been resolved, and even some sixteen months later, in December 1940, he was still worrying: 'My letters to China haven't been answered; it is bad news if the university has had to move again, but they were sturdily trying to get out of it.'

He had first considered taking a year's home leave early in 1939. He had no intention whatever of permanently forsaking Lianda, only to recuperate from the rigours of wartime China and if possible to finish his book of criticism: 'I hanker after glitter, because the material [for the book that eventually became *The Structure of Complex Words*] seems so unreal unless pleasing…,' he wrote on 22 February; 'there isn't a great deal more I can spin out of my bowels, I don't believe'.[177] Stagnation and harassment had taken their toll of his morale, leaving him feeling 'slack and submerged,' he wrote home in May.[178] 'I seem to be drinking too much, too much brandy alone, I keep healthy and good humoured but seem to stop thinking altogether.' That same month he was granted a year's furlough, to begin at the end of the current academic session— 'with a chain on the leg, promising to come back',[179] and with a one-way passage to be afforded by the university. But Chiang Monlin, the Chancellor of Peking University, compassionately made it known to him that his leave would be deemed to be 'indefinite' if the war broke out in Europe.

'Bill Empson is leaving here tomorrow,' the kindly Pollard-Urquhart wrote to I. A. Richards. 'He says the place has got on his nerves, and indeed he has become very queer. He is going to the States but will eventually go on to Europe. Naturally he will look you up in Harvard. I shall miss him, as he is the only really intelligent foreigner here.' He departed from Kunming for Indo-China just after the middle of August, leaving behind all his books and gramophone records for use by Lianda. With his friend Norman France he stayed for a few days in Hanoi at the well-proportioned and coolly shuttered elegance of the Hotel Metropole (subsequently famous for accommodating Graham Greene twenty years later, it is now the Thong Nhat Hotel), where he hoped to unbutton himself. But the newspapers announced the signing of the Molotov–Ribbentrop Pact, and at once it became obvious that the European war was imminent. Another guest at the hotel, on leave from Hong Kong, was Arthur Cooper, who had known Empson through his friendship with Humphrey Jennings (Jennings had in fact married Cooper's sister Cicely) and with other mutual acquaintances including Kathleen Raine and Charles Madge. Across the crowded hotel dining-room, in a sudden pause of French conversations, Cooper heard what at the time he termed 'Cambridge noises' and immediately recognized Norman France's haughtily high-class tone of voice saying 'end they hed *nothing* but messahs and messahs of sausageahs'. Glad to hear peculiarly English voices on a day of such dreadful news, Cooper went over to their table. Empson treated him as a good friend, as a friend of his friends, and for the rest of the week Cooper hugely enjoyed his stimulating and entertaining conversation on every conceivable subject—'some of which he knew about and some very little,' Cooper recalls, 'but that hardly mattered, if at all, to the enjoyment derived.' Cooper, who could speak Chinese, was visiting the École Française d'Études d'Extrême Orient, and he introduced Empson to a distinguished French friend, François Géoffroy-Dechaume (later French Ambassador in Rangoon, and Ambassador-designate to Washington at the time of his death in a road accident), who happened to be doing his military service and so wearing uniform. Cooper was amused that Empson talked engrossingly about his own ideas on Buddhist iconography—illustrating his exposition with his collection of photographs and occasionally turning to Géoffroy-Dechaume with polite remarks about the weather— and never realized that Géoffroy-Dechaume, whose father was a celebrated painter, and who was a painter himself, was in fact deeply informed on the subject of Buddhist images.

Bill was, anyway in those days, very Cambridge and very English abroad; or at least played that part, as when in the mornings he used to shout louder and louder for shaving water in English and then come along to my room with interesting theories about why the natives took no notice whatever! He was, of course, great fun and wonderful company. I remember drinking with him one evening and emerging at the top of some steps into the street, where a throng of 'poussespousses', rickshaws and trishaws, rushed up to the foreigners with cries of 'Femme français, femme annamite, femme métis!' and Bill swaying on the top step, bawling in appalling French: 'Je ne veux *rien*, qu'un sergeant négre *énorme* de régiment sénégale!!'[180]

Whether playing the convivial clown or simply paying his social dues, Empson was yet drawing on very low reserves of nervous energy. He was in a wretched condition by the time he reached Hong Kong in the first week of September. There he stayed for three days with another friend, Hugh Williamson—whose servant was horrified at Empson's destitute and dirty appearance—and then again for a while at Norman France's beautiful house, before sailing for America on a Norwegian-registered freighter. The passage seemed more like a cruise than a crossing, as he wrote home from on board, just short of Shanghai.

Very soothing . . . with nobody much to talk to . . . The other passengers are mainly American ladies, nice friendly goodlooking people who spend their whole time acting like small children at a tea party: they have to scream with pleasure all the time or they would feel they weren't good mixers. I have been on the boat three or four days and none of them has yet mentioned the war at all. Of course everybody I knew in Hongkong was volunteering and talking strategy and hardly able to talk about anything else, so it is a fine rest cure. We get just the essential news but no more.[181]

On 14 October he landed in Los Angeles, and even twenty-two years later he had a clear recollection of what he did next:

there is a park in that city which rises to a fairly bluff summit. I went to the top of it and screamed; this was in 1939, so my feelings need not all be blamed upon Los Angeles. After I had been screaming for a bit I found I was being shot at by boys with air-guns; this satisfied me in some way; I came down the hill, and took the train to San Francisco.[182]

He had very good reason to try to purge himself with that primal scream. He had just spent two years trudging through the Chinese war—which even he, who never indulged in overstatement, once described as 'the savage life and the fleas and the bombs'[183]—and was about to enter its sequel, the war in Europe. No one could tell when peace would come again.

17

Postscript

England I think an eagle flight
May come too late, may take too long.
What would I teach it? Where it could
The place has answered like a gong.

'Autumn on Nan-Yueh'

I N the face of all the personal and professional difficulties he had shouldered in China, and with his vexed view of the country's political and military situation, what had ultimately kept him going for those two years? 'China is extremely short of trained men in all the departments necessary to her defence and reorganisation, and cannot let the training lapse during a war which may take a very long time,' he had written in his unpublished essay on 'Students in China'. But would it not therefore be proper, he had often asked himself, to sacrifice his own lectures on English literature for the duration of the war? 'The old savage notion is still retained here that teaching students is next door to charity, though charity itself is the first duty of any decent man,' he added. But not even that observation fully reassured his conscience. Was he, as an Englishman, serving any genuinely useful purpose by staying in China at all?

Two answers had sustained him above all else. The first took the form of a heartfelt conviction that he had been lucky beyond all expectations to live and work with a group of extraordinary colleagues (and pupils), and to have been able to contribute in some measure to their community of scholarship. He believed he could never speak too highly of their personal and intellectual gifts, and it was with them in mind that he wrote this simple formulation:

The object of a university is not to train officers or political lecturers (not even in the bleakest war) but firstly to teach men who are capable of being made better as individuals by the teaching (a small number in any class) and secondly to collect from the students a body of men who can claim to be a university, when they are put on the staff, that is, a group competent to answer what any sensible man might choose to ask. The idea of a university (though of course the perfect one is in the clouds) is quite a simple thing. It is what good talkers talk about. When Boswell and Johnson were in the Hebrides it struck them that their own club of personal friends would make a nearly complete university; they had a mathematician before, but he had died. Before his death the list of what the club could teach covers nearly all the knowledge of the time.[1]

The other answer he found valid and genuinely satisfying had been given him quite by chance early in 1938, as he recalled in 'A Chinese University':

A student of economics [Chang Chiu-tse] brought this up in Mengtzu while we were swimming in a rather insanitary little pool used by the villagers for bathing their water-buffalo, and in passing I must tell any millionaire among my readers that no rubber toy for the bath has anything approaching the charm of a water-buffalo. It is curiously slimy, so that to hold on to its tail and try to climb on to its back as it heaves forward is one of the major sports. This student remarked that the opinions of a Middle School boy are always wrong; while he was a Middle School boy he had considered how best to serve his country, and had thought that the best thing to go in for was economics. But now, he said, we can see that the economists have been totally useless, while the literary students who can do Propaganda are very important.[2]

'Given this attitude,' he affirmed in a draft of the published article, 'even the literary teacher can reasonably be asked to carry on through the war.'[3] It seemed to him 'a respectable defence' of his own role, especially since the Chinese placed a high value upon propaganda; and even science students needed to acquire at least one European language in order to keep up with their subjects. 'Hence good language teaching is much more needed here than in Europe. It is hard to deny that even practical or newspaper English is tricky enough to make an English literary training useful for the teacher. It is quite unsafe to read a political article in English if you can't spot an irony. You might well make other demands from the overworked and underpaid teacher (about methods of teaching) but some literary training has to be demanded [for teachers in the Middle Schools].'

He must have felt fully vindicated in that conviction when Pollard-Urquhart presently wrote to tell him that only seventeen students from the province had passed into the various universities in 1940. The Commissioner for Education had 'lost a lot of face and is more furious than ever with the Universities,' Pollard-Urquhart observed. Consequently the Commissioner asked the Basic English Institute for a report on why the standard of English teaching in the province was so bad, and they responded in no uncertain terms, with the recommendation that a Teacher's Institute should be established under their direction.[4] The reconstruction of English teaching duly began with the inauguration in Yunnan of a Basic English Experimental College advised by I. A. Richards.

But on 6 October, soon after writing his affectionate letter to Empson— 'I miss you very much . . . At Chinese dinners we liven the table by *Empson stories*, of which there are many,' he added[5]—Pollard-Urquhart died from a blood infection leading to gangrene after being injured in an accident involving a car during an air raid.[6] 'I do feel very bad about Pollard; he got to be an intimate friend of mine,' wrote Empson to Richards. The Experimental College was subsequently headed by Robert Winter (1887–1987), a flamboyant, gifted, and gossipy American expert on Basic English who had once, while studying at Wabash College, Crawfordsville, Indiana, been acquainted with Ezra Pound, and who had taught English literature at Tsinghua University since the 1920s; his circle of friends included the writer Emily Hahn. Empson came to know Winter well in Peking after the war.[7]

A belief in the value of propaganda had run through Empson's mind a great deal during his last months in China. It was almost as if he was training his attention to the next stage of his career, when he would join the BBC and in due course lead the Chinese Section of the Far Eastern Service. 'We are slowly learning,' he wrote in his unpublished 'Letter from Yunnan', 'that the technique of rival or counter propaganda is the only straight answer to the recent appalling discoveries in the technique of propaganda. President Roosevelt is an impressive figure in Europe because he understands this simple truth.'

He had even found a local occasion to test that proposition. Shortly before his departure from Kunming, the School of Arts organized an 'English Evening' in a classroom on the third floor of the Agricultural Institute, with George Yeh as master of ceremonies. Students of English appropriately staged a performance of W. B. Yeats's nationalistic play *Cathleen ni Houlihan*. In addition, according to a reliable account, Empson happily contributed to a programme of readings by virtually 'singing' one of his own poems.[8] And then he chose to recite from memory a speech that he later characterized as 'sheer splendour'; it was Satan's first address to the fallen angels from Book I of *Paradise Lost*, including these lines:

> that fixt mind
> And high disdain, from sense of injured merit,
> That with the mightiest raised me to contend,
> And to the fierce contention brought along
> Innumerable force of spirits armed
> That durst dislike his reign, and me preferring,
> His utmost power with adverse power opposed
> In dubious battle on the plains of Heaven,
> And shook his throne. What though the field be lost?
> All is not lost; the unconquerable will,
> And study of revenge, immortal hate,
> And courage never to submit or yield...

The passage was brilliantly chosen, for his students could immediately see its applicability to their own predicament in the war against Japan. 'His recitation filled us with hope and renewed confidence,' Professor Li Fu-ning recalled for me.[9] Twenty-two years later, in *Milton's God* (1961), Empson glossed the same speech with the questionable observation that it showed 'an impressive degree of sincerity, in a politician': it proved 'that Satan's cause is just,' he contended. Whether or not any of his Chinese students shied at the irony of being identified with Satan, albeit a Satan vindicated, Empson's reading certainly spoke to their political mood; and again in *Milton's God* he remembered the occasion at Lianda as having positively convinced him that the speech had 'a powerful direct impact':

It was received with fierce enthusiasm, but also with a mild groan from some of the older hands, who felt they had been having enough propaganda already. I am not sure how familiar it would be with that audience, but I know at least that it goes over as a direct political speech, which is what Mr Eliot said the style of Milton could not do. The audience, you understand, really did mean to resist to the end however powerless, exactly like Satan and with the same pride in it; also, not being Christian, they would not require a separate theological argument before they could sympathize with him.[10]

Theology aside, Empson's classroom exercise in moral reinforcement— a sincere and stirring performance—further promoted in his mind a belief in the value and effectiveness of good propaganda that would direct his career throughout the war. By the time he had travelled across America on his way home to England, he had gathered plenty of evidence to support the conviction, and he soon found that he needed to put propaganda into practice, both on behalf of Basic English and for swaying political opinion.

When passing through the 'legendary' Chicago he thought to save money by staying for 35 cents a night in yet another 'cubicle', at what he called 'a lovely doss house' (for men only). But the economy measure did not pay off, for he was presently robbed of 100 dollars, leaving him with nothing but his rail ticket. Happily in New York he called on W. H. Auden, who had no hesitation in lending him 50 dollars. He recalled the visit in an obituary tribute to Auden entitled 'Wartime Recollections' (1975):

The picture window of his flat looked across the water to the tremendous view of the skyscrapers at night, and Chester [Kallman] was already present. Auden was white and drawn, with small shining eyes, like Edmund Blunden. 'Of course you can't have friends here,' he said. 'Nobody does. No food—you live on sandwiches. As to drink, if you touch the stuff you fall like a stone.' I explained that I had no money for my boat, and when you consider that all money from England was frozen, and he was certain that I could not repay him, his behaviour should be recognized as noble. 'We would be foolish not to be afraid' he said. 'There are many things we ought to be afraid of. But to be afraid of money too, no, that is asking too much.' I was very thankful that I could astonish him by repayment before I got on this boat.

   I did not ask any questions, but it seemed plain that he could not have stayed in Engand to be Churchill's laureate, since he believed that England was imperialist but America wasn't, whereas I could safely go home and do the minor propaganda jobs which would be required of me, having no such fame. I now realise that a great wave of revulsion was coming over him, purely social and not religious or political, which convinced him that all that left-wing stuff, everything he had written when he was a great poet, was just in frightfully bad taste; he must say he had no idea what it meant or was sure it was wrong. But the practical reason for leaving England, that he really would have found his political situation embarrassing, too full of prickly enemy-making and useless decisions, was enough to settle it.[11]

However, remembering that Auden had been gleaming with social success when he had last seen him in Hong Kong, Empson reported too in a contemporary letter, 'now all the flesh is off the bones on the white face'; and he expostulated: 'but good heavens, why is the man choosing to live in the most expensive town in the world? Richards says he must have seen a bit of war in China after all this writing about it and got the horrors. All rather shocking, I think; he is a very amusing chap and extremely kind to me, but left me with a feeling I had better get back to England not take a job here.' As for himself in general, he found it 'a very rackety business travelling all the time', even though he wanted to lay down a store of useful contacts and possibly even land a lecturing job—'but America seems rather too full of English literary chaps, just now, explaining why they have left home . . . '[12]

He wrote to Allen Tate, hoping to be able to meet him—'it seems Princeton is quite near Boston,' he vaguely ventured[13]—but first sought out I. A. and Dorothea Richards in Cambridge, Massachusetts, where he arrived on 4 November. He looked shabby beyond words; as Dorothea Richards noted in her diary, 'v. fit but in the same overcoat he slept in in Central China & in a suit which had belonged to [George] Rainer!' Just days later she had the satisfaction of recording in a letter, 'Fortunately we've managed to get the suit he borrowed...cleaned (& mended) or Harvard's horror at such a particularly ghastly "bum" would have boiled over.' ('There seems some chance of his getting a job at Yale,' she added to her note.) I. A. Richards was working as a general adviser on education at Harvard University, and sat in his office swamped by unreadable pamphlets. 'The real question is, are these men merely unable to write?' he groaned with weariness. 'Is there something I ought to get out of these monographs, or is it just a professional habit here to put out a pompous monograph that says nothing?' Empson teased him, 'Which would you rather?'; and went on to reflect, far more sarcastically than was his wont: 'The point is that solemn official written English is anyway a long way from how *we* talk, but it is so far from how most Americans talk that they write like the famous Babus or like Chinese students.'[14] (That last phrase seems something more than merry; it is most revealing about the secret sense he must have acknowledged to himself of sometimes feeling patronizing—or contemptuous?—towards his students.)

Empson seized the opportunity to try to correct the errors of the new American way of writing when he gave a lecture on 'Basic English in Criticism' at Princeton University—where he finally met both Allen Tate and Richard Blackmur ('a fine chap')[15]—splendidly driving home to an audience of literary academics what he called 'this main idea':

that a good working sentence has one point of emphasis or of difficulty or of precise appreciation or whatever it is. Some such technique [as using the Basic English list of words] at least might grapple with this new and alarming disease of filling the whole of your sentence with diffuse intellectual terminology. The root of it is a failure to keep the normal living connection between the written language and the spoken one. It is a question of politeness; if there is *one* puzzling word the attention can handle it, but not if there are six. And though it *looks* as if the situation is better in writing, because a man can take the written sentence slowly and go back, in another way it is even worse. Because with two or three puzzling words in the *written* sentence the reader does not even know (so to speak) which is meant to be puzzling. He cannot guess from the print what is the accent of the spoken voice, which would tell him where the special advance made by this sentence is supposed to be made. And if he cannot guess that he is merely tossing about on the sea of this author's verbal produce. All becomes one. Nor does he toss long; he stops. But we *must* have free communication between the expert and the outsider, who may be an expert at something else, or the whole business of forward development and democracy and so on will stop.[16]

Expounding and illustrating the virtues of Basic English also enabled him to earn the money to repay W. H. Auden, for (at Richards's suggestion) he presently took a temporary job writing radio scripts in Basic English for short-wave broadcast by Station WRUL in Boston. His scripts included 'Basic English and Wordsworth' (later published in *Kenyon Review*, Autumn 1940), as well as a series on the history of science.[17] Into one of the science scripts he introduced this timely, if too simply idealizing, political homily:

The history of science is not, like most history, a story of the bad acts of foolish men. It is a story of men living at different times and places, all over the earth, but all working together and building up one system of knowledge, a thing good in itself and able to do good to men. And it may be a good thing, at this time, to keep that picture in mind.

The question of whether or not America would expeditiously work together with Great Britain in prosecuting the war seemed to be everywhere in doubt. In America, he discovered, there were as many sharply opposed political views as there were voters, making it almost impossible to foresee which way the USA would swing. He feared both that the country might not use its weight to the best strategic advantage, so that the nations already at war would be forced sooner rather than later to reach a 'decent and lasting peace', and that America was anyway riddled with dangerous lobbies and *faux amis*. Even on the train from Chicago to Boston he had fallen into conversation with an old Irish businessman who warned him that the Irish element in Boston was bitterly anti-British—they would object to his accent, to say the least—and insisted on conducting him to a decent hotel for his first night in town. Sure enough, in Boston and Cambridge, Empson felt he had to talk to the Americans 'with about as much watch on the words all the time as you take in talking to Japanese, much more than in talking to Chinese.'[18] In one Boston bar an Irish-American started to take his coat off for a fight just as soon as Empson opened his mouth: Empson had to talk fast to avoid a scrap. The war in Europe seemed to make everyone jittery about their mixed and self-defensive political postures. When Professor Theodore Spencer and his wife entertained him on Christmas day, for example, Mrs Spencer casually

remarked that their Christmas tree had come from England and then
hastened to correct herself, 'No, of course, I was mixing it up with
Germany.' Empson noticed that she blushed 'to the roots of her ears',
and he later commented that 'she visibly felt that TACT had broken down
here to an appalling degree'.[19] At social gatherings, Empson himself drank
too much and allowed the burning truth about what he had witnessed in
China to come pouring out of him. Unbottling the bile he had somehow
contained for two years as a refugee-academic, he yelled at anyone who
did not comprehend the full scale of China's experience: the suffering, the
horror, the heroism. Dorothea Richards noted on 8 November, for example, 'Bill got very drunk & shouted & became quarrelsome...about
Chinese being starved & getting goitre—& shouting about being "bloody".
Just on the verge of monstrous. Ted [Spencer] & all of us very distressed—
at such force running to waste. Kind of hatred & contempt coming up—.'
While the Richardses tut-tutted at the fact, as they saw it, that Empson was
drowning himself in alcohol and so behaving badly, of course he was
actually bombinating at everyone because of his devout sense of loyalty
to China. His Chinese friends were just surviving, labouring to sustain
intellectual culture and university life in the face of the worst that
Japan threw at them; and yet here were the sophisticates of Harvard—
more concerned with keeping up appearances, social propriety...and
indifference.

As far as Empson was concerned, the end in view was not to preserve
good manners but to win the war. The problem was how best to influence
opinion 'in a country of nervous restlessness and wild freedom of untested
assertion in the press'. Unlike in Great Britain, he astutely observed, the
general public in America were all too susceptible to propaganda and for
that very reason all the more anxious to guard themselves against unwanted pressures:

Americans easily feel that belief produces its object, and their politicians in
speeches continually say 'I believe' (some comforting belief) with an effect of
labouring to make it true. All this makes them good subjects for propaganda. But
they know all this, and they are very much afraid of being dragged into the
war...To be sure, it is recognized that the [British] Ambassador is simply doing
his usual job, but simple avowed propagandists come up against a good deal of
hatred as public seducers, trying to kill our [American] boys, and tend to get the
rather false idea that the country is full of anti-British feeling.[20]

The point, which he published in an article entitled 'Passing through
U.S.A.' (*Horizon*, June 1940), was well made; and Empson had come across

just such opposition in his personal encounters. On the other hand, to judge from the evidence of newspaper journalism, the USA seemed to be possessed of so much self-regard, to see itself as the inevitable arbiter of world affairs simply because of being so powerful, that many Americans spoke of themselves as being fated to settle the war rather than positively willing to aid their allies: 'it is hard to separate the worthy feeling of being somehow responsible for the rest of the world from the feeling of being helplessly caught in some kind of machine,' wrote Empson.[21] In print he expressed his analysis firmly but diplomatically; in private, he felt annoyed and disdainful of the Americans' sense of superiority in that respect. As he wrote in a letter to his mother, dated 3 January 1940, 'All that line of spoiled-child squealing seems really disagreeable to me. It is probably true that if they could make up their minds for it they could be world police and put down any warmonger, but as no President can make a normal treaty with other countries without knowing that the Senate may break it next month, because they won't keep their word in fact, they can't expect to be important.'[22]

If America looked both helpless before its own power and likely to resist the influence of direct propaganda, he decided, the British should at least rebuff what he construed as the 'dangerous amount of sub-Nazi propaganda disguised as pacifist and anti-imperialist'.[23] Even sincere pacifists he regarded as 'twisted' and 'squeamish' in their morality:

If, when talking to American young men who argue, not merely that all wars are wicked, but that no war ever achieves its object, you say 'How about the American War of Independence?' they are honestly astonished. It would never occur to them to test so holy an ideal by examples. The American papers are a bit sensitive about selling scrap-iron to Japan, but not because this helps Japan to defeat China, merely because those same bits of scrap-iron may be made into guns, and that would be shocking.[24]

The pacifists' argument was not illogical, he granted; their idealism just seemed to him nothing more than misprision of principle.

He was not a warmonger himself, as the contemporary reader might have been tempted to think, but he was fired by his own patriotism and obviously exasperated that America would not yet take a decisive stance alongside Britain. In any event, he concluded, 'America looks like drifting towards the only really important thing wanted of her at present, and that is holding the Far East set-up while Europe is fighting.'[25] Whilst recognizing that America and other 'secret allies' would have to intervene if the Allies looked like losing the war, he felt insulted at the prospect of seeing the USA belatedly sweeping onto the stage, claiming the victory, and then expecting repayment for its charitable support. Though never a Little Englander, he clearly felt unabashed pride that Great Britain did not shilly-shally like America but straightforwardly set out to fight the just war.

'The only important thing is the general political set-up,' he wrote to his mother from America. 'And I have to be rather apologetic about coming home and being a nuisance, because as I sit here it seems clear that I am not needed. But still, carrying a little butter in the suitcases, and bacon, it seems fair to turn up and have a look round.'[26]

He reached Liverpool on 28 January 1940, and went directly home to rest for a while in York. Old friends found the 33-year-old Empson unusually withdrawn; Julian Trevelyan remarked to John Davenport upon Empson's flat, reserved demeanour. Davenport responded with kindly but limited understanding of the hardships that Empson had stoically endured for two years: 'I think Bill always does seem a little shy & reserved after these long oriental interludes. Not unnaturally I suppose.'[27]

Severe myopia debarred Empson from enlisting in the armed forces, but within just a few weeks he had applied for work at Broadcasting House. 'I had returned feeling that the defeat of Hitler was of immense importance, to be sure,' he recalled with his characteristically unassuming air many years later,

but also feeling reasonably confident that I would be allowed an interesting war by being let into the propaganda machine; and, then again, I was protected by my obscurity, unlike the poet Auden who, I still think, was right in refusing to become the laureate of Churchill. For that matter, my Chinese university had simply assumed that I would require indefinite wartime leave (the Chinese were already regarding our war as a part of their war); it would have been embarrassing to act otherwise.

Neither while working in China nor afterwards did it ever occur to him that his students had grown to revere him as a loyal and large-hearted hero, an exemplary 'Elder Born' with true *han yang* ('elevated nurture'). Nor did he know that his efforts in the years 1937–9 in great part determined the future development of the study and teaching of English literature in China. His pupils from those years were to become the country's leading literary academicians, and they unanimously acknowledged their debt to Empson as their mentor. As far as he was concerned, he had just carried on doing the job he had undertaken to do, no matter how punishing the circumstances. Back in England, still the same trooper, he simply determined to do what needed next to be done. Anything else would have seemed bad faith, though he had certainly been tempted to take up other kinds of work—such as an academic appointment in America. At the BBC he would fight for the Chinese interest just as resolutely as he would propagandize against Japan.

His convictions had utterly solid foundation, for his Chinese colleagues and students went on to suffer more dreadful privations with every year of the war. John King Fairbank, who visited Kunming for the American Office of War Information three years after Empson's departure, found himself profoundly shocked by the deteriorating conditions at the National South-west Associated University. As he reported in a dispatch dated 23 September 1942, the faculty were 'seriously threatened with extinction' because of 'continued malnutrition, illness, and eventual demoralization':

The present Minister of Education, Dr. Ch'en Li-fu, in working toward the regimentation of intellectual life in China has made persistent efforts to gain control over the policies of Tsing Hua, as well as of other universities... The result is a continuing struggle, in which the power of the Ministry and of the Kuomintang, with their financial backing, is matched against the determination of the faculty to preserve their freedom of teaching...

Specifically, the effort of the Kuomintang and the Ministry has taken the following forms: younger faculty members have been urged to join the Party...; the assistance given to the University as a whole (and this applies to the S. W. Assoc. Univ. generally) has been less than would be justified by its academic standing in China—it has been aided by the Government on a quantitative rather than a qualitative basis; in Kunming the provincial Yunnan University has received extensive funds and is a good deal better off than Lienta [Lianda] although the latter contains the cream of the Chinese academic world in the faculties of Nankai, Peita, and Tsing Hua.

Examples of this struggle could be multiplied, and it is unnecessary to describe how the faculty members are living in bare garrets, selling their books and clothes, going into debt, and developing nutritional ailments...

If it be admitted that China is one battlefield in the world struggle between regimentation and freedom in which we profess to be engaged, then it is clear that failure to help these people will be a shameful stain upon the American record in this struggle.[28]

Even when official reports suggested that the effect of BBC transmissions to China was unequal to the effort involved in supplying them, Empson insisted on maintaining the essential service of broadcasting good news to Free China, and on ensuring both that the Chinese universities were kept supplied with scientific digests and that Chinese news should be regularly reported over the BBC Home Service. However small the provision, that form of service would help to sustain Chinese morale, he believed; it would clearly demonstrate that Great Britain respected the Chinese front against the common enemy.

APPENDIX:
FURTHER FAMOUS FOREBEARS

───◆───

Branches of the family Empson, Emmeson, or Emson, have lived in York-shire and Lincolnshire since time immemorial, though they could not quite trace their descent from Deucalion. (Emmeson seems to have been the original spelling of the name, derived from either 'son of Emma' or 'son of Emery' and then contracted to Emson; the 'p' is a later intrusion.) There are Emsons in the Yorkshire Lay Subsidy Rolls of 1297; Empsons figure in the West Riding Poll Tax Returns for 1379; and there are several Empsons and Emsons in the City of York Rolls of Freemen—the earliest recorded being Richard Emson de London, in 1424.

But the documented history of the Empsons of Yorkshire really begins with the brothers George and Richard (albeit that there appears to have been an inter-marriage in an earlier year, when a William Jefferson Edwin Empson married Isabel, daughter of Giles Empson of Yokefleet, gentleman, in 1594). The brothers George and Richard, grandsons of the said William and Isabel, were at odds during the Civil War. Born in about 1619, George the gentleman, who inherited Southam Grange from his grandfather, saw service as a lieutenant of Horse for the King against Parliament: he fought at the Battle of Marston Moor in 1644, and was taken prisoner at the fall of Sandall Castle. As part of the penalty for his 'severall crimes committed against the Parleament', his personal property was plundered by the Roundheads, with the remainder being seized by sequestrators and sold for the sum of £40; furthermore, the cost of his 'Delinquencie' was a fine of £100 levied against the estates he held in fee simple in Goole: lands which had formerly yielded an income of £50 a year 'before this Unnaturall warr' but which were worth no more than £30 in 1645. Thus, on 29 November that year, having taken both the 'National Covenant' and the 'Negative oath', he entered a petition for mitigation— 'having...long since disserted the Enemies quarters & for the space of six moneths liued at home,' he claimed—but there is no record as to whether or not he was granted leniency.[1] We do know, however, that by 8 August 1665, when he was said to be 46, he was married to Elizabeth (daughter of John

Anby of Sherwood Hall), by whom he had two children, George and Mary. After Elizabeth's death, when their children were still under age, he married anew, to Anne (whose maiden name is not known), and took into the family his sister-in-law Jane, who was a widow. At his death on 7 April 1677, George was plainly not a wealthy man, though seized of certain lands which he willed to be divided between his relict ('in full satisfaction of her dower') and his son; the 'first of the profitts' of the land bequeathed to the son were to be put towards 'raising a portion' for Mary until George reached the age of 14. The widow Anne was young enough to think of getting married again, and George was accordingly decent enough to specify in his will that Anne should not be burdened with the tuition of her stepchildren, George and Mary, in the event that she did make a new match. Mary Empson, whom he had named as co-executrix of his will, outlived her father by just five years, and she died a spinster. George the younger, who was 7 when his father died, did not happen upon a match until he was in his late thirties, when he married Margaret, widow of Francis Nevile of Chevet. But then, a year or so later, in 1710, the poor fellow died.

But now the plot shifts over to Richard the Parliamentarian—'Stiff Dick'—younger brother of George the Royalist. Eight generations were to run in the male line from Richard the Roundhead to Sir William Empson, poet and critic. And a question that remained in what would appear to have been a state of misapprehension down through all those generations was the true armorial status of this family. At Dugdale's Visitation of Yorkshire in August 1665, George Empson, who officially resided in Osgodcrosse Wapentake, had been recorded as claiming the right to bear arms, with his blazon described as 'Azure a chevron between 3 crosses formy argent'—though with the crucial proviso: 'Respite given for proofe of these Armes, but no proofe made'. In other words, the arms that this branch of the Empson family professed had not at that time been vouchsafed a legal endorsement. Likewise, in his will dated 8 July 1675, George Empson took pains to stipulate that his son should receive 'my silver seale with my Coat of Armes on it'. And yet there was another, thriving (and breeding) branch of the family which, throughout the seventeenth century, laid claim to that self-same coat of arms: the Empsons of Boston in Lincolnshire. In the 1634–5 Visitation of Lincolnshire, there is a pedigree of four generations of Boston Empsons, with those selfsame Arms allowed to them (Francys, who signed the pedigree in 1635, had a son and heir of 16, alive at that date); and an unofficial manuscript volume known as Larkin's Lincolnshire Pedigrees carries this family a little further, down to about 1650, with the collaterals somewhat elaborated: all of them appear to have been settled at Boston.[2] Also, a work entitled *The Union of Honour*, by James Yorke of Lincoln, Blacksmith,[3] assigns the Arms as described above to the Empsons of Lincolnshire (the Revd John Empson, who turned up this work in 1832, took pleasure in finding his family's supposed Arms depicted there, for he did not realize that his branch of the family did not descend from the rightful holders);[4] and *Lincolnshire Pedigrees* (*Harleian Society Publications*, vol. 50, 1902) endorses the attribution to the Empsons of Boston, not to the Empsons of Goole in Yorkshire. Thus the sorry conclusion to be drawn from the available evidence (as R. P. Graham-Vivian, Windsor Herald, informed William Empson's brother as late in the saga as 1949) was that, even if the most recent generation of Yorkshire Empsons could prove and register their descent in the direct male line from George Empson, the self-declared 'gentleman' of Goole, that would still not establish their right to the Arms—'as the proof for which they were respited was, so far as we know, never made.'[5] Yet we may not assume from all this that George Empson was simply continuing the tradition of chicanery begun by his supposed ancestor, the legendary Sir Richard Empson, though such a very sharp practice would have been worthy of Sir Richard's natural heirs; George might well have been acting in good faith, and merely perpetuating the mistake of some peasant who had not appreciated the legal niceties of heraldry. There can be little doubt, however, that the succeeding generations of the Yorkshire Empsons were often enough persons of proud pretensions (to borrow the Revd John's innocent phrase); if they were not actually living a lie, they were assuredly intent upon thrusting themselves up and up the social ladder—to the point where the family had developed such a high regard for the gentleman's code of honour that it was ultimately forced to confront a Victorian tragedy from which it never recovered. The twentieth century saw the disintegration and dispersal of the Empson family of Yorkshire. It is a thoroughly English tale.

'Stiff Dick', Richard Empson the Roundhead, George's estranged brother, was never guilty of pretending to Arms, for all that he assuredly prospered under the Commonwealth. On 19 June 1649 he was able to buy from Dr William Parker and his wife Judith 'a messuage or tenement at Goole in the Co. of York',[6] and over the next few years he engrossed not only the 'Closes, lands, grounds, moores, woods and other... premisses' bounded by the River Ouse to the north and the Blackwater to the south, and abutting the lands of Sir Thomas Redstone on the east and those of William Empson (probably a cousin) on the west, but also sundry other closes, pastures, and arable lands. He married *circa* 1655 Mary Clarke, and had four sons and three daughters; but Mary predeceased him, and at his death in 1675 he had a second wife, Ann. Yet in his will he left his estates not to his first-born but to the three younger sons, Cornelius, Charles, and Jonathan, but only on condition that they educate and bring up a grandchild by the strange name of Bononi until he reached the age of 22—'and when he shall attayne to the Age of two and twenty yeares that they pay him the said Bononi Empson the sum of fifty pounds of good and lawful money of England for a portion.'[7] The rather odd name Bononi may indicate that the child was a bastard; if that is so, whose love child was it (the only grandchild to be mentioned in the will) that the grandfather should not only charge his sons upon pain of disinheritance that they bring up this by-blow with every possible advantage but also honour him with the family surname? The most likely answer is that Bononi was the illegitimate offspring of James, the eldest son; which would also explain why Richard sought to snub his son by willing him a mere twenty pounds—the largest part of which James would have to call in: 'viz, thirteene pounds eighteen shillings thereof is in the hands and due from Thomas Cawood of Arkworth and Six pounds one shilling sixpence to be payd him by my Executor in full satisfaction of his child's portion.' (Even the married daughters, who would expect to receive less than the eldest son, were given a minimum of £20 each.) The fact that Richard Empson short-changed his son by sixpence may indicate the measure of his deep contempt for James's scurvy behaviour. Whatever else, we may judge that Richard Empson, the stiff parliamentarian, was a figure of considerable probity and pride—with a head for human nature ('Item I give to Elizabeth Richardson my daughter three score pounds of lawful money of England to be paid her within ffourty weekes after my decease provided and not unlesse her husband or his ffrinds doe make to her an estate for her life of lands worth ffive or six pounds a yeare'). He was clearly just as proud to know full well (probably in contrast to the false pretensions of his brother the Royalist) that he lived and died a yeoman—and not a step higher. Richard Empson was veritably the founding father of the dynasty of the Empsons of Yorkshire.

If James his first-born was indeed the black sheep and so spurned by his father,[8] that fact may go a good way to explaining why James's children, and his children's children, felt a sense of being excluded from the Empson family proper; and why, five generations down their line (which had died out in the male succession), a gentleman who married into the family elected to adopt the patronymic Empson. In 1842, Robert Cornelius Lister, Esquire, of Ousefleet Grange and Goole Hall, married Elizabeth, the only daughter and heir of Jarvis Empson, Esquire, of Goole Hall, and thereupon changed his own name to Lister Empson and called his only son James Empson Lister Empson. (Nonetheless, this change of name was effected not by Royal Licence but by Deed Poll, with the consequence that the Arms he then assumed—Empson and Lister, quartered— were never in fact registered or recognized by the College of Arms.) On the other hand, John Henry Empson, Esq., of Yokefleet Hall, the eldest son and heir in direct male line of succession from Richard the Roundhead, must have enjoyed a virtually mystical sense of fulfilment, a sense of twofold completion, when he came to be married in 1867—for his chosen bride was none other than his own cousin at a remarkable remove, Alice Lister, the only daughter of Robert Cornelius Lister (Empson). This intermarriage meant a consummation devoutly to be wished: it closed a circle, reuniting a family that had been divided for two centuries. Within two years, however—as recounted in Chapter 1—all family joy was laid waste.

Cornelius Empson, the second son of Richard Empson the Roundhead, won himself a place in history by crossing the Atlantic not long after the death of his father. (Oddly enough, the very first Empson in the United States was one William Empson, who went to Maryland—Lord Baltimore's 'plantation'—in about 1637).[9] Cornelius, who was born *circa* 1660 in the hamlet of Booth, between

Goole and Howden in Yorkshire, acquired a share of the lands in West New Jersey and so journeyed to America in 1684. He was evidently a man of means, for although he retained his title to the lands in West New Jersey, he presently purchased (for £625) a substantial tract of land on Brandywine Creek, New Castle County, near the present-day site of Wilmington, Delaware, where he became a dependable friend of William Penn. Immediately after settling in Penn's province, he was selected as an officer of the government: in 1685 he was commissioned Justice of the Peace and Judge of the Courts of New Castle County, and he was still a judge in 1701. By 1690 he had been appointed Collector and Receiver for William Penn in New Castle County, and he was a member of the legislative Assembly of Pennsylvania. In addition, he was a judge of the Provincial Court of Chester County, and, to crown a career of public service, a Justice of the Supreme Court of Pennsylvania from 1698 to 1701. In 1701, Cornelius, with twenty other families, acquired and made a settlement on a 15,000-acre site called the Notting-ham Tract; lying about halfway between Delaware and Susquehanna, this estate eventually formed part of Maryland. A Quaker, Cornelius got through four wives in all (the second wife was in fact the sister of the first, recently deceased; so the Newark Meeting to which he belonged disowned him after he went ahead and married her without their prior consent; but as soon as he condemned his own o'erhasty action and received a formal reprimand 'very gladly and with great content', honour was satisfied on both sides); and he had a total of four sons and four daughters by those four wives. He died in 1710, after making a will in which a number of negroes and mulattos naturally figured high on the list of the posses-sions he devised to his family. And in memory of his first, forsaken home he signed his last will and testament from the American mansion he had chosen to call Goole Grange. (Among his talented descendants, perhaps the best known—in his day— was Robert Montgomery Bird (1806–54), physician and author, who made his name by turning out adventure stories not unlike those of James Fenimore Cooper and who won great applause for plays including *The Gladiator* and *The Broker of Bogota*.) William Empson, who assuredly knew that his collateral ancestor was a colonialist and slave-holder, must have heard more about Cornelius Empson from his friend Bonamy Dobrée, who in 1932 published a good monograph on William Penn.[10]

Of the four sons of Richard the Roundhead, therefore, James was possibly disinherited by his father (and in any case his immediate offspring produced no male heir), and Cornelius departed for the New World (it is notable that the memorandum quoted above altogether omits the name of Cornelius from the genealogy of the family). Which leaves just Charles and Jonathan. Yet it is actually from Jonathan, Stiff Dick's youngest son, that the line descends, truly if precar-iously, to the present generation, though we may certainly not presume that Charles was gelded of his patrimony by his younger brother. (Charles did have sons, but he may have died before Jonathan.) Jonathan prospered; while his father bought a 'messuage' in Goole, Jonathan did even better by acquiring Goole Hall (we know this because he was able to re-inter on his own land both his father and his eldest brother: Richard in 1710 and James in 1715). So, after all is said and done, maybe it was Jonathan who felt it desirable to snaffle the Arms of the Empsons to his side of the family.

But it was Jonathan's son and heir, Amaziah (1692–1776), who brought the family to the fullness of its landed estate. A wealthy man on the make, he was quite ravenous for property and busied himself with buying up lands in the parish of Howden, to the north of the River Ouse—a great plain of reclaimed 'marish land' stretching eastwards to the Walling Fen—though he usually lived with his wife Sarah Wressel at Luddington, near Brigg. Most notably, in 1758 he purchased from Francis Smith the Manor of Yokefleet, an ancient estate fronting the river (it appears thrice in the Domesday Book, as 'Iugufled'—the name being derived from 'Iugu', or 'Yoke', and 'fled', or 'flcct'), together with a fishery. The Ouse at that time abounded in salmon (they 'cannot be surpassed in flavour,' it was said), as well as trout, smelts, and lampreys (in 1726 an Act was passed to improve the navigation of the river, though it 'produced no adequate result').[11] The estate at 'Youckfleet' or 'Yoakfleete' (as it was variously written at first), with its attendant joys and conflicts, has remained in the family ever since. In addition, Amaziah energetically negotiated with the Charterhouse in London to buy the estate at Blacktoft, downriver from Yokefleet; but it turned out that because the land actually belonged to a charity (Sutton's Hospital, as the Charterhouse had become), it was inalienable, so it required an Act of Parliament 'for enabling the governors of the Charterhouse to sell and convey the manor of Blacktoft to Mr Amaziah Empson' (Geo II 1757)—for which Amaziah had to meet the rather considerable fees and costs amounting to £161 10s.[12] The full process of this elaborate piece of conveyancing took almost a quarter of a century (Amaziah could hardly write, and became quite acrimonious at times), but the result was to enlarge the estate to what is virtually its size today—4,200 acres—for more than two centuries. And finally Amaziah Empson applied his empire-building assiduity to the estates of another neighbour with a title of ancient rank, Sir George Metham (the family of Metham had been eminent since medieval times), an improvident and destitute figure who had little option but to sell the Metham Estate to Amaziah in 1769.[13] A memo by Sarah Empson, the doughty aunt of William Empson's great-grandfather John, records that Amaziah actually bought Waterside House farm (which no longer exists), with the Metham foreshore, on 2 March 1769, although there seem to have been a number of farms in Metham and Yokefleet vested in 'Sr. George Metham and the Heirs Male of his Body' from time immemorial—all of which fell to Amaziah's appetite.[14]

As if in reaction to the worldly acquisitiveness of his father, John Empson, the elder son and heir of Amaziah (who died in 1776, at the good age of 84), was the first of the family to enter the Church (he was in any case nearly 50 by the time he succeeded his father, and outlived him by only eleven years). John became vicar of Scawby in Lincolnshire, where a tablet on the wall of his church records the fact—which is interesting for the student of his lineal descendant—that the Revd John Empson was 'distinguished in the early part of Life for his literary Attainments' at Cambridge, where he was a scholar of St Catharine's Hall; also distinguished 'Through each succeeding Period,' the tablet goes on, 'by the Cultivation of every Moral and Christian Excellence, Displayed in the Devotion of his Talents to the Service, the Comfort, The Edification of His Family, his Flock and all within his Influence.' (William Empson would have been gratified to remark that, no matter his ministry, his flock did not glibly identify 'Moral' with 'Christian'.) The Revd John married in 1750 Ann Wharam of Wath, who bore him five children, two sons and three daughters. But the elder son died at the age of 37 in 1787, the same year as his father. So Amaziah—named for his grandfather, the great aggrandizer—inherited the family estates, although he too lived *in absentia*, since he succeeded his father as curate of Scawby and sublet at a substantial profit the farms at Yokefleet and its environs. (Notwithstanding his living in Lincolnshire, his formal address was normally given as Yokefleet Hall—just as it had been for his father.) An idea of the size of the estates amassed by his grandfather and father that had come down to him, and which he diligently augmented, is provided by his will (signed in 1798), in which he not only left to his wife a tax-free annuity of £600, plus £100 among other gifts, but also bequeathed to his five sons several farms and other hereditaments in Swinefleet and Reedness (in the parish of Whitgift), and other lands at Cotness, Metham, Thorntoft, Blacktoft, Staddlethorpe, and Bishopsoil, as well as the Yokefleet estate. But Amaziah did not have long to enjoy his temporal possessions, for he died betimes, at the age of 44, leaving his afflicted widow Ann (daughter of John Kelk of Brigg), whom he had married in 1786, to bring up five infant sons—'to lament his loss and teach them to follow his example,' as his memorial in Scawby church has it.

The eldest son, the spirited and eccentric Flying Parson, would recollect his rum mother—who seems to have been rather silly, a hopeless parent and a hypochondriac—in a letter to his son written soon after her death in 1835 at the age of 73: 'For some constitutional maladies Time & Perseverance are needful. My mother told me that she had considered herself to be absolutely well at no period during about the last 50 years of her life, yet she could do everything as well as an healthy Person, tho' in a certain sense She was a Valetudinarian, & still had outlived three fourths of the medical men who had been by her consulted; having plenty of money which allowed her to travel to the Sea or the Watering Places, & having a good House & Table at which she of course could command Society, she never was Alone, & never was in Solitude the victim of Low Spirits, & the daily act of swallowing medicinal draughts or Pills was often her amusement.'[15]

If the widow Ann did not really suffer from the vapours, even though she lived in such a very vaporous place as Yokefleet Hall, in the fens of the Ouse, she was greatly aided in the task of bringing up her sons by her redoubtable sister-in-law,

Sarah, a spinster of excellent intelligence, initiative, and energy, a formidable little body with a steely satirical eye, who would not yield up her own full and selfless life till she was 97. Aunt Sarah was at all times a ministering angel to the Revd John Empson and his brothers. An idea of her direct, commonsensical character can be gauged from this passage in a letter to her great-nephew, John William (the Revd John's son and heir), on his reaching his majority in 1838: 'I think all young men should see their own Country before they go on the Continent lest they should feel as the late Lord Chesterfield did, when he was asked respecting the beauties of St. Stephens Walbroke & was obliged to own that he had never seen it.'[16]

In another well-angled letter, written some twenty-two years earlier to her eldest nephew, the Revd John Empson himself, she fired off a reprimand that would return to haunt him—with shame for his improper fame—four years later: 'I am glad to hear your Wife is better & hope Saxby will agree with her; & that you will not leave her to follow Hounds as you did at Rempstone. If you limit yourself to one or two Hunters it will not be your occupation, & as you will have the care of a Parish you would not like to be called a Hunting Parson.'[17] She had reason to feel urgent in her anxiety for his good conduct: she had already taken charge of his brother James, who had turned out to be a drunk and a debtor. She was concerned too that the youngest of the brothers, Richard, who was just graduating from Cambridge—where, being a Regency blade, he had almost inevitably contracted some kind of venereal disease[18]—should be resolute about choosing a profession. In fact, Richard duly went into the Church and became curate of the Lincolnshire parish of Scotton; he got married, but died without issue at the age of 43. 'Our Dicky ever made rare fun,' said his brother John in a loving Yorkshire idiom.[19]

Born in 1787, the year which also saw the death of his grandfather John, vicar of Scawby, the young John Empson took his MA at St John's, Cambridge, and became deacon and priest at Norwich and Lincoln before being assigned the benefice of Rempstone Lodge, near Loughborough—where, as his aunt noted with disdain, he preferred the thrills of the chase to the cure of souls, so earning his apt *nomme de chasse* 'The Flying Parson' (he was also styled 'The Lincoln Crow' and, less charismatically, 'The Man in the Waterproof Hat'). Before leaving for Rempstone he married Margaret Hunt (a ward in Chancery), who bore him a son, John William, as well as two daughters who died in infancy. However, while his aunt chided him to get out of the saddle and to look to his family and flock, the removal to Saxby in Leicestershire saw no change in his ways; rather, he rode all the harder, joining the finest hunts of the Midlands—the Quorn, Belvoir, Cottesmore—and being extolled for his hunting prowess by the sporting writers of the day. Major Guy Paget described his 'crack runs' in a rather sentimental monograph of 1934 to which all his descendants, including William Empson, dutifully subscribed (Rudyard Kipling did so too): 'Being a light weight, he was able to ride extremely cheap horses, and though never keeping more than three or four, was always in the first flight, and saw the end of a run with one horse better, and more often, than many who had two. He appears in several of the big sporting pictures painted by J. Ferneley'[20]—including *A Run with the Pytchley Hounds* (Duke of Portland's Collection, no 716), in which Empson appears mounted on his horse 'Malvern'. The Flying Parson was the first man to appear at a Leicestershire hunt with a clipped horse, called 'Shaven'; and among the other 'capital Hunters' he owned were 'The Mare', 'Morven', 'Spectre', 'Grog', and 'Traveller'—all of them tended by his groom (and gossip) named Fowler.

The Revd John Empson—this bantam cleric and sportsman, with his quick mordant wit, no respecter of persons—relished every single aspect of the sport of hunting; he would roister way into the small hours, strutting his fanfaronade with the best of them; he also showed skill as a gallant and ad hoc courtly versifier. In sum, he was point-device an old-style gentleman—and this in an age which saw the upsurge of radicalism and reform. It could not even be said in his defence that he entered Holy Orders in the first place out of family custom rather than true vocation, for at Cambridge a friend had remarked upon his singular ambition for a 'station' in life: 'a good Country parson & Justice of Peace'. His selfish dedication to hunting was perhaps a symptom of delayed adolescence. In any event, he knew that he was born out of his time, the mid-eighteenth century (though he would in due time become a keen Whig): Fielding's Squire Western might have been his model. Among his miscellaneous writings is this prescription for a thoroughbred sportsman which amply illustrates his flagrant nostalgia:

HOW TO RIDE *AFTER* HOUNDS, AND TO DO THE THING WELL

Take a real sportsman, never mind his Dress, put him upon a decent Nag, and place him at the cover-side; first goes away the fox; secondly goes away the body of the Hounds; thirdly goes out FRIEND; He steers straight as an arrow, observes the Hounds, and neither presses nor over-rides them; keeping his horse together, does not blow him in ten minutes; perseveres without any notion of Jealousy at a certain rate, and with the pack, coming to a wood, enters a riding, and rides to the Cry; goes away (as before) and especially notices the leading Dogs, and watches the conduct of all in any temporary difficulty; as he was careful not to screech, interfere, and spoil sport at the beginning, does the same towards the end of the run; when the fox is killed, keeps his horse at a distance from the hounds, looks at his watch, calculates the whole extent of ground gone over, as well as the length of the chase from point-to-point; he talks over the Thing, is overjoyed himself, and by civility and a display of old English character imparts Joy to all around him. If the Hounds try again, he stays for a second fox, and sees the whole of the Day.

Our said friend returns home at a gentle trot, sits down with his family to a joint of meat and a pudding; in a pint of Port, honest, genuine, old Port, toasts the Master of the Hounds, the King, the fair sex, fox-hunting, and the unrivalled Nimrod of the age; he retires to bed, wishing every Englishman to partake of public diversions suited to his taste, and fervently desiring, that the ancient reign of good humour, benevolence, hospitality, etc., which marked the era of Sir Roger de Coverley, may speedily return.[21]

Such was his obsolescent ideal of civility.

It is also interesting to discover, however, that one of William Empson's pastimes was actually a hereditary hobby: the Revd John had a proclivity for doodling with sums, as in this typical example dated 7th November 1825:

A HUNTING MAN'S RISKS.

1st in the course of a long day's hunting it is 10–1 in favour of a bold and good rider well mounted that he meet any accident at all. 2nd supposing he falls, it is 8–1 that he or his horse is materially hurt, 3rd it is 6–1 the horse is hurt and the rider. 4th if the rider is hurt it is 12–1 that no Bone is broken. 5th it is 20–1 if a bone is broken that the wound is not mortal.

$$10 \times 8 \times 6 \times 12 \times 20 = 115{,}200$$
$$: 1 \times 1 \times 1 \times 1 \times 1 \times 1 = 1$$

and 115,200 = 1—thus started—it details that he has no fall is 10 1 : that himself and horse is not hurt 80–1 : that it is horse not self 480–1, no bone is broken 5,760–1 : that the hurt is not mortal 115,200–1.[22]

The ease of his talent for mathematics had become apparent during his time at Cambridge, where a friend wrote after a conversation with him in 1808:

[L]ike the orator who gained immortal Glory by showing the futility of all glory, he evinced some knowledge of Mathematics ... by endeavouring to prove to me how impossible it was that he should ever make a Mathematician. 'For' says he, 'It is universally allowed that they who can *get* a thing the quicker *forget* it also the soonest. Now Henry Walter [a Fellow of St John's, son of yet another Lincolnshire parson, and cousin of Jane Austen who in 1813 was pleased to learn that he was 'considered as the best classick in the University'] allows that he never knew anyone who could get him three or four Pages of Hydrostatics so quick as I can: of course I forget them as quick; & as it is absolutely necessary for being high at the Examination that I should remember them, it follows as an immediate Consequence of the quickness of my Apprehension that I can never be high at a Mathematical Examination.'[23]

His great-grandson William would have good cause to say something rather similar at Cambridge exactly 120 years later.

In a sense, of course, the whole tribe of Empsons, from the patriarchs to the recent run of clerics, were clever calculators—not least at land-grabbing. This family facility is again apparent in 'A Bill of Costs' that the Revd John sometime submitted to his brother Richard on account of having journeyed north so as to perform a local christening at his request:[24]

The Revd. J. Empson to the Revd. R. Empson	Dr.		
	£	s.	d.
April 4th Journey to Yokefleet, Ferries, etc.	10	0	
April 5th To carving, smoking shag, playing the agreeable			
to T. Jacques and N. Gardham, drinking punch,			
etc.	1	0	0

April 6th	To riding with Array, attending the Courts, drinking punch, falling from my horse, tearing my coat and getting drunk	1	15	0
April 7th	To talking with Mr. Weddall, christening J. Stephenson's grandson, and journey home	1	0	0
		4	5	0
	Without wine 4 days	1	8	0
		5	13	0
	Arrears	20	10	0
		£26	3	0

Of course he was spoofing his brother—the invoice is first and foremost a pretty good jest—but we may suspect there was a close part of the parson that really did mean business.

There is a portrait of the Revd John still in the possession of the Empson family. It shows a very august, middle-aged figure in clerical habit, tending to stoutness, with a broad bald pate and square jowly face; the nose long, aquiline, possibly broken. The gaze is clear-eyed, intense, almost but not quite stern; the mouth is small, thin-lipped, and crimped slightly to one side, as if about to snarl or sneer a sarcasm—or, at a second glance, to smirk or even (perhaps) to break into a grin. Taken for all in all, one has to say, the demeanour is self-centred, opinionated, and overbearing. It is not the face of a runagate priest, a tearaway curate, a negligent husband and father. It is the face of a sombre personage. How do we reconcile the Flying Parson, with his devotion to the fox-hunting fraternity, to high fences and high jinks, with the gravity of this clerk in holy orders? Why and when did he come to mend his ways? He had often been warned off his irresponsible, hedonistic carry-ons, even from the first years of his priesthood—not least by his Aunt Sarah. As early as 1813 he received the following evangelical exhortation—almost an imprecation—from someone who obviously kept close watch over his licentious conduct; it is almost worthy of Jonathan Edwards (or, better still, the Low-Church Mr James Colley in William Golding's *Rites of Passage*):

> Disdain not, Sir, I entreat you, once more to peruse what is dictated not by the Impulse of a Moment, but a serious and fervent Desire for the eternal Welfare of your better Part, the immortal, immaterial essence: I should not venture to intrude my Sentiments upon you, were I not convinced that they are agreeable to the Word of God and Truths which are inculcated by your own Church, and interwoven in all her Services; and I am the more emboldened to presume upon your Patience since I heard the elegant and scriptural Lecture you delivered on the 19th of last April. Oh, how am I grieved to find the Hopes inspired by that valedictory Address were far too sanguine; I vainly imagined what you there expressed was the Experience of your Soul, pierced by the barbed Arrows of Conviction, and thought you were enlightened and inspired to preach the pure Gospel, and to prove by an exemplary Life that, however your deluded Brothers around you might have perjured themselves at the solemn Season of Ordination,

you were indeed called to the important Work of the Ministry. How ardently did I supplicate the God of Grace that your Absence during the Summer might be the happy Opportunity to wean you from your carnal Pleasures, and that you might return with a new Heart, and be annointed with Unction from the Holy One to preach Christ crucified in a City where (exclusive of the Dissenters) vital Godliness is nearly a total Stranger, whose Inhabitants together with their Ministers, are immersed in sensual Delights, trusting in their boasted Deeds of public Charity to procure them an Admission into the Mansions which are prepared for those alone who are born of the Spirit.

But alas Sir, what a sad Reverse has presented itself to View! No sooner did November return, than you resumed your Amusements with Avidity, and again plunged in the Vortex of Dissipation (be not indignant at the Term, for those Pleasures which alienate the Mind from God, deserve no better appellation); and, notwithstanding you have for a Time been entrusted with the Care of Souls for whose Welfare you appeared solicitous, you scrupled not to manifest by your Life, that you lightly esteemed the Rock of Salvation, and were only possest of Head-Knowledge. No wonder that on all Sides, by Plebeian Tongues, as well as those who are elevated as far above vulgar Prejudices as yourself, you are called a consummate Hypocrite. They admire your Preaching but condemn your Example; they are loud in your Praise as a Scholar and Orator, but just in censuring your Conduct; and they can scarcely credit that you desire your Exhortations to Holiness to be indelibly graven upon their Hearts, since your Practice is directly contrary to the revealed Will of God.

O Sir, you are indeed a Monument of Long suff'ring Mercy! Reflect but on the providential Interferences you have experienced, and you must with Gratitude acknowledge it. Remember the imminent Danger your Life was in the Winter before last, when the Pit received you whilst partaking of your favorite Diversion: had your Soul been there summoned to quit its earthly Tenement, whither would it have fled? or had the iron Grasp of Death arrested you whilst entertaining your sporting Companions, when called upon for the Lesson of the Day, with a most disgraceful Song: what would have been your Portion? or had the infinite Wisdom required your Spirit on the day you repaired from the Altar to the Race-Course, what Account could you have given? or even on the 22nd of December, whilst present at your Friend's Scene of Folly: was this the Preparation for the approaching Ordinance which on the preceeding Sabbath you so strenuously recommended as fitting your Hearers for Heaven? Methinks Gethsemane Garden would have afforded a far nobler and more profitable Subject for the Contemplation of one who was about to receive, and administer, the sacramental Cup on the Saviour's natal Morn: I shall include but one more Instance in this retrospective View, to prove how abundantly kind the Lord had been to you in a Way of Providence; and which ought, and I trust will, make a lasting Impression upon your Mind. You can never surely forget God's watchful Care over you on the twentieth of February: And yet you continue to slight his Mercy and despise his Warnings, by walking still in the same broad Road: you have begun this Year as you ended the last; and dishonoured your Name by placing it in the Page of Vanity with those of the thoughtless and unconscious Multitude, who cannot in this Case shield themselves under the Wing of Charity.

And so it goes on, for a further six big paragraphs of froth and fume penned into two-and-a-half pages of foolscap, concluding aptly:

I am conscious of having been too prolix, but I hope you will pardon me, as the subject is of Infinite Importance. Plucking Sinners as Brands from the Fire is the most delightful Work Man can be employed in, and if I am so happy as to be the honoured humble Instrument of bringing but one to a saving Acquaintance with the ever blessed Immanuel, I shall have abundant Cause for Thankfulness. I solemnly promise you, Sir, that I will never again thus intrude upon you. Yet I will never cease to supplicate my God to lead you into all Truth, to be your unerring Pilot in Life's stormy Ocean, and at length to conduct you safely to the Haven of immortal Rest.

The Revd John must have dismissed that curious mixture of recrimination and unctuousness, which is signed, almost appeasingly, 'A Fellow Sinner', as confounded impudence, since he carried on being the hearty hunter and bibber for a few years yet. No, what eventually pierced his conscience was not the warnings of his fellows, nor even of his noble maiden aunt; it was something that just smote his heart: the death of his wife Margaret in 1820 at the age of 27. 'Her death so greatly affected him,' wrote Major Paget, 'that in 1823 he gave up both his curacy in Leicestershire, and his hunting, and having no love for his Yorkshire home, calling the village a nest of dissent and the house Mud Hall, he spent the rest of his life in London.' These tributary verses on her gravestone (in Fulham, London), which he must have written himself, are far more awkwardly, unhappily expressive than any conventional eulogy:

> Could clasped hands & streaming eyes delay
> An angel's flight, we had not lost Thee here
> Our heart's own friend, and if poor tears could pay
> Thee honor, they should hallow still thy Bier.
> A holier Mass, dear Saint, we'll celebrate
> Loving thy Memory with patient Mind,
> Teaching that darling Child to imitate
> The blest example thou hast left behind;
> So may we humbly hope to meet again
> Where friends assembled dread no second parting pain.

His sudden bereavement finally brought home to him the value of the wife he had lost—just as such a loss would do for Thomas Hardy a century later. While there may be a portion of mawkishness in any such belated and guilt-laden expressions of affection, we can be sure that the Revd John experienced not just a short-winded misery but a sorrowing that bore down upon him for the remainder of his life. As his verse inscription quoted above points out, Margaret Empson's death left the Revd John with a sprig of a son to bring up: John William—William Empson's grandfather—was just 3 years of age. The Revd John lived on for forty years, and it was that son of his who knew better than anyone else the quality of grief his father endured through those long years: he clearly appreciated the release, the bliss, that death meant to his father when he wrote these verses for his grave (also in Fulham).

For Forty Years thy Pilgrimage yet lasted
And thou didst see and bless that dear Son's Sons
Who reverently thy tired form and wasted
Bear now to the same Tomb—so thou art once
Again united Gentle Souls and Kind,
Watch for the Mourners ye have left behind.

A remark by W. B. Yeats seems all too applicable to the fate of the Revd John: 'no tragedy is legitimate unless it leads some great character to his final joy' (*Explorations* (1962), 448–9).

Fortunately, the ever-dependable Aunt Sarah stepped in to supervise the early education of the child. But that is not to say that the Revd John turned out to be a distant and uninvolved parent, indifferent or negligent; on the contrary, he was a fond, delightful father, always looking for ways to instruct and entertain his son and to bestow on him an unspoiling kind of generosity. He also became a devout and practical Christian; for while he was already a cleric in name, after his wife's death he really underwent what can best be described as a kind of Pauline conversion. In December 1832, for example, he drew the attention of the 15-year-old John William ('Jack')—'my respected and right dearly beloved Son'— to the agreeable excellence of Addison's essays in the *Spectator*, in particular his writings on the 'Immortality of the Soul'. Then he added his own further thoughts on the subject, so his epistle became a gentle lesson in faith and wise conduct for the benefit of his son: 'Without reference to a future State I think that it can be proved that in the majority of Cases the Practise of Virtue will give to a man greater happiness than the Practise of Vice during his existence on Earth; add to this present certainty of Happiness Here the probability only of eternal happiness hereafter, & the inducements to virtuous conduct becomes strengthened. I can additionally & to my own conviction PROVE the existence of a future State, & at some future day shall submit such proof to your eye. Why Happiness here is not universal I do not know, but I am satisfied that the leading object of the Supreme Being has been, & is, to produce Happiness, & I am positive that Hereafter will be given an Explanation which will justify the Governor, & carry conviction to the minds of the Governed.' (What proof of immortality he believed he possessed, I do not know.) Yet he did retain some of the keen and sparky ways of the Flying Parson of old; his great-grandson would have enjoyed the almost epigrammatic deftness with which he dismissed the corruptions of the Roman Catholic Church: 'I have frequent interviews with a sensible, liberal, & well read Catholic; & he explained away most of the nonsense of his creed; & I told him that as the mass of the People did not hear, or hearing did not receive, such explanation, the evil to them remained; & the system at bottom was radically defective, being a premium on vice, & throwing money into priestly coffers to procure remittance from even the mortal Price due to Crime . . . Many Catholics are sceptics: from believing too much they finish with believing Nothing, just as a high Calvinist has finished with Socinianism.'

Nevertheless, such was the intensity of his grief at his wife's death that he was prevailed upon to go on a European tour to get over it. The cultural life of Paris, Milan, and Naples in the mid-1820s brought him much relief; in particular the opera simply thrilled him, and he presently became entranced to the point of besottedness by Giuditta Pasta, the outstanding soprano of the day (one of the busts still at Yokefleet Hall is of pale Madame Pasta). 'Some Performers have given additional force to their natural representation from identifying themselves with the character. Pasta's representation of Romeo arises from her own domestic history,' he noted; '& such has been the effect on her mind that Mr Allen tells me that he has frequently at the end of the Opera assisted in carrying her off the stage; and Mlle. Naldi said that in the Tomb Scene Pasta was, whilst hanging over the tomb, dissolved in tears.' It seems fair for us to assume that he too identified with the soul-searing pitch of such scenes of death. Haunting the opera houses of Europe as fervently as he formerly hunted the foxes of Leicestershire, the Revd John Empson thus transformed himself into the complete stage-door Johnny, a connoisseur of stage and song. Knowledge and familiarity heightened his pleasure and his critical insight, so that his avid, perspicacious critiques of certain performers have some lasting value. Here, for example, is his comparative evaluation (dated 12 April 1830, in London) of the acting talents of Fanny Kemble and Madame Pasta, which is worth quoting at length (despite its pompous style of address, and the shortcomings of its critical vocabulary). We need not be at all surprised to discover that La Pasta's attributes and accomplishments—not to mention her especial 'Attitudes'—outshone those of the English star (whom he was remembering from a good many years earlier), for Empson admitted that he much preferred dumbshow to voice on the stage:

It is difficult to say in which of the characters, hitherto sustained by Fanny Kemble, she appears to the best advantage. Miss [Eliza] O'Neill had not F.K.'s voice, neither had she her enunciation of passages, but she had a great degree the play of countenance & the charms of attitudes. Mrs Siddons [née Sarah Kemble, Fanny's aunt] was a Mannerist, always the Actress, dignified, formal, and theatrically tragic; there was less of nature & more of art in her performance than there is in that of her niece,[25] whilst Miss O'Neill has been reproached with being too true to nature in death-scenes, & was thought by the gurgling in the throat & by convulsive gasps to give unnecessary pain to the Spectator. Each of these persons have been exhibited talents of the first order: Mrs Siddons, as Lady Macbeth, had no rival; Juliet was the triumph of Miss O'Neill; & perhaps neither of them could have surpassed F.K. in the part of Belvidera.

F.K. is plain, & her delineation of Passions simply by the expression of emotion, & by the force of attitudes is not particularly striking; great is the power of language, as the Revd. R. Hall shews without advantages of person or of voice; & great is the power of music, as Madame Pisaroni proves without any aid from person, & with an imperfect voice; but J. J. Rousseau thought that Signs are more forcible than words, &, giving examples in proof of his position, he maintained that there are Passions which cannot be pourtrayed by language so powerfully as by the expression of countenance, & by Attitudes. One chief merit in F.K. is her voice; in rank it comes second; the voice, taken by itself, is a natural gift, a bodily perfection, &, as mind ranks higher than body, we must place F.K.'s greatest merit in her conception of characters, in her inimitable delivery of sentences, & in the exercise of that taste & judgment which never over-step nature's limits. Nothing can surpass her articulation; her emphasis is faultless; after hearing from her lips 'The Quality of Mercy etc.' it may be safely asserted that in the delivery of an able discourse from the pulpit no living Preacher could make a greater impression. This Speech in her hands is a calm, authoritative & powerful Sermon on the injunction to 'be merciful & to forgive, as we hope to be forgiven.' In a short sentence, as well as in a longer speech, her tones produces a remarkable effect & her Emphasis in the brief address to Beverley's pretended friend, 'Your absence, Sir, will please me' justifies this remark, whilst her pronunciation of the word 'banished' in the character of Juliet must be heard to be appreciated. Notwithstanding this success, it ought to be admitted that the Individual who by a delineation of the Passions can make the *strongest* impression, & who by the varied expression of countenance, by the beauty of attitudes, & by a judicious combination of these external Signs (all true to nature) can convey to others in the most *powerful* degree those Passions which the assumed character is meant to represent, deserves the first place in the Profession. We will endeavour to ascertain to whom this place belongs.

In prosecuting this inquiry we shall notice certain Italian operas: in the 1st act of Semiramide [by Rossini, who conducted the performance] the Queen is in love with Arsace; in the 2nd act she learns that he is her Son & the sentiments of Love become then exchanged for maternal affection; the nice discrimination made by La Pasta between these two Passions cannot be exceeded; in the first instance she paints by her counten-ance Human Love, & in the second, & by the same means, the affection of a Mother; a discrimination equally effective could not be produced by Words. In another Opera no language could give such an accurate idea of the state of Nina's mind as we derive from the expression of the countenance. In the last act of Otello her attitudes & countenance throw all verbal expression into the shade, & the assertion of innocence & the accusation of ingratitude seem to be almost superfluous. In the 1st act of Zingarelli's Romeo & Juliet, & in the Duet 'O cari palpiti' the words appropriate & the music charming are inferior in their effect when compared with the expression of the Tragedian's countenance, & even after the Interest & touching Effect produced by 'Ombra adorata' her countenance, her attitudes & the whole piece of Acting (fruits of mental Talent & put forth with the best judgment) shew how utterly unequal any words would be to produce a similar expres-sion.

As instance of the Effect worked upon Members of the Profession by the talents of Made. Pasta, the following may be mentioned. On the morning after the performance of Otello at Naples, Giovannina di Vecchii, who belonged to the company at San Carlo, assured the writer of these pages that from the excitements produced by la Grande Tragedienne in the Character of Desdemona, she had been unable to sleep during the night; in London Made. Caradori Allan told him that when she performed Juliet the Acting of La Pasta as Romeo deprived her of the power to do justice to her Part. The Neapolitans will long remember the effect produced at the end of the 2nd act of Otello upon the Soldier who is posted on the stage with orders not to turn his eyes from the Royal Box [he quite forgot his orders and could not take his eyes off La Pasta, his musket resting negligently on his arm], & an English audience will not soon forget the impression made upon one of the two children who are introduced in the Opera of

Medea. [The child took fright and tried to run off the stage, but was forcibly restrained by the Nurse; whereupon, as the Revd John amusingly reported on another page, La Pasta 'put an arm round her Neck, held her tightly & looked at her with a Smile, & then the said child dropped a few Tears, next smiled, & then played with Medea's Girdle. This little incident produced an effect upon the Spectators, & was more agreable to witness than any other Part of the representation.'] The authority of Talma shd. be decisive but, as the writer of these lines will advance only what he heard from the parties themselves & what he himself saw, he can merely state that during the last year of this celebrated man's career, & when he was in a declining state of health, Talma rarely lost an opportunity of witnessing the talents of Made. Pasta at the Salle Favant.

That Mrs. Siddons or Miss O'Neill could have given, or that Miss F.K. could give such effective representations is hardly credible, & since in Italy, in Austria & in France the first place in the Profession has been assigned to Guiditta Pasta, we may conclude that in the highest department of histrionic art all living candidates for theatrical fame in Europe must yield to Her the Precedence.

But his infatuation with Madame Pasta could not go on, and presently he stopped traipsing round Europe in her train and ensconced himself at no. 17 Cecil Street, by the Strand in London (the Savoy Hotel now stands more or less on the very site), where he would spend the next thirty years living as something of a recluse and amateur scholar. (He refused to live at Yokefleet Hall, which he did indeed call 'Mud Hall'. It was not that the place had any associations with his tragic marriage, for he and his wife never lived there, and he had grown up in Lincoln; he simply disliked it intensely and desired to live somewhere else altogether—like the majority of its owners. In any case, a landscape that is flat and dank when not beset by slicing cold winds is an acquired taste, despite the occasional sparkling of sunlight on the river, the cry of fowl, mice in the wainscot, and the prospect of dim distant hills—the Lincolnshire Wolds.) Nevertheless he continued to watch the world with an observant, particular eye, and with a progressive social conscience, all the time writing numerous letters and little essays—such as this piece dated 25 September 1831, in eager anticipation of the Reform Bill:

Low Debauchery is at a greater Height in London in 1831 than in any European Metropolis & now the no. of children (ie of persons of tender age) in the Profession is monstrous, whilst shops for sale apparently of fruit are kept in fact for another purpose & chiefly by Jews; the sale of books of an indecent character is extensive, & they are in Italian, French & English, & publicly exhibited whilst the sale of irreligious books is small. In the heart of London at this time an infant school, a shop with indecent books in the window & a house of ill-fame are within 500 yds. of each other; & some of the great Schools are Hotbeds of vice & of tyranny, whilst at the Universities the Quantity of Learning obtained bears an inverse Proportion to the Sum of Money expended. In solidity the middle Rank in England contains, as in most countries, the greatest Quantity of valuable Properties, & the 3d. Rank has shown during the past 12 months a more accurate knowledge on political Questions than the highest Rank, whilst the representatives of the 3d. Rank in the Hse. of Commons have met the expectations of their constituents (the People) &, seconded by the King, must eventually triumph over the House of Lords who reluctantly will be obliged to give up certain Sources of Money & of Power hitherto held under a corrupt System which had its origin in the Administration of Wm. Pitt.

He felt he had reason to misgive the profligacy of university life within a few years, when his son John William went up to Brasenose College, Oxford, and showed himself inclined to live up to a fashion way beyond his means. Like Lord Chesterfield the previous century, the Revd John began to send his son a series of expansive, wise, witty letters: cautionary tales artfully salted with humorous anecdote and observation. He was a very keen bibliophile, and had accumulated hundreds of volumes, including first editions, from the booksellers of Covent Garden—he called his collection 'a solid library' of 'old English standard Authors' (he had no taste at all for contemporary literature, which—like Francis Jeffrey, to whom he would soon be related by marriage—he thought 'flimsy or mystical')—so he would season his missives with old saws and modern instances. A letter of 20 October 1836, for example, hints to his son (perhaps too heavily in this case, since John William had recently graduated from Eton to Oxford)—'Sir Henry Wotton, Provost of Eton, writing to the Queen of Bohemia in 1636, & speaking of a newly appointed Lord Treasurer says "There is in Him no Humour, no distraction of thoughts, but a quiet mind, patient care, free access, & mild answers." Such qualities would adorn any man'—before gradually inclining towards the major plaint of the day (which puts to fair use the family knack for mathematics): '£40: may have been paid for entrance into rooms inferior to yours, but 'tis paid for furniture, which might be in Quality superior to your furniture . . . At Oxford you can get a dark coloured Gambroon warmly lined Shooting Jacket, & I will have a Closet Audience with Monsr. Mette about Yellow Valencia Waistcoats with Brass Buttons for a brasen-nose Student! Best would it be to send your list for books, some of which I may have; we have such a quantity of books already that I would abstain from addition of a Superfluous Kind. You say that your £35 is reduced to £12; at rough calculation that expenditure in one week makes £1300 per annum, & at that rate with other Payments the annual Expence would be at least two thousand Pounds Per Annum. I cannot know how far such expence is customary, or necessary, but I do know that there are few Men in any rank of life in England who with a House to keep, & a family of children for whom provision must be made, could for any continuance of years support such cost.' A year later, he was inspired by a set of questions 'of a prudential character' printed in *Old Moore's Almanac* to pen this characteristically witty inquisition for the unthrifty John William:

> In my mind, as soon as I opened my eyes this morning, were the following questions in regard to the station of an Undergraduate in his Minority at an University.
> 1. Is Sparkling Champagne a necessary Appendage to a Cellar?
> 2. Is Champagne to be drunk at dinner in the College Hall, or in private rooms after dinner, or at Luncheon, or at Supper?

3. Given the number of which the Party consists, name the number of bottles of Sparkling Champagne which should be sufficient.

4. What sort of red wine should follow Still Champagne?

5. Name the number of glasses of any kind of Champagne likely to clear the Brain for a Rubber of Whist, for talking Common Sense, & for being in the Double First Class.[26]

As much as he felt the need to chide and chivvy his son, however, he clearly doted on his sole surviving offspring ('Dear Montresor', 'Dear Euclid', 'My Dear Student'), to whom he signed himself 'yr. obliged father & friend'; and to whom he would spontaneously send fine gifts, including pheasant in season. 'To ascertain condition of Game, 'tis the custom to part the feathers on the neck and to examine the colour of the skin, & when the skin there is white, the animal is known to be fresh, & therefore fit for a Journey even to a Fresh Man in an University; consequently I procured for your Honour a brace of fresh birds, which with this note will, I trust, safely reach B.N.C.'[27] It is even possible that his generosity inspired the extravagant expectations of his son, for the business of setting him up in college apparently required regular benisons such as this:

I have ordered to be sent to you by Waggon
  3 dozen of old Port
  2 dozen of Brown Sherry
  1 dozen of Pale Sherry
To prevent the Crust of the old Port being shaken from the sides of the bottle into the body of the wine, and thereby rendering the wine thick, the Old Port will be decanted out of the old Bottles into the New bottles, & I am informed that thereby the flavour of the red wine will not be deteriorated on the road to the College of Brazen Nose.
  I remain faithfully & affect. yrs.
    John Empson, Senior[28]

Yet the Revd John, the reformed socialite and sinner, was constantly afflicted by depression, which he fought to command with a philosophical resignation. Day after day, his kindness and wit went hand-in-hand with a most frightful sense of the joylessness in his life—which on one occasion he could not resist describing with an old hunting metaphor: 'During the 4 Mile Beacon Course of Life I've been over-rode during the first part, over-weighted during the 2nd Part, & brought to a standstill during the last Part.' All the same, being *anima naturaliter theologica*, he cast every pain into a parable; every woe should serve for a source of wisdom. On the same day, 19 October 1936, that he merrily sent his son the supplies for his cellar itemized above, for instance, his mood swung so far that he could not stop himself from posting off a second letter—'Private, Confidential & Immediate'—to describe how

during the last 5 years I have had a worse & more incurable disorder than any bodily ailments, which at worst can only bring Peace by an early demise, & when I reflect on the Deaths at an early date of my father, my wife & my daughters I'm persuaded that God could not shew to them greater proofs of his Mercy & his Acceptance, than by a

Translation to his Kingdom, whither, if I did not think that I could be here useful to you, I should be Right Glad to go before I can finish this Sheet.

My Time during the last 5 years has been spent in buying solid authors, & next in reading them, & also in visiting the Sick Poor. But I have no taste for paying visits & for receiving Callers, & dine Alone every day in the Year, & neither desire to receive nor to give a Dinner. This Habitual Seclusion had its source in the long continued Ill Treatment from an unprincipled & ungrateful Man, & very possibly the dark visitation of Providence may prove a secret blessing, could it eventually be proved to have been the school of wisdom. Some writers have called worldly adversity a profitable school, & even better lessons may be learned in mental adversity, if they be wisely practised. With full reliance on Providence, & acting according to the dictates, & naturally possessing High Spirits, it must have been no ordinary Trials which have generated habitual Melancholy, & for so long a Time Dreams by night & Visions by day which none could see in a Play, none read in Romance, without Pain. These dreams, visions & reflexions are not capable of being vanquished or controlled by me, any more than I could be able to avoid the sound of a Cannon should it be fired under my windows, & facts which experimentally I know to be Realities my reason will not allow me to regard as delusions & fancies of the Brain. I find Cowper & several virtuous Persons to have been tormented with depressed spirits which are not always the off-spring of a Guilty Conscience, the stings of which God has not inflicted on me; why the Great God should have afflicted the amiable Poet Cowper is a mystery with which I have no right to meddle, but I am permitted to draw from such affliction an invincible argument in favour of an eternal & spiritual state where pains of mind & of body, & suffering from human wickedness, will be Unknown, & where the vicious shall cease from troubling, & the weary shall be at Rest, & where God shall wipe from the Eyes of his servants all Tears, & condescend to justify his ways to his obedient Children.

In regard to Old Satan & to his Subjects, I will now say little, yet the Bible is clear on this Topic, as far is needful for us to know; & Bishop Jeremy Taylor's Holy Living & Holy Dying justly describes the difference hereafter between the Servants of a Gracious God & of His Perfect & Good Son on the one hand, & on the other side the Devil's Darlings.

His great-grandson William Empson would wholly endorse his appreciative sympathy for the poet Cowper ('it really is hard for us to understand why Cowper went on struggling when he was certain that the end would be the worst possible,' he said in a radio broadcast of 1955, 'and even more how he could go on writing his playful, cultivated little poems'), but he could never share his trust in the Christian Providence, nor the specious logic of his belief that all suffering in this life affords an 'invincible argument' in favour of a fulfilling state of immortality. The Revd John sent his son that sad profession of faith not at the point of his death but twenty-five years before the end he desired.

A year later, in 1837, he would write again to his son, rehearsing the best moments of his life in a way that must have seemed to John William to be turning into a tiresome refrain by his ageing, odd papa—and yet simply to review such memories must have refreshed him no end:

As I do not like new faces I have chosen to indulge in retirement, to live with Old Authors, & to play with children, & could find no pleasure in the amusement of early days, nor in going to dinners & routs, nor in receiving Callers nor in making Calls. I have no wish to go to the Philharmonic Concert, & there is not a pack of hounds after which I shd. desire to ride, albeit I've ridden many miles in rough weather to follow Mr Asheton-Smith over the country, & to see Mr Musters perform the office of a Scientific Huntsman.

The Prospects of Italy, the Sculpture at Rome, the Paintings at Milan & Florence, some Galleries at Venice, & at Amsterdam & at Paris, the acting of Pasta, the Singing of Pisaroni, the Dancing of Tallioni (spelt Taglioni), the comic powers of Madlle. Mars & the tragic efforts of Monsieur Talma, the abilities of Koecken the Dentist, the Lisp & the earliest words of some favourite children, George the 3rd when blind in the Chapel at Windsor, my father in his Pulpit, Sir Matthew Hale on Religion, Paley on any Topic, the Eloquence, humility & piety of Robert Hall, the practical Christianity of Aunt Sarah's life & the benignity of yr. Mother's disposition, of whose present & eternal happiness I am as positive as I can be certain of the plainest fact submitted to any of my five senses... Thoughts upon these & upon other subjects enter my mind from day to day, yet a father is best employed when a pen is in his hand, if he transcribes for the eye of his child useful knowledge from the works of the most solid authors upon subjects either of general utility or, of the greatest importance, sound writings on Practical Christianity being the most important portion of literature which can be published in any Country.[29]

Bouts of valedictory melancholia, without self-pity, seem to have been both fuelled and quenched by his never-failing memories, as well as a sense that his earthly service was not yet done. His great-grandson too, when he felt afflicted by depression or neurosis, pulled himself up by recalling his duty.

The final third of the 'Beacon Course' of the Revd John Empson's life was not destined to be merely a gently lugubrious, passive period. Although he loathed the idea of living at Yokefleet in Yorkshire, he remained active to the last in securing the most profitable management of the estates there. He knew, for example, that the act of 'warping'—the periodic breaching of the artificial dykes of the Ouse, which has tides running as high as 20 feet, in order to flood the low-lying farmlands with fertile silt—cost a great deal in the short term but meant an excellent longer-term investment. In 1844, when his son had been married for less than two years to Maria (daughter of John Henry Allen, of The Rhydd in Worcestershire), who promptly produced a first child—he was christened only for her father, John Henry—the family heir and his paternal grandfather's joy ('Mother of our Wonder,' he would address his daughter-in-law),[30] the Revd John therefore duly arranged for the land to be warped and asked his son to share in the expense of the work. But Maria, who obviously had a good deal of George Eliot's Rosamond Vincy in her make-up, claimed to know better about good husbandry in Yorkshire after taking counsel from her father in Worcestershire. The Revd John's tart response to his daughter-in-law's impertinence perfectly illuminates his own integrity and selflessness; his letter is a model of the rebuke dry and direct:

London May 15. 1844

Dear Maria,

I did never feel distrust in your father; I never considered his language or letters disrespectful; I never hold an ill-opinion of any one without positive proof.

You say that you do not wish your good husband to sell Stock & thereby diminish his income; I never wished that his income should be lessened; however it may be his Personal interest to sell out, because should I desire him to sell out Stock for my warping Payment, & shd. pay to him Twice as much interest annually for the Cash as he could get in the market, he would be a Gainer; & the Principal Money wd. be for him as safe as is my estate to the possession of which he will arrive!

The act of warping has been for the interest of yr. husband & his Son; as to benefit to myself, I care not a Pin's head about my Estate, whilst I can live by any fair means on a small Pittance, but I wish that my Son, you & the Grandson shd. not be stinted.

Yrs. affectly. J. E. Senr.

On the Revd John's side at least, this spat left no ill will; nor did he allow it to sour his feelings for his beloved John William.

During vacations from school and university, John William often stayed with his uncle Amaziah, the Revd John's next eldest brother, who lived with his family at Spellow Hill—where he was warden of Staveley, near the Great North Road, between Knaresborough and Boroughbridge (to the north-west of York and Wetherby). Amongst letters still in the family, there is one from John William thanking Uncle Amaziah for the gift of a gun, and for a lovely holiday spent learning how to use it. Amaziah was a genuine countryman who very nobly, in addition to his work at Staveley, undertook to manage his brother's estate at Yokefleet: it meant that often he would have to climb into his gig and go on a round-trip journey of about 100 miles. He behaved like the authentic squire, that is to say, whereas the real owner of Yokefleet was a Doctor of Divinity who hated the place and would not go near it. However, when the sterling Amaziah's daughter Marianne, his first child, came of age, she had what he considered a very expensive season in London; at the same time, his eldest son William Henry went up from Harrow to Cambridge, and his second son Arthur John was enrolled in a public school (Amaziah had five children in all). All these expenses obliged him to close the house at Spellow Hill for a time and to live with his family at Blacktoft Grange, near Yokefleet (it still formed part of the Revd John's estate: it was the property, the lonely outlying farm, that had been purchased through an act of parliament by his great-grandfather seventy years earlier), where they were able to save money by living a much simpler life. (Interestingly, Amaziah's first two sons followed the family tradition in taking Holy Orders. The eldest, William Henry, was for many years vicar of Wellow in Hampshire, where he was acquainted with Florence Nightingale. Two letters dating from the 1860s, now in the British Library, from a young Marian Empson—probably a niece of William Henry—speak of her gratitude for the inspiring example of Nightingale: 'the name I have so long loved and reverenced—in common with every English woman.')

But the Revd John Empson, the former Flying Parson, must have felt it to be a particularly piercing irony of his solitary last years that his brother Amaziah was killed in an accident on the hunting field, in 1848, at the age of 60. He was brought home on a gate, and was buried at Staveley. The Revd John would unwillingly outlive him by a further thirteen years. William Henry inherited most of his father Amaziah's property, including Blacktoft Grange, although—like so many of his predecessors—he would never live on it. But then, at the death of his only surviving son, Charles William, who had taken the Members' Prize for an English Essay at Trinity College, Cambridge, before being called to the bar by Lincoln's Inn, and who died without issue in 1919, it was willed back to his cousins—the Empsons of Yokefleet.

NOTES

———◆———

1. Introduction

1. WE, letter to John Hayward, 4 May 1939 (courtesy of Theodore Hofmann).
2. Letter to Philip Hobsbaum, 2 August 1969 (copy in Empson Papers).
3. Untitled review of Elizabeth Holmes, *Studies in Elizabethan Imagery*, in *Criterion*, 9 (July 1930), 771.
4. WE, 'Still the Strange Necessity' (1955), in *Argufying*, 123, 125.
5. I. A. Richards, 'Semantic Frontiersman', in Gill, 98.
6. Kingsley Amis, 'Bare Choirs?' (a review of *Argufying*), *Sunday Telegraph*, 29 November 1987.
7. Barbara Hardy, 'William Empson and *Seven Types of Ambiguity*', *Sewanee Review*, 90 (1982), 432, 438–9.
8. Jonathan Bate, 'Disaste for Leavis' (a letter to the editors), *London Review of Books*, 24 January 1991, p. 4. Anthony Powell, who tackled Empson for the first time at the age of 86, recorded that he enjoyed the 'knockabout humour' of *Ambiguity* (*Journals: 1990–1992* (London: Heinemann, 1997)).
9. Alan Ansen, *The Table Talk of W. H. Auden*, ed. Nicholas Jenkins (London: Faber & Faber, 1991), 3, 44.
10. Undated letter (*c.*1973) to Roger Sale (copy in Empson Papers).
11. *Ambiguity*, 2nd edn., 1947, p. x.
12. Ibid., p. xv.
13. *Pastoral*, 14.
14. WE, 'Herbert's Quaintness' (1963), in *Argufying*, 257.
15. Letter to *New Statesman*, 31 March 1967, p. 437.
16. John N. Morris, 'Empson's Milton', *Sewanee Review*, Autumn 1962, p. 676.
17. John Bayley, '. . . The Ways of Man to Man', *The Spectator*, 30 July 1965.
18. Letter to Karunakar Jha, 20 June 1971 (copy in Empson Papers). Cf. Harold Beaver: '[Empson] is at heart a generous critic, on the look-out for "decent feelings", temperamentally averse to ironic or aesthetic closures, persuaded that an author's intention (be he Milton or Joyce) "is inherently likely to be the best possible, the richest or most humanly responsive, construction we

can place upon his work"' ('Tilting at Windbags', *New Statesman*, 11 August 1978, pp. 185–6).

19. Letter to 'Mr Montague', n.d. (copy in Empson Papers).

20. WE, letter to Christopher Ricks, 19 January 1975.

21. WE, 'Still the Strange Necessity' (1955), in *Argufying*, 126.

22. WE, letter to Qien Xuexi, 7 September 1947 (Qien Xuexi). 'The advances of science in our time, though very likely to cause disaster,' Empson was to argue in the 1970s, 'have been so magnificent that I could not wish to have been born earlier; and I estimate that most of the poets worth study who were in fact born earlier would have felt so if they were alive now' (*'The Ancient Mariner*: An Answer to Robert Penn Warren', in *SSS* 146).

23. Kathleen Raine, 'And Learn a Style from a Despair', *New Statesman & Nation*, 5 November 1955.

24. E. M. Forster, *The Hill of Devi and Other Writings*, ed. Elizabeth Heine (London: Edward Arnold, 1983), 71.

25. 'William Empson in Conversation with Christopher Ricks', *the review*, 6 and 7 (June 1963), repr. in *CP*, 33.

26. Empson in interview with Christopher Norris and David Wilson (typescript copy kindly supplied by Christopher Norris and David Wilson).

27. T. S. Eliot, letter to A. L. Rowse, 3 March 1941 (Exeter University Library).

28. I. A. Richards, 'Semantic Frontiersman', in Gill, 98.

29. 'Volpone' (1968), *Essays on Renaissance Literature*, ii: *The Drama*, ed. J. Haffenden (Cambridge: Cambridge University Press, 1994), 72.

2. In the Blood

1. *Empson's Folly: A Collection of Letters*, ed. C. C. Empson (Seaton: Empson Publications, 2000), 217.

2. Tablet in Scawby Church, Lincolnshire. Quoted in *Empsons' Peace*, ed. C. C. Empson (Bishop Auckland: The Pentland Press, 1996), 5.

3. The Revd John Empson, letter to Amaziah and Ellen Empson, 24 July 1832 (C. C. Empson).

4. WE, 'The Variants for the Byzantium Poems', *Using Biography* (London: Chatto & Windus, 1984), 176–7.

5. Andrew White, letter to JH, 5 July 1985.

6. British Library, Lansdowne 978, fo. 127 (102) (Bishop Bennett's Collections, vol. xliv): Notes on the Trials and Executions of Empson and Dudley.

7. Mark R. Horowitz, 'Richard Empson, Minister of Henry VII', *Bulletin of the Institute of Historical Research*, 55/131 (May 1982), 35–49. William Empson did not know of Horowitz's documented research; but he had read with interest earlier documents such as the 'Plumpton Correspondence' (ed. T. Stapleton, 2 vols., 1838–9). See also Charles Henry Cooper and Thomas Cooper, *Athenae*

Cantabrigienses, 1859; *The Lisle Letters*, ed. Muriel St Clare Byrne, vol. i (Chicago: University of Chicago Press, 1981), 11–12; C. R. N. Routh, *Who's Who in Tudor England*, rev. Peter Holmes (London: Shepheard-Walwyn, 1990).

8. See Dylan Thomas and John Davenport, *The Death of the King's Canary* (London: Hutchinson & Co., 1976), 18–19.

9. *Selection from the Correspondence of the Late Macvey Napier, Esq.*, ed. Macvey Napier (London: Macmillan, 1879), 198.

10. Judith Anne Merivale, *Autobiography and Letters of Charles Merivale, Dean of Ely* (Oxford: Horace Hart, 1898), 54.

11. Lord Cockburn, *Life of Lord Jeffrey*, vol. ii (Edinburgh: Adam & Charles Black, 1852), 387.

12. Cf. *The George Eliot Letters*, ii, ed. Gordon S. Haight (London: Oxford University Press/Geoffrey Cumberlege, 1954), 315–16. Lewes believed that Jeffrey had interfered with his article on *Shirley*, but his extenuating letter to Mrs Gaskell was written more than seven years after the event: he must have forgotten that the editor of the *Edinburgh* in 1850 was no longer Jeffrey but his son-in-law William Empson.

13. Letter to Susan Darwin, 1 April 1838, *The Correspondence of Charles Darwin*, vol. ii: *1837–1843* (Cambridge: Cambridge University Press, 1986), 80–1.

14. Carlyle's eulogy features in a letter to Goethe, 10 June 1831, adverting to Empson's review of *Correspondence with Schiller* in *Edinburgh Review*, 53 (March 1831): see *Correspondence between Goethe and Carlyle*, ed. Charles Eliot Norton (London: Macmillan & Co., 1887), 282–3; *The Collected Letters of Thomas and Jane Welsh Carlyle*, vol. v: *January 1829–September 1831*, ed. Charles Richard Sanders (Durham, NC: Duke University Press, 1976 [1977]), 288.

15. Obituary in *Hertford Mercury*, 18 December 1852, quoted in *Memorials of Old Haileybury College*, ed. F. C. Danvers et al. (London: Constable & Co., 1894), 173.

16. Anonymous student quoted in *Memorials of Old Haileybury College*, 69.

17. Merivale, *Autobiography and Letters of Charles Merivale*, 53.

18. *Memorials of Old Haileybury College*, 171 n. 1.

19. 'Professor Empson' (obituary), *Gentleman's Magazine*, 39/194, NS 1 (January 1853), 100.

20. Quoted in *Memorials of Old Haileybury College*, 172.

21. It is possible that in an earlier year he had been engaged to the sister of a long-established neighbour, Philip Saltmarshe VI; see Colonel Philip Saltmarshe, *History of the Township and Family of Saltmarshe in the East Riding of Yorkshire* (privately printed, 1910), 185: 'His second sister, Henrietta Maria, who was engaged to Mr William Empson, a Cambridge professor . . .' (Goole Library, YE/SAL/942.)

22. Thomas Carlyle, *Reminiscences*, ed. J. A. Froude (London: Longmans, Green & Co., 1881), 34–5. All the same, Charlotte Weekes Empson managed to outlive her husband by no less than forty-five years: she died in June 1897, in

Dawlish, where she had lived in a house called 'The Cottage' with two spinster daughters since at least 1874 (as reported by the *Dawlish Times* of that date). Ann Sarah Empson, who died in March 1906, is also buried in Dawlish Cemetery. 'The Cottage' subsequently passed into the hands of Lady Violet Cavendish-Bentinck, an aunt of the late Queen Mother; it is now a hotel. 'Empson's Hill' commemorates the ladies named Empson.

23. *Empsons' Peace*, 13–14.
24. William Empson, letter to Margaret, Sarah, John, and Anne Empson, 21 December 1814.
25. Much of the following paragraph is indebted to an interview with C. C. Empson, September 1991.
26. J. T. Ward, *East Yorkshire Landed Estates in the Nineteenth Century* (York: East Yorkshire Local History Society, 1967), 63, 72.
27. C. C. Empson, letter to William Empson, 5 February 1982.
28. Cuthbert Brodrick of Leeds left England for France in 1869; so it seems much more likely, unless Cuthbert left designs for Yokefleet Hall before his departure, that his nephew, a partner in a Hull firm, was the architect. See also John Hutchinson, 'Yokefleet Hall and Sand Hall', *York Georgian Society Annual Report* (1979), 55–6; *Bulmer's History and Directory of East Yorkshire* (1892), 672–3.
29. A notice of death occurs in the *Yorkshire Gazette*, 6 February 1869, p. 3.
30. Quoted in Samuel Hull, letter to John William Empson, 27 February 1869.
31. C. C. Empson, letter to WE, 5 February 1982.
32. The story may be apocryphal; Lady (Monica) Empson told me she heard it from WE's brother Arthur.

3. 'A HORRID LITTLE BOY, AIRING MY VIEWS'

1. See 'The Coast Erosion Commission: Warping Experiments in Howdenshire', *Yorkshire Post*, 16 May 1907.
2. 'Out of Joint', *The Granta*, 17 February 1928, p. 286.
3. The town of Howden is about 2 miles from Yokefleet; it was famous in its day for the Horse Fair, the largest in Great Britain; in 1875, 16,000 horses were traded for the huge sum of not less than £200,000.
4. As reported in an interview with C. C. Empson, September 1991.
5. Humberside County Record Office, Beverley: PE 91/16.
6. As reported by her son C. C. Empson, September 1991.
7. Interviews with Mrs Vera Yorke, 4 October 1985; Mrs Grace Margery Key, 4 January 1989.
8. As related by Air Marshal Sir Richard Atcherley in a letter to William Empson dated 'August 6th' (Empson Papers).
9. Ardsley House became a hotel in 1973; in 1985 it was purchased by the Queens Moat House Group.
10. 'The Will of the Late Mr Richard Micklethwait', *Barnsley Chronicle*, 6 October 1888.

11. Obituary in *Barnsley Chronicle*, 18 April 1908.
12. ' "Squire of Ardsley" dies, 79', *Barnsley Chronicle*, 8 July 1976; see also *Burke's Landed Gentry*.
13. Humberside County Record Office, Beverley: PE 90/12—Blacktoft register (copy).
14. Interview with Lady (Monica) Empson, 1983.
15. *Empsons' War: A Collection of Letters*, ed. C. C. Empson (Bishop Auckland: Pentland Press, 1995), 29.
16. Reported in an unidentified newspaper cutting, 'Coming of Age Festivities at Yokefleet'; *Empsons' War*, 30.
17. *Empsons' War*, 33.
18. Sir Walter Raleigh, quoted in John Pudney, *A Pride of Unicorns: Richard and David Atcherley of the R.A.F.* (London: Oldbourne, 1960), 14.
19. Laura Empson, quoted in Pudney, *A Pride of Unicorns*, 10.
20. The disaster was widely reported in newspapers; e.g., *Morning Post*, 16 May 1914. See also an article reprinted in *Empsons' War*, 33–9; Ted Dodsworth, *Wings over Yorkshire* (Beverley: Hutton Press, 1988), 47.
21. Interview with Grace Margery Key, 4 January 1989.
22. Pudney, *A Pride of Unicorns*, 12. Pudney gives an account of Jack Empson's disaster on pp. 9–12.
23. Obituary in *The Times*, 20 April 1970.
24. *DNB. 1961–1970*, 44–5.
25. Death certificate of Arthur Reginald Empson.
26. Interview with Grace Margery Key, 4 January 1989.
27. District Probate Registry, York; probate was granted on 8 July 1916. The terms of the Settled Land Act, 1882, are elucidated by R. Megarry and H. W. R. Wade, *The Law of Real Property*, 4th edn. (London: Stevens & Sons, 1975), 288–95. The current legislation is the 1925 Settled Land Act.
28. John Poynder Dickson-Poynder was created Baron Islington in 1910; he was Conservative MP for Chippenham, 1892–1910, and Governor of New Zealand, 1910–12; later appointments included a stint as Parliamentary Under-Secretary for India, 1915–18, and as chairman of the National Savings Committee, 1920–6. See *DNB 1931–1940* and *Who Was Who, 1929–1940*.
29. Small notebook, with Empson's handwritten notes and comments on his parents' wills and settlements (Empson Papers).
30. In a draft of the review, he asked simply and pertinently, 'why did he [Eliot] never mention his father?'
31. Undated draft TS letter to 'Mr Green' on the subject of 'A. R. Empson Will Trust'.
32. WE wrote to his accountant, for example, on 24 August 1968:

> the entail I think could be and should be looked up. Are you prepared to send a young man to Somerset House to examine the wills of my father and grandfather and report on a specific point, the mode of inheritance laid down in the entail

(it might involve great-grandfather, but probably not). I am willing to spend twenty pounds on learning what I want to know, but not more. Does Yokefleet descend through daughters, like royalty, or through sons, like an earldom?...If it goes through the male line, Mogador is the eventual heir, or his elder son is at any rate. If not, it goes to the son of the daughter of my elder brother Charles, as he seems to assume it will do.

Surely all these entails are written down plainly a long time before and not hidden, so that I can ask to be informed. On second thoughts, the entail is perhaps not part of the will; I only want to know one fact about the entail. Is it a secret?

See also a TS draft letter to 'Mr Green', 8 February 1981:

Thank you very much for your letter, which surprised me very much. I had no idea that my brother Arthur had rearranged the estate in 1960 so that a disentailing deed could be executed. It seemed impossible; surely he would need to get some acquittal from me, as I would be the next heir after my nephew Charles.

Then I remembered that there had been a kind of meeting at Yokefleet, when I was sent for and found my two elder brothers sitting among papers. I thought this was merely to get my assent to the renouncement of the estate by old Charles in favour of young Charles, a saving in death duties, and a case where it seemed over-scrupulous to get my consent. But I expected my brother Arthur to behave scrupulously like that. I remember saying as I came in: 'I won't make any difficulty; I accept the rule of primogeniture'. This seems worth recalling, as it proves (to me at least) that I had no idea I had been brought in to break the rule of primogeniture. If I signed anything disastrous on that occasion please let me know; I do not remember signing, and surely I would not do it without even feeling curiosity. If I did I behaved very badly towards my elder son, so please let us know.

There was in fact a 1960 settlement, arranged by Arthur to avoid double death duties, which involved brother Charles to the extent that he had to renounce his life interest. Arthur set up a Discretionary Trust; and William was angry at Arthur when it was divulged, quite unexpectedly, that Mogador, William's son, had been cut out. Charles Empson, William's nephew, received no money when he inherited the estate after his Uncle Arthur's death: it all went to pay death duties, and he was taxed from the start at 82 per cent, the highest rate.

33. WE, letter to his brother Charles, n.d. (?1973), in possession of his son Jacob Empson. In another undated draft letter, to 'Mr Green', Empson stated: 'My brother Arthur was a very conscientious man...'
34. Arthur Empson, undated letter to mother (C. C. Empson).
35. Arthur Empson, undated letter to mother (C. C. Empson).
36. *Empsons' War*, 58.
37. Arthur Empson, letter to mother, 9 December (1915); *Empsons' War*, 64.
38. Arthur Empson, letter to mother, 11 January (1916); *Empsons' War*, 65.
39. Arthur Empson, letter to mother, 31 July (1917); *Empsons' War*, 77–8.
40. Arthur Empson, letter to father, 5 December (1915); *Empsons' War*, 60–1.

41. Arthur Empson, letter to mother, n.d.; *Empsons' War*, 69.
42. Arthur Empson, letter to mother, n.d. (C. C. Empson).
43. Arthur Empson, letter to mother, 29 July 1917; *Empsons' War*, 82–3.
44. *Empsons' War*, 83.
45. Ibid. 84.
46. Ibid. 85.
47. Arthur Empson, letter to mother, 14 September (1917); *Empsons' War*, 86.
48. Arthur Empson, letter to mother, 11 November 1918; *Empsons' War*, 95.
49. Arthur Empson, letter to mother, 23 November 1918; *Empsons' War*, 98–9.
50. Arthur Empson, letter to mother, Cologne, 11 December 1918; *Empsons' War*, 100.
51. Arthur Empson, letter to mother, 27 November 1918; *Empsons' War*, 99.
52. Arthur Empson, letter to Charles, 12 November (1917); *Empsons' War*, 89–90.
53. Arthur Empson, letter to mother, 1 February 1918: *Empsons' War*, 102.
54. Interview with C. C. Empson, September 1991.
55. Interview with Lady (Monica) Empson, 1983.
56. Interview with Vera Yorke, 4 October 1985.
57. Interview with C. C. Empson, September 1991; and article '150,000 see Queen's Trooping the Color', *New York Times*, 12 June 1953, which includes a four-paragraph Reuters report headed 'Duke Has Rough Ride':

   > A disrespectful horse named Yokefleet gave the Duke of Edinburgh a rough ride today.
   >
   > Yokefleet bucked. He pranced. He walked sidewise like a crab. But the Duke hung on gamely. Once the 13-year-old Yokefleet jerked his head around and tried to take a bite out of the Duke's leg . . .
   >
   > As the seventy-five-minute parade ended, Queen Elizabeth turned to her husband and with a straight face made a remark. The Duke grinned and replied with a comment that made the Queen bite her lip to suppress a smile.

58. 'Infans Pervers' (a review of *Dreams Fade*, by Godfrey Winn), *The Granta*, 3 February 1928, p. 250.
59. Interview with Grace Margery Key, 4 January 1989; and Margery Key, letter to JH, 21 January 1989.
60. WE, '*Volpone*', in *Essays on Renaissance Literature*, vol. ii: *The Drama*, ed. J. Haffenden (Cambridge: Cambridge University Press, 1994), 68.
61. TS draft, dating from the 1970s, of an essay subsequently published as 'The Spirits of *The Dream*'.
62. *Coleridge's Verse: A selection*, ed. William Empson and David Pirie (London: Faber & Faber, 1974), 73.
63. WE, letter to W. D. Maxwell-Mahon, n.d. (Derek Roper).
64. Interview with M. F. Micklethwait, 9 August 1992.
65. Interview with Hetta Empson, 14 January 1990; also a letter to JH from Andrew White, 5 July 1985: 'I do remember his once remarking over some meal in Hall [at Winchester]—but, in what context, I forget—that he was the

youngest of his parents' brood & understood that his arrival—some years after the youngest of his siblings—had *not* been intended.'

66. See 'Donne and the Rhetorical Tradition', in *Essays on Renaissance Literature*, vol. i: *Donne and the New Philosophy* (Cambridge: Cambridge University Press, 1993), 65.

67. *Ambiguity*, 198.

68. Interviews with Lady (Monica) Empson, 1983; C. C. Empson, September 1991.

69. Interview with Margery Key, 4 January 1989.

70. In an interview with Christopher Norris and David Wilson, Empson was to remark that a friend of his—a sailor, Josh Avery—'and sailors are always afraid of cows'—once said to him, 'You really aren't afraid of cows, are you? I've been watching.' Empson went on: 'Well, I was brought up to believe that the good man simply could not fear cows, you see. It was unthinkable as they liked to say. And I gaped at him in astonishment: "How could you suppose I would be in fear of cows?" And I feel this in much the same way that when I see people writing down what I meant in poems I feel that again and again: "How could you have supposed I was wrestling with cows?" Still, mind you, I feel it's very sensible to be afraid of the sund'ring herds. As a matter of fact they can trample you into the mud perfectly well. But the way to handle cows is to refuse to let them know you're afraid of them. That much I know at any rate.'

71. Interview with Vera Yorke, 4 October 1985.

72. Interview with C. C. Empson, September 1991.

73. From the bare beginnings of a memoir written by Sir Charles Empson; quoted in a letter to JH from Lady (Monica) Empson, 16 May 1983.

74. Interview with C. C. Empson, September 1991.

75. Interview with Vera Yorke, 4 October 1985.

76. Interview with Hetta Empson, 14 January 1990.

77. Arthur Empson, letter to mother, n.d.; *Empsons' War*, 73.

78. Even in the boys' society of Winchester, Empson spoke with enthusiasm about his sister (Miriam MacIver, letter to JH, 3 October 1987).

79. *Milton's God*, 319.

80. 'Bastards and Barstards', *Essays in Criticism*, 17/3 (July 1967), 407.

81. Empson took a lively interest in accents and pronunciation, and was concerned that authentic dialects should not be trimmed into a standard, 'Received Pronunciation' or even 'BBC English', though he himself spoke with an unmistakably upper-middle-class voice. He must have been drawing on personal knowledge, particularly his experience of growing up in rural Yorkshire, when he wrote in 1937, for an American audience: 'the point about dialects in England is that most villagers have a wide range between standard English and the dialect or indeed the several dialects, and put a great deal of weight on varying the talk with the person addressed and the feeling towards

him . . . Nobody puts this into dialect novels except for the crude change to standard English (which is hardly used except for rudeness) because the novel-reading public would not understand it; I wouldn't myself. In fact if you are expected to talk standard English you are not allowed to learn this game; the old style squire still does a bit, but it seems patronising' ('A London Letter', *Poetry*, 40 (1937), 220). Presumably, in that last, rather pejorative remark, he was thinking of his father or (more likely) his brother as being just the sort of 'old style squire' who would think to assume a regional voice when addressing their tenants.

82. Letter to Phyllis Chroustchoff (*c.* Christmas 1930); in possession of Igor Chroustchoff.

83. Loose leaf from diary, dated 'Sunday 3rd'. The preceding passage of this diary-entry is just as entertaining: 'My Mother turns back the sittingroom carpet from the fire at night because hot cinders might roll out, and locks the door, I suppose because my grandmother did it. Twice on coming into it after my bath I have found her arranging the carpet on her knees, with the lights out and the door shut. Returning tonight the mangled Observer I was frightened by the fancy I might find her in the dark, with the door locked on the outside, muttering to herself and crawling quietly about the carpet on all fours. To lock the door on the outside is a quintessence of witchcraft, and to get out again and become my admirable mamma before morning may stand well enough for the odd rule of sanity; the effect of other people, and practical business, and regular observances, on the human soul. Actually I think she does it in the dark as a businesslike way of showing that she's got it nearly all done, anyway.'

84. WE, letter to 'Mr McMahon' (W. D. Maxwell-Mahon), 21 August 1973.

85. A quondam inn, the White House was said to be haunted (Mrs Empson and Molly witnessed a ghost in the bathroom, it was said); folklore had it that the olde inne-keeper had murdered some of his wealthy patrons.

86. Unpublished memoir by the late Sir Desmond Lee.

87. Interview with Lady (Monica) Empson, 1983. Charles Empson married Monica (b. 1909) in 1931. Daughter of a dean of Canterbury Cathedral, she was fond of her brother-in-law and always called him 'Willum'; she liked to claim that his poem 'Camping Out' was about her, but this is unlikely—if only because of the date of the poem: published in February 1929, it must refer back to a camping trip in the summer of 1928; in any event, we are to infer that the pair in the poem are lovers.

88. Unfinished draft review of Wilbur Sanders's *The Dramatist and the Received Idea* (Cambridge, 1968); Empson Papers.

89. WE to John Hayward, 4 May 1939 (T. Hofmann).

90. *Milton's God*, 111.

91. WE, letter to mother, 15 March 1938 (Empson Papers).

92. *Milton's God*, 246.

93. WE, letter to 'Mr McMahon' (W. D. Maxwell-Mahon), 21 August 1973 (copy in Empson Papers).

94. Undated draft letter to the editor of the *Hudson Review* (in response to Roger Sale's article 'The Achievement of William Empson', *Hudson Review*, 19 (Autumn 1966), 369–90). See also WE's published letter, *Hudson Review*, 20 (1967), 434–8.

95. S. G. F. Brandon, *The Judgment of the Dead* (London: Weidenfeld & Nicolson, 1967), 104, 108, 98, 134–5, 196.

96. Interview with Grace Margery Key, 4 January 1989.

4. 'OWL EMPSON'

1. WE, letter to Molly Empson, 13 June 1915.
2. Arthur Empson, letter to Mrs Empson, 13 June 1915.
3. WE, letter to Molly Empson, 13 June 1915.
4. WE, letter to his mother, 28 November 1915.
5. WE, letter to his mother, 30 May 1915.
6. John A. Simson, letter to JH, 29 March 1985.
7. John A. Simson, letter to JH, 20 April 1985.
8. WE, letter to his mother, 6 June 1915.
9. WE, letter to mother, 24 September 1916.
10. WE, letter to his mother, 28 November 1915.
11. WE, letter to his mother, 6 June 1915.
12. WE, letter to his mother, 5 December 1915.
13. WE, letter to his mother, n.d.
14. Undated memorandum by Geoffrey Hazelden (courtesy of Derek Roper).
15. Memo by G. Hazelden.
16. WE, letter to mother, 24 September 1916.
17. Maurice Roderick, letter to Mrs Empson, 18 May 1919.
18. Maurice Roderick, letter to Mrs Empson, 16 April 1920.
19. WE, postcard to his mother, 11 June 1920.
20. Revd A. T. P. Williams, letter to Mrs Empson, 12 June 1920.
21. WE, letter to mother, 13 June 1920.
22. John A. Simson, letter to JH, 20 April 1985.
23. J. D'E. Firth, *Rendall of Winchester: The Life and Witness of a Teacher* (London: Oxford University Press, 1954), 163; Christopher Dilke, *Dr Moberly's Mint-Mark: A Study of Winchester College* (London: Heinemann, 1965), 60–1.
24. Dilke, *Dr Moberly's Mint-Mark*, 125.
25. J. D'E. Firth, *Winchester* (London: Blackie & Son, 1936), 145–6. 'It will surprise my Wykehamist readers to learn', wrote John D'E. ('Budge') Firth as late as 1949—nearly 25 years after Empson became a Wykehamist—'that "notions examina" and "spanking" have been abolished on the highest authority for the last seventy-five years' (Firth, *Winchester College* (London: Winchester Publications, 1949), 169).

26. Empson Papers. See also Firth, *Winchester*, 144; Dilke, *Dr Moberly's Mint-Mark*, 132–3; James Sabben-Clare, *Winchester College: After 600 Years, 1382–1988* (Winchester: P. & G. Wells, 1989), 144.

27. Firth, *Winchester*, 144; Dilke, *Dr Moberly's Mint-Mark*, 11, 62, 92–3.

28. R. H. S. Crossman, 'Highland Light Reading', *The Guardian*, 15 June 1962.

29. Firth, *Winchester College*, 83; Dilke, *Dr Moberly's Mint-Mark*, 132.

30. Sir William Hayter, interview with JH, August 1985.

31. Firth, *Winchester College*, 104.

32. Undated draft letter (*c*.1955) to Desmond Lee ('My dear Desmond').

33. *The Wykehamist*, 630 (27 February 1923), 300. For US readers, a 'public' school in the UK is a private, fee-paying school.

34. Undated draft letter (*c*.1955) to Desmond Lee.

35. WE, ' "Just a Blond" ' (book review), *The Granta*, 30 April 1926, p. 365.

36. Undated holograph letter (Empson Papers).

37. Douglas Jay, letter to JH, 5 July 1985.

38. Andrew White, letter to JH, 5 July 1985.

39. Colin Clark, letter to JH, 12 August 1985.

40. Michael Hope, letter to JH, 1 July 1985.

41. Andrew White, letter to JH, 5 July 1985.

42. Sir William Hayter, interview with JH, August 1985. With regard to the common assumption that 'boys' boarding-schools must be hotbeds of homosexuality,' Hayter wrote in his memoirs: 'There was a good deal of talk about this in College, as there was on every other subject, but not so far as I was aware much more than talk' (*A Double Life* (London: Hamish Hamilton, 1974), 8).

43. Dilke, *Mr Moberly's Mint-Mark*, 116.

44. Firth, *Winchester*, 160–1.

45. Firth, *Rendall of Winchester*, 250.

46. Dilke, *Dr Moberly's Mint-Mark*, 111–12.

47. Kenneth Clark, *Another Part of the Wood: A Self-Portrait* (London: John Murray, 1974), 60–1.

48. Michael Hope, letter to JH, 1 July 1985.

49. Firth, *Rendall of Winchester*, 53, 118; Dilke, *Dr Moberly's Mint-Mark*, 115–16.

50. Firth, *Rendall of Winchester*, 146–7.

51. Interview with E. A. Radice, July 1985. In General Division, there was equally enormous stress on learning English poetry by heart.

52. Firth, *Winchester*, 160–1; *Rendall of Winchester*, 121.

53. Firth, *Winchester*, 161; Sabben-Clare, *Winchester College*, 84.

54. Colin Clark, letter to JH, 12 August 1985.

55. Firth, *Rendall of Winchester*, 131.

56. Colin Clark, letter to JH, 12 August 1985.

57. The Revd H. P. Kingdon, letter to JH, 2 July 1985.

58. *Milton's God*, 106–7.

59. *The Wykehamist*, 633 (18 May 1923), 337.

60. Firth, *Rendall of Winchester*, 127, 73–4.

61. 'The day after my father's death, my mother asked me to go round and see Rendall about a funeral service for him in Winchester College Chapel. Rendall was a man for whom I felt fear rather than respect; my father, who had known him all his life, did not like him, and I found his Corsican-brigand style unattractive and rather synthetic. When I visited him on that August morning we quickly sorted out the details about the funeral service. He then settled down in his armchair and indicated that I should sit on his lap. Much surprised, I did what I was told, and he then began to kiss me, his black bristly moustache scratching my cheek, talking religion all the time. I found the situation, though not traumatic, very distasteful. I was too afraid of him to protest (a great boy of eighteen!) and accepted the situation passively. A day or two later I had to see him again and the same performance was repeated. Never at any time did he actually say anything that referred to the way he was behaving; his talk was all of his highest religious and moral plane' (Hayter, *A Double Life*, 10). See also Anthony Howard, *Crossman: The Pursuit of Power* (London: Jonathan Cape, 1990), 17. Hayter told me that he regarded Rendall as 'a flamboyant, perhaps phoney figure'.

62. Dilke, *Mr Moberly's Mint-Mark*, 117.

63. John Willis, letter to JH, 1 August 1985; Miriam McIver (widow of Arthur McIver, an Empson contemporary who went on to become Professor of Philosophy at Southampton University), letter to JH, 3 October 1987; the Revd H. P. Kingdon, letter to JH, 2 July 1985.

64. Colin Clark, letter to JH, 12 August 1985.

65. Firth, *Winchester College*, 39; Sabben-Clare, *Winchester College*, 35.

66. Dilke, *Dr Moberly's Mint-Mark*, 112, 137.

67. Firth, *Winchester*, 142; Sabben-Clare, *Winchester College*, 10; Dilke, *Dr Moberly's Mint-Mark*, 132.

68. This and many further details are taken from a typescript memoir in the Second Chamber Annals, Winchester College.

69. *Spencer Leeson, Shepherd: Teacher: Friend, a Memoir by some of his Friends* (London: SPCK, 1958), 37–8.

70. Anonymous contributor, in *Spencer Leeson*, 43–4. See also Hayter, *A Double Life*, 11.

71. Michael Hope, letter to JH, 1 July 1985.

72. *Spencer Leeson*, 71.

73. Undated draft letter (*c.*1955) to Desmond Lee.

74. WE went on, however: 'I don't quite like seeing him in purple and Dick Crossman plotting together in the Athenaeum. They have the same tiny grudge: we were both given the best education of all, and we still pretend we were wronged. Now the fundamental idea of all administration, as you well realise, is not to have people think they were wronged. It does seem to me

tiresome to see these characters sit together in the Athenaeum and say they were both wronged. There are very real troubles in the world but a decent education is not one of them. Winchester invented both these characters; it seems to me bad tempered of them to be cross about it.'

75. *Spencer Leeson*, 21.
76. Firth, *Winchester College*, 207.
77. Sabben-Clare, *Winchester College*, 58.
78. Firth, *Rendall of Winchester*, 138–9, 142–3.
79. Sabben-Clare, *Winchester College*, 62.
80. Andrew White, letter to JH, 5 July 1985.
81. Ibid.
82. Interview with Dr E. A. Radice, July 1985.
83. Sabben-Clare, *Winchester College*, 69.
84. E. A. Radice, letter to JH, 2 July 1985.
85. School report for Common Time, 1925 (Empson Papers).
86. A. S. Ramsey, letter to Mrs Laura Empson, 18 December 1924 (Empson Papers).
87. E. A. Radice, letter to JH, 2 July 1985.
88. School report for Common Time, 1925 (Empson Papers).
89. *The Wykehamist*, 660 (27 May 1925), 85.
90. 'Second Chamber Annals, begun Cloister Time 1920' (courtesy of Winchester College), and A. L. Rowse, 'John Sparrow', in *All Souls in My Time* (London: Gerald Duckworth, 1993), 199.
91. George Watson has related, in a memoir of Empson, 'it was amazing to hear him talk of Sparrow as a youthful radical. Once, I recall his telling, at a speech-day at Winchester, the boy Sparrow had turned to him and asked him to stand up and look around at a large assembly of parents. Empson wonderingly did as he was told. "Now, Empson," said Sparrow, "when in years to come you are asked to appoint a Wykehamist or to overlook a fault in one, just remember what you have seen today." But now, Empson went on savagely, a life spent in Oxford had turned Sparrow into "the trusted family butler—and that is just the matter with Oxford: it turns people into trusted family butlers"' (*Never Ones for Theory? England and the War of Ideas* (Cambridge: Lutterworth Press, 2000), 66).
92. Colin Clark, letter to JH, 12 August 1985.
93. Ibid.
94. Sir William Hayter, letter to Sir Jeremy Morse, 20 July 1989; Douglas Jay, letter to Morse, 19 May 1989 (courtesy of Sir Jeremy Morse); Morse, letter to JH, 3 February 1990.
95. E. A. Radice, letter to JH, 2 July 1985.
96. Christopher Hawkes, letter to JH, 25 December 1989: 'his repute, in line with his demeanour, was that of a somewhat perky, but occasionally witty, bespectacled eccentric; and as such wasn't the boy just the father of the man?

Quiet though he usually was, he knew he was something of a clown, and acted up to it.'

97. *The Wykehamist*, 647 (23 May 1924), 490.

98. Christopher Hawkes, letter to JH, 8 November 1989; interview with Professor Hawkes, July 1985.

99. Colin Clark, letter to JH, 12 August 1985.

100. Sir William Hayter, interview with JH, August 1985.

101. School report for Common Time, 1925 (Empson Papers).

102. Firth, *Winchester*, 176–7.

103. Patrick Clapham, letter to JH, 6 July 1985: 'My memory of him is of a *very* reserved man with, I would say, no close friends.'

104. Undated draft letter (*c.*1955) to Desmond Lee.

105. John Willis, letter to JH, 1 August 1985.

106. Michael Hope, letter to JH, 1 July 1985.

107. 'Second Chamber Annals'. According to Stephen Spender, Crossman remarked at Oxford in the late 1920s: 'Even if I become Prime Minister, I'll never be as great as I was at Winchester' (Howard, *Crossman*, 20).

108. Michael Hope, letter to JH, 1 July 1985.

109. Colin Clark, letter to JH, 12 August 1985.

110. E. A. Radice, letter to JH, 2 July 1985.

111. *The Wykehamist*, 655 (22 December 1924), 41.

112. Ibid. 657 (25 February 1925), 60.

113. Ibid. 654 (2 December 1924), 34.

114. Undated draft letter (*c.*1955) to Desmond Lee.

115. 'Second Chamber Annals'.

116. Undated draft letter (*c.*1955) to Desmond Lee. 'We then had the loathsome spectacle,' he went on, 'of a teacher, the then Second Master, head of the College, leeringly approaching elder children and saying it would be in accordance with tradition if they choose to torture younger children. This we thought filthy . . .'

117. Quoted in Howard, *Crossman*, 16.

118. WE, 'Wykehamist' (letter to the editor), *New Statesman*, 25 September 1954. On the other hand, the future Earl Waldegrave, who was Empson's senior by a year, would later be quoted as saying: 'All the young masters were in the trenches in the war and a lot of them were killed. It was very rough indeed for small boys like myself' ('Extramural', *Daily Telegraph*, 25 March 1992, p. 19).

119. Undated draft letter (*c.*1955) to Desmond Lee. Elsewhere in the same letter, Empson remarked, he felt most surprised, at a recent meeting with Crossman, to find him 'sincere or at least barefaced in insisting that he had to fight, when we were boys together, for what really everybody gave him with both hands.'

120. Firth, *Winchester*, 91.

121. Geoffrey McDermott, *Leader Lost: A Biography of Hugh Gaitskell* (London: Leslie Frewin, 1972), 14.

122. Firth, *Winchester*, 25; *Winchester College*, 59, 75.

123. Firth, *Winchester College*, 95, 200.

124. Undated draft letter (*c.*1955) to Desmond Lee.

5. 'DID I, I WONDER, TALK TOO MUCH?'

1. For a full account of Magdalene, see Peter Cunich, David Hoyle, Eamon Duffy, and Ronald Hyam, *A History of Magdalene College, Cambridge, 1428–1988* (Cambridge: Magdalene College Publications, 1994).

2. In 1928, to mark the 500th anniversary of this displaced beginning, *Magdalene College Magazine* sported an article on 'How to celebrate the Quincentenary by one who will not be there'. Since Empson had become renowned for his fervid interest in psychology, poetry, and anti-Christian sentiment, the article included this apt if arcane passage: 'At 3.45 p.m. Will Epsom is to present his topical song-scena entitled "An Experiment with Monks' Hostel, a psycho-septico papal-nuncio analysis of the history of the College"' (*Magdalene College Magazine*, 58 (June 1928), 186).

3. Owen Chadwick, *Michael Ramsey: A Life* (Oxford: Clarendon Press, 1990), 16.

4. The terms of provision of the Milner Scholarships express a preference for scholars from Leeds, Halifax, and Heversham Schools; perhaps it was enough for Benson that Empson stemmed from Yorkshire.

   Empson later had the opportunity to write about both men; with a mixture of respect and impudence he reviewed *Cressage*, a fiction by A. C. Benson, and David Pye's memoir of George Leigh Mallory: 'These are both dead generations; it is too soon to judge them. In the last of Benson's flowing slightly imagined novels one finds the anxiety of the natural celibate, has he the right to withdraw himself from those who need him; and in the biography of Mallory, the later of these charming self-tortured people, the anxiety of the moth before the candle, had he the right to throw up a too difficult world, and died in the fascination of the mountains. "All sound plans are abandoned for a last dash to the top"—he did not know whether it was suicide; nor do I. But at least they will never be judged in the future more harshly than they judged themselves' ('Mustard and Cress', *The Granta*, 2 December 1927, p. 194).

5. Benson quoted in Cunich *et al.*, *A History of Magdalene College*, 235.

6. 'Ramsay was a kindly man, as I can testify from personal experience' (Christopher N. L. Brooke, *A History of the University of Cambridge*, iv: *1870–1990* (Cambridge: Cambridge University Press, 1993), 47 n. 83).

7. Francis Mc. C. Turner, 'In Memoriam: Allen Beville Ramsay', *Magdalene College Record*, 4 (1955–6), 4.

8. Cunich *et al.*, *A History of Magdalene College*, 235–6.

9. Peter Joyce, 'A Day-Boy's Magdalene Memories, 1925', *Magdalene College Magazine and Record*, 33 (1988–9), 30.

10. Frank West, 'Magdalene Memories, 1928–31', *Magdalene College Magazine and Record*, 33 (1988–9), 27.

11. Ibid.

12. D. C. R. Francombe, 'Reminiscences: (1) Magdalene, 1924–1927', *Magdalene College Magazine and Record*, NS 35 (1990–1), 41; letters from Francombe to JH, 3 and 9 September 1993.

13. Ramsey's textbooks in applied mathematics sold over 100,000 copies in his lifetime (Cunich *et al.*, *A History of Magdalene College*, 229).

14. Don Francombe has recalled of Michael Ramsay: 'He read Classics for Pt 1 of the Tripos with, if I remember aright, no more distinction than I. He was immensely entertaining and a very good mimic. He talked a great deal to himself and always addressed me as "my boy". One of his memorable acts was to preach a sermon in the style of a Methodist minister. One text I recall was "Under a Juniper tree" extracting somewhat bogus significance from every word. I could almost repeat it!' (letter to JH, 9 September 1993).

15. Chadwick, *Michael Ramsey*, 4, 6.

16. I. A. Richards's contribution to the radio programme *The Ambiguity of William Empson* (produced by David Perry), BBC Radio 3, 22 October 1977.

17. 'I never met Wittgenstein,' said Empson late in life. 'We all thought the Tractatus very important somehow' (letter to David Wilson, 5 November 1970).

18. John D. Solomon, letters to JH, n.d. (1991), 17 March 1991, 29 March 1991.

19. John D. Solomon, letter to JH, n.d. (1991).

20. WE, 'The Romantic Rationalist', *The Granta*, 12 June 1926; *EG* supplement.

21. P. Sargant Florence, 'The Cambridge Heretics (1909–1932)', *The Humanist Outlook* (London: Pemberton, 1968), 238.

22. See John Paul Russo, *I. A. Richards: His Life and Work* (London: Routledge, 1989), 54 and 702.

23. Cf. ibid. 123.

24. D. H. Lawrence, letter to John Hayward, 22 January 1926 (Hayward Papers, King's College Cambridge: DHL/JDH/1).

25. 'I remember him [Wittgenstein] lecturing to the Heretics, of which I was secretary for a time, on Ethics, which he considered a huge nonsense' (Julian Trevelyan, *Indigo Days* (London: MacGibbon & Kee, 1957), 18).

26. George Watson, 'The Cambridge Lectures of T. S. Eliot', *Sewanee Review* (Fall 1991), 579.

27. Ibid.

28. Richards Collection, Old Library, Magdalene College, Cambridge.

29. He missed the last of Eliot's audiences simply because he overslept. The night before, he had attended an odd sort of Magdalene dining club (run by a friend, Mark Hartland Thomas) at which the participants performed party pieces and cod speeches. To judge from Empson's morning-after account, they made a great display of themselves: 'Very funny, vodka. Curtis-Brown

[the future literary agent] did iggety-piggety mysticism with relapses into coarse Chaucer and commonsense; I have not seen it done before; capable. [Guy] Mayfield [future Archdeacon of Hastings], "Sadism, my alternative to athleticism", followed by my sadist play; harmonious. [A. C.] Townsend upon the social unrest in Southern Patagonia and Wigglesworth, revivalist for astrology; the president "was made up better than usual" and turned out a Joyce drunken scene in the historical-popular style. Did I, I wonder, talk too much in the supper stages?

'But why, wailing, did I sleep uncarefully and not go to the last, a well worth hearing, T. S. Eliot grande levée? I had forgotten, and it is too late. They were together, and he fell. Carammbo.'

30. WE, 'Donne the Space Man' (1957); *Essays on Renaissance Literature*, i. 127.

31. WE, 'The Style of the Master', in Richard March and Tambimuttu (eds.), *T. S. Eliot: A Symposium* (London: Editions Poetry London, 1948), 36–7.

32. 'Editor's Introduction', in T. S. Eliot, *The Varieties of Metaphysical Poetry*, ed. Ronald Schuchard (London: Faber & Faber, 1993), 14.

33. Ibid. 15. Schuchard notes too: 'Empson did not attribute the discussion so directly to Eliot in the first edition (London: Chatto & Windus, 1930), writing more obliquely that Shelley's poem "has received much discussion recently. I am afraid more points will have been brought out than I have noticed" (p. 197).' Eliot was to publish his remark on Shelley's 'To a Skylark' in his essay, 'Note on Richard Crashaw', in *For Lancelot Andrewes: Essays on Style and Order* (London: Faber & Faber, 1928), 96. See also George Franklin, 'Instances of Meeting: Shelley and Eliot: A Study in Affinity', *ELH* 61 (1994), 955–90.

34. WE, letter to Gareth Jones, 22 December 1973 (Trinity College, Cambridge).

35. D. R. Thorpe, *Selwyn Lloyd* (London: Jonathan Cape, 1989), 27. (Gilbert Harding was later to achieve fame and some notoriety as a 'personality' on the TV panel game *What's My Line*.)

36. 'Union Notes', *The Granta*, 35 (29 June 1926).

37. *Cambridge Review*, 29 January 1926, p. 216.

38. *Cambridge Review*, 5 February 1926, pp. 230–1.

39. 'Union Notes', *The Granta*, 28 May 1926, p. 413.

40. *Cambridge Review*, 28 May 1928, p. 446.

41. Judging from internal evidence, this was probably in February 1926, when 'the religious groups in the university agreed, after much difficulty, upon the common organization of a mission to the university' (Chadwick, *Michael Ramsey*, 23).

42. *Cambridge Review*, 48 11 February 1927, 264.

43. P.M.J., 'Completely Inverted', *The Granta*, 12 June 1926, p. 473.

44. 'Those in Obscurity', *The Granta*, 12 June 1926, p. 465.

45. Guy Clutton-Brock (b. 1906) read History at Magdalene and was later an Honorary Fellow; his elder brother, Alan Francis (b. 1904), who was up at

King's, would in due course become Art Critic for *The Times* and Slade Professor of Fine Art at Cambridge University.

46. This is not necessarily to Empson's discredit; as D. R. Thorpe has pointed out, 'Magdalene was a comparatively small college at a time when Union votes came mainly from College connections' (Thorpe, *Selwyn Lloyd*, 27).

47. 'The Union Society', *Cambridge Review*, 12 November 1926, p. 98. Interestingly, Lord Devlin remarked in a letter to JH (8 April 1991): 'The invitation to Empson to speak "on the paper" shows that he must previously have spoken successfully...'

48. 'Neither [R. A.] Butler nor [Selwyn] Lloyd...had the rapier-like agility in meeting, destroying and ridiculing a preceding speaker which Patrick Devlin, now Mr Justice Devlin, possessed,' wrote Michael Ramsey in a later year. 'Devlin of Christ's outstripped all rivals in the oratory of the *advocate*: he was the F. E. Smith of the Union in the 1920's' ('"Time to begin anew"', in *Recollections of the Cambridge Union*, ed. Percy Cradock (Cambridge: Bowes & Bowes, 1953), 123).

49. 'Union Notes', *The Granta*, 12 November 1926, p. 99.

50. 'Those in Authority: William Empson (Magdalene)', *The Granta*, 31 May 1929, p. 485.

51. *The Granta*, 28 October 1927, pp. 65–6.

52. Frank West, who went up to Magdalene three years later than Empson, would write in after years: 'I recall a certain amount of harmless bawdy talk, but serious sex topics do not seem to have played a significant part in our conversation. None of us had what is now called a "steady" girlfriend...We had all been conditioned by the quasi-celibate life of a public school.' West's experience seems to have differed from Empson's only in this particular: 'There was not the faintest suggestion of homosexuality either in conversation or practice' (West, 'Magdalene Memories, 1928–31', 28). Likewise J. E. H. Blackie, who entered Magdalene in 1922: 'Women...played curiously little part in our lives...[M]ost of us led a masculine existence in masculine company, in which the College provided the setting and our rooms the focal point' ('Cambridge in the Twenties', *Magdalene College Magazine*, 31 (1986–7), 24).

53. 'The Union', *The Granta*, 7 May 1926, p. 368.

54. WE, undated letter to John Wain (copy in Empson Papers). 'I forget the circumstances of writing it completely...,' he added. 'I expect the sexual situation was bad.'

55. WE, letter to J. A. Stephens, 28 October 1957.

56. WE, letter to W. D. Maxwell-Mahon, 6 November 1967.

57. WE, letter to David Wilson, 5 November 1970 (David Wilson).

58. Compare *Paradise Lost*, iv. 372–3: 'this high seat your Heaven | Ill fenced for Heaven to keep out such a foe | As now is entered.'

59. G. Karl Galinsky, *Ovid's 'Metamorphoses': An Introduction to the Basic Aspects* (Berkeley and Los Angeles: University of California Press, 1975), 67.

60. *Complete Poems of William Empson*, 116.

61. 'One prime concern felt by the General Council was to remain respectable in public eyes. It was rather an embarrassment for them to learn that there had been widespread demonstrations in support of the strike in the Soviet Union, that collections were being taken in all industrial centres, that many Russian workers had voted to contribute part of their wages towards a strike donation, and that all British ships in Russian ports had been held up. This embarrassment was increased by the offer of the All-Russian Trade Union Council to contribute 2 million roubles towards strike funds. Their reaction was immediate. As the *British Worker* put it: "The Council has informed the Russian Trade Unions, in a courteous communication, that they are unable to accept the offer and the cheque has been returned."' (Julian Symons, *The General Strike: A Historical Portrait* (London: Cresset Press, 1957), 136.)

62. 'Those in Authority: William Empson (Magdalene)', 485.

63. Symons, *The General Strike*, 189.

64. 'Ba! Ba! Barbara', *The Granta*, 24 February 1928, p. 304.

6. The Multiple Man of Letters

1. 'Hermetically Shelled', *The Granta*, 17 February 1928, p. 285. He was not repeating the joke when he wrote in 'Double Plots': 'a work of art is a thing judged by the artist and yet a thing inspired which may mean more than he knew—as may a mathematical formula for that matter' (*Pastoral*, 68).

2. *Cambridge University Reporter*, 11 August 1926, p. 1357.

3. Empson's friend Mark Hartland Thomas won a similar college bounty for his performance in Classics; though P. H. Vellacott outran everyone else with the Gill Prize for Classics of £100.

4. The third play performed on the bill was *The Tragedy of Mr Punch*, by Russell Thorndike and Reginald Arkell.

5. Interview with Basil Wright, April 1983. (Humphrey Trevelyan, who read *Dragons* in manuscript, had pressed for it to be staged.) Wright thought Empson's play 'startlingly provocative, interesting, and surprising; and it certainly created a sensation'.

6. 'Birth at the A.D.C.', *The Granta*, 11 February 1927, p. 238.

7. Guy Naylor, 'A.D.C. Nursery Productions', *Cambridge Review*, 11 February 1927, p. 250.

8. John Ruskin, *Sesame and Lilies* (London: George Allen, 1893), 90–1, 109, 113, 117–18, 119, 123.

9. 'Jacobean Sodomy', a letter to the *London Review of Books*, 5/16 (1983), p. 4.

10. See John Paul Russo, *I. A. Richards: His Life and Work* (London: Routledge, 1989), 127–9.

11. In an undated diary entry, WE essayed this piece of wry self-reckoning: 'Peter Jack told me today my acting was out of place, that in the otherwise wholly

amateur chattering of the Marlowe Society my professional precision jarred. Fancy going about making up that sort of thing to say to people, the sinking feeling you have hearing it done to somebody else, how pleased I am even by such frankly comical flattery. Surely as a social device elaborate and much neglected.'

12. Interview with Basil Wright, April 1983.
13. James Jensen, 'Some Ambiguous Preliminaries: Empson in "The Granta"', *Criticism*, 8 (Fall 1966), 350.
14. See Christopher Ricks, 'Empson's *Granta*', *The Granta* (Easter term, 1978).
15. 'Cinema Notes', *The Granta*, 14 October 1927, p. 18; in *EG* 72.
16. 'The Circus', *Cambridge Review*, 4 May 1928, p. 396.
17. 'The King of Kings', *Cambridge Review*, 19 October 1928, p. 34.
18. Martin Dodsworth, 'Empson at Cambridge', *The Review*, 6 & 7 (June 1963), 5.
19. *Pastoral*, 30–1.
20. 'The Magic Flame', *Cambridge Review*, 19 October 1928, p. 33.
21. *Pastoral*, 42–3.
22. Ibid. 80.
23. Compare his use of the term in a review of Bernard Shaw's *Heartbreak House*: 'the point of the satire ... is the effect of the War on rather expatriated intellectuals ...' (*The Granta*, 19 October 1928, p. 42).
24. *The Granta*, 4 November 1927, p. 84; *EG* 72–3.
25. 'Berlin', *Cambridge Review*, 27 April 1928, p. 375.
26. 'Correspondence', *Cambridge Review*, 11 May 1928, pp. 412–13.
27. 'Puff Puff Puff', *The Granta*, 27 April 1928, p. 375; *EG* 50.
28. Untitled review of *Diversion* by John Van Druten, *Cambridge Review*, 8 March 1929, p. 355.
29. 'The Festival Theatre', *Cambridge Review*, 25 May 1928, p. 452.
30. Julian Trevelyan, *Indigo Days* (London: MacGibbon & Kee, 1957), 19.
31. *The Granta*, 8 June 1928, p. 515; *EG* 79.
32. Empson engaged in something of a running battle with Terence Gray's policy vis-à-vis the Festival Theatre; as he wrote in another place, 'of course, Mr Gray wants critics to talk about producing, not literary form' (*The Granta*, 19 October 1928, p. 42; *EG* 81).
33. *The Granta*, 16 November 1928, p. 120; *EG* 86–7.
34. 'The Moke from his Stall', *The Granta*, 30 November 1928, p. 197; *EG* 89–91.
35. 'Forster-Mother', *The Granta*, 28 October 1927, p. 61; *EG* 21–2.
36. 'Worried Butterfly', *The Granta*, 28 October 1927; *EG* 22.
37. 'Others Supplied', *The Granta*, 4 November 1927, p. 89; *EG* 24.
38. 'Strained Glass', *The Granta*, 11 November 1927, p. 105; *EG* 27.
39. 'Where the Body is ...', *The Granta*, 2 December 1927, p. 193; *EG* 31–2.
40. 'The Missing Meta-Link', *The Granta*, 4 November 1927, p. 89; *EG* 23–4.
41. 'Little Mairet', *The Granta*, 8 June 1928, pp. 519–20; *EG* 61–2.
42. 'Mind the Step', 2 December 1927; *EG* 32–3.

Notes to pp. 148–54

43. 'Skipper's Guide', *The Granta*, 1 June 1928, p. 481; *EG* 60.
44. 'Pontifical Death', *The Granta*, 9 March 1928, p. 339; *EG* 44.
45. 'Dorian Greyer', *The Granta*, 9 March 1928, p. 339; *EG* 44.
46. 'More Barren Leaves', *The Granta*, 18 November 1927, p. 123; *EG* 27.
47. 'Forster-Mother', *The Granta*, 28 October 1927, p. 61; *EG* 21–2.
48. 'Baby Austin', *The Granta*, 11 May 1928, p. 419; *EG* 54–5.
49. Jensen, 'Some Ambiguous Preliminaries: Empson in "The Granta"', 360.
50. *Cambridge University Reporter*, 16 June 1928, p. 1134.

7. THE *EXPERIMENT* GROUP

1. 'Notes & Bars', *The Cambridge Gownsman and Undergraduate*, 16/1 (13 October 1928), 6. For good detailed accounts of *Experiment*, see Jason Harding, '*Experiment* in Cambridge: "A Manifesto of Young England"', *Cambridge Quarterly*, 27/4 (1998), 287–309; Kate Price, 'Finite But Unbounded: *Experiment* magazine, Cambridge, England, 1928–31', *Jacket Magazine*, 20 <http://jacketmagazine.com/20/price-expe.html>
2. When Ennismore published in the first number of *Experiment* a piece entitled 'Beauty: A Problem and Attitude to Life', an undergraduate reviewer commented, 'I simply do not know what on earth the author is talking about' (*The Gownsman*, 17 November 1928, p. 6).
3. Letter, Max Black to JH, 12 July 1985.
4. *The Granta*, 23 November 1928, p. 148.
5. See Thomas R. Sawyer, 'Experiment', in *British Literary Magazines: The Modern Age, 1914–1984*, ed. Alvin Sullivan (Westport, Conn.: Greenwood Press, 1986), 177–9. I am indebted too to John Vice for sharing with me a draft copy of chapter 3—'Lamentably clever young men talking claptrap'—of his forthcoming biography of Jacob Bronowski.
6. T. H. White quoted in John Vice's draft biography of Bronowski.
7. 'A Note on W. H. Auden's *Paid on Both Sides*', *Experiment* 7 (Spring 1931); in *Argufying*, 370–1.
8. Jacob Bronowski, 'Time of my Life', BBC radio 4 broadcast (tape transcript), 16 December 1973.
9. Sir Desmond Lee, upublished memoirs. Bronowski became director of the Council for Biology and Human Affairs at the Salk Institute in California; and he presented the BBC TV series *The Ascent of Man*.
10. See Ian MacKillop, *F. R. Leavis: A Life in Criticism* (London: Allen Lane, 1995), 88–91.
11. Bronowski, 'Time of my Life'.
12. Julian Trevelyan, *Indigo Days* (London: MacGibbon & Kee, 1957), 15–16.
13. J. Bronowski, 'Poetry at the Universities', *Cambridge Review*, 30 November 1928, p. 169.
14. Bronowski won a chess Blue by playing for Cambridge in autumn 1928, and represented the university several times over the following months.

15. Kathleen Raine, *The Land Unknown* (London: Hamish Hamilton, 1975), 50.

16. Bronowski, 'Time of My Life'.

17. Ibid.

18. See 'Roses Round the Door', *The Granta*, 8 June 1928; reprinted in *EG* 63: 'Intolerable; I am almost tempted to say [call] it morbid, so I suppose it catches me on the raw for some quite private reason...*Antic Hay*, to which this is comparable, both in wit and in the painful state of nervous tension disclosed, was less painful reading...'

19. 'Those in Authority: William Empson (Magdalene)', *The Granta*, 31 May 1929, p. 485.

20. Hugh Sykes Davies, 'He Was Different from the Rest of Us', in Gordon Bowker (ed.), *Malcolm Lowry Remembered* (London: Ariel Books/BBC, 1985), 44. Richard Eberhart considered Sykes Davies 'the most brilliant of the very young students' (quoted in Joel Roache, *Richard Eberhart: The Progress of an American Poet* (New York: Oxford University Press, 1971), 57). See also George Watson, 'Remembering Prufrock: Hugh Sykes Davies 1909–1984', *Sewanee Review* 109/4 (Fall 2001), 573–80.

21. Raine, *The Land Unknown*, 48.

22. T. S. Eliot wrote to I. A. Richards on 3 April 1934: 'I am rather at a loss to know what to do about Jennings and his article on Gray. It is extremely ingenious and rather fascinating but it is much too long for a periodical and too short for anything else' (I. A. Richards Collection, Magdalene College).

23. Bronowski, 'Time of My Life'.

24. Jacob Bronowksi, 'Recollections of Humphrey Jennings', *The Twentieth Century*, 165/983 (January 1959), 46.

25. Trevelyan, *Indigo Days*, 17–18.

26. See also Anthony W. Hodgkinson and Rodney E. Sheratsky, *Humphrey Jennings—More Than a Maker of Films* (Hanover, NH: Published for Clark University by University Press of New England, 1982).

27. Untitled memoir of Humphrey Jennings, written for Colin Moffat; in possession of Mary-Lou Jennings, who kindly loaned me the typescript.

28. Bronowski, 'Recollections of Humphrey Jennings', 46–7.

29. T. S. Eliot, letters to I. A. Richards, 18 October 1950 and 3 April 1934 (I. A. Richards Collection, The Old Library, Magdalene College, Cambridge).

30. Except where otherwise stated, quotations in these two paragraphs are taken from a memoir by Elsie Elizabeth Phare, 'From Devon to Cambridge, 1926: or, Mentioned with Derision', *Cambridge Review*, 103/2267 (26 February 1982), 144–9.

31. Interview with E. E. Duncan-Jones, 10 August 1983.

32. Trevelyan, *Indigo Days*, 16.

33. Raine, *The Land Unknown*, 38.

34. Ibid. 42. See also Raine, *Defending Ancient Springs* (London: Oxford University Press, 1967), 106.

35. Raine, *The Land Unknown*, 44–5. See also a profile of Raine by Maggie Parham: ' "I don't think he had any wish to dominate, but he spellbound us," she says. "He gave one the impression of perpetual, self-consuming mental energy. I see now that he was impressive because he was so terribly intimidating. I remember him reciting poetry as if he were *possessed* " ' ('She will not cease from mental flight', *The Times Saturday Review*, 18 April 1992, p. 13).

36. Raine, *The Land Unknown*, 45.

37. Ibid. 39. See also James Reeves, 'Cambridge Twenty Years Ago', in Richard March and Tambimuttu (eds.), *T. S. Eliot: A Symposium* (London: Editions Poetry London, 1948), 38–42.

38. Raine, *The Land Unknown*, 19.

39. Ibid. 62.

40. In later years, relations between Empson and Raine deteriorated. She could no longer tolerate what she considered his exclusive emphasis on the cognitive intelligence; he could not stand what he saw as her pietistic mysticism. In *Defending Ancient Springs*, she disclaimed his early influence in favour of aesthetics and the metaphysical imagination: 'What William Empson, in his subtle, brilliant, and influential critical writings gave his generation was a theory of poetry consistent with the positivist philosophy which flourished in Cambridge; the Cambridge of Darwin and the Cavendish Laboratory, of Russell and Wittgenstein and their successors. His theory of ambiguity lacks nothing in conceptual subtlety but dispenses with the imagination and disregards the metaphysical roots of poetic thought . . . Then, I thought (as we all did) that it was our outstanding intelligence which compelled us to forgo beauty and lyricism at the bidding of intellect . . . ' (p. 107).

41. Raine, *The Land Unknown*, 48.

42. Edward M. Wilson, letter to WE, 2 June 1930. (The other dedicatee was Dámaso Alonso, literary critic and expert on Góngora.)

43. M. J. Tilby, 'Céline's letters to his translator', *TLS*, 2 April 1982, p. 385.

44. 'Those in Obscurity', *The Granta*, 7 June 1929, p. 524.

45. Michael Redgrave, *In My Mind's Eye: An Autobiography* (London: Weidenfeld & Nicolson, 1983), 63.

46. John Lehmann, *The Whispering Gallery: Autobiography I* (London: Longmans, Green & Co., 1955), 150–1.

47. E. K. Bennett, letter to E. E. Phare, 2 May 1930 (E. E. Duncan-Jones).

48. Redgrave, *In My Mind's Eye*, 63.

49. Ibid. In a letter to Elsie Phare, Redgrave admitted he felt 'hustled by *Experiment*' (quoted in Harding, '*Experiment* in Cambridge', 296).

50. Trevelyan, *Indigo Days*, 16.

51. Lehmann, *The Whispering Gallery*, 151.

52. Of the three editors of *Cambridge Poetry 1929*, the name of Kit Saltmarshe appears first on the title-page. (See obituary of Saltmarshe by John Davenport in *The Times*, 26 February 1966, p. 10.) Advertisements in *The Gownsman*

and *The Granta* made it clear that he was the prime mover; and *The Granta* (23 November 1928, p. 153) printed by way of annunciation some verses entitled 'Lines for Long-Hairs', including:

> Than writing verses what is sillier?
> —Though it's really not my fault
> If they print my juvenilia
> And Kit's taste is worth its salt.

Eberhart lamented in a letter: 'Because I am unknown, perhaps a little out of self-protection too, Salty saw to it that three of my poems were cut out; he notified me in January [1929]. And it did make me feel as contentious and little-with-wrath as a schoolboy, hurt at the simpering personalism connected with a book' (Roache, *Richard Eberhart*, 61).

Saltmarshe later wrote to Julian Trevelyan, in a different connection: 'if you only knew how Bill [Empson] and I denied ourselves . . . Let me tell you that we made it a rule to pay for ourselves except upon one occasion a term' (29 October 1929; Trinity College, Cambridge).

53. Only six pamphlets were issued in the series: poems by Julian Bell, T. H. White, John Davenport, Michael Redgrave, and Jacob Bronowski.

54. Trevelyan, *Indigo Days*, 17. Michael Wharton, who knew Davenport after the war, described him thus: 'A man of note in his day and of considerable influence as a teacher, perhaps the greatest non-writing writer of the twentieth century (he had a literary reputation although he never published a book, and could truly be said to "know everybody") . . . He was a very strong, barrel-shaped man with an incongruous, high-pitched voice of extreme refinement' (*The Missing Will* (London: Chatto & Windus, 1984), 203). See obituary in *The Times*, 28 June 1966, p. 14.

55. In 1940 Empson and Thomas would together visit Davenport at his home in Marshfield, near Bristol. At the end of the Second World War, Empson was to leave in Davenport's care the copy of a monograph (with irreplaceable illustrations) that he had been fashioning for more than ten years, *The Faces of Buddha*; and it appears Davenport lost it in a taxi.

56. See also Judith Adamson, *Charlotte Haldane: Woman Writer in a Man's World* (Basingstoke: Macmillan Press, 1998), esp. 72–88. Charles Madge told me that he considered Charlotte 'a singularly unlikeable person . . . She was a dangerous and unpleasant person: spiteful, always gossiping about people in a destructive kind of way.'

57. 'To Charlotte Haldane', *TLS*, 17 August 1989; *CP*, p. 42.

58. Draft typescript. The edited version of Empson's contribution to 'Portrait of J. B. S. Haldane' (*The Listener*, 78 (2 November 1967), 565–8) makes nonsense of part of the passage quoted. On Haldane, see also a centenary essay by John Durant, 'Plain speaking with a world to win', *Times Higher Education Supplement*, 3 April 1992, p. 15.

59. Raine, *The Land Unknown*, 51.

60. Ibid. 51–2.

61. WE, letter to John Hayward, 8 October 1933 (King's College, Cambridge: WE/JDH/4).

62. WE quoted in Tony Kilgallon, *Lowry* (Erin, Ont.: Press Percepic, 1973), 19. Gordon Bowker comments: 'But in his expressions of taste Lowry was nothing if not extravagant' (*Pursued by Furies: A Life of Malcolm Lowry* (London: HarperCollins, 1993), 107. For the 'lasting, if dispersed, effect' of *Ambiguity* upon Lowry, see *'Sursum Corda!' The Collected Letters of Malcolm Lowry*, i: *1926–1946*, ed. Sherrill E. Grace (London: Jonathan Cape, 1995), 417, n. 14; 'Empson's book was an important part of a formative intellectual and artistic milieu for Lowry.'

63. John Davenport, in Bowker (ed.), *Malcolm Lowry Remembered*, 47.

64. Mark Thompson, 'Notes on meetings with William Empson' (unpublished typescript), June 1986.

65. Richard Eberhart, 'Empson's Poetry', *Accent*, 4/4 (Summer 1944); repr. in Eberhart, *On Poetry and Poets* (Urbana: University of Illinois Press, 1979), 117–18.

66. Eberhart's letters to Richards are in the Old Library, Magdalene College, Cambridge.

67. F. R. Leavis, 'Cambridge Poetry', *Cambridge Review*, 1 March 1929, p. 318. I. A. Richards sounded the same cautiously Romantic caveat: 'We may value this adroitness in emotional logic variously, but we cannot deny it. And enough sensibility may be suspected beneath the startling compression of his verses to carry him some distance if he should later find a direction in which to travel. He may be merely bottling a contemporary atmosphere—but he may have an explosive mixture of his own' ('Cambridge Poetry', *The Granta*, 8 March 1929, p. 359).

68. F. R. Leavis, *New Bearings in English Poetry* (London: Chatto & Windus, 1932; repr. with 'Retrospect 1950', 1950; Harmondsworth: Penguin Books, 1963), 159–61.

69. Leavis, *New Bearings in English Poetry*, 159–61. Leavis did much in the early 1930s to promote Bottrall's poetry (MacKillop, *F. R. Leavis*, 116–18). Empson too would help to push Bottrall's work; he related in a letter to Bottrall (26 January 1937), 'I have taken Crooked Eclipses to Ian Parsons, who said he hadn't understood or "got on with" your earlier stuff and that he doubted whether he would like this, but would try. I think it would do Chatto's good to have an author. Eliot was very regretful to me about refusing it and suggested Hamish Miles if Chatto refuse. There is a lot of good stuff in it, I thought . . . ' (Harry Ransom Humanities Research Center, University of Texas at Austin).

70. Randall Pope wrote to E. E. Phare on 3 December 1929: 'The Empson cultus is ubiquitous. Public readings of his poems are given, as you probably know. Leavis mentions him in every lecture. Some poem of his is to be found in

nearly everyone's rooms; even in the possession of people who would not dream of reading the work of an ordinary poet' (courtesy of E. E. Duncan-Jones).

71. F. R. Leavis, 'Criticism of the Year', *Bookman*, 81 (December 1931), 180.

72. F. R. Leavis, letter to Ian Parsons, 12 August 1931 (Reading).

73. F. R. Leavis, *How To Teach Reading: A Primer for Ezra Pound* (Cambridge: Gordon Fraser: Minority Press, 1932), 26. By 1943 Leavis had moderated his praise of *Ambiguity*: 'A useful exercise for the moderately seasoned student would be to go through W. Empson's *Seven Types of Ambiguity*, or parts of it, discriminating between the profitable and the unprofitable, the valid and the vicious. Empson's extremely mixed and uneven book, offering as it does a good deal of valuable stimulus, serves the better as a warning—a warning against temptation that the analyst whose practice is to be a discipline must resist. It abounds in instances of ingenuity that has taken the bit between its teeth' (*Education and the University: A Sketch for an 'English School'* (London: Chatto & Windus, 1943; 2nd edn., 1949; Cambridge, 1979), 71.

74. F. R. Leavis, *The Critic as Anti-Philosopher*, ed. G. Singh (London: Chatto & Windus, 1982), 144–5. See also MacKillop, *F. R. Leavis*, 396. Richard Eberhart recalled, in a letter to JH (16 June 1983): 'Bill and I would go to high tea tutorial on a Thursday afternoon with F. R. Leavis, my tutor, I would read a paper on Wordsworth never to be published and Empson would read a chapter of what was coming to be Seven Types of Ambiguity, seminal for half a century.' But there is no other evidence to corroborate the suggestion that Empson ever attended a Leavis tutorial. Eberhart described Leavis, in a contemporary letter, as 'a light, lithe, nervous [don] who sleeps not . . . and is now a seething mass of brains, often very jumbled, I think. Erratic . . . [Y]ou see the fallacies in Leavis; a biting iconoclast, unbalanced. I have had him for supervisions this year, and go to war about once a fortnight' (from an undated letter quoted in Roache, *Richard Eberhart*, 58–9).

75. WE, undated notebook, Empson Papers.

8. THE MAKING OF *SEVEN TYPES OF AMBIGUITY*

1. M. C. Bradbrook, 'I. A. Richards at Cambridge', in Reuben Brower, Helen Vendler, and John Hollander (eds.), *I. A. Richards: Essays in His Honor* (New York: Oxford University Press, 1973), 69.

2. E. M. W. Tillyard, *The Muse Unchained: An Intimate Account of the Revolution in English Studies at Cambridge* (London: Bowes & Bowes, 1958), 101.

3. Quoted in Hugh Carey, *Mansfield Forbes and his Cambridge* (Cambridge: Cambridge University Press, 1984), 69. As of 1919, as Carey notes, 'The official establishment consisted of two professors (Chadwick and Q) and one lecturer, a position left vacant after the death of its holder in 1914' (p. 66).

4. The full complement of University Lecturers in English created by the Initial Appointments Board was A. L. Attwater (Pembroke), H. S. Bennett

(Emmanuel), J. M. de Navarro (Trinity), B. W. Downs (Christ's), M. D. Forbes (Clare), F. L. Lucas (King's), Miss Hilda Murray (Girton), Miss A. C. Paues (Newnham), Miss B. S. (later Dame Bertha) Philpotts (Girton), I. A. Richards (Magdalene), and E. M. W. Tillyard (Jesus).

5. John Paul Russo, *I. A. Richards: His Life and Work* (London: Routledge, 1989), 727; Richards is quoted from G. S. Fraser, *The Modern Writer and His World* (London, 1964), 384.

6. The other Probationary Faculty Lecturers were Mrs H. S. (Joan) Bennett, T. R. Henn, L. J. Potts, Enid Welsford, and Basil Willey.

7. F. R. Leavis, *English Literature in our Time and the University* (London, 1969); quoted in Carey, *Mansfield Forbes and his Cambridge*, 73.

8. Compare a review of Tillyard's tome by W. W. Robson, 'The English Tripos', *The Spectator*, 31 October 1958, pp. 586–7.

9. Tillyard, *The Muse Unchained*, 81, 88–9.

10. Joan Bennett, ' "How It Strikes a Contemporary": The Impact of I. A. Richards' Literary Criticism in Cambridge, England', in Brower *et al.* (eds.), *I. A. Richards*, 49.

11. Christopher Isherwood, *Lions and Shadows: An Education in the Twenties* (1938) (London: New English Library/Signet Classics, 1968), 74–5. Likewise Frances Partridge: 'Amongst the dons who taught me English, the outstanding stimulus came from I. A. Richards, who not only had a lot that was interesting to say but gave the impression of thinking as he talked, which added greatly to the freshness of his ideas and compared favourably with the obviously oft-repeated dronings, delivered with glazed eyes, of some of the lecturers. Richards would stand in front of a blackboard on which he made cabalistic marks with immense delicacy and dedication, thus elucidating some subtle complex of ideas both to himself and us. There was a strong vein of abstract thinking in his talk which . . . diverted my mind from English literature . . . ' (*Memories* (London: Robin Clark, 1982), 64–5).

12. 'I usually saw that the bad poems were bad, but not always that the good were good,' E. E. Phare (Duncan-Jones) has written. 'Longfellow's "In a Village Churchyard", for instance—the best account of that poem, baffling if one didn't know that the churchyard was in America, since the lady in the poem was buried with her slaves, I think is from the pen of T. S. Eliot, but I don't know how I know' ('From Devon to Cambridge, 1926: or, Mentioned with Derision', *Cambridge Review*, 103/2267 (26 February 1982)', 147). Cf. Joan Bennett, ' "How It Strikes a Contemporary" ', in Brower (ed.), *I. A. Richards*, 52–3.

13. M. C. Bradbrook, 'I. A. Richards at Cambridge', in Brower (ed.), *I. A. Richards*, 62.

14. Alistair Cooke, letter to John Constable, 15 June 1988 (John Constable).

15. Russo, *I. A. Richards*, 299.

16. Ibid. 299; Joan Bennett, ' "How It Strikes a Contemporary" ', 57.

17. 'I. A. Richards and Practical Criticism' (1930), *Argufying*, 194–5.
18. Cooke, letter to Constable, 15 June 1988.
19. Bennett, ' "How It Strikes a Contemporary" ', 55.
20. Hugh Carey, *Mansfield Forbes and his Cambridge* (Cambridge: Cambridge University Press, 1984), 72.
21. WE, 'The Hammer's Ring', 73; *Argufying*, 216.
22. WE, 'I. A. Richards', *Magdalene College Magazine and Record*, NS 23 (1978–9), 5; *Argufying*, 227.
23. WE, letter to David Wilson, 5 November 1970 (courtesy of David Wilson).
24. Notes in Empson Papers, Houghton Library, Harvard University. F. R. Leavis, who also attended Forster's lectures in 1927, expressed himself 'astonished at the intellectual nullity' of the series (quoted in MacKillop, *F. R. Leavis*, 97).
25. WE, letter to Gareth Jones, 31 March 1973 (Trinity College Library, Cambridge).
26. E. M. W. Tillyard recorded, in his memoir of Cambridge English, the regrettable popularity of lectures in the late 1920s: 'As a supervisor I used…to have to stop pupils from going to too many' lectures (*The Muse Unchained*, 118).
27. See T.W., 'The Book of the Play', *The Granta*, 9 March 1928, 340.
28. Phare, 'From Devon to Cambridge, 1926', 146.
29. Carey, *Mansfield Forbes and his Cambridge*, 86.
30. For an account of Stein at Cambridge, see Harold Acton, *Memoirs of an Aesthete* (London: Methuen, 1948), cited in Geoffrey Elborn, *Edith Sitwell: A Biography* (London: Sheldon Press, 1981), 56–7.
31. One of I. A. Richards's key words was 'equilibrium'; but he did not care to use the noun 'equilibration' or the verb 'equilibrating'—as Stein did. Empson used both of Stein's forms in reviews published in *The Granta* on 6 May and 14 October 1927; for example, conflating the influence of *Science and Poetry* and *Composition as Explanation*, when writing off a film as 'half-baked, it gave you half-heartedly whatever you looked for: an equilibration of magical attitudes, or a tiresome sentimental film.'
32. Basil Willey, *Cambridge and Other Memories, 1920–1953* (London: Chatto & Windus, 1968), 20–1.
33. Gwendolyn Freeman, 'Queenie at Girton', in Denys Thompson (ed.), *The Leavises: Recollections and Impressions* (Cambridge: Cambridge University Press, 1984), 14; quoted too in Carey, *Mansfield Forbes and his Cambridge*, 71.
34. Graham Hough, 'Idols of the Lecture-Room' (a review of *Mansfield Forbes and his Cambridge* by Hugh Carey, and Thompson (ed.), *The Leavises: Recollections and Impressions*), *TLS*, 23 November 1984, p. 1329.
35. 'The Last Word', *The Granta*, 9 March 1928, p. 340; *EG* 46.
36. WE, letter to Gareth Jones, 31 March 1973 (Trinity College, Cambridge).
37. 'The Romantic Rationalist', *The Granta*, 12 June 1926, p. 477; *EG*, supplement.

38. Richards (8 May 1978), quoted in Russo, *I. A. Richards*, 178.

39. I. A. Richards, *Principles of Literary Criticism* (1924, 2nd edn. 1926; reset edition, London: Routledge & Kegan Paul, 1967), 230, 46.

40. Ibid. 42, 38.

41. I. A. Richards, *Practical Criticism: A Study of Literary Judgment* (London: Routledge & Kegan Paul, 1929), 249, 252.

42. Richards, *Principles of Literary Criticism*, 229.

43. Russo, *I. A. Richards*, 190.

44. C. K. Ogden, I. A. Richards, and James Wood, *The Foundations of Aesthetics* (London: Allen & Unwin, 1922), 75, 91. E. D. Hirsch Jr. is not alone in his significant misrepresentation: 'Psychologically, the most beneficial literature, in Richards's view, is the kind that harmonizes a large number of different and conflicting psychic impulses. Thus, a formal or purely literary criterion of excellence, according to the kind proposed by Coleridge, is altogether concordant with Richards's psychological criterion. Literature that is formally rich and complex, and brings into unity a great many opposite and discordant elements achieves excellence both as literature and as therapy. Since the two kinds of criteria coincide, the psychological values of literature can be accommodated to literary categories' (*The Aims of Interpretation* (Chicago: University of Chicago Press, 1976), 125).

45. Empson too believed that the critic should address both the act of creation and the reader's response; in 1930, when defining the 'mode of action' of a poem (in an article defending Richards against the attack by John Sparrow), he wrote, 'I think that people mean by the phrase . . . both the devices which a poet has employed to convey what he does convey, and the way those devices come to convey to the reader what they do. Evidently you cannot know this without knowing some part of what happens in the mind of the reader, and some part of what happens in the mind of the author; and some "analysis of the poem", so far as it is different from this, will also be necessary to it. I suggested these different sorts of analysis, not as different objects, but as different elements of one act' (*Argufying*, 202).

46. Russo, *I. A. Richards*, 91.

47. Jerome P. Schiller, *I. A. Richards' Theory of Literature* (New Haven: Yale University Press, 1969), 57.

48. WE wrote to Richards on 29 January (?1931): 'Nor am I sure what an impulse is: apparently it need not be a conscious impulse, so it cannot easily be recognised. The Freudian point of view would seem to be that there are very few fundamental impulses, and that they are not originally impulses to do anything in particular: they are made into definite impulses by circumstances—by beliefs formed and by training, particularly.' Richards jotted in the margin: 'My "impulse" physiological rather than psychological[,] microscopic not macroscopic' (Richards Collection).

49. John Needham, *The Completest Mode: I. A. Richards and the Continuity of English Literary Criticism* (Edinburgh: Edinburgh University Press, 1982), 35.

50. Russo, *I. A. Richards*, 262. Russo observes too, 'While Richards was reluctant to sever the poem from the experience of it, both romantic organicism and the exigencies of textual analysis gradually led him to make a strong case for poetic autonomy.' (Ibid.)

51. 'Beginnings and Transitions: I. A. Richards Interviewed by Reuben Brower', in Brower (ed.), *I. A. Richards: Essays in His Honor*, 20.

52. Russo, *I. A. Richards*, 178–9.

53. Ibid. 183. Russo observes too, 'The power of impulse in Richards' system appears to extend from crude sensation to the driving force behind civilization itself. He was perhaps trying too hard to squeeze the universe into a ball.' (Ibid.) Christopher Isherwood, who attended the lectures that became *Principles of Literary Criticism*, would rhapsodize over Richards's teaching: 'Poetry wasn't a holy flame, a fire-bird from the moon; it was a group of interrelated stimuli acting upon the ocular nerves, the semi-circular canals, the brain, the solar plexus, the digestive and sexual organs. It did you medically demonstrable good, like a dose of strychnine of salts.' (*Lions and Shadows: An Education in the Twenties* (1938; repr. London: New English Library, 1974), 75.)

54. Russo, *I. A. Richards*, 217.

55. Needham, *The Completest Mode*, 49. Cf. Russo, *I. A. Richards*, 250.

56. I. A. Richards, *Speculative Instruments* (London: Routledge & Kegan Paul, 1955), 9.

57. Note Russo, *I. A. Richards*, 91.

58. I. A. Richards, *Poetries and Sciences*, 60–1. Cf. Russo, *I. A. Richards*, on the pseudo-statement controversy, pp. 246–51.

59. T. S. Eliot, 'Literature, Science, and Dogma', *Dial*, 82/3 (March 1927) (239–43), 243, 241. See also Russo, *I. A. Richards*, 194–5. For further information about Eliot's problem, see John Constable (ed.), *Selected Letters of I. A. Richards, CH* (Oxford: Clarendon Press, 1990), p. xxxix.

60. See also Russo, *I. A. Richards*, 194–5: 'Richards was piqued by Eliot's mockery...On the basis of a few illustrative metaphors, Eliot misconstrued his theory as quantitative and mechanistic; whereas the entire tenor of his commentary had been organic and qualitative...

   'Even if Richards' pragmatic theory of value were better constructed, it could hardly have met with Eliot's approval. Yet Richards made Eliot's (and other critics') case against him that much easier by his brevity of treatment and gaps in argument. He often elided the number and quality of impulses without much ado, and "impulse" itself stood for too wide a variety of mental and physical happenings.'

61. Frank Day, *Sir William Empson: An Annotated Bibliography* (New York: Garland, 1984), pp. xxix–xxx.

62. Richards, *The Foundations of Aesthetics*, 75.

63. *SCW* 424–5. Cf. WE's footnote in *Ambiguity* (3rd edn., 1953), 193, which I quote in part: 'One could, of course, also introduce much philosophical puzzling about the reconciliation of contradictions. The German tradition in the matter seems even based on Indian ideas, best worked out in Buddhism.'

64. Harold Beaver, 'Tilting at Windbags' (rev. of *William Empson and the Philosophy of Literary Criticism*, by Christopher Norris), *New Statesman*, 11 August 1979, p. 186.

65. Empson wrote in a published letter, 'Basic gives a natural English for careful plain statement, but that is not always the natural way to talk... But... Basic itself is a dignified and rational means of expression, quickly learned and at once widely understood' ('Basic English', *The Spectator*, 2 August 1935, p. 191).

66. See *Beyond the Pleasure Principle*, in *The Standard Edition of the Complete Psychological Works of Sigmund Freud*, ed. James Strachey (London: Hogarth Press, 1953–74), vol. xviii. Cf. Russo on Richards and Freud (*I. A. Richards*, 196–7).

67. Richards, *Principles of Literary Criticism*, 197–8.

68. *SCW* 425.

69. Cf. Russo's protestations: 'Richards was not a behaviorist; he used behaviorist elements; he was an instrumentalist and behaviorism was one of his instruments'; and, 'the evidence is overwhelmingly against his ever having been a behaviorist' (*I. A. Richards*, 125, 175).

70. Richards, *Principles of Literary Criticism*, 36, 40.

71. WE, 'The Hammer's Ring', 75.

72. Richards on Dante: 'How can a poem so dependent on such principles be justly read by those who think them among the most pernicious aberrations men have suffered?' (*Beyond* (New York: Harcourt Brace Jovanovich, 1974), 108–9, 112; quoted in Russo, *I. A. Richards*, 210).

73. Day, *Sir William Empson*, p. xxix.

74. Michael Roberts, untitled rev. of *Pastoral*, *Criterion* (January 1936), 345.

75. WE, 'The Hammer's Ring', 74.

76. WE, letter to Mark Roberts, 8 February 1959 (copy in Empson Papers). F. R. Leavis, though he applauded Richards's social criticism in 1930, later scoffed at the 'pseudo-scientific pseudo-psychological' trappings of the theory of value ('I. A. Richards', *Scrutiny*, 3 (1935), 366–400).

77. Richards quoted in Russo, *I. A. Richards*, 201.

78. WE, letter to John Paul Russo, 24 March 1982, quoted in Russo, *I. A. Richards*, 202, 732 n. 96.

79. WE, 'Remembering I. A. Richards', *Argufying*, 226–7. (Further page references are given in the text.)

80. Many other readers shared his doubts about this quasi-scientific input. His friends of the time included James Smith (1904–72), a brilliant, charming, feline scholar of Trinity who graduated with firsts in both the English Tripos and the Modern and Medieval Languages Tripos (French and German); he also reaped the Oldham Shakespeare Scholarship along with other prizes.

He became known as the 'Dr Johnson' of Empson's circle. In 1925–6 he had skippered *The Granta* (and was thus responsible for printing Empson's first literary review—the one praising Richards's theory of value at the expense of Herbert Read). Among his other accomplishments was the rare ability to relate Wittgenstein's work to literary criticism. Also, as it was noted in a profile in *The Granta*, he had revived the Cam Literary Society 'and even presided over it for a year, in order to introduce Cambridge to T. S. Eliot'. As for the future, *The Granta* pointedly went on, 'His immediate prospects are difficult to prophesy. He may seek out a corner and live the life theoric, thinking about God and the devil and all . . .' (He actually went on in the 1930s, among other things, to write some fine essays for *Scrutiny*, one of which—on metaphysical poetry—gave Empson a significant impetus in his work on *Some Versions of Pastoral*. But he would also take Empson to task, in *The Criterion* in 1931, for the extravagances of *Seven Types of Ambiguity*.) He was a Catholic, as *The Granta* hinted, so his devotion to Christianity and to T. S. Eliot set him at odds with 'scientism'. Empson would write to I. A. Richards in 1932: 'I wish I could get poor James Smith to send you his thesis for a Trinity fellowship [he had failed to win a research fellowship], where he did for Aristotle very much what you have done for Mencius; I copied out some into my book, and it has always been my intellectual capital on these matters; but I expect the (rather repulsive) petulance which made him annoy Trinity and refuse to get into touch with you at the time will make him refuse to send it you, though I will ask him to, as somebody ought to see it' (Richards Collection). See also a memoir by Edward M. Wilson, 'James Smith (1904–1972)', in a posthumous collection by Smith, *Shakespearean and Other Essays* (Cambridge: Cambridge University Press, 1974).

81. 'I didn't realise that Richards was right till after he had stopped teaching me—my friends thought him absurd and regarded me as a source of comic anecdotes about my tutorials under him. The young are always wrong and I suppose need to be' (WE, letter to David Wilson, 5 November 1970).

82. WE, 'The Hammer's Ring', 73–4.

83. John Paul Russo, with whom I shall be quarrelling later, agrees with my argument to this extent: 'Richards wrote mainly theoretical books; Empson, a continuous series of practical essays' (*I. A. Richards*, 533).

84. I. A. Richards, *Science and Poetry* (1926); repr. as *Poetries and Sciences* (London: Routledge & Kegan Paul, 1970), 32–3.

85. Russo, *I. A. Richards*, 157–8.

86. Ibid. 239.

87. Richards had first differentiated referential from 'emotional' language in 'On Talking' (ch. 10 of the co-authored *The Meaning of Meaning*).

88. WE, Answers to a questionnaire on criticism, *Agenda*, 14/3 (Autumn 1976), 24.

89. Richards's copy of *The Structure of Complex Words* is in the Old Library, Magdalene College, Cambridge.

90. See W. H. N. Hotopf, *Language, Thought and Comprehension: A Case Study of the Writings of I. A. Richards* (London: Routledge & Kegan Paul, 1965), esp. 169–76. For a brief account of Richards's career, see John Paul Russo, 'I. A. Richards in Retrospect', *Critical Inquiry*, 8 (Summer 1982), 743–60.

91. Isherwood, *Lions and Shadows*, 75.

92. Edward Upward, *No Home but the Struggle* (1977, repr. London: Quartet Books, 1979), 190–1.

93. Letter to Philip Hobsbaum, 2 August 1969 (copy in Empson Papers).

94. Russo, *I. A. Richards*, 532.

95. *Argufying*, 196. Empson went on, marvellously: 'At a moment you may be conscious of either side in any proportion; you are more conscious of thought, for instance, if the thing in hand is a novelty; more conscious of feeling if it is urgent and not unusual. But if what you are conscious of as a feeling is badly thought, that is part of what you feel; you wish then to be conscious of it as a thought, and put it right.'

96. Richards, *Practical Criticism*, 180.

97. Richards, *Practical Criticism*, 217.

98. *Ambiguity*, 3rd edn., 238. (Further references are given in the text.) In an undated letter (early 1930), Empson endeavoured to palliate Richards in advance of the publication of his book: 'I have just offered *a* finished version of Ambiguity to Chattos, to ask them how it might be altered. It is a very amateurish sort of book, I don't understand the difference between Thought and Feeling, and you have got to have some way of using that distinction if you are to know where you are' (Richards Collection). Since he was about to publish a monograph which took issue with his mentor on this very score, the letter has to be seen as disingenuous.

99. I. A. Richards, 'Semantic Frontiersman', in Gill, 100–1.

100. Russo, *I. A. Richards*, 216.

101. Ibid. 719.

102. For a critique of Richards on practical criticism, and of his false deductions from the 'protocols' he collected from his unfortunately uninformed students, see Gerald Graff, *Professing Literature: An Institutional History* (Chicago: University of Chicago Press, 1987).

103. Bennett, ' "How It Strikes a Contemporary" ', 59.

104. Russo, *I. A. Richards*, 216.

105. Richards, *Practical Criticism*, 215.

106. Russo, *I. A. Richards*, 280–1.

107. I am grateful to John Vice, biographer of Jacob Bronowski, for supplying me with this information (letter to JH, 24 February 1990).

108. Edward M. Wilson, letter to WE, 25 August 1957. Wilson went on: 'My debt to Owst, Chambers, Seznec, Curtius and Tuve is that they—coming after Eliot—showed me that what you had helped me to see was part of something much larger than the work of one man, one period or one century.' In

a notebook dated 5 February 1933, WE would write of attending a 'No play' in Tokyo; his remarks include this observation: 'Delightful young lad at the practice dances, like E. Wilson . . . '

109. To corroborate the argument that WE had determined upon his categories of ambiguity by early 1929, it is enough to cite an autograph copy of his poem 'Myth' (written 1929) which includes this enumeration:

The seven classes of ambiguity.
1. Mere richness; (a metaphor valid from many points of view).
2. Two different meanings conveying the same point.
3. Two unconnected meanings, both wanted but not illuminating one another.
4. Irony: two apparently opposite meanings combined into a judgement.
5. Transition of meaning; (a metaphor applying halfway between two comparisons).
6. Tautology or contradiction, allowing of a variety of guesses as to its meaning.
7. Two meanings that are the opposites created by the context.

110. I. A. Richards, *Principles of Literary Criticism*, 162.
111. Ibid. 232.
112. Russo, *I. A. Richards*, 279.
113. Richards, *Practical Criticism*, 214.
114. *Ambiguity*, 81.
115. Russo, *I. A. Richards*, 793. 'Richards objected to psychoanalytic criticism on antibiographical grounds.'
116. Margaret Gardiner, 'In and out of Cambridge', in *A Scatter of Memories* (London: Free Association Books, 1988), 70–1. Gardiner adds a further good memory in the next paragraph (p. 71): 'One day when I had called to go with Richards to some meeting or other, we met T. S. Eliot coming up the stairs to visit him. Richards introduced me and I sat on a step while the two of them stood and talked about *The Waste Land*. I remember that Eliot said, "I write about the Thames but I think about the Mississippi." '
117. Richards, 'Semantic Frontiersman', in Gill, 102.
118. I. A. Richards, 'William Empson', *Furioso*, 1/3 (1940), supplement following p. 44. René Wellek considered Richards's *Furioso* piece 'a somewhat condescending, avuncular reminiscence' (*A History of Modern Criticism: 1750–1950: English Criticism, 1900–1950* (London: Jonathan Cape, 1986), 275).
119. Roger Sale, 'The Achievement of William Empson', in *Modern Heroism: Essays on D. H. Lawrence, William Empson, & J. R. R. Tolkien* (Berkeley and Los Angeles: University of California Press, 1973), 117.
120. WE, letter to Elsie Phare, postmarked 4 September 1928.
121. Soon Peng Su suggests that WE's notion of full contradiction 'may, perhaps, be further refined as [a] kind of disjunctive ambiguity . . . ' (*Lexical Ambiguity in Poetry* (London: Longman, 1994), 8). Nevertheless, Su believes Empson created a 'muddle' in his overall conceptualization of ambiguity.

122. Sigmund Freud, ' "The Antithetical Sense of Primal Words" ' (1910), in *Collected Papers*, iv, trans. Joan Riviere (London: Hogarth Press and the Institute of Psycho-Analysis, 1925), 184–91.

WE was to write to C. K. Ogden, in an undated letter: 'I found a dictionary of hieroglyphs in the British Museum; perhaps you would be interested to hear about the opposites that Freud claimed in Egyptian. It is true about *black* and *white*; they are pronounced the same but with a different determinative to show which is which. But they mean "dead white" and "dead black", and are derived from the idea of "strong"; there are other words for the shades in between. It is hard to see how there could be a conflict in the mind of an Egyptian as to whether he was dead white or dead black; however one might appeal to a more primitive language from which the word was derived. There are two pairs of words, pronounced nearly the same, for "young" and "old"; one pair is defined by the dictionary as "childhood" and "second childhood", the other is derived from the idea of "shaking" and feebleness. Thus in each case the words are similar because the things are thought of as similar, not because they are thought of as opposite. At the same time it is odd that black and white should be thought of as similar; it may have something to do with interpreting the colours on a ceremonial wall-painting, but that only takes the oddity one step further back.' (McMaster University Library).

123. WE, letter to Elsie Phare, postmarked 7 October 1928.

124. Cf. Richards, *Principles of Literary Criticism*: 'The effect of a word varies with the other words among which it is placed. What would be highly ambiguous by itself becomes definite in a suitable context' (p. 138).

125. Richards, *Practical Criticism*, 304.

126. 'The Negation of Negation', *The Granta*, 9 March 1928, 340; *EG* 46.

127. *Ambiguity*, 224.

128. Ibid. 226.

129. Ibid. 231.

130. Ibid. 226–7.

131. *Practical Criticism*, 285.

132. *Ambiguity*, 227.

133. Russo, *I. A. Richards*, 528.

134. The phrase 'state of composure' is adopted from Richards (*Principles of Literary Criticism*, 198).

135. *Principles of Literary Criticism*, 46.

136. Russo, *I. A. Richards*, 216.

137. I. A. Richards, 'Gerard Hopkins', *The Dial*, 81 (1926), repr. in *Complementarities: Uncollected Essays*, ed. John Paul Russo (Cambridge, Mass.: Harvard University Press, 1976; Manchester: Carcanet New Press, 1977), 143, 147.

138. Russo, *I. A. Richards*, 267.

139. *Ambiguity*, 225–6. It is characteristic of WE's challenging mentality that in a letter postmarked 14 September 1928, he urged Elsie Phare: 'Do send along your Hopkins article, it would be rather a smack at Richards if we got somebody to say something quite different.' In the event, WE had his own different say—just such a smack at Richards—in *Ambiguity*.

140. See Russo, *I. A. Richards*, 266.

141. Laura Riding and Robert Graves, *A Survey of Modernist Poetry* (London: William Heinemann, 1927), 74–5, 80. See also Giorgio Melchioro, ch. 4: 'Th'expense of spirit: Sonnet 129 and the Ethics of Sex', in *Shakespeare's Dramatic Meditations: An Experiment in Criticism* (Oxford: Clarendon Press, 1976); also Jeffrey Walsh, 'Alternative "Modernists": Robert Graves and Laura Riding', in Gary Day and Brian Docherty (eds.), *British Poetry, 1900– 50: Aspects of Tradition* (Basingstoke: Macmillan Press, 1995), 131–50.

142. 'Curds and Whey', *The Granta*, 11 May 1928, p. 419; *EG* 55–6.

143. WE, 'Ambiguity in Shakespeare: Sonnet XVI', *Experiment*, 2 (February 1929), 33.

144. WE, 'Some Notes on Mr. Eliot', *Experiment*, 4 (November 1929), 6–8.

145. The first printing of *Ambiguity* ran to 2,000 copies, of which 500 went to Harcourt Brace Inc. in New York. Following the initial Graves–Riding complaint, an erratum slip was inserted in all copies of the Chatto & Windus edition; but it seems possible that the slip was not included in the USA.

146. Quoted in Deborah Baker, *In Extremis: The Life of Laura Riding* (London: Hamish Hamilton, 1993), 142–3. Baker gives credit to Riding as the initiator of the critical approach used in *A Survey of Modernist Poetry*; and she disparages WE's achievement, incorrectly categorizing him as a New Critic and snidely remarking, 'Being an aspiring mathematician, Empson set out to prove that there were, in fact, exactly seven varieties of linguistic ambiguity' (p. 143). ' "Ambiguity" and "indeterminancy" [*sic*] remain the language of a critic; a poet would be more likely to insist, as Riding did, on the existence of congruent meanings or "manifold precision" ' (p. 145).

147. 'Empson is as clever as a monkey & I do not like monkeys,' wrote Graves in a later year (1944)—though he apparently came to like Empson a good deal better as the years passed (Martin Seymour-Smith, *Robert Graves: His Life and Work* (London: Bloomsbury, 1995), 147).

148. Laura Jackson, letter to WE, 31 October 1970.

149. Laura Jackson, letter to WE, 11 November 1970.

150. Laura Jackson, letter to WE, 13 December 1970.

151. Laura (Riding) Jackson, 'Correspondence', *Modern Language Quarterly*, 32 (1971), 447–8.

152. Laura (Riding) Jackson, 'Some Autobiographical Corrections of Literary History', *Denver Quarterly*, 8/4 (Winter 1974), 12. Riding had written also to Chatto & Windus, on 19 May 1970: 'my "firstness" was not a formality, and especially not so in the case of that analysis'; again on 12 June 1970, when she

called herself 'the actual originator of this technique' of analysis; and so too on 8 August 1970: 'The method, as anyone familiar with my work, my thinking, my laborings with other poets for their better attention to the requirements of linguistic responsibility, is of my formation—there is much general and particular testimony to this' (Chatto & Windus Archive, Reading University Library).

153. Joyce Piell Wexler, *Laura Riding's Pursuit of Truth* (Athens, Oh.: Ohio University Press, 1979), 8. John Carey made a similarly pungent point in a review of Baker's *In Extremis: The Life of Laura Riding* (1993), remarking that 'it never seems to occur to [Baker] that the apparent blackout of Laura's brain the moment she left Graves may reflect adversely on the supposition that she was the mastermind during their association' ('Chasing eternal verities', *Sunday Times*, 24 October 1993, section 6, p. 6).

154. Laura Riding, letter to WE, 7 May 1971.

155. See also, for further falsifications of her own, 'Laura (Riding) Jackson in Conversation with Elizabeth Friedmann', *PN Review*, 17/4 (March/April 1991), 68. The place of WE's work in relation to the New Criticism is equally often misrepresented: Harold Fromm, for example, incorrectly asserts, 'the New Critics carefully took in Graves and Riding's *Survey of Modernist Poetry* (1927), whose close reading of Shakespeare set the model for Empson and his followers while promulgating the view of a poem as an autotelic, self-existent substance unbeholden to the outside world or to history' ('Myths and Mishegaas: Robert Graves and Laura Riding', *Hudson Review*, 44/2 (Summer 1991)).

156. Cf. Baker's comments on Graves's early work, *In Extremis*, 139–40.

157. Richards, *Principles of Literary Criticism*, 20–1.

158. 'Note for the third edition', *Ambiguity* (1953), p. xvii.

159. Ibid., p. ix.

160. Robert Graves, *Poetic Unreason and Other Studies* (London: Cecil Palmer, 1925), 82. Indeed, it is possible too that a remark in Graves's early work may have prompted WE's later essay 'Alice in Wonderland: The Child as Swain': while touching on the topic of 'dream-machinery' in *On English Poetry*, Graves remarks that *Alice in Wonderland* 'is founded on dream-material' (*On English Poetry* (London: William Heinemann, 1922), 121).

9. CRISIS, EXPULSION, AND AFTERMATH

1. A.S. (Arthur Sale), 'Sir William Empson (1906–1984)', *Magdalene College Magazine and Record*, 28 (1983–4), 9. See obituary of Sale (1912–2000) in the *The Times*, 4 May 2000, and by Bamber Gascoigne in *The Independent*, 26 April 2000.

2. The Minutes of a meeting of the Governing Body of Magdalene College held on 16 May 1928 record: 'It was agreed that if Mr Empson made application to come into residence for a fourth year continuation of his

scholarship should be conditional on his obtaining a first class in the Tripos and subsequently taking another Tripos.'

Forty years on, Empson was to recall: 'I got tired of mathematics and only got a second. As a result I lost my scholarship, so my patient mother had to pay for me in my fourth year. It was not so unusual combining mathematics with literature in those days. However, I was one of the weak sisters who fell by the way' (quoted in John Horder, 'William Empson, Straight', *The Guardian*, 12 August 1969).

3. I. A. Richards speaking in *Some Versions of Empson*, produced by David Perry (BBC Radio 3, 22 October 1977).

4. Robert Lazarus, letter to JH (April 1989); John D. Solomon, letter to JH (n.d.).

5. See also Nick Clarke, *Alistair Cooke: The Biography* (London: Weidenfeld & Nicolson, 1999), 34.

6. M.S.R., 'The Cambridge Mummers', *Cambridge Review*, 19 April 1929, p. 380. See also Michael Redgrave, *In My Mind's Eye* (London: Weidenfeld & Nicolson, 1983), 76.

7. A.R.P., 'The Moke from his Stall', *The Granta*, 38/860 (19 April 1929), 378. 'Mr Cooke was a villain of the deepest dye and the first water...'

8. Alistair Cooke, letter to JH, 18 June 1991.

9. Alistair Cooke, letter to John Constable, 15 June 1988.

10. *Magdalene College Magazine*, 59 (9/1) (December 1928), 14.

11. Lee was one of Wittgenstein's favourite pupils during his second period at Cambridge (from 1929). In 1930 he went to stay with the philosopher at his home in Austria. Lee was for some years a university lecturer in Classics, and for fourteen years, from 1954, Headmaster of Winchester. He married Elizabeth Crockenden on 23 March 1935 (the occasion is commemorated in Empson's poem of the same date, 'Letter VI: A Marriage'), and had a son and two daughters. He was knighted in 1961.

12. A. S. Eddington, *The Nature of the Physical World* (Cambridge: Cambridge University Press, 1928), 81–2; *Stars and Atoms* (Oxford: Clarendon Press, 1927), 67.

13. WE, 'A Doctrine of Aesthetics', *Hudson Review*, 2 (Spring 1949), 95; *Argufying*, 212.

14. J. B. S. Haldane, *Possible Worlds* (London: Chatto & Windus, 1929), 290.

15. Eddington, *The Nature of the Physical World*, 251.

16. Ibid. 257.

17. Empson uses the phrase to explain the poem—'more intimacy for less hope'—in a draft letter to W. D. Maxwell-Mahon, 6 November 1967.

18. *Selected Poems* (Marvell Press: *Listen* LPV 3, 1959).

19. 'The Metaphysical Foundations of Empirical Knowledge', *Criterion*, 3/15 (March 1941), 222–3; *Argufying*, 583–4.

20. See Christopher Ricks's notes on 'The Love Song of St. Sebastian', in T. S. Eliot, *Inventions of the March Hare: Poems 1909–1917* (London: Faber & Faber, 1996), 267–70.

21. I am grateful to the late Sir Desmond Lee for his 'Autobiographical Notes'; and to the late Lady Lee.

22. WE, answers to a questionnaire, *Agenda*, 14/3 (Autumn, 1976), 24. Empson was sanguine about the critic's business of enquiring into the unconscious. When W. K. Wimsatt Jr., in his essay 'The Intentional Fallacy', questioned whether it would be a legitimate proceeding to ask T. S. Eliot if he had Donne or Marvell in mind when writing *The Waste Land*, Empson wrote in the margin of the copy he had to hand: 'the poet may mean more than he knew—easily may not want to tell. No reason for not asking' (Wimsatt, *The Verbal Icon: Studies in the Meaning of Poetry* (Lexington: University of Kentucky Press, 1954), 18). Where Wimsatt objected (p. 17), 'And Eliot himself, in his notes, has justified his poetic practice in terms of intention,' Empson answered: 'how could he not?' And against Wimsatt's remark (p. 3), 'The poem is not the critic's own and not the author's (it is detached from the author at birth and goes about the world beyond his power to intend about it or control it)', Empson commented: 'But both author and critic are part of the world.'

23. WE, 'Still the Strange Necessity', *Sewanee Review*, 63/3 (Summer 1955); *Argufying*, 125.

24. *Cambridge Review*, 23 November 1928, p. 161.

25. WE, 'Foundations of Despair', *Poetry*, 49/4 (January 1937), 230–1; *Argufying*, 419.

26. M. C. Bradbrook, 'Sir William Empson (1906–84)', in *Shakespeare in his Context: The Constellated Globe*, The Collected Papers of Muriel Bradbrook, vol. iv (Hemel Hempstead: Harvester Wheatsheaf, 1989), 193 (first published in *The Kenyon Review*, 7/4, Fall 1985). Interview with Muriel Bradbrook, 16 September 1992.

27. Interview with Hugh Sykes Davies, 9 August 1983.

28. This account of Elizabeth Wiskemann owes much to interviews with Elizabeth Jenkins (17 September 1992) and E. E. Duncan-Jones (11 August 1992); and to an obituary by L. K. Duff, 'Elizabeth Meta Wiskemann, 1899–1971', *Newnham College Roll*, January 1972, pp. 70–4.

29. Richards diary (Magdalene), 1 March 1934: 'Bradbrook to tea. Pathetic & mousey but acutely intelligent & remarkable memory. Pleasant.' In January 1935, after entertaining WE and Bradbrook to lunch in Cambridge, Richards lamented to his wife that 'Brad is hard to get anything out of.' Muriel Bradbrook's publications include *Elizabethan Stage Conditions* (1932), *Themes and Conventions of Elizabethan Tragedy* (1935), and four volumes of *Collected Papers* (1981–9). See the bibliography of her writings in *English Drama: Forms and Development*, ed. Marie Axton and Raymond Williams (Cambridge: Cambridge University Press, 1977); Leo Salingar, *Professor M. C. Bradbrook, Litt.D., F.B.A., F.R.S.L.* (privately printed: Trinity College, Cambridge, n.d.).

30. *Cambridge University Examination Papers*, lviii (Cambridge: Cambridge University Press, 1929).

31. E. M. W. Tillyard to Professor Potter, Registrar's Department, University of Sheffield, 14 December 1952. See Basil Willey, 'Eustace Mandeville Wetenhall Tillyard 1889–1963', *Proceedings of the British Academy*, 49 (1963), 387–405.

32. W. G. Shepherd, letter to JH, 30 March 1993.

33. *College Orders and Memoranda 1907–1946*, 208 (Old Library, Magdalene College, Cambridge).

34. See *C. K. Ogden: A Collective Memoir*, ed. P. Sargant Florence and J. R. L. Anderson (London: Elek Pemberton, 1977).

35. 'William Empson was effectually "sent down" in the summer of 1931 [*sic*] when his bye fellowship at Magdalene was withheld' (M. C. Bradbrook, 'Lowry's Cambridge', in Sue Vice (ed.), *Malcolm Lowry: Eighty Years On* (London: Macmillan Press, 1989), 139–40).

36. *College Orders and Memoranda 1907–1946*, 210.

37. See R. Luckett and R. Hyam, 'Empson and the Engines of Love', *Magdalene College Magazine and Record*, NS. 35 (1990–1), 33–8.

38. The college historians agree that 'the particular punishment adopted' in Empson's case 'was perilously close to being vindictive' (Peter Cunich et al., *A History of Magdalene College, Cambridge, 1428–1988* (Cambridge: Magdalene College Publications, 1994), 245). The sole item that escaped the purge is a small card recording the simple details of his scholarships and prizes, terms kept, and dates and results of examinations (Old Library, Magdalene College). See also a letter from Malcolm Lowry in 1940, in Sherrill E. Grace (ed.), *Sursum Corda! The Collected Letters of Malcolm Lowry*, vol. i: *1926–1946* (London: Jonathan Cape, 1995), 282; Anthony Powell in 1986, *Journals 1982–1986* (London: Heinemann, 1995), 263.

39. Richards, letter transcribed in diary for 29 September 1929 (Magdalene).

40. Letter in I. A. Richards Papers, Magdalene College. Dean until 1927, then Tutor, F. R. Salter was regaled in *Magdalene College Magazine* (7/56 (December 1927), 129), in one of a doggerel series of 'Biographies for sinners': 'Frank R. Salter | Is never known to falter. | His hurricanic pragmatism | Is impregnible to criticism.' See obituary by F. McD. C. Turner, *Magdalene College Magazine and Record*, 12 (1967–8), 2–6.

41. 'Fairfax Scott was a younger man who had served in the War as a subaltern. Then a bachelor, he lived permanently in College, taking an indulgent view of the sometimes rather juvenile escapades of the undergraduates. He was the only one of the Tutors who never drew his pupils' attention to their failure to attend Chapel' (Frank West, 'Magdalene Memories, 1928–31', *Magdalene College Magazine and Record*, 33 (1988–9), 29).

42. D. C. R. Francombe, 'Reminiscences (1) Magdalene, 1924–1927', *Magdalene College Magazine and Record*, NS. 35 (1990–1), 42.

43. 'Some old College MSS.', *Magdalene College Magazine*, 61 (June 1929), 81.

44. 'Election Interviews', *Magdalene College Magazine*, 61 (June 1929), 90.

45. Stephen Garrett, letter to Empson, 1 January 1979; letter to JH, 9 October 1987.

46. 'Those in Authority: William Empson (Magdalene)', *The Granta*, 31 May 1929, 485.

47. Francombe, 'Reminiscences: (1) Magdalene, 1924–1927', 42.

48. 'Those in Authority: William Empson (Magdalene)', 485.

49. M.S.R. (Michael Redgrave), 'The Great Frost: What They are Saying', *Magdalene College Magazine*, 60 (March 1929), 44.

50. There is a sorry irony in this sitation, for Empson was not above nosing into his friends' letters. In an undated diary entry from 1926 he records looking round his friend Carew Meredith's rooms, ostensibly in search of a programme for the Heretics: 'I found his Ulyssean diary, and read it furtively with an eye on the door. Imitations of Ulysses' abrupt analytical manner poor; touches of descriptive "confession" at times excellent; also a religio-homosexual ecstasy was rather impressive; some undistinguished verses ... Ought I to be ashamed of myself? Am not.'

51. A further irony resides in the report that, if a published contemporary (satirical) account is to be believed, Empson himself, no lilywhite, was not above 'inventing gossip which is, often unfortunately, repeated' ('Those in Authority: William Empson (Magdalene)', 485).

52. Interview with Muriel Bradbrook, 16 September 1992. Bradbrook, 'Lowry's Cambridge', 140.

53. Michael Tanner, 'Some Recollections of the Leavises', in Denys Thompson (ed.), *The Leavises: Recollections and Impressions* (Cambridge: Cambridge University Press, 1984), 135–6.

54. John D. Solomon, letter to JH (n.d.).

55. 'The Pride of Othello', *Kenyon Review*, 16 (Winter 1954), 165. In 1935, undergraduates were to petition for 'an automatic machine for the supply of "rubber goods"'; a condom-vending machine was finally installed in the college in the mid-1980s (Cunich *et al.*, *A History of Magdalene College*, 241).

56. Interview with Julian Trevelyan.

57. Kathleen Gibberd, letter to JH, 18 July 1991.

58. Elizabeth Wiskemann, *The Europe I Saw* (London: Collins, 1968), 9.

59. See also *Ludwig Wittgenstein: Cambridge Letters: Correspondence with Russell, Keynes, Moore, Ramsey and Sraffa*, ed. Brian McGuinness and G. H. von Wright (Oxford: Blackwells, 1995), 247.

60. Redgrave, *In My Mind's Eye*, 63.

61. 'News & Notes', *Cambridge Review*, 1 November 1929, p. 69.

62. Ralph Parker to E. E. Phare, 15 November 1929 (E. E. Duncan-Jones).

63. Max Black, letter to JH, 12 July 1985.

64. See Richard Holmes, *Shelley: The Pursuit* (London: Weidenfeld & Nicolson, 1974), 50–60.

65. See John Halperin, *Gissing: A Life in Books* (Oxford: Oxford University Press, 1982), 15–19.

66. WE, letter to Julian Trevelyan, n.d. (the late Julian Trevelyan).

67. David Garnett to Julian Bell, 4 September 1929 (School Library, Eton College). For Bell on Empson's poetry: 'The Progress of Poetry: A Letter to a Contemporary', *Cambridge Review*, 7 March 1930, pp. 321–2.

68. WE, letter to Richards (n.d.) summer 1929 (Magdalene College).

69. Robert Lazarus, letter to JH, April 1989.

70. Walter Allen, *As I Walked Down New Grub Street: Memoirs of a Writing Life* (London: Heinemann, 1981), 37–8.

71. See Ian MacKillop, *F. R. Leavis: A Life in Criticism* (London: Allen Lane, 1995), 105–6.

72. J. D. Solomon, letter to JH, 29 March 1991.

73. Charles Hobday, *Edgell Rickword* (Manchester: Carcanet Press, 1989), 152–3.

74. Ralph Parker to E. E. Phare, 15 November 1929.

75. Thanks to Gordon Bowker for this information.

76. Quotation kindly supplied by Claire Harman; copyright Susanne Pinney and William Maxwell.

77. Bottrall, 'William Empson', Gill, 50.

78. John Lehmann, *Thrown to the Woolfs* (London: Weidenfeld & Nicolson, 1978), 18. See also *A Portrait of Michael Roberts*, ed. T. W. Eason and R. Hamilton (College of S. Mark and S. John, Chelsea, 1949).

79. WE, letter to R. Fukuhara, 28 February 1934.

80. J. H. Willis, Jr., *Leonard and Virginia Woolf as Publishers: The Hogarth Press, 1917–41* (Charlottesville: University Press of Virginia, 1992), 200.

81. Denise Hooker, *Nina Hamnett: Queen of Bohemia* (London: Constable, 1986), 211.

82. WE, 'Edgell Rickword', in *Argufying*, 428.

83. *A Reflection of the Other Person: The Letters of Virginia Woolf*, iv: *1929–1931*, ed. Nigel Nicolson (London: Hogarth Press, 1978), 140–1. Empson later referred to Julian Bell as 'a man I undervalued at Cambridge' (draft TS letter to mother, 11 August 1938; Empson Papers).

84. WE, 'Wartime Recollections', in *SSS* 195; Barry Webb, *Edmund Blunden: A Biography* (New Haven: Yale University Press, 1990), 190.

85. Joy Grant, *Harold Monro and the Poetry Bookshop* (London: Routledge & Kegan Paul, 1967): Drinkwater quoted on p. 3.

86. WE, 'Harold Monro', *The Rising Generation* (Tokyo), 67/5 (1 June 1932), 151.

87. *Selected Letters of I. A. Richards, CH*, ed. John Constable (Oxford: Clarendon Press, 1990), 52–3. It was no doubt in consequence of Richards's tip-offs that T. S. Eliot wrote to Julian Bell on 2 January 1930 that he was keeping an eye on Empson, Bronowski, and T. H. White (Julian Bell Papers 2/15, Modern Archive Centre, King's College, Cambridge; also quoted in Harding, 'Experiment in Cambridge', 297).

88. WE, 'My God, man, there's bears on it', a review of *The Waste Land: A Facsimile and Transcript of the Original Drafts*, ed. Valerie Eliot), *Essays in Criticism*, 22/4 (October 1972); in *Using Biography* (London: Chatto & Windus, 1984), 199. Empson's amusement at the sexual lives of other writers is evident in a letter

to Katherine Sansom on his return to London: 'It was exciting to look at the London telephone book. One saw at once that Mrs Quennell has left Peter, who is living with a rather grisly young beauty and seems much the same' (Empson Papers).

89. WE, 'The Style of the Master', in Richard March and Tambimuttu (eds.), *T. S. Eliot: A Symposium* (London: Editions Poetry London, 1948); *Argufying*, 361. Eliot wrote in his introduction to Ezra Pound, *Selected Poems* (London: Faber & Faber, 1928): 'The poet who wishes to continue to write poetry must keep in training; and must do this, not by forcing his imagination, but by good workmanship on a level possible for some hours' work every week of his life' (p. 16). See also another version of the anecdote by Empson, 'A London Letter', *Poetry*, 49 (1937); *Argufying*, 417.

90. WE, 'In Eruption' (a review of Robert Graves, *The Crowning Privilege*), *New Statesman*, 1 October 1955), in *Argufying*, 130–1.

91. Telephone interview with Mrs Sybil Meredith, 10 July 1991.

92. See obituaries of Alice Stewart in *The Guardian*, 28 June 2002, p. 18; *The Independent*, 9 July 2002, p. 18; *The Times*, 27 June 2002, p. 36.

93. Gail Vines, 'A Nuclear Reactionary', *Times Higher Education Supplement*, 28 July 1995, p. 16. This and the following three paragraphs are indebted to an interview with Dr Alice Stewart on 23 March 1991. See also *Half a Century of Social Medicine: An Annotated Bibliography of the Work of Alice M. Stewart*, ed. C. Renate Barber (Wisborough Green, Billingshurst: Piers Press, 1987); and Clive Cookson, 'Unsung Heroine', *Financial Times*, 19 January 1995.

94. Ludovick Stewart's father, a French scholar, was a Fellow of Trinity College, Cambridge; his mother Jessie, a classicist and Fellow of Newnham College.

95. The phrase 'nostrum-plastered' is from Empson's poem 'The Ants', which compares the chambers of the termites to the tube in London.

96. Gayle Greene, *The Woman Who Knew Too Much: Alice Stewart and the Secrets of Radiation* (Ann Arbor: University of Michigan Press, 1999), 48.

97. *The New York Times*, 3 May 1990.

98. Quoted in Greene, *The Woman Who Knew Too Much*, 229.

10. SEVEN TYPES OF AMBIGUITY

1. The source of this account of the correspondence between Empson and Ian Parsons is the archive of Chatto & Windus; now located in the Library of the University of Reading.

2. 'John Carey's Books of the Century', *Sunday Times*, 13 June 1999, p. 12.

3. WE, letter to Ian Parsons, received 2 July 1929.

4. Undated letter; the Richards Diary (at Magdalene) reveals that Richards received this letter on 12 December: 'today from Empson himself who has done 60,000 words on ambiguity.' Apropos the Cambridge débacle, Richards added: 'He doesn't clear up anything more.'

5. Ian Parsons, letter to Christopher Ricks, 24 February 1966.

6. Ian Parsons, letter to WE, 13 April 1930.

7. Ian Parsons, letter to WE, 24 July 1930.

8. The print run of the second (revised and completely reset) edition, which appeared in February 1947, was 3,500; 1,500 of them went to the imprint of New Directions, New York, which sold 4,169 copies between 1947 and 1954. Further impressions came out in the UK in March 1949, July 1953, December 1956, and October 1963; Peregrine paperback editions appeared in 1962 and 1965. The Noonday Press, New York, published a Meridian paperback edition (with an advance on royalties of $1,000, divided between Empson and New Directions), which sold between 7,000 and 8,000 copies by October 1959.

9. Ian Parsons, letter to WE, 7 November 1930. (So far from sitting back to await the critical reception of his first book, Empson promptly moved on to some of the work that would be collected in his second volume, *Some Versions of Pastoral* (1935): he was teasing out the psychological implications of *Alice in Wonderland* by that autumn, as a letter from Parsons of 7 November 1930 indicates: 'Meanwhile I hope you are progressing with "Alice".'

10. According to Lisa A. Rodensky, in her useful preface to the Penguin edition of 1995, *Ambiguity* received seventeen reviews in 1930, sixteen in 1931. Edmund Blunden joked in his review of the book, 'I expect I am late, as usual, in imparting a fresh secret—the arrival of William Empson . . . I cannot even produce a ballad myself to the glory of our present critics; but if I could, I should unambiguously include the name of Empson' ('The Oracular Poets', *The Nation & Athenaeum*, 22 November 1930, p. 267). See also Christopher Ricks, 'Seven Types of Ambiguity' (in a series, 'How well have they worn?—8'), *The Times*, 24 February 1966).

11. F. R. Leavis, 'Intelligence and Sensibility', *Cambridge Review*, 52/1275 (6 January 1931), 187. Ian Parsons, in a letter to Empson (20 February 1933), acknowledged that Leavis's praise of the work had done much to promote Empson's interests: ' "Ambiguity" has now established a certain reputation (the Leavis propagand it steadily, though only among the elect, and it might be a good plan to follow up with some poetry pretty soon. How do you feel?' (*sic*).

12. *Selected Letters of I. A. Richards*, ed. Constable, 60 (letter dated 30 November 1930). According to the, uncorroborated evidence of E. W. F. Tomlin, Eliot sometime said of *Ambiguity* 'he thought Empson ought to re-write it from start to finish' (*T. S. Eliot: A Friendship* (London: Routledge, 1988), 45).

13. James Smith, 'Books of the Quarter', *The Criterion*, 10/41 (July 1931); reprinted in John Constable (ed.), *Critical Essays on William Empson* (Aldershot: Scolar Press, 1993), 43; hereinafter abbreviated as 'Constable'. 'I don't remember any review except James Smith's,' Empson was to write even 35 years later (letter to Christopher Ricks, 31 January 1966). So seriously did he take Smith's critique that he dedicated a large portion of the preface to the second edition

to answering him.) Likewise, Muriel Bradbrook, in 'The Criticism of William Empson' (*Scrutiny*, 2/3 (December 1933), 254), lamented the lack in Empson's criticism of 'judgements of comparative values' (Constable, 54).

14. WE, letter to Christopher Ricks, 31 January 1966 (Christopher Ricks).

15. Undated letter (*c*.1973) to Roger Sale (copy in Empson Papers).

16. [John Middleton Murry], 'Analytical Criticism', *TLS* 29/1507 (18 December 1930), 1082; reprinted in Constable, 30.

17. T. Earle Welby, 'Time to Make a Stand', *Week-End Review*, 3/43 (3 January 1931), 18.

18. Elder Olson, 'William Empson, Contemporary Criticism and Poetic Diction', *Modern Philology*, 47/4 (May 1950), 227, 233–4. More recently, Soon Peng Su asserts that Empson's definition of ambiguity is 'indiscriminately accommodating, with no constraint whatsoever on declaring any expression ambiguous'; Empson's 'weakness is to allow the reader an unbridled liberty to project ambiguity on to any word or part of a text . . . This gives rise to the danger of overreading, with no criterion given for how far or in what direction the meanings of words can be stretched' (*Lexical Ambiguity in Poetry* (London: Longman, 1994), 8.

19. 'What claim do I make for the sort of ambiguity I consider here,' he wrote in the preface to the second edition, 'and is all good poetry supposed to be ambiguous? I think that it is; but I am ready to believe that the methods I was developing would often be irrelevant to the demonstration' (*Seven Types of Ambiguity* (London: Chatto & Windus, 1947), p. xv). Perhaps surprisingly, John Middleton Murry conceded in his review: 'Ambiguity, in the wide and generous sense in which Mr Empson uses the word, is almost essential to poetry' (p. 29).

20. E. D. Hirsch Jr., *The Aims of Interpretation* (Chicago: University of Chicago Press, 1976), 116, 122.

21. Philip Wheelwright, *The Burning Fountain* (Bloomington: Indiana University Press, 1954), 61.

22. WE, letter to Karunakar Jha, 20 June 1971 (copy in Empson Papers).

23. 'It is incontinent . . . ,' wrote Middleton Murry in the *TLS* (18 December 1930). 'It is the work of an exceedingly able young man, who has not learned to control his abilities, and perhaps sees no reason why he should control them. One has the impression that he has been turned, or has turned himself, loose on to poetry; and that poetry has no particular importance to him save as an opportunity for a free exercise of his abilities' (p. 31).

24. WE, 'Explaining Modern Poetry' (1937); *Argufying*, 103.

25. WE, 'Still the Strange Necessity' (1955); *Argufying*, 123.

26. WE, 'The Verbal Analysis' (1950), *Argufying*, 104.

27. René Wellek, *A History of Modern Criticism: 1750–1950: English Criticism, 1900–1950* (London: Jonathan Cape, 1986), 205–6.

28. WE, 'The Verbal Analysis', *Argufying*, 106. Cf. E. D. Hirsch Jr.'s justifiable claim that 'the goal of a definitive, literary evaluation of literature is actually a mirage masked by a tautology. The ideal of a privileged "literary mode" of evaluation is rendered hopeless by the impossibility of deducing genuinely privileged, literary criteria of evaluation. I make this statement categorically, because an analysis of the various types of evaluative principles which have evolved in the history of criticism reveals that such criteria have never been successfully formulated, and, in the nature of the case, never could be' (*The Aims of Interpretation*, 114).

29. Ibid., p. xv.

30. Geoffrey Strickland, 'The Criticism of William Empson', *Mandrake*, 2 (Winter 1954–5), 322–3.

31. 'Answers to Comments', *Essays in Criticism*, 3/2 (1953), 120.

32. WE, 'I. A. Richards and Practical Criticism' (1931); *Argufying*, 201.

33. *Ambiguity*, p. x.

34. R. G. Cox, *Scrutiny* (Spring 1948).

35. See e.g. R. G. Cox, 'Ambiguity Revised', *Scrutiny*, 15 (Spring 1948), 148; Newell F. Ford, 'Empson's and Ransom's Mutilations of Texts', *Philological Quarterly*, 29 (January 1950), 81–4. Among all of his supposedly creative misquotations, one of the most heavily criticized cases found him discussing the possibilities of the syntax of T. S. Eliot's 'Whispers of Immortality', in which, he claimed (*Ambiguity*, 79), the less obvious grammatical construction is insisted upon by the punctuation. Unfortunately, as Robert Beare has explained ('Notes on the Text of T. S. Eliot: Variants from Russell Square', *Studies in Bibliography*, 9 (1957), 27–8), those particular ambiguous possibilities were licensed only by the editions of Eliot's poetry issued between 1920 and 1932—including *Poems 1909–1925* (London, 1925), the edition Empson must have used—in which the relevant lines were mispunctuated; the mistake in Eliot's text was put right only in *Collected Poems 1909–1935* (London, 1936).

Two years after the appearance of Beare's article on the Eliot texts, Fredson Bowers, in his important study *Textual and Literary Criticism* (Cambridge, 1959)—which has assumed the status of a modern classic—positively crowed with derision at Empson's interpretative 'gaffe': 'The truth is that Empson studied Eliot, and spun his finely drawn theories about Eliot's literary art . . . from either the third or the fourth edition . . . [I]t was the faulty printer—and not the poet—who introduced the syntactical ambiguity that Empson so greatly admired and felt was the point of the whole poem. I should dearly like to know whether Eliot blushed, or laughed, when he read Empson on this poem and its non-existent point' (pp. 31–2). Quite apart from the fact that Beare's article does not actually attribute the mispunctuation to the printer (Beare says only that 'the poem was completely revised for the Knopf edition in 1920'), it is difficult to know why Empson should have been accused of comical misconstruction when he had directly based his interpretation of the poem on the canonical collection *Poems 1909–1925* (London, 1925)—which was the only edition that was readily available to an English reader in 1929–30.

A few years later again, Roger Sale, in 'The Achievement of William Empson', complained that Empson had 'mispunctuated "Whispers of Immortality" so as to give the poem a reading not available to readers of the correct version'; and in general, it seemed to him, Empson manifested an 'almost incredible penchant to be lax about details' (*Hudson Review*, 19 (Autumn 1966)). The obvious answer to Sale's accusation is to say again that it was not in fact Empson who 'misquoted' Eliot, it was the editions of Eliot published between 1920 and 1932; the very notion of a 'correct' text is anyway in doubt, as more recent bibliographical authorities maintain.

Empson, who angrily rejected the insinuation that he must have misquoted on purpose (for the sake of a false, inventive argument), took the trouble to respond to Sale's canard (*Hudson Review*, 20 (Winter 1967–8)):

> I am very bad at correcting proofs of my own writing, always seeing what I meant to write and considering whether it should be improved, and in my first book I foolishly imitated Hazlitt in what seemed a civilised practice, making incidental quotations as I remembered them, which was sufficient for the purpose. The effect of the combination was that a close study of an odd bit of punctuation in a poem would sometimes appear with the punctuation wrong, and nearby there were evidently careless quotations. My paragraph would make nonsense until the punctuation was put right, and I struggled to do this as soon as possible, but my opponents were already saying that I had cheated; I had misquoted the text in order to make it fit my interpretation, they said, and they have continued to do so. Now, in dealing with a long poem, I can see, one might be tempted to fudge a detail to fit an overall interpretation; but here I was dealing almost entirely with short lyrics. I was keen on explaining why they were so beautiful, and of course I was not interested in faking the text; almost any other form of our mortal frailty would then have tempted me more. And what I had written about the text did not apply to the erroneous version which had got printed. For years I have sometimes looked up the facts about these accusations, and they would always seem to me such obvious lies that I need not refute them. It has cured me of feeling any great reverence for textual scholars. (*Hudson Review*, 20 (Winter 1967–8))

(De Quincey, in a review of Thomas Noon Talfourd's biography of Charles Lamb (1848), lamented what he called Hazlitt's 'habit of trite quotation... which places the reader at the mercy of a man's tritest remembrances from his most school-boy reading' (*The Collected Writing of Thomas De Quincey*, vol. v, ed. David Masson (London: A. & C. Black, 1897), 236–7).)

A genuine and more unfortunate example of an Empson mistake, which should almost certainly be put down to his 'Hazlitt habit', occurs on p. 173, where he attributes to Carew the following two-and-a-half lines:

> that jewel in your ear…
> Shall last to be a precious stone
> When all your world of beauty's gone.

In fact, the passage in question is taken from Herrick, and should run:

> When as that Rubie, which you weare,
> Sunk from the tip of your soft eare,
> Will last to be a precious Stone,
> When all your world of Beautie's gone.

36. F. W. Bateson, 'The Function of Criticism at the Present Time', *Essays in Criticism*, 3/1 (January 1953), 8–9; WE's 'Answers to Comments', 114–20; and a final exchange, ' "Bare Ruined Choirs" ', 357–63. Despite dutifully baiting Empson on Shakespeare, Bateson privately informed him: 'The embarrassing point about it all is that I know in my bones that you're much the best living lit. critic (now that T.S.E. has gone out of business). Only if you're *wrong* I must say so, mustn't I?' (Bateson letter to Empson, 24 January 1953); he sought to reassure him again on 2 April 1953, 'I'm sorry we are having this row, because—in spite of all my reservations—I really do admire you a lot more than any other living critic' (Empson Papers). See also Tom Paulin, 'The Art of Criticism: 2 Ambiguity', *Independent on Sunday*, 15 January 1995, p. 36.

37. Empson's antagonist apropos Herbert was Rosemond Tuve: see her 'On Herbert's "Sacrifice" ' (*Kenyon Review*, 12 (Winter 1950)), 51–75; *A Reading of George Herbert* (London: Faber & Faber, 1952). By WE: 'George Herbert and Miss Tuve' (1950), *Argufying*, 250–5; 'Herbert's Quaintness' (1963), *Argufying*, 256–9; 'Last Words on George Herbert', *SSS* 119–28; also, 'Hopkins's "The Windhover": A Controversy' (1954–5), *Argufying*, 330–7. For a judicious evaluation of the controversy over George Herbert, see Philip Hobsbaum, *A Theory of Communication* (Basingstoke: Macmillan Press, 1970), 131–4.

38. Though often associated with the New Criticism, Empson never saw his own critical procedures as adhering to the same principles as the criticism of Cleanth Brooks, John Crowe Ransom, or W. K. Wimsatt; he was always insistent, for example, that the work of literature, so far from being autotelic—an aesthetic object to be analysed only in and for itself—was for him necessarily related to historical occasion, to context and creative intention.

39. John Carey, 'Burnt-Out Case', *Sunday Times*, 30 November 1986, p. 53. In a later year, Carey unequivocally praised *Ambiguity* as one of the 'Books of the Century'; Empson as 'a matchlessly sensitive and ingenious reader' (*Sunday Times*, 13 June 1999, p. 12).

40. WE, 'Still the Strange Necessity' (1955), *Argufying*, 127.

41. 'When I returned to England from communist China in 1952,' Empson wrote in response to criticisms by Roger Sale, 'I was frequently told that I obviously didn't know any history, so I have had to look into the evidence for the

opinions I was taught at school, and I found every time that they stand up like a rock' (*Hudson Review*, 20/4 (Winter 1967–8)). Likewise, to 'Mr Miller' (19 November 1974): 'Insisting that I did attend to the context, though I often took it for granted in the printed criticism, seemed to need saying in letters to magazines at some point . . . ' (copy in Empson Papers).

42. WE, 'The Love of Definition' (1979), *Argufying*, 270. In his inaugural lecture, 'The Critic as Vandal', John Carey had stated: 'We take it as an axiom that paraphrase inevitably alters meaning. To reword is to destroy.' As one of his specific (and well-chosen) examples of criticism that separates form and content by paraphrasing a poem, he cited Empson's discussion of George Herbert's 'Affliction' (from chapter 6 of *Seven Types of Ambiguity*), commenting: 'Empson wants to deter his readers from the way of understanding the line that will probably have occurred to them, and accordingly he reduces it to a comic paraphrase so that they will feel ashamed of thinking the line meant that, and be readier to believe Empson's less likely alternative' ('The Critic as Vandal—1', *New Statesman*, 6 August 1976, p. 178). Empson produced a fighting defence including the following remarks:

> The poem outlines the life of Herbert, saying he had desired the ruling-class career which was open to him but had also felt God was calling him to religion; yet now, having obeyed the call, he feels that God no longer wants him. He is plucky about being jilted in this way, and plans to take up some other line of life:
>
> > Well, I will change the service, and go seek
> > Some other master out.
> > Ah, my dear God, though I be clean forgot,
> > Let me not love thee, if I love thee not.
>
> Clearly there is an interval before the final couplet, while he finds that he cannot bring himself to go. The last line may express total self-abandonment: 'I will love you however badly you treat me', and then *let me not love thee* has to become, very oddly, a kind of swearing—he invokes the worst penalty he can think of. 'Damn me if I don't stick to the parsonage', I am blamed [by Carey] for writing down, but it does bring out the queer logic or syntax of this version. Another version would follow more naturally from the lines just before, by making a practical appeal: 'Stop calling me if I have no real vocation. Do not make me love you in desire if I am incapable of loving you in achievement.' There is no conflict between the two meanings; he hardly knows which he can afford to say; but unless he means both there is no reason for giving the final line its peculiar form, that of a paradox or riddle. Very likely I phrased the alternatives clumsily, but that is a minor matter. As to the main point, if a man calls me a cheat for saying it I think he is practically deranged' (*New Statesman*, 13 August 1976, p. 208).

See also Empson's fierce and maybe unforgiving ' "There Is No Penance Due to Ignorance" ' (a review of *John Donne: Life, Mind and Art*, by John Carey), *New York Review of Books*, 28/19 (3 December 1981), 42–50.

43. WE, 'The Love of Definition', *Argufying*, 270–1. Carey's piece in *Approaches to Marvell: The York Tercentenary Lectures* he found 'magnificent' (p. 269).
44. Letter to Roger Sale, n.d. (copy in Empson Papers).
45. *Ambiguity*, p. xiii; quoting Smith, 'Books of the Quarter' (Constable, 44). Edward M. Wilson was to report in a memoir of James Smith: 'At William Empson's request I sent [Smith] the draft preface to the second edition of *Seven Types of Ambiguity*, in which the author replied to some of the criticisms made in the review in *The Criterion* in 1931; Smith read, but did not comment, on it' ('James Smith (1904–1972)', in James Smith, *Shakespearean and Other Essays* (Cambridge: Cambridge University Press, 1974), 345).
46. WE, ' "The Ancient Mariner" ' (1964), *Argufying*, 317.
47. Cf. WE, 'The Verbal Analysis', *Argufying* 105: 'Another trouble that seems to crop up is the idea that poetry is good in proportion as it is complicated, or simply hard to construe; it seems quite a common delusion, and always shocks me when expressed. And yet I suppose it is very near my own position; in any case it joins onto I. A. Richards's Theory of Value as the satisfaction of more impulses rather than less, and T. S. Eliot's struggle to find a poetic idiom adequate to the complexities of modern life.'
48. Hugh Kenner, 'Alice in Empsonland', *Hudson Review*, 1 (Spring 1952), 138.
49. Letter to 'Mr Miller', 19 November 1974 (Empson Papers).
50. *Ambiguity*, p. viii.
51. WE, 'Herbert's Quaintness', *Argufying*, 257.
52. Ibid., 258.
53. In an undated notebook from a later year (*c.*1960), Empson reflected: '[Graham] Hough said the effect of disapproving Christianity would be to make me unable to appreciate Eng. Lit.—a drive at my professional competence. I don't think this usually true, but it does seem true about Herbert's *Sacrifice*. I now feel that he [Herbert] was an ass if he was ignorant of the ambiguities of the poem, and at best perverse if he wasn't. He ought not to have put up with such a disgusting doctrine—to this extent I agree with my opponents of a third of a century ago. Can one get further evidence from the manuscripts that he screwed up the ambiguity in later drafts? But what use would it be anyway?' (Empson Papers).
54. John Crowe Ransom, *The New Criticism* (Norfolk, Conn.: New Directions, 1941), 102.
55. WE, letter to Sylvia Townsend Warner, 4 June 1932 (Reading). 'I shall stay here two more years, if I can. Of course it's very deadening but I am less hysterical than I got in Bloomsbury.'
56. Arthur Empson, letter to WE, 18 November 1930 (Empson Papers).
57. WE, undated letter to T. S. Eliot (courtesy of Faber & Faber Ltd.)

II. THE TRIALS OF TOKYO

1. Sumie Okada, *Western Writers in Japan* (Basingstoke: Macmillan Press, 1999), 44; Kyohei Ogihara, 'About Emp-san' (the title is a pun on the polite form of address in Japan), *Eigo-Seinen* (*The Rising Generation*), 106/10 (1 October 1960), 32; interview with Professor F. Narita, 9 April 1984.
2. WE, undated letter (*c.* late 1931) to his mother (Empson Papers).
3. See Sir Robert Craigie, *Behind the Japanese Mask* (London: Hutchinson & Co., 1945); Shunsuke Tsurumi, *An Intellectual History of Wartime Japan: 1931–1945* (London: KPI, 1986), ch. 5: 'Greater Asia'; Ikuhita Hata, 'Continental Expansion, 1905–1941', in *The Cambridge History of Japan*, vol. vi: *The Twentieth Century*, ed. Peter Duus (Cambridge: Cambridge University Press, 1988), esp. pp. 290–8.
4. Richard Storry, *The Double Patriots: A Study in Japanese Nationalism* (London: Chatto & Windus, 1957), 124.
5. Peter Quennell, *A Superficial Journey through Tokyo and Peking* (1932; repr. Oxford: Oxford University Press, 1986), 99.
6. WE, letter to Michael Roberts, 2 April 1933 (Janet Adam Smith). This is not to say that Empson did not project a book about his experiences, but whereas Quennell incontinently and wittily blows the gaff on Japan, like an anthropologist writing up some curiously silly tribe, Empson must have thought he might attempt to write a work of mediation, a book addressed in some sort to Japan. Here are a few passages from the handful of typed pages with holograph emendations that survive amongst the Empson Papers:

> I am writing now on the assumption that Japanese people will be interested to hear a foreigner on Japan; an English or French public would not care what a foreigner thought of them, unless he knew enough to be quite piercingly rude, and then they would only be amused and think 'that's all he's made of it' . . . I chatter here in the dark; I do not know what is worth saying to 'Japan', that false assumption of unity; but it may be worth pointing out that England did not become part of 'Europe' till her best work was done, that there has never been a racial criterion for Europe; that the poor Hitler, trying to be European, has seized on the swastika, which if it means anything means the East; that Europe was hardly unified at all by its international language of Latin before that language imported from the Arabs a memory of Plato and the sciences.
>
> When a literary Englishman takes a comfortable job in Japan, he is warned (if he isn't he should be) that it is a very severe strain on the 'nerves'—an obscure term but plain in its context; if my own nerves had not survived it I shouldn't be writing this. A number of rude books about 'Japan' have been written by Englishmen whose nerves could not pass the test, and an intelligent Japanese teacher may extract from them many profound truths with which to scold his pupils. No book advertising 'Japan' can possibly do anything but make the strain worse for such a man, and he is astonished to find his pupils (it is hard to say this strongly enough; my sort of

Englishman is *frightened* to find his pupils) talking like the advertisements, *asking* him to admire Fujisan. He has seen a hundred pictures of it, and admired them; can they be such fools as to want him to *say* so; what do *they* admire, other than the obvious, in Japan? The fundamental misunderstanding is that the Englishman takes for granted his admiration for Japan, and that the Japanese he speaks to dare not do so; I am not speaking of myself but of at least three men I have known. This is the puzzle of the international situation. All the Japanese patriotism I have met with has been vanity...

    The difficulty is only the embarassment, which seems a specially difficult matter in Japan. It seems to be polite according to the conventions of this country to make a display of embarrassment when one feels that respect is demanded; now I believe my own feelings here are as common in China as Europe; I often show embarrassment when among people I respect, but both I and they think it an involuntary rudeness... I have heard foreigners in Japan puzzled to decide whether the Japanese are rude or overpolite; the answer is that by our conventions to be overpolite is to be rude. (Empson Papers)

7. Quennell, *A Superficial Journey*, 115.
8. WE, letter to I. A. Richards, 13 October 1931 (I. A. Richards Collection). The grotesquerie of the first paragraph is presumably a case of insult by anticipation, since he made thrifty use of the same terms in a letter to John Hayward: 'I am just looking through your Donne [Hayward's edition of the works of John Donne for the Nonesuch Press], wondering what I can say in my first lecture tomorrow. Apparently they are all Christians, with the spaniel like eyes of the convert. (As for the dons, they are so absurdly English that you can tell which are Presbyterians and which Anglicans.)' (Undated letter to John Hayward, King's College, Cambridge: WE/JDH/5.)
9. WE, letter to I. A. Richards, 13 October 1931.
10. WE, letter to I. A. Richards, 23 April 1932.
11. WE, undated letter (*c.*1931–2) to his mother (Empson Papers).
12. WE, undated letter to John Hayward, ?March 1932 (King's College, Cambridge: WE/JDH/6).
13. WE, undated letter (*c.*1931–2) to his mother (Empson Papers).
14. Quennell, *A Superficial Journey*, 166.
15. WE, undated letter to John Hayward, ?March 1932 (King's College, Cambridge: WE/JDH/6). 'I am clutching round for somewhere I can work free from noise. I have taken a room in an apartment house as well as my Jap house: they have different noises and so are a relief, but I can't work in either' (letter to I. A. Richards, 23 April 1932: I. A. Richards Collection).
16. WE, holograph notes written on Christmas Day 1937 (Empson Papers).
17. WE, letter to C. K. Ogden, 31 August 1932 (McMaster University Library); Ryuichi Kajiki, letter to JH, 22 September 1984.
18. *The Japan Biographical Encyclopedia and Who's Who*, 3rd edn. (Tokyo: The Rengo Press, 1964–5). Empson paid tribute to Fukuhara in *The Rising Generation*,

1 June 1981, p. 168: 'I admired Fukuhara very much. He was my boss when I was employed in Japan . . . and gave me much help and good advice . . . '

19. Rintaro Fukuhara, 'Mr William Empson in Japan', in Gill, 22.

20. WE, letter to Sylvia Townsend Warner, 4 June 1932 (Reading University Library, MS 1399/1/2).

21. WE's incidental comment on an essay by Kyo Nogawa on Gray's 'Elegy', quoted in Fukuhara, 'Mr William Empson in Japan', in Gill, 25; previously quoted in Fukuhara, 'Empson and/on Gray', *Essays in English Language and Literature* (Otsuka English Association), iv (November 1936), 159.

22. Kai Yuzuru, 'Two Old Familiar Faces', 32; Ogawa Kazuo, 'My Impression of Prof. Empson', *The Rising Generation*, 1 September 1960 (article in Japanese).

23. G. C. Allen, *An Appointment in Japan* (London: Athlone Press, 1983).

24. Professor Kai Yuzuru, letter to JH, 20 February 1986.

25. Telephone conversation with Kajiki Ryuichi, Tokyo, 11 April 1984; Kajiki, letter to JH, 22 September 1984.

26. Interview with Professor F. Narita and Professor Y. Irie, Tokyo, 9 April 1984.

27. Fukuhara, 'Mr William Empson in Japan', 22.

28. Kazuo Ogawa, letter to JH, 28 April 1984.

29. Naritoshi Narita, cited in Okada, *Western Writers in Japan*, 44.

30. The swimming anecdote is the substance of an article written in Japanese by Irie Yukio, 'Swimming together with William Empson', *A Flower Basket*, 14 September 1933 (copy kindly supplied by Professor Irie); also interview with Narita and Irie, 9 April 1984.

31. Quennell, *A Superficial Journey*, 96, 102,

32. Fukuhara, 'Mr William Empson in Japan', 23.

33. WE, draft article/broadcast, 4 pp. typescript (Empson Papers).

34. Quennell, *A Superficial Journey*, 99.

35. Sumie Okada, *Edmund Blunden and Japan: The History of a Relationship* (Basingstoke: Macmillan Press, 1988), 200; see also Barry Webb, *Edmund Blunden: A Biography* (New Haven: Yale University Press, 1990). A brief biography of Professor Ichikawa Sanki may be found in *The Japan Biographical Encyclopedia and Who's Who*, 3rd edn.

36. Interview with Narita and Irie, 9 April 1984.

37. WE, Introduction to T. S. Eliot's *Selected Essays* (Tokyo: Kinseido, 1933); reprinted in *Argufying*, 568–9.

38. Notes on an essay, 'On Shakespeare's Attitude to Life', by Irie Yukio. 'The comic characters agree with you,' Empson went on, '(the puns on *sense*, which perhaps I talked about too much, are ironical jokes) but Shakespeare's own ideas were more contradictory or more complete.' Remarkably, Empson was lecturing on the substance of his own essay 'Sense in *Measure for Measure*' as early as 1932, six years before a version of it first appeared in *Southern Review* in the autumn of 1938 (it was revised for inclusion in *The Structure of Complex Words*, 1951). Even though he had yet to complete the essays in *Some Versions of*

Pastoral (1935), Empson was thus already at work on pieces that would become his next big book. Another of Irie Yukio's essays addressed the topic 'Is a Theory of Criticism necessary or useful? Has a good writing been written without one?', and ended up by arguing: 'A good writing is derived from the author's good (rich) life, which can do without a Theory of Criticism. A good writing, therefore, can do without a Theory of Criticism and has been written without it naturally.' Empson's comment was as succinct as it was logical: 'Well, you may not be able to make a rich life without some beliefs about what it is, and for that you may need a Theory of Criticism.' (Courtesy of Professor Irie.)

39. Quennell, *A Superficial Journey*, 96.
40. WE, letter to John Hayward, ?March 1932 (King's College, Cambridge: WE/JDH/6).
41. WE, 'Teaching Literature', *Argufying*, 97.
42. WE, letter to I. A. Richards, 9 January 1933 (I. A. Richards Collection).
43. Ishikawa Rinshiro, testimonial for WE, 15 December 1936 (Empson Papers).
44. Ogawa Kazuo, 'A reminiscence of William Empson', written 1952; source unknown (photocopy kindly supplied by Professor Ogawa). Empson had modified his view of Wordsworth's mature poetry by the time he came to write 'Sense in *The Prelude*' (*SCW*, 1951).
45. Quennell, *A Superficial Journey*, 101–2.
46. WE, letter to I. A. Richards, 23 April 1932 (I. A. Richards Collection).
47. *Pastoral*, 49, 159.
48. Dilys Powell, 'Elusive "Pastoral"', *Sunday Times*, 9 February 1936.
49. 'Mrs Dalloway', *Eigo Seinen* (*The Rising Generation*), 68/6 (15 December 1932), 182; repr., as '*Mrs Dalloway* as a Political Satire', in *Essays in English Language and Literature* (Tokyo), 1 (April 1933); in *Argufying*, 451.
50. '*Mrs Dalloway* as a Political Satire', *Argufying*, 450–2.
51. WE, 'Calling the West Indies: Close-Up', BBC broadcast script, 14 December 1941 (BBC Written Archives Centre); published in 'Did You Hear That?—How the Japanese student thinks', *The Listener*, 1 January 1942, p. 9. WE reiterated these observations in an article 'Puzzle of the Jap' published in the periodical *John Bull* at the close of the Second World War (vol. 78, no. 2045, 25 August 1945, p. 10): 'At Tokyo the students were constantly under the eye of the police. The system was so strict that if the least suspicion of a liberal opinion popped out in my lectures the students would giggle... A large number of these "liberal" Japanese youngsters were in due course killed by the political police. What kept them even more in check was the knowledge that if they came under the least breath of political suspicion they would never be able to get a job. They would simply have to starve.'
52. WE, 'Teaching English in the Far East and England', *SSS*, 216.
53. WE, undated letter to John Hayward, ?March 1932 (King's College, Cambridge: WE/JDH/6).

54. WE, 'Calling the West Indies: Close-Up'. Empson was genuinely shocked by the students' response to Housman; he returned to the matter again and again, in his private thoughts and in his writings. In a BBC radio talk, 'The Traps of Idealism' (broadcast on 3 September 1936), for example, he recalled of his time in Japan in the winter and spring of 1932: 'Before the end of term several of the class were drafted to Shanghai, where there was a row at the time; one of them was killed, but I am thankful to say that he left early in the term, so that I cannot have pumped much of this poison into him, otherwise I might feel partly responsible for his death . . . It really is what Housman says, if you read him as a source of direct advice; a thing it had never occurred to me to do. What he meant, of course, is that this would be a fine thing for a man to feel under special circumstances; the man has gone to war thinking he had a good cause, and he dies disillusioned about the cause, but he still feels that his life was a fine one. For a man to *start* on a war in this spirit, not from patriotism but from the flat ideal of death, seemed to me painful and actually rather slavish. Even if you were to grant that at bottom death is the best, this was not the right way to bring in the ideal. Of course these cultivated young Japanese were drawing on Buddhism more than on Housman, and just what levels of thought are at work under the crucial desire for death in Buddhism is the last thing you would learn about that great religion.' (Empson Papers.) Cf. Empson's poem 'Ignorance of Death', which was perhaps drafted at the same time.

55. WE, undated letter to John Hayward, ?March 1932 (King's College, Cambridge: WE/JDH/6).

56. S.T.U., 'Farewell to Empson' (in Japanese), *Eibungaku-Fukei* (*English Literary Scenes*, a Bunrika graduate periodical), August 1934, pp. 50–1. Empson would tease one of his quondam students in a later year, 'I do not remember what I said in the lectures, and hope you have not all had to struggle to get rid of my mistakes. None of you told me I was wrong, and I have remained very opinionated ever since' (letter to Professor Kai Yuzuru, 10 August 1978; courtesy of Kai Yuzuru).

57. The passage on Gray's elegy appeared in August 1933, in the Japanese periodical *New English and American Literature* (Rodensky, p. xiv).

58. *Pastoral*, 11–12.

59. Fukuhara, 'Mr William Empson in Japan', 25–6; Empson's jottings were previously quoted (in English) by Professor Fukuhara Rintaro in his article in Japanese, 'Empson and/on Gray', *Essays in English Language and Literature* (Otsuka English Association), iv (November 1936), 155–63.

60. *Pastoral*, 12. J. Brian Harvey took Empson to task in *Left Review*: 'But to think that one must always accept the injustice of society is not to establish a permanent truth, and Mr Empson in taking this attitude shows that he cannot understand one of the basic principles of dialectical materialism— that a quantity of changes in degree will ultimately comprise a quantitative

change. Thus his scholarly attempt to meet the Marxists on their own ground is invalid from the beginning' ('Proletarian or Pastoral?', *Left Review*, February 1936, p. 231). But Empson was not applying himself in any concerted way to outfacing Marxist theory.

61. Interview with Professor Irie Yukio, 9 April 1984.

62. Telephone interview with Professor Kajiki Ryuichi, Tokyo, 11 April 1984; and Kajiki, letter to JH, 22 September 1984.

63. Telephone interview with Professor Eitaro Sayama, Tokyo, 9 April 1984.

64. Kazuo Ogawa, letter to JH, 28 April 1984.

65. See *The Japan Biographical Encyclopedia and Who's Who*.

66. *Argufying*, 96.

67. WE, letter to John Hayward, 7 March 1933 (King's College, Cambridge: WE/JDH/7).

68. Ibid.

69. Quennell, *A Superficial Journey*, 101.

70. WE, letter to I. A. Richards, 2 September 1932 (I. A. Richards Collection). He was gratified to find a personal response in one student's essay, though this must have been exceptional; as he wrote home in 1932: 'I don't think them so very inscrutable: one man in the course of an essay about satire and Pope set to work to explain how hard he found it to love his father' (letter to John Hayward, ?March 1932; King's College, Cambridge: WE/JDH/6).

71. WE, portion of a letter, or notes, written on writing paper from the Kyoto Hotel, Kyoto, where he was stuck for a few days after his return from Korea (Empson Papers).

72. Bottrall, 'William Empson', Gill, 50.

73. WE, letter to C. K. Ogden, n.d. (1933).

74. WE, letters to Ogden, 16 March 1933, [?8 June] 1933, and 31 August 1931 (McMaster University Library); Harold E. Palmer, letter to WE, 12 November 1932 (McMaster); WE, draft letter to Palmer, 13 November [1933] (Empson Papers). 'Fukuhara seems to have backed out of wanting words in *ing* and *ed* to be verbs and now wants to have no qualifiers in *ing* or *ed*,' Empson wrote to I. A. Richards on 2 September 1932. 'But you haven't gained anything when you make them apparently agree with you in conversation, of course.' (I. A. Richards Collection.)

75. WE, letter to C. K. Ogden, n.d. (1933).

76. WE, 'The learning of English' (letter), *The Japan Chronicle*, 25 November 1931, p. 5.

77. WE, 'The Hammer's Ring', in Reuben Brower, Helen Vendler, John Hollander (eds.), *I. A. Richards: Essays in His Honor* (New York: Oxford University Press, 1973), 79.

78. Report in *Japan Times*, 20 October 1931.

79. *The Japan Chronicle*, 29 October 1931.

80. Dorothée Anderson, 'Harold E. Palmer: A Biographical Essay', in Harold E. Palmer and H. Vere Redman, *This Language-Learning Business* (1932) (Oxford: Oxford University Press, 1969), 153. Details in this and the following paragraph are taken from Anderson's essay on her father.

81. WE, letter to Sylvia Townsend Warner, 10 October 1933 (Reading University Library).

82. H. Bongers, *The History and Principles of Vocabulary Control* (Woerden: Wocopi, 1947), quoted by Dorothée Anderson in Palmer and Redman, *This Language-Learning Business*, 152.

83. Palmer quoted by Anderson, in Palmer and Redman, *This Language-Learning Business*, 141.

84. A full obituary of Professor Okakura is given in 'International Notes', *The Basic News*, 1 (January–March 1937), 11–14.

85. 'I was talking about Basic today (16th) to some teachers' congress,' Empson wrote to Richards in a letter begun on 13 October 1931, 'and old Ishikawa said after that he and the Advisory committee (is it that?) are not *not* in favour of it, and after all are only waiting for our text book, and have to consider where they can fit it in—and I think of him as honest, though sly: so I suppose there are some prospects' (I. A. Richards Collection).

86. WE, letter to C. K. Ogden, 31 August 1932 (McMaster).

87. Ibid.

88. A. S. Hornby, letter to WE, 22 February 1947 (McMaster).

89. WE, letter to A. S. Hornby, 19 February 1947 (McMaster).

90. WE, letter to C. K. Ogden, 10 June 1933.

91. WE, letter to C. K. Ogden, 31 August 1932 (McMaster).

92. WE, letter to I. A. Richards, 2 September 1932 (I. A. Richards Collection).

93. WE, letter to C. K. Ogden, n.d. (1933).

94. WE, letter to John Hayward, 12 July 1933 (King's College, Cambridge: WE/JDH/3).

95. WE, letter to Sylvia Townsend Warner, 10 October 1933 (Reading University Library). He was given his due tribute in 'International Notes', *The Basic News*, 1 (January–March 1937), 7: 'Professor Empson and others kept Basic well before the public by their letters in *The Japan Chronicle* in answer to certain English teachers of the old school and the I.R.E.T.'

96. Nakano Yoshio, 'A Visit to the Noh Drama with William Empson', *The Rising Generation* (Tokyo), 1 September 1981, p. 383 (original in Japanese).

97. Okada, *Western Writers in Japan*, 45.

98. WE, letter to Sylvia Townsend Warner, 4 June 1932 (Reading University Library: MS 1399/1/2).

99. WE, postcard to Phyllis Chroustchoff, 'New Year's Night' 1932 (courtesy of Igor Chroustchoff).

100. In a later draft essay (written in China), Empson added: 'I cooed with pleasure and began saying how German this was, a thing that seemed

sufficiently true and tactful, but my Japanese friends were already burning with resentful blushes. The convention is that you assume cowardice as a source of contract; as soon as anything goes wrong you put it on duty or a romantic interest in death or something like that. An English group of course would have extracted courage from swearing at the nuisance of the thing. Their convention seems rather less untrue than ours, and certainly gives you more emotional exercise; but one would think it made the group liable to break earlier, even though not the individual. The Chinese seem to have no convention on this issue, and probably we all need one.'

101. WE, letter to John Hayward, 7 March 1933 (King's College, Cambridge).

102. WE, untitled review of Dylan Thomas's *Collected Poems* and *Under Milk Wood*, in *New Statesman & Nation*, 15 May 1954, p. 635; *Argufying*, 392.

103. WE, letter to George Sansom, (?September) 1934 (Empson Papers).

104. WE, untitled review of Dylan Thomas, as n. 102 above.

105. Undated version of letter published as 'Mr Empson and the Fire Sermon', *Essays in Criticism*, 6/4 (October 1956), 482–3 (Empson Papers).

106. WE, letter to John Hayward, 7 March 1933 (King's College, Cambridge: WE/JDH/7).

107. Ibid. The second paragraph is echoed in a letter to Michael Roberts (2 April 1933): 'The chief thing I feel in this very agreeable place is that worship of the state claimed as universal is bound to come back—these great altars like football stadiums will be used again. But what one's "feelings" are worth is another thing' (courtesy of Janet Adam Smith).

108. WE, letter to Sylvia Townsend Warner, 4 June 1932 (Reading University Library, MS 1399/1/2).

109. WE, letter, or notes, written on writing paper headed Kyoto Hotel, Kyoto (Empson Papers).

110. WE, letter to George Sansom, 2 September 1934 (Empson Papers). George Sansom (1883–1965) joined the Consular Service in the Far East in 1904, at the age of 20; by 1907 he was Private Secretary to the British Ambassador in Tokyo. Sir Charles Eliot, British Ambassador from 1919 to 1926, wrote of him in 1921: 'For sheer intellectual power he is in all probability easily first in the Government Service in Japan' (quoted in Katharine Sansom, *Sir George Sansom and Japan: A Memoir* (Tallahassee, Fla.: Diplomatic Press, 1972), 13). In 1926–39 he was commercial counsellor in Tokyo. He was knighted in 1935, and in 1947 elected Knight Grand Cross of the Order of the British Empire. After the War, he became first Director of the Far Eastern Institute at Columbia University. His publications include *Historical Grammar of the Japanese Language* (1928), *Japan: A Short Cultural History* (1931), and *History of Japan* (3 vols., 1958–64). See also Gordon Daniels, 'Sir George Sansom (1883–1965): Historian and Diplomat', in Sir Hugh Cortazzi and Gordon Daniels (eds.), *Britain and Japan 1859–1991: Themes and Personalities* (London: Routledge, 1991), 277–88.

111. Dorothea Richards journal, Old Library, Magdalene College, Cambridge.

112. Langdon Warner (1881–1955): assistant curator of Oriental Art, Museum of Fine Arts, Boston, 1906–1913; he was field fellow of the Fogg Museum, Harvard University, at the time when Empson talked to him in Boston in 1939. Katharine Sansom characterized him as 'a jolly sort of buccaneer... the gentlest of men and a passionate aesthete. We already knew of his amazing journeys in China, where he discovered lost caves filled with superb sculpture and paintings' (*Sir George Sansom and Japan*, 20).

113. WE, 'These Japanese', *The Listener*, 5 March 1942, p.293.

114. WE, letter to Sylvia Townsend Warner, 10 October 1933 (Reading University Library, MS 1399/1/1).

115. Edward Seidensticker, *Tokyo Rising: The City since the Great Earthquake* (New York: Alfred A. Knopf, 1990), 36.

116. WE, letter to Michael Roberts, 12 November 1932 (Janet Adam Smith).

117. WE, letter to John Hayward, 8 October 1933 (King's College, Cambridge: WE/JDH/4).

118. Bottrall may have unconsciously relocated the place of this pub crawl. Bottrall did make one vacation trip to visit Empson in Tokyo, and that might have been the occasion on which Empson was 'taken drinking with some Able-Bodies'—although there is no reason to suppose that it did not happen on more than one occasion. Otherwise, this shared night on the town must have taken place by the early part of August 1934, when Empson stopped off in Singapore on his way home to England.

119. WE, undated draft letter to Molly Kitching (notebook in Empson Papers).

120. WE, 'These Japanese', 294.

121. Much of the information in the following four paragraphs is taken from an article in Japanese by Sato Nobuo, 'Remembering Mr Empson', in *Eibungaku-Fukai* (2/1, 1934); translation courtesy of Gordon Daniels.

122. WE, 'These Japanese', 294.

123. WE, letter to John Hayward, 12 July 1933 (King's College, Cambridge: WE/JDH/3).

124. WE, letter to I. A. Richards, 9 January 1933 (I. A. Richards Collection).

125. WE, letter to John Hayward, 8 October 1933 (King's College, Cambridge: WE/JDH/4).

126. It was quite common for European visitors to become involved with Japanese women; one of the best-known cases is that of Edmund Blunden (see Okada, *Edmund Blunden and Japan*; Webb, *Edmund Blunden*).

127. WE, *Complete Poems*, 69.

128. S. F. Bolt, letter to the editor, *The London Review of Books*, 15/16 (19 August 1993), 5.

129. S. F. Bolt, letter to JH, 26 August 1993.

130. Bottrall, 'William Empson', Gill, 50.

131. WE, letter to Katharine Sansom, 13 January [1935?] (Empson Papers).

132. David Wevill's letter is quoted in Okada, *Western Writers in Japan*, 48.

133. Notebook kept while working for the BBC in 1942 (Empson Papers). According to Charles Madge (who believed he had heard it from Kathleen Raine), the gossip went that the woman had 'followed' Empson to England; and there was 'some vague story about their being together in the country, with Bill trying to get away from her round a haystack—it's probably what he told Kathleen' (JH, interview with Madge, June 1983).

134. WE, letter to Sir George Sansom, 11 October 1935 (Empson Papers).

135. WE, letter to Sir George Sansom, 13 November 1935 (Empson Papers).

136. John Davenport, letter to Trevelyan (Julian Trevelyan Papers, Wren Library, Trinity College, Cambridge: JOT 4/16). Earlier, Davenport had entertained Empson at his home near Andover; he wrote to Trevelyan on 15 November 1935: 'Bill Empson & the Bonham Carters—excluding Charlotte of comic memory—are coming on Saturday for the day, which will be amusing' (Julian Trevelyan Papers).

137. WE, letter to Robert Herring, 14 July 1938 (Empson Papers).

138. WE, letter to Ronald Bottrall, 23 July 1940 (Humanities Research Center, University of Texas at Austin).

139. The following account of WE's relations with Chikoyo Hatakeyama is indebted to Peter Robinson's article 'Very Shrinking Behaviour', *TLS*, 18 July 2003, pp. 13–15. Robinson has also very kindly supplied me with his own typed transcript of the correspondence between WE and Hatakeyama.

140. *Complete Poems*, 322–3.

141. Hiroshi Hirai, who went on to gain a doctorate, taught at Fukushima University; he published poems and a biography of Oscar Wilde (1960).

142. WE, undated letter to Hatakeyama, 1933?

143. WE, letter to Hatakeyama, 15 June 1933.

144. WE, letter to Hatakeyama, 23 December (1933).

145. WE, undated end to a letter, possibly written after their meeting on 26 March 1934.

146. Extracts from Hatakeyama's diary by courtesy of Peter Robinson.

147. Quoted in Peter Robinson, 'Ice cream with Empson' (letter), *TLS*, 24 October 2003, p. 19.

148. WE, undated end to a letter, perhaps after meeting on 26 March 1934.

149. WE, undated letter to Hatakeyama, June 1934?

150. Robinson, 'Very Shrinking Behaviour', 14.

151. Quotation from WE's poem 'Aubade'.

152. Tamotsu Sone, quoted in Robinson, 'Very Shrinking Behaviour', 14.

153. Quoted in Robinson, 'Very Shrinking Behaviour', 14.

154. 'Here,' notes Robinson, 'Empson is fending off the misapprehensions produced by Japanese student–teacher hierarchy expectation, and equally the misleading patronage that can be concealed in the British student–teacher equality ideal' (ibid. 15).

155. Quoted ibid.

156. Ibid. 15.

157. WE, letter to Michael Roberts, 7 December 1932 (Janet Adam Smith). Sherard Vines taught in Japan for many years; his books include *YOFUKU, or Japan in Trousers* (London, 1931). Empson had reviewed *Triforium* in the *Cambridge Review*, 23 November 1928, p. 161: 'his peace of mind is based, not on renouncing anything, but on that solid and learned variety of gratification which one associates with a High Table. The fully digested despair, the habit of writing poetry about a profound nervous dissatisfaction, the Byronism of the scholar which Mr Eliot has cultivated, is not Mr Vines's game at all . . . [H]ow seldom the bald head of our epoch shows through [in Vines's verse], or seems buried, a cenotaph, under bunches of plucked flowers.'

158. *Pastoral*, 9.

159. Gordon M. Berger, 'Politics and Mobilization in Japan, 1931–1945', in *The Cambridge History of Japan*, vi: *The Twentieth Century*, 109.

160. This statement is given on the authority of John Vice, Bronowski's biographer.

161. 'C.-B.' (Jacob Bronowski), 'Japan Rampant', *The Granta*, 10 May 1933, p. 415.

162. Crowley, *Japan's Quest*, quoted in Berger, 'Politics and Mobilization in Japan, 1931–1945', 112.

163. See Ikuhiko Hata, 'Continental Expansion, 1905–1941', in *The Cambridge History of Japan*, vi: *The Twentieth Century*, 295–8.

164. 'Paradoxically,' Peter Duus and Irwin Scheiner point out, 'Marxism gained intellectual force and influence in the late 1920s and early 1930s even as the government intensified its crackdown on the Communist Party and defections from the movement increased. The intellectual significance that Marxism attained as a principium can be explained in part by the totality with which its theory of dialectical and historical materialism explained human social, economic, and political behaviour' ('Socialism, Liberalism, and Marxism, 1901–1931', in *The Cambridge History of Japan*, vol. vi: *The Twentieth Century*, 709). See also Quennell, *A Superficial Journey*, 108; Shunsuke Tsurumi, *An Intellectual History of Wartime Japan: 1931–1945*, ch. 8: 'Germs of Anti-Stalinism'.

165. WE, 'Moralising over Japan', *World*, 2/3 (March 1935), 292–3.

166. Lenin quoted in Leszek Kolakowski, *Main Currents of Marxism: Its Origins, Growth and Dissolution* (Oxford, 1978), ii. 386; cited in Duus and Scheiner, 'Socialism, Liberalism, and Marxism, 1901–1931', 701.

167. WE, 'Teaching Literature', *Argufying*, 93.

168. Fukuhara, 'Mr William Empson in Japan', 28.

169. WE, 'Teaching Literature', *Argufying*, 95.

170. See FO 262/1878/ 151. 158081 (Public Record Office, London).

171. WE, letter to Michael Roberts, 28 March 1934 (Janet Adam Smith).

172. Interview with Ronald Bottrall.

173. Peter F. Alexander, *William Plomer: A Biography* (Oxford: Oxford University Press, 1989), 357 n. 99; Alexander, letter to JH, 24 April 1991. Professor Kajiki wrote to me on 3 April 1991: 'It is true that there was a rumor of his homosexual activity, but we could not ascertain this fact. I am sure he had no trouble with any of his pupils in that respect. . . . Fortunately, however, it was never reported in newspapers'; and on 8 May 1991, 'it is true I told you in my last letter that there was a rumor about it which I could not verify, but I do not mean that it was a groundless rumor. There was no denying that he had homosexual inclinations and most probably had a few chances to accomplish his desire. We can easily imagine that the Japanese police must have been worried when they received some report of the matter, but they could do nothing in their power, because it was not a criminal offense. At any rate, nobody in the circle of my acquaintance criticized Empson for his behavior which became a sort of open secret among us.' According to another report, the incident did hit the newspapers (Nakano Yoshio, 'A Visit to the Noh Drama with William Empson', *The Rising Generation*, 127/6 (1 September 1981), 383).

174. WE, letter to John Hayward, 18 May 1948 (King's College, Cambridge: WE/JDH/13).

175. WE, letter to George Sansom, 13 November 1935 (Empson Papers).

176. Fukuhara, 'Mr William Empson in Japan', 31; and S.T.U., 'Farewell to Empson', 51.

177. FO 371/24742 Political: Far Eastern—Japan 1940; files 953-1559; Public Record Office, London (letter from Tokyo Chancery, British Embassy, Tokyo, to Far Eastern Department, Foreign Office, 4 December 1939).

178. All the same, curiouser and curiouser, a strange piece of autobiographical writing survives among Empson's papers that does seem to suggest that he really had been trailed while in Chungking in 1937:

> The most alarmingly magical thing in my life occurred just before getting onto the boat at Chungking, when I spent some time wandering about the town. It looks much more European than Changsha, with open streets and natty department stores, though you can certainly buy much more in Changsha; the look of the streets depends on governors of provinces. As I looked at my watch and turned round to go home I was jostled against by a small snotty boy with a squint and a cap on one side, who was looking earnestly up, not at me, but at something just behind my head. I pushed away with an obscure fear of skin diseases and walked briskly forward, dodging the dawdling crowd on the pavement, for about a hundred yards, and then I was held up; and at once I was jostled against by exactly the same small boy doing exactly the same thing. I thought he was inquisitive about foreigners, or liable to beg, or anyway disagreeable for some reason, and walked on as briskly as I could. I only knew one roundabout way through the town which took about two hours fast walking; it must have been an absurd route, but it would just fill in my time and asking the way is always useless. After the same thing had happened five times at five enforced pauses I began

telling myself that this was quite a magical incident that had happened to me, and I kept a sharp eye on the road behind me, as well as walking pretty fast, in order to make sure that the incident was closed. We are all pleased with magic as a story, and I was quite pleased to half-believe in it as a thing that had happened. It happened three times more. I am sure that I can get through a crowded pavement faster than that decrepit small boy, and he was very recognisable. I stood waiting and watching for him, and I could see a good way back, he was only in sight when I was stopped involuntarily; and he was always looking in exactly the same wrong place, and always touching me. Whatever really happened I was pushed out of thinking I had made the thing up.

While Empson thus theorized about his own magical Oliver Twist, perhaps the incident really does lend hilarious credence to the suggestion that he was followed in Chungking at the bidding of the Japanese secret police.

179. WE, 'Living in Japan' (unsigned), *The Listener*, 4 November 1936, p. 876.
180. Small notebook (Empson Papers).

12. *POEMS* 1935

1. Ian Parsons, letter to WE, 6 June 1929. 'Before putting you to the trouble of preparing elaborate notes, etc.,' Parsons added, 'would it not be best for you to send us a typescript of the twenty odd poems, without any notes, which you intend to include.'

2. F. R. Leavis, 'Intelligence and Sensibility', *Cambridge Review*, 16 January 1931, p. 187.

3. Ian Parsons, letter to WE, 20 February 1933 (Reading). 'How do you feel? . . .' Parsons asked. 'It would be nice, anyway, to have a book of your poems on the stocks.'

4. A year in advance of WE's first British volume, *Poems* (1935), fourteen of the early poems were bound in marbled covers for private circulation, likewise with the bare title *Poems*, by The Fox & Daffodil Press, at Kinuta-mura, near Tokyo. A note written in Japanese and signed by 'Members of the Fox and Daffodil Press'—Tamotsu Sone, Yoshitaka Sakai, and Tsuneo Kitamura (who were presumably among WE's students at the Tokyo Bun-rika Daigaku)—translates as follows: 'This collection of poems was printed with the author's approval on the limitation of 100 copies, so as to be distributed among his acquaintances and pupils. Mr Empson will return to England before long, and we shall be very happy if this small volume becomes a good memento of his sojourn in Japan. We are deeply indebted to Mr Shinobu, head of the Kairyudo Publishing Company, for this publication.'

5. See obituary of Trekkie Parsons by Janet Adam Smith in *The Independent* (29 July 1995); and *The Times* (2 August 1995).

6. By way of contrast, Auden's first volume, *Poems* (1930), which was likewise first issued in a printing of 1,000 copies, sold more than 6,500 in the decade;

Look, Stranger! (1936) sold out an initial printing of 2,350 copies within two months. Auden's sales were quite exceptional in the 1930s.

7. 'Donne in our Time', in Theodore Spencer (ed.), *A Garland for John Donne* (Cambridge, Mass.: Harvard University Press, 1931).

8. WE, 'Argufying in Poetry', *The Listener*, 22 August 1963, p. 277; *Argufying*, 167. In a later year (?1984) he would put it to his editor in another way, pseudo-dyspeptically: 'Nowadays it is usual for a poet to present himself as a lost bunnyrabbit' (draft letter to Andrew Motion; Empson Papers).

9. Rosemund Tuve, *Elizabethan and Jacobean Imagery* (1947; repr. Chicago: University of Chicago Press, 1961), 419.

10. See Ronald Schuchard, *Eliot's Dark Angel: Intersections of Life and Art* (New York: Oxford University Press, 1999), ch. 2: 'Hulme of Original Sin', 52–69.

11. T. E. Hulme, *Speculations* (London: Kegan Paul, 1924), 127, 152, 154, 164.

12. WE's slightly impaired appreciation of Virginia Woolf, prompted by traditional narrative expectations of the novel, led him for much the same reasons to criticize the fallaciousness of her 'impressionist method': 'it tries to substitute for telling a story, as the main centre of interest, what is in fact one of the by-products of telling a story; it tries to correlate sensations rather than the impulses which make the sensations interesting ... All one can say against the wilful and jumping brilliance of Mrs Woolf's descriptive passages is that, as part of a design, they come to seem unsatisfying ... [I]f only these dissolved units of understanding had been co-ordinated into a system ... [I]f only these materials for the metaphysical conceit, poured out so lavishly, had been concentrated into crystals of poetry ...' ('Virginia Woolf', in Edgell Rickword (ed.), *Scrutinies*, 2 (London: Wishart & Co., 1931), 214–16; *Argufying*, 448–9).

T. S. Eliot's concentration on the local 'verbal conceit' of metaphysical poetry and the unified sensibility it conveyed can be seen to have neglected the formal or structural character of the best of metaphysical verse. As WE protested of Marvell's 'The Coronet', for example, 'if the technique is not used to say something, it is not used at all ... [I]t was hammered out to carry a firm and passionate mental operation ...' ('The Love of Definition', *Cambridge Review*, 25 May 1979, p. 145; *Argufying*, 267).

On the question of 'visual images', WE wrote further: 'I should confess to a prejudice here, in that I am a nonvisualizer, never getting a row of pictures when I read a line of verse; though I can see visions as well as the next man, especially after an eye operation. But anyway the mere existence of nonvisualizers is enough to refute most of the cluster of Imagist beliefs' ('Yeats and the Spirits', *The New York Review of Books*, 13 December 1973, p. 43; *Argufying*, 353).

13. WE, 'More Barren Leaves' (review of *Proper Studies*, by Aldous Huxley), *The Granta*, 18 November 1927, p. 123; *EG* 28.

14. 'Argufying in Poetry', *The Listener*, 22 August 1963, pp. 277, 290; *Argufying*, p. 167–70. WE paraphrases Graham Hough's observation, 'To attempt to explain to an intelligent person who knows nothing about twentieth-century

poetry how *The Waste Land* works is to be overcome with embarrassment at having to justify principles so affected, so perverse, so deliberately removed from the ordinary modes of communication' (*Image and Experience* (London: Gerald Duckworth, 1960), 28). The extended argument of Hough's opening chapter, 'Reflections on a Literary Revolution', supports WE in baiting the significance of the Imagist 'school', as in this declaration: 'I should like to commit myself to the view that . . . the collocation of images is not a method at all, but the negation of method. In fact, to expose myself completely, I want to say that a poem, internally considered, ought to make the same kind of sense as any other discourse' (p. 25). WE quotes T. E. Hulme by way of Herbert Read, *The True Voice of Feeling* (London: Faber & Faber, 1953), 109: 'Thought is prior to language and consists in the simultaneous presentation to the mind of two images.' The aphorism was originally quoted from Hulme by Michael Roberts in *T. E. Hulme* (London: Faber & Faber, 1938), 281. See further WE's review, 'Jam Theory and Imagism', in *Argufying*, 113–16.

15. Hugh Kenner, 'Son of Spiders', *Poetry*, June 1950.
16. A. Alvarez, '"A Style from a Despair": William Empson', *The Twentieth Century*, April 1957.
17. F. W. Bateson, 'Auden's (and Empson's) Heirs', *Essays in Criticism*, January 1957.
18. Denis Donoghue, 'Reading a Poem: Empson's "Arachne"', *Studies*, 45 (1956), 220.
19. *Metaphysical Lyrics and Poems of the Seventeenth Century*, ed. H. Grierson (Oxford: Clarendon Press, 1921), p. xxvi.
20. 'Donne the Space Man', *Kenyon Review*, 19 (Summer 1957), 344, 350; *Essays on Renaissance Literature*, 1, p. 84.
21. 'Donne the Space Man', 339, 341; *Argufying*, 79, 81.
22. WE, 'Donne and the Rhetorical Tradition', *Kenyon Review*, 2 (1949), 581; *Argufying*, 71.
23. WE, 'Donne and the Rhetorical Tradition', 580; *Argufying*, 71.
24. WE, 'Donne the Space Man', 347; *Argufying*, 86.
25. WE, *Complete Poems*, 257.
26. 'The Union,' *The Granta*, 28 October 1927, p. 66.
27. WE, letter to Qien Xuexi, 7 September 1947 (courtesy of Qien Xuexi).
28. Lewis Wolpert in conversation; also Wolpert, 'Let there be enlightenment' (a review of *The Faber Book of Science*, ed. John Carey), *Sunday Times*, 17 September 1995, book supplement, p. 4.
29. Monroe K. Spears, 'Cosmology and the Writer', *Hudson Review*, 47/1 (Spring 1994), 37.
30. T. R. Henn, 'Science and Poetry', *Nature* (5 August 1961), 534–9.
31. Kathleen Raine, 'And Learn a Style from a Despair', *New Statesman & Nation*, 5 November 1955.
32. Review of Elizabeth Holmes, *Aspects of Elizabethan Imagery*, in *Criterion*, 9/37 (July 1930), 770; repr. in *SSS* 68.

33. WE, 'Playne but Worthy' (rev. of *The Pre-War Mind in Britain*, by C. E. Playne), *The Granta*, 27 April 1928, p. 376; *EG* 51.

34. In Hesiod's *Theogony*, Styx is seen as a ninefold barrier which 'traverses that desolate place where are the sources and limits of the Earth . . .' (quoted in F. M. Cornford, *From Religion to Philosophy* (London: Edward Arnold, 1912), 24); it is a fence or Oath, a symbolic representation of Taboo.

35. WE, 'The Just Man Made Innocent', *New Statesman*, 19 April 1963; *Argufying*, 378.

36. 'The Metaphysical Foundations of Modern Science', *Criterion*, 10/38 (October 1930), 169; *Argufying*, 531.

37. James A. Coleman, *Relativity for the Layman* (Harmondsworth: Penguin, 1969), 126.

38. Coleman, *Relativity for the Layman*, 62.

39. *Experiment*, 4 (November 1929), 8.

40. *The Criterion*, 14 (1934–5), 483.

41. WE, 'Ballet of the Far East', *The Listener*, 7 July 1937, p. 16; *Argufying*, 577.

42. 'Buddhism obviously deserves respect; for one thing, though not only, as an extreme; it needs to be remembered when one tries to survey what the human mind could think about a subject. But I naturally would not want to present myself as a believer by mistake' ('Everything, beggars, is on fire', *Arrows* (Sheffield University), New Year edition 1957, p. 6; *Argufying*, 600).

43. WE, 'Ballet of the Far East', 16; *Argufying*, 577.

44. WE, undated letter (1929–30) to Julian Trevelyan (courtesy of the late Julian Trevelyan, whose papers are now in the Wren Library, Trinity College, Cambridge).

45. WE, *Argufying*, 70–87.

46. WE, undated letter to Ian Parsons, received 6 June 1929.

47. Grover Smith, *The Waste Land* (London: George Allen & Unwin, 1983), 81 (Unwin Critical Library).

48. In 1929, WE took this view: 'When Mr Eliot writes notes to *The Waste Land* so as to imply "well, if you haven't read such and such a play by Middleton, you had better go and do it at once"—the schoolmaster's tone is an anachronism, it belongs to a time when knowledge could be treated as a unified field. An odd reference does not even show that the writer is learned on a subject; it may merely be a piece of information that had stuck in his head, and become useful as a metaphor. Everybody's reading is miscellaneous and scrappy, like his' ('Obscurity and Annotation', *Argufying*, 71).

49. T. S. Eliot, *On Poetry and Poets* (London: Faber & Faber, 1957), 109–10. The publication history of *The Waste Land* is now known to be more complicated than Eliot liked to maintain: see Lawrence Rainey, 'The Price of Modernism: Publishing *The Waste Land*', in Ronald Bush (ed.), *T. S. Eliot: The Modernist in History* (Cambridge, 1991), 91–133.

50. WE, undated letter to Ian Parsons, received 14 June 1929 (Reading). He would make use of the same joke in his paper on 'Obscurity and Annotation', *Argufying*, 72.

51. WE, 'A London Letter', *Poetry*, 49 (1937), 222; *Argufying*, 417.

52. WE, 'To Understand a Modern Poem', *Strand*, March 1947; *Argufying*, 383.

53. Steven Connor, *Postmodernist Culture: An Introduction to Theories of the Contemporary* (Oxford: Basil Blackwell, 1989), 99.

54. Hilary Corke, 'Riding a Hare', *The Listener*, 54/1388 (6 October 1955), 565.

55. S. Sultan, *Ulysses, The Waste Land, and Modernism* (Port Washington, NY, 1977), 41; cited in Smith, *The Waste Land*, 80. J. H. Willis Jr. notes: 'Never providing exact documentation, Empson's notes, while explanatory, are often self-contained. Contrapuntal in effect, usually providing another dimension to the poem, they expand the meaning, or add the pleasures of prose to poetry' (*William Empson* (New York: Columbia University Press, 1969), 28–9). Jean-Jacques Lecercle has some interesting things to say about the 'strangeness' of WE's notes, in 'William Empson's Cosmicomics' (Christopher Norris and Nigel Mapp (eds.), *William Empson: The Critical Achievement* (Cambridge: Cambridge University Press, 1993), 269–93). 'Empson's notes are not at all like Eliot's,' Lecercle writes. 'They do not indicate sources but provide explanations in the etymological sense of unfolding of meaning. Besides, we do need them. They often provide meaning which is so close to Wittgenstein's "private language" (that notorious impossibility) that we could hardly have expected to recover it . . . There is a teasing aspect to the notes: more information is proffered than we could reasonably have expected, and yet some of the information we did expect—at times, most of it—is withdrawn. Nor is this, of course, a criticism of Empson: complete explanation would reduce the reader's effort towards understanding to nothing, insufferably constrain his or her freedom of interpretation, and make the act of reading somewhat boring' (pp. 273–4).

56. Robert Lowell, letter to WE, 29 January 1958 (Empson Papers). John Betjeman, reviewing *Complete Poems* in the *Daily Telegraph*, 1955, remarked: 'William Empson's "Collected Poems" are few and difficult, and to me reluctantly fascinating. I turn to them again and again.'

   Roy Campbell, in 'William Empson: Contemporary English Poet and Scholar' (an undated article produced during the war by the Central Office of Information and circulated in agreement with the British Council [S.6547]), offered these generous personal remarks:

   > In the notes you meet Mr Empson himself, and that is a charming experience. You meet a man with a radiant human curiosity and an erudition about non-academical things which counterbalances the very learned scholar who is also inherent in Empson. Little chips and splinters of personal experience and reminiscence fit into the main outlines of his more impersonal and philosophic utterance. You feel that the annotator is intensely human, although the poet may be completely

impersonal. But the annotator certainly breaks the ice in introducing you personally to the poet. Empson's poetry is full of doom and disillusion, but for all that there is an uncommon witty gaiety about it. . . .

Mr Empson is one of the few English writers whose conversation is on a level with his writing. It is rare nowadays for anyone except an Irishman to speak English in complete sentences without hesitating; but when Empson gets well launched into one of his celebrated monologues he takes one back to the great days of English conversation in the eighteenth century. In listening to Empson's conversation one gets a key to the amazingly mathematical construction which underlies his poetry, for although his conversation sparkles with all the incidental brilliancies which are the delight of all convivial company, one is even more struck by the architectural design of his reasoning and the control which he exerts over the most abstruse and complicated matters.

57. Ian Hamilton, 'A Conversation with Robert Lowell', *The Review*, 26 (Summer 1971), repr. in *Robert Lowell: Interviews and Memoirs*, ed. Jeffrey Meyers (Ann Arbor: University of Michigan Press, 1988), 154. Philip Booth, 'Summers in Castine: Contact Prints, 1955–1965', *Salmagundi*, 37 (Spring 1977), repr. in *Robert Lowell*, ed. Meyers, p. 196. Robert Lowell, 'Digressions from Larkin's 20th-Century Verse', *Encounter*, 40/5 (May 1973), 68.

When Christopher Ricks approached Lowell to see if he would contribute to the WE Festschrift which Roma Gill was then editing (*William Empson: The Man and His Work*, 1974), Lowell replied on a postcard postmarked 16 January 1973: 'Doing something on William has long defeated me, I'm afraid. No poem comes; a considered critical essay is beyond my uncritical talents; I can't somehow catch hold of him briefly in a paragraph or two. My kind of judgment edged out of reminiscence would be impertinent in a festschrift. I've been through this with my old friend Allen Tate, and finally did nothing. William is one of the few (only?) people I read every scrap of and am never disappointed. I don't want to disappoint by promising a piece I won't write' (courtesy of Christopher Ricks).

58. Robert Fitzgerald speaks of the influence of WE on Lowell's *Lord Weary's Castle*, in 'The Things of the Eye', *Poetry*, 132 (May 1978), repr. in *Robert Lowell: Interviews and Memoirs*, ed. Meyers, p. 225.

59. John Berryman's copy of *Complete Poems* (1949) is in Special Collections, Wilson Library, University of Minnesota. Berryman and Lowell's contemporary Randall Jarrell was to write: 'I have not written about the hard or dry or "classical" tendencies of some modern verse—what Empson and Marianne Moore have in common, for instance . . . ' ('The End of the Line', *The Nation*, 21 February 1942; repr. in *Kipling, Auden & Co.: Essays and Reviews 1935–1964* (New York: Farrar, Straus & Giroux, 1980; Manchester: Carcanet Press, 1980), 83).

60. MacNeice, entry for WE in *The Concise Encyclopedia of English and American Poets and Poetry*, ed. Stephen Spender and Donald Hall (London: Hutchinson & Co., 1963), 128. MacNeice concluded strangely, 'And of his generation he is probably unique in that he has not a trace of self-pity.'

61. WE, letter to A. Alvarez, 29 August 1956 (courtesy of A. Alvarez). Alvarez was to write the following year, in 'A Style from a Despair: William Empson': 'the poetry is an outcome of a peculiarly strong and sensitive feeling for the intellectual tone of the time. Empson seems to create less out of personal situations than out of an emotional response to something he has already known with his wits, intellectually ... It is as a stylist of poetry and ideas that, I think, Empson is most important' (*The Twentieth Century*, 161 (April 1957), 346). G. S. Fraser was astute to note of WE's verse, 'There is a sense of an intricate, witty, and deliberately puzzling form being imposed on a massive and almost unbearable personal unhappiness' (*Contemporary Poets*, ed. James Vinson (London: Macmillan Press, 1970; 3rd edn., 1980), 439). Likewise Graham Hough, in an obituary article on WE: 'It is often the case that what comes across to most readers as an intricate intellectual puzzle was experienced as a painful knot of feeling' (*The London Review of Books*, 21 June–4 July 1984, p. 17). Compare David Perkins's good remarks: 'Intricate, ironically poised, sardonic, and disintoxicated, Empson's poems appealed because of their intellectual excitement, complexity, and honest bleakness ...

    'Yet strong emotion was present. If his style was witty and "metaphysical" in some ways, his hurt was Hardy's. He accused God for not existing and man for his mortality ... We may be tempted to justify Empson's style by New Critical considerations, but the state of mind and the psychological struggle embodied in his poems are what fascinates and holds us' (*A History of Modern Poetry: Modernism and After* (Cambridge, Mass.: Harvard University Press, 1987), 100–1).

62. See Anthony Hartley, 'Poets of the Fifties', *The Spectator*, 193 (1954), 260–1. Aspects of WE's poetry had an influence too on certain poems by Auden, most notably 'Time will say nothing but I told you so' (1940; entitled 'Villanelle' on first publication in 1941); 'Sometimes we see astonishingly clearly' (1949); and 'All that which lies outside our sort of why' (1956): see John Fuller, *W. H. Auden: A Commentary* (London: Faber & Faber, 1998), 400, 409, 467. Sylvia Plath also took lessons from WE, in her juvenilia of the early 1950s, in poems such as 'To Eva Descending the Stair: A Villanelle': see *Collected Poems*, ed. Ted Hughes (London: Faber & Faber, 1981), 303.

63. WE, 'Literary Opinion' (broadcast 20 October 1954); copy in Empson Papers. The villanelle-parody to which he referred was Patric Dickinson's 'At the Villa Nelle', which concludes: 'That the young have taken Empson for a master | One cannot but regard as a disaster' (*Encounter*, 3/1 (July 1954), 63). An article entitled 'Double Target', in the *TLS* (10 September 1954), was to remark: 'Poets of smaller stature than Mr Eliot or Mr Pound, poets in some ways much more "traditionalist" like Mr Empson or Mr Graves, today provide young poets with more practical working models than the two great experimental masters.' In a letter to the *TLS* (1 October 1954), Robert Graves took exception to that observation: 'Let us ... hope that your reviewer

does not envisage Mr Empson and myself as respectively the Waller and Denham of a new Augustan age.' Anthony Thwaite disputed the notion of undue indebtedness in a letter, 'Young Writers', published in *Encounter*, 2/5 (May 1954), 67–8. For an example of direct (and acknowledged) influence, see John Wain's 'The Marksman'.

Other parodies of WE include Dylan Thomas's incomplete villanelle, written in 1940, 'Request to Leda: Homage to William Empson', first published in *Horizon*, 6/31 (July 1942), 6; D. J. Enright, 'Underneath the Arches', *Essays in Criticism* (October 1956); Richard Kell, 'Empsonium', *London Magazine*, 6/10 (October 1959), 55–6; and L. E. Sissman, 'Just a Whack at Empson', *The Review* (June 1963), 75. See also Babette Deutsch, 'Just a Smack at Empson's Epigoni', *Poetry London-New York*, 1/3 (Winter 1957), 47. G. S. Fraser, in his introduction to *Poetry Now: An Anthology* (London: Faber & Faber, 1956, p. 23), remarked that Empson's epigoni found in him 'a mind of the first order ... exercising an ironic control over an inner core of passion'. Edwin Muir, in a review of Fraser's collection (*The Observer*, 14 October 1956), disputed Fraser's claim with this tribute to WE: 'The passion in Mr Empson's poetry is uncomfortably real, almost raw (*Slowly the poison the whole blood-stream fills*), and the control is difficult. He moves us by the spectacle of a shocking struggle for control. In his followers the control is almost complete; the passion is stifled before it has a chance to be born.' In a review of the anthologies *The Chatto Book of Modern Poetry*, ed. C. Day Lewis and John Lehmann (London: Chatto & Windus, 1956), and *New Lines*, ed. Robert Conquest (London: Macmillan, 1956), Ian Gregor concluded: 'In the austere Pantheon of the new poets two prominent niches are occupied by George Orwell and Mr Empson. The hatred of theoretical systems of the one and the tense verbal exactness of the other have blended to influence a body of poetry which is notably different from that of recent decades. Decorous, ironical, ratiocinative, it is verse which the eighteenth century would have understood, and if we fail to respond to it, it is because the ethos of the Coffee Shop has become irretrievably lost in that of the Espresso Bar' (*The Tablet*, 10 November 1956).

64. Quoted (with my ellipsis) in TS letter from John Hayward to Frank Morley— 'Tarantula's Special News Service. Letter V'—October 1939 (King's College Library, Cambridge).

13. SCAPEGOAT AND SACRIFICE

1. WE, letter to Katherine Sansom, 13 January 1935 (Empson Papers).
2. WE in undated interview with Christopher Norris and David Wilson (courtesy of Christopher Norris).
3. Andrew Ettin, *Literature and the Pastoral* (New Haven: Yale University Press, 1984), 189; quoted in Annabel Patterson, *Pastoral and Ideology: Virgil to Valéry* (Berkeley and Los Angeles: University of California Press, 1987), 7.

4. For a review of the development of the volume, and its critical reception, see Lisa A. Rodensky, 'Prefatory Note: On Origins, Revision and Reception', in *Some Versions of Pastoral* (Harmondsworth: Penguin, 1995), pp. vii–xxviii; John Constable (ed.), *Critical Essays on William Empson* (Aldershot: Scolar Press, 1993). 'Empson explicitly names pastoral as a concern [for the first time] in his October 1933 article on Shakespeare's Sonnet 94,' remarks Rodensky (p. xiii).

5. WE, 'Some Versions of Pastoral', *TLS*, 7 December 1935, p. 838.

6. G. W. Stonier complained in a review, 'Mr Empson avoids even mentioning the more straightforward forms of pastoral . . . and this flight from the obvious seems to me a weakness, because it deprives his book of the norm which it so plainly needs. He deals only with exceptions, with remote variations' ('Complexity', *New Statesman and Nation*, 10/243 (19 October 1935)). Christopher Norris reasonably remarks that pastoral for Empson may figure 'as a cover-term or conveniently loose generic description for the kinds of text that enabled Empson to address matters of depth-psychology (or downright conflicts of motive and meaning) . . . ' ('For Truth in Criticism: William Empson and the Claims of Theory', in *The Truth about Postmodernism* (Oxford: Basil Blackwell, 1993), 115).

7. Compare Norris's justifiable comment that 'Empsonian pastoral is not so much a *genre* or literary "form" as a standing possibility for endless variations on a basic structure of feeling, a technique of self-complicating irony . . . ' ('For Truth in Criticism', 111).

8. Compare Empson's commentary on the image of Christ in Herbert's poem: 'scapegoat and tragic hero; loved because hated; hated because godlike; freeing from torture because tortured; torturing his torturers because all-merciful; source of all strength to all men because by accepting he exaggerates their weakness; and, because outcast, creating the possibility of society' (*Ambiguity*, 233). In short, Empson was already defining Herbert's Christ in terms of the Frazerian sacrificial cult hero.

9. In an undated letter (1930) to Julian Trevelyan (who had succeeded him as secretary of the Cambridge Heretics and who had bravely invited him back to Cambridge to address the society), Empson wrote from London: 'it now occurs to me that I could read a paper . . . about whether poems ought to be annotated, whether it is important, and why it is hard. If you want a bright caption I suggest "Sphinx, or the future of exegesis"; and I can do that as soon as you want it. If it is too short for a paper (it is too long for a life) I could give examples from the Bentley edition of Milton, and the answers to Bentley, which I have been being very excited about (not because any of them are any good, of course, but they raise the crucial questions, and the answers by contemporaries are sometimes illuminating)' (Wren Library, Trinity College, Cambridge).

10. See Robert E. Bourdette, Jr., ' "To *Milton* lending sense": Richard Bentley and *Paradise Lost* ', *Milton Quarterly*, 14/2 (May 1980), 37–49; R. Gordon

Moyles, 'Iconoclast and Catalyst: Richard Bentley as Editor of *Paradise Lost*', in A. H. de Quehen (ed.), *Editing Poetry from Spenser to Dryden* (New York: Garland Publishing, 1981), 77–98; John K. Hale, 'Notes on Richard Bentley's Edition of *Paradise Lost* (1732)', *Milton Quarterly*, 18/2 (May 1984), 46–50; Joseph M. Levine, 'Bentley's Milton: Philology and Criticism in Eighteenth-Century England', *Journal of the History of Ideas*, 50/4 (October–December 1989), 549–68; Simon Jarvis, *Scholars and Gentlemen: Shakespearian Textual Criticism and Representations of Scholarly Labour 1725–1765* (Oxford: Oxford University Press, 1995).

11. The only immediately preceding study was an essay by J. W. Mackail, *Bentley's Milton*, Warton Lecture, XV (London, 1924). The most severe critic of Empson on Milton and Bentley has been Robert Bernard Adams, 'Empson and Bentley: *Scherzo*', in his *Ikon: John Milton and the Modern Critics* (Ithaca, NY: Cornell University Press, 1955), 112–27.

12. See *Paradise Lost*, ed. Alastair Fowler (Harlow: Longman, 1971), 301–2.

13. In some notes taken during the 1930s Empson enjoyed spotting a nice ambiguity in some lines from a late nineteenth-century translation of Dante's *Paradiso*; is Adam or Satan being referred to here?: '. . . that first proud being, | who was the summit of all creation, because | he would not wait for light, falling unripe' (The Revd Philip H. Wicksteed, *The Paradiso of Dante* [Temple Classics], London: J. M. Dent & Co., 1899, p. 231).

> Ambiguity by vagueness for both Adam and Satan, thus treating them as the same [Empson decided]. This is an opposite conception to Milton's of the Fall: here it is from seeking to know too much; there it was from forgetting what was known.
>
> Another important vagary from Christianity which the poets always tumble into is the treatment of Christ as the scapegoat, as himself in some sense really sinful and so fitted to his functions. (Empson Papers)

14. See also Jonathan Goldberg, *Sodometries: Renaissance Texts, Modern Sexualities* (Stanford, Calif.: Stanford University Press, 1992), 152–73.

15. Compare Giorgio Melchiori, 'Lilies that fester: The Strategy of Sonnet 94 and the Ethics of Power', in *Shakespeare's Dramatic Meditations: An Experiment in Criticism* (Oxford: Clarendon Press, 1976), 35–69. Norris remarks that Empson's account of Shakespeare's tribute to his patron is 'savagely double-edged': 'Indeed it is one of the great ironies of this book that it breezily flouts the New Critical veto on paraphrasing poems—most often by offering multiple attempts at prose summary—while its own interpretations are so complex (or so hedged about with qualifying ironies) that no paraphrase could possibly do them justice' ('For Truth in Criticism', 124).

16. Compare Norris's fair comment: 'Many readers have felt that the essay, like the poem, has a sense of quiet exhilaration which comes of its somehow holding these antinomies in a state of rapt, near-mystical repose, a mood seldom to be found in Empson's criticism' ('For Truth in Criticism', 112). See

also Philip Hobsbaum's review of the controversy apropos 'The Garden', in *A Theory of Communication* (Basingstoke: Macmillan Press, 1970), 135–41.

17. As Mark Thompson remarks, Empson was possessed of 'a large comparative approach, heroic and fundamental, formed at a moment when the cultural impact of Freud, Marx and Frazer was first widely felt... For Empson, psychoanalysis and anthropology were, like linguistics, always empirical, exploratory and humane' ('"On the borderland"', *Edinburgh Review*, 85 (1991), 102). On Frazer, see John B. Vickery, *The Literary Impact of 'The Golden Bough'* (Princeton: Princeton University Press, 1973); Robert Fraser, *The Making of 'The Golden Bough': The Origins and Growth of an Argument* (New York: St Martin's Press, 1990).

18. René Girard, *The Scapegoat* (1982), trans. Yvonne Freccero (Baltimore: Johns Hopkins University Press, 1986), 50. See also Robert Parker, *Miasma: Pollution and Purification in Early Greek Religion* (Oxford: Clarendon Press, 1983), ch. 9: 'Purifying the City'.

19. Girard, *The Scapegoat*, 120.

20. Wyndham Lewis, *The Lion and the Fox: The Rôle of the Hero in the Plays of Shakespeare* (London: Grant Richards, 1927), 135.

21. Rodensky notes: 'Smith's review carries a special significance for *Some Versions* because it helps Empson better describe his idea of pastoral in Shakespeare and Marvell. Empson's essay on double plots predates Smith's on metaphysical poetry, and what is striking... is that by connecting the double plot to metaphysical poetry and then to questions of the one and the many, Empson has begun to define his pastoral' (p. xiii).

22. James Smith, 'On Metaphysical Poetry', *Scrutiny*, 2/3 (December 1933), 227–8, 234–5. Compare Aldous Huxley's remarks in 'One and Many': 'Man can and does conceive of himself and of the world as being, now essentially many, and now essentially one. Therefore—since God, for our human purposes, is simply Life in so far as man can conceive it as a whole—the Divine is both one and many' (*Do What You Will: Essays* (London: Chatto & Windus, 1929), 46–7).

23. See Ben Jonson, *Works*, ed. C. H. Herford and P. Simpson (Oxford: Clarendon Press, 1925), i. 133.

24. 'Apart from Empson,' remarks Mark Thompson, 'the writers who were taking Lewis Carroll seriously in the thirties were the French surrealists' ('"On the borderland"', 103). 'Among literary critics... Empson was unique in using and synthesizing the intellectual discoveries of his day to build a coherent, historical worldview. His filigree interpretations of English poetry were earthed in a quirky, polymathic knowledge of the interplay, patterns and differences of world cultures' (p. 109).

25. Paul Alpers noted Empson's 'obliqueness in argument, his casualness about the unity of the book, his wit, colloquial ease and abruptness' ('Empson on Pastoral', *New Literary History*, 10/1 (Autumn 1978), 102). See also Paul Alpers, *What is Pastoral?* (Chicago: University of Chicago Press, 1996), 37–43.

26. The American critic René Wellek among others felt Empson had pushed 'Freudian allegorization very hard' (*A History of Modern Criticism: 1750–1950: English Criticism, 1900–1950* (London: Jonathan Cape, 1986), 283). Two of the foremost critics of Carroll, Lancelyn Green and Morton Cohen, have been 'dismissive about Empson as a commentator', report J. Elwyn Jones and J. Francis Gladstone. 'Cohen cannot even bring himself to mention the name of this great critic' (*The 'Alice' Companion: A Guide to Lewis Carroll's 'Alice' Books* (Basingstoke: Macmillan Press, 1998), 85). Jones and Gladstone nonetheless affirm: 'Empson's essay was the most serious attempt of its day to build contextual meaning into *Alice* criticism.'

27. The first English edition (price 8*s*. 6*d*.) ran to 1,750 copies; W. W. Norton distributed 1,600 copies in 1937; the second impression of 4,250 copies (of which 1,500 went to New Directions in the USA) appeared in 1949.

28. The term 'circumventory' is taken from a review by 'J.K.' in *The Granta*, 45 (30 October 1935), which remarked too: 'The association of both heroic and pastoral with the sacrificial cult idea is good, but, I feel, results in undue suggestion of the identity of pastoral and comic' (pp. 71–2). On the other hand, Dilys Powell, in a mostly laudatory review, felt there was 'an appalling amount of misplaced ingenuity' in the book, including the attempt to interpret Macheath in terms of mock-heroic, mock-pastoral, Dying God, and Christ (*Sunday Times*, 9 February 1936).

29. John Crowe Ransom, 'Mr Empson's Muddles', *Southern Review*, 4/2 (July–April 1938–9), 322–39.

30. Desmond Hawkins, 'Illuminated Texts', *The Spectator*, 95/5603 (15 November 1935); in Constable, 65. Compare H. A. Mason: 'The pastoral theme only imperfectly binds the eight essays together...The initial unity of the book being so slight the author has little scruple about pursuing digressions whenever (and it is not seldom) they invite' ('W. Empson's Criticism', *Scrutiny*, 4/3 (March 1936), 432; in Constable, 79).

31. G. W. Stonier, untitled review in *New Statesman and Nation*, 10/243 (19 October 1935), in Constable, 61, 63.

32. [J. Middleton Murry], 'Pastoral and Proletarian: In Search of All Possible Meanings', *TLS* 34/1765 (30 November 1935), 798; in Constable, 67.

33. WE, 'Some Versions of Empson', *TLS* 34/1776 (7 December 1935), 838; in Constable, *Critical Essays on William Empson*, 68. In an undated draft letter Empson emphasized, 'I followed my nose about what seemed interesting, with long interruptions, and did not realize how connected the result was till I fitted it together; but then I thought it all did fit together, surprisingly and reassuringly' (Houghton Library; quoted in Rodensky, p. ix). Alpers represents *Pastoral* only in terms of what he calls 'the two main ideas that run through it: first, that "the pastoral process" consists of "putting the complex into the simple", and second, that pastoral has a unifying social force, as a means of bridging differences and reconciling social classes' (p. 101)—though

both of those ideas are the starting point of Empson's enquiry rather than the conclusion. Similarly, John Constable, in his introduction to *Critical Essays on William Empson*, characterizes 'the book's thesis' as being 'the representation of the complex in terms of the simple' (p. 8), so overlooking the deeper thesis which connects the pastoral figure to the scapegoat and the sacrificial tragic hero, to the key dilemma of metaphysics, and to the detached intelligence. Constable does his subject a further disservice with the following remarks: 'Viewed as a series Empson's four books eddy about one another. *Some Versions of Pastoral* differs from *Seven Types of Ambiguity* merely in raising the level of examination from the sentence and the word to that of narrati- ve . . . [H]e is a critic with only a handful of closely knit subjects' (p. 11).

34. Denis Donoghue, 'Some Versions of Empson', *TLS*, 7 June 1974, pp. 597–8.
35. Alpers, 'Empson on Pastoral', 119. (Compare Thompson: 'his ideas are always historical, cultural-materialist' [' "On the borderland" ', 108].) Alpers misun- derstands Empson's remarks on the subversive and blasphemous implications of the way in which a writer such as Donne nominates a secular figure as 'Logos': 'There is only one hero in Empson who fully takes on the conflicts of other men and experiences them as his own. That is Christ himself, who, as Sale points out, stands as "a unifying figure in the background" of Empson's account of human culture' (p. 118). The quotation comes from Roger Sale, 'The Achievement of William Empson', in *Modern Heroism* (Berkeley and Los Angeles. University of California Press, 1973), 107–92.
36. 'I have sometimes expressed a solemn interest in the ancient craving for human sacrifice and its protean reappearances,' said Empson in 1961, 'but this does not imply Christian belief' (*Milton's God*, 10).
37. The sentiment is akin to Empson's remark: 'life is essentially inadequate to the human spirit, and yet . . . a good life must avoid saying so . . . ' (*Pastoral*, 114).

14. POLITICS, POETS, AND MASS-OBSERVATION

1. I. A. Richards, letter to T. S. Eliot, 29 October–7 November 1934, in *Selected Letters of I. A. Richards C.H.*, ed. John Constable (Oxford: Clarendon Press, 1990), 84. 'I should think he could tear up my Coleridge [in a review for *The Criterion*] pretty thoroughly if it needs it,' Richards added gamely.
2. I. A. Richards, letter to Eliot, 21 November 1934; *Selected Letters*, 85.
3. I. A. Richards, letter to D. Richards, 26 November 1934 (Magdalene).
4. F. R. Leavis, letter to Ronald Bottrall, 19 January 1935 (Harry Ransom Humanities Research Center, University of Texas at Austin); Ian MacKillop, *F. R. Leavis: A Life in Criticism* (London: Allen Lane, 1995), 205–6.
5. F. R. Leavis, letter to Ronald Bottrall, 26 March 1935 (HRC, Texas).
6. Leo Salingar, letter to Haffenden, 21 September 1987.
7. F. R. Leavis, letter to Ronald Bottrall, 5 December 1936 (HRC, Texas); MacKillop, *F. R. Leavis*, 157–9, 181.

8. I. A. Richards, letter to D. E. Richards, 26 November 1934 (Magdalene).

9. Richards, letter to D. E. Richards, 28 January 1936 (*Selected Letters*, 87).

10. Charles Hobday, *Edgell Rickword* (Manchester: Carcanet Press, 1989), 153.

11. Interview with Margaret Bottrall, 25 March 1991. Margaret Bottrall had been introduced to WE in 1928, at a hunt ball where Charles Empson—an imposing but shy figure—was trying to get engaged to a charming, pretty young woman named Monica Tomlin (who lived in Canterbury where her father was a canon). Charles brought his brother along to the ball, with the consequence that WE and Margaret (Monica's friend) ended up chatting very happily about metaphysical poetry.

12. During the war, as a Russian citizen, Igor Vinogradoff was not allowed to enlist in the British forces; instead, he worked as a scriptwriter for the BBC on such programmes as *The Shadow of the Swastika* (and on some features co-written with Empson), and later on the official history of the BBC. He became a naturalized British citizen after the war. Later, with the help of his son-in-law Anthony Hobson, he became a consultant to Sotheby's on Russian manuscripts; among other tasks, he catalogued the library of Serge Lifar for a sale in Monte Carlo. He also wrote many book reviews on Russian history for the *Daily Telegraph* and the *TLS*. He died in August 1987, the year before his daughter Tanya died of cancer. His papers on Russian history are now at Leeds University. The happiest eventuality of his life was that in 1923, on a visit from Oxford to Garsington, he fell in love with Julian, daughter of Philip and Lady Ottoline Morrell, but the parents, who rightly thought him a wild and penniless young man, forbade them to marry; later, having met again by chance in 1939 (she had married someone else in 1928), they carried on an affair throughout the war until 1946 when she finally divorced her husband and married Igor. (Information kindly supplied by Adrian Goodman.)

13. WE, 'A London Letter', *Poetry* (Chicago), 49 (1937); in *Argufying*, 415–16. He wrote similarly to Ralph Hodgson in Japan, on 20 August 1935: 'What I notice in London is that they have thrown out a lot of the Aliens' restaurants—a Chinese meal used to be as cheap a fill as you could get. But that won't stir your blood much. Also this eerie patience of everybody—they feel any sort of row will make things worse. I believe too that I have seen several Indians walking about with negroes—now that if true is very pregnant' (Ralph Hodgson Papers, Yale University: GEN MSS 245: Box 9, folder 177).

14. WE, 'The Collected Dylan Thomas', *New Statesman and Nation*, 15 May 1954; in *Argufying*, 393.

15. WE, 'A London Letter', *Argufying*, 416.

16. WE always admired Auden's genius; his review of Auden's early work, *Paid on Both Sides*, offers this encomiastic peroration: 'One reason the scheme [of the play] is so impressive is that it puts psychoanalysis and surrealism and all that, all the irrationalist tendencies which are so essential a part of the machinery of present-day thought, into their proper place; they are made part of the

normal and rational tragic form, and indeed what constitutes the tragic situation. One feels as if at the crisis of many, perhaps better, tragedies, it is just this machinery which has been covertly employed. Within its scale (twenty-seven pages) there is the gamut of all the ways we have of thinking about the matter; it has the sort of completeness that makes a work seem to define the attitude of a generation' ('A Note on W. H. Auden's *Paid on Both Sides*' (1931); *Argufying*, 371).

In an unpublished essay on pacifism drafted sometime after 1941, WE chose to defend a famous line of Auden's poetry that would be subject to attack from various quarters, most notably by George Orwell: 'Voigt was saying in a political book that the poets are all warmongers now, and illustrated this by a line from Auden's *Spain*: "The conscious acceptance of guilt in the necessary murder". Of course a paradox can always be read several ways: *murder* says this act of killing is wicked, and *necessary* (for the ends considered) says it is good, so you don't know what sorts of killing the poet has in view. But surely it comes from a conscience sensitive about war rather than brutalised. Cf. the song of Deborah, for real warmongering. But maybe there is a kind of German-philosophic quality in the line, which Voigt might feel more of a Nazi weapon than Auden did. The more striking thing about Auden is the horror of Power, e.g. The Ascent of F6. All power corrupts . . . It is remarkable to me that nobody has yet turned the epigram of Lord Acton backwards. All impotence corrupts; absolute impotence corrupts absolutely. This is quite as true as the other, but maybe they only recommend the same thing, a wide spreading of power through the country. It is always hard to translate the wisdom of the literary into political plans.' (Empson Papers)

17. WE, 'Early Auden' (1963), in *Argufying*, 375.
18. Auden quoted in Humphrey Carpenter, *W. H. Auden: A Biography* (London: Allen & Unwin, 1981), 153; Louis MacNeice in Jon Stallworthy, *Louis MacNeice* (London: Faber & Faber, 1995), 153. See also Justin Replogle, 'Auden's Marxism', *PMLA*, 80 (December 1965), 584–95.
19. 'Early Auden', in *Argufying*, 375–6.
20. 'Just a Smack at Auden' was first published in *Contemporary Poetry and Prose* (Autumn 1937), 24–6; it was reprinted in *The Year's Poetry 1938* (London, 1938). WE may have learnt about Benda's counter-campaign from reading a piece by T. S. Eliot, 'The Idealism of Julien Benda', that appeared in the *Cambridge Review*, 49 (6 June 1928, pp. 485–8), directly alongside WE's poem 'Letter' (later 'Letter II').
21. WE in *The Ambiguity of William Empson*, BBC Radio 3 (22 October 1977), produced by David Perry (National Sound Archive, The British Library: T1726W).
22. WE, letter to Andrew Motion, 14 August 1983 (Chatto & Windus Archive, University of Reading Library).

23. WE, letter to Christopher Ricks, 19 January 1975 (courtesy of Christopher Ricks). In 'Early Auden' (1975), he remarked too: 'I have sometimes known later critics say, "Oh, well, Empson wasn't so much of a mug as to be a pylon poet; he may have very little to say, but at least he didn't say that." Well, of course, I agreed with the pylon poets entirely. I've always felt I ought to make that point plain whenever I had the opportunity: I think they were quite right, I just didn't know how to do this kind of poetry' (*Argufying*, 375–6).

24. Janet Adam Smith quoted in *The Ambiguity of William Empson*. On Janet Adam Smith (1905–99), see obituaries in the *Daily Telegraph*, 14 September 1999; *The Guardian* (by Nicolas Barker), 14 September 1999; *The Independent* (by Leonard Miall), 13 September 1999; and *The Times*, 13 September 1999.

25. Interview with Arthur Calder-Marshall, 19 June 1988.

26. Courtesy of Theodore Hofmann. WE was wittily echoing the White Knight's exchange with Alice, in chapter 8 ('It's my own Invention'), of *Through the Looking Glass, and What Alice Found There*:

> '. . . The name of the song is called "*Haddocks' Eyes*".'
>
> 'Oh, that's the name of the song, is it?' Alice said, trying to feel interested.
>
> 'No, you don't understand,' the Knight said, looking a little vexed. 'That's what the name is *called*. The name really *is* "*The Aged Man*".'
>
> 'Then I ought to have said, "That's what the *song* is called"?' Alice corrected herself.
>
> 'No, you oughtn't: that's another thing. The *song* is called "*Ways and Means*": but that's only what it's *called*, you know!'

27. John Hayward, letter to Frank Morley, October 1938 (Hayward Collection, King's College, Cambridge: JDH/FVM/15).

28. Interview with Julian Trevelyan.

29. Undated interview with Christopher Norris and David Wilson.

30. David Gascoyne, *Journal 1936–37* (London: Enitharmon Press, 1980), 59. David Gascoyne (1916–2001) was a poet, translator, essayist, and diarist, and first chronicler of surrealism. See obituaries in the *Daily Telegraph* and *The Guardian* (both 27 November 2001), *The Times* (28 November 2001).

31. Desmond Hawkins, *When I Was: A Memoir of the Years between the Wars* (Basingstoke: Macmillan Press, 1989), 118. Julian Trevelyan, in conversation with me, remembered once going with Davenport, WE, and Thomas to Hampstead Heath—and Thomas telling smutty stories into the small hours.

32. 'London Letter', *Argufying*, 417.

33. Ibid. 416–17.

34. WE, 'Some More Dylan Thomas', *The Listener*, 28 October 1971; in *Argufying*, 408. 'I remember his telling me how frightening it was always to have nothing to do next day,' WE elsewhere recalled of Thomas: 'sometimes, he said, "I buy a Mars Bar, and I think tomorrow I will eat that, so then I can go to sleep, because I have a plan." I did not much like this highly polished bit of tear-jerking, but there is little doubt that unemployment would have driven

me to drink too.' Still, everything would be forgiven Thomas because of his sense of humour: 'He was so immensely entertaining that many people felt themselves adequately repaid. Drink was necessary to screw him up to the duty of entertainment, and because the whole party (however assembled) must be seduced into joining the feast of wit' ('Dylan Thomas in Maturity', a review of *The Life of Dylan Thomas*, by Constantine FitzGibbon, in *The New Statesman*, 29 October 1965; *Argufying*, 407.

35. E. W. F. Tomlin, *T. S. Eliot: A Friendship* (London: Routledge, 1988), 91.

36. T. S. Eliot, letter to I. A. Richards, 24 September 1935: 'your two best pupils are too disreputable to get jobs . . . ' (Richards Papers). WE liked to purvey an item of gossip that arose from one visit to Faber & Faber, where he discovered Eliot hunched in irritation over a copy of Leavis's periodical *Scrutiny*: 'how *disgusting* the behaviour of Leavis was, what mob oratory his arguments were, couldn't something be done to stop him?—and then, with cold indignation, "Of course, I know it's going to be me next?" At that time, Leavis was adulating Eliot with all the breath he had to spare from denouncing Richards. I was not an intimate friend, as the anecdote may seem to claim, but neither was I eavesdropping; he just accepted anyone who was in the office as an honorary member of the conversation. Being a disciple of Richards, I was already sure of the truth of what Eliot was saying, but I was surprised to hear him say it, and thought it did him great credit, as I still do' ('The Hammer's Ring' [1973], *Argufying*, 217). However, WE was indiscreet or provocative enough to pass on Eliot's comments even to Leavis himself: WE 'unguardedly (he's not humanly intelligent) let on about that Russell Square glimpse to me in the 1930s,' wrote Leavis at the time (quoted in MacKillop, *F. R. Leavis*, 207).

37. T. S. Eliot to John Hayward, 13 October 1936 (Hayward Bequest, King's College, Cambridge: 1/12/1/5).

38. Interview with Igor Vinogradoff, 1985.

39. Interview with Julian Trevelyan.

40. WE, 'The Style of the Master', in Richard March and Tambimuttu (eds.), *T. S. Eliot: A Symposium* (London: Editions Poetry London, 1948); in *Argufying*, 362–3.

41. Ibid., 362.

42. WE, from a TV film *The Mysterious Mr Eliot*, directed by Stephen Cross (New York: McGraw-Hill Films, n.d.), cited in Russell Kirk, 'Eliot's Christian Imagination', in *The Placing of T. S. Eliot*, ed. Jewel Spears Brooker (Columbia: University of Missouri Press, 1991), 139.

43. The following five paragraphs are indebted to Janet Adam Smith's memoir, 'A is B at 8,000 feet', in Gill, 34–40.

44. This and the following paragraph are indebted to an interview with Igor Chroustchoff, 1 January 1991.

45. WE, interview with Norris and Wilson. Boris's friend Cecil Gray later invoked him as 'a descendant of the *boyar* mentioned in the Boris Godounov

of Pushkin and Moussorgsky, an eminent bibliophile and the greatest living authority on edible fungi, who hates work even more than Norman Douglas and I, and with whom I once walked from Bayonne to Carcassone...' (*Musical Chairs: or Between Two Stools: Being the Life and Memoirs* (London: Home & Van Thal, 1948), 291).

46. His son Igor Chroustchoff told me in 1991 that many years later he was working for a period in the post room at the Royal Free Hospital in London; once, he spotted a telegram for WE and took it up to his room. 'Boris! Yes! A wonderful voice! I should have kept up,' exclaimed WE.

47. See Barry Smith, *Peter Warlock: The Life of Philip Heseltine* (Oxford: Oxford University Press, 1994); and British Library Add. MS 57794.

48. *Contemporary Poets Reading Their Own Poems*, British Council (National Sound Archive, British Library: 10226 WR).

49. J. H. Willis, Jr., 'The Poetry of William Empson' (unpublished Ph.D. thesis: Columbia University, New York, 1967), 291.

50. 'George Herbert and Miss Tuve' (1950), in *Argufying*, 253.

51. WE, interview with Christopher Norris and David Wilson.

52. On Madge (1912–96), see obituaries in *The Times*, 25 January 1996; *The Guardian* (by Angus Calder), 20 January 1996; *The Independent* (by Michael Young), 24 January 1996.

53. Edith Sitwell was to praise WE's poetry, along with that of Ronald Bottrall and Dylan Thomas, in her Northcliffe Lecture—'Three Eras of Modern Poetry' (which drew on her book *Aspects of Modern Poetry*)—at the University of London in 1937 (John Lehmann, *A Nest of Tigers: Edith, Osbert and Sacheverell Sitwell in Their Times* (London: Macmillan, 1968), 134–5).

54. Of the great fire at the old Crystal Palace, David Gascoyne observed: 'For most of us,—we Mass-Observationists that is to say—it represented in a sort of symbolic way an image of the world-conflagration which we were already beginning to think of as about to break out, and we felt that it meant this, unconsciously, to the general public...' (*Journal 1936–37*, 9).

55. Jeremy MacClancy, 'Brief Encounter: The Meeting, in Mass-Observation, of British Surrealism and Popular Anthropology', *Journal of the Royal Anthropological Institute*, 1/3 (September 1995), 498.

56. Kathleen Raine, *Defending Ancient Spring* (London: Oxford University Press, 1967), 47.

57. Gascoyne, *Journal 1936–37*, 60. 'But what a bore!' Gascoyne went on. 'His poems get steadily duller and more wooden; though some of his early ones, like "Arachne" or "The proper scale" ["The Scales"], apart from their intellectual crossword-puzzle ingenuity (or their famous ambiguity) are, in a certain way, decoratively or evocatively, quite exciting.' However, in 1980 he reflected (p. 12): 'I no longer feel in the least as I did then either about Empson, or his poetry, which I now much appreciate, while greatly admiring also his critical writings.'

58. WE, unpublished memoir of Jennings (courtesy of Mary-Lou Jennings). Kevin Jackson confirms WE's understanding of his friend's purposes: 'Jennings was trying to seek out small but telling clues to the unacknowledged semi-pagan beliefs and idols of his fellow-countrymen' (*The Humphrey Jennings Film Reader* (Manchester: Carcanet, 1993), p. xv).

59. Interview with Madge, June 1983. Soon after Jennings's death, T. S. Eliot wrote to I. A. Richards in praise of what he called Jennings's 'extraordinary liveliness of mind and conversational powers' (18 October 1950; Richards Papers).

60. *May the Twelfth* (London: Faber & Faber, 1937), 347.

61. MacClancy, 'Brief Encounter', 500.

62. Ibid. 501.

63. *May the Twelfth*, 92.

64. MacClancy, 'Brief Encounter', 502.

65. *Britain by Mass-Observation*, arranged and written by Tom Harrisson and Charles Madge (reissued London: The Cresset Library, 1986, pp. 157–8). The book sold 100,000 copies in ten days.

66. Charles Madge, letter to JH, 20 March 1991.

67. JH interview with Madge, June 1983.

68. See Anthony W. Hodgkinson and Rodney E. Sheratsky, *Humphrey Jennings— More Than a Maker of Films* (Hanover, NH: Published for Clark University by the University Press of New England, 1982), 39.

69. Tom Harrisson, letter to a friend, quoted in MacClancy, 'Brief Encounter', 502.

70. Gascoyne, *Journal 1936–37*, 10.

71. Madge interview; and letter to JH, 20 March 1991. On Harrisson and Mass Observation, see also Judith M. Heimann, *The Most Offending Soul Alive: Tom Harrisson and his Remarkable Life* (Honolulu: University of Hawai'i Press, 1988), esp. ch. 13: 'Mass-Observation', and ch. 15: 'M-O in Bolton'. Jeremy MacClancy, a lecturer in anthropology at Oxford Brooks University, has written in a review of Heimann's biography that there can be no doubt that Harrisson's 'contribution to Mass-Observation was truly original. For its liberating programme is an unequalled example of proto-postmodernism: the creation of a plural text, the questioning of ethnographic authority, the recognition of the need for reflexivity, the realization of the subversive potential of anthropology, the irreducibly literary nature of ethnography, the study of Western industrialized societies, and the recognition of the essentially contested nature of the codes and representations which compose culture. All these factors were present in the early years of M-O, and Harrisson was one of its three main movers' ('Cage me a Harrisson', *TLS*, 16 August 2002, p. 3).

72. Julian Trevelyan, *Indigo Days* (London: MacGibbon & Kee, 1957), 83.

73. Tom Harrisson, letter to Trevelyan, 7 June 1937 (Julian Trevelyan Papers, Trinity College, Cambridge). 'Bolton art awaits you! You will enjoy it, I swear,' Harrisson exhorted his friend.

74. Trevelyan, *Indigo Days*, 84. 'Mass-Observation is . . . a marvellously impossible project, unfettered by any notion of method other than a vague, all-encompassing idea of participant-observation. Harrisson might dispatch a full-time observer to report on the contents of sweet-shop windows . . .' (MacClancy, 'Cage me a Harrisson', 3).

75. Interview with Christopher Norris and David Wilson.

76. WE, letter to C. K. Ogden, 14 February 1940 (McMaster University Library).

77. Compare Woodrow Wyatt's endorsement in a biographical entry on Tom Harrisson: 'In 1939 the validity of Mass-Observations reports was so well accepted that the Ministry of Information employed it for detailed studies on civilian morale during World War II. These have become important historical documents . . .' (*DNB 1971–1980*).

78. '. . . I choose to go where honest, downright barbarity is professed; where men devour one another like generous, hungry lions and tigers, not like crocodiles . . .' (William Wycherley, *The Plain Dealer* [1676], I. i. 612–16).

79. WE, letter to Madge, dated by Madge 16 March 1936 (courtesy of the late Charles Madge).

15. China, 1937–1938

1. WE, letter to mother, 15 March 1938 (Houghton).

2. WE, letter to T. Tunnard Moore, The British Council, 3 September 1945 (Houghton carbon).

3. WE, letter to Michael Roberts, 22 February 1939 (Janet Adam Smith).

4. WE, letter to T. S. Eliot, n.d., 1937 (Faber & Faber).

5. WE, loose-leaf holograph diary notes, 22 December 1937 (Empson Papers).

6. C. K. Ogden, letter to WE, 9 August 1937 (Empson Papers).

7. Richards diary: letter drafted/transcribed as for 11 July.

8. Richards diary: entry for 17 July.

9. Richards diary entry recorded as for Saturday, 21 August.

10. See John Greenway, 'R. D. Jameson (1895–1959)', *Western Folklore*, 19/3: 153–4. 'Jim' Jameson studied at Chicago and at Montpellier, and at King's College, London; after a period as a newspaperman he taught at Rensselaer Polytechnic Institute, the University of Idaho, and Grinnell College, before leaving the USA for China. A productive scholar, he published (before the age of 40) *The Concert and Other Studies* (1917), *Trails of the Troubadours* (London, 1926, under the *non de plume* 'Ramon de Loi'), a five-volume *Short History of European Literature* (Shanghai, 1930), *Three Lectures on Chinese Folklore* (Shanghai, 1932), and *A Comparison of Literatures* (London, 1935). After leaving China in 1938 he became a consultant at the Library of Congress in Washington,

1938–42; and from 1948 until his death he was Professor of English at the New Mexico Highlands College, Las Vegas. I am grateful to Professor Herbert Stern (Department of English, Wabash College, Crawfordsville, Indiana) for showing me draft chapters from his study of Robert Winter, I. A. Richards, the Orthological Institute, and the Rockefeller Foundation; his chapter provisionally entitled 'OIC and the RF' is informative about Jameson's resourceful commitment to Basic in China.

11. Wu Fu-heng, letter to JH, 14 April 1984.
12. Shui Tien-tung, letter to JH, 4 April 1984. Shui Tien-tung had already, by the mid-1930s, prepared a collection in Basic English of 'Good Stories from Greece and Rome', as well as a Basic English version of *Black Beauty*.

    For a comprehensive account of the Basic English project in China, see Rodney Koeneke, *Empires of the Mind: I. A. Richards and Basic English in China, 1929–1979* (Stanford, Calif.: Stanford University Press, 2004).
13. WE, letter to John Hayward, n.d. (King's College, Cambridge: WE/JDH/8).
14. See S. Bernard Thomas, *Season of High Adventure: Edgar Snow in China* (University of California Press, 1996); *China Remembers Edgar Snow*, ed. Wang Xing (Beijing: Beijing Review, 1982).
15. Edgar Snow, *The Battle for Asia* (New York: Random House, 1941), 24.
16. WE, letter to Julian Trevelyan, 10 September 1937 (Trinity College, Cambridge); letter to John Hayward, 15 September 1937 (King's College, Cambridge: WE/JDH/7).
17. WE, letter to Hayward, 15 September 1937 (King's College, Cambridge: WE/JDH/7).
18. I. A. Richards to David H. Stevens, Director of the Humanities Program, Rockefeller Foundation, 10 September 1937 (Rockefeller Archive Center, 1/601, box 48, folder 400). See also V. W. W. S. Purcell, 'The Teaching of Basic', *The Basic News*, 5 (January–March 1938), 12–22. After the Second World War, Purcell would become UN Consultant on Asia. His publications include *The Problems of Chinese Education* (1936), *Chinese in Southeast Asia* (1951), and *The Memoirs of a Malaysian Official* (1965).
19. Victor Purcell, *Chinese Evergreen* (London: Michael Joseph, 1938), 36–49.
20. JH interview with Dorothea Richards, 1983.
21. Interview with Professor Li Fu-ning, Peking University, 16 March 1984.
22. Richards diary, 23 September 1937.
23. Purcell, *Chinese Evergreen*, 58.
24. Yeh Kung-Chao (Ye Gongchao) (1904–81) later joined the Chinese Ministry of Information first in Singapore and then in London, where he was also counsellor to the embassy. After the defeat of the Nationalists, he became Minister of Foreign Affairs for the government of Nationalist China, Taiwan; and in 1958–61 he was Taiwanese Ambassador to Washington; an adviser to President Chiang Kai-shek; and then a minister without portfolio (1962–78). In 1978 he was named senior adviser to Chiang's son and successor, Chiang

Ching-kuo. Author of books on literature and culture, he was the recipient of several medals and citations.

25. I. A. Richards, letter to David H. Stevens, 1 September 1937 (Rockefeller Archive Center, 1/601, box 48, folder 400).

26. Purcell, *Chinese Evergreen*, 60.

27. WE, letter to Professor Richard Wilson, 15 December 1955.

28. Purcell, *Chinese Evergreen*, 71.

29. WE, undated TS letter (Empson Papers). See also letter from R. D. Jameson to D. H. Stevens, with a 13-page memorandum 'On the Work of the Subcommittees', 10 September 1937; and letter from I. A. Richards to Jameson, 27 September 1937: both in Rockefeller Archive Center, RG1, series 601, box 48, folder 400. 'The experience of having Empson and Purcell come along justified itself.'

30. WE, 'Letter from China', *Night and Day*, 25 November 1937, p. 20; reprinted in *SSS* 183. Koeneke (*Empires of the Mind*, 148) gives the name of the Vice-Minister of Communication as Hsu En-tseng; the confusion may have arisen because Purcell gave him a *nom de guerre*.

31. 'Letter from China', 20.

32. Purcell, *Chinese Evergreen*, 103.

33. Ibid. 113–15.

34. Ibid. 109.

35. Ibid.

36. Ibid. 122–4.

37. Letter, Dorothea Richards to John G. Pilley, 12 October 1937; quoted in John Paul Russo, *I. A. Richards: His Life and Work* (London: Routledge, 1989), 424.

38. Purcell, *Chinese Evergreen*, 121.

39. Dorothea Richards quoted in Russo, *I. A. Richards*, 423–4.

40. Purcell, *Chinese Evergreen*, 131.

41. Ibid. 135.

42. Ibid. 144–5.

43. 'Letter from China', *Night and Day*, 25 November 1937, p. 20; in *SSS* 184. See also an optimistic letter from I. A. Richards to David Stevens, 15 October 1937 (Rockefeller Archive Center, RG 1, series 601, box 48, folder 400).

44. 'Letter from China', *Night and Day*, 25 November 1937, p. 20; *SSS* 184.

45. Ibid. 184–5.

46. Purcell, *Chinese Evergreen*, 166.

47. 'I feel it is only sensible to cash in on the travelling,' Empson wrote to Ian Parsons on 11 February 1939. 'But it would have to be light and thin; I dont want to pretend to know about politics and be "frank" about people.' To John Hayward on 4/16 May 1939: 'Ian Parsons wants a travel book and maybe if I can take some kind of purgative I can tell all my polite funny stories once for all and then stop' (courtesy of T. Hofmann).

48. WE, letter to Ian Parsons, 16 May 1939 (Reading University Library).

49. TS draft of unpublished article 'Letter from Yunnan'.

50. WE, letter to mother, 11 August 1938 (Empson Papers). Empson wrote also to Lady Sansom (27 September 1938), 'It seems that Victor Purcell has written a book about the journey across China he and I did with the Richards, which I need to get hold of; he was heading for a quarrel with Dowwofea all the way and it burst out at the end . . . It struck me at the time it would make a real funny novel but I only saw him as a character and certainly wouldn't have written it myself. The truth is that illnatured jokes about your companions are very nearly all you think of while travelling, so naturally that has to be the material of the travel book. But what Purcell has put in I don't yet know' (Empson Papers). Empson's remarks reveal as much about himself as about Purcell. In fact, Purcell managed to compose a book that is at once genial and understanding, candid and compassionate; jokes he tells, but none of them truly ill-natured. Purcell would write to Richards on 19 December 1938: 'Did you read my "Chinese Evergreen"? I was a little anxious about your reactions but Bill Empson [who had just visited Purcell in Malaya before rejoining his Chinese university-in-exile in Kunming] says he thought I treated us all "very kindly". I hope you think so too' (I. A Richards Papers, box 50; Magdalene College, Cambridge).

51. Purcell, *Chinese Evergreen*, 250–1.

52. Ibid. 252.

53. 'Letter from China', *Night and Day*, 25 November 1937, p. 21; *SSS* 185.

54. Russo, *I. A. Richards*, 425.

55. Russo mistakes the situation: 'Realizing (well before Richards) the hopelessness of the political situation, Empson now decided to leave China[,] and Dorothea duly noted his plane taking off on 19 October' (*I. A. Richards*, 425–6). Alan M. Hollingsworth, in an earlier essay on Richards's work in China, claimed, 'Richards was the only influential critic/scholar/teacher/poet of his generation from the Western World (with the exception of his student, William Empson) to actually live and teach in China'; but he is mistaken here: 'Of significant and influential critic-scholar-teacher-poets of his generation, Richards alone actually went to China to teach and to learn' ('I. A. Richards in China and America', in *R.O.C. & U.S.A.: 1911–1981: Collected Papers of an International Conference Held by the American Studies Association of the Republic of China in November 21–23, 1981*, ed. Tung-hsun Sun and Morris Wei-hsin Tien (Taipei: American Studies Association of the Republic of China, 1982), 126, 140.

56. Purcell, *Chinese Evergreen*, 175. Not long after Purcell's death in 1965, Richards wrote of him to the Empsons: 'I wish I could have been more patient with him! He was a sort of door-god of a man, with much more talent than his judgement could afford' (*Selected Letters*, 169).

57. Purcell, *Chinese Evergreen*, 77–8.

58. WE, letter to mother, 11 August 1938; undated TS diary notes (Empson Papers).

59. WE, typescript notes on journey.

60. WE, letter to Professor Wilson, 15 December 1955: 'I did cross China alone . . . '

61. Holograph notes, written Christmas Day 1937.

62. Theodore H. White and Annalee Jacoby, *Thunder out of China* (New York: William Sloane Associates, 1946), 52.

63. Ibid. 56.

64. Ibid. 58.

65. Lloyd E. Eastman, 'Nationalist China during the Sino-Japanese War 1937–1945', in John K. Fairbank and Albert Feuerwerker (eds.), *The Cambridge History of China*, vol. xiii: *Republican China 1912–1949, Part 2* (Cambridge: Cambridge University Press, 1986), 564–5.

66. Percy Maude Roxby, *China* (Oxford: Oxford University Press, 1942), Oxford Pamphlets on World Affairs, no. 54, p. 28.

67. WE, 'A Chinese University', *Life & Letters Today*, 25 (June 1940), 239; reprinted in *SSS* 190.

68. Han Suyin, *Birdless Summer: China: Autobiography, History*, Book 3 (London: Jonathan Cape, 1968; Triad/Panther, 1982), 46. See also Han Suyin, *Destination Chungking* (London: Jonathan Cape, 1942), ch. 6: 'Nanyu—Heart of China'.

69. WE, TS draft of a 'Letter from China'.

70. Ibid.

71. Ibid.

72. WE, 'A Chinese University', 243; *SSS* 192–3.

73. See also John Israel, *Lianda: A Chinese University in War and Revolution* (Stanford, Calif.: Stanford University Press, 1998), 157–8. 'Because [Jin] allegedly dwelt on the heights of abstraction, avoiding political issues, a left-wing journal dubbed him a representative of "the hermit faction," yet in the classroom, he displayed a worldly wit. He told his students that they could understand philosophy better by reading novels than by studying the writings of philosophers, and his favorite illustrations came from Ingrid Bergman films' (p. 158). This chapter draws at length on Professor Israel's indefatigable research. I am grateful to John Israel for sharing with me drafts of his work-in-progress, and for his good cheer and tolerance while sharing a room with me in Kunming in 1988.

74. Draft TS notes, written at Christmas 1937.

75. WE, draft TS letter to mother, 11 August 1938 (Empson Papers).

76. Interview with Jin Yue Lin, Peking, April 1984. In 1938 Empson wrote home, 'I am friends again with the professor of philosophy here (I was fool enough to say what I thought of his philosophy)' (undated letter to mother).

77. WE, letter to T. Tunnard Moore, The British Council, 3 September 1945 (Houghton carbon).

78. WE, 'Chinese Food', foreword to Kenneth H. C. Lo, *Peking Cookery* (London, 1971); *SSS* 180–1.

79. Draft TS 'Letter from China'.
80. Quoted in John Israel, 'Southwest Associated University: Preservation as an Ultimate Value', in Paul K. T. Sih (ed.), *Nationalist China during the Sino-Japanese War, 1937–1945* (Hicksville, NY: Exposition Press, 1977), 136.
81. 'A Chinese University', *SSS* 190.
82. 'Teaching English in the Far East and England', *SSS* 211.
83. Ibid. 211–12.
84. Professor Li Fu-ning, for example, in 'William Empson As I Remember Him—A Young Teacher of English in China': essay by Li Fu-ning dated 26 January 1986; confirmed in interview with Li Fu-ning, 16 March 1984.
85. TS draft of a 'Letter from China'.
86. Draft TS notes, written at Christmas 1937.
87. TS draft of WE's 'travel book' on China.
88. TS draft of article on 'Students in China'. I. A. Richards recalled that his class at Tsinghua University 'burst into loud applause when the black flag went up telling that Tess of the D'Urbervilles had been hanged. (I was reading the page aloud to them.) They had been waiting all through the book for the lack of respect Tess had shown for her father to be suitably punished' ('Sources of our Common Aim', *Poetries: Their Media and Ends*, ed. T. Easton (The Hague: Mouton, 1974), 172).
89. TS draft of WE's 'travel book' on China.
90. 'Basic and Communication', *SSS* 165–6.
91. *SCW* 22–3, 25.
92. Quoted in Israel, *Lianda*, 23.
93. 'I set out to read Othello's last speech from the carbon copy merely to show how it scanned,' he further reported, 'but it must have got fairly noisy; at the end the peculiar titter spread over the class that apparently means pleasure in a dramatic performance.'
94. TS draft article 'The Combined South Western Universities'.
95. Han Suyin, *Birdless Summer*, 53, 60.
96. Ibid. 57.
97. TS diary notes.
98. See Israel, *Lianda*, 23.
99. See obituary of Hong Qian, by A. C. Grayling, *The Guardian*, 24 April 1992.
100. WE reported that he had actually begun his 'silly novel' by 10 September 1937, while staying with the Richardses in Hong Kong.
101. Richards diary, 8 September 1937.
102. Lord Zuckerman, letter to JH, 7 April 1986.
103. S. Zuckerman, *The Social Life of Monkeys and Apes* (London: Kegan Paul, 1932), 51.
104. Ibid. 54.
105. S. Zuckerman, *Functional Affinities of Man, Monkeys and Apes* (London: Kegan Paul, 1933), 93.

106. Zuckerman, *The Social Life of Monkeys and Apes*, 63, 311.

107. Ibid. 304.

108. WE, 'Animals', *The Spectator*, 30 October 1936, p. 768.

109. 'Ask a Policeman', *The Granta*, 21 October 1927, p. 47; *EG* 19.

110. 'Donne the Space Man', *Kenyon Review*, 19/3 (Summer 1957), 339, 341; *Essays on Renaissance Literature*, i. 79, 81.

111. Ibid. 339–40.

112. WE, 'Literary Criticism and the Christian Revival', *Rationalist Annual* (London, 1966); *Argufying*, 634. See also Frances A. Yates on Giordano Bruno in *Renaissance and Reform: The Italian Contribution* (London: Routledge & Kegan Paul, 1983). Empson's conjecture that Christ might die on (and for the inhabitants of) other worlds helps to explain an otherwise obscure line— 'No star he [i. e. Christ] aimed at is entirely waste'—in his poem 'Reflection from Anita Loos'.

113. 'Senator Milton' (rev. of *Five Essays on Milton's Epics*), *The Listener*, 28 July 1966. For Milton's interest in Galileo's researches, see *Paradise Lost*, ed. Alistair Fowler (Harlow: Longman, 1971), notes to i. 286–91; iii. 589–90; v. 261–3; also Marjorie H. Nicolson, 'A World in the Moon', *Smith College Studies in Modern Languages*, 17 (1936).

114. 'Dylan Thomas', *Essays in Criticism*, 13/2 (April 1963), 206; *Argufying*, 397.

115. 'Resurrection', *Critical Quarterly*, 6/2 (1964), 178; *Argufying*, 617.

116. 'Donne the Space Man', 353; *Essays on Renaissance Literature*, i. 91.

117. *Milton's God*, 261.

118. *Complete Poems*, 119.

119. U Myint Thein (1900–94), lawyer and diplomat, studied at Rangoon University and at Queen's College, Cambridge, and was called to the Bar by Lincoln's Inn in 1925. In 1948 he became Burma's first Ambassador to China, where he remained in post until 1953. He was Chief Justice of Burma from 1957 to 1962, when he was imprisoned for six years by the revolutionary government. See obituary in *The Times*, 6 October 1994.

16. CHINA, 1938–1939

1. WE, letter to Julian and Ursula Trevelyan, 'May 15?' 1938 (Empson Papers).

2. WE, letter to John Hayward, 23 May 1938 (T. Hofmann).

3. WE, letter to mother, 15 March 1938 (Houghton). The real Governor of Hong Kong, Empson considered 'a very sturdy intelligent old boy'.

4. Christopher Isherwood, *Christopher and His Kind: 1929–1939* (London: Eyre Methuen, 1977), 223.

5. WE, loose leaf of MS notes.

6. WE, letter to mother, 15 March 1938.

7. WE, draft TS article, 'Letter from China' (Empson Papers).

8. 'Angkor seemed to me to divide into the Hindu stuff (e. g. the Vat) which was dignified and in good taste, and the Buddhist stuff (the Bayon) which has a noble and wonderful imagination; it is very bad luck that they got mucked up with Hinduism from the start' (letter to Michael Roberts, 'end of May' 1938; courtesy of the late Janet Adam Smith).

9. See also 'Lyrical Harmonies in Spring City: Remembering Southwest Associated University: Special Issue in Honor of the Fiftieth Anniversary of Southwest Associated University', ed. John Israel, *Chinese Education*, 21/2 (Summer 1988).

10. Gerald Reitlinger, *South of the Clouds* (London: The Travel Book Club, 1941), 29.

11. WE, letter to Julian and Ursula Trevelyan, 'May 15?' 1938 (Empson Papers).

12. John Israel, *Lianda: A Chinese University in War and Revolution* (Stanford, Calif.: Stanford University Press, 1998), 64. See also Israel, '50th Anniversary of a Special Wartime University', *China Reconstructs* (November 1988), 44–7.

13. Israel, *Lianda*, 65.

14. Reitlinger, *South of the Clouds*, 30.

15. WE, letter to Michael Roberts, 'end of May' 1938 (Janet Adam Smith); letter to John Hayward, 23 May 1938 (T. Hofmann).

16. WE, letter to John Hayward, 23 May 1938 (T. Hofmann).

17. WE, draft TS letter to mother, 11 August 1938 (Empson Papers).

18. WE, letter to Julian and Ursula Trevelyan, 'May 15?' 1938 (Empson Papers).

19. Undated draft letter to Michael Roberts, written in Mengtzu (Empson Papers).

20. WE, letter to John Hayward, 23 May 1938 (T. Hofmann).

21. WE, letter to mother, 6 June 1938: 'We have a swimming pool, a deeper bit dug in the lake; my colleagues are too proud to swim in it because it is muddy, but I think it's all right.' (Empson Papers)

22. WE, letter to Robert Herring (editor of *Life and Letters*), 6 June 1938. It remained a backwater for many years; Professor Israel, who visited the town in June 1980, discovered that he was the first Caucasian American to set foot there for thirty years (Israel, *Lianda*, 74).

23. Li Fu-ning, 'William Empson As I Remember Him'; interview with Li Fu-ning, 16 March 1984.

24. WE, letter to John Hayward, 23 May 1938 (T. Hofmann).

25. Interview with Li Zhiwei, Kunming, 4 November 1988.

26. Interview with Li Fu-ning, 16 March 1984.

27. WE, letter to Julian and Ursula Trevelyan, 'May 15?' 1938 (Empson Papers). The students 'have to read after dark by nightlights and coastguard lanterns, or they would go blind,' Empson wrote in a draft 'Letter from China'; also, 'The only lamps to be bought in Changsha were patented in New York in 1880, and create a draught by clockwork.'

28. Jonathan D. Spence, *The Gate of Heavenly Peace: The Chinese and Their Revolution, 1895–1980* (London: Faber & Faber, 1982), 276. For an authoritative account of the students' trek, see Israel, *Lianda*, ch.2: 'Lianda's Long March'.

29. Anonymous diary, entry for 29 April 1938, quoted by Israel in draft ch. 3, 'From Changsha to Kunming': 2: 'Slow Train to Mengzi', p. 3; abbreviated in *Lianda*, 64.

30. TS draft of article on 'Students in China'.

31. WE, letter to John Hayward, 23 May 1938 (T. Hofmann).

32. WE, letter to Julian and Ursula Trevelyan, 'May 15?' 1938 (Empson Papers).

33. WE, letter to John Hayward, 23 May 1938 (T. Hofmann).

34. Ibid.

35. Ibid.

36. WE, letter to Jin Di, 13 March 1980 (courtesy of Professor Jin Di).

37. WE, undated draft letter to John Hayward, 1938 (Empson Papers).

38. Yang Zhouhan, letter to JH, 22 July 1985.

39. WE, letter to John Hayward, 23 May 1938 (T. Hofmann); undated draft letter to Hayward, 1938 (Empson Papers).

40. WE, 'Chinese Bandits', *SSS* 188–9.

41. WE, letter to mother, 11 August 1938 (Empson Papers).

42. Israel, *Lianda*, 67.

43. WE, letter to mother, 11 August 1938 (Empson Papers).

44. Undated TS draft of a 'Letter from China'.

45. Draft TS of a 'Letter from China'.

46. Israel, 'Southwest Associated University', 145.

47. See also Spence, *The Gate of Heavenly Peace*, 282.

48. WE, letter to mother, 15 March 1938.

49. WE, undated draft letter to John Hayward, 1938 (Empson Papers).

50. WE, letter to Michael Roberts, 'end of May' 1938; to Robert Herring, 6 June 1938; undated draft 'Letter from China'; and a draft TS article on 'Yunnan' (Empson Papers).

51. Fitzgerald would much later publish a book about Tali and its people, *The Tower of Five Glories* (1972).

52. Reitlinger, *South of the Clouds*, 83, 122.

53. 'Fourth Report on the Yunnan Situation, 10/12/38': Rockefeller Archive Center: Orthological Institute, May–December 1938, 1/601/Box 48, folder 402.

54. H. G. Wells, Julian Huxley, G. P. Wells, *The Science of Life* (1931), 572, quoted in Philip and Averil Gardner, *The God Approached: A Commentary on the Poems of William Empson* (London: Chatto & Windus, 1978), 212.

55. WE, TS draft letter to Robert Herring, 14 July 1938; TS draft of a 'Letter from China' written from Mengtzu, China (both in Empson Papers).

56. WE, undated letter to mother, 1938.

57. WE, undated TS draft letter to John Hayward, 1938 (Empson Papers).

58. TS draft letter to mother, 11 August 1938 (Empson Papers).

59. WE, letter to Robert Herring, 6 June 1938 (Houghton).

60. See Chiang Monlin, *Tides from the West: A Chinese Autobiography* (New Haven: Yale University Press, 1947). Chiang Monlin had studied at Berkeley, where he helped to edit the Chinese Free Press (being advised in person by the 'inspiring' Sun Yat-sen); then at Columbia University, New York, where he worked, together with Hu Shih, under John Dewey.

61. WE, fragment of draft letter to mother, n.d., p. 4.

62. WE, TS draft letter to Robert Herring, 14 July 1938 (Empson Papers).

63. Quoted in 'China on the March', broadcast on the BBC Home Service, 27 April 1942 (uncut text in Empson Papers).

64. WE, letter to Michael Roberts, 'end of May' 1938 (Janet Adam Smith); letter to Julian Trevelyan, 1 November 1938 (Trinity College, Cambridge).

65. Undated TS draft of a 'Letter from China', from Mengtzu (Empson Papers).

66. WE, letter to mother, 11 August 1938 (Empson Papers).

67. Compare a draft letter to Michael Roberts, written from Mengtzu in 1938: 'It is silly to write and not talk politics. I will not be like Mrs Richards though and call myself We who love China' (Empson Papers).

68. WE, letter to Julian and Ursula Trevelyan, 'May 15?' 1938 (Empson Papers).

69. WE, undated draft letter to I. A. Richards (? September 1948) (Empson Papers).

70. TS draft article 'The Combined South Western Universities'.

71. TS diary notes (Empson Papers). A year later, on 29 June 1939, he wrote to Michael Roberts from Kunming (where he was sharing a house with western visitors): 'It is the European household that makes the strain, as far as I can see; I was far better camping out in a heap of Chinese' (The late Janet Adam Smith).

72. WE, letter to Lady Sansom, 27 September 1938 (Empson Papers).

73. 'Graham Hough thinks about William Empson and his work', *London Review of Books*, 21 June–4 July 1984, p. 16. George Watson relates a story that Hough had told him: 'In the 1930s, at a dinner in Hanoi . . . [Empson] remarked to Graham Hough . . . shortly after the death of D. H. Lawrence: "You know, I think I see what Lawrence's novels are about: they are about *coming* at the same time", adding even more disconcertingly: "I have once or twice managed it myself" ' (*Never Ones for Theory? England and the War of Ideas* (Cambridge: The Lutterworth Press, 2000), 64).

74. WE, letter to Michael Roberts, 4 December 1938 (Janet Adam Smith).

75. Interview with Professor Yang Zhouhan, Peking, 13 March 1984. John Israel compares it to Santa Fe (*Lianda*, 81).

76. Clair Lee Chennault, *Way of a Fighter* (New York: Putnam's, 1949), 73; quoted in Israel, *Lianda*, 82.

77. Theodore H. White and Annalee Jacoby, *Thunder out of China* (New York: William Sloane Associates, 1946), 160.

78. Israel, *Lianda*, 87–90; also 'General Report on the Province of Yunnan: The Education and the Possibilities for the Future' (Rockefeller Archive Center, 1/601, box 48, folder 403).

79. White and Jacoby, *Thunder out of China*, 160.

80. Israel, *Lianda*, 83.

81. Ibid. See also Owen Lattimore, *China Memoirs: Chiang Kai-shek and the War against Japan* (Tokyo: University of Tokyo Press, 1990), 126–30.

82. WE, letter to mother, 7 April 1939 (Empson Papers).

83. Israel, 'Southwest Associated University', 145.

84. Milla Gapanovich, unpublished essay 'Life in a Chinese town and in a Village in the Time of the Japanese War', July 1985 (privately supplied). Mrs Gapanovich lived throughout the war in Kunming. Her husband was Professor Ivan Ivanovich Gapanovich—'Ge Bangfu'—a White Russian aristocrat, Petersburg University graduate, and Qinghua professor who taught historiography, ancient history, and the history of Russia. When students sought other professors for political advice, Gapanovich enunciated sentiments common to foreign residents in China since the time of Marco Polo: "Don't treat me as a foreigner; I too understand Chinese affairs"' (Israel, *Lianda*, 153).

85. WE, letter to Michael Roberts, 4 December 1938 (Janet Adam Smith).

86. WE, letter to I. A. Richards, 8 August 1939 (Richards Papers).

87. TS draft of a 'Letter from China'.

88. Quoted in Israel, 'Southwest Associated University', 144.

89. WE, letter to Michael Roberts, 4 December 1938 (Janet Adam Smith); 'A Chinese University', 240; *SSS*, 191.

90. Interview with Professor Chao Chao-hsiung, Peking, 21 March 1984.

91. Wu Fu-heng, letter to JH, 14 April 1984; a similar story is related by Li Fu-ning in 'William Empson As I Remember Him'; interview with Li Fu-ning, 16 March 1984; interview with Yang Zhouhan, Peking, 13 March 1984.

92. WE, letter to John Hayward, 4 March 1939 (T. Hofmann).

93. Israel, 'Southwest Associated University', 142.

94. WE, letter to John Hayward, 4 March 1939 (T. Hofmann).

95. WE, letter to Ian Parsons, 11 February 1939 (Reading?).

96. Israel, *Lianda*, 88.

97. Ibid. 85.

98. TS draft of a 'Letter from China'.

99. Draft TS article on 'Yunnan'.

100. *Milton's God*, 81.

101. Richard P. Dobson, *China Cycle* (London: Macmillan, 1946), 120.
102. Compare Israel, *Lianda*, 91.
103. Ibid. 87.
104. Draft TS essay on life in Yunnan. To his mother Empson wrote, 'The price of rice is kept steady in these parts, but the price of opium is steadily going up, and now about double prewar. You must think of that as like the price of beer. I mean the ordinary opiumsmoker is a steady and healthy worker; only different in an important way; that a regular beerdrinker can keep quite cheerful on rather less, but a regular opiumsmoker needs a fixed amount. I have never bothered to try opium because it takes a month or so before you get any effect, but it is not a terrible drug like the heroin that the Japanese use as a weapon of war. People in England would probably be shocked to hear it is on open sale in Singapore and Hongkong, let alone Macao; the Chinese forbid it officially because so many of them smoke too much, but plenty of competent people do; we have a famous heavy smoker on the faculty, and it is exactly as if he was a rather heavy drinker. I doubt if I could tell the difference. Well then, the rise of the price of opium in this place forces a large number of physically very able people into getting the money for their extra bit of opium. If the drug made them ill they would be harmless; because it doesn't they become bandits.' (TS draft letter to mother, 11 August 1938.)
105. Han Suyin, *Birdless Summer: China: Autobiography, History*, Book 3 (London: Jonathan Cape, 1968; Triad/Panther, 1982), 112.
106. Harold B. Rattenbury, *China, My China* (London: Frederick Muller, 1944), 222.
107. C. P. Fitzgerald, letter to Dorothea Richards, 19 May 1937 (I. A. Richards Papers, Magdalene College, Cambridge).
108. Undated TS fragment of a 'Letter from China'.
109. WE, undated (?July 1939) and unposted letter to mother (Empson Papers).
110. WE, undated draft letter to Peter Fleming (*The Times*), enclosing a 1,700-word article about the situation in China (not published), n.d. (Empson Papers). 'Busy I am not, indeed the lack of conversation makes it hard to write anything, a fact that I have only seen written down by the later Walter Raleigh.'
111. WE, letter to John Hayward, 4/16 May 1939 (T. Hofmann).
112. WE, letter to Anthony and Kitty West, 10 January 1939 (Empson Papers); letter to Michael Roberts, 12 January 1939; Reitlinger, *South of the Clouds*, 36.
113. Israel, *Lianda*, 82–3.
114. See 'China's Economic War', *The Spectator*, 18 October 1940, p. 385.
115. WE, letter to 'Anthony and Kitty', 10 January 1939 (Empson Papers).
116. John King Fairbank, *The Great Chinese Revolution: 1800–1985* (New York: Perennial Library, 1987), 243. See also Kai-yu Hsu, 'The Life and Poetry of Wen I-to', *Harvard Journal of Asiatic Studies*, 21 (1958), 134–79.

117. See also A. Doak Barnett, *China on the Eve of Communist Takeover* (London: Thames & Hudson, 1963), 282–5.

118. WE, draft TS article on 'Yunnan'.

119. Eastman, 'Nationalist China during the Sino-Japanese War 1937–1945', in John K. Fairbank and Albert Feuerwerker (eds.,) *Cambridge History of China*, xiii, Part 2 (Cambridge: Cambridge University Press, 1986), 565.

120. WE, draft TS article on 'Yunnan'.

121. WE, undated letter to mother, 1938; Spence, *The Gate of Heavenly Peace*, 274. See also Frank Moraes, *Report on Mao's China* (New York: Macmillan, 1953), 93.

122. Draft TS article on 'Yunnan'.

123. In contrast (according to *Cambridge History of China*, xiv (1987), 105), 'the KMT regime, influenced by Western concepts of nationalism, followed an assimilationist approach denying minority autonomy...'

124. WE, letter to mother, 7 April 1939 (Houghton).

125. WE, 'A Chinese University', 243–4; *SSS* 193.

126. WE, letter to T. Tunnard Moore, The British Council, 3 September 1945 (Houghton carbon).

127. E-tu Zen Sun, 'The Growth of the Academic Community 1912–1949', in *Cambridge History of China*, xiii, Part 2, 416.

128. White and Jacoby, *Thunder out of China*, 109.

129. Ibid.

130. Chin Yueh-lin, in Harley Farnsworth MacNair (ed.), *Voices from Unoccupied China* (Chicago: University of Chicago Press, 1944), p. liii; quoted in Israel, 'Southwest Associated University', 137; Israel, *Lianda*, 99.

131. White and Jacoby, *Thunder out of China*, 109.

132. WE, letter to mother, 7 April 1939 (Empson Papers). 'Chinese money is dropping steadily and prices going up,' he told his mother on 25 July (Empson Papers). See also Chiang Monlin: 'When we came there [Kunming], in the second year of war, rice per Chinese bushel (eighty kilograms) cost $6 in Chinese currency. When it had increased by degrees to $40 a bushel one of our professors predicted that it would rise to $70. People laughed at him. But it did go to $70' (*Tides from the West*, 226).

133. Israel, 'Southwest Associated University', 143.

134. WE, 'A Chinese University', 244; *SSS* 193.

135. WE, letter to mother, 2 June 1939 (Empson Papers).

136. White and Jacoby, *Thunder out of China*, 60.

137. John Israel, 'Random Notes on Wartime Chinese Intellectuals', *Republican China*, 9/3 (April 1984), 10–11, 12.

138. WE, letter to Michael Roberts, 8 August 1939 (Janet Adam Smith).

139. WE, 'Madame Chiang', *The Spectator*, 15 March 1940.

140. WE, 'A Chinese University', 242; *SSS* 192. See also Pei-sung Tang, 'Chinese Universities on the March', *American Scholar*, 10/1 (1940–1), 41–8.

141. WE, letter to Michael Roberts, 12 January 1939 (Janet Adam Smith).

142. WE, 'A Chinese University', 241; *SSS* 191.

143. TS draft article 'The Combined South Western Universities'.

144. Interview with Professor Yang, Department of German, Peking University, 4 April 1984.

145. WE, letter to Michael Roberts, 4 December 1938 (Janet Adam Smith).

146. Undated draft letter to Michael Roberts, from Mengtzu (Empson Papers).

147. WE, letter to John Hayward, 4 March 1939 (T. Hofmann).

148. Li Fu-ning, 'William Empson As I Remember Him'.

149. TS draft of an article headed 'Students in China'.

150. TS draft of an article headed 'The Refugee Peking Universities'.

151. WE, letter to John Hayward, 4/16 May 1939 (T. Hofmann).

152. WE, letter to Ian Parsons, 16 May 1939 (Reading University Library).

153. WE, letter to Ian Parsons, 11 February 1939 (Reading University Library).

154. WE, letter to Michael Roberts, 12 June 1939 (Janet Adam Smith).

155. WE, letter to Michael Roberts, 22 February 1939 (Janet Adam Smith).

156. WE, undated (?July 1939) and unposted letter to mother (Empson Papers).

157. WE, undated (?July 1939) and unposted letter to mother (Empson Papers).

158. WE, letter to John Hayward, 4 March 1939 (T. Hofmann).

159. WE, undated (?July 1939) and unposted letter to mother (Empson Papers).

160. Gapanovich, 'Life in a Chinese Town and in a Village in the Time of the Japanese War'.

161. WE, letter to John Hayward, 4 March 1939 (T. Hofmann); a similar letter, virtually word for word, to mother, 4 March 1939.

162. WE, letter to John Hayward, 4/16 May 1939 (T. Hofmann).

163. For a detailed report on appropriations by the Rockefeller Foundation, and the course of Basic English in China, see 'Orthological Institute, China': Rockefeller Archive Center, RG 1, series 601, box 48, folder 397.

164. WE, letter to Michael Roberts, 12 January 1939 (Janet Adam Smith).

165. WE, letter to John Hayward, 4 March 1939 (T. Hofmann).

166. WE, undated (?July 1939) and unposted letter to mother (Empson Papers).

167. WE, undated draft TS letter to I. A. Richards (Empson Papers).

168. WE, letter to mother, 4 March 1939 (Empson Papers).

169. WE, TS draft unsigned letter to mother, 12 June 1939 (Empson Papers).

170. WE, undated (?July 1939) and unposted letter to mother (Empson Papers).

171. WE, TS letter to I. A. Richards, undated draft (Empson Papers). Chao Chao-hsiung told me he considered Empson the best stylist of Basic English, even better than I. A. Richards (interview, Peking, 21 March 1984).

172. WE, (?unposted) TS letter to mother, 12 June 1939 (Empson Papers). 'I feel fond of this letter, can't you put it into a drawer,' he added at the head of the letter, even after taking breath in the middle of gossiping about Basic in China: 'I don't believe you'll read this. Your last letter says how dull it must be, so it seemed worth putting down a little politics.'

173. WE, undated draft TS letter to I. A. Richards (Empson Papers).
174. 'Basic and Communication', *SSS* 163–4, 169.
175. WE, letter to Michael Roberts, 8 August 1939 (Janet Adam Smith).
176. WE, letter to mother, 25 July 1939 (Empson Papers); to I. A. Richards, 8 August 1939; Israel, 'Southwest Associated University', 142–3.
177. WE, letter to Michael Roberts, 22 February 1939 (Janet Adam Smith).
178. WE, letter to Michael Roberts, 16 May 1939 (Janet Adam Smith).
179. Ibid.
180. Arthur Cooper, letters to JH, 21 September 1983, 3 October 1983.
181. WE, letter to mother, 23 September 1939 (Empson Papers).
182. *Milton's God*, 67.
183. TS draft of an unpublished 'Letter from China'.

17. POSTSCRIPT

1. TS draft of an unpublished 'Letter from China'.
2. *SSS* 193–4.
3. TS draft of article headed 'The Refugee Peking Universities'.
4. From an undated letter from Pollard-Urquhart to WE (Empson Papers).
5. Loose page of undated letter (Sept. 1940) from Pollard-Urquhart to WE. 'The University authorities hope you will come back,' he went on, before chaffing Empson: 'If you do you had better bring a nice sensible wife to look after you, and then I think you would be quite happy here. I have been told that your fur was stolen in Haiphong as well as some hundreds of piastres, and I am not surprised!' (Empson Papers). T. T. Shui wrote to I. A. Richards on 20 October 1940 with an account of Pollard-Urquhart's horrible and untimely death: after being knocked down by a vehicle during an air raid, when people and vehicles were crushed together in a desperate effort to get out of Kunming's narrow East Gate, his wound began to fester and turn black with gangrene; and he died two weeks later (Richards Papers, box 55).
6. Interview with Professor Chao Chao-hsiung, Peking, 21 March 1984.
7. Robert Winter was to write to a student, Wang Rujie, on 9 January 1982: 'In one of [Ezra Pound's] letters he said that I was the most civilised person in Crawfordsville ... Without Pound I probably would now be an idiot crawling about in Crawfordsville. As it is, I am a belligerent atheist in China' (quoted in James J. Wilhelm, 'On the Trail of the "One" Crawfordsville Incident or, The Poet in Hoosierland', *Paideuma*, 13/1 (Spring 1984), 25; also quoted in Herbert Stern, unpublished TS 'OIC III', 8; privately supplied). I. A. Richards, who met Winter in 1927, extolled him in the mid-1930s as 'a great increase in our strength ... an excessively gifted man who seems to have almost been waiting for Basic to give him his proper work to do' (letter to David H. Stevens, Rockefeller Archive Center, RG1, series 601, box 48, folder 398). Richards inscribed a copy of his volume *New and Selected Poems*

(1978) to Winter as '*the* reader who knows my verse best'. Dorothea Richards was vividly to recall, 'Winter's knowledge of China was deep, varied, and witty. He taught us much of old Chinese culture—these were the days when rickshaw coolies still wore pigtails and white socks and ran the 14 miles from Tsinghua to Peking and return in all weathers and at great speed. He had a reputation for knowing the coolies' most uninhibited forms of swearing well beyond the average foreigner's range' (quoted in Stern, op. cit., p. 9). See also Israel, *Lianda*, 162.

8. Interview with Xu Yuan-zhong, Peking University, 6 April 1984.
9. Li Fu-ning, 'William Empson As I Remember Him'. I. A. Richards was to write to Richard Eberhart on 13 March 1969: 'Did you ever hear Empson reciting those speeches? One of the supreme and most unforgettable of poetic experiences' (courtesy of John Constable).
10. *Milton's God* (1961, 1981), 44–5.
11. WE, 'Wartime Recollections', *Harvard Advocate*, 108/2–3 (1975); in *SSS* 195–6.
12. WE, TS draft letter to mother, 8 November 1939 (Empson Papers).
13. WE, letter to Allen Tate, 31 October 1939 (Allen Tate Collection, Box 19, Princeton University Library).
14. WE, TS draft letter to mother, 8 November 1939 (Empson Papers). The collocation of Babus and Chinese students must have been spurred by a recent conversation; Empson related in a TS draft of a 'Letter from China' written in Kunming: 'local, even sub-provincial, politics is the strength of China, and ... that chief and unsolved problem (both for running the war and for the aftermath) is to gear that life onto the ample products of the higher education. We had a British officer through here on some mission who insisted on calling the students Babus. He meant something which is nearly not true, but still it is the danger to avoid.'
15. WE, letter to Allen Tate, 18 December 1939 (Princeton University Library).
16. A few weeks before, Empson had met up in Chicago with the critic Ronald Crane—as Crane himself later told the Cambridge critic George Watson: 'He sat where you are sitting now and told me he had been teaching Basic English to the Chinese. "Do you mean to tell me," I said, "that you believe everything can be said in less than a thousand words?" Empson said he did. "I challenge you to pick a book off that shelf at random, open it and translate it into Basic English."

'Empson put out a hand blindly and, as chance had it, pulled out Coleridge's *Biographia Literaria*, opened it at a venture and read silently for a minute or two. Then he raised his eyes. "Of course," he said humbly, "it does rather make nonsense of Coleridge"' (*Never Ones for Theory? England and the War of Ideas* (Cambridge: The Lutterworth Press, 2000), 68).
17. John Paul Russo, *I. A. Richards: His Life and Work* (London: Routledge, 1989), 432, 775 n.13.

18. WE, (?unposted) letter to mother, 3 January 1940 (Empson Papers). This letter formed the basis of his later article 'Passing through U.S.A.'

19. WE, (?unposted) letter to mother, 3 January 1940 (Empson Papers).

20. WE, 'Passing through U.S.A.', *Horizon*, 1/6 (June 1940), 426–7.

21. Ibid. 428.

22. WE, (?unposted) letter to mother, 3 January 1940 (Empson Papers).

23. WE, 'Passing through U.S.A.', 430.

24. Ibid. 428.

25. WE, (?unposted) letter to mother, 3 January 1940 (Empson Papers).

26. Ibid.

27. John Davenport, letter to Julian Trevelyan, 16 February 1940 (Trinity College Library, Cambridge: JOT 4/41). On 29 June 1939, WE wrote to Michael Roberts from Kunming: 'There is a lot of fun going on really, only I am mental to the point of swallowing brandy before trying to do anything. What my plans are really depends on how I heal up' (Janet Adam Smith).

28. Report quoted in John King Fairbank, *Chinabound: A Fifty-Year Memoir* (New York: Harper Colophon, 1983), 197–9.

Appendix

1. *The Yorkshire Archaeological Society, Record Series vol. XV*; Yorkshire Royalist Composition Papers, I (1893), 214–15. Thomas Empson, a yeoman, who was seized of lands in Whitgift and Goole, also 'adhered to the King's party' and was likewise obliged to submit himself to the parliamentary sequestrators in 1645 (he took the oath and covenant in 1646); in 1652 he entered the plea that he had lately become 'very aged and inform' and was 'never in arms or in any service against the Parliament, though for the preservation of his life he was forced to fly to a garrison of the enemies to avoid the fury of the soldiers that at the same time killed a neighbour of your petitioner's at his own doors; his estate having been now about 7 years under sequestration and all his personal estate taken away at the first and nothing left him to buy himself bread he prayeth your honours to commiserate his sad condition and to allow him the fifths of his small estate for his livelyhood.' He was denied the fifth of his estate, though he had told no lie in his petition: he died within the year, whereupon William Empson, his cousin and heir, paid off his fine and had the estate—'a mess[uage] or mansion house in Goole in the parish of Snaith'—discharged.

2. *Harleian Society Publications*, 50 (1902): *Lincolnshire Pedigrees*, vol. i.

3. Notwithstanding his lowly trade, James Yorke's work is regarded as authoritative on the subject of his subtitle: *The Arms, Matches & Issues of Kings & of Nobility of England from the Conquest to 1640. With the Arms of the Gentry of Lincolnshire.*

4. John Empson, letter to Amaziah and Ellen Empson, 24 July 1832.

5. R. P. Graham-Vivian, letter to Arthur Empson, 19 September 1949.

6. *A Descriptive Catalogue of the Legal and Other Documents in the Archives of the Royal College of Physicians of London* (1924): Box 9, BDL. 13.

7. Will of Richard Empson of Goole, county York, yeoman, dated 20 April 1675; proved York, 27 September 1675.

8. This argument supposes that the father was a severe Puritan, in every sense. Not many seventeenth-century fathers would have been outraged over a bastard; the Empson seed was probably planted all over the parish.

9. See Donald Lawrence Empson and Amy Eileen Empson, *The Empson Families in America* (St Paul, Minn., 1984).

10. Bonamy Dobrée, *William Penn: Quaker and Pioneer* (London: Constable & Co., 1932).

11. *History of the Church, Parish and Manor of Howden* (Howden: W. F. Pratt, 1850), 75, 79. The Ouse was a major salmon river up to the Second World War.

12. C. C. Empson, letter to WE, 5 February 1982. See also Robert Thompson (Gilberdyke Local History Group), *Historic Blacktoft*, privately printed (1993), 44–5. There is a memorandum in the family papers, and another in the County Archives at Beverley, which indicates that on 24 November 1761 Amaziah bought the Manor at Blacktoft from Mr Charles Pelham; but it may be that Amaziah purchased either Pelham's lease or his 'messuage' on the property (as distinct from the estate lands which were vested in the Charter-house). It was Amaziah who initiated the ambitious process of engineering awesome drains for 'warping' the land.

13. *Handbook for Tourists in Yorkshire* (Leeds: Richard Jackson, 1891), 659.

14. 'Sir Thomas Metham, who had married a Constable, commanded at Flodden; his descendant, another Sir Thomas, who had also married a Constable, was slain at Marston. The family became greatly impoverished in the time of Sir George, the last who bore the name. He sold the estate and lived some years at North Cave, where he died, a reckless and improvident man, subsisting upon a small pension from the Crown' (*Handbook for Tourists in Yorkshire*, 659). The Revd John Empson wrote to his son John Henry on 27 May 1839: 'The ancient & famous family of Metham near Howden is extinct; the last of the family was Sir George Metham, a gay & expensive man, whose extravagance obliged him to sell his Estate to my Great-Grandfather, by whose Economy the chief part of the Lands now possessed by his descendants was acquired' (*Empson's Folly: A Collection of Letters*, ed. C. C. Empson (Seaton: Empson Publications, 2000), 309).

15. The Revd John Empson, letter to John William Empson, 19 October 1836; *Empson's Folly*, 209.

16. Sarah Empson, letter to the Revd John Empson, 29 June 1838; *Empson's Folly*, 293.

17. Sarah Empson, letter to John Empson, 10 October 1816; quoted in *Empsons' Peace*, ed. C. C. Empson (Bishop Auckland, Durham: Pentland Press, 1996), 75.

18. JH, interview with C. C. Empson, September 1991.

19. The Revd John Empson, letter to John William Empson, 5 October 1837; *Empson's Folly*, 261.

20. Major Guy Paget, DL, and Lionel Irvine, MA, *The Flying Parson and Dick Christian* (Leicester: Edgar Backus, 1934), 4.

21. Ibid. 69–70.

22. Ibid. 91.

23. T. Cautley, letter to William Empson, 28 April 1808.

24. *Empson's Folly*, 78.

25. 'The gods do not bestow such a face as Mrs Siddons' on the stage more than once in a century,' said Sydney Smith, the wit of the century. 'I knew her very well, and she had the good taste to laugh heartily at my jokes; she was an excellent person, but she was not remarkable out of her profession, and never got out of tragedy even in common life. She used to *stab* the potatoes; and said "Boy, give me a knife!" as she would have said, "Give me the dagger!"' ' (*A Memoir of the Rev. Sydney Smith* by his daughter Lady Holland (London: Longman, Green, & Co., 1855), 242).

26. The Revd John Empson, letter to John William Empson, 5 October 1837.

27. The Revd John Empson, letter to John William Empson, 26 November 1836.

28. The Revd John Empson, letter to John William Empson, 19 October 1836.

29. The Revd John Empson, letter to John William Empson, 5 October 1837.

30. The Revd John Empson, letter to Maria, his daughter-in-law, 19 August 1844.

INDEX